U0593334

欧亚历史文化文库

总策划 张余胜

兰州大学出版社

三夷教研究

——林悟殊先生古稀纪念论文集

丛书主编　余太山

主　　编　张小贵

副 主 编　王媛媛　殷小平

图书在版编目（CIP）数据

三夷教研究 ：林悟殊先生古稀纪念论文集 / 张小贵主编. -- 兰州 ：兰州大学出版社，2014.12
（欧亚历史文化文库 / 余太山主编）
ISBN 978-7-311-04663-7

Ⅰ. ①三… Ⅱ. ①张… Ⅲ. ①祆教－中国－文集②摩尼教－中国－文集③景教－中国－文集 Ⅳ. ①B983-53 ②B989.1-53③B976-53

中国版本图书馆CIP数据核字(2014)第299669号

策划编辑 施援平
责任编辑 钟 静 施援平
装帧设计 张友乾

书 名 三夷教研究——林悟殊先生古稀纪念论文集
丛书主编 余太山
作 者 张小贵 主编
出版发行 兰州大学出版社 （地址:兰州市天水南路222号 730000）
电 话 0931-8912613(总编办公室) 0931-8617156(营销中心)
0931-8914298(读者服务部)
网 址 http://www.onbook.com.cn
电子信箱 press@lzu.edu.cn
网上销售 http://lzup.taobao.com
印 刷 兰州人民印刷厂
开 本 700 mm×1000 mm 1/16
印 张 33.25(插页2)
字 数 489千
版 次 2014年12月第1版
印 次 2014年12月第1次印刷
书 号 ISBN 978-7-311-04663-7
定 价 100.00元

出版说明

随着20世纪以来联系地、整体地看待世界和事物的系统科学理念的深入人心，人文社会学科也出现了整合的趋势，熔东北亚、北亚、中亚和中、东欧历史文化研究于一炉的内陆欧亚学于是应运而生。时至今日，内陆欧亚学研究取得的成果已成为人类不可多得的宝贵财富。

当下，日益高涨的全球化和区域化呼声，既要求世界范围内的广泛合作，也强调区域内的协调发展。我国作为内陆欧亚的大国之一，加之20世纪末欧亚大陆桥再度开通，深入开展内陆欧亚历史文化的研究已是责无旁贷；而为改革开放的深入和中国特色社会主义建设创造有利周边环境的需要，亦使得内陆欧亚历史文化研究的现实意义更为突出和迫切。因此，将针对古代活动于内陆欧亚这一广泛区域的诸民族的历史文化研究成果呈现给广大的读者，不仅是实现当今该地区各国共赢的历史基础，也是这一地区各族人民共同进步与发展的需求。

甘肃作为古代西北丝绸之路的必经之地与重要组

成部分，历史上曾经是草原文明与农耕文明交汇的锋面，是多民族历史文化交融的历史舞台，世界几大文明（希腊—罗马文明、阿拉伯—波斯文明、印度文明和中华文明）在此交汇、碰撞，域内多民族文化在此融合。同时，甘肃也是现代欧亚大陆桥的必经之地与重要组成部分，是现代内陆欧亚商贸流通、文化交流的主要通道。

基于上述考虑，甘肃省新闻出版局将这套《欧亚历史文化文库》确定为 2009—2012 年重点出版项目，依此展开甘版图书的品牌建设，确实是既有眼光，亦有气魄的。

丛书主编余太山先生出于对自己耕耘了大半辈子的学科的热爱与执著，联络、组织这个领域国内外的知名专家和学者，把他们的研究成果呈现给了各位读者，其兢兢业业、如临如履的工作态度，令人感动。谨在此表示我们的谢意。

出版《欧亚历史文化文库》这样一套书，对于我们这样一个立足学术与教育出版的出版社来说，既是机遇，也是挑战。我们本着重点图书重点做的原则，严格于每一个环节和过程，力争不负作者、对得起读者。

我们更希望通过这套丛书的出版，使我们的学术出版在这个领域里与学界的发展相偕相伴，这是我们的理想，是我们的不懈追求。当然，我们最根本的目的，是向读者提交一份出色的答卷。

我们期待着读者的回声。

总序

本文库所称“欧亚”(Eurasia)是指内陆欧亚,这是一个地理概念。其范围大致东起黑龙江、松花江流域,西抵多瑙河、伏尔加河流域,具体而言除中欧和东欧外,主要包括我国东三省、内蒙古自治区、新疆维吾尔自治区,以及蒙古高原、西伯利亚、哈萨克斯坦、乌兹别克斯坦、吉尔吉斯斯坦、土库曼斯坦、塔吉克斯坦、阿富汗斯坦、巴基斯坦和西北印度。其核心地带即所谓欧亚草原(Eurasian Steppes)。

内陆欧亚历史文化研究的对象主要是历史上活动于欧亚草原及其周邻地区(我国甘肃、宁夏、青海、西藏,以及小亚、伊朗、阿拉伯、印度、日本、朝鲜乃至西欧、北非等地)的诸民族本身,及其与世界其他地区在经济、政治、文化各方面的交流和交涉。由于内陆欧亚自然地理环境的特殊性,其历史文化呈现出鲜明的特色。

内陆欧亚历史文化研究是世界历史文化研究中不可或缺的组成部分,东亚、西亚、南亚以及欧洲、美洲历史文化上的许多疑难问题,都必须通过加强内陆欧亚历史文化的研究,特别是将内陆欧亚历史文化视做一个整体加以研究,才能获得确解。

中国作为内陆欧亚的大国，其历史进程从一开始就和内陆欧亚有千丝万缕的联系。我们只要注意到历代王朝的创建者中有一半以上有内陆欧亚渊源就不难理解这一点了。可以说,今后中国史研究要有大的突破,在很大程度上有待于内陆欧亚史研究的进展。

古代内陆欧亚对于古代中外关系史的发展具有不同寻常的意义。古代中国与位于它东北、西北和北方，乃至西北次大陆的国家和地区的关系,无疑是古代中外关系史最主要的篇章,而只有通过研究内陆欧亚史,才能真正把握之。

内陆欧亚历史文化研究既饶有学术趣味,也是加深睦邻关系,为改革开放和建设有中国特色的社会主义创造有利周边环境的需要，因而亦具有重要的现实政治意义。由此可见,我国深入开展内陆欧亚历史文化的研究责无旁贷。

为了联合全国内陆欧亚学的研究力量，更好地建设和发展内陆欧亚学这一新学科,繁荣社会主义文化,适应打造学术精品的战略要求,在深思熟虑和广泛征求意见后,我们决定编辑出版这套《欧亚历史文化文库》。

本文库所收大别为三类:一,研究专著;二,译著;三,知识性丛书。其中,研究专著旨在收辑有关诸课题的各种研究成果;译著旨在介绍国外学术界高质量的研究专著;知识性丛书收辑有关的通俗读物。不言而喻,这三类著作对于一个学科的发展都是不可或缺的。

构建和发展中国的内陆欧亚学,任重道远。衷心希望全国各族学者共同努力,一起推进内陆欧亚研究的发展。愿本文库有蓬勃的生命力,拥有越来越多的作者和读者。

最后,甘肃省新闻出版局支持这一文库编辑出版,确实需要眼光和魄力,特此致敬、致谢。

余太山

2010年6月30日

目录

林悟殊先生与中古三夷教研究

张小贵　李清波

林悟殊先生，1943 年生于广东潮州，1962—1967 年入中山大学历史系读书，1978 年复入中山大学历史系攻读硕士学位，主要跟随蔡鸿生先生研习摩尼教东渐史，自此开始中古三夷教的研究。有关中古三夷教，林先生均有系列性的论文发表，且分别修订整合成专著出版（详见本书所附作者论著目录）。先生一以贯之的研究风格，乃以求真为目的，以考证为主要方法，即在前人研究基础上，对有关三夷教研究的疑难专题进行深入考察。如中华书局资深编辑李解民先生在评论《中古三夷教辨证》一书时所言："［该书］以陈寅恪先生的文化传播变异论为指导，围绕三夷教，即袄教（火祆教、拜火教）、摩尼教（明教）、景教（大秦教）的华化，梳理文献，考证文物，探赜索隐，辨疑正误，沟通中外，融汇古今，作多角度深层次具体考察，勾勒三夷教在古代中国传播演化的轨迹。"〔1〕诚为先生研究工作的真实写照，即并非面面俱到地撰写中古三夷教史，而是针对若干专题进行深入探讨，同时注意各专题之间的内在联系。同时，先生又不仅仅局限于考镜源流，而是力图在专题研究基础上获得对三夷教入华传播史的通性认识。

一、摩尼教及其东渐

（一）对摩尼教入华传播史的重新梳理

现代意义上的摩尼教入华史研究，无疑始于 20 世纪初我国敦煌吐鲁番地区的考古发现。自 1911 年伯希和、沙畹发表有关汉文摩尼教经

〔1〕《书品》2005年第5辑。

典释读和研究的长文以来，各国学者有关摩尼教的研究一直方兴未艾。先生首先回顾了 20 世纪初以来世界各地有关摩尼教文献和文物的发现及各国学者的研究概况，[1] 然后在广泛参考国内外学界有关研究成果的基础上进行摩尼教的研究。作者 80 年代有关摩尼教研究的文章收入《摩尼教及其东渐》一书，于 1987 年由中华书局正式出版。这一阶段，作者的研究重点是考察摩尼教入华史领域的经典问题，澄清传统认识的某些误区，虽不说体系完备，却大致勾勒出摩尼教入华传播的史实脉络。

摩尼教起源于萨珊波斯，其入传中亚地区，“乃是摩尼教徒对其教主的世界宗教思想的自觉实践，是忠实地执行摩尼宏伟的传教计划的一个具体行动”。[2] 然而“摩尼教能在中亚地区广为传播，这固然是其教徒自觉实践教主的世界宗教思想、主观努力的结果，但亦是和当地的社会历史条件分不开的”。[3] 而摩尼教徒们则利用了这些有利条件，充分运用其固有的灵活的传教方式，而终于在该地区获得了最大的成功。先生亦通过对三部汉文摩尼教经典的语言学分析，认为“唐代中国流行的摩尼教直接渊源于具有浓厚佛教色彩的中亚摩尼教团，而又在这个教团的佛教色彩上进一步加深佛化”。[4] 而确认唐代中国内地流行的摩尼教与中亚摩尼教的近亲血缘关系，则是为了“更大胆地利用这两者资料的互相印证和补充，来进一步弄清古代东方摩尼教的‘庐山真面目’”。[5]

摩尼教自唐武后时，在中国内地公开、合法地传播；安史之乱后，更借助回鹘势力，盛极一时；后虽遭唐武宗镇压，但仍在民间流传。回鹘人把摩尼教奉为国教，显然是摩尼教入华史的辉煌篇章。先生分析了这一事件的特定社会历史根源，认为乃源于回鹘助唐平定安史之乱后，

[1]《本世纪来摩尼教资料的新发现及其研究概况》，此据林悟殊：《摩尼教及其东渐》，北京：中华书局，1987年，第1–11页。（以下所引先生诸论文，皆根据论文集所收版本，详细版本信息请参考本书附录论著目录。）

[2]《摩尼教及其东渐》，第39页。

[3]《摩尼教及其东渐》，第40页。

[4]《唐代摩尼教与中亚摩尼教团》，参见《摩尼教及其东渐》，第73页。

[5]《唐代摩尼教与中亚摩尼教团》，参见《摩尼教及其东渐》，第73页。

在国家事务和宗教信仰上对信仰摩尼教的粟特人的依赖，并得出一个朴素的结论："透过回鹘奉摩尼教这个历史现象，我们进一步看到，古代任何一种宗教的传播，与当时社会经济的发展是有着不可分割的联系的。"〔1〕先生以吐鲁番考古发现的摩尼教资料，证以其他有关资料，论证了摩尼教在高昌回鹘的封建化。在封建化的过程中，教徒除了在行动上渐渐背离古训外，势必亦要在经典上修改古训。进而提示我们注意，必须甄别在吐鲁番发现的大量摩尼教手抄残片中，哪些是经过当地封建摩尼教僧侣所篡改的，哪些是当地封建摩尼教僧侣自己新撰的？如此才能正确地认识摩尼教本来的面目及其后来的演变。〔2〕

在宋代中国东南沿海广为流行的明教，是源自唐代中原的摩尼教，是唐代摩尼教在宋代条件下高度华化的产物。先生对宋元时代东南沿海地区的四所摩尼教寺院进行考察，指明摩尼教经过了唐季的宗教迫害后，内部发生了根本性的分化：上层僧侣遁入山林，进一步发展寺院制度，把宗教活动局限于寺院之内，把摩尼教进一步向超世绝俗、自我修炼的方向发展；而下层教徒则走向民间，与农民反抗运动相结合。社会条件不同，分化的结果自然亦就相异。〔3〕有关前者，先生重新考察了传统将敦煌本《老子化胡经》中言及摩尼和二宗三际的内容，解读为当时道家依托摩尼教的误解，指出："《化胡经》之出现摩尼教的内容，原来并非为了宣传或依托摩尼教，而是像道家窃取他家材料一样，只是为了增加自己经典的力量，玄化自己的教义，抬高自身的地位，以与佛家抗衡罢了。"〔4〕而且由于《化胡经》吸收了摩尼教的成分，这就为后来（主要是宋代）摩尼教依托道教大开了方便之门。这也符合古代各种宗教在思想材料上，往往互相渗透、互相吸收、互相混杂、互相利用的规律。〔5〕有关摩尼教下层教徒走向民间，与农民反抗运动相结合的情况，学界常将其与宋代吃菜事魔等同，先生指出：在宋代，吃菜事魔

〔1〕《回鹘奉摩尼教的社会历史根源》，参见《摩尼教及其东渐》，第98页。

〔2〕《从考古发现看摩尼教在高昌回鹘的封建化》，参见《摩尼教及其东渐》，第100–110页。

〔3〕《宋元时代中国东南沿海的寺院式摩尼教》，参见《摩尼教及其东渐》，第156页。

〔4〕《摩尼教及其东渐》，第81页。

〔5〕《〈老子化胡经〉与摩尼教》，参见《摩尼教及其东渐》，第76–86页。

一词之专用于摩尼教（明教），只局限于一些佛教徒；而统治者鲜有用该词来专指明教者。因此，历史上被称为吃菜事魔的人，可能与摩尼教有关，亦可能无关。在考察宋代的一些农民起义军或农民起义领袖与摩尼教的关系时，如果没有找到确属摩尼教所特有的东西，而只凭其被称为吃菜事魔这一点就认定其为摩尼教徒，这很可能会远离本来的实际。[1]

敦煌汉文摩尼教文献是摩尼教入华史研究的重要资料基础。先生除了利用该等经典进行传播史的考察外，也对经典本身，结合宗教学、文献学、历史学等方面进行了深入的综合研究。如对京藏《摩尼教残经》的原名，英法藏《摩尼光佛教法仪略》的缀合，其产生的原因，及所反映的三圣同一论，《下部赞》的汉译年代等等进行了系统考察，既是敦煌写本研究的典型个案，又为深入利用这些内典资料奠定了基础。如先生质疑了西方学者关于唐宋时代中国摩尼教徒流行《三际经》的说法，认为当时流行的是《二宗三际经》，或简称为《二宗经》；汉文摩尼教经典中，并不存在一部与《二宗经》或《二宗三际经》不同的《三际经》；敦煌卷子 P.3847 所提到的《三际经》不会是摩尼教经典，它应属于景教经典。[2]

值得注意的是，在从事摩尼教研究的第一阶段，先生已开始对汉文摩尼教经典的词汇作专门研究。如对“慕阇”一词的考察，先生认为其系一音译的外来语，盖源自中古波斯语，为摩尼教高级僧侣的称呼。而粟特语的 mozak、回鹘语的 možak 都是从中古波斯语衍化音译来的。其他的一些汉文摩尼教音译术语，只要在摩尼教的原始语言中找到相同意思的词语，而对音又近似，那就应把它说成是源自那种原始语言，而不应在其他民族语言中去寻找它的原型。[3] 同时考出中亚摩尼教团设有慕阇 12 位，并对他们在中国内地传教的史实进行了勾勒。

（二）对宋元时代东南沿海摩尼教走向的探讨

《摩尼教及其东渐》一书出版后，先生并未停止对摩尼教的研究，

---

〔1〕《吃菜事魔与摩尼教》，参见《摩尼教及其东渐》，第143页。

〔2〕《唐宋〈三际经〉质疑》，参见《摩尼教及其东渐》，第159–167页。

〔3〕《慕阇考》，参见《摩尼教及其东渐》，第113页。

除继续对汉文摩尼教经进行探讨外，还主要从文物、文献、历史等各方面对宋元时代滨海地域，尤其是福建摩尼教的流行状况，特别是其走向进行了专题考察。如《福建明教石刻十六字偈考释》一文[1]，就中国摩尼教术语“清净”一词，指出许多西方学者依据希腊文、中古波斯文、帕提亚文、拉丁文及科普特文种的摩尼教文献，将其比对为“神”，并把“清净，光明，大力，智慧”与希腊文“父的四面尊严”一一对号入座的机械“互证”方法，乃是西人不熟悉中国古代译经格义法之故。其实，汉文经典中的一些思想内容，在中亚文献中并不可能有。从文化变异的角度看，中亚的经典教义传入中国后，必须经过很大的改装方可为汉人所接受。对一种外来文化专有术语的翻译，一般而言，应当先有音译才有意译；摩尼教的翻译同样是先有音译，再通过“格义”，用本土语文意译而成。该文立意乃受陈寅恪先生“格义”论启发，[2]无疑具有方法论的意义。先生最近完成的《摩尼教“拂多诞”名辨》一文，便是利用“格义”理论继续研究中古三夷教入华传播问题的力作。文章针对西方学者认为其为中亚摩尼教第二教阶称号的看法，认为该词并非源于来华摩尼僧之简单音译，而是延载元年（694）某位西域摩尼高僧朝觐则天女皇的产物。朝廷为便于与该僧打交道，并示恩宠，特为其取“拂多诞”这一汉文名号，寓去除荒诞之意，谐胡语某些宗教尊号之音。由于该名号来自朝廷，而名号受者适属第二品阶摩尼僧，教会遂以其作为该教阶之汉文称号。[3]

早在 1985 年，先生就在《宋元明教与唐代摩尼教》一文中对宋元摩尼教的渊源进行了释疑，认为其乃源于唐代北方的摩尼教。但近些年来，在现实利益的驱动下，某些人无视历史发展的事实和逻辑，大力鼓吹海上传入说。先生以泉州摩尼教为个案，深入地挖掘《闽书》等文献的历史信息，以文物和文献相印证，论证了泉州摩尼教与唐代摩尼教一

〔1〕《福建明教石刻十六字偈考释》，参见《中古三夷教辨证》，北京：中华书局，2005年，第5–32页。

〔2〕蔡鸿生:《从支愍度学说到支愍度话题》，收入《仰望陈寅恪》，北京：中华书局，2004年，第59–65页。

〔3〕《摩尼教“拂多诞”名辨》，载于《中华文史论丛》2014年第1期，第287–309页。

脉相承，而其间的差异则是由于“宗教传播过程中因应当地社会环境嬗变所造成”。就此一问题，先生又专门撰写《宋元滨海地域明教非海路输入辨》一文，论证宋元时期福建滨海地域流行的明教，并非海路输入，而是由陆路传入的唐代摩尼教华化变异而来。〔1〕

先生不仅对宋元摩尼教做了溯本清源的工作，还努力挖掘滨海摩尼教华化的种种表现。如摩尼教经典如何提炼出以“瞑颂”为形式的“十六字偈”，“佛身道貌”的泉州摩尼光佛雕像如何不同于吐鲁番的摩尼画像〔2〕，温州明教徒“日每一食”所反映的宋元摩尼教对教规的坚持及对现实的适应〔3〕，以及摩尼教如何吸收佛道思想发展为偶像崇拜〔4〕。先生以选真寺为个案，指出到立碑时（至正十年）的选真寺，其建筑规模、生活设施等，已非昔日的选真寺所可伦比，其时居住其中的“苏邻国之教者”，恐也今非昔比了，殆与佛教僧人没有多大的区别，选真寺已经或正在变成一所附有宗族祠堂的民间私家佛教寺院或庙宇。如是，选真寺为宋元明教的最终走向提供了鲜明个案。

《摩尼教华名辨异》可算是一篇有关摩尼教华化问题的总结性文章。本篇旨在考定该教的正式华名，在此基础上，将其他有关的称谓进行梳理，本着循名责实的原则，就其与摩尼教之间的实际关系，一一试加考辨，以窥见摩尼教华化的真正形态。〔5〕学界所认为的摩尼教诸多其他称谓中，大概唯有与教主诞生地相联系的“苏邻法”或“苏邻教”，乃确指该教。其他的称谓，诸如宋代“吃菜事魔”“妖幻邪人”之类的叫法，是官方对于带有宗教色彩的民间群体组织的恶称，在官方心目中，摩尼教当然是包括其中，但实际则并非单指该教。宋代之“二襘子”“牟尼教”“四果”“金刚禅”“揭谛斋”等名号下的群体组织，可能吸收、效法摩尼教的某些成分，但不大可能是直接脱胎于该教。至今传统认为

〔1〕《宋元滨海地域明教非海路输入辨》，参见《中古夷教华化丛考》，兰州：兰州大学出版社，2011年，第40–50页。

〔2〕《泉州草庵摩尼雕像与吐鲁番摩尼画像的比较》，参见《中古三夷教辨证》，第33–41页。

〔3〕《元〈竹西楼记〉摩尼教信息辨析》，参见《中古三夷教辨证》，第142–160页。

〔4〕《元代泉州摩尼教偶像崇拜探源》，参见《中古三夷教辨证》，第399–417页。

〔5〕《摩尼教华名辨异》，参见《中古夷教华化丛考》，第51页。

明代的明尊教就是明教，实际只是就名字的推测，两者之间即便有联系，也不能替代。此外，或认为福建明教最后易名为师氏法，则可能是缘于原始文献表述欠明晰所导致的误会。[1]

（三）霞浦文书带来的新问题

有学者曾言林先生论著鲜见使用新资料者。其实，这与其说是作者的写作风格，毋宁说乃由于研究主题本身的局限所致。其实，在霞浦文书现世之前，福建泉州晋江的文博工作者粘良图先生已经就福建当地的明教遗迹调查有所斩获。先生及时关注了这些新的田野调查资料，如指出草庵境主宫所供奉秦皎明使和都天灵相或许就是从何乔远所披露的明代泉州晋江明教徒所拜“二圣”先意和夷数演变而来。此二神称谓和形象的产生不会早于何氏《闽书》撰成的万历四十七年（1619）。这表明原始摩尼教义中的先意和夷数二神，从名字到相貌，以致功能的彻底华化，成为中国民间的地方保护神，是在其入华千年之后，即在明末清初之际或更晚后些。在此基础上，作者进一步指出，在何乔远撰写《闽书》的年代，泉州的摩尼教显然已进入转型的最后阶段，即彻底华化，融入当地的民间宗教中。其主要表现，乃在于行为方式上向中国传统道教和民间宗教完全看齐、靠拢，即行“符咒”和签诗求卜活动。本属摩尼教的草庵，至迟在明末清初时便已出现签诗求卜活动，这从外表的行为方式看，实与当地其他宗教或民间信仰并无二致；但就签诗中的具体内容而言，却明显保持着本教的理念和习惯用语，尤其是教主摩尼明暗二宗的基本义理。通过晋江新发现的摩尼教遗迹，证明该教在明清之际，其诸神从形象到功能，与中国传统民间信仰的诸神，已融成一体；而其所流行的符咒之术、签诗求卜等活动，就行为方式而言，则与中国传统的民间宗教殆无差别。[2]

近年，霞浦明教遗迹调查屡有创获，其中尤以科仪文书引人注目。针对霞浦的新发现，先生有公允的评论：“近年，由林鋆先生主导、陈

[1]《摩尼教华名辨异》，参见《中古夷教华化丛考》，第92页。

[2]《泉州晋江新发现摩尼教遗迹辨析》，参见《中古夷教华化丛考》，第20–39页。

进国先生积极参与的霞浦明教遗迹调查所得科仪抄本，多有涉及明教术语词章者。就已披露的科册看，涉及斋醮仪式的文疏格式颇为齐备，学界或言该等即为明教科典，传承自宋代，甚至唐代，并据该等新资料，演绎有关宋代明教甚至唐代摩尼教之种种新见。窃以为，该等新发现的资料，于追踪失传的明教、摩尼教信息，认识摩尼教在华的最后归宿，无疑有重要的价值。不过。该等抄本为私家世传秘藏，如果要作为历史文献使用，自应依历史文献学的规范，就文本本身形成年代，藉助相关学科的知识，进行一一考实。”[1]

黄佳欣《霞浦科仪本〈乐山堂神记〉再考察》一文，[2]即在林悟殊先生指导下，对《乐山堂神记》文本之性质、用途、产生年代等重新考察。作者将《神记》与另一科仪本《明门初传请本师》做比，推断《神记》为清季民国时期之作。作者认为《神记》所依托之乐山堂，依现有资料，尚不足以确认其为明教遗址；《神记》所标榜明门，在所请众多神灵中，如学者所揭示的，确有若干名可与唐代摩尼教或宋代明教挂钩，这倒有助于说明波斯摩尼教在华夏的最后历史归宿：汇入乡土民间信仰。但若将霞浦文书认为是传承自宋代明教内典，并据此演绎立论，显不足取。林悟殊先生肯定了黄文的考证，并指出“透过《明门》和《神记》这两个科仪本，不难看到，就霞浦‘新明门’之神谱而言，其特色在于奉摩尼光佛为教主，而以林瞪为教门‘祖师’、‘都统’，在当地传统信仰的神谱上，添加若干衍化自唐代摩尼教、宋代明教甚或其他夷教之神灵。通向历史实际有种种门径，窃意从新门派的角度，去解读霞浦科仪本之明教遗迹，或不失为门径之一”。[3]对霞浦文书研究实有导向作用。

[1]《霞浦科仪本〈奏教主〉形成年代考》，载于《九州学林》第31辑，2013年，第102–135页。

[2] 黄佳欣:《霞浦科仪本〈乐山堂神记〉再考察》，提交“海陆交通与世界文明”国际学术研讨会论文，广州·中山大学，2011年12月4—5日；刊陈春声主编《海陆交通与世界文明》，北京：商务印书馆，2013年，第229–255页。

[3]《跋〈乐山堂神记〉再考察》，刊陈春声主编《海陆交通与世界文明》，第256–260页。

林悟殊先生比较了霞浦所发现的三个版本的科仪本《下部赞》[1]与敦煌本《下部赞》诗文的异同，指出“即便某些文字差异含义有别，但各诗文所表达的主体思想并无二致。因此，无论出自霞浦科册，抑或敦煌石窟，毫无疑问，都应源自唐代‘道明所翻译’（敦煌本《下部赞》第 417-418 行）的同一摩尼教赞诗。”[2]“唐代摩尼教《下部赞》的一些完整诗文，竟出现在霞浦的科仪本上，证明了尽管摩尼教在会昌初元遭到迫害，外来摩尼僧被杀害、驱逐殆尽，但其汉文经典，尤其是像《下部赞》这样佛味浓厚、表达通俗之宗教仪式用经，却仍长期在华夏民间传播。而福建、两浙在宋代以盛行明教著称，霞浦位于福建东北部，距著名的宋代道化摩尼寺崇寿宫所在地四明（宁波）仅 40 多公里，而离曾因明教之盛遭官方点名的温州则仅 90 公里，其地处明教流播区域，遗存《下部赞》诗文，自不为奇。”[3]敦煌本《下部赞》423 行，而被采入陈法师藏《摩尼光佛》科册者，依次是第 11、30、42、119、127、135、140、169-172、206、301、303、410-414 行。就其所撷《下部赞》诗文于敦煌卷之分布，可推测科册制作者所接触的《下部赞》，应是比较完整者，而非残篇断简，否则不可能如此全卷式的遴选其诗文。不过，其所据者未必是唐写本，而应是被唐后明教徒修订过的新版。这从第六组首句的差异就可看出。敦煌本作“又启普遍忙你尊”，而陈摩本中，“忙你尊”作“摩尼光”；诸如“五佛摩尼光”“末号摩尼光”的提法，不可能始于唐代，而应是华化成明教之后。[4]而陈摩本所据《下部赞》抄本既出自明教会，那么其所录文字如与敦煌本有实质性差异，在排除出于唐代不同版本和明教会修改的可能性后，问题自出在科仪本制作者本身，或误录，或误改，或刻意修改。先生分析了霞浦本出于不谙教理之笔误、霞浦本不谙教理之误改、霞浦本之刻意修改等几个方面，指出：“从采录《下部赞》诗文这个角度，陈摩本科册版的制作要比其它两个

〔1〕即陈姓法师“存修”并题的《摩尼光佛》科册，其保藏的《兴福祖庆诞科》及谢姓法师保有的《点灯七层科册》。

〔2〕《霞浦科仪本〈下部赞〉诗文辨异》，载于《世界宗教研究》2012年第3期，第170-178页。

〔3〕《霞浦科仪本〈下部赞〉诗文辨异》，第174页。

〔4〕《霞浦科仪本〈下部赞〉诗文辨异》，第174-175页。

科册为早，成为后两者编撰的参考物。亦正因为如此，霞浦三个版本与敦煌本之比较始见多有共同的差异。这也就提示吾辈，田野调查所发现的有关科仪本，未必是同一时期的批量产物，彼等之形成或有先有后，若后者参考前者，亦属常理。学界或把霞浦科仪本直当北宋明教遗书，本文考察上揭抄本中采录《下部赞》诗文之异同，辨释其差异产生之诸多原因，庶几有助于澄清有关之认识。”〔1〕

在《霞浦科仪本〈奏教主〉形成年代考》一文中〔2〕，先生指出，《奏教主》制作于清初百年之内，文检虽标榜明门法嗣所用，但制作者于真正的明教经典并未多所涉猎。所奏三位主神名号：“电光王佛”，直接间接地变造自佛门的“电光佛”，现有唐宋文献未见，明代始用于指代摩尼教之最高神，以避“明尊教”之嫌；“摩尼光佛”，作为摩尼的名号，仅见于敦煌摩尼经 S.3969，但于唐宋时期并未普遍使用；“夷数和佛”，仅见于霞浦科册，变造自唐宋文献所见的“夷数佛”。摩尼教并无以“三”为吉的数字崇拜，其在唐宋中国传播时期，亦未见有以三为度拼组本教神灵的习俗。上揭“三佛”的拼组，源于明代后期制作的《奏三清》，而后者则效法道教之“三清”崇拜。至于《奏教主》所显示的荐亡斋醮模式，唐代摩尼教和宋代明教都不可能流行。因此，无论文检本身的制作，或其所谓“内核”之形成，都无从上溯唐宋，其与唐代的摩尼教会或宋代的明教会不存在什么承传关系，其制作者很可能假明门之名，依道教荐亡科仪之格式，参合前代遗存的某些明教资讯而撰成。

林悟殊先生通过对文本形成年代的考实，虽然否定了多数霞浦文书的摩尼教“内核”，但是并没有否定文书对明教研究的重要意义。《明教五佛崇拜补说》一文〔3〕，即利用霞浦文书对宋代的“五佛”崇拜进行考察。认为云五佛的“五雷子”属荐亡词，五佛乃源于摩尼语录。文章认为宋代明教徒曾依傍道教神谱，冠第一佛明尊佛以“元始天尊”之

---

〔1〕《霞浦科仪本〈下部赞〉诗文辨异》。

〔2〕《霞浦科仪本〈奏教主〉形成年代考》。

〔3〕《明教五佛崇拜补说》，载于《文史》2012年第3期（总第100辑），第385-408页。

号，事过境迁，当明尊佛被易为那罗延佛后，该名号仍被无意残留下来。从霞浦抄本五佛规避明尊佛来看，其产生年代当不可能早于明朝。而那罗延佛取代明尊佛之因缘则是职业法师制作科仪本随意附会之举。文章利用霞浦文书对明教在晚近时代的传播进行了生动的说明。《敦煌摩尼教〈下部赞〉"电光佛"非"光明处女"辨》一文[1]，针对论者多把霞浦科仪本的"电光王佛"直当唐代摩尼教的"电光佛"，而"电光佛"则直当西域摩尼教那个色诱雄魔的女神"光明处女"的情况，指出："在中国的主流宗教和民间信仰中，神灵盖以男性为主体，在较成体系的宗教中，被崇拜的女性神灵毕竟不多，且多不扮演重要角色，希见被奉为主神者。……诸如'光明处女'这样的异域女神，即便没有违背中国传统伦理之色诱行为，也很难进入中国信仰之主神殿。"

霞浦文书并非是明教科典，传承自宋代，甚至唐代；其应为明清时代某些职业法师将原有经典、神谱渐次利用改造成道教模式的科仪文书，成为该等法师的谋生工具。该等标榜明门的科仪本，均属若干法师的世传秘本，不敢流传他人，亦证明了这些法师并未主动利用秘传科册以劝民入教。因此，与其将霞浦文书定性为摩尼教民间化、地方化的产物，毋宁将其定性为民间宗教吸收某些明教讯息而成。如《奏申牒疏科册·[奏]昊天》的主旨在于通过上奏昊天玉皇大帝，希望他大发慈悲，颁布圣旨，以赦免阴司亡灵之罪。再如《奏三清》，通过上奏夷数和佛、电光王佛和摩尼光佛，祈求诸位神祇能够保禾苗以求五谷丰登，祛天灾以佑民平安。与其说这是"摩尼教在霞浦流播过程中，因应形势的不同而有所变革，未拘泥于原始经典之窠臼，而是朝着人生化、现实化和世俗化的方向转变"，毋宁说这是当地民间信仰借用了摩尼教的某些成分，更符合逻辑。霞浦文书多为科仪书和表文，用于斋戒祭祀、祈福禳灾和超度亡灵，具有浓厚的民间色彩。如《兴福祖庆诞科·召符官文》，其中的兴福雷使、顺懿夫人，都是霞浦当地民间所信奉的地方神祇，为原始摩尼教经典所不具。在奉请诸神之前，要设置寿诞，修整法坛，而且

[1]《敦煌摩尼教〈下部赞〉"电光佛"非"光明处女"辨》，载于《文史》2013年第1辑（总第102辑），第175-196页。

需在"筵前祠中焚香三炷"，这些显然都是民间所为。将此类资料直当摩尼教在霞浦演变的证据，似乎夸大了其对摩尼教研究的价值；当然，其对当地民间宗教研究的价值却值得进一步探究。最近，先生新撰成《霞浦抄本元代天主教赞诗辨释——附霞浦抄本基督教〈吉思呪〉考略》一文[1]，考"信礼夷数和"唱词源于元代天主教赞诗，倘此论得实，则显示霞浦抄本的学术资料价值，绝不止于摩尼教、明教研究领域。

二、唐代景教再研究

（一）敦煌汉文景教文献的辨伪与质疑

20 世纪初敦煌出土的汉文景教写经无疑开启了中国景教研究的新时代。作者有关景教的研究始于 1992 年与荣新江先生的合作，对早年曾被认为是李氏旧藏的景教真迹《大秦景教大圣通真归法讃》和《大秦景教宣元至本经》，即所谓小岛文书进行辨伪，考证其为近人制作的赝品。[2]这一发现也被近年来洛阳新出的考古发现所进一步证实。而后，作者又对所谓的高楠文书和富岗文书进行质疑。[3]对《景教三威蒙度讃》《尊经》《志玄安乐经》《大秦景教宣元本经》作为景教真迹的价值进一步肯定，并对其中蕴涵的信息在前人研究基础上进一步阐发。

1995 年，他发表《敦煌遗书〈大秦景教宣元本经〉考释》，根据《羽田博士史学论文集》下卷所刊图版做了释文，并就其篇幅、来源及作者问题加以探讨[4]。2001 年，他发表《敦煌本景教〈志玄安乐经〉佐伯录文质疑》，指出后人所依据的佐伯好郎对该经前 10 行录文的臆补是不可依据的。[5]十年后，他又发表《景教〈志玄安乐经〉敦煌写

[1]《霞浦抄本元代天主教赞诗辨释——附霞浦抄本基督教〈吉思呪〉考略》，待刊。

[2] 林悟殊、荣新江：《所谓李氏旧藏敦煌景教文献二种辨伪》，参见《唐代景教再研究》，北京：中国社会科学出版社，2003年，第156–174页。

[3] 林悟殊：《富冈谦藏氏藏景教〈一神论〉真伪存疑》，《高楠氏藏景教〈序听迷诗所经〉真伪存疑》，参见《唐代景教再研究》，第175–228页。

[4]《唐代景教再研究》，第175–185页；《林悟殊敦煌文书与夷教研究》，上海：上海古籍出版社，2011年，第248–258页。

[5]《唐代景教再研究》，第146–155页；《林悟殊敦煌文书与夷教研究》，第284–293页。

本真伪及录文补说》，根据杏雨书屋刊布的全卷照片，从该经的承传关系、《尊经》之著录、写本篇幅及内容、作者的推测等角度，推断写本为唐代景教徒真迹。又据原件照片，参考羽田亨录文，做出新的释文本。[1]

（二）景教传播史的再研究

相比摩尼教、祆教来说，有关中国景教的研究要早得多，可追溯至明季天启年间（1621—1627）西安府大秦景教流行中国碑的出土。时隔三百余年，景碑之研究，还有多少胜义？先生撰写《西安景教碑研究述评》一文，通过总结评论三百多年来众多学者的研究，指出："就碑文的研究，国人倘能注意上揭所整理的伯希和研究成果，或许可以避免某些不必要的重复劳动。像景教碑这样一块'中西文化交流的丰碑'、世界考古发现史上'四大石碑'之一、'众碑之魁'的古碑，在新世纪的研究中，除了从历史学、语言学、宗教学等角度，更深入地解读碑文内涵外，更加艰巨的任务是，根据碑文所记述的景教在华流行状况，深入发掘新的资料，揭示碑文所颂扬的景教在中国社会的影响。因为在这方面的研究，迄今仍相当薄弱。"[2]

西安景教碑中记有若干之词句，似关其时寺院的数量。对这些词句的正确理解，与客观评估唐代景教传播的情况，密切相关。《西安景教碑有关景寺数量词句考释》一文，对高宗时期"于诸州各置景寺""法流十道""寺满百城"解读，对肃宗"灵武等五郡，重立景寺"考释，及对"每岁集四寺僧徒"的考辨，并非拘泥于字面意思，而是参照整个碑文的精神，并结合当时中西历史背景，进而对景教传播的历史做实质性的考察。[3]

《唐代首所景寺考略》一文，以文献和文物资料为依据，就唐代景教寺院的称谓、首所景教寺院建置的年代，及长安义宁坊大秦寺的重要地位略作考察。寺院是宗教徒从事宗教活动的场所、中心，往往又是各

[1]《林悟殊敦煌文书与夷教研究》，第294–323页。

[2]《西安景教碑研究述评》，参见《唐代景教再研究》，第26页。

[3]《西安景教碑有关景寺数量词句考释》，参见《唐代景教再研究》，第27–47页。

级宗教领袖、高级僧人的驻锡地。正确评估义宁坊大秦寺在唐代景教会中的崇高地位，有利于想象当时中国景教徒组织活动的运作情况，深化对基督教在华早期传播史的认识。〔1〕

《西安景碑有关阿罗本入华事辨析》一文认为，景碑记载阿罗本于贞观九年到达长安事，不过是景士一面之词，尚缺乏其他资料支撑。把教会的传说作为基督教最早入华的依据，从学术研究的角度看，显然有欠严谨。……就景教入华滥觞之标志，与其据景碑所云贞观九年事，倒不如以贞观十二年诏为妥。〔2〕基督教之首期入华，既有像摩尼教那样经由陆路的间接传播，又有像明季耶稣会士那样经由海路直接来华传播。……由是，基督教在唐代中国的表现未必千孔一面。不同地区、不同时期的景教群体，难免自多所差异。这一差异，对于我们解读新近发现的唐代洛阳景教经幢的浓郁佛味，揭示其与西安景碑迥异的原因，或许会有所帮助。因此，本篇辨析阿罗本入华的真相，其学理价值就不止局限于恢复历史的本来面目，而且更有助于我们对历史复杂性、多样性的深化认识。〔3〕

《唐代景教传播成败评说》一文，讨论景教在唐代中国的传教活动，指出我们首先要注意到的一个特点是：该教与其他两个夷教不同，既不借助任何外来的政治、军事或经济的势力，也不借助众多信徒移民的优势，全靠本教僧侣对自身信仰的执着。〔4〕

《李白〈上云乐〉景教思想质疑》一文则指出：“有鉴于此，如果我们能找到唐代景教影响当时思想文化的某些蛛丝马迹，甚或明确证据，固然是好事，是成绩；但找不到，实在也不必去凑合或附会。窃以为，与其勉强去寻找唐代基督教影响当时思想文化的痕迹，毋宁去深入探索其对当时思想文化难以产生大影响的原因。”〔5〕

〔1〕《唐代首所景寺考略》，参见《唐代景教再研究》，第48–64页。

〔2〕《西安景碑有关阿罗本入华事辨析》，参见《中古夷教华化丛考》，第135页。

〔3〕《西安景碑有关阿罗本入华事辨析》，参见《中古夷教华化丛考》，第136页。

〔4〕《唐代景教传播成败评说》，参见《唐代景教再研究》，第85–105页。

〔5〕《李白〈上云乐〉景教思想质疑》，参见《中古夷教华化丛考》，第114页。

（三）洛阳新出土唐代景教经幢研究

2006 年 5 月，洛阳面世一残半的唐代景教经幢，是为近年国内景教文物的最重大发现，无疑为唐代景教研究增添了不可多得的宝贵资料。而洛阳经幢的面世，亦证明经幢本《宣元至本经》对应的是敦煌本《宣元本经》，所谓李氏旧藏的小岛文书并非敦煌真迹，盖可定谳。就此问题，多位作者都一致予以肯定，相关论文收入葛承雍先生主编《景教遗珍》一书，极便参考。[1]这一结果，相信也会引起学界重新关注富冈文书《一神论》和高楠文书《序听谜诗所经》的真伪问题。由此看来，中国景教研究所依据的汉语“内典”资料数量有限，因此任何新资料的发现都显得弥足珍贵。

从经文内容看，经幢所刻《宣经》共计 19 行。其第 1 至 11 行的残文，对应了敦煌残本，而文字间有差异；余行内容则为现存敦煌残本所缺录。因此，洛阳经幢本的发现，无疑为《宣经》研究提供了不可多得的新资料，使对整个经文的了解，得以跨进一大步。就如何正确认识经幢本《宣经》的价值，先生与殷小平合撰《经幢版〈大秦景教宣元至本经〉考释——唐代洛阳景教经幢研究之一》一文所论较为客观，“根据录文比勘，可以发现《宣经》的经幢本和敦煌本不惟题目有一‘至’字之差，内容若干词句亦有异”，表明“两者很可能是各有所本”。“由于经幢本中‘民’字出现凡两次（见第 3、14 行），均无缺笔避讳；而敦煌本虽只出现一次，但却像多数唐代写本那样避讳缺笔。这使我们至少相信：敦煌本的粉本应早于经幢的制作”。[2]作者分析了当今论者就《宣经》全名有无“至”字，多以经幢本为是的原因，令人信服地指出“说不定《宣经》的原始版本就没有一个‘至’字”。[3]也就是说，虽然经幢本《宣经》篇幅多于敦煌本，但从文献学角度看，敦煌本实有其不可替代的版本价值。

---

〔1〕葛承雍主编:《景教遗珍——洛阳新出土唐代景教经幢研究》，北京：文物出版社，2009年。

〔2〕《经幢版〈大秦景教宣元至本经〉考释——唐代洛阳景教经幢研究之一》，参见《景教遗珍——洛阳新出土唐代景教经幢研究》，第72–73页；《中古夷教华化丛考》，第173–174页。

〔3〕《景教遗珍——洛阳新出土唐代景教经幢研究》，第74页；《中古夷教华化丛考》，第176页。

由于《宣经》并无传世完整本，因此其篇幅问题也颇有争议。《遗珍》一书的作者们就提出了至少三种不同的观点。其实，《宣经》的篇幅问题，需要经幢残缺部分的重新发现始能有望解决，而并不能简单认为其已因洛阳景教经幢的发现而解决。客观估量"新资料"的价值无疑为进一步研究奠定了坚实基础。

洛阳景教经幢带来此前不为学界所知的崭新资讯，即唐代洛阳存在着比长安更加华化的景教群体。诚如蔡鸿生教授在《景教遗珍》一书扉页推介辞中所指出："作为唐代景教遗珍，洛阳新出的《宣元至本经》及幢记究竟'新'在哪里？如果着眼于时、地、人，似乎可以形成这样的印象：第一，反映出'安史之乱'后到'会昌法难'前的景教状况，为长安《大秦景教流行中国碑》续新篇；第二，洛阳的景教是在佛教文化的强势之下生存的，其教阶和礼仪散发出浓烈的佛味，经刻于幢，就是'景'与'佛'的矛盾性结合；第三，景士和信众来自胡姓（米、康、安），其人物称谓和人际关系，隐约表露出洛阳景教还是以华化胡裔为社会基础的。"

洛阳经幢"新"在揭示了唐代后期景教在华传播的华化命运。就景教华化问题，既往的研究多集中于讨论敦煌景教文献中术语及表述方式的佛教化与道教化。如敦煌本《尊经》的表达形式即踏袭了佛教忏法敬礼文敬礼诸佛、诸经、诸菩萨的形式。〔1〕敦煌本《宣元本经》亦含有浓厚的道释色彩。〔2〕然而，有关华化的具体史实却多隐晦不清。就景教的华化问题，新发现的洛阳景教经幢所带来的宝贵资讯，可以说刷新了我们的认识。殷小平、林悟殊先生合撰《幢记若干问题考释——唐代洛阳景教经幢研究之二》一文，集中讨论了对宗教史研究更具历史价值的幢记部分，尤其注重理清有关人物称谓与人际关系。如作者重新对幢记撰人"于陵文翼"进行解读，认为其是信奉景教之胡裔，且是早已华化的胡裔，除继承先人夷教信仰，其文化背景殆与汉族士人无异。"而其被遴选为幢记人，当然不只是因为其与幢主同为教友，或华文造诣特

〔1〕松本荣一：《景教〈尊经〉の形式に就て》，刊东京《东方学报》8，1938年，第21–32页。

〔2〕《唐代景教再研究》，第175–185页。

高，其本人必定在社会，或在教内颇有声望地位，足以匹对甚或超过幢主。”[1]而幢记内容则暗示立幢人自幼所受家庭教育便是儒家的孝伦理，其先祖虽来自西域，但在中土已历世代，后世渐次华化，及至其父母辈，华化程度已极深，始有以儒家孝伦理、尊师重道之精神教诲子女。立幢人为亡妣、亡师（或师伯）修建墓茔，并隆重迁葬，这纯属地道的儒家行为。至于刻经立幢，则是效法中国主流宗教——佛教，亦为华化的典型表现。[2]

先生另撰《经幢版“三位一体”考释——唐代洛阳景教经幢研究之三》一文，从解读经幢版“三位一体”的表述入手，进而解释景教入华传播的文化史。“三位一体”乃基督教的基本信条，传入唐代中国后，其汉文的表述至少产生过两个版本。其一，即《尊经》所见的“妙身皇父阿罗诃，应身皇子弥师诃，证身卢诃宁俱沙，已上三身同归一体”。由于抄录《尊经》的敦煌写本 P.3847 卷子已被证明是唐亡后制作，意味该版本一直流行于唐时中国西北的景教徒中。[3]其二，即洛阳景教经幢所勒的“清净阿罗诃，清净大威力，清净大智慧”。先生指出，这个版本比前者无疑更加佛化、民间化、通俗化，显更易为那些华化胡裔教徒所理解接受。这个版本应在经幢营建时，即已为洛阳当地的景教徒所熟知，表明唐代后期的洛阳地区，确实存在着一个华化程度比西北地方更深的景教群体。[4]

《唐代景僧名字的华化轨迹——唐代洛阳景教经幢研究之四》一文，从洛阳经幢《幢记》所见若干僧人的称谓，以摩尼僧为参照，考察景教华化的深度，并参比景碑和教外文献所存景僧名字，追溯、勾勒唐代景僧名字华化的轨迹，冀以此一斑，窥景教华化历程之全豹。[5]可谓利用洛阳经幢新资料考察景教华化问题的力作。

〔1〕《景教遗珍——洛阳新出土唐代景教经幢研究》，第98页；《中古夷教华化丛考》，第199页。

〔2〕《景教遗珍——洛阳新出土唐代景教经幢研究》，第100页；《中古夷教华化丛考》，第202页。

〔3〕《唐代景教再研究》，第123–145页。

〔4〕《景教遗珍——洛阳新出土唐代景教经幢研究》，第120页；《中古夷教华化丛考》，第225页。

〔5〕《唐代景僧名字的华化轨迹——唐代洛阳景教经幢研究之四》，参见《中古夷教华化丛考》，第226–268。

正是在诸多个案研究基础上，先生又发表《唐代“景僧”释义》一文，从“景僧”含义角度综论唐代景教华化问题。文章指出唐代景教之称僧，并非局限于古代翻译的“格义”，即不是仅仅借用一个佛教名词而已。聂斯脱里教徒在中土浓烈之佛教氛围下，得以称僧，敢于称僧，实际暗示着该教的教阶制度、教士戒行制度等已发生微妙的变化。看来，景教为了与佛教、道教并存发展，除了学者们业已注意的一些华化表现外，更实质的是：其不得不遵华情、循华俗，效法佛教，在神职人员以及有志献身于神的虔信徒中，推行禁欲主义，像佛僧那样出家，过独身的生活，以取得僧人的资格，扩大本教的社会影响。[1]

三、对入华火祆教民俗化走向的探索

（一）对波斯琐罗亚斯德教的关注

对中国学者来说，琐罗亚斯德教的研究要比摩尼教的研究难度高很多。因为迄今为止，学界并未发现中古时期该教较为完整的汉文经典，所发现的有关实物资料也颇多争议，文献记载相对模糊。自陈垣先生以来，学界一般将祆教比定为源于波斯的琐罗亚斯德教。随着研究的深入，学者们逐渐认识到波斯琐罗亚斯德教与中亚祆教之间的区别。因此，作者有关祆教的研究是从追溯波斯本原的琐罗亚斯德教开始的。作者自1987 年发表介绍文章开始，撰写了一系列有关波斯琐罗亚斯德教经典、礼仪的文章，相关论文于 1995 年在台湾结集出版。在此之前，国内学界有关该教知识的了解，主要见诸《宗教辞典》《中国大百科全书·宗教卷》的简单介绍。以琐罗亚斯德（Zoroaster）的生平为例，这位古伊朗先知究竟生于何时，自始就是一个聚讼纷纭的问题。实际上有关这个问题，一直是西方学界争论不已的重大问题，20 世纪下半叶国际琐罗亚斯德教史研究的领袖 Mary Boyce 教授，就至少提出过公元前 1200 年、前 1700 年等几种不同观点。[2]1980 年，意大利著名的伊朗学家 G. Gnoli

〔1〕《唐代“景僧”释义》，参见《中古夷教华化丛考》，第167页。

〔2〕Mary Boyce, Zoroastrians, Their Religious Beliefs and Practices, London: Routledge, 2001, p.xiii.

出版了一本著作，专门讨论这个问题，他基本同意 Boyce 的观点，即公元前 1000 年前后。[1]但是时隔 20 年，也就是 2000 年，Gnoli 又出版了 *Zoroaster in History* 一书，完全否定了自己 20 年前的观点，转而认同早在 1949 年，Boyce 的老师 W. B. Henning 提出的公元前 6—7 世纪的观点。[2] 当然，Gnoli 的新观点并未得到学界的普遍认同。有关琐罗亚斯德生平的问题非常复杂，其关涉对这一人物的定性，这一古伊朗宗教的起源、性质等等许多关键性问题。西方学界的相关研究并未停止。而时至今日，有关该教创立的时间，国内多数学者还沿袭 20 世纪上半叶西方学界的传统观点，认为其是公元前 6—7 世纪，这显然并未了解学界研究的进展。

学者们在引用该教经典时，多依据 19 世纪末的《东方圣书》版，而实际上林先生早已根据国际学界的研究成果，指出《东方圣书》所收录的诸多《阿维斯陀经》译本已经过时。[3]以阿维斯陀经中最古代的部分之一《伽萨》圣诗（Gathas）为例，早在 1959 年，德国伊朗学家洪巴赫（Helmut Humbach）就推出了两卷本的 Gāthās 德译本[4]，对《伽萨》进行系统研究，改变了学界长期依赖 1905 年巴托洛梅译本的旧格局。[5]洪氏 1991 年又推出了两卷本的英译本，1994 年又推出了英文简译本。时隔 16 年，也就是在 2010 年，他又出版了该经新的英文与德文译本。每次的翻译均存在不同程度上的差异。[6]1975 年耶鲁大学的 Insler 就出版了大著 *The Gāthās of Zarathustra*[7]，1988—1991 年，法兰西学院的 J. Kellens 与 Pirat 合作，出版了三卷本的法译本及研究[8]等等。学

[1] Gh. Gnoli, *Zoroaster's Time and Homeland. A Study on the Origins of Mazdeism and Related Problems*, Istituto Universitario Orientale. Seminario di Studi Asiatici, Series Minor 7; Naples, 1980.

[2] Gh. Gnoli, *Zoroaster in History*, Biennial Yarshater Lecture Series 2; New York, 2000.

[3]《琐罗亚斯德教徒的圣经》，收入《波斯拜火教与古代中国》，第23-30页。

[4] Helmut Humbach, *Die Gathas des Zarathustra*, Heidelberg, 1959.

[5] Chr. Bartholomae, Die Gatha's des Awesta, Zarathustra's Verspredigten, Strassburg, 1905.

[6] Humbach, H. in collaboration with Elfenbein, J. and Skjærvø, P. O., *The Gāthās of Zarathushtra and the the Other Old Avestan Texts:I–II*. Indogermanische Bibliothek. Heidelberg, 1991. Humbach, H. And Klaus Faiss. *Zarathushtra and His Antagonists*. Wiesbaden: Dr. Ludwig Reichert Verlag, 2010.

[7] Insler, *The Gāthās of Zarathustra*, Leiden: E. J. Brill, 1975.

[8] J. Kellens & Pirat, *Les texts vieil-avestiques*, Vol.I–III, Wiesbaden, 1988–1991.

者们针对阿经所做的研究，不但包括利用不同写本对其进行文献校勘，也包括从比较语言学的角度探讨词义词源，以及从宗教学、历史学角度探讨经文的内涵。由于各自的学术背景与学术旨趣的差异，各家对经文理解不同，翻译也就千差万别了。即使同一个人在不同时代也易对经文产生不同的理解。而这些最新的研究成功并未出现在有关论著的注解中。

（二）有关祆教入华走向的探讨

正是对波斯本原的琐罗亚斯德教深入了解，作者很早认识到传入中亚地区的祆教与波斯本教的不同。《中古琐罗亚斯德教葬俗及其在中亚的遗痕》一文[1]，即是作者探讨不同地区流传的祆教差异的力作。也正由于此，作者考察火祆教始通中国的时间、高昌俗事天神的性质、唐代长安的火祆与大秦寺、唐人信奉火祆教的状况等祆教入华史的经典问题时，往往得出与前人不同的新认识。[2]

先生认为，琐罗亚斯德教作为一个古老的世界性宗教，随着时间、空间的推移，不断在发生变异，由是，在历史上的不同时期、不同区域，产生了不同的版本："中国人所接受的琐罗亚斯德教，主要是民俗成分甚浓的粟特版宗教。唐会昌灭佛，祆教也受牵连而遭取缔。但根据宋代的文献，祆庙、祆祠已被纳入官方轨道，与泰山、城隍等传统祠庙一样，享受官方规定的祭祀标准。这说明了祆神已进入了中国的万神殿，列位于民间诸神。"[3]虽然就民俗中的游神赛会、七星剑的使用、驱魔赶鬼的迷信活动等所包含的粟特祆教因素，已有学者关注，但深入探讨琐罗亚斯德教东传过程中的传播与变异，仍需学界的长期努力。先生所论对有关问题的探讨，显然有导向的作用。

在先生有关祆教研究的文章中，最受学界注目的一篇恐怕是《波斯

---

〔1〕《中古琐罗亚斯德教葬俗及其在中亚的遗痕》，收入《波斯拜火教与古代中国》，第85–97页。

〔2〕详见《火祆教始通中国的再认识》《论高昌"俗事天神"》《唐代长安火祆大秦寺考辨》《唐人奉火祆教考辨》等，收入《波斯拜火教与古代中国》，第105–164页。

〔3〕《〈伊朗琐罗亚斯德教村落〉中译本序》，参见《中古三夷教辨证》，第432–439页。

琐罗亚斯德教与中国古代的祆神崇拜》。[1]文章首先从分析元代俗文学中有关“祆庙”的诸多记载入手，阐明元代俗文学中以祆为典的现象，从而推断“祆神”崇拜在宋代的广泛流行。接着又进一步追溯了宋代祆神崇拜的流行及其与唐代火祆教的渊源。是文重点论证了中国的祆神崇拜并不等同于波斯的琐罗亚斯德教，认为“波斯琐罗亚斯德教并没有在深层文化上对中国产生重大的影响。但其体系中粟特版的祆神崇拜，作为西域胡人的习俗，却为中国人所吸收，并中国化，成为中国古代民间信仰之一”。从理论上厘清了波斯琐罗亚斯德教与中国祆神崇拜的关系。

《唐季“大秦穆护祆”考》[2]是一篇极见考证功夫和思维力度的文章。该文小题大做，对大秦究竟是教名还是地名、穆护祆与回教有无关系、回教在唐代中国的实际地位、“穆护”可能的含义都作了详细的讨论。最后指出：大秦乃指景教徒，“穆护”是来自波斯的琐罗亚斯德教僧侣，祆指中亚的琐罗亚斯德教教徒，即火祆教徒；“大秦穆护祆”应该点断为“大秦、穆护、祆”；并进一步指出应重视波斯琐罗亚斯德教与中亚祆教的区别。

《火祆教在唐代中国社会地位之考察》[3]一文，从探讨“祆”字的创立窥见火祆教在唐人心目中的地位，并以摩尼教、景教为参照坐标，为唐代火祆教定位。此文眼界广阔，从多方位考察，文物文献互证，阐明了唐代火祆教优于摩尼、景教的社会地位。

自1999年虞弘墓、2000年安伽墓、2003年史君墓出土以来，入华粟特人的研究引起中外学界的广泛关注，其中所蕴含的祆教信息尤为引人注目。《西安北周安伽墓葬式的再思考》一文，基本反映了先生对彼等新资料的态度：“如否认其曾被盗扰，按所发现的现状，其葬式显然更与琐罗亚斯德教冲突”，“假如我们仍界定安伽、康业以及本篇提到的史君等北周胡姓人士为中亚祆教徒的话，则其葬式与波斯琐罗亚斯德

[1]《波斯琐罗亚斯德教与中国古代的祆神崇拜》，原刊余太山主编《欧亚学刊》第1辑，北京：中华书局，1999年；收入傅杰编《二十世纪中国文史考据文录》，昆明：云南人民出版社，2001年。

[2]《唐季“大秦穆护祆”考》，参见《中古三夷教辨证》，第284-315页。

[3]《火祆教在唐代中国社会地位之考察》，参见《中古三夷教辨证》，第256-283页。

教无疑是有区别的，决不能划一等号，而移居中土的中亚祆教徒，与本土的祆教徒同样也不能简单划一等号”。[1]

诚如蔡鸿生先生在《中外交流历史文丛·总序》中所言：“精神生产的历史经验教导人们，要与时俱进，继往开来，才无愧于自己的时代。学海无涯，我们应当奋力潜研，敢于浮游的弄潮儿是没有出息的。”此处的潜研，也就是甘心坐冷板凳的精神。先生是一位甘于寂寞、奋力潜研的学者，近年发表的《宋代明教伪托白诗考》[2]、《“宋摩尼教依托道教”考论》[3]、《摩尼教“裸葬”辨》[4]、《佛书所载摩尼僧始通中国史事辨释》[5]、《〈夷坚志〉明教纪事史料价值辨释》[6]诸文旧题新作，正是奋力潜研的结晶。这启发我们，在学术研究上，只有长期坚持不懈，方能在认识上有所深化，甚至突破。

刘知几提倡史家必备“史才、史学、史识”三才，为多数历史工作者所认同。“识”是三才中最高境界。一个历史学家有无“识”见，关键看他是否有历史的思维。中古三夷教不是主流宗教，资料非常有限。先生的多数文章，实际都没有什么稀见材料，但他能够深入思考，竭力从全方位、深层次对文献和史实进行考察，故能有所创新，发表独到见解。三夷教研究属于历史研究中的专史，但先生在研究过程中十分注重专中求通。在具体研究过程中，先生十分注意运用比较宗教学的方法，不仅将三夷教互相参照，与中亚、波斯本教进行比较，更将其与佛教、道教，及至印度教、民间宗教等多种宗教相联系、比对，体现了广阔的学术眼界。由此，专门史终获“通”的关照，避免走上由专入偏的歧途。

---

〔1〕《西安北周安伽墓葬式的再思考》，参见《中古夷教华化丛考》，第269–292页。

〔2〕《宋代明教伪托白诗考》，载于《文史》2010年第4辑（总第93辑），第175–199页。

〔3〕《“宋摩尼教依托道教”考论》，参见张荣芳、戴治国主编：《陈垣与岭南：纪念陈垣先生诞生130周年学术研讨会论文集》，北京：中国社会科学出版社，2011年，第81–107页。

〔4〕《摩尼教“裸葬”辨》，参见刘东主编：《中国学术》第32辑，北京，商务印书馆，第244–264页。

〔5〕林悟殊、张淑琼：《佛书所载摩尼僧始通中国史事辨释》，参见余太山、李锦绣主编：《丝瓷之路：古代中外关系史研究 I》，北京，商务印书馆，2011年，第279–297页。

〔6〕林悟殊、殷小平：《〈夷坚志〉明教纪事史料价值辨释》，载于《中华文史论丛》2012年第2期（总第106期），第255–283页。

这方面，《唐朝三夷教政策论略》[1]、《唐代三夷教的社会走向》[2]可谓代表作。

三夷教是中古时期传入中国的外来宗教，若要对其进行深入认识，必须具备宗教史的知识，对原教旨的宗教及其在中亚、中国的传播有整体的把握；由于其经典（主要是摩尼教、景教）曾被译成各种语言文字，因此要具备历史比较语言学的知识；而涉及对霞浦文书的解读，则需要用传统的历史文献学方法，首先对文本进行考实的工作。当然，三夷教入华史亦是中外文化交流史的重要课题，在探讨相关问题时，亦需谨记陈寅恪先生当年倡导的“译经格义”“文化交流发生变异”等理论。先生对于近年的诸多新发现，尤其是唐代洛阳景教经幢，东南沿海地区的摩尼教遗迹，霞浦民间科仪文书的解读，益证明从华化的角度去考察，乃研究古代外来精神文明在中土传播的不二法门。

〔1〕《唐朝三夷教政策论略》，参见《唐代景教再研究》，第106–119页。

〔2〕《唐代三夷教的社会走向》，参见《中古三夷教辨证》，第346–374页。

1 《注疏集》摩尼教章节译释*

芮传明
（上海社会科学院历史所）

叙利亚语文书《注疏集》（*kᵉṯāḇā deskōlyōn*，Book of Scholia）是公元 8—9 世纪的聂斯脱里教派教士提奥多里·巴库尼（Theodore bar Khoni）撰写的一本书，成于 791—792 年。该书共分 11 讲，总的来说，是以问答形式，谈论基督教的教义，以及综论异端的教义，诸如占星学、希腊信仰和波斯异教信仰等。该书的第十一讲对于伊朗研究来说最为重要，其中涉及与伊朗相关的各个异端教派和宗教，既有基督教的，也有非基督教的；而所有这些段落中，最为重要者则是有关摩尼教的部分。

尽管作者是带着批判"异端"，维护"正统基督教"的观念和口吻行文的，但是显然也因此比较客观地反映了诸"异教"的教义和观念。所以，有关摩尼教的一节，不仅体现了摩尼教神学中的宇宙创生观，还直接引用了摩尼本人的一些话，从而使这段资料更具价值。

对于巴库尼《注疏集》中的这段摩尼教资料，前人作过不少翻译和注释，如早在 19 世纪末波尼翁的法文译本〔1〕、20 世纪初居蒙的法译文〔2〕、20 世纪 20 年代谢德尔的德译文〔3〕，以及 20 世纪 30 年代杰克逊的英文

---

* 本文为复旦大学"985"哲学社会科学创新基地资助课题的研究成果之一；在文史研究院访问期间完成。

〔1〕H. Pognon, Inscriptions mandaïtes des coupes de Khouabir Ⅱ, Paris, 1899.

〔2〕F. Cumont, Recherches sur le manichéisme I: La cosmogonie manichéenne d'après Théodore bar Khôni, Brussels, 1908.

〔3〕H. H. Schaeder, "Iranische Lehren," in R. Reitzenstein and H. H. Schaeder eds., *Studien zum antiken Synkretismus aus Iran und Griechenland*, Leipzig and Berlin, 1926, repr. Darmstadt, 1965, pp. 203ff.

译注和嗣后其他学者的译释[1]。本文主要根据杰克逊的英译本[2]转译，有些注释也多所参考，除了必要的说明之外，下文不再逐一标明。

有关他（指摩尼——译者）的古怪教义

我们有必要在本书中录入一些那不敬神的摩尼的虚伪[3]教义和亵渎神明的言词，以羞辱一下这些摩尼教教徒。因为：

他（指摩尼——译者）说道，有两种原质[4]，一种为善良、另一种为邪恶，它们在苍天和大地及其包含的所有事物创生之前就已存在。善良原质居于光明之界，他（指摩尼）称他为伟大父尊[5]。他们（指摩尼教教徒）说道，在他（指明尊）之傍还居住着他的五

---

〔1〕A. V. W. Jackson, *Researches in Manichaeism*, New York, 1932。此后尚有 A. Adam, *Texte zum Manichäismus*, Berlin, 1954；A. Böhlig with the collaboration of J. P. Asmussen, *Die Gnosis* III: *Der Manichäismus*, Zurich and Munich, 1980；等等。

〔2〕当然，所谓的“杰克逊的英译本”，实际上是由他的助手 Abraham Yohannan 博士从叙利亚文翻译的，并且包括不少注释，从开始到完成，历时5年之久；有关这点，杰克逊已在其著述中指出，见 *Researches*, p.221, note 1。

〔3〕叙利亚语 *bedyā*，原义为伪造的、欺骗的、空虚的、愚蠢的等，经常被基督教用来形容异端的教义。

〔4〕叙利亚语 *k^{e}yānīn*，原义为本性、本质、性质等。在此所言的两种 *k^{e}yānīn* 即是摩尼教汉语文书（如《摩尼光佛教法仪略》）中所谓的“二宗”，也就是光明与黑暗两种原质，英语通常译作 two principles。为尽量体现原文书的措辞，在此的汉译不直接作“二宗”。

〔5〕叙利亚语 *'Abhā d^{e}Rabbūthā* 意为“伟大的父亲”。具有这类含义的称呼经常出现在非汉语的摩尼教文书中，用以指称摩尼教的最高和最原始的神灵；而在摩尼教汉语文书中，则称明父、明尊、明王、明主、明宗祖、明尊父、慈父、大明、大圣等等。

荣耀[1]，即智慧、知识、推理、思维、熟虑[2]。他称邪恶原质为黑暗王[3]；他说道，他（指黑暗王）居住在他的五个世界，即烟界、火界、风界、水界、暗界。[4]

他说道，当黑暗王故意侵入明界时，五荣耀战栗了。他又说道，此时，伟大父尊经过深思熟虑后声称："我不会派遣五荣耀中的任何一位离开我的五界，前去作战，因为他们是我为了安宁与和平而创造出来的；我将亲自前去，进行这场战斗。"

---

〔1〕叙利亚语 *š^ekhīnthā*（复数 *š^ekhīnāthā*）义为居所、帐篷、临时房屋、圣体龛等，也义为荣耀、最高权威等。在叙利亚文的圣经《旧约》中，此词用以指称神圣的荣耀。在涉及摩尼教的各类文书中都谈到过这五种神灵，但是其称呼颇不相同，有五种荣耀、五种居所、五种领域、五种国土、五种品性、五种肢体等各种名号；至于摩尼教汉语文书中，则更有五妙身、五净体、五体、五城、五地等称，分别称呼，则为"相""心""念""思""意"。有关这些名号的辨析和含义，可参看拙文《摩尼教"五妙身"考》（载《史林》2004年第6期）、张广达《唐代汉译摩尼教残卷——心王、相、三常、四处、种子等语词试释》（载〔日〕《东方学报》第77册，2005年3月）、马小鹤《"相心念思意"考》（载《中华文史论丛》2006年第4辑）等。

〔2〕这五种"荣耀"的叙利亚语分别为 *haunā*、*madd^e'ā*、*re'yānā*、*maḥšabhthā*、*tar'īthā*，见于 *Researches*, p.223的英译文分别作 Intelligence、Knowledge、Reason、Thought 和 Deliberation，故译如正文。但是，更早的布尔基特对它们的释义则有所不同，他说道："*Haunā* 意为判断力（sense）或心智健全（sanity），是疯狂（madness）的反义词；……*Mad'ā* 意为辨别人类的推理能力（reason）；……*Re'yānā* 是意为思想（thought）或心智（mind）的最普通的叙利亚词；我将 *Maḥshabthā* 译成想象力（imagination），因为它通常似乎包含了创造新事物之意；……*Tar'ithā* 一般是意图（intention）之意，被视作意愿（will）。"（见 *Manichees*, p.33）。不仅如此，在其他诸多文书和研究著述中，对这五者的排列顺序及具体含义还有许多不同的说法，在此不赘，只是提请读者注意。

〔3〕在摩尼教汉语典籍中，通常将这"黑暗之王"称为"贪魔"或"魔王"；学界则多以"暗魔"称呼之。

〔4〕有关暗魔所居"五界"的名称，各记载有所不同，如阿拉伯语的《群书类述》，分别列为云（clouds）、火焰（flame）、瘟疫风（pestilential wind）、毒（poison）、晦阴（obscurity）（见 Fihrist, p.777）。即使可将"晦阴"视同于"黑暗"，"火焰"视同于"火"，也仍然有"云"与"水"，"毒"与"烟"的较大区别。

他说道，伟大父尊召唤[1]出了生命母[2]；生命母则召唤出了初人[3]；而初人又召唤出了他的五个儿子[4]，犹如一个人穿上了其甲胄去作战。

他还说道，有个名叫纳哈希巴特的天使[5]来到他（指初人）的面前，手中拿着一顶胜利桂冠。他说道，初人在天使面前散发出光明。黑暗王见到这光明后就思考了，并说道："我一直在远方寻觅的事物却在我身边找到了。"于是，初人本身以及他的五个儿子都成为了黑暗五子的食物，恰如一个人把掺有致命毒药的糕饼送给其敌人一样。[6]

他又说道，当他们（即黑暗五子）吞吃了初人的五明子后，五明神的智慧被夺走了。由于黑暗诸子的毒液侵入，五明神变得就像

---

〔1〕叙利亚语 qᵉrā 义为"召唤"（英文通常作 evoke），在摩尼教神学中，此词专门用以指高级神灵创造出次级神灵的行为。与之用法完全相同的另一个专用术语则是"发射"（英文通常作 emanate），例如，科普特语文献《赞美诗》载云："（明尊的）第三次发射（προβολή）形成了第三使，即是第二（伟）大，是为这些世界之王、神界之主、真实主的形貌。还有他的十二少女、他的十二台阶。"（Psalm-Book, 138⁵⁹⁻⁶⁶）。这些被"召唤"或"发射"出来的次级神灵往往都称其创造者为"父"，因此，这样的"召唤"或"发射"就相当于人类通常所谓的"生育""繁殖"等。然而，摩尼教在谈及神灵创造时，却完全避免使用可以令人联想到"性交繁殖"之类的任何词汇。这是摩尼教性观念的特色之一。有关摩尼教的"性观念"，可参看拙文《摩尼教性观念源流考》（载《社会科学》2006年第2期）。

〔2〕叙利亚语'emmā dᵉḥayyē 义为"生命之母"，英文通常作 the Mother of Life；在摩尼教汉语典籍中则称"善母"。

〔3〕叙利亚语'enāšā qadmāyā 义为"最初的人，古老的人"，英文通常译作 the Primal Man 或 the First Man；在摩尼教汉语文书中则称"先意"。

〔4〕在此所谓的初人的"五个儿子"即是在摩尼教神学中占有重要地位的光明五要素，是为五种形态：气（ether，亦称"以太"；此概念在古代的宇宙构成学说中占有重要地位）、风（wind）、光（light）、水（water）、火（fire）。摩尼教汉语文献通常称之为"五明子""五明"等；在许多情况下，这"五明子"等同于被暗魔囚禁在肉体中的"灵魂"，或者亟待拯救的"光明分子"。

〔5〕叙利亚语名 Nḥšbṭ，通常读作 Naḥashbaṭ，但是，杰克逊认为此词的读音是可以再探讨的。他在一个长注中谈及了此词的来源、含义等，见 *Researches*, p.225, note 13。

〔6〕文书在此欲表达的意思当是：初人（先意）以自身及其五子（光明分子）为饵，故意让暗魔吞食。而其他资料则表明，似乎是明界神灵与暗魔交战时失败而被暗魔"吞食"或囚禁的，如《群书类述》称："于是，古魔装备了他的五要素——烟、火焰、晦阴、瘟疫风、云，用它们武装自己，使之作为他的防护。他来与初人接触，他们长时间地交战。古魔制服了初人，吞食了他的光明，用自己的原质和要素围困了光明。"（*the Fihrist*, p.779）。所以，摩尼教的神学在这个方面究竟想表达什么样的观念，还是值得再作详细探讨的。

被疯狗或毒蛇咬过的人一样。[1]

他又说道，当初人恢复理智后，他便起身，向伟大父尊作了七次祈祷。于是，他（即伟大父尊）作了第二次召唤，召唤出光明之友[2]；光明之友则召唤出大建筑师[3]；大建筑师又召唤出生命神[4]。生命神也召唤出他的五个儿子：从他的智慧召唤出辉煌监护者，从其知识召唤出伟大光荣王，从其推理召唤出光明阿达马斯，从其思维召唤出荣耀王，从其熟虑召唤出负载者。[5]

这些神灵来到黑暗之地，发现初人及其五子都被暗魔吞食了。于是，生命神用他的声音呼唤起来，生命神的声音就像一把锋利的剑，揭示了初人的形体，[6] 并且对他说道："祝你和平安宁，身处邪恶中的正直者，身处黑暗中的发光者，居于毫无荣耀之感的狂兽中的神灵。"随即，初人对他作出回应，说道："你为了濒死者的宁静而来！啊，来吧，你是宁静与和平的宝藏！"他（指初人）又问他道："明界中我们的父尊们，光明之子的情况如何？"呼唤

---

〔1〕这里所描绘的，即是人类心智被邪恶思想所控制的象征性表达。类似的描写亦见于摩尼教汉语典籍《摩尼教残经》，并且更为详细："其五明身，既被如是苦切禁缚，废忘本心，如狂如醉。犹如有人以众毒蛇，编之为笼，头皆在内，吐毒纵横；复取一人，倒悬于内，其人尔时为蛇所逼，及以倒悬，心意迷错，无暇思惟父母亲戚及本欢乐。今五明性在肉身中，为魔束缚，昼夜受苦，亦复如是。"（第43–48行）

〔2〕叙利亚语 ḥabbībh nahīrē 的字面意义为"光明的热爱者"，但是英文通常都译作"光明之友"（the Friend of Light）；不过，汉语文书《下部赞》却译作"乐明"，颇符合此名的原义。

〔3〕叙利亚语 bān 义为建筑师，故此神的英译名往往作 Great Builder；但是也常将后一词音译，从而作 Great Bān，以至汉译相应地作"大般"。在汉语文书《下部赞》中，此神作"造相佛"，则基本上为意译名。

〔4〕是为摩尼教的重要神灵之一，英文名通常作 the Living Spirit。汉译本来可作"活灵"，但是，由于用以指称人类灵魂或光明分子的 the Living Soul 亦可汉译作"活灵"，故将前者译作"生命神"。

〔5〕在此，生命神所召唤出的五个儿子的叙利亚语名分别为 *ṣaphath zīwā*、*malkā rabbā dᵉīqārā*、*Ādāmōs nūhrā*、*mᵉlekh šūbhḥā*、*sabbālā*；对应的英译名则分别作 the Custody of Splendor、the Great King of Honor、the Adamas of Light、the King of Glory、the Supporter。文书声称他们是分别从智慧、知识等等创造出来的；而"智慧"等五者正是前文提及的"五荣耀"，也就是汉语文书提到的"五妙身"相、心、念、思、意。但是，前后两种"五荣耀"似乎又有所不同：前一种"五荣耀"早在生命神被创造之前就已存在；而后一种"五荣耀"则显然只属于生命神本身。当然，在此只是顺便指出这一现象，而不欲对该问题进行深入的探讨。

〔6〕在此，生命神利用其声音揭示了初人的形体云云之语，含义不太清晰。但是按杰克逊的理解，似乎是指生命神发声呼唤之后，确定了初人在暗界的位置。见 *Researches*, p.230, note 29a。

者[1]答道："他们的情况很好。"呼唤者和应答者[2]联合起来，登升至生命母和生命神处。[3]然后，生命神穿上了呼唤者，而生命母则穿上了应答者，[4]她所热爱的儿子。于是，他们（即生命母和生命神）下临黑暗之地，即初人及其诸子的所在。[5]

随后，生命神对诸子中的三个儿子下达命令：一个去斩杀暗魔诸子，另两个将众魔剥皮，并把它们交给生命母。[6]生命母则用

〔1〕叙利亚语 *qāryā* 义为呼唤者，在此显然已经成为明界的一位神灵，而他即是因生命神"呼唤"初人而创造出来的。在汉语典籍《摩尼教残经》中，由于其主要范本来自帕提亚语文书，故此神之名译自帕提亚语 Xruštag，称"呼嚧瑟德"，意译名则称"说听"。

〔2〕叙利亚语 *'ānyā* 义为应答者，如同"呼唤者"一样，是因初人回应生命神的话而创造出来的神灵。在汉语典籍《摩尼教残经》中，此神之名译自帕提亚语 Padwāxtag，称"嚧嘍嘞德"，意译名则称"唤应"。

〔3〕对于此语的含义，杰克逊是这样解释的：由于初人陷于黑暗深渊，生命母与生命神只是在渊边向下"呼唤"，初人也只是凭借"应答"与之交流。所以，嗣后是"呼唤""应答"二神"向上登升"才与上方的生命母、生命神二位神灵会合。

〔4〕叙利亚语 *l^ebhaš* 为"穿上（甲胄、衣服等）"之义，但是文书在此所言的是"穿上"呼唤、应答两个神灵，似乎语意不通，故有必要略作解释。盖因摩尼教曾从基督教等古代宗教观念中承袭和发展了"衣服神学"，即是在某些场合用"衣服"来作为最神圣之精神存在的象征符号；就摩尼教而言，则光明原质便可视作"衣服"或"妙衣"。而众所周知，摩尼教的一切善良神灵都是明尊直接或间接创造（"召唤"或"发射"）出来的，他们全都源自同一本质"光明"。因此，利用光明神灵来防护或净化自身，与"穿上光明衣服作为甲胄"之类的意思是没有区别的。于是，摩尼教文书中经常出现"穿上某某神灵"的表达方式，如本文书最初提到初人创造出其五子的情节，在其他文书中则描绘成"初人穿上五子，作为甲胄"之类。这里提到的生命神"穿上"呼唤者，生命母"穿上"应答者，也是同样的意思。有关摩尼教的"衣服神学"，马小鹤曾有专文讨论，可参看其《摩尼教宗教符号"妙衣"研究》一文（载《中华文史论丛》第59辑，1999年）。

〔5〕本文书在这段记述之后就直接谈到诸神创造宇宙之事了，而对于生命神等如何将初人拯救出来之事却只字未提，显然有所遗漏。在此则据见于吐鲁番的突厥语文书 T II D 173 b[1]对此内容略作补充："呼唤神与应答神向上登升，脱离初人所在的暗狱后，急忙前赴生命神和生命母处。二神帮助初人向上登升，脱出暗狱，他们又把他送往神圣的天界。嗣后，生命母和生命神又将五明神（即是与暗质混杂在一起的原光明分子——引者）与初人分离开来，并利用它们创造了大地和苍天。"（原文、拉丁转定和德译文见 *Türk.Man. I*, pp.13–14）

〔6〕按照杰克逊之见，在此所言斩杀诸魔和剥诸魔之皮的三位"生命神之子"，应该是生命神五个儿子中的这样三神：英勇善战的阿达马斯负责斩杀诸魔，荣耀王和光荣王则负责剥诸魔之皮。（见 *Researches*, p.233, note 45）

诸魔之皮铺成了苍天，共计十一层天；[1]他们并将众魔的尸体抛入黑暗之地，他们建造了八层大地。[2]于是，［生命神的］五个儿子便各司其职。辉煌监护者握住了五明神的腰部；在他们的腰部之下散布着诸天。负载者一膝跪下，支撑着诸地。伟大光荣王则在诸天诸地被创造之后，踞坐在苍天的中央，守护着所有的天地。

然后，生命神向黑暗诸子显露了自己的形相；净化了被诸魔吞食的五明神的光明，创造了太阳、月亮和成千上万的光明星辰。[3]

他（指生命神）制造了三轮，即风轮、水轮与火轮；他降临下方，制作了它们，并使之在负载者下方的附近运行。荣耀王召唤出一个覆盖物，置于它们（指三轮）的上方，以使它们可以升至被征服于各层大地的魔众之上，帮助五明神免遭魔众毒液的烧灼。

他（指摩尼）又说道："然后，生命母、初人及生命神站在一起，祈祷和恳求伟大父尊；伟大父尊倾听了他们的祈祷，遂作了第三次召唤，召唤出了使者。[4]

相应地，使者又召唤出了各具礼服、桂冠和品性的十二少女。

---

〔1〕在此，叙利亚文书的原语作 *ḥᵉdh'sar*，则确是义为"十一"。但是，其他的相关文书都称当初创造的是"十天八地"，如阿拉伯语《群书类述》谓"明界之王命令他的天使之一创造了这个世界，用这些混杂的微粒建造了它，以将光明分子从暗质中解救出来。他们就这样建造了十层天和八层地"。（*the Fihrist*, p.781）。又，汉语文书《摩尼教残经》称"净风明使以五类魔及五明身，二力和合，千万世界，十天、八地"。（第11–12行）有鉴于此，叙利亚文书之"十一"当是"十"之讹。

〔2〕对于"抛尸体"和"造大地"行为的主体，文书都使用了"他们"这样的复数形式。杰克逊认为这是指生命神的三个儿子，即是此前斩杀和剥诸魔皮的三位神灵；至少，除了生命神、生命母这样的高级神灵外，还包括这三位次级神灵。（见 *Researches*, pp.234–235, notes 49, 53）此说有理。所以，严格地说，生命母、生命神只是"创造天地"领导者，而非独自创造者。

〔3〕在此，文书声称生命神"显露形相"之后，就紧接着说他"净化"了光明分子，在语意上似有突兀之感。实际上，恐怕确是删略了一段描述。即，犹如下文的描绘那样：第三使向众魔"显露（裸体男女）形相"，诱发雌雄诸魔泄出包含光明分子的精子或胎儿，从而将光明分子与罪孽分离出来云云。那么，生命神用以制造日月星辰的光明分子，显然也是通过裸露自己的形相，诱发众魔的性欲，泄出包含光明分子的精液、胎儿，再加以"净化"而获得的。叙利亚语文书的作者之所以在此有所删略，或许是为了避免与下文的描述重复，或许是不愿意过分直白地谈及"色诱"情节。

〔4〕在此所言的"使者"，由于是明尊第三次召唤所创造的一位高级神灵，故通常又称"第三使"（the Third Messenger），其特性与古波斯的太阳密特拉（Mithra）很接近。在汉语文书中，则称"三丈夫""三明使"等（见《下部赞》第126、141行等）。

第一品性是王权；第二品性是智慧；第三是胜利；第四是顺从；第五是纯洁；第六是真理；第七是信仰；第八是忍耐；第九是正直；第十是仁慈；第十一是公正；第十二是光明。〔1〕

使者来到这些舟船〔2〕后，他命令三位随从驱使这舟船运行〔3〕。他并命令大建筑师建造新地，以及用以登升舟船的三轮。当舟船向上，抵达苍天的中央后，使者便显现了男身和女身的形相，让一切

〔1〕文书在此所言的十二种良好品性是与第三使创造的“十二少女”联系在一起的；但是在经过演变和发展的摩尼教东方文书中，这十二种良好品性便与更高级的“十二大王”联系在一起了，如《下部赞》载云：“一者无上光明王，二者智惠善母佛，三者常胜先意佛，四者欢喜五明佛，五者勤修乐明佛，六者真实造相佛，七者信心净风佛，八者忍辱日光佛，九者直意卢舍那，十者知恩夷数佛，十一者齐心电光佛，十二者庄严惠明佛。”（第169-171行）。有关摩尼教推崇的十二种品德与十二种神灵之关系的探讨，可参看马小鹤《摩尼教“十二大王”和“三大光明日”考》（载《西域历史语言研究集刊》第1辑，科学出版社，2007年12月）。

〔2〕叙利亚语*'elpē*义为舟船，在摩尼教文书中，多为日、月的象征符号。但是，摩尼教东、西方文书对于日月的象征符号略有不同，即，西方文书多称为“船”，而东方文书则多称为“车”或“宫（殿）”。例如，拉丁文的《阿基来行传》谓耶稣、生命母、明女等神灵居于“小船（指月亮）”中，生命神等居于“大船（指太阳）”中（见*Acta*, 13.2, p.57）。科普特语《赞美诗》称：“我发现了航船，这航船即是太阳和月亮，它们运渡我，直抵我的城池。”（见*Psalm-Book*, 168$^{5-8}$）中古波斯语文书《沙卜拉干》称“然后，密特拉神（Mihryazd，指生命神——引者）将从太阳车上下来，走向宇宙”。突厥语《忏悔词》称：“第二，是对于日月神，是对居于二光明宫中的神灵所犯的罪过。”（见*X^{u}āstvānīft*, p. 194）。汉语文书《下部赞》称：“又启日月光明宫，三世诸佛安置处，七及十二大船主，并余一切光明众。”（第127行）。诸如此类。有关摩尼教“舟船”象征符号的详细讨论，可参看拙文《摩尼教文献所见“船”与“船主”考释》（载《欧亚学刊》第1辑，1999年12月）。

〔3〕在此所称驱使日月运行的“三位随从”（叙利亚语*t^{e}lāthā ʿabhdīn*）究竟是何等神灵，是可以探讨的。从文义看，这三者似乎是第三使的“随从”。然而，似乎未见其他文书提到过第三使的“随从”。故杰克逊认为，这三名“随从”当是生命神的三个儿子，因为同一叙利亚文书在谈及生命神创造天地时，曾提到他命令其五个儿子中的三个儿子（阿达马斯、荣耀王和光荣王）去宰杀诸魔，用其尸体建造天地。他们的事迹颇为突出，故可能在此被移植到第三使名下，作为三名“随从”，来推动天体的初始运转（见*Researches*, p.233, note 45和p.242, note86）。

但是，若谓这三位“随从”是生命神的三个儿子，那么，派遣他们的主神很可能并非第三使，而当是其父生命神，因为生命神偕其五子与第三使分属大明尊第二次和第三次“召唤”出的两批不同神灵。另一方面，在摩尼教的帕提亚语和中古波斯语文书中，myhr（常为太阳之称）一词有时指称生命神，有时亦指称第三使，所以在某些情况下，亦不无可能混淆了二者。

另外还有一种可能是：这“三位随从”恐怕也非生命神之子，而是在大明尊第三次“召唤”中诞生的另外三位次级神灵，即是由第三使本身“召唤”出的光耀柱（Pillar of Glory，汉语文书称相柱）、耶稣（Jesus，汉语文书称夷数）和光明少女（Virgin of Light，汉语文书称电光佛）。这三位神灵与第三使的关系，恰如五子与生命神的关系，故若言他（她）们奉第三使之命去办某事，较诸生命神之子奉第三使之命办事更加合乎情理。有关论述，可参看拙文《摩尼教“宇宙创生论”探讨——以M 98、M 99和M 178 II文书为中心》（载《丝瓷之路》第二辑，商务印书馆，2012年9月）。

暗魔，无论雌雄，都看见此身。一切诸魔见到使者俊美的身形后都充满了欲望，雄魔因女身之神而起欲念，雌魔因男身之神而起欲念，于是他们全都将此前吞食的五明神的光明射泄出来。幽闭在他们体内的罪孽犹如毛发混合在面团中一样，随着光明而泄出诸魔体外。他们欲图再次进入光明，但是使者隐蔽了其形相，并将五明神的光明与诸魔的罪孽分离开来。来自诸魔的罪孽归还诸魔，但是他们拒绝接纳，犹如一个人厌恶自己的呕吐物一样。

于是，罪孽降落大地，一半落入湿处，一半落入干地。落入湿处者变成了恐怖的怪物，其状宛如暗魔之王；光明的阿达马斯被派去对付她。[1]他与她格斗，打败了她，把她掀翻得仰面朝天，用其长矛刺进她的心脏，用其护盾按在她的嘴上，用其一足踩在她的大腿上，另一足踏在她的胸膛上。而落在干地的罪孽则长成了五类树木。[2]

他（指摩尼）又说道：黑暗的这些女儿们此前都怀了孕，但是见到使者的美妙形相后，她们的胎儿都堕落了，落到地上，吞食了树木的嫩芽。这些堕胎物一起思考，回忆起他们曾经见过的使者的形貌，他们说道："我们所见的形貌如今在哪里？"黑暗王之子阿沙克龙[3]对堕胎物说道："把你的子女们给我，我将为你们创造

---

〔1〕在摩尼教文书中，凡是象征罪孽的魔怪往往都用阴性名词表示，甚至邪恶的阴性角色往往是暗界方面的最高掌控者。例如，帕提亚语文书 M 183 I 载云："……还有……阿赫尔曼（Ahrmēn，借用自琐罗亚斯德教，为善神 Ormazd 的主要对手）以及诸魔在五洞穴（即暗界的五个部分）展开了战斗，一个洞穴深于一个洞穴。阿缁（Āz，义为贪欲），即诸魔之母，一切罪孽从她而出。她来自五洞穴，那里拥有五毒泉以及咸、酸、辛、甜、苦五味……拥有五……"（见 *Literature*, p.119）

〔2〕这里所言的"五类树木"当即汉语文书《摩尼教残经》描述的"五毒死树"，用以禁锢光明分子，系由暗魔所造："魔见是已，起贪毒心，以五明性，禁于肉身，为小世界。亦以十三无明暗力，囚固束缚，不令自在。其彼贪魔，以清净气，禁于骨城，安置暗相，栽莳死树；又以妙风，禁于筋城，安置暗心，栽莳死树；又以明力，禁于脉城，安置暗念，栽莳死树；又以妙水，禁于肉城，安置暗思，栽莳死树；又以妙火，禁于皮城，安置暗意，栽莳死树。贪魔以此五毒死树，栽于五种破坏地中，每令惑乱光明本性，抽彼客性，变成毒果。是暗相树者，生于骨城，其菓是怨；是暗心树者，生于筋城，其果是嗔；其暗念树者，生于脉城，其果是淫；其暗思树者，生于肉城，其果是忿；其暗意树者，生于皮城，其果是痴。如是五种骨、筋、脉、肉、皮等，以为牢狱，禁五分身。"（第29–40行）

〔3〕此即叙利亚语 Ašaqlūn 的汉译名。按摩尼教神学，是为诞育最初人类亚当、夏娃之雄魔的名号。希腊语和拉丁语作 Saklas；中古波斯语则称 *āsrēštār*（上文汉译作阿斯雷什塔）。

你们见过的那形貌。”于是，他们将其子、女交给了他。然而，他只吞食了雄性者，而将雌性者给其配偶纳姆里尔。[1]随后，纳姆里尔和阿沙克龙一起交合，她因而怀孕，遂生下一个儿子，起名为亚当。她又怀孕，生下一个女儿，起名夏娃。

他（指摩尼）又说道：光辉者耶稣走近清白者亚当，把他从死亡睡眠中唤醒，以使他可以摆脱那两个凶灵。正如一个正直之人发现有人被恶魔所困时，他就会用其法术使之缓解一样，这位深受爱戴者（指耶稣）发现他沉睡时，就把他唤醒，抓住他，摇晃他；他把诱惑他的暗魔从他身边驱走，使他脱离了厉害雌魔的束缚。然后，亚当审视了自己，认清了自己的真相。他（指耶稣）向他展示了高空中的诸位父尊，以及他自己是如何落入虎豹的利牙中，落入猛象的口中，以及如何被贪婪的嗜食怪兽所吞食，被群狗所吃，以及被混杂和禁锢在一切物质之中，被束缚在黑暗的污秽之中。

他（指摩尼）又说道：他（指耶稣）将他（指亚当）提升，让他品尝生命之树。此后，亚当观望，并且悲泣起来。他用力提高嗓门，犹如狮子吼叫一般；他解开胸口的衣襟，捶打着自己的胸脯，说道：“唉，唉，该死的，我肉体的制造者，我灵魂的束缚者，还有那奴役我的背叛者！”[2]

如本文开首所言，在此译释的，是有关摩尼教神学的一份重要资料；并且，撰写的时间较早（公元8世纪末），所以具有很高的参考价值。但是，它毕竟不是摩尼教本身的专门典籍，而只是《注疏集》的十余讲之一，是作为“批判资料”而转述的。这样的“转述式”记载，尽管比较客观，却仍然难免或多或少的失真；这或许是本文书的一个不足之处。

另一方面，本文书对于摩尼教情况的介绍实际上并不全面，至少与稍晚撰成（公元10世纪下半叶）的，同样为“转述式”记载的阿拉伯

[1] 叙利亚语 Namrāēl 即是诞育最初人类亚当、夏娃之雌魔的名号，但按教父著述，似乎更宜称 Nebrōēl。在帕提亚语和粟特语文书中，此魔则称 Pēsūs。

[2] 提奥多里·巴库尼有关摩尼的说教，录引到这里便突然截止了。但从其他文书可以得知，这份叙利亚文书只是选择性地转述了摩尼教的若干神学。

语典籍《群书类述》（*The Fihrist of al-Nadim*）第9章相比，缺少了许多方面的内容。例如，后者曾谈到摩尼的出生、其父亲和母亲的情况、摩尼的创教经过、暗魔的形貌等细节和明尊的数次召唤、宇宙的创生、人类的创造、耶稣的拯救、暗狱的情况、摩尼教的戒律、摩尼之死亡、摩尼的著述，以及摩尼之后的诸多摩尼教领袖等。所以，严格地说，本文书只是主要集中于摩尼教的"宇宙创生"神学，作了一定的描绘。当然，它依然具有重要的资料价值。

略语表

Acta　Hegenonius, *The Acta Archelai*, tr. by Mark Vermes, com. by Samuel N.C.Lieu, Manichaean Studies IV, Lovanii, 2001.

Fihrist　Bayard Dodge, *The Fihrist of al-Nadīm——A Tenth-Century Survey of Muslim Culture*, Volume 1, Chapter IX, Section I, "Manichaeans", Columbia University Press, 1970.

Literature and Art　Manfred Heuser & Hans-Joachim Klimkeit, *Studies in Manichaean Literature and Art*, Leiden, E.J.Brill, 1998.

Manichees　F. C. Burkitt, *The Religion of the Manichees*, London, Cambridge University Press, 1925.

Psalm-Book　C. R. C. Allberry, *A Manichaean Psalm-Book (Part II)*, Stuttgart, 1938.

Researches　A. V. Williams Jackson, *Researches in Manichaeism with Special Reference to the Turfan Fragments*, New York Columbia University Press, 1932.

Türk. Man.,　A. von Le Coq, *Türkische Manichaica aus Chotscho* (I, II, III), APAW, 1911, Nr.6; 1919, Nr.3; 1922, Nr.2.

X^{u}āstvānīft　Jes P. Asmussen, *X^{u}āstvānīft, Studies in Manichaeism*, Copenhagen, Prostant apud Munksgaard, 1965.

2 “吃菜事魔”名实再探*

杨富学 史亚军
（敦煌研究院民族宗教文化研究所；
西北民族大学历史文化学院）

2.1 “吃菜事魔”诸说评议

《宋会要》记：“宣和三年（1121 年）闰五月七日，尚书省言契勘江浙吃菜事魔之徒，习以成风。”[1]庄绰《鸡肋篇》载：“事魔食菜，法禁甚严。”[2]王质《论镇盗疏》言：“是则食菜事魔，盖生于愚民求福之无厌也。”[3]这里的“吃菜事魔”“事魔食菜”或“食菜事魔”是宋代史籍中出现的一个专有名词。由于这一术语与摩尼教及宋以来农民起义关系密切，故深受学界重视。20 世纪初，研究摩尼教的前贤普遍指认“吃菜事魔”是摩尼教的异名，并将有关“吃菜事魔”的史料都归为摩尼教史料加以运用。[4]后来，随着研究的深入，有学者们属意谨慎处理两者关系，不再等同视之，认为“吃菜事魔”所指的不仅

* 基金项目：国家社科基金项目“回鹘摩尼教研究”（07BZS003）、西北民族大学研究生科研创新项目“从新发现摩尼教文献看摩尼教与宋元农民起义之关系”（ycx13140）。

〔1〕〔清〕徐松辑《宋会要辑稿》刑法二之八一。

〔2〕〔南宋〕庄绰《鸡肋篇》卷上，北京：中华书局，1983年，第11页。

〔3〕〔南宋〕王质《论镇盗疏》，载于《雪山集》卷3，上海：商务印书馆，1935年，第26页。

〔4〕王国维：《摩尼教流行中国考》（《亚洲学术杂志》第11期，1921年）始将有关“吃菜事魔”材料看作摩尼教史料。遵其说者有吴晗《明教与大明帝国》，载于《清华学报》第13卷，1941年，第49–85页；方庆瑛《白莲教的源流及其和摩尼教的关系》，载于《历史教学问题》1959年第5期，第34–38页；星月《宋代明教与农民起义》，载于《历史教学》1959年第6期，第39–42页，等。

仅是摩尼教，也被用来指一切邪教异端。[1]尤有进者，更认为“吃菜事魔”与摩尼教无关。[2]总而言之，学界对“吃菜事魔”的观点有三：一者指为摩尼教；二者认为指包括摩尼教在内的所有异端团体的总称；第三种意见认为与摩尼教无涉，而是当时佛教异端团体的总称。

其中最后一种观点是王见川先生所倡导的，认为“吃菜事魔”的原意并不是官方对信奉摩尼教者的恶谥，而可能是指包括二襘子、金刚禅等在内的佛教异端团体。[3]此观点虽有新意，但由于论述时缺乏对这一概念出现时代的关照，难以成立。因为，官方提出查禁“吃菜事魔”是北宋宣和三年的事，而二襘子、金刚禅等名称直到南宋才出现，焉有一开始提出便包括后出现者的道理？况且王先生在否认两者关联的同时，又说明教被冠上“吃菜事魔”称号是不足为奇的，也显得比较矛盾，所以这个论点是站不住脚的。但反过来说，如果又像第一种观点那样不加分辨便将两者完全等同，也是不能成立的。

第二种观点，较为折中谨慎，有一定道理，但难称得的之见。作为该观点的倡导者，竺沙雅章先生通过对“吃菜事魔”史料的梳理，并结合当时政府的统治，认为宋代的“吃菜事魔”随着时间的推移而有不同的意义[4]，这个看法颇得鹄的。遗憾的是，在“吃菜事魔”出现的源头上，竺沙先生并未多作有益之探讨。林悟殊先生最新的观点认为“‘吃菜事魔’应是官方对带有宗教色彩的民间结社群体的统称，其中当然亦

〔1〕如陈垣：《摩尼教入中国考》，载于《国学季刊》第1卷第2号，1923年，第203–239页；竺沙雅章：《吃菜事魔について》，载于《青山博士古稀纪念宋代史论丛》，东京：创文社，1974年，第239–262页；陈高华：《摩尼教与吃菜事魔——从王质〈论镇盗疏〉说起》，载于《中国农民战争史论丛》第4辑，郑州：河南人民出版社，1982年，第97–106页；林悟殊：《吃菜事魔与摩尼教》，载于《文史》第26辑，北京：中华书局，1985年，第149–155页（收入氏著《摩尼教及其东渐》，北京：中华书局，1987年，第135–144页）。

〔2〕说见王见川：《从摩尼教到明教》，台北：新文丰出版公司，1992年，第233–258页。

〔3〕王见川：《从摩尼教到明教》，第250–258页。

〔4〕竺沙雅章：《吃菜事魔について》，载于《青山博士古稀纪念宋代史论丛》，东京：创文社，1974年，第279页（收入氏著《中国佛教社会史研究》，京都：同朋舍，1982年，第211页。汉译文载《日本学者研究中国史论著选译》，北京：中华书局，1993年，第381页）。

包括摩尼教群体，现在学界对此的看法已渐趋一致”。[1]持该观点的学者们大都认为“魔”字是当时对摩尼教之“摩”的恶称而加以抹黑，“吃菜事魔”包括摩尼教而不等同。在对待史料方面，学者们谨慎的态度是可取的，但对于“吃菜事魔”一词本身所做的解释则显得有些苍白。诚然，历史上出现的“吃菜事魔”并不一定都是指摩尼教而言，对两者关系的看法也在趋向一致。但“吃菜事魔”作为官方的称呼，其出现的历史背景是什么？又何以用“菜”和“魔”二字称？这两个字在当时是否又特定所指？针对这些问题，我们拟在前贤研究的基础上，结合近期不断发现于福建各地及日本的摩尼教新资料，给出自己的解答，冀以对“吃菜事魔”一称循名而责实。

2.2 “吃菜事魔”究为何指？

林悟殊先生言，“吃菜事魔”之“魔”字是一个贬义词，中国的宗教徒，尤其摩尼教徒是不会自称为“魔”的。[2] 此诚不易之论。是故，“吃菜事魔”是他称，而非教徒的自称，当无疑义。上文已提到，在对“魔”字的理解上，学界意见大体一致，即“魔”是对摩尼教的恶称。《佛祖统纪》述及拂多诞持《二宗经》来朝之事，曰“此魔教邪法，愚民易于渐染”。[3]《释门正统·斥伪志》云：“此所谓事魔妖教者也”；“今之魔党，仍会昌配流之后，故不名火祆；仍贞明诛斩之余，故不称末尼，其教法则犹尔也”。[4]此之“魔”显然是指摩尼教而言。所以吴晗先生有“其教又为历来政府及佛徒所深嫉，佛徒每斥异己者为魔，易摩为魔，斥为魔王，为魔教”之论。[5]林悟殊先生亦云：中国佛教

---

〔1〕林悟殊：《摩尼教华名辨异》，载于《九州学林》第5卷1期，2007年春季号，第180–243页（收入氏著《中古夷教华化丛考》，兰州：兰州大学出版社，2011年，第70页）。

〔2〕林悟殊：《吃菜事魔与摩尼教》，载于《文史》第26辑，北京：中华书局，1985年，第149页（收入氏著《摩尼教及其东渐》，第136页）。

〔3〕〔南宋〕志磐《佛祖统纪》卷39，《大正藏》卷49《史传部》，No. 2035，页370a。

〔4〕〔南宋〕宗鉴《释门正统》卷4，《续藏经》卷75《史传部》，No. 1513，页314c。

〔5〕吴晗：《明教与大明帝国》，载于《清华学报》第13卷，1941年，第57页（氏著《读史札记》，北京：三联书店，1956年，第243页）。

徒以“魔”字妖化摩尼教，其手法与西方基督徒对摩尼教的丑化，可谓异曲同工。[1] 另外，在南宋士人眼里，“魔教”亦是对明教的称谓。如陆游对赴明教会的士人宗子诘问“此魔也，奈何与之游？”[2] 朱熹的私淑门人真德秀（1178—1235 年）于嘉定十四年（1221 年）再任泉州知府时发布的《再守泉州劝农文》力劝泉民“后生子弟，各为善人，各守本业……莫习魔教，莫信邪师”。[3] 这里的“魔教”，显然是对明教的恶称。

但对于“吃菜”一词，前贤多不认为是对摩尼教的专指，言其应概指许多宗教。[4] 芮传明先生通过对佛教与摩尼教在根本教义上的探微及分析，指出：“自唐宋以降（尤其是南宋时期），盛行于中国各地的以‘吃菜’为号的大众信仰的主要观念，很可能来自中亚的摩尼教。”[5] 这提醒我们对摩尼教徒自称“吃菜”还有再行探讨的必要。

近期，一幅藏于日本大和文华馆的绢画引起了学术界的关注。该绢画内容分作五层，着色，2007 年日本泉武夫教授首次揭櫫其内容，泉武夫教授虽疑其可能为摩尼教画像，却未下断语。[6] 后经美国学者古乐慈（Z. Gulácsi）教授和日本学者吉田丰先生考定，指认其宗教属性应

〔1〕林悟殊：《吃菜事魔与摩尼教》，载于《文史》第26辑，北京：中华书局，1985年，第149页（收入氏著《摩尼教及其东渐》，第138页）。

〔2〕〔南宋〕陆游《老学庵笔记》卷10，北京：中华书局，1979年，第125页。

〔3〕〔南宋〕真德秀《西山文集》卷40（《景印文渊阁四库全书》第1174册），台北：台湾商务印书馆，1986年，第634页。又见《乾隆泉州府志》卷20《风俗》（《中国地方志集成·福建府县志辑》22），上海：上海书店出版社，2000年，第496页。

〔4〕说见林悟殊：《吃菜事魔与摩尼教》，载于《文史》第26辑，北京：中华书局，1985年，第150页（收入氏著《摩尼教及其东渐》，第136页）。

〔5〕芮传明：《论古代中国的“吃菜”信仰》，载于《中华文史论丛》2000年第3辑（总第63辑），第15页。

〔6〕泉武夫：《景教圣像の可能性——栖云寺藏传虚空藏画像について》，载于《国华》第1330号（第112编第1册），2007年，第7-17页。

为摩尼教，只不过古乐慈认为该画的创作年代可能在13世纪上半期，[1]而吉田丰则将其推定在南宋期间（大约在1127—1129年之间）。[2]笔者将此绢画的照片示诸福建霞浦县上万村村民，识者指其应为上万村祖传圣物之一。绢画全帙应为12幅（一说8幅），惜在抗战时尽皆流失。现存绢画第二层的大像为摩尼光佛，两侧所坐，右边身白衣者为明教教主身份的林瞪，左边身红衣者为宰相身份的林瞪。[3]这里需申明的是该摩尼教绢画第四层祥云下方的5行题字，书于形似风幡的白色方框内，模糊不清吉田丰氏释读为："东乡茂头保弟子张思义/偕郑氏辛娘喜舍/冥王圣［帧］恭入/宝山菜院永充供养祈保/平安愿（圣？王？）□□（安？）日。"[4]尤其是文末之字最为模糊，经笔者详加辨认，应读作"愿重生卯年二月"。如是，对于该题记，我们可做如下断句：

东乡茂头保弟子张思义，偕郑氏辛娘，喜舍冥王圣［帧］，恭入宝山菜院，永充供养，祈保平安，愿重生。卯年二月。

是证张思义与郑辛娘曾将"冥王圣帧"恭敬置入"宝山菜院"供养，以求平安，并获得重生。"冥王"职司地狱，内容正相契合。将该绢画属

〔1〕Z. Gulácsi, "A Visual Sermon on Mani's Teaching of Salvation: A Contextualized Reading of a Chinese Manichaean Silk Painting in the Collection of the Yamato Bunkakan in Nara, Japan",《内陆アジア言语の研究》第23号，中央ユーラシア学研究会，2008年，p. 2, n. 6; ibid, "A Manichaean '*Portrait of the Buddha Jesus*'(*Yishu Fo Zheng*). Identifying a 13th–century Chinese Painting from the Collection of Seiun–ji Zen Temple, near Kofu, Japan", *Artibus Asiae* 69/1, 2009, 2009, p. 102（〔美〕古乐慈著，王媛媛译《一幅宋代摩尼教〈夷数佛帧〉》，载于《艺术史研究》第10辑，广州：中山大学出版社，2008年，第148页）。

〔2〕Y. Yoshida, "A Newly Recognized Manichaean Painting: Manichaean Daēn Japan", Mohammad A. Amir – Moezzi, J. – D. Dubois, Ch. Jullien – F. Jullien (eds.), *Pensée Grecque et Sagessed'Orient Hommage à Michel Tardieu*, Brepols, 2010, pp. 694–714; 吉田丰《マニの降诞图について》附录，《大和文华》第124号，2012年，第8页。

〔3〕杨富学：《林瞪及其在中国摩尼教史上的地位》，载于《中国史研究》2014年第1期，第119–120页。

〔4〕吉田丰：《マニの降诞图について》附录，载于《大和文华》第124号，2012年，第8页。这是吉田丰先生的最新录文，此文英文版"A Newly Recognized Manichaean Painting: Manichaean Daēn Japan"(Mohammad A. Amir – Moezzi, J. – D. Dubois, Ch. Jullien – F. Jullien(eds.), *Pensée Grecque et Sagessed'Orient Hommage à Michel Tardieu*, Brepols, 2010, p. 704.)一文中有较早的版本，录文为："东乡茂头保弟子张思义/偕郑氏辛娘喜舍/冥王圣（图）（恭）入/宝（山菜）院永充供养祈（保）/平安（愿）□□□存。"

性既为摩尼教，则题记中的“弟子”张思义自为摩尼教徒无疑。泉武夫教授在首次提到该画时，称其为白莲宗所有，于是，“菜院”就用于指代白莲教了。[1]王媛媛通过对历史上白莲教徒聚众之所命名的梳理与分析，正确地指出白莲教聚众之处多以“××堂”命名，而不是“菜(茶)院”。[2]但此处的“宝山菜院”究为何指呢？既然这里是明教徒祈福之所，则“菜院”自为摩尼教寺院（至少为摩尼教斋堂）无疑。那么，历史上摩尼教徒曾否将自己的寺院（斋堂）称作“菜院（堂）”呢？答案是肯定的，在近期福建晋江发现的民间族谱资料中，就有摩尼教徒将自建摩尼教（族谱中称为“苏邻法”）斋堂称为“菜堂”的例证。嘉靖年间续修之《青阳庄氏族谱》（以下简称《庄氏族谱》）抄本中有庄惠龙“晚年厌观世谛，托以苏邻法，构萨坛以为娱宾优游之所”和“天德，惠龙三子，从空，葬菜堂地基”之语。[3] 该族谱之集外篇还收录有元至正年间晋江县主簿欧阳贤记所撰《庄惠龙墓志铭》，其中亦言庄氏“晚年厌观世谛，托以苏邻法，构摩萨坛于其里之右，往来优游，自适己志而已”，而且志中有“天德为晛达”之语，颇令人关注。可知庄惠龙晚年信仰的就是明教，并建有明教活动场所摩萨坛。庄惠龙第三子天德被称作“晛达”，即明教神职人员，死后葬于自家所建“菜堂地基”处。[4]近期，庄氏后人庄汉城先生言，青阳庄氏先祖曾建有两处“菜堂”：一处是惠龙“有菜堂地基一所”；还有一处是庄氏四世祖谦架造的“塔上堡斋堂”。另据庄氏族人回忆，该家族还有“石鼓山菜堂”一所，隘门头村道入口不远处原也有“菜堂”一所，只是这两处现已无存。这些“菜堂”都是庄氏先祖开辟的明教活动场所，同时对在“菜堂”中或家中的信徒也称为“菜姑”。[5]这些都足以说明至迟于南宋时期，“菜

[1] 泉武夫：《景教圣像の可能性——栖云寺藏传虚空藏画像について》，第8页。

[2] 王媛媛：《再论日本大和文华馆藏摩尼教绢画》，载于《唐研究》第18卷，北京：北京大学出版社，2012年，第388–390页。

[3] 李玉昆：《20世纪福建摩尼教的新发现及其研究》，载于《福建宗教》1999年第1期，第37页。

[4] 粘良图：《晋江草庵研究》，厦门：厦门大学出版社，2008年，第49–50页。

[5] 庄汉城：《青阳庄氏先祖明教活动寻踪》，见粘良图《晋江草庵研究》，厦门：厦门大学出版社，2008年，第60–62页。

堂（院）”“菜姑”就作为对明教斋堂和明教徒的称谓，而非他指。这也使我们对宋代史籍中的“食菜”一词有了明确的认识。洪适言：

先君登政和五年进士第，主台州宁海簿……方腊反，台之仙居民应之，踪捕反党及旁县。一日驱菜食者数百人至县，丞尉皆曰可杀，先君争不得，丞尉用赏秩。不逾年，相继死，皆见所杀为历云。[1]

“菜食者”显指摩尼教徒，殆无疑义。洪适所谓“方腊反，台之仙居民应之”，而后“驱菜食者数百人至县”之载，说明“菜食者”是累于方腊起义而被下狱并遇害的。此事发生于方腊起义之后，宣和三年臣僚请求颁布禁“吃菜事魔”条法之前，而在这期间（宣和二年十一月四日）便出现了臣僚言温州明教徒之情况：

宣和二年（1120年）十一月四日，臣僚言：一温州等处狂悖之人，自称明教，号为行者。今来明教行者各于所居乡村建立屋宇，号为斋堂，如温州共有四十余处，并是私建无名额佛堂……

奉御笔：仰所在官司根究指实，将斋堂等一切毁拆。所犯为首之人依条施行外，严立赏格，许认陈告。今后更有似此去处，州县官并行停废，以违御笔论，廉访使者失觉察，监司按劾与同罪。[2]

该疏很显然是官员对明教的一份调查报告，其背景抑或与上述洪适所言事件有关，尤其是“菜食者”参与的方腊起义。报告内容非常全面，由是以观，当时明教徒的活动应该是公开且场面很大的，[3] 如若不然，如此翔实之报告书就成了无源之水。翌年，又出现了臣僚请求禁止“吃菜事魔”法令的条状：

宣和三年闰五月七日，尚书省言契勘江浙吃菜事魔之徒，习以成风。自来虽有禁止传习妖教刑赏，既无止绝吃菜事魔之文。

〔1〕〔宋〕洪适《盘洲文集》卷74《先君述》(《景印文渊阁四库全书》第1158册)，台北：台湾商务印书馆，1986年，第742页。

〔2〕〔清〕徐松辑《宋会要辑稿》刑法二之七八—七九。

〔3〕这也可从考古发现的“明教会”碗反映出来，参见庄为玑《泉州摩尼教初探》，载于《世界宗教研究》1983年第3期，第80页；黄世春《福建晋江草庵发现“明教会”黑釉碗》，载于《海交史研究》1985年第1期，第73页。

即州县监司不为禁止，民间无有告捕，遂致吃菜事魔之人聚众山谷，一日窃发，倍费经画。若不重立禁约，即难以止绝，乞修立条。从之。[1]

在报告后便有乞禁“吃菜事魔”之请和禁“吃菜事魔”条法的颁布。林悟殊先生认为《摩尼光佛教法仪略》当写成于唐玄宗颁诏禁摩尼教之前，旨在令在华摩尼教师向其书面说明该教的整体情况。[2] 唐代先有摩尼教徒上呈《摩尼光佛教法仪略》，而后有法禁事，宋代在禁明教前也有官员的调查报告。两者之原委何其似也！

该疏所谓“吃菜事魔”在史料中首见，其中言当时虽有禁止传习妖教的刑赏条文，但由于没有“吃菜事魔”之禁令，致使其活动官不究、民不举，致使其愈演愈烈。仔细玩味其文，深层原因应是“吃菜事魔”的活动在此之前是被允许的，与“妖教”并非一码事，但其活动对社会安定确有危害，亟待严禁。条文言“吃菜事魔”之徒活动于江浙地带，而此前的方腊起义及对明教会的调查恰好也集中于同一区域，当非巧合，而是确有所指。联系前文所述“菜”“魔”都是指明教的，可见此时的“吃菜事魔”完全是官方出于对明教的摘发而对其的恶称。由于这个上疏，官方也于宣和三年八月二十五日颁布了禁“事魔”之条法：

[宣和三年]八月二十五日，诏：诸路事魔、聚众、烧香等人所习经文，今尚书省取索名件，严立法禁行，下诸处焚毁。令刑部遍下诸路州军，多出文榜于州县城郭、乡村要会处，分明晓谕，应有逐件经文等，限令来指挥到一季内，于所在州县首纳。除《二宗经》外并焚毁，限满不首杖一百，本条私有罪重者自从重。仍仰州县严切觉察施行，及仰刑部、大理寺，今后诸处申奏案内如有非道释藏内所有经文等，除已追取到声说下本处焚毁外，仍具名件，下诸路照会出榜，谕人户依今来日限约束，首纳焚毁施行。[3]

---

〔1〕〔清〕徐松辑《宋会要辑稿》刑法二之八一。

〔2〕林悟殊：《敦煌本〈摩尼光佛教法仪略〉的产生》，载于《世界宗教研究》1983年第3期，第76页（收入氏著《摩尼教及其东渐》，第175页）。

〔3〕〔清〕徐松辑《宋会要辑稿》刑法二之八三。

条文“除《二宗经》外并焚毁”一句，说明《二宗经》就是“吃菜事魔”之徒所习的经文，更说明此时遭官方查禁的“吃菜事魔”非明教莫属。不过由于某种原因，《二宗经》被排除在禁毁经典之外。同样的条文也见于《释门正统·斥伪志》：“唯祖宗法令，诸以《二宗经》及非藏经所载不根经文传习惑众者有罪。”此处又说《二宗经》是不根经文，与前说悖。王见川先生认为官府诏文中的《二宗经》与《释门正统》中的《二宗经》只是同名而已，实非一经，前者确属明教，而后者则是事魔教的不根经文。[1] 如是处理缺乏依据，显得有点儿轻率。缘《释门正统》是南宋僧人宗鉴编订成书的，其文中言“祖宗法令”，应是上述宣和年间的法令，[2] 之所以说《二宗经》是不根经文，很可能是出于佛教徒对明教的嫉恨与抹黑（不排除宗鉴时《二宗经》已不见于《道藏》之可能）。官府之所以未将《二宗经》列入禁毁之列，概因为《二宗经》确为《道藏》所收典籍之一，而且还是经真宗、徽宗二帝御批入藏的。是故，不能仅凭此条法令未禁《二宗经》而断言“吃菜事魔”与明教无干。

“吃菜”“魔教”在当时都是针对华化的摩尼教即明教而言的，而“吃菜事魔”一词出于政府之口，以妖魔化其查禁对象，依北宋民间秘密宗教状况推论，只能是明教，这也符合政府对危害其统治的宗教结社痛恨的心理。所以，“吃菜事魔”一出现就是当时政府对明教会带有污蔑性的称呼。

2.3 “吃菜事魔”指代范围之扩大

南宋庆元二年，监察御史沈继祖弹劾大儒朱熹，云其“剽张载、程颐之余论，寓以吃菜事魔之妖术，以簧鼓后进”。[3] 另明代万历年间，徐州人马登儒祈雨显灵而被称为神仙，凤阳巡抚李三才上奏云：“马登

〔1〕王见川：《从摩尼教到明教》，第266页。

〔2〕当然也可能不是北宋宣和年间所颁法令，而是在宗鉴生活的年代所颁布的法令，只是史籍阙如。如果是这个情况，也更能说明官方对“吃菜事魔”和摩尼教关系的态度。

〔3〕束景南《朱熹年谱长编》卷下，上海：华东师大出版社，2001年，第1272页。

儒吃斋事魔，而造《推背图》《阵法图》，惑众有证。”[1] 两处均提到“吃菜事魔”，这使人不禁要问：朱熹是明教徒吗？及至明代还将摩尼教恶称为“吃菜事魔”吗？

作为被官府力除的对象，明教从北宋宣和三年起被官方持续立法查禁，且越来越严，至南宋绍兴年间更甚，频频颁布有关法令，见于《宋会要辑稿》刑法二之一一一至一一三。

据载，绍兴七年十月二十九日，枢密院曾上奏曰：“宣和间，温、台村民多学妖法，号吃菜事魔，鼓惑众听，劫持州县。朝廷遣兵荡平之后，专立法禁，非不严切。访闻日近又有奸猾改易名称，名称‘结集社会’，或曰‘白衣礼佛会’，及假天兵号‘迎神会’。千百成群，夜聚晓散，传习妖教。州县坐视全不觉察。诏令浙东帅宪司，温、台州守臣，疾速措置，收捉为首鼓众之人，依条断遣。今后遵依见行条法，各先具已，措置事状以闻。”接着，奏章列举了此前所颁法令，分别颁于绍兴三年四月十五日、四年五月四日、六年六月八日和七年三月二十四日。从中不难看出朝廷对明教的关注及相关法令的密集。接着，南宋政府又于绍兴十一年正月九日、十一年正月十七日、十二年七月十三日接连颁令禁止吃菜事魔。

尽管诏令频频，但效果似乎不大。南宋绍兴四年五月癸丑，起居舍人王居正言：

> 伏见两浙州县，有吃菜事魔之俗。方腊以前，法禁尚宽，而事魔之俗犹未至于甚炽；方腊之后，法禁愈严而事魔之俗愈不可胜禁。州县之吏，平居坐视，一切不问则已。间有贪功或畏事者，稍纵迹之，则一方之地流血积尸。至于庐舍积聚，山林鸡犬之属，焚烧杀戮，靡有孑遗。自方腊之平，至今十余年间，不幸而死者，不知几千万人矣。[2]

这种禁不胜禁的状况反使“吃菜者”继续流传，甚至流入军队和

[1]《神宗实录》卷345“万历二十八年三月甲辰朔”条，台北：中央研究院历史语言研究所，1962年，第6419页。

[2]〔南宋〕李心传《建炎以来系年要录》卷76，北京：中华书局，1956年，第1248页。

政府官员中。绍兴十五年二月四日，“上曰：近传闻军中亦时有吃菜者”，[1] 绍兴二十六年又有两浙西路提点刑狱公事谢邦彦“吃菜”之事，[2] 陆游亦记士人宗子辈赴明教斋会之事，足见南宋时教流传范围之广。这种局面是政府始料未及的，为进一步查禁明教会，政府开始加大了对地方官吏的责任。绍兴十一年正月九日：

臣僚乞黜责婺州东阳县官吏，以不能擒捕事魔之人，诏自今州县守令能悉心措置，许本路监司审覆以闻，除推赏外，量加奖擢。[3]

可见官吏查禁事魔之业绩直接关系到自身的推赏奖擢。绍兴十二年七月十三日时，政府“仍令提刑司责据州县，有无吃菜事魔人月具奏闻”。[4] 在对地方官员施压的同时，政府也允许“诸色人”相互检举，并给予赏钱。利之所在，使得不少地方官员有意将查禁“吃菜事魔”的对象扩大化，而前述王居正所言连累无辜的现象也就在所难免。洪迈《夷坚志》载：

张才甫太尉居乌戍，效远公莲社，与僧俗为念佛会，御史论其白衣吃菜。遂赋《鹊桥仙词》云：“远公莲社，流传图画，千古声多犹在。后人多少继遗迹，到我便失惊打怪。西方未到，官方先到，冤我白衣吃菜。龙华三会愿相逢，怎敢学他家二会。”[5]

该词反映了地方官将远公（庐山慧远）莲社念佛会冤为白衣吃菜即明教会而予以纠察之案例，南宋理宗时期的一通书判——吴雨岩《痛治传习事魔等人》［时间大约在南宋理宗淳祐（1251 年）之后］——更能反映出当时白莲与事魔的关系。[6] 书判有云：

---

〔1〕〔清〕徐松辑《宋会要辑稿》刑法二之一一三。李心传《建炎以来系年要录》卷153（第2464页）亦载：“绍兴十五年二月庚辰，上曰：‘闻军中亦有吃菜者。’”

〔2〕〔南宋〕李心传《建炎以来系年要录》卷172（第2832页）载：绍兴二十六年四月己卯，“左朝请郎两浙西路提点刑狱公事谢邦彦……邦彦、邦哲顷与妖人交游，论列放罢，因钟世明荐与魏良臣，复得起用，尚不知自新……今又赴云吃菜之会……”

〔3〕〔清〕徐松辑《宋会要辑稿》刑法二之一一二。

〔4〕〔清〕徐松辑《宋会要辑稿》刑法二之一一三。

〔5〕〔南宋〕洪迈《夷坚志》（三）己七《善虐诗词》，北京：中华书局，1981年，第1353页。

〔6〕陈智超：《南宋〈吃菜事魔〉新史料》，载于《北京师院学报》1985年第4期，第31页。

> 白佛载于法，已成者杀；黄巾载于史，其祸可鉴。饶（今江西省鄱阳县）、信（今江西上饶市信州区）之间，小民无知，为一等妖人所惑，往往传习事魔，男女混杂，夜聚晓散。惧官府之发觉，则更易其名，曰我系白莲，非魔教也。既吃菜，既鼓众，便非魔教亦不可，况既系魔教乎？若不扫除，则女不从父从夫而从妖，生男不拜父拜母而拜魔王、灭天理，绝人伦，究其极则不至于黄巾不止。何况绍兴间，饶、信亦自有魔贼之变，直是官军剿灭，使无噍类，方得一了。若不平时禁戢，小不惩，大不戒，是罔民也。[1]

此前，该书判被学者当作白莲教的材料加以使用，但仔细玩味，实觉不妥。书判中谓“传习事魔、男女混杂、夜聚晓散”者，因怕官府查抄，便改易名号，“曰我系白莲，非魔教也”，此为欲盖弥彰之举，更使人清楚他们不是“白莲”，而正是官府所要查抄的“魔教”。反过来说，他们之所以要自称“白莲”，只能说明“白莲”是被官府允许的，于是才有附会之举。但事与愿违，此时官宪是“既吃菜，既鼓众，便非魔教亦不可”，何况他们“既系魔教”。可见在当时只要是“吃菜”“鼓众”，不管是“白莲”还是“魔教”，都要查抄，“白莲”实受累于“魔教”。

白莲教为茅子元于南宋初创建，脱胎于佛教。据其教徒普度记载，该教在茅子元的努力下受到当时身为太上皇的高宗赵构的赏识，并准其传教。正因其合法，才有后来像“曰我系白莲，非魔教也”之句的辩护。至于该教何时被禁，1207 年台州知州李谦所作《戒事魔诗》中有“金针引透白莲池，此语欺人亦自欺”一句，或可窥其端倪。上文所引材料也反映其因“事魔”而遭禁。白莲教在南宋前后期的境遇更能说明南宋时“吃菜事魔”一词所指的扩大。

就在官府不加细究而欲将“吃菜事魔”一网打尽时，佛教徒也乘机发难，将其异端白云宗和白莲宗徒恶称为“白云菜”和“白莲菜”，并将其归入“事魔邪党”之列，从而欲借官府之手来达到清理门户之目的。但他们也很清楚，不管是“白云”还是“白莲”，归根结底都是佛教的

〔1〕中国社会科学院历史研究所宋辽金元史研究室点校：《名公书判清明集》，北京：中华书局，1987年，第537页。

异端，所以又云“实不可与事魔妖党同论”。[1] 而对什么是“吃菜事魔”，他们也有清醒的认识。南宋志磐《佛祖统纪》卷 48 引洪迈《夷坚志》云：

尝考《夷坚志》云，吃菜事魔，三山犹炽。为首者紫帽宽衫，妇人黑冠白服，称为明教会。[2]

其中明言“吃菜事魔”为明教会而非他指。除佛教徒外，当时的道教徒亦持此种看法，南宋道士白玉蟾与彭耜有关明教的对话堪为明证：

耜曰：“乡间多有吃菜持斋以事明教，谓之灭魔，彼之徒且曰太上老君之遗教，然耶？否耶？”

答曰：“昔苏邻国有一居士号曰慕阇，始者学仙不成，终乎学佛不就，隐于大那伽山。始遇西天外道有曰毗婆伽明使者，教以一法，使之修持，遂留此一教，其实非理。彼之教有一禁戒，且云尽大地山河草木水火，皆是毗卢遮那法身，所以不敢践履，不敢举动，然虽如此，却是毗卢遮那佛身外面立地。且如持八斋、礼五方，不过教戒使之然尔。其教中一曰天王，二曰明使，三曰灵相土地。以主其教，大要在乎清净光明、大力智慧八字而已。然此八字，无出乎心。今人著相修行，而欲尽此八字可乎？况曰明教，而且自昧！”[3]

众所周知，宋代明教极力附会道教。[4] 而白玉蟾既知明教大要“清净光明，大力智慧”，可见他对明教的了解不尽皮毛而是实质，对当时吃菜持斋之“灭魔”就是明教的回答亦至为清楚。可见佛道高僧一方面对政府查禁“吃菜事魔”表示赞同，另一方面又对政府的扩大化查禁之

[1]〔南宋〕宗鉴《释门正统》卷4，《续藏经》卷75《史传部》，No. 1513，页314c。

[2]〔南宋〕志磐《佛祖统纪》卷48，《大正藏》卷49《史传部》，No. 2035，页431a。这段文字不见于现存《夷坚志》中。林悟殊《〈夷坚志〉明教纪事史料价值辨析》（载于《中华文史论丛》2012年第2期，第255－283页）考证认为实出自洪迈手笔，可信。

[3]〔北宋〕谢显道编《海琼白真人语录》卷1，《道藏》第33册，文物出版社、上海书店、天津古籍出版社影印，1988年，页114下－115上。参见饶宗颐《穆护歌考》，《选堂集林·史林》（中），香港：中华书局，1982年，第501–502页。

[4] 林悟殊：《“宋摩尼依托道教”考论》，参见张荣芳、戴治国主编：《陈垣与岭南：纪念陈垣先生诞生130周年学术研讨会论文集》，北京：中国社会科学出版社，2011年，第81–107页。

举深以为忧，担心引火烧身而极力撇清与“魔教”的关系。

南宋绍兴年间对“吃菜事魔”的高压政策成效不大，不过地方官员出于仕途之计，将查禁范围尽量扩大，以便更多地获取朝廷的青睐。在如此氛围下，当时的官员、儒士，如陆游、庄绰等亦大造舆论，将所有不利于统治的人员团体统统划入“吃菜事魔”之列而呼吁政府加以查禁。正如有学者言“南宋时代，吃菜事魔被认为是含有扰乱社会的最邪恶者之意”。〔1〕所以，当时的禅宗高僧宗杲〔2〕、儒学大成朱熹，以及地方“道民”〔3〕，都被冠以“吃菜事魔”，足以反映这种扩大化的现象。而在明代的史料中亦将有妖术者称为“吃菜事魔”，那就更不足为奇了。

2.4 结论

会昌法难后，摩尼教在中土文献中多称作明教，辗转流传于东南沿海一带，并不断地与地方信仰相融合，渐次成为地方化和民间化信仰。〔4〕在转型过程中，由于在地方大建斋堂、菜院等场所，举行不合于当时礼法的法事活动，且又与方腊起义扯上关系，遂不受容于宋王朝的统治。宋政府在真宗、徽宗时期对摩尼教的传播持鼓励与支持态度，直至宣和三年，因方腊起义与明教会有关，臣僚上言予以查禁。查禁过程中，宋政府根据当时明教会的特点而将其恶称为“吃菜事魔”。不过政府的查禁非但没有将明教会连根拔除，反致其愈演愈烈。及至南宋，政府更加大了打击力度，不仅对地方官员施行摘发的高压，同时也奖励其他人告发或教内人相互检举。佛道徒众也相机发难，意欲将明教这一“异教”置之死地而后快。如是一来，官员出于自保，下层百姓为得到

〔1〕竺沙雅章：《吃菜事魔について》，氏著《中国佛教社会史研究》，京都：同朋舍，1982年，第246页（许洋主汉译文载刘俊文主编《日本学者研究中国史论著选译》第7卷，北京：中华书局，1993年，第378页）。

〔2〕〔南宋〕薛季宣《浪语集》三三《先大夫行状笺》。宗杲被秦桧诬为主战派张九龄一党而被流放岭南，在流放途中，有人“欲以危法加之，用茹素事魔告之”。

〔3〕有关“道民”的资料见《宋会要辑稿》刑法二之一三〇；〔南宋〕志磐《佛祖统纪》卷48，《大正藏》卷49《史传部》，No. 2035，页430c。

〔4〕杨富学：《〈乐山堂神记〉与福建摩尼教——霞浦与敦煌吐鲁番等摩尼教文献的比较研究》，载于《文史》2011年第4期（总第97辑），第173页。

赏银，佛道徒为纯洁队伍，均不遗余力地围剿“魔教”。势之所使，原本恶称明教会的“吃菜事魔”外延逐步扩大，用以概称一切不利于政府统治或是对自己不利的民间信仰，久而久之，逐步成为南宋以后历代对邪教的代名词。[1] 质言之，“吃菜事魔”一开始是对摩尼教的恶称，大约在南宋时期，原本恶指明教的“吃菜事魔”一词，在各方力量的推波助澜下，范围被有意扩大，尤其是政府官员，只要对不利于统治的团体，概以“吃菜事魔”称之。

〔1〕清人钱大昕在谈及朱熹被沈继祖诬为“吃菜事魔”者时，就云“乃知吃菜事魔，即今人所谓邪教也”。见钱大昕《十驾斋养新录》卷8《吃菜事魔》，南京：江苏古籍出版社，2000年，第175页。

3 Manichaeism meets Chinese Buddhism: Some comments on the 'sutrafication' of the Sermon on the Light-Nous

Gunner Mikkelsen
(Macquarie University, Australia)

In the absence of a title in the extant part of the scroll[1], the famous Chinese version of the Manichaean *Sermon on the Light-Nous* from Dunhuang is usually given the provisional title *Treatise on the Light-Nous* in English. The 'treatise' part of this title derives from the name "Traitémanichéen" given by its first translators, the eminent French Sinologists Édouard Chavannes and Paul Pelliot, whose richly annotated French translation appeared in the *Journal asiatique* in 1911.[2] At that time many fragments of more 'original' Parthian versions of the *Sermon* had been discovered at Turfan but were yet to be identified and edited. Ernst Waldschmidt and Wolfgang Lentz discussed a few of these in 1926 in their major study "Die Stellung Jesu im Manichaïsmus". They identified words in the partly preserved titles of two versions, *sxwn*, *wyfr's'* and *mnwhmyd rwšn* which they translated as "Rede, Auseinandersetzung", "Belehrung" and

[1] The opening words are lost, and the title is not repeated at end as the main text fills the entire final sheet of the scroll. The scroll is kept in the National Library of China (BD00256). High-resolution images are accessible in the *International Dunhuang Project Database* (http://idp.bl.uk; http://idp.nlc.gov.cn).

[2] Édouard Chavannes and Paul Pelliot, "Un traité manichéen retrouvé en Chine", *Journal asiatique*, 10ème sér., 18 (1911), 499-617.

"lichte Monuhmēδ" respectively.[1] The fuller title of one of the versions, reconstructed as *mnwhmyd rwšn wyfr's'* was rendered as '(die Lehrschrift über die) lichte Monuhmēδ'.[2] In 1984, Werner Sundermann translated this title as "Traktat/Sermon/Homilie vom Lichtnous"[3] before deciding on "Der Sermon vom Licht-Nous" for his major edition, published in 1992, of all known fragments of the text in Parthian and Sogdian.[4] Sundermann translated the second partly preserved title '*mnwhmydrwšnsxwn'* as "Die Rede vom Licht-Nous".[5] According to the *Dictionary of Manichaean Middle Persian and Parthian* by Desmond Durkin- Meisterernst *wyfr's* and *sxwn* both carry the meaning "sermon"; *wyfr's* may mean "teaching", "instruction", "sermon" or "homily", and *sxwn* "chapter" or "sermon".[6] The Parthian versions may have been based on a sermon of Mani, but only their titles seem to indicate this. The Chinese version from Dunhuang, on the other hand, is explicitly presented as a sermon of the "Apostle/ Envoy

[1] Ernst Waldschmidt and Wolfgang Lentz, *Die Stellung Jesu im Manichäismus*, Abhandlungen der Preussischen Akademie der Wissenschaften, Phil.-hist. Kl., No. 4 (Berlin: Verlag der Akademie der Wissenschaften, in Komm. bei Walter de Gruyter, 1926), 44.

[2] Ibid. 44.

[3] Werner Sundermann, "Der chinesische Traité Manichéen und der parthische Sermon vom Lichtnous", *Altorientalische Forschungen* 10 (1983), 232.

[4] Werner Sundermann, Der Sermon vom Licht-Nous. Eine Lehrschrift des östlichen Manichäismus. Edition der parthischen und soghdischen Version, Berliner Turfantexte 17 (Berlin: Akademie Verlag, 1992), 44 and 63.

[5] Ibid. This title occurs on one fragment only.

[6] Desmond Durkin-Meisterernst, Dictionary of Manichaean texts III. Texts from Central Asia and China, Part 1. Dictionary of Manichaean Middle Persian and Parthian, Corpus Fontium Manichaeorum, Subsidia (Turnhout: Brepols, 2004), 352 and 311.

of Light" (*mingshi* 明使), i.e. Mani.[1] As noted by Chavannes and Pelliot this version is modelled on Buddhist *sūtras*, i.e. (mostly) canonical scriptures containing sermons/discourses of the Buddha – it is "…rédigé à la manière des *sūtra* bouddhiques".[2] Accordingly, the title of the text is likely to have contained the term *jing* 经, as this is the standard Buddhist Chinese term for *sūtra*. The standard Buddhist Chinese term *lun* 论 for *śāstra* or "treatise" is in this context not applicable. The title of the Chinese version of the *Sermon on the Light-Nous* is likely to have contained both the name for "Light-Nous", *Huiming* 惠明, corresponding to Parthian *mnwhmyd rwšn*, and the term *jing* 经 which we may translate as "*sūtra*" or, more neutrally (as the text is not Buddhist) as "scripture" or "book".

The large number of recovered fragments of various versions of the *Sermon on the Light-Nous* in Parthian,[3] Sogdian,[4] Old Turkish[5] and

[1] The equivalent Parthian term is *fryštgrwšn*; cf. edition by Sundermann, op.cit., 1992, §14. In the Chinese Manichaean *Hymn-scroll* from Dunhuang (British Library, S.2659), col. 338b, *mingshi* is an epithet of Mani: *Mangni mingshi* 忙你明使 "Mani, the Envoy of Light". In the *Compendium of the Teachings of Mani the Buddha of Light*, also found at Dunhuang (British Library, S.3969), it is explained that "*Foyisede wulushen* (original gloss; transliterated from the author's native speech) in translation of Apostle of Light, is also called the King of Law (*dharmaraja*) of Perfect Wisdom, and again Mani, the Buddha of Light" 佛夷瑟德乌卢诜者（本国梵音也）译云光明使者，又号具智法王，亦谓摩尼光佛 (cols. 5-6).

[2] Chavannes and Pelliot, op.cit., 500; see also 509 n. 2.

[3] Sundermann, op.cit., 1992, §§2-79.

[4] Ibid., 62-73.

[5] Albert von Le Coq, *Türkische Manichaica aus Chotscho. III. Nebst einem christlichen Bruchstück aus Bulayïq*, Abhandlungen der Preussischen Akademie der Wissenschaft, Phil.-hist. Kl., no. 2 (Berlin: Akademie der Wissenschaften, 1922), 15-22; Peter Zieme, "Neue Fragmente des alttürkischen Sermons vom Licht-Nous", in Christiane Reck & Peter Zieme (eds.), *Iran und Turfan. Beiträge Berliner Wissenschaftler, Werner Sundermann zum 60. Geburtstag gewidmet*, Iranica 2 (Wiesbaden: Harrassowitz, 1995), 251-76; Jens Wilkens, "Der manichäische Traktat in seiner alttürkischen Fassung – neues Material, neue Perspektiven", *Ural-Altaische Jahrbücher*, N.F., 17 (2001/2), 78-105.

Chinese[1] bear testimony to its importance and popularity in the Eastern Manichaean church. It may well have had semi-canonical status here. Several scholars, including Sundermann,[2] Sam Lieu[3] and Ma Xiaohe[4] have argued that the *Sermon* contains material from the canonical *Book of the Giants* (Chinese title: *Dalishi jing* 大力士经 *Scripture of the Heroes of Great Strength*), and our distinguished honorand 'Lin Wushu' has linked it to the canonical *Pragmateia* (Chinese title: *Zhengming guoqu jiao jing* 证明过去教经 *Scripture on Instruction Testifying the Past*)[5]. Among other *jings* with which the Chinese *Sermon* may share content is the *Erzong sanji jing* 二宗三际经 *Book of Two Principles and Three Times* (also titled *Erzong jing* 二宗经 *Book of Two Principles*). This book is mentioned in several Chinese sources. In 1923, Chen Yuan suggested that the *Erzong jing* might, in fact, be the Dunhuang *Sermon*.[6] This received support from Antonino Forte in recent times: "...there is no convincing reason to renounce the old hypothesis of Chen Yuan. On the contrary, the fact that until now the *Traité manichéen* remains the only Manichaean text which we know for certain to have existed during the Zhou dynasty (690-705),

---

[1] Chavannes and Pelliot, op.cit.; Gunner Mikkelsen, "The fragments of Chinese Manichaean texts from the Turfan region", in Desmond Durkin-Meisterernst et al. (eds.), *Turfan revisited – the first century of research into the arts and cultures of the Silk Road*, Monographien zur indischen Archäologie, Kunst und Philologie 17 (Berlin: Dietrich Reimer Verlag, 2004), 214, 217.

[2] Werner Sundermann, "Ein weiteres Fragment aus Manis Gigantenbuch", *in Orientalia J. Duchesne-Guillemin emerito oblata*, Acta Iranica 23, Hommages et Opera Minora IX (Leiden: Brill, 1984), 498ff.; idem, op.cit., 1992, 15f.; idem, "Mani's 'Book of the Giants' and the Jewish books of Enoch. A case of terminological difference and what it implies", *Irano-Judaica* 3 (1994), 48.

[3] Samuel Lieu, "From Parthian into Chinese – some observations on the *Traktat (Traité) Pelliot*", in idem, *Manichaeism in Central Asia and China*, Nag Hammadi and Manichaean Studies 45 (Leiden-Boston-Köln: Brill, 1998) (first publ. in *Orientalistische Literaturzeitung* 90, 4 (July/August 1995), 357-72).

[4] 马小鹤，《摩尼教残经一》改编《大力士经》考，传统中国研究集刊 7 (2010), 211-221.

[5] 林悟殊，《摩尼教残经一》原名之我见，in idem, 摩尼教及其东渐，世界文化丛书 33 (Taibei: 淑馨出版社, 1997), 211-26.

[6] 陈垣，摩尼教入中国考，国学季刊 1/2 (1923), 206; Chen Yuan, "Manichaeism in China", Catholic University of Peking, Bulletin 4 (1928), 63; 陈垣学术论文集 (Beijing: 中华书局, 1980-82), I, 333.

precisely when the *Scripture of the Two Principles and Three Times* was introduced, should be a matter for reflection".[1]

The 'sutrafication' of the *Sermon on the Light-Nous* in the Dunhuang version is particularly evident in the framework of the text. The prologue and parts of the epilogue to the sermon closely follow the pattern, style and language of popular Chinese Mahāyāna *sūtras*. It is unfortunate that the first few columns of text are missing. These may have provided a short description of the scene of the sermon as *sūtras* normally do, and possibly, at the very beginning, the phrase "Thus I have heard" (*rushi wowen* 如是我闻, Skt. *evaṃ mayā śrutam*), i.e. the opening words of most sūtras and traditionally attributed to the Buddha's disciple Ānanda, or a similar phrase. Mani's sermon is delivered in response to questions posed by a disciple. The initial master-disciple dialogue of the *Sermon* is strongly reminiscent of master-disciple dialogues in the prologues of popular Buddhist *sūtras*. Mani, the "Apostle/Envoy of Light" takes the place of the Buddha, and Addā (Atuo 阿驮), one of Mani's principal, disciples takes the place of one of the Buddha's ten principal disciples, Subhūti or other. Addā asks Mani several profound questions, and Mani commends him for these and then proceeds to give his lecture.

Prologue of the Chinese *Sermon on the Light-Nous* from Dunhuang (cols. 1-8)[2]

[…] should one not encounter the opportunity, there is no way to

[1] Antonino Forte, "The Chinese title of the Manichaean Treatise from Dunhuang", *Annali dell' Istituto Orientale di Napoli* 62 (2002), 241; also idem, "Il titolo cinese del Traité manichéen", in Ugo Marazzi (ed.), *Turcica et Islamica. Studi in memoria di Aldo Gallotta* (Napoli: Università degli Studi di Napoli "L'Orientale"; Roma: dist. Herder, 2003), 237.

[2] This and other passages cited here derive from an *editio major* of the text by Sam Lieu and me in collaboration with Lance Eccles. Thanks to a major research grant from the Australian Research Council (2013-15) this is now in preparation for the *Series Sinica* of the *Corpus Fontium Manichaeorum* (Turnhout: Brepols).

free oneself or strive towards deliverance [...] the carnal body and the original nature, are they single or dual? Which skilful means did all the various hallowed ones who ever appeared in the world employ to rescue the Light-nature and free it from the multitude of sufferings so that it might finally achieve peace and happiness? After he (sc. Atuo) had asked these questions, he bowed respectfully and stood to one side.

□□□□□□□若不遇缘，无由自脱，求解□□□□ 肉身本性，是一为是二耶？一切诸圣，出现于世，施（何）[1]方便，能救明性，得离众苦，究竟安乐？作是问已，曲躬恭敬，却住一面。

Then the Envoy of Light spoke to Atuo (Addā) thus: Excellent, excellent! It is in order to benefit the countless living beings that you are able to ask these questions of such profound and mysterious significance. You are now a great knowledgeable friend of all the blind and confused creatures living in the world. I will explain everything point by point, so that the net of your doubts should be forever sundered, leaving nothing behind.

尔时明使告阿驮言：善哉善哉！ 汝为利益无量众生，能问如此甚深秘义。汝今即是一切世间盲迷众生大善知识。我当为汝分别解说，令汝疑网永断无余。

This heavily Buddhicised dialogue preceding Mani's sermon is unparalleled in the surviving fragments of Parthian, Sogdian and Old Turkish versions. Clearly, those versions are not modelled on Buddhist *sūtras*. One of the Parthian versions begins with a Trinitarian doxology: "Homage (be) to the F[ather], bles[sing to the Son], honour to the Holy Spirit, [... to] the Glory of the Religion, praise to the Light-No[us]!"[2]

In 1915, Herbert Giles noted that Mani in the Chinese *Sermon* "began

[1] Only a small part of this character is preserved. The interrogative *he* 何 is a likely reconstruction here (cf. prologue of the *Zhixuan anle jing, infra*) rather than *zuo* 作 as proposed by previous editors.

[2] Cf. Sundermann, op.cit., 63, §1.

his reply in the very words of Buddha in the *Diamond Sûtra*, the Chinese characters being the same in both cases".[1] The master-disciple dialogue is certainly reminiscent of that of the *Diamond Sūtra* and may very well have been inspired by this *sūtra*. The wide popularity of the *Diamond Sūtra* in Chinese Mahāyāna is evidenced amply in the number of copies recovered from the Mogao 'library' cave at Dunhuang. Close to two thousand copies of this text were found, surpassed only by the number of copies of the *Lotus Sūtra* (*Miaofa lianhua jing* 妙法莲华经) and the *Great Perfection of Wisdom Sūtra* (*Mohe bore boluomiduo jing* 摩诃般若波罗蜜多经).[2] However, only the initial four characters in Mani's reply to Addā correspond directly to the Buddha's reply to Subhūti (Xuputi 须菩提, Shanbao 善宝) in various translations of the *Diamond Sūtra*, including those by Kumārajīva (401/2), Bodhiruci (509), Paramārtha (562) and Dharmagupta (590), namely *shanzai shanzai* 善哉善哉 "Excellent, excellent!" or "Good indeed, good indeed!" (Skt. *sādhu*, *sādhu*). In the earliest and by far most widely consulted and copied (but not necessarily most accurate)[3] translation by Kumārajīva, the Buddha begins his reply with the following words:

Excerpt of the prologue of the *Diamond Sūtra* (*Jingang boreboluomiduo jing* 金刚般若波罗蜜多经; trans. Kumārajīva)[4]

Excellent, excellent! Subhūti, it is as you have said. The

[1] Herbert Giles, *Confucianism and its rivals. Lectures delivered at the University Hall of Dr. William's Library*, London, October-December, 1914, Hibbert lectures (London: Williams & Norgate; New York: C. Scribner's Sons, 1915), 191.

[2] Cf. Yongyou Shi, *The Diamond Sutra in Chinese culture* (Hacienda Heights: Buddha's Light Publ., 2010), 43ff.

[3] Cf. Paul Harrison, "Resetting the Diamond: reflections on Kumārajīva's Chinese translation of the Vajracchedikā", *Xiyu lishi yuyan yanjiu jikan* 西域历史语言研究集刊 / *Journal of historical and philological studies of China's Western Regions* 3 (2010), 233-48.

[4] T.235, vol. 8, 748c29-749a4.

Thus-come (*Tathāgata*) is well mindful and protective of all bodhisattvas and skilful in entrusting to all bodhisattvas. Now listen carefully, and I shall explain for you how good men and good women who set forth to attain a mind of unsurpassed complete enlightenment (*anuttara-samyak-saṃbodhi*) should abide and subdue their thoughts.

善哉善哉！须菩提，如汝所说。如来善护念诸菩萨、善付嘱诸菩萨。汝今谛听，当为汝说，善男子、善女人，发阿耨多罗三藐三菩提心，应如是住如是降伏其心。

Well over half of all manuscripts found at Dunhuang contain copies of common Buddhist *sūtras*, and a very large proportion (some 90%) of all manuscripts are Buddhist and mainly in Chinese. That the Manichaean authors and translators adopted and adapted formats, stylistic elements, terms and phrases of the scriptures of the predominant religion is hardly surprising. The Dunhuang *Sermon on the Light-Nous* is in many passages of the sermon itself quite parallel to the versions in Parthian and Old Turkish and quite un-Buddhist in its terminology or phraseology, but its prologue would have led many readers to believe that it was a Buddhist *sūtra*, at least at first sight. Paul Pelliot, on his visit at the Mogao Caves of Thousand Buddhas at Dunhuang and the 'library' cave in 1908, was highly selective in his collection of manuscripts, removing only copies of common texts like the *Diamond Sūtra* if they were of special interest (e.g. had colophons, dedications, etc.). However, he was completely deceived by the *sūtra* prologue of the Manichaean *Sermon*, and this unique manuscript was therefore left behind in the cave, much to his later regret. [1]

The Manichaean strategy of 'sutrafying' sermons in Chinese was

〔1〕Cf. Gunner Mikkelsen, "Skilfully planting the trees of light: the Chinese manichaica, their Central Asian counterparts, and some observations on the translation of Manichaeism into Chinese", in Søren Clausen, Roy Starrs and Anne Wedell-Wedellsborg (eds.), *Cultural encounters: China, Japan, and the West. Essays commemorating* 25 *years of East Asian Studies at the University of Aarhus* (Aarhus: Aarhus University Press, 1995), 92-93.

shared by the 'Church of the East' Christians, the so-called Nestorians. In their *Book* (*Sūtra*) *on the Attainment of Mysterious Peace and Happiness* (*Zhixuan anle jing* 志玄安乐经),[1] which probably dates to the eighth century, Jesus' sermon is prompted by questions from his disciple Simon (Cenwen 岑稳). Less than half of the prologue has survived (cols. 2-9), but the opening words *wen shi zhiyan* 闻是至言 "(I have) heard these profound words", quite similar to the opening words of Buddhist *sūtras*, are extant. Some description of the scene of the sermon is preserved. The sermon was delivered by the Messiah (Mishihe 弥施诃) to a large crowd of followers by a river and at the "Hall of Purity and Emptiness" (Jingxu tang 净虚堂). Remarkably parallel to Addā's question in the *Sermon* is Simon's question "by which skilful means (are you able) to rescue sentient beings?" (*he fangbian jiuhu youqing* … 何方便救护有情…), and like Mani in the *Sermon* the Messiah begins his reply with the exclamation "Excellent!" (*shanzai* 善哉)[2] and then focuses on the topic of attainment of the "nature of peace and happiness" (*anle xing* 安乐性).

The concluding words of both texts describe the reaction of the "members of the great gathering" to the sermon they had just heard. More

---

〔1〕The original manuscript of the *Zhixuan anle jing* is unavailable. Photographs of the beginning and end (and not the main part) of the manuscript are published in: Haneda Tōru 羽田亨, 羽田博士史学论文集 / *Recueil des Œuvres posthumes de Tôru Haneda*, II. *Études religieuses et linguistiques* (Kyōto: Tōyōshi kenkyūkai, Société pour l'étude de l'histoire de l'Extrême-Orient, Université de Kyōto, 1958, pl. 6, and Lin Wushu 林悟殊, 唐代景教再研究 (Beijing: 中国社会科学出版社, 2003), 344-45. For discussion of editorial problems with the prologue of this text, see idem, 敦煌本景教《志玄安乐经》佐伯录文质疑, 中山大学学报(社会科学版) 41 (2001), 1-7 (revised version in Lin Wushu, op.cit., 2003, 146-55) and Gunner Mikkelsen, "Haneda's and Saeki's editions of the Chinese Nestorian *Zhixuan anle jing* – a comment on recent work by Lin Wushu", in Roman Malek (ed.) in connection with Peter Hofrichter, *Jingjiao – the Church of the East in China and Central Asia*, Collectanea Serica, Sankt Augustin: Institut Monumenta Serica; Nettetal: Steyler 2006), 143-48. For technical reasons all Chinese characters in my article had to be re-entered by the editorial team at a late stage. This led to several errors (beyond my control), and readers are therefore advised to consult the list of Errata and Corrigenda for the volume (insert or on the website http://www.monumenta-serica.de).

〔2〕The repeat of the exclamation is lost in a lacuna.

than half of the words are the same in the two texts.

Concluding words of the Chinese Book on the Mysterious Attainment of Peace and Happiness (col. 159)

> When all the members of the great gathering had listened to this lecture, they humbly accepted it and were overjoyed. Respectfully they withdrew and put it into practice.
>
> 时诸大众闻是语已，顶受欢喜。礼退奉行。

Concluding words of the Chinese *Sermon on the Light-Nous* from Dunhuang (cols. 344-45)

> When all the members of the great gathering had heard this holy text (*sūtra*), they accepted it as law with faith and put it into practice with cheerfulness.
>
> 时诸大众闻是经已，如法信受，欢喜奉行。

The epilogue of the *Sermon* is far more elaborate (cols. 316-45). Parts of it are strongly Buddhicised, and it alternates between prose and verse as is the case in some *sūtras*. The epilogue is unparalleled in the Turfan versions of the *Sermon*.

Excerpt of the epilogue of the Chinese *Sermon on the Light-Nous* from Dunhuang (cols. 316-20)

> And so, when the *mushe* (i.e. Manichaean teachers) in the gathering had heard this holy text professed, they leapt for joy and cried out that there had never been anything like it. The gods and the good spirits, the limited and the unlimited, all the kings, the multitude of magnates, and the four categories of men and women, infinite and countless, having heard this holy text, were all overjoyed. They were all able to bring forth the desire for unsurpassed perfection, just as the

plants and trees which, without exception, develop and thrive when the life-giving spring arrives, unfolding their flowers and putting forth their fruits to achieve maturity; only those roots that are damaged and torn are unable to develop and grow.

尔时会中诸慕阇等闻说是经，欢喜踊跃，叹未曾有。诸天善神，有碍无碍，及诸国王、群臣、士女四部之众，无量无数，闻是经已，皆大欢喜。悉能发起无上道心，犹如卉木值遇阳春，无不滋茂，敷花结果得成熟；唯除败根不能滋长。

Very similar reactions to the Buddha's sermons are described at the end of several popular *sūtras*.

Concluding words of the *Diamond Sūtra* (trans. Kumārajīva) [1]

When the Buddha had preached this *sūtra*, the elder Subhūti and all the monks (*bhikṣus*) and nuns (*bhikṣunīs*), laymen (*upāsakas*) and laywomen (*upāsikās*), and all the gods (*devas*), humans, and *asuras* of the world, having heard what the Buddha had said, were overjoyed. They accepted (his teaching) and put it into practice.

佛说是经已，长老须菩提及诸比丘、比丘尼、优婆塞、优婆夷、一切世间天、人、阿修罗，闻佛所说，皆大欢喜。信受奉行。

Concluding words of the *Lotus Sūtra* (*Miaofa lianhua jing* 妙法莲华经; trans. Kumārajīva) [2]

When the Buddha preached this *sūtra*, Universal Worthy (Samantabhadra) and the other *bodhisattvas*, Śāriputra and the other hearers (*śrāvakas*), along with the gods (*devas*), dragons (*nāgas*),

---

〔1〕T.235, vol. 8, 752b30-c2. Herbert Giles noted the similarity of these words with the concluding words of the Manichaean *Sermon*; Giles, op.cit., 195.

〔2〕T.262, vol. 9, 62a27-29. The translation largely follows Burton Watson, *The Lotus Sutra* (New York: Columbia University Press, 1993), 324.

human and non-human beings, and all others in the great assembly were overjoyed. Accepting and upholding the Buddha's words, made salutation to him and withdrew.

佛说是经时，普贤等诸菩萨，舍利弗等诸声闻，及诸天、龙、人非人等，一切大会，皆大欢喜，受持佛语，作礼而去。

Concluding words of the *Longer Sukhāvatīvyūha Sūtra* (*Wuliangshou jing* 无量寿经; trans. Kang Sengkai 康僧铠)[1]

As the Buddha had preached this *sūtra*, the *bodhisattva* Maitreya and the assembly of *bodhisattvas* who had come from the ten directions (of the universe), together with the elder Ānanda and other great hearers (*śrāvakas*), all in this vast crowd, having heard what the Buddha said, all without exception rejoiced.

佛说经已，弥勒菩萨及十方来诸菩萨众，长老阿难诸大声闻。一切大众，闻佛所说靡不欢喜。

Whilst there is no doubt that the translators and authors of the Church of the East and the Manichaean church in China modelled their sermons directly on Mahāyāna *sūtras*, it is important to point out that the textual format of sermons as part of or following a dialogue between master and disciples was well established at an early stage in both churches. Jesus' sermons as recorded in the Gospels usually follow a dialogue between him and his disciples (and descriptions of scenes and backgrounds for the sermons), and Mani's sermons are delivered in a very similar manner in the Coptic *Kephalaia of the Teacher*. In fact, the format of the Coptic version of the *Sermon on the Light-Nous*, the 38th *kephalaion, Concerning the Light-Nous and the Apostles and the Saints*, which is the longest and most complex of all of the *kephalaia*, resembles the Chinese version in several

[1] T.360, vol. 12, 279a26-28.

ways. Mani's sermon is framed by a series of questions posed by a disciple at the beginning and the reaction of the audience at the end. Parts of the concluding passage are similar to the Chinese:

Concluding words of the Coptic *Kephalaia of the Teacher, keph.* 38 [1]

> Then, after his disciples had heard all these sayings, which he (i.e. Mani) proclaimed, his disciples answered. They said to him: Gre[at] and mighty are all these things that you have uttered to us; which [you] have [do]ne by your power, and the power of the one who sent you. Who could fully recompense you for the grace that you have done us, except this one who sent you? Still, the on[l]y gift available to us, to repay you, is this: that we will make ourselves strong in y[our] faith; and persevere in your commandments; and also be per[s]uaded of your word, which you have proclaimed to us.

In his *Sermon vom Licht-Nous*, Sundermann is unsure how to interpret the similarities between the Coptic and Chinese versions – "Mir ist nicht klar, wie man diese frappierende Ähnlichkeit beurteilen soll". [2] He finds it possible that the two versions had developed independently, that their structural similarities may be sheer coincidence – "zufälligen Parallelenent-wicklung" – and he also finds that the Chinese dialogue format may reflect a traditional format as seen in the *Kephalaia of the Teacher*. As the *Kephalaia* dates back to the early years of the Manichaean church, the Chinese version may have been based on a more original version of Mani's sermon than the Parthian versions of which fragments have been found at Turfan: "Der chinesische Traité wurde dann in dieser Hinsicht eine den

[1] Keph. 38, p. 102.4-12; Iain Gardner, *The Kephalaia of the Teacher: the edited Coptic Manichaean texts in translation with commentary*, Nag Hammadi and Manichaean studies 37 (Leiden–New York–Köln: Brill, 1995), 105.

[2] Sundermann, op.cit., 1992, 19.

Ursprüngen nähere Version als der parthische Text überliefern".[1] Sam Lieu supports this view in his review article of Sundermann's work: "It is therefore entirely possible that what we have in Chinese is a translation of the prologue of a different Parthian version based on the style of interlocution in the *Kephalaia*. (...) As Manichaean texts came under Buddhist influence in Central Asia, the Christian-gnostic dialogue form readily assumed a Buddhist guise."[2]

It is certainly possible that the Chinese *Sermon* is a Buddhicised translation of a lost Parthian version that is older than the Turfan versions and includes a master-disciple dialogue, especially in the light of the fact that only a relatively small number of the surviving fragments of Parthian versions are closely parallel to the Chinese version. It is equally possible that the dialogue format was more common in Coptic and Chinese, in predominantly Christian and Buddhist environments, and that there was no 'original' *Sermon on the Light-Nous* in this format. The only firm conclusion we can draw from the extant evidence is that the Manichaean *Sermon on the Light-Nous*, as it was translated into Chinese was given a new format modelled directly on popular Chinese Mahāyāna *sūtras*.[3]

〔1〕Ibid., 19.

〔2〕Lieu, op.cit., 1998, 68.

〔3〕For further discussion of the indroduction and conclusion of the Chicese *Sermon on the Light-Nous*, see now also Lin Wushu's own study (published after the submission of my article):京藏摩尼经开篇结语辨释，西域研究（2013）2，41-50.

4 A Manichaean Sogdian hymn in two scripts

Nicholas Sims-Williams
(SOAS, University of London)

It is well known that the Sogdian Manichaeans made use of two scripts for writing their texts, the Manichaean script and the native Sogdian script (sometimes referred to as the "National script").[1] Unfortunately it is very rarely the case that copies of the same text survive in both scripts, a notable exception being the Tale of the Pearl-borer, the two versions of which were published by W. B. Henning (1945, 465-9). Another such biscript text is a prayer for the Uygur Qagan, the two versions of which are published in Yoshida 2001, 111-14. In addition, I was recently able to establish that one side of M 1060 (in Manichaean script) and one side of So 10100m (in Sogdian script) contain copies of the same text. It is a pleasure to offer a first, tentative edition of these interesting but enigmatic fragments to Professor Lin Wushu, who has done so much to keep alive the study of Manichaeism in the country where it survived for the longest time as a living religion.

So 10100m, the text in Sogdian script, is described in Reck 2006, 37. As Reck points out, it belongs to the same manuscript as the folio So

[1] The Manichaean Sogdian literature in Sogdian script can now be conveniently surveyed in the catalogue of Reck 2006. Only brief details of the Sogdian texts in Manichaean script are given in the catalogues of Boyce 1960 and Morano 2008.

10100g(2), which contains the Tale of the Monkey and the Fox.[1] A few lines are damaged or missing at the top and bottom of the page. The Recto side contains the end of an unidentified text in Sogdian (R1-7), with the Turkish name of the copyist, sponsor or owner of the manuscript filling the space at the end of line 7. A new text begins on R8 with the Parthian invocation "Be thou blessed, Apostle Mar Mani!" written in red ink. From R9 onwards, in black ink, we have the Sogdian text of a hymn or poem, which continues on the Verso. It is part of this text, from V4 onwards, which has a parallel in Manichaean script. The words "I pay homage, Mar Mani" in V12, the last line of the Verso, probably belong to the introductory invocation of another hymn.[2]

M 1060, the fragment in Manichaean script, is briefly described in Boyce 1960, 64, and Morano 2008, 252. Both catalogues state that the Recto is in Sogdian and the Verso in Middle Persian, but since the fragment has no margins there is in fact no way of distinguishing Recto from Verso. I therefore prefer to label the Sogdian side as "Side A" and the Middle Persian side as "Side B". The Sogdian text on Side A, with the possible exception of the last few fragmentary words, is entirely parallel to So 10100m, V4ff.

The following edition is based on So 10100m as the better preserved of the two texts. The parallel text in Manichaean script, M 1060, Side A, is printed *in italics* between the lines of the Verso of So 10100m, thus reversing the practice introduced by Henning in his edition of the Tale of the Pearl-borer, where the text in Sogdian script is printed in italics and the better-preserved text in Manichaean script in Roman. For the sake of completeness, the Middle Persian text of M 1060, Side B, is included at the

[1] Tale F in Henning 1945, 474–5, re-edited in Sims-Williams 2010.

[2] At any rate, the language of V12 seems to be Sogdian, rather than Parthian as suggested by Reck, since Pth. *br'm* would probably have been written **pr'm* in Sogdian script (cf. *pw'* for Pth. *bw'ẖ*, R9).

end of this paper.[1]

Text and translation of So 10100*m* (*with M* 1060, *Side A, as interlinear text*)

R1 [..](....t') o ms m'x[ ]

R2 [n]y's γwtk'n o kšy L' •[...y](m)

R3 xyry p(r) '(y)[.....](ky)' o šyr'kty'

R4 kwny-m rw'ny pt(s)t't' tnp'r

R5 prnxwnty rw'n nwš xwrty-yh

R6 pryk 't myšy wγš'nty pr

R7 'z̤-w'nt-δ'm o 'nwk cwr 'yn'l

R8 (red) nm' pwstw'ny nw'k xw o

R9 (black) ''pry-δ pw' m'rm'ny pry-št'

R10 kr'n 'wswγt' cs't pwtyšt

R11 (nyx)tr' o 'ys γwβ'ym'n

R12 'x(wr)m(z)t' βγ('y •)[

R1 ... Also for us

R2 it will be necessary to take ... Now, let us not

R3 ... foolish in ..., let us perform righteousness.

R4 O support of the soul, (O) body,

R5 the fortunate soul feeds on ambrosia,

R6 ... and always(?) rejoicing in

R7 the world of the living. (Tk.) Änük Čor Ïnal.

R8 (Sogd.) This is (to) the *pwstw'ny* tune.

R9 (Pth.) Be thou blessed, Apostle Mar Mani!

R10 (Sogd.) O pure, purified one, wiser(?) than

---

[1] Photographs of both manuscripts are easily available on the web-site of the Berlin- Brandenburgische Akademie der Wissenschaften:

http://www.bbaw.de/forschung/turfanforschung/dta/index.html

I would like to take this opportunity to express my thanks to Professor Yutaka Yoshida (Kyoto), who kindly read a draft of this paper and made many valuable suggestions referred to below.

R11 all buddhas! Come, let us praise

R12 God Khurmazt ...

V1 [ ]m'x wrt[n]•m[ ]

V2 [ ]... xy(r o) tys kw xwr wrt(n)

V3 cxwr wr(tn)[ ]•r[ ](pr)

V4 'nwšy '(wc''wt) s'r pcδ'

'w](c')w(t s)['r](k)t(y

V5 't z'yh wrδyh pr'kn' 't

')ṭ z'yy[w](r)[δyẖ ...

V6 yxsβwδn š'š o kwwt m'ny

β]w(δ)'n š'š kwwṭ m'n[y

V7 xr'mt' twrny prkyn s't

... t](w)rnyẖ prqyyn s'[ṭ

V8 wβrk'rty 'prw o γrβw skt' š'š

... *]oo γrf skṭ' š'š oo*

V9 kt βr'm't šyšt' synktnc

q*ṭ[ ]oo syngṭync*

V10 sk'r s't kwβ'nty pryw o wyz-trγ

sk'r oo s'ṭ[ ]• oo wyjṭrγ

V11 nxwy-δ kwwt šmnw [']('z̤-)t' o

nxwyδδ oo qw[wṭ ...

V12 [n](m')c βr'm (m)rm'ny

]....ẖ nm'c [ ](•tz o) qr(')[

V1 ... moon chariot ...

V2 ... go ..., enter into the sun chariot,

V3 [alight](?) from the sun chariot ... in(?)

V4 eternal(?) justice(?) take your ease(?),

V5 and plant the earth (with) roses, and

V6 scatter the scent of musk where Mani

V7 has trodden. Dig out ... with all

V8 ..., scatter many thorns

V9 so that they may ripen (and) be scattered(?),

V10 with all mallets pound embers of jujube (wood)

V11 (into) lye where Satan was born(?).

V12 ... I pay homage, Mar Mani ...

Philological commentary

R2 *[n]y's* "to take", present infinitive governed by the following *γw-* "to be necessary, ought". Cf. *βxšy γwṭ* (Tale B, lines 45-6, cited in GMS, §909). — In view of other 1st person plural forms in the context (*m'x*, R1; *kwny-m*, R4), the last word in this line should probably be restored as a 1 pl. form in *-ym*, perhaps, as Yutaka Yoshida kindly suggests, an optative with a hortative sense ("Let us ...").

R4 *pt(s)t't'* "support". Although the end of the word is smudged, it seems impossible to read **ptst'th*, as *-h* has a very particular form in the handwriting of this scribe. The final -' is either a vocative ending (GMS, §1222) or the "invocatory *aleph*" which is peculiar to poetical texts (GMS, §974; cf. also Durkin-Meisterernst 2004, 1-2, for a long list of examples in Middle Persian and Parthian). Either explanation is also possible for *(nyx)tr'* "wiser" in R11, but *'wswyt'* in R10 is presumably a vocative (GMS, §1253).

R6 The phrase *pryk 't myšy wγš'nty* "... and always rejoicing" seems to give us two previously unknown words, of which *myšy* could well be the Sogd. equivalent of MP *hamēšag*, *mēšag* "always". Sogdian has at least two words spelt *pryk*, one meaning "witch, fairy", and one meaning "remaining, other", but neither seems suitable here. What seems to be required is either an adverb parallel with *myšy* (e.g. "*henceforth and always", cf. perhaps MP *fr'y* "more, further" etc.?) or an adjective parallel with *wγš'nty* (e.g. "*blessed and always rejoicing").

R7 On the Turkish name Änük Čor İnal see Reck 2006, 37 n. 2. In Zieme 2006, 116, to which Yutaka Yoshida has drawn my attention, the first word is read *ʾnwr* instead of *ʾnwk*, but this seems impossible.

R8 *nmʾ* "this" is a characteristically late Sogd. form, see Sims-Williams–Hamilton 1990, 42-3. — The name of the tune, *pwstwʾny*, is unknown. It is not even clear to what language it belongs.

R9 In theory *pwʾ* could represent Pth. *pwʾg* "pure", as it does in a fragment of *Huyadagmān* (Sims-Williams 1989, 322, R5), but several other hymns beginning with the phrase *ʾfryd bwʾẖ* "Be thou blessed" are attested, e.g. Müller 1913, 23, lines 327-8. — *pry-štʾ* can hardly be read *pry-štk* with Reck. In Sogdian script, Western Middle Iranian *-ag* is transcribed either by *-k* or by *-ʾ* (see Henning 1958, 76, on Sogd. *ʾzγwlʾ* for Pth. *ʿzgwlg*), so there is no reason to doubt that *pry-štʾ* represents Pth. *fryštg* "Apostle". It is much less likely that *pry-štʾ* is a Sogdian vocative form, since this would imply a change of language in the middle of the invocation.

R10 Since there is no punctuation after *krʾn*, it probably belongs with the following words, in which case it must be understood as Sogd. *krʾn* "pure". It is less likely that it represents Pth. *klʾn* "great" or "pure" (Sims-Williams 1989, 329) and belongs with the preceding sentence. — The phrases *csʾt pwtyšt* "from/than all buddhas" and *cxwr wr(tn)* "from the sun chariot" (V3), both cited in GMS, §1611, are late forms in which the final nasal of the preposition *cn* "from" is lost before a fricative.

R11 I am grateful to Yutaka Yoshida for suggesting the reading *γwβʾymʾn* "let us praise". For the 1 pl. ending *-(ʾ)ym(ʾ)n* see GMS, §721.

R12 *ʾx(wr)m(z)tʾ βγ(ʾy •)[*: since there is only one "God Khurmazt", the restoration *ʾxwrmztʾ (β)γ(ʾyš)[t* (Reck 2006, 37) does not seem likely.

V2 The forms *xyr* and *tys* are ambiguous, either 2 sg. imperative or 3 sg. imperfect, as are several other verbal forms in the following text (*prʾknʾ* or *prʾkʾn*, V5; *šʾš*, V6, V8). Others, however, seem to be unambiguous imperatives (*pcδ'*, V4; *prkyn*, V7; *nxwyδ*, V11), so it is probably best to understand them all in this way.

V3-4 The "circumposition" *pr* ... *s'r* is rather uncommon. Three instances are cited in Sims-Williams–Durkin-Meisterernst 2012, 173b, glossed approximately as "in, for".

V4 This line, the first with at least a partial parallel in M 1060, is the most problematic in the whole text. In the first place, if *'nwšy* is a variant of *nwšy* "eternal", the apparent preservation of the initial vowel of Old Iranian **an-auša-* (Avestan *anaoša-*) is extremely unusual and probably only comprehensible as a result of the influence of the Western Middle Iranian equivalent *'nwšg*. A reading *''wšy* is also possible, but no such word is known. — The following word was read *'(βc'npt)* by Reck (2006, 37 with n. 3), who took this to be an otherwise unattested variant spelling of *'βc'npδ* "world". My admittedly hypothetical reading *'(wc''wt)* is based on the occurrence of a similar word, possibly to be read *'wc'wṭ*, in M 1828, R7. This text was published by Sundermann (2001, 813-25), who preferred the reading *('yc)'w(ṭ)* (ibid., 825), but allowed that *('wc)'w(ṭ)* would be a possible alternative (ibid., 816 n. 18, referring to an unexplained *'wc'w* in M 776, V6). As Sundermann shows, M 1828 contains a quotation from St. John's Gospel, Chapter 16, verse 8, where Greek δικαιοσύνη, Syriac *zdyqwt'* "justice, righteousness" appears the most likely equivalent of *'wc'wṭ*. If *'wc'wṭ* is in origin an abstract noun in **-tā-* or **-tāt-*, then *'wc'w* in M 776 might be the underlying adjective "just, righteous". — Finally, *pcδ'* is another unknown word, presumably 2 sg. imperative (see above on V2) of a verb *pcδ-*. Though such a verb is not yet attested, it would be an expected outcome of **pati-šad* "to sit down, rest, take one's ease", which has been reconstructed as the base underlying the well-attested noun *pṭš'δṭy'*, Christian Sogd. *ptš'dty'*, *pc'dty'* "rest, ease" and the adjective *ptš'dy*, *pc'dy* "at rest" (Sims-Williams 1985, 54). — An additional problem is the fact that the two versions do not seem to correspond exactly here. Though M 1060 contains traces which are at least compatible with a reading *[ʾw](cʾ)w(t s)[ʾr]*, what follows cannot by any means be equated with the clearly legible *pcδʾ* of So 10100m. It seems therefore that there must be a mistake in one version or the other, or that they contain two different recensions of the text.

V5 I have adopted the reading *prʾknʾ* (suggested by Yutaka Yoshida), though *prʾkʾn* is not out of the question. The latter would be the simple 2 sg. imperative, while the former would be the same with added "invocatory *aleph*", cf. below on V7.

V6 The compound *yxs-βwδn* "scent of musk" is new, but *yxs-* "musk" is attested in the Manichaean Sogdian poem M 137 (see GMS, §807) as well as in the "Ancient Letters". — *kwwt* or *kwwṭ* "where" (also in V11) is an unusual spelling for what is usually written as two words, *kw ZY* (and variants) in Sogdian script, *kw ʾṭy* (and variants) in Manichaean script.

V7 The verb *xrʾmtʾ* looks like a 2 pl. form, but a 3 sg. is clearly required. Possibly the final -ʾ is here the "invocatory *aleph*" mentioned above on R4 and V5. In that case, *xrʾmtʾ* is most probably 3 sg. intransitive preterite. The same explanation may apply to *[ʾ](ʾẓ-)tʾ* "was born" in V11, if this is correctly restored. See also below on *šyštʾ* in V9. — *twrny* is another new word, presumably a noun, object of the verb *prkyn*. The latter is also unknown, but is presumably cognate with the attested noun *prkʾyn* "ditch" (Sundermann 1985, 51) from the root **kan* "to dig".

V8 *wβrkʾrty*, perhaps oblique pl. of a noun **wβrkʾr*, may contain *wβr-* "snow" but is otherwise unclear. — Two words are sometimes spelt *ʾprw*: an adverb meaning "then, afterwards" (GMS, §1142 n. 1) and the combination of the preposition *pr* with the definite article (Henning 1943, 70, Text H, line 1). Since neither of these fits here, I suspect a variant spelling of the postposition meaning "with", elsewhere spelt *pryw* (as in

V10), *'pryw*, *'pr'yw*, *pr'w*, *prw*, etc. — The phrase *γrf skṭ' š'š* was cited from this text by Gershevitch 1985, 53, q.v. on *skṭ'* "thorns".

V9 For Buddhist Sogdian *βr''mt* "ripe" (= Christian *fr'm[t]*) and *βr'mty'* "harvest" see Sims-Williams 1995, 299-300. The present passage may attest the underlying verb *βr'm* "to ripen", here in the 3 sg. subjunctive *βr'm't*. In that case the following *šyšt'* is probably 3 sg. subj. likewise, either an error for the expected **šyš't*, or yet another verbal form with "invocatory *aleph*" (*šyšt-'* shortened from **šyš't-'*?), cf. above on V7. On the verb *šyš-* "to be scattered, dispersed" see GMS, §540, 706.

V9-10 *syngṭync* "made of jujube" is cited from this text in GMS, §1053. Since *sk'r* means "coals, embers" (see Sims-Williams 1985, 225, s.v. *sq'r*), presumably "made of jujube (wood)" is implied.

V10 *kwβ'nty* is another new word, perhaps oblique pl. of **kwβ'n*. If this is a word for some implement for pounding, as the context suggests, it could be a loanword from a Western Middle Iranian form cognate with Persian *kōban* "mallet", a derivative of the root **kaup* "to pound". Note the parallelism between the phrases *s't kwβ'nty pryw* here and *s't wβrk'rty 'prw* in V7-8. — The meaning of *wyjṭrγ* "alkali" was established by Gershevitch in GMS, p. 249 (Addendum to §1056).

V12 The texts in Sogdian and Manichaean script do not seem to correspond, although both contain the word *nm'c* "homage". (I owe the reading *nm'c* in M 1060, A8, to Yutaka Yoshida; it implies extended writing of *-c* at the end of the line.) So 10100m, V12, looks like the introductory invocation of a hymn; that it belongs to a new text is also suggested by the change to the first person singular ("I pay homage") as opposed to the first person plural (*γwβ'ym'n* "let us praise") in R11.

A note on the content of the biscript hymn

The hymn begins clearly enough with conventionally worded invocations, first to Mani (R9) and then (R12) to "God Khurmazt". At this point in the manuscript a few lines are missing, and it is not clear to me whether or not the text which follows on the Verso is actually addressed to Khurmazt, the Primal Man. At any rate, the goal of the journey via the moon chariot and the sun chariot which is described in V1ff. must be the New Paradise, the realm ruled by the Primal Man, and it is presumably the "earth" of the New Paradise which is referred to in V5. The following lines (V5-7) exhort the addressee to embellish this earth "where Mani has trodden" with roses and musk. It may be significant that the verb used here with Mani as subject, *xrʾm* "to walk, step, tread", is the same which is used of the righteous soul entering the "fragrant, wonderful Paradise" in the famous Manichaean "Daēnā" text.[1] Although many details are unclear, the final lines of the hymn (V7-11) present a stark contrast, calling for the place "where Satan was born(?)" to be made a desolation.

Text of M 1060, with translation of Side B

A1 *traces*

A2 ʾw](cʾ)w(t s)[ʾr](k)t(y ʾ)ṭ zʾyy[w](r)[δyẖ]

A3 yxsβ]w(δ)ʾn šʾš kwwṭ mʾn[y]

A4 t](w)rnyẖ prqyyn sʾ[ṭ]

A5]oo γrf skṭʾ šʾš oo qṭ[]

A6]oo syngṭync skʾr oo sʾṭ[]

A7]• oo wyjṭrγ nxwyδδ oo qw[wṭ]

A8]....ẖ nmʾc []

A9](•tz o) qr(ʾ)[

〔1〕Henning 1945, 476–7, lines 12, 13, 18; Reck 2003, 336–8, lines 17, 18, 23.

A10 *traces*

B1 *traces*

B2]ʾ(x)šyʾd h[nʾ]m p(d)[

B3 [ʾ]w wyspʾn ʾwd(h)rw •[

B4 [ʾ](wd) bwrzʾnd ʾwd pd fryẖ [

B5 []dwšʾrmyy ʾwd nyzʾr ʾʾ•[

B6 [d]rmʾngr ʾwd hwgʾmg q•[

B7 [ʾ]wd p(d)[1] hwjstgyy ʾw(d nyrw)[g

B8](• dyn) wzrgyhʾ (wys)[p

B9](•r)w prwx(yyẖ)[

B2 ... will be heard, limb(?) ...

B3 to(?) all and every ...

B4 and(?) they will honour, and with love ...

B5 tenderness, and the weak ...

B6 healer and benevolent ...

B7 and with good fortune and strength(?) ...

B8 ... religion(?) greatly all ...

B9 ... prosperity ...

References

Boyce 1960 = M. Boyce, *A catalogue of the Iranian manuscripts in Manichean script in the German Turfan collection*, Berlin.

Durkin-Meisterernst 2004 = D. Durkin-Meisterernst, *Dictionary of Manichaean Middle Persian and Parthian* (Dictionary of Manichaean Texts, Vol. III, Part 1), Turnhout.

Gershevitch 1985 = I. Gershevitch, *Philologia Iranica* (Beiträge zur Iranistik 12, ed. N. Sims-Williams), Wiesbaden.

[1] This word is followed by an unexplained mark like a reversed letter *d*.

GMS = I. Gershevitch, *A grammar of Manichean Sogdian*, Oxford, 1954.

Henning 1943 = W. B. Henning, "The Book of the Giants", *BSOAS* 11/1, 52-74.

Henning 1945 = W. B. Henning, "Sogdian tales", *BSOAS* 11/3, 465-487.

Henning 1958 = W. B. Henning, "Mitteliranisch", *Handbuch der Orientalistik* I/IV/1, Leiden-Cologne, 20-130.

Morano 2008 = E. Morano, "A working catalogue of the Berlin Sogdian fragments in Manichaean script", *Iranian languages and texts from Iran and Turan. Ronald E. Emmerick memorial volume* (ed. M. Macuch et al.), Wiesbaden, 2007 [2008], 239-270.

Müller 1913 = F. W. K. Müller, "Ein Doppelblatt aus einem manichäischen Hymnenbuch (Maḥrnâmag)", *APAW* 1912, No. 5, Berlin, 1913.

Reck 2003 = C. Reck, "Die Beschreibung der Daēnā in einem soghdischen manichäischen Text", *Religious themes and texts of pre-Islamic Iran and Central Asia. Studies in honour of Professor Gherardo Gnoli* (ed. C. G. Cereti et al.), Wiesbaden, 323-338.

Reck 2006 = C. Reck, *Mitteliranische Handschriften*, Teil 1: *Berliner Turfanfragmente manichäischen Inhalts in soghdischer Schrift* (VOHD XVIII/1), Stuttgart.

Sims-Williams 1985 = N. Sims-Williams, *The Christian Sogdian manuscript C2* (Berliner Turfantexte XII), Berlin.

Sims-Williams 1989 = N. Sims-Williams, "A new fragment from the Parthian hymn-cycle *Huyadagmān*", *Études irano-aryennes offertes à Gilbert Lazard* (Cahiers de Studia Iranica 7), Paris, 321-331.

Sims-Williams 1995 = N. Sims-Williams, "Christian Sogdian texts from the Nachlass of Olaf Hansen, II: Fragments of polemic and prognostics", *BSOAS* 58, 288-302.

Sims-Williams 2010 = N. Sims-Williams, "A haunch of meat: A fable of Aesop in Sogdian and Old Turkish", *Papyri graecae Schøyen (PSchøyen II). Essays and texts in honour of Martin Schøyen* (Papyrologica Florentina XL, ed. D. Minutoli & R. Pintaudi), Florence, 197-201.

Sims-Williams–Durkin-Meisterernst 2012 = N. Sims-Williams & D. Durkin-Meisterernst, *Dictionary of Manichaean Sogdian and Bactrian* (Dictionary of Manichaean Texts, Vol. III, Part 2), Turnhout.

Sims-Williams–Hamilton 1990 = N. Sims-Williams & J. Hamilton, *Documents turco-sogdiens du IXe–Xe siècle de Touen-houang* (Corpus Inscriptionum Iranicarum, Part II, Vol. III/3), London.

Sundermann 1985 = W. Sundermann, *Ein manichäisch-soghdisches Parabelbuch* (Berliner Turfantexte XV), Berlin.

Sundermann 2001 = W. Sundermann, *Manichaica Iranica. Ausgewählte Schriften*, 2 vols., Rome.

Yoshida 2001 = Y. Yoshida, "On the Sogdian fragments of the St. Petersburg collection", *Contributions to the Studies of Eurasian Languages*, Series 3, *Issues in Eurasian Languages* 1, 105-17.

Zieme 2006 = P. Zieme, "Hybrid Names as a Special Device of Central Asian Naming", *Turkic-Iranian contact areas. Historical and linguistic aspects* (ed. L. Johanson and Ch. Bulut), Wiesbaden, 114-127.

5 The Iconographical Affiliation and the Religious Message of the Judgment Scene in the Chinese Manichaean Cosmology Painting

Gábor Kósa

(ELTE University, Budapest)[1]

The Cosmology painting (colours on silk, 137.1 cm x 56.6 cm, Japanese private collection, Japanese *uchū zu* 宇宙圖, Chinese *yǔzhòu tú* 宇宙図) is one of the nine Chinese Manichaean paintings preserved in Japan.[2] This unique painting, which might go back to Mānī's *Eikōn*[3] and which was

〔1〕The present paper was completed with the financial support received from the Chiang Ching-kuo Foundation for International Scholarly Exchange (PD003-U-09). I thank Prof. Yutaka Yoshida and Prof. Imre Galambos for reading and commenting on my paper. I am grateful for Dr. Lilla Russell-Smith and Furukawa Shoichi for allowing me to use copyrighted material of the Museum für Asiatische Kunst, Staatliche Museen zu Berlin (Berlin) and the Yamato Art Museum (Nara), respectively. My special thanks go to Sara Toso at British Museum Images, who was patiently replying to all my questions on copyrights, and kindly helped me to obtain permission for 1919,0101,0.80 (Fig. 8). The images of these manuscripts can also be found at the homepage of the Gallica website (http://gallica.bnf.fr) and the International Dunhuang Project (http://idp.bl.uk/). I gave a talk with the same title, but partly different content, at the "Symposium on the Newly Discovered Chinese Manichaean Paintings in Japan", Yamato Art Museum, Nara City (Japan), June 5–6, 2011.

〔2〕The currently identified paintings include the following ones: the Seiun-ji 栖云寺 image, the Sandōzu 三道図 (or Yamato Bunkakan Rokudōzu 六道図) painting, five paintings from a private collection (including two fragments of the Realm of Light, two missionary paintings and the Cosmology Painting discussed in this paper), the so-called Kokka 国華 image, and a further painting depicting the birth of Mānī. On the secondary literature of the new Chinese Manichaean paintings, see Kósa 2011.

〔3〕Yoshida 2015, Kósa 2014a.

identified by Prof. Yutaka Yoshida 吉田豊,[1] contains the third version of a pictorial Manichaean judgment scene, the other two being MIK III 4959 V (Museum für Asiatische Kunst, Berlin) and the Sandōzu 三道図 painting[2] (Yamato Bunkakan 大和文華館, Nara). In a former study, I endeavoured to demonstrate that the two latter paintings carry dissimilar messages.[3] Interestingly, as will be clear later on, the same is true for the judgment scene in the Cosmology painting (hence abbreviated as CP): in my interpretation, this painting again seems to convey a message that is different from those of both previously known judgment scenes.

In the present study, I will first offer my view of the iconographical affiliation of the CP judgment scene, and then proceed to offering some possible interpretations of this highly sophisticated scene. I am extremely grateful to the Japanese private collector, who wants to remain anonymous, for granting me the permission to use certain details of the Cosmology painting.

5.1 The Iconographical Affiliation of the Judgment Scene in the Cosmology Painting

The judgment scene in the lower register of the Sandōzu painting (hanging scroll, colours on silk, 142 cm×59.2 cm, Yamato Bunkakan 大和文華館,

[1] The Coptic *Psalm-book* is quoted from Allberry 1938; the *Kephalaia* from Böhlig and Polotsky 1940, and Gardner 1995. The Chinese Manichaean scriptures are abbreviated as T = *Traité* (*Bosi jiao canjing* 波斯教残经, BD00256) and H = *Hymnscroll* (*Monijiao xiabu zan* 摩尼教下部赞, S.2659). These Chinese texts, which were also included in the *Taishō shinshū daizōkyō* 大正新修大藏经 (*Traité*: T.54.2141b: 1281a–1286a; *Hymnscroll*: T.54.2140: 1270b–1279c), are quoted according to the column of the manuscript. For the sake of simplicity, here I use a simplified way of transcription of the Chinese characters; on a more precise and faithful transcription of the original Chinese texts, see Prof. Lin Wushu's editions (1997: 268–316, and his most recent edition of the Dunhuang texts).

[2] See Yoshida 2009.

[3] Kósa 2015.

Nara) applies the Ten Kings of Hell iconography to convey its Manichaean message.[1] For the present analysis, I divided the extant Ten Kings of Hell paintings into four principal categories.[2]

The first is intimately related to the 32 handwritten copies of *The Scripture on the Ten Kings* or *Ten Kings sūtra* (*Shiwang jing* 十王经),[3] all deriving from 10–11th century Dunhuang,[4] six of which also contain illustrations.[5] The birth of the concept of the Ten Kings can be followed from the 7th century to the currently extant, first dated copy from AD 908.[6] Although the *Ten Kings sūtra* did not enjoy a canonical status, several surviving manuscripts attest to its popularity.[7] As for the relation of the text and the images in this type, there are two poles (only pictures [e.g. P.4523], only text [e.g. P.5580]) and forms in-between with texts (prose or hymns) and images alike (e.g. P.2003, P.2870).[8] In these handscrolls, each

---

[1] Gulácsi 2009: 16, 2009a: 27. On the iconography of the Ten Kings of Hell paintings, see e.g. Tokushi and Ogawa 1963, Miya 1990, 1992, 1993, Ebine 1986, Kajitani 1974, 1979, Takasu 1993. This basic introduction to the Ten Kings of Hell tradition is taken from Kósa 2015: 208-209.

[2] Cf. Miya 1990: 83, Miya 1992: 1–3, Phillips 2003: 127. On Sichuan sculptures of the Ten Kings, which seem to be related to the second category above, see e.g. Zhang and Liao 2007, Suchan 2003, Kucera 1995. Here I do not treat material which is much later than the late Yuan or early Ming Manichaean paintings, since they could not influence the present paintings (for an interesting collection of 19–20th century images, see K.E. Brashier's site: http://academic.reed.edu/hellscrolls/).

[3] The complete title of the text is *Fo shuo Yanluo wang shouji sizhong yuxiu shengqi wangsheng jingtu jing* 佛说阎罗王授记四众预修生七往生净土经 ["The Scripture Spoken by the Buddha to the Four Orders on the Prophecy Given to King Yama Concerning the Sevens of Life to Be Cultivated in Preparation for Rebirth in the Pure Land", Teiser 1994: 7], but it is sometimes abbreviated as *Yanluo wang shouji jing* 阎罗王授记经, *Yuxiu shengqi wangsheng jingtu jing* 预修生七往生净土经 or *Shiwang jing* 十王经. On the various manuscript copies, see Teiser 1994: 239–241, on a list of those containing illustrations, see Teiser 1994: 228–229, on the Japanese version of the scripture, see Teiser 1994: 58–61. I will use a short title (*Ten Kings sūtra*) throughout.

[4] Teiser 1999: 177. Most copies attribute the authorship to Zangchuan 藏川, who lived in Dashengcisi 大圣慈寺 in Chengdu 成都 (Sichuan).

[5] Teiser 1994: 228–229.

[6] Teiser 1999: 177, Ledderose 2000: 176.

[7] Teiser 1994: 80–81, 239–241.

[8] Teiser 1999: 179–182. On the various versions of the text of the sūtra, see e.g. Du 1989.

image of the Ten Kings is followed by a eulogy of the respective king. The influence of this type was not confined to the Dunhuang region, but was also present in the northern and southwestern (e.g. Sichuan) parts of China, the text itself being widely used later on in other regions as well.[1]

The second type of 10th century paintings also comes from the Dunhuang region, but it envisages the Ten Kings as flanking Kṣitigarbha in the middle on a single hanging scroll.[2] In contrast with the narrative Dunhuang scrolls, Cheeyun Kwon labels the 'Kṣitigarbha and the Ten Kings' type as iconic.[3] A possible prototype of this arrangement might have been the frontispiece of some narrative Dunhuang scrolls, where Śākyamuni (P.2003) or Kṣitigarbha (P.4523) appears in a central position while the Ten Kings are seated on his two sides.[4]

The third important type of Ten Kings tradition was present in southeast China, especially the Ningbo 宁波 region (Zhejiang), during the $12–13^{th}$ centuries.[5] In Ningbo, this type of painting enjoyed such popularity that they were mass-produced for overt commercial purposes,[6] as it is evidenced, among others, by the fact that they bear "commercial" inscriptions: "Painted by Lu Xinzhong in Flagstone alley, Cartbridge ward, Qingyuanfu",[7] or "The Great Song [dynasty], at Mingzhou [Ningbo], the Carriage Bridge, West, painted at the house of Jin Chushi".[8] As Qingyuanfu 庆元府 was the official name of Ningbo only between 1195

〔1〕Teiser 1994: 79. On the fragments of its Uighur version, which was translated from the Chinese between 1050–1250 (Teiser 1994: 56), see von Gabain 1973, Zieme 1996.

〔2〕Matsumoto 1937.II: Figs. CVIII–CXII, Watanabe 1984: 7–16, 77–81. pls. 1–5; Teiser 1994: 230–232.

〔3〕Kwon 2005: 28.

〔4〕Cf. Teiser 1999: 185, Soymié 1981: 171–172.

〔5〕On the secondary literature on these paintings, see e.g. Hirasawa 2008: 13–14. n.55. Cheeyun Kwon (2005) assumes that the Packard set is the "missing link" between the Dunhuang and the Ningbo paintings.

〔6〕Ledderose 1981.

〔7〕Ledderose 1981: 34.

〔8〕Fong 1992: 342.

and 1276/77, thus the paintings are generally considered to be the products of the 13th century. Though there are many paintings that bear Lu Xinzhong's 陆信忠 (fl. ca. 1195–1276) name, the quality of these works vary, thus, as Ledderose notes, "they must have been produced by ateliers with many employees."[1] They were especially favoured by Japanese merchants, who brought many of them to Japan, where they sold them, triggering a unique and intensive fascination with the topic among later Japanese painters.[2] The paintings by Jin Chushi 金处士 and Lu Xinzhong were intensively copied, and examples from their ateliers are currently housed in various collections of Japan, Europe and the United States.[3]

In the present classification, the last category contains the non-Chinese Ten Kings of Hell paintings: these include the Uighur,[4] the Korean[5] and the Japanese[6] ones. They represent different traditions: while the first closely follows the Chinese version,[7] the two latter ones are more elaborated compared to the Chinese tradition. Nevertheless, since they were not antecedents of the CP, here I categorized them in one group.

In the following, I will make use of paintings of the Dunhuang narrative style and the Ningbo individual style, and will refer to the two other types only when they offer a good analogy. While in Dunhuang the figures of the Ten Kings illustrated the scrolls of *Ten Kings sūtra*, in Ningbo

---

〔1〕Ledderose 1981: 34. Also see Ledderose 2000: 163–185.

〔2〕Teiser 1993: 129: "By the fourteenth century pictures of the ten kings were a familiar sight throughout China and were gaining popularity in Korea and Japan." On a summary of the Japanese concepts of hell, including the Ten Kings paintings, see Hirasawa 2008.

〔3〕Teiser 1993: 129.

〔4〕See von Gabain 1973, Teiser 1994: 55–57, 235–236, Zieme 1996.

〔5〕E.g. Kwon 1999.

〔6〕E.g. Shi 1985, Teiser 1994: 57–62, on the most important secondary studies, see Phillips 2003: 144. n.1.

〔7〕Zieme 1996: 408.

the individual kings were painted on individual scrolls, and except for the name of the king, no written reference to the sūtra is included in the paintings. There are, however, more differences between the Dunhuang and the Ningbo types of Ten Kings of Hell paintings (compare e.g. 4/d).

1. The Dunhuang scenes are usually simpler and more schematic, while the Ningbo paintings are more detailed and elaborated in the depiction of the kings' robe, the various clerks, the wards and the general environment.[1]

2. The kings' courts of the Dunhuang paintings lack the hellish torture scenes,[2] while they are frequently depicted in the Ningbo paintings.[3]

3. Various motifs that were present in the Dunhuang scrolls (River Nai, the scale of *karma*, or the six paths of rebirth) are missing from the Ningbo paintings.[4]

4. In the Dunhuang paintings, the king is usually flanked by one or two young, feminine assistants, while in the Ningbo paintings middle-aged male clerks help him in his judgment.

The Manichaean Sandōzu (SD) and the CP judgment scenes also have various differences (see Fig. 4/c and Fig. 3):

1. They are positioned in different parts of the painting: lower register (SD), middle section (CP);

2. They differ in their degree of stylization: hardly stylized, more realistic (SD) and rather stylized (CP);

3. The judge is flanked by middle-aged male clerks (SD) and young feminine assistants (CP) with the scrolls of deeds;

---

〔1〕Kwon (1999: 70) characterizes the Ningbo paintings as expressing "sensual realism".

〔2〕However, this motif appears in a separate image of hell at the end of the manuscripts.

〔3〕Phillips 2003: 129, although Uighur representations in A. von Gabain's study (1973: 60. Fig. 76 [MIK III 4690a], p. 62. Fig. 78 [MIK III 6332]) seem to contain such scenes.

〔4〕Kwon 2005: 31.

4. A scene of torture is visible below the judgment scene (SD); on the other hand, the CP does not feature any torture scene.

However, the Manichaean Sandōzu painting and the "Buddhist" Ningbo paintings share several common features (compare Fig. 4/c and Fig. 4/d):

1. Figures are not stylized.

2. Judge is in three-quarter[1] profile.

3. Attendants holding a scroll of paper are always male adults, sometimes with monster-heads.

4. Tortures of the convicts are depicted in the same painting.

These preceding four features are in turn not characteristic of the CP judgment scene (Fig. 3).

1. The figures of CP are stylized.

2. Judge is shown in a full frontal view, and not in three-quarter profile.

3. The two attendants with the scroll are young people, they are not adults and do not have a monster-head.

4. Tortures of the convicts are depicted neither in the surroundings of the judgment scene, nor anywhere else in the painting.

In sum, the Ningbo Ten Kings paintings are indeed good analogies to the Sandōzu judgment scene, but do not have any stylistic characteristics of the CP judgment scene. The question naturally arises: do we possess better analogies to the judgment scene of the CP?

As mentioned before, there is another set of Ten Kings: the illustrations of the Dunhuang copies. At a first glance, they seem to be both geographically and temporally distant from the CP, which is currently regarded as originating from 14–15th century southeast China,[2] very close

[1] For the sake of simplicity, I always use the expression "three-quarter" view, though certain figures might be in two-thirds (or other) views between profile and full frontal view.

[2] Furukawa 2010.

in time and place to the production of the Ningbo paintings, which are, despite the proximity, not appropriate analogies. Among the Dunhuang Ten Kings illustrations there is one set which reveals a remarkable analogy to the CP judgment scene: P.2870 (ink on paper, ca. 30 x 615,2 cm, 10th c., Bibliothèque nationale de France). This manuscript (*Fo shuo shiwang jing* 佛说十王经),[1] which is attributed to Zangchuan 藏川 from Dashengci 大圣慈 monastery (Chengdu),[2] the supposed originator of the *Ten Kings sūtra*, contains 34 eulogies (*zan* 赞) and 14 images.[3] Together with the manuscript from the Satō Han'ai 佐藤汎愛 collection (10th c., Dunhuang),[4] this manuscript belongs to Group B in Stephen Teiser's classification.[5] Here I summarize some of the similarities between the illustrations of P.2870 and the CP judgment scene (Fig. 1/a–c).

1. Similarly to the CP judge, the majority of P.2870 judges (1st, 3rd–8th) are seated on raised platform with roof supported by poles,[6] with three, visually divided compartments (unique among the Dunhuang manuscripts, only the fifth court of Yama has a similar background in S.3961).

2. Similarly to the CP platform, the P.2870 platforms have stairs in the middle leading to the judge (unique among the Dunhuang manuscripts, only the fifth court of Yama has a similar background in S.3961).

3. Similarly to the CP judge, the P.2870 judges are usually shown in a full frontal view (1st, 3rd–7th, 8th [except for head], 9th).

---

〔1〕Fo shuo Yanluo wang shouji sizhong yuxiu sheng qi wangsheng jingtu jing 佛说阎罗王授记四众预修生七往生净土经.

〔2〕Teiser 1999: 177. Chengdufu Dashengci si shamen Zangchuan shu 成都府大圣慈寺沙门藏川述.

〔3〕See www.idp.bl.uk.

〔4〕Kubosō Kinen Bijutsukan 久保惣记念美术馆 (Izumi 和泉).

〔5〕Teiser 1993: 126, 1994: 228.

〔6〕Teiser 1994: 228. Because of the ostensibly more solid roof, the CP building seems to be closer to a real house.

4. Similarly to the CP attendants, the P.2870 attendants are not male adult officers (like in the Ningbo paintings), but young people, furthermore, there is no monster-headed attendant (this feature is general among Dunhuang scrolls, but different from the Ningbo paintings).

Fig. 1/a. Cosmology painting (detail)
Copyright © Japanese private collection

Fig. 1/b. The court of Qin Guangwang 秦广王
Ten Kings sūtra, P.2870 (detail) 10th c., ink on paper, ca. 30.7 cm × 615.2 cm.
Copyright © Bibliothèque nationale de France
Fig. 1/a–b. The Judge and his attendants in the CP (Fig. 1/a) compared with the first (Fig. 1/b) court of the P.2870 Dunhuang manuscript

None of these similarities between P.2870 and the CP is in turn shared by the Ningbo paintings. Thus, P.2870 seems to be a fitting analogy, but is it a perfect one? At a first glance, there are also some differences between P.2870 and the CP judgment scene, the rationale of which I will clarify one by one.

1. The Manichaean Judge has a halo (*nimbus*), while none of the judges in P.2870 (or any other scrolls or paintings) has one. This difference can be explained by the fact that in the CP almost all divine figures have a halo (see Fig. 2/b), the Manichaean Judge, who is considered as a divine emanation, is thus simply no exception to this general rule.

2. The face of the Manichaean Judge is different from the judge of P.2870, who has a moustache and beard. This difference can be explained by the feature that in the CP the faces of the various divine emanations are practically identical, as a rule they have no beard or moustache (see Fig. 2/b),[1] the judge is therefore again no exception to this general rule.

3. The robes of the Manichaean Judge and the attendants are different from those of the judge and his attendants of P.2870. This can be explained by the fact that in the Cosmology painting, the robes worn by various divine figures differ only in colouring, but they are otherwise rather similar (see Fig. 2/b), the judge and his attendants are therefore once again no exceptions to this general feature.

---

[1] There is one exception: a huge head between the Sun and the Moon, whom I identify with the Perfect Man (Column of Glory), does have a thin moustache and beard, but this figure is highly dissimilar from all other divine figures, including the Righteous Judge.

Fig. 2/a–b. The similarity of robe and halo, the lack of moustache and beard in the CP: the Righteous Judge (left) and the Father of Greatness with the Twelve Aeons (right) compared
Cosmology painting (details)
Copyright © Japanese private collection

In sum, P.2870 is a much better analogy of the CP judgment scene than the Ningbo Ten Kings paintings or the Sandōzu judgment scene. Although there are some differences between the P.2870 and the CP judgment scene, these can be explained by the accommodation of the Dunhuang-type judgment scene to the entire Manichaean Cosmology painting. All seemingly differing features (halo, attire, moustache and beard) might therefore be the result of this process of accommodation (Fig. 2/a–b). It must be emphasized that I do not claim that the painter of the CP judgment scene copied P.2780, but that among the currently available manuscripts and paintings, the iconography of P.2780 stands closest to the CP judgment scene. Therefore, it can be assumed that the painter of the CP judgment scene might have had a similar Dunhuang-type image in mind.

Consequently, the similarity between the P.2870 manuscript and the CP allows at least two theoretical possibilities. The first is that the CP, which most probably arrived in China along the Silk Road, was produced in several stages, thus at an earlier stage, the 10th century P.2870 or a similar manuscript from Dunhuang served as a prototype of the CP judgment scene. The second option is that the manuscript type which is at present exemplified by the P.2870 were known not only in 10th century Dunhuang, but also in 14–15th century Zhejiang or Fujian, thus they could exert a local influence at the time of the production of the currently known CP version. As for the second option, as far as I know, there is only one surviving Dunhuang-type manuscript from around Ningbo (the Huangyan Bowuguan 黄岩博物馆 Ten Kings scroll[1]), but this is a 10th century copy and is rather dissimilar from the P.2870. Furthermore, the second option is eclipsed by the first one not only because of the essential lack of Dunhuang-type manuscripts from the 14–15th century Ningbo, but also because at this time in southeast China, according to our present knowledge, the Ningbo type of paintings were in absolute vogue. As far as we know, Manichaeans always attempted to apply the locally and temporally most

〔1〕NNM 2009: 84.

fashionable religious and artistic trends in order to reach the widest audience, therefore the Ningbo-style judgment scene must have been more appropriate for their missionary purposes in the 14–15th c. southeastern Chinese environment.

In sum, although the second option cannot be excluded, I would opt for the first one, i.e. the judgment scene of the CP is the remnant of an earlier phase of the CP, which can be approximately traced back to 10–11th century Dunhuang.

5.2 A Possible Interpretation of the Judgment Scene in the Cosmology Painting

The CP judgment scene is a rather complex unity of various motifs, which I will attempt to clarify one by one in order to arrive at a possible, comprehensive interpretation. First, I will concentrate on the position of the scene in the CP, and then proceed to the analysis of the various groups of figures appearing in it.

5.2.1 The Positon of the Judgment Scene and the Two Types of Judgment

The judgment scene in the CP is placed on the viewer's right side of the CP, above the horizon line and under the lowest firmament held up by two angels (Fig. 3). This position in the air ("atmosphere") can be paralleled with the descriptions in some Coptic sources that place the Righteous Judge ("the Judge of truth") in the air.[1]

> This is the sign of the Bema of the judge, who is in the air.[2]
>
> The judge himself that is in the air will give thee his three gifts.[3]

〔1〕Cf. Sundermann 1979: 124. n.132, Yoshida 2010: 12b.

〔2〕*Psalmbook* 21,1–2: πεϊ πε πμεϊνε / м̅πβημα μπκριτης ετϩп̅παηρ.

〔3〕*Psalmbook* 22,12–13: πκριτης ϩωωϥ [ετϩη] / παηρ [ϥ]ⲁϯ πε м̅πεϥϣαμτ̅ п̅ϩмaτ.

The second power whom Jesus summoned is the gre[at Jud]ge, who gives judgment on all the souls [of] mankind, [his] dwelling being established in the atmosphere under [… / …] wheel […] stars. [1]

The tenth judge is [the Jud]ge who dwells in the atmosphere, judging all mankind. He [ma]kes a separation between they who are good and they who are evil, setting [apart] the righteous from the sinners. [2]

The eighth throne is established in the atmosphere. The Judge of truth sits upon it, he who judges all mankind. Three paths shall be distinguished be[f]ore him: one to death, one to life, on[e] to the mingling. [3]

[Bef]ore sin had multiplied and had made a kingdom in the flesh, before the acquitted and the condemn[ed] were set apart from each other, the Judge [w]as sent forth and revealed. His throne was created and placed [i]n the living atmosphere, so that he would be [a] just Judge, so that there the righteous and the sinners would be set apart and tested [a]nd separated from each other. [4]

Especially intriguing is the fact that the Judge's position in the air is thus detected in two distant sets of sources: the 4–5th century written Coptic

---

〔1〕Trans. Gardner 1995: 39–40. *Kephalaia* 35,24–27: ⲧⲙⲁϩⲥⲛ̄ⲧⲉ ⲛ̄ϭⲁⲙ ⲉⲧⲁ ⲓ̄ⲏ̄ⲥ̄ ⲧⲁϩ/ [ⲙ]ⲉⲥ ⲡⲉ ⲡⲛⲁ[ϭ ⲛ̄ⲕⲣⲓ]ⲧⲏⲥ ⲉⲧϯϩⲉⲡ ⲁⲛⲯⲩⲭⲁⲩⲉ ⲧⲏⲣⲟⲩ / [ⲛ̄]ⲛ̄ⲣⲱⲙⲉ ⲉⲣ[ⲉ ⲧⲉϥ]ⲥⲕⲏⲛⲏ ⲥⲙⲁⲁⲛⲧ̄ ϩⲛ̄ ⲡⲁⲏⲣ ϩⲁ . . . / [. .] ⲧⲣⲟⲭⲟⲥ . [. .]ⲥⲓⲟⲩ.

〔2〕Trans. Gardner 1995: 82. *Kephalaia* 80,29–32: ⲡⲙⲁϩⲙⲏⲧ ⲛⲕⲣⲓⲧⲏⲥ ⲡⲉ [ⲡⲕⲣⲓ] /ⲧⲏⲥ ⲉⲧϩⲙⲉⲥⲧ ϩⲙ̄ ⲡⲁⲏⲣ ⲉϥϯϩⲉⲡ ⲁⲛⲣⲱⲙⲉ ⲧⲏⲣⲟⲩ ⲉϥ[ⲉⲓ]/ⲣⲉ ⲛ̄ⲟⲩⲡⲱⲣϫ ⲁⲃⲁⲗ ⲟⲩⲧⲉ ⲛⲉⲧⲁⲛⲓⲧ ⲙⲛ ⲛⲉⲧϩⲁⲩ ⲉϥⲛⲟⲩ[ϩⲉ] / ⲛ̄ⲛ̄ⲇⲓⲕⲁⲓⲟⲥ ⲁⲃⲁⲗ ⲛ̄ⲛ̄ⲣⲉϥⲣⲛⲁⲃⲉ.

〔3〕Trans. Gardner 1995: 85. *Kephalaia* 83,4–8: ⲡⲙⲁϩϣⲙⲟⲩⲛ ⲛⲑⲣⲟⲛⲟⲥ ⲡⲉ ⲡⲉⲧⲥⲙⲁⲁ/ⲛⲧ̄ ϩⲙ ⲡⲁⲏⲣ ⲉⲣⲉ ⲡⲕⲣⲓⲧⲏⲥ ⲛⲧⲉ ⲧⲙⲏⲉ ϩⲙⲉⲥⲧ ⲁϫⲱϥ ⲉ/ⲧⲉ ⲛ̄ⲧⲁϥ ⲡⲉⲧϯϩⲉⲡ ⲁⲛⲣⲱⲙⲉ ⲧⲏⲣⲟⲩ ϣⲁⲣⲉ ϣⲁⲙⲧ̄ ⲙ̄ⲙⲁⲓ̈ⲧ / ⲡⲱⲣϫ ⲁⲃⲁⲗ ϩⲓ[ⲧ]ⲉϥⲉϩⲏ ⲟⲩⲉ ⲁⲡⲙⲟⲩ ⲟⲩⲉ ⲁⲡⲱⲛϩ̄ ⲟⲩ[ⲉ] ⲁ/ⲡⲧⲱⲧ.

〔4〕Trans. Gardner 1995: 124. *Kephalaia* 117,22–28: [ϩⲁ]ⲑⲏ ⲉⲙⲡⲉ ⲡⲛⲁⲃⲉ ⲁϣⲉⲓ̈ⲧⲉ ⲛ̄ϥⲣ̄ⲣ̄ⲣⲟ ϩⲉ ⲧⲥⲁⲣⲝ ⲉⲙⲡⲁ/ⲧⲟⲩⲛⲁϩ ⲛⲉⲧϭⲣⲁⲓ̈ⲧ ⲙⲛ̄ ⲛⲉⲧⲧⲁϫⲁ[ⲓ̈ⲧ] ⲁⲃⲁⲗ ⲛ̄ⲛⲉⲩⲉⲣⲏⲩ / [ⲁ]ⲩⲧⲛⲛⲁⲩ ⲁⲃⲁⲗ ⲙ̄ⲡⲕⲣⲓⲧⲏⲥ ⲁϥⲟⲩⲱⲛϩ̄ ⲁⲃⲁⲗ ⲁⲩⲥⲱⲛⲧ / ⲙ̄ⲡⲉϥⲑⲣⲟⲛⲟⲥ ⲁⲩⲕⲁⲁϥ [ϩ]ⲙ̄ ⲡⲁⲏⲣ ⲉⲧⲁⲛϩ̄ ϫⲉϥⲛⲁⲣ / [ⲟⲩ]ⲕⲣⲓⲧⲏⲥ ⲛ̄ⲇⲓⲕⲁⲓⲟⲥ ϫⲉⲕⲁⲁⲥ ⲉⲩⲛⲁⲛⲟⲩϩⲉ ⲁⲃⲁⲗ ⲛ̄ / [ϩ]ⲏⲧϥ ⲛ̄ⲥⲉⲇⲟⲕⲓⲙⲁⲥⲉ ⲛⲛⲇⲓⲕⲁⲓⲟⲥ ⲙⲛ̄ ⲛ̄ⲣⲉϥⲣⲛⲁⲃⲉ / [ⲛ̄]ⲥⲉⲡⲁⲣϫⲟⲩ ⲁⲃⲁⲗ ⲛ̄ⲛⲉⲩⲉⲣⲏⲩ.

sources in Egypt and the 14–15th Cosmology painting from southeast China (Fig. 3).

Fig. 3. The judgment scene of the Cosmology painting in the air above the horizon and below the lowest firmament
Cosmology painting (detail)
Copyright © Japanese private collection

It is evident that in the Coptic descriptions above, the eschatological Righteous or Just Judge appears who announces the final, "collective" judgment for humanity. Both his position in the air and the statements that he judges "all mankind" or "all the souls of mankind" support this identification. This eschatological scene is most exhaustively described in the Middle Persian *Šābuhragān*[1] (supposedly 3rd c. AD, the only work that Mānī wrote in a Middle Iranian language) and the *Sermon on the Great War* of the Coptic *Homilies* (4–5th c.).[2] It should be emphasized, however, that the Manichaeans also professed another type of judgment, the individual one. There are both differences and similarities between these two types of judgment. While the universal judgment takes place in the eschatological future, the individual judgment is meted out after the death of the individual at any time. While the universal judgment is closely related to Jesus and *Matthew* 25,31–46, the individual judgment does not seem to follow this pattern.

Notwithstanding the differences, there are also several similarities: in both cases, the human soul is judged, and this judgment opens three possible ways for him/her: Paradise, Hell or reincarnation(s).[3] In both cases, the past behaviour towards the elect (the Manichaean "priest") is the standard of the judgment. According to the Arabic *al-Fihrist*, which describes an individual judgment, the auditor (the Manichaean layman) makes known "what he has accomplished in the form of righteous behaviour and caring for the cult and the Elect,"[4] and the evil man is

---

[1] MacKenzie 1979: 505–509.

[2] E.g. Gardner and Lieu 2004: 224–225.

[3] See e.g. "The eighth throne is established in the atmosphere. The Judge of truth sits upon it, he who judges all mankind. Three paths shall be distinguished be[f]ore him: one to death, one to life, on[e] to the mingling." These three possible destinations are visually depicted in the Sandōzu painting as three registers in the uppermost, middle and lowermost parts of the painting.

[4] Dodge 1970: 796.

reproached of his evil deeds, and some deities "substantiate proof of his [sinner's] having neglected to aid the Elect". [1] Similarly, the *Šābuhragān*, which describes the collective, final judgment, states: "And Xradešahr [Jesus] says to them, 'You, (by) those (things) which the religious have *recounted – there(by) you have harmed me [and] I had reason to complain of [you]. And you are sinners, for you have been deceitful enemies of the religious [elects, GK], and you have distressed (them) and had no mercy on them." Moreover, it seems that both judges bestow three gifts, "the three victories", to the righteous (Coptic *Psalmbook* 22,12–13 [collective]; Chinese *Hymnscroll* 396–400 [individual]).

Furthermore, it also seems probable that Manichaeans labelled the two judges with the same name: the Chinese invariably used *Pingdeng wang* 平等王 (though we have examples only in the context of the individual judgment), while the Egyptian Manichaeans used, among others, the appellation 'Judge of Truth' (ⲡⲕⲣⲓⲧⲏⲥ ⲛⲧⲉ ⲧⲙⲏⲉ) for both judges. Here I quote from the Coptic *Kephalaia* to substantiate my second assertion.

> The eighth throne is established in the atmosphere. The Judge of truth sits upon it, he who judges all mankind. [2]
>
> You shall [come f]rom your body and see these things that I have recou[nted to] you; that they occur in truth before the Jud[ge] of truth, the one who shall not favour anyone. [3]

The first quotation refers to the collective judgment, while the second citation clearly refers to the individual one; nevertheless, the designation of the judge is the same (the Judge of truth, ⲡⲕⲣⲓⲧⲏⲥ ⲛⲧⲉ ⲧⲙⲏⲉ). In addition,

[1] Dodge 1970: 796.

[2] Trans. Gardner 1995: 85. *Kephalaia* 83,4–6: ⲡⲙⲁϩϣⲙⲟⲩⲛ ⲛⲑⲣⲟⲛⲟⲥ ⲡⲉ ⲡⲉⲧⲥⲙⲁⲁ/ⲛⲧ̄ ϩⲙ ⲡⲁⲏⲣ ⲉⲣⲉ ⲡⲕⲣⲓⲧⲏⲥ ⲛⲧⲉ ⲧⲙⲏⲉ ϩⲙⲉⲥⲧ ⲁϫⲱϥ ⲉ/ⲧⲉ ⲛ̄ⲧⲁϥ ⲡⲉⲧϯϩⲉⲡ ⲁⲛⲣⲱⲙⲉ ⲧⲏⲣⲟⲩ.

[3] Trans. Gardner 1995: 289. *Kephalaia* 288,15–18 (Böhlig 1966: 288): ⲉϣⲁⲛⲧⲉⲧⲛ̄[ⲉⲓ ⲁ] /ⲃⲁⲗ [ⲙ]ⲡⲉⲧⲛⲥⲱⲙⲁ ⲧⲉⲧⲛⲁⲛⲉⲩ ⲁⲛⲉϊ ⲉⲧⲁϊⲧⲉⲟ[ⲩⲁⲩ ⲛⲏ] /ⲧⲛ̄ ϫⲉ ⲥⲉϣⲟⲟⲡ ϩⲛ̄ ⲟⲩⲙⲏⲉ ⲙⲡⲙⲏⲧ ⲁⲃⲁⲗ ⲙⲡⲕⲣⲓⲧ[ⲏⲥ] / ⲛ̄ⲧⲉ ⲧⲙⲏⲉ ⲡⲉⲧⲉⲙⲁϥϫⲓϩⲟ ⲛ̄ⲗⲁⲟⲩⲉ.

there is also an apparently minor motif that coincides in the descriptions of the two different types of judgment scenes: following the initial joy of seeing the deities or the gift of the elects, the evil people become disappointed after they realize their own, not so felicitous fate. The first quotation comes again from the *al-Fihrist* (individual judgment), while the second comes from the *Homilies* (collective judgment):

> When death comes to an evil man (…) As those [good] deities are also present with the same garments, the evil man supposes that they have come to save him. But, instead, they have come to reproach him, to remind him if his evil deeds, and to substantiate proof of his having neglected to aid the Elect.[1]
>
> But the goats [sinners, GK] which are on his left [will] see the "hope" which he [the Judge, GK] has given to those who are on his right side. [Their] heart will rejoice for a moment because they [think that the] victory of the sheep [the righteous, GK] will also come to them. Then he will [turn to those] on the left side, and he will speak and say to them: "……… me, you that are accursed! Go to the fire [of the] Devil and his powers."[2]

In sum, it cannot be excluded that an average Manichaean envisaged only one Judge.[3] In the same way, I am not completely convinced that the painter of the CP,[4] or at least the Chinese Manichaean believers who were

---

〔1〕*Al-Fihrist* (Dodge 1970: 796).

〔2〕Trans. Pedersen 1996: 353–354. *Homilies* 38,16–22 (Pedersen 1996: 354. n.566): ⲛ̄ⲃⲁⲙⲡⲉ ϩⲱϥ ⲉⲧⲥⲁ ϭⲃⲟⲩⲣ ⲙ̄ⲙ[ⲁϥ] / [ⲛⲁⲛ]ⲟ ⲁⲡⲕⲁϩⲧⲏϥ ⲉⲧⲁϥⲧⲉϥ ⲛ̄ⲛⲉⲧⲥⲁ ⲟⲩⲛⲉⲙ / / [ⲡⲟⲩϩ]ⲛⲧ ⲛⲁⲣⲉϣⲉ ⲡⲣⲟⲥ ⲟⲩⲁⲡⲣⲏⲧⲉ · ⲉⲩⲙ[ⲉ]ⲩ[ⲉ]/ [ϫⲉ ⲡϭ]ⲣⲟ ⲛ̄ⲛⲉⲥⲁⲩ ⲛⲁⲉⲓ ⲛⲉⲩ ϩⲱⲟⲩⲉ · ⲧⲟⲧⲉ ϥⲁ/[ⲛⲁⲩϩϥ ⲁⲛ]ⲉⲧⲥⲁ [ϭ]ⲃⲟⲩⲣ · ⲛ̄ϥⲥⲉϫⲉ ⲛ̄[ϥ]ϫⲟⲥ ⲁⲣⲁⲩ [. .] / [. . . . . .] . . . ⲁⲣⲁï ⲛⲉⲧⲥϩⲟⲩⲁⲣⲧ · ⲃⲱⲕ ⲁ ⲧⲥⲉ/ⲧⲉ . . [ⲡⲇⲓⲁⲃⲟⲗ]ⲟⲥ ⲙ̄ⲛ̄ ⲛⲉϥϭⲁⲙ.

〔3〕The 28th *kephalaion* of the rather sophisticated *Kephalaia* differentiates between the seventh judge, whose name was not preserved, and who seems to be the judge of the individuals, and the tenth Judge, "the Judge who dwells in the atmosphere, judging all mankind" (Gardner 1995: 82).

〔4〕Even if the CP as a whole might be traced back to the *Eikōn* (Kósa 2014), I think that this particular scene of the judgment is obviously a later, and pronouncedly Chinese, replacement of the original judgment scene.

viewing it, made a distinction between the two different types of judgment. It is possible that the painter conflated these two types into one single scene. While the judge is seated in the atmosphere, and therefore he must be equated with the judge of the final judgment, the judgment itself is principally directed at one single individual (the naked figure), and we do not see the crowds of people who should appear at such a collective judgment.[1] One of the important points in which a collective judgment differs from the individual one is obviously the presence of the entire humanity,[2] but this is conspicuously absent in the CP.[3]

Nils A. Pedersen, who wrote a book on the topic, voiced a similar opinion on the intimate interrelatedness of the individual and the collective eschatology.[4] The reason I mention the blurred borders of the two types of judgment is twofold. Firstly, I will mainly use material from texts that describe the universal judgment, but sometimes I will use written material that report on individual eschatology. Secondly, the Buddhist Ten Kings of Hell paintings, which will play a pivotal role in my analysis, only know of the individual eschatology, though, as I argue, they are applied to express the Manichaean universal eschatological notions as well.

---

[1] The identification of the three figures in ornate garment on the Judge's right is not secure, see later.

[2] E.g. *Šābuhragān* (MacKenzie 1979: 505): "And the men who will be rulers in the world will go running before him and pay homage and accept his commands. And lustful [and] wicked and *tyrannous men will repent. And then god Xradešahr will send messengers to east and west, and they will go and [bring] the religious with (their) helpers, and those wicked ones [together] with (their) accomplices, before Xradešahr."

[3] Though the absence of a multitude is evident, it must be also added that later on I will argue that the naked figure in fact represents the entire humanity.

[4] "The passage also shows how the Manichees united "individual" and "collective" eschatology" (Pedersen 1996: 352–353). "...in various ways it [individual eschatology, GK] corresponds to or has influenced the 'collective eschatology'" (Pedersen 1996: 341). "There are clear analogies between on the one hand the judgment after death and the associated judge (...), and on the other hand Jesus' "collective" end-time judgment..." (Pedersen 1996: 341).

5.2.2 Mānī and his attendants

On the viewer's left side of the judgment scene, Mānī appears with two attendants standing on a red-pink cloud that is meandering upwards. Mānī is clad in his usual white attire with a red border, which makes his figure easily recognizable in the CP and the other new paintings from the same private collection. Both Mānī with a green halo and his attendants with a golden crown are depicted in *añjali mudrā.* Since this triad appears frequently in the CP, it seems probable that it is not specifically related to the judgment scene.

Mānī never appears at the lower part of the CP (under Mount Sumeru): unlike in the missionary paintings, in the CP Mānī does not appear in earthly settings. While he apparently witnesses the activities of the Sun and the Moon, the two figures of Rex Honoris in the seventh firmament, the Virgin of Light or the Righteous Judge, he does not appear beside the equally significant figures of Adamas, Primal Man, Atlas or Gloriosus Rex (all appearing in the two lower sections of the CP). Based on a legend of Mānī's celestial journey preserved by Mīrkhwānd (15th c.),[1] Y. Yoshida assumes that the numerous appearances of Mānī in the CP refer to the notion that during his visions Mānī personally observed the upper parts of the cosmos.[2]

Borrowed from Buddhist iconography, the meandering "tail" of the cloud, on which this triad stands, clearly indicates the direction from where the figures on them arrived. This feature is present in the entire CP. The four divine groups of three figures, for example, who arrive at the four continents around Mount Sumeru, all have the tails of their cloud "vehicle" meandering upwards, which signifies that they arrive from the upper regions. Similarly, in all cases when Mānī appears on a cloud, it is implied that he

〔1〕Reeves 2011: 122–123.

〔2〕Yoshida 2010: 9b–10a.

arrives from the upper regions. This in turn would mean that these appearances in the CP claim that he was first taken for a journey to the Realm of Light, and from there did he descend to the other celestial regions with two divine attendants. The figure of Mānī is indeed visible in the uppermost section of the painting, the one which depicts the Realm of Light, where three angel-like figures, all seated on clouds, are facing him, and the figure in the middle seems to grant him a crown.

Whatever the exact meaning of the triad of Mānī and his two attendants is, it is evident that they are only witnessing the act of judgment. As it was frequently emphasized previously,[1] the CP also testifies to the notion that the Righteous Judge is not identical with Mānī, they are two independent figures.

5.2.3 The Judge and his attendants

As mentioned before, Ten Kings judges are usually depicted in a three-quarter profile and seated behind a table. The motif of table is missing only in the later Dunhuang-type Huangyan Bowuguan 黄岩博物馆 scroll[2] and in a very few courts of the Ningbo kings, otherwise it is present in both the Dunhuang and the Ningbo paintings. Although the seated judge (king) here evidently follows the Ten Kings of Hell tradition, it coincides with the fact that the Righteous Judge, who is the emanation of Jesus or sometimes perhaps Jesus himself,[3] also takes a seat to judge mankind.[4]

---

[1] Franzmann 2003: 89–97, Rui 2003, Gardner and Lieu 2004: 138. n.59.

[2] NNM 2009: 84.

[3] Lindt 1992: 195: "As an emanation of Jesus, his function is in the *Psalm-Book* often attributed to Jesus himself."

[4] Heuser 1998: 84: "Jesus takes his place on the judgment seat in order to judge humanity." *Psalm-book* 42,5: "The great Judge is seated"; *Psalm-book* 34,23–24: "For Jesus my judge it is that sits upon it and judges the man …"; *Kephalaia* 83,4–6 (Trans. Gardner 1995: 85): "The eighth throne is established in the atmosphere. The Judge of truth sits upon it, he who judges all mankind."

Following the original position of the judges around Kṣitigarbha, the three-quarter profile is ubiquitous in the Ningbo paintings, and usual in the Dunhuang ones, though the P.2870 manuscript, which most closely resembles the CP judgment scene, has only the 2nd and the 10th judges shown in three-quarter profile; all the others are in full frontal view. As also mentioned above, even more distinctive is the presence of a rather stylized building with the three visually divided compartments. This kind of stylized building appears exclusively on P.2870 and the CP. The house of the CP judgment scene has red columns and a golden roof, and seems to be accommodated to the stylistic features of the other buildings in the CP (the 28 buildings along the vertical axis of the painting, the 120 buildings in the firmaments, and a further building on the top of Mount Sumeru). The stairs leading to the judge are not depicted at other buildings of the CP.

The judge has both a halo and a crown (Fig. 2/a), which is a relatively rare combination in the CP. Among the ca. 300 divine figures, it occurs only in the following cases: the Father of Greatness, some non-identified divine figures in the Realm of Light (one seated on a lotus throne behind Mānī, two groups of figures on the two sides of the Realm of Light), Splenditenens above the firmaments in the middle, six figures seated on the columns on the two sides of the painting, a god in the first firmament, the Virgin of Light, two gods (probably the Living Spirit and the Mother of Living) encountering the Primal Man, and Gloriosus Rex on the fifth earth. This combination of the halo and the crown most probably stresses the importance of the Judge's figure.

Though the facial expression of the Judge seems to be very close to the rather simplicistic depiction of all non-demonic figures, the hand gesture is rather similar to some of the Dunhuang and Ningbo paintings: the right hand is raised in front of the chest, while the left hand is gently placed on the table (Fig. 4/a–d). Although the right hand does not hold a pen, which frequently appears in other Ten Kings paintings, the gesture itself clearly shows the moment before the final verdict is written on a paper spread in front of the Judge. The raised right hand and the left one resting on the table appear, for example, in almost all courts of the Dunhuang P.2003, an even closer analogy of the gesture is visible in the 1st, 4th, 8th and 9th courts of the P.2870 scroll (Fig. 4/b), though here the judges sometimes hold a pen in their right hand (4th and 8th courts). Unlike the Dunhuang cases, where more than one judge exhibit this gesture, among the more elaborated Ningbo versions, it is only the seventh king who displays the same gesture in a scroll from Lu Xinzhong's workshop (Fig. 4/c).[1] In the CP judgment scene (Fig. 4/a), however, neither the pen, nor the paper appears, and the orange-red oblong rectangle with a beige contour stripe on the table clearly resembles the surface of Dunhuang tables (e.g. Or. 8210 [= S.3961]). The lack of pen, paper, and similar accessories on the table, all enhance the degree of stylization, while all these objects are always realistically shown in the Ningbo paintings.

---

〔1〕This hanging scroll (ink and colour on silk, 13th c., 85 cm × 50.5 cm), preserved in the Museum für Ostasiatische Kunst (Berlin), belongs to the Kōtōin 高桐院 set of Kyoto (Ledderose 2000: 162. Fig. 7.1, 165). Another version of this hanging scroll (ink and colour on silk, 80.6 cm × 45.7 cm), which derives from the same atelier, is preserved at Nara National Museum (Ledderose 2000: 168. Fig. 7.8). Two further scrolls also exhibit the same king with the same gesture (Ledderose 2000: 170. Fig. 7.14: painting formerly on loan to Princeton University Art Museum, Princeton, 86.2 cm × 39.1 cm; Ledderose 2000: 171. Fig. 7.15: Zendō-ji, Hakata, 39.5 cm × 25 cm).

Fig. 4/a. The gesture of the CP judge
Cosmology painting (detail)
Copyright © Japanese private collection

Fig. 4/b. The gesture of Qin Guangwang
Ten Kings sūtra, P.2870 (detail) 10th c., ink on paper, ca. 30.7 cm × 615.2 cm.
Copyright © Bibliothèque nationale de France

Fig. 4/c The gesture of the Sandōzu Judge
The Yamato Bunkakan silk painting (detail). 13–14th century.
Complete hanging scroll, colours on silk, 142 cm × 59.2 cm.

Fig. 4/d. The gesture of a Ningbo Judge
Lu Xinzhong (studio of): The Seventh King of Hell (detail)
13th century. Hanging scroll, ink and colours on silk, 85 cm × 50.5 cm, Object No. 1962-14,
 [1]

Fig. 4/a–d. The same gesture of four Judges: two (4/a–b) in full frontal view (CP and P.2870), and two (4/c–d) in three-quarter view (Sandōzu and Ningbo)

〔1〕Cf. Ledderose 1981: Pl.1; Kyōto Kokuritsu Hakubutsukan 1992: 90.

A unique motif of the CP judgment scene is a small, seated figure travelling on a white-red cloud on the Judge's right side (Fig. 5/a). The cloud seems to leave the mouth of the Judge, since the tail of the cloud, which transfixes the Judge's halo, points to his mouth, even if the latter is closed. In the tenth king's court of P.2003, the armoured Wudao zhuanlun wang 五道转轮王[1] has a small portion of cloud leaving his mouth, which might represent his final and unappealable verdict.[2]

---

〔1〕Despite the obvious Yama imagery of the CP judge, which will be elaborated later on, the function of the Manichaean Righteous Judge is in fact closer to the function of the tenth king, who utters the final decision and determines the subsequent fate of the people.

〔2〕Tenth King in the *Ten Kings sūtra*, P.2003 (ink and colours on paper, 29.4 cm × 760 cm, Bibliothèque nationale de France), see at the IDP (International Dunhuang Project) website (http://idp.bl.uk). There is another seemingly similar motif of cloud in the same manuscript (P.2003: Biancheng wang 变城王): a woman and a man, whose upper part is only visible, travel on red and greenish clouds, which are positioned obliquely upwards. The tail of the cloud is placed in front of the judge's desk. This scene evidently illustrates the content of the poem: "Day in and day out all they see is the power of merit, how the difference between the halls of heaven and the prisons underground lies in a kṣana" (Teiser 1993: 214). The woman and the man obviously refer to the people travelling to heaven, while below them the underground prison (hell) as an alternative destination is depicted (cf. Teiser 1999: 193). A very similar cloud is visible in P.2870 (Wudao zhuanlun wang 五道转轮王), where it refers to the best, i.e. divine, reincarnation. A division between those travelling to the heavens and those who would suffer an unfortunate reincarnation is present in Taishan's (Taizan's) seventh court of the Japanese Jōfuku-ji 净福寺 (Kyoto) scroll (97 cm × 42.1 cm) by Tosa Minobu 土佐光信 (dated 1489), see Phillips 2003: 128. fig. 7. and p. 140: "A small female figure ascends on a cloud above two *torii*. Dressed in regal Chinese garb and clasping hands in prayer, she probably represents those who achieve special salvation and need not face further time as an incarnated being, particularly in the underworlds. In contrast, the demons below transform men in dogs as a suggestion both of the further suffering the dead who remain will encounter and of the likelihood of rebirth into a lower realm." Consequently, this motif of the Dunhuang scrolls and the Jōfuku-ji Taishan hanging scroll can be paralleled with the ten CP figures travelling on colour clouds above the firmaments towards the heavens, and not with the single figure seated on a cloud in the judgment scene.

Fig. 5/a–b. The judgment as a living word leaving the mouth of the Righteous Judge (5/a) and Rex Honoris in the 7th firmament (5/b)
Cosmology painting (details)
Copyright © Japanese private collection

Although small human figures seated on clouds do appear in some cases in the CP, a cloud originating from the lower part of a divine figure's halo, and thus suggesting his mouth as the source, occurs only in two other cases: a currently unidentified figure[1] on the right side above the firmaments, whose mouth seems to be the source of twelve seated figures, and Rex Honoris on the right side of the seventh firmament (Fig. 5/b).[2] Interestingly, in all three cases, the small figures seated on cloud face and greet the figure of Mānī, and all of them are in *añjali mudrā*. Theoretically, such figures could mean some kind of emanation from the deity in question, but neither the Rex Honoris, nor the Righteous Judge has any emanations. Thus a small figure apparently leaving the mouth of a deity, even if in all cases the mouths are closed, might perhaps denote an important and living utterance. Its living nature is aptly expressed by the fact that it is depicted as a small human figure. Indeed, there is an important moment in the eschatological future when the universal judgment leaves the mouth of the Righteous Judge as a living word (Coptic ⲥⲉϫⲉ ⲉⲧⲁⲛϩ).[3]

> Then the great shining one will open his mouth and he . . . the great and blessed king of kings. By his sweet blessed mouth he can proclaim his glorious word. And by the sound of his living word all the languages will understand that he is …each country and language.[4]

---

[1] Y. Yoshida (2010: 17b–18a) originally identified this figure as Splenditenens, whom I equated with the figure under the Perfect Man (Kósa 2012a), thus for the time being (August of 2012) I regard this figure unidentified.

[2] On the left side of the Virgin of Light in the middle left part of the painting, there is a further similar figure (red upper garment, bluish halo) but in this case, the cloud on which he is seated seems to originate from the left elbow of this divine figure. The fourth example is a tiny figure (red upper garment, white halo) whose cloud comes from the bottom part of the golden throne, on which the middle of the three divine figures in the Sun is seated.

[3] Cf. Pedersen 1996: 346.

[4] Trans. I. Gardner (Gardner and Lieu 2004: 224). *Homilies* 37,14–18: ⲧⲟⲧⲉ ⲡ[ⲛⲁ]ϭ ⲙ̄ⲡⲣ̄ⲓ̈ⲉ ⲛⲁⲟⲩⲉⲛ ⲛ̄ⲣⲱϥ ⲛϥ . [. . .] / ⲡⲛⲁϭ ⲛⲣⲣⲟ [ⲛ̄]ⲣⲣⲁⲓ̈ ⲉⲧⲥⲙⲁⲙⲁⲁⲧ/ ϩⲛⲧⲉϥ[ⲧⲁ] /ⲡⲣⲟ ⲉⲧϩⲁⲗϭ ⲉⲧⲥⲙⲁⲙⲁⲁⲧ · ϥⲁⲧⲉⲟⲩⲟ ⲙⲡ[ⲉϥ]/ⲥⲉϫⲉ ⲉⲧⲟⲓ̈ ⲛⲉⲁⲩ/ ϩⲛ̄ ⲧⲥ̄ⲙⲏ ⲇⲉ ⲙ̄ⲡⲉϥⲥⲉϫ[ⲉ ⲉ] /ⲧⲁⲛϩ · ⲛ̄ⲉⲥⲡⲉ ⲧⲏⲣⲟⲩ ⲛⲁⲙⲙⲉ ⲇⲉ ⲉⲉϥ ⲧⲙ[.

The equation of the small figure with an important judgment might be corroborated by the similar figure in the seventh firmament emanating from the mouth of Rex Honoris (Fig. 5/b), who, perhaps only accidentally, also has the function of judging. [1]

> The King of Honour, the strong God, who is in the seventh heaven, judging the demons, the creatures of abyss(?). [2]

> The [fif]th [j]udge is the great King of Honour, he who dwells and is established in the seventh firmament. He is the judge of all the firmaments who gives a true judgment, according to [a] judgment of righteousness, upon all powers and all the [king]doms [of the] firmaments. [3]

Even more interestingly, the figures of these two judges (the Righteous Judge and Rex Honoris) in the CP are positioned precisely along the same axis on the right side of the painting. What is more, the small figures leaving their mouth are not simply clad in very similar robes (lower part of which is red in both cases) and sit on very similar clouds (red and white), but the small figures and the clouds are accurately positioned along the same axis again. [4]

A further motif appearing in both the Ten Kings of Hell paintings and

---

〔1〕It must be noted that the 28th *kephalaion* lists twelve judges, the majority of whom has no such motif in the CP.

〔2〕*Psalmbook* 2,9–11: ⲡⲣⲣⲟ ⲙ̄ⲡⲧⲁⲓ̈ⲟ ⲡⲛⲟⲩⲧⲉ ⲛ̄ϫⲱⲣⲉ ⲡⲉⲧϣⲟⲟⲡ . . . . / . . ⲧⲙⲁϩⲥⲁϣϥⲉ ⲙ̄ⲡⲉ ⲉϥϯϩⲉⲡ ⲁⲛⲓϩ ⲛ̄ϫⲡ[ⲟ ⲙⲡ/ⲛⲟⲩ]ⲛ.

〔3〕Trans. Gardner 1995: 82. *Kephalaia* 80,5–9: ⲡ[ⲙⲁϩ]ϯⲟⲩ [ⲛⲕ]ⲣⲓⲧⲏⲥ ⲡⲉ ⲡⲛⲁϭ ⲛⲣⲣⲟ ⲛ̄ⲧⲉ ⲡⲧⲁⲓ̈ⲟ ⲡⲉⲧⲟⲩⲏϩ / [ⲉⲧ]ⲥⲙⲁⲛⲧ ϩⲙ ⲡⲙⲁϩⲥⲁϣϥ̄ ⲛⲥⲧⲉⲣⲉⲱⲙⲁ ⲛⲧⲁϥ ⲡⲉ ⲡⲕⲣⲓ/ⲧⲏⲥ ⲛ̄ⲛ̄ⲥⲧⲉⲣⲉⲱⲙⲁ ⲧⲏⲣⲟⲩ ⲡⲉⲧϯ ⲛ̄ⲟⲩϩⲉⲡ ⲙ̄ⲙⲏⲉ ⲕⲁⲧⲁ / [ⲟⲩ]ϩⲉⲡ ⲛ̄ⲇⲓⲕⲁⲓⲟⲥⲩⲛⲏ ⲁⲛϭⲁⲙ ⲧⲏⲣⲟⲩ ⲙⲛ ⲛ[ⲙⲛⲧ]ⲣⲣⲁⲓ̈ ⲧⲏⲣⲟⲩ / ⲛ̄ⲛ̄ⲥⲧⲉⲣⲉⲱⲙⲁ.

〔4〕The importance of various axes in the CP are conspicuous; see, for example, the position of the forty angels, the golden roofed houses, the celestial boats, or the relation of Splenditenens and Atlas (on this latter, see Kósa 2012a). There are only two differences between these two seated figures: the colour of their halo (the small figure beside Rex Honoris has a red inner stripe in his halo) and the meandering of the tail of the cloud. In the case of the figure beside the Righteous Judge, this latter feature can perhaps be explained by the presence of the attendant standing beside him).

the CP judgment scene are the two assistants flanking the judge. As for the Ten Kings paintings, it is usually assumed that beside the judge two young boys are standing. Lothar Ledderose, for example, notes generally, and more specifically about the Kṣitigarbha with Ten Kings image preserved in Musée Guimet (10th c., Dunhuang, hanging scroll, 84 cm × 53.6 cm): "The sutra mentions two spirit boys of good and evil, who seem to be descendants of a species called "spirits born at the same time" (*jusheng shen* [俱生神, Jap. *dōshōjin* 同生神, GK]), which are mentioned in literature as early as A.D. 457. The two spirit boys constantly accompany a human being throughout life. One boy records all good deeds, the other all evil deeds, and then they report to the underworld officials. (...) All [judges, GK] but one are attended by the twin boys of good and evil, who are recognizable by the circular pigtails behind their ears."[1] The *Ten Kings sūtra* says in S.F. Teiser's translation: "The balance of actions (...) in the five offices is suspended in the air; to the left and the right the Twin Boys complete the logbook of actions."[2] Similarly, Ch. Kwon calls them boys,[3] and Michel Soymié uses 'garçons du Bien et du Mal'.[4] Nevertheless, I do not see any reason to translate *tong* 童 as boys, since this word refers only to adolescent age, and does not imply sex.[5] Therefore, based on other Dunhuang manuscripts (P.4523, P.2003, P.2870), which show a great similarity between these young attendants and the female figures in the scroll, I am not convinced that these figures are indeed male figures, thus I

---

〔1〕Ledderose 2000:177–178.

〔2〕Teiser 1994: 213. X01, 0021: p0409b23–24: 五官业秤向空悬，左右双童业簿全。

〔3〕Kwon 1999: 115–116: "They are standard iconography in the Ten Kings painting tradition in China, and are usually shown as young boys in buns holding scrolls."

〔4〕Soymié 1966: 46, 1967: 143. On the possible female aspects of at least one of the attendants, see Soymié 1966: 47–51.

〔5〕Cf. Soymié 1966: 47: "Le mot *t'ong* [*tong,* GK] a le sens d'adolescent, de l'un et l'autre sexe. L'expression *t'ong-tseu* [*tongzi*, GK] est en principe réservée aux garçons, mais peut s'employer aussi pour les filles. Le sens est souvent assez équivoque."

agree with Y. Yoshida who calls them female helpers.[1]

5.2.4 The mirror on the right side of the Judge

On the onlooker's right side of the building, a standing golden mirror is placed with a cock, a quadruped, a snake and a crab within.[2] The presence of mirror does not simply generally reflect the tradition of Ten Kings of Hell paintings,[3] but more specifically evokes one of the Ten Kings.

Since the expression Righteous King (*Pingdeng wang* 平等王) occurs in connection with the Manichaean judge, it is sometimes assumed that it was *Pingdeng wang*, the eighth among the Ten Kings of Hell, with whom the Chinese Manichaeans specifically linked their judging deity.[4] These textual occurrences can be found in the *Hymnscroll* (H099, H131, H152, H255, H394) and the *Traité* (Tr.307), the former being convincingly dated by Yu Wanli to not earlier than the 2nd half of the 8th century.[5] Unfortunately, scholars do not clearly see the roots of the Ten Kings of Hell tradition; therefore, it is not evident if this system of the Ten Kings in its present form was already an integral part of the Chinese religious concepts by AD 760s. The first copy of the *Ten Kings sūtra* derives from AD 926,[6]

---

〔1〕Yoshida 2010: 12a. Cf. Soymié 1966: 47: "Sur les représentations mentionnées ci-dessus les deux garçons sont vêtus de la même façon, parfois d'une tunique cachant à demi des pantalons blancs, costume masculin (exemple, Matsumoto, planche 107a), le plus souvent d'une robe ample, costume apparemment féminin. (…) Dans le cas, le plus fréquent, où leurs coiffures sont différentes, on est tenté de croire qu'ils sont un garçon (cheveux sur les oreilles) et une fille (cheveux en cornes). (…) Quoiqu'il en soit de leur coiffure, leur vêtement et leur physionomie leur donnent le plus souvent un aspect féminin." Also cf. Kwon 1999: 116: "The consistent rendering of the Boys of Good and Evil as female courtiers with sumptuous hairdos and costumes [in the Seikadō paintings, GK] parallels the distinctively female rendering of the "Boys" in the Haein-sa frontispiece." At the Baodingshan site, two kings explicitly have a female attendant (Kucera 1995: 87).

〔2〕Yoshida 2010: 12b.

〔3〕Yoshida 2010: 12b.

〔4〕Rui 2009. Based on a reference in the *Yiqie jing yinyi* 一切经音义 (T54, 2128: p0338c) Teiser (1993: 124, 1999: 195) claims that *pingdeng* 平等 (righteous, just) was originally an epithet of Yama.

〔5〕Yu 1995.

〔6〕Teiser 1993: 120–121.

which naturally does not mean that the concept originated from this period,[1] 150 years later after the translation of the *Hymnscroll*.

There is perhaps one clue that would suggest that the Chinese translators of the original Parthian text (both the *Hymnscroll* and the *Traité* are translations from a Middle Iranian original) had an already existing Chinese concept in mind when they rendered the name of the Manichaean figure in Chinese. The name of this figure in the non-Chinese sources basically always refers to a judge, not a king: Parthian *d'db(')r r'štygr*,[2] Sogdian *rštyy 'xṯw*,[3] Coptic пкрітнс нте тмне,[4] Latin *iustus iudex*,[5] Greek δίκαιος κριτής[6] all mean Righteous Judge,[7] and although this figure evidently has royal attributes,[8] the appellations themselves do not contain the word 'king'. Nevertheless, even if Daoming 道明, the 8th century Chinese translator, had associated *Pingdeng wang* with the Manichaean Righteous Judge, it does not seem to have a direct influence on a Yuan or early Ming painting.

The judge of the Sandōzu painting does not show the peculiarities of any of the Ten Kings, he does not have a scale, for example, which was a usual attribute of the fourth king (King of the Five Offices, Wuguan wang 五官王) in the sūtra[9] and its illustrations in the Dunhuang manuscripts.[10] This lack of attribute can perhaps be attributed to the fact that the Sandōzu evidently follows the Ningbo tradition, and between Dunhuang and Ningbo

---

[1] S.F. Teiser (1993: 121) mentions two earlier (late 7th c.) references.

[2] M 6032 V (Sundermann 1981: 115), M6598/4–5.

[3] M501 g/I/R/2 (Sundermann 1979: 100).

[4] *Homilies* 6,27; 35,24; *Kephalaia* II.288,17–18.

[5] Contra Fortunatum 2.

[6] Capita VII contra Manichaeos 3,76; HHF 1461 C/D.

[7] *Homilies* 87,18 also has the Great Judge (пнаб п̄крітнс).

[8] Franzmann 2003: 97.

[9] Teiser 1994: 213.

[10] S.3961, P.2003, P.2870, P.4523.

the majority of the kings' specific attributes were lost. "The scene of River Nai, the scale of *karma*, and the six paths of rebirth, for example, vanish from the iconographic repertoire..."[1]

One attribute, however, is preserved throughout the entire history of the Ten Kings of Hell paintings: the karmic mirror (*yejing* 业镜, *jōhari no kagami* 净玻璃镜), which is a constant attribute of Yama (Yanmo [Jap. Enma] 阎魔, Yanluo 阎罗), the fifth king.[2] In all Dunhuang, Ningbo and other types of Ten Kings paintings, Yama's fifth court invariably features a conspicuously positioned karmic mirror. It must be emphasized that this karmic mirror, in which, as an irrefutable evidence, the person under judgment is forced to inspect his former sins, never appears in any other court. Thus the kamic mirror is an invariable attribute of Yama.

This karmic mirror is clearly visible beside the building of the CP judgment scene and thus unambiguously associates the figure of the CP judge with Yama, who is perhaps the most important, most well-known and "most Buddhist" among the Ten Kings (see Fig. 1/a–b).[3] Although the position of the mirror and the motifs in it, as will be clear later on, carry a

〔1〕Kwon 2005: 31. The Korean-type Seikadō images (SBB 1999: 43. Pl. 6-4: Scales in the 4th court [also in the 8th court, SBB 1999: 47, Pl. 6-8; SBB 1999: 49. Pl. 6-10: paths of reincarnations]) and the Packard collection (Kwon 2005), however, preserved some of these attributes.

〔2〕Cf. Tokushi and Ogawa 1963: 275; Watanabe 1984: 23; Miya 1990: 106–107, 1992: 39–44, Shi 1985: 584, Kwon 1999: 54. The Daoist adaptation of the Ten Kings scripture also contains a reference to the karmic mirror in Yama's (Daoist: Zuisheng yaoling zhenjun 最圣耀灵真君) palace. The *Difu shiwang badu yi* 地府十王拔度仪 (Daozang 3:598a) says: "When one arrives at this palace, the karmic mirror shows the forms (of previous deeds), the karmic causes (incur) retaliation" (当至此宫，业镜现形，随缘报对), cf. Teiser 1993: 137, 1994: 226. In the sculptural representations of Ten Kings from Sichuan, the karmic mirror, probably for spatial reasons, is usually placed under Kṣitigarbha, not in front of one of the kings (see e.g. Zhang and Liao 2007: 47). In addition to the Ten Kings paintings, Yama (Enma) and the karmic mirror also make appearance in Japanese mandalas, such as the *Tateyama mandara* 立山曼荼羅 or the *Kumano kanjin jikkai mandara* 熊野观心十界曼荼罗.

〔3〕Teiser (1994: 175): "Yama is the highest ranking among the ten kings." Teiser (1993: 131) also warns against calling the Ten Kings of Hell tradition as a whole a Buddhist one, but Yama is evidently of Indian origin and does not belong to the local Chinese religious tradition (as some other kings).

special Manichaean message, the shape of the mirror can be clearly traced back to Dunhuang and Ningbo mirrors of Yama. An interesting case of a rather specific analogy is the cloth hanging from the back upper part of the mirror, which also appears, for example, in a judgment scene in Yulin 榆林 (10th c., Cave 33, eastern wall), in the Huangyan Bowuguan 黄岩博物馆 Ten Kings scroll,[1] in the Satō Han'ai scroll,[2] Seiju-ji 聖寿寺 (Kōyasan 高野山) scroll,[3] the Yuanjue dong 圓覺洞 niche 60 (84, Anyue 安岳 Sichuan),[4] the Ningbo painting by Lu Xinzhong (NNM),[5] the Ningbo painting by Lu Zhongyuan 陆仲渊(NNM),[6] the Haein-sa and the Hōju-in 宝珠院 scrolls.[7]

The presence of the karmic mirror thus contributes to our understanding of the identity of the judge,[8] since it unquestionably

[1] NNM 2009: 84.

[2] Teiser 1993: 123. Fig. 4.2, Miya 1990: 110. Fig. 8.

[3] Tokushi and Ogawa 1963: 292. Fig. 504/D.

[4] Zhiru 2007: 155. Figs. 29–30.

[5] NNM 2009: 86.

[6] NNM 2009: 92.

[7] Kwon 1999: 255. Figs. 38–39.

[8] Despite the obvious iconographical similarity of the mirror in the CP and the mirror in Yama's court, it is interesting that we have some Coptic Manichaean references to mirrors in an eschatological context, even if these mirrors do not necessarily belong to the Judge, and might have a different function. Nevertheless, the third citation does associate the Righteous Judge with a mirror. *Psalm-book* 9,4–7: "Let us bless our Lord Jesus who has sent to us the Spirit of Truth. He came and separated us from the Error of the world, he brought us a mirror, we looked, we saw the Universe in it." *Psalm-book* 21,17–21: "Thou didst not leave us lacking anything to find defence in the presence of the judge of Truth; thou didst bring us a mirror from thy kingdom, we looked and saw the universe in it, the things that have been and that shall be and that are, all of them…"; *Psalm-book* 83,21–23: "Hail, righteous Judge, strong power, path of Truth, clear mirror that separates the victorious and the condemned…" There is another mirror-like object in the Manichaean cosmology, the wheel in front of the King of Honor (Rex Honoris) in the seventh firmament, about which the *Kephalaia* (88,27–33; Gardner 1995: 92) says: "This is also the case for all the rulers who are in the firmaments, and every power of the zone: If they should wish to escape, they shall be recognized and revealed by that wheel. [As] the wheel is like a great mirror, for [the di]scrimination of all things [… is] in it." In addition to the small figure seated on a cloud and emanating from a divine mouth, interpreted above as a living word of judgment, this mirror-like object is the second similarity between the Righteous Judge and Rex Honoris.

associates the Manichaean Judge with Yama. There is one further clue that also supports this association. The presence of animals in front of the judge, a motif to be investigated later on, is also a recurring, though not constant, attribute of Yama, which does not occur in other courts of the Chinese Ten Kings paintings.〔1〕

As for the mirror itself, two features will be discussed here: its position and its "content". The position of the mirror is unique, since in the majority of the cases the karmic mirror is placed somewhere in front of the judge, and it is more specifically put in front of the person whose sins it is supposed to reveal.〔2〕 The hair of the sinner is usually held tight by a ward (human or monster), who compels the sinner to look at the scene that the mirror shows.〔3〕

What the karmic mirrors of the Ten Kings paintings usually show is a man hitting or killing an animal,〔4〕 or harming another person.〔5〕 The Manichaean depiction of the mirror is peculiar in this respect as well, since it has four animals in it and does not exhibit the agent of the aggression, the agent who is otherwise invariably depicted in the Ten Kings paintings. It

---

〔1〕In a Fujianese example, animals with scroll in their mouth do occur in front of *Pingdeng wang* (NNM 2009: 236). However, this set of 17 pieces from the 15th century belongs to the *shuilu* 水陆 images, not those of the Ten Kings (it features only six of them), even if during the Ming dynasty the Ten Kings became part of the former *shuilu* set. An Edo period Japanese set (Kanazawa Bunko 1991: 29. fig. 5-4, 102.3 x 44.3 cm) contains a painting where the animals (duck, goose, cow, horse etc.) with scroll appear in the fourth court (Wuguan wang 五官王).

〔2〕E.g. [Dunhuang-type] Or.8210/S.3961, P.2870; [Ningbo-type:] Metropolitan Museum of Art painting.

〔3〕E.g. [Dunhuang-type:] Or.8210/S.3961, P.4523, Huangyan Bowuguan (NNM 2009: 84); [Ningbo-type:] Lu Xinzhong [NNM] (NNM 2009: 86), Lu Xinzhong [Shiga–Eigenji] (NNM 2009: 90), Metropolitan Museum of Art painting (NNM 2009: 83).

〔4〕E.g. [Dunhuang-type:] P.2003, P.4523, P.2870, Satō Han'ai scroll (Teiser 1993: 123. Fig. 4.2, Miya 1990: 110. Fig. 8.); [Ningbo-type:] Lu Xinzhong 陆忠信 [Shiga–Eigenji] (NNM 2009: 90), Lu Zhongyuan 陆仲渊 [NNM] (NNM 2009: 92); other: Seikadō image (SBB 1999: 44. Pl. 6-5), Yuanjue dong niche 60 (84), Anyue, (Sichuan) (Zhiru 2007: 155. Figs. 29–30).

〔5〕[Dunhuang-type:] Or.8210/S.3961; [Ningbo-type:] Metropolitan Museum of Art painting (NNM 2009: 83).

seems rather likely that the position of the mirror (i.e. it is not placed in front of a sinner) and the fact that it does not reveal any particular crime and consequently the agent of any crime, are somehow interrelated.

Here I would like to offer a possible explanation for the unusual position of the karmic mirror ("mirror of actions"), since it is evident that in this lateral position, where neither the judge, nor the potential sinner can see it, it cannot fulfil its original function: to reveal the various sins committed by the human figure.

As mentioned above, yanking the hair (*ce fa* 策发) of the sinner by a monster ward is a recurring motif in all types of Ten Kings paintings, and its function is clearly recorded in the *Ten Kings sūtra*:

> The fifth. After seven days they pass before King Yama rāja. The hymn goes: During the fifth seven, Yama rāja puts an end to sounds of dispute, but in their hearts sinners are resentful and unwilling, with their hair yanked and their heads pulled up to look in the mirror of actions, they begin to know the affairs from previous lives are rendered distinct and clear.[1]

It is clear from the citation that certain sinners deny their former sins, therefore, in addition to the records of the good and bad deeds, the king at this court, and only at this one, can use a secondary device, the karmic mirror, to confront the sinner with their previous sins. The karmic mirror thus becomes an infallible witness: a human witness might err, but that can never happen with the mirror: it reveals the past event as if a photo was taken at the moment of the crime.

From the analysis of the Ten Kings pictorial tradition, it seems that the king has a further assistance: the animals against which the crime was committed may also appear in front of Yama to submit their pleas (Fig. 6/b).

---

〔1〕Teiser 1994: 213–214. X01n0021: p0409c02–04: 第五七日过阎罗王。赞曰：五七阎王息诤声，罪人心恨未甘情，策发仰头看业镜，始知先世事分明。

Therefore, the animals function as a second group of possible witnesses, but, unlike the mirror, they do not appear in all cases. Thus Yama has both the documents recording the good and bad deeds of the person under judgment (this is present at all courts), furthermore, he can force the person obstinately denying the charges to face the witness of the karmic mirror, and, if it is still not sufficient, Yama can listen to "the aggrieved party", i.e. the animals.

The presence of animals as witnesses also offers a new possibility for the painters of the Ten Kings paintings: to express that the person in question committed various sins against various animals. Otherwise, this would be hard to express merely with the help of the mirror, since karmic mirrors only show one act or one type of crime, they have no "split screen" to show more crimes together.

What are the consequences of this analysis of the Ten Kings paintings for the CP judgment scene (Fig. 6/a)? It seems to me that the placement of the mirror beside the building and the appearance of the representatives of vegetation (to be explained later on) and animals in front of the Manichaean Judge mean that the Judge relies solely, or at least primarily, on the witnesses of the aggrieved party, who line up in front of the stairs of the building. This might perhaps mean that the sinner, who represents the entire mankind here (also to be detailed later on), committed various sins which cannot be expressed by the display of a single (type of) act, which invariably appears in Ten Kings mirrors. Since the Ten Kings paintings visualize individual judgments, and the acts appearing in the karmic mirror

Fig. 6/a. Cosmology painting (detail)
Copyright © Japanese private collection

Fig. 6/b. The court of Yama (detail)
Illustrations to the *Ten Kings sūtra*, P.4523 (detail). 10th c., ink on paper, ca. 30 cm × 300.3 cm.
Copyright © Bibliothèque nationale de France

Fig. 6/a–b. The presence of animals in front of the Judge in the CP (6/a) and P.4523 (Dunhuang), the animals in the latter holding accusation in their mouth and beak (6/b)

are often related to certain professions and typical habits,[1] thus, in comparison with the universal nature of the Manichaean judgment scene of the CP, their scope of application is restricted. Manichaean confessional texts frequently refer to the great amount of possible sins; here I quote only a Uighur and a Chinese example:

> My God, we are encumbered with defect and sin, we are great debtors. Because of the insatiable and shameless Āz demon we in

[1] It should be noted that the images appearing in the karmic mirror most probably expresses recurring acts in certain professions, cf. Hirasawa 2008: 16: "Aside from cardinal sins such as murdering monks or setting fire to temple property, the mirrors reflect killing associated with vocational and culinary customs such as the butchering of animals, fishing, and hunting game. Animals gather around some mirrors, accusatorily facing their slaughterers. Other mirrors depict warriors engaged in battle. Such iconography prompted consciousness of the retribution awaiting those engaged in certain professions and primed them to consider their options for salvation."

thought, word, and deed, likewise looking with its (i.e. Āz's) eyes, hearing with its ears, speaking with its tongue, seizing with its hand, (and) walking with its feet, incur constant and permanent agony on the light of the Fivefold God in the dry and wet earth, the five kinds of living beings (and) the five kinds of herbs and trees.[1]

(If we) moreover harmed against the five parts of the dharma body [i.e. the Five Lights of the Living Soul, GK], permanently wasting them, if we sometimes cut and fell the five kinds of grasses and trees, or made the five types of living beings our slaves, and had other innumerable faults, now let them all be washed away as we repent.[2]

(…) if I harmed the body of Vairocana and the five light-sons (…) I wish that my sins would be abolished![3]

Both confession texts contain a list of various sins, especially those committed against other living beings (vegetation and animals), which groups, as will be explained later on, can roughly be equated with the five heads on green stalks (vegetation) and the five animals behind them. The injury of Vairocana (the Chinese equivalent of the Living Soul) and the Five Lights (together also called the Living Soul) in the Chinese text also refers to the sins that were committed against the members of the created universe, where the Five Lights, i.e. the Five Sons of the Primal Man, suffer in every living being, but especially in vegetation.[4] This importance is perhaps symbolized by the position of vegetation that appears closer to the

〔1〕Trans. J. Asmussen (1965: 198–199). *X^u āstvānīft* XV C (Asmussen 1965: 179): t(ä)ŋrim ägsüklüg yazuqluγ / biz ötägčii birimčibiz / todunčsuz uwutsuz suq / yäk üčün : saqïnčïn sözin / qïlïnčïn ymä közin körüp / qulqaqïn äšidip tilin sözläp / älgin sunup adaqïn yorïp / ürkä üzüksüz ämgätirbiz : / biš t(ä)ŋrii y(a)ruqïn quruγ öl / yirig biš türlüg tïnl(ï)γ(ï)γ biš / türlüg otuγ 'ïγačïγ. A similar reference is found in *X^u āstvānīft* III C.

〔2〕H392–393: 又损五分法身，恒加费用；或斩伐五种草木，或劳役五 / 类众生，余有无数愆违，今并洗除忏悔!

〔3〕H412, 413–414: (…) 或损卢舍那身兼五明子 (…) 愿 / 罪销灭！

〔4〕Jackson 1925: 258. n.55 (also p.264. n.70.): "Observe that, in the Manichaean system throughout, insentient plant life is regarded as standing on a higher plane than active animal life."

Righteous Judge than the animals.

This might also be a further possible explanation for the position of the mirror: it seems that this karmic mirror, just like mirrors in Ten Kings paintings, can only show sins committed against animals (and humans), but are apparently unable to show those committed against vegetation, which is, however, a primary topic for the Manichaeans. Indeed, the mirror besides the building only shows animals. Thus, if the Manichaean Judge wants to obtain a complete picture of the sins committed by somebody, then he must put the "Buddhist" mirror aside as a non-sufficient tool for a Manichaean judgment, and must resort to the second standard method: listening to the witnesses. Since the number and types of witnesses are not restricted, this method would in turn provide him with all necessary information to give an impartial judgment.

In sum, in my interpretation, the mirror is put aside because not one single sin of one individual is examined, but all types of sins are scrutinized; therefore, instead of one image of one act that the mirror can show, the Judge can listen to the witnesses of all living beings.[1]

The contents of the mirror, I think, support the hypothesis above. In the mirror, one can spot various animals, the types of which are easy to equate with those standing in front of the judge. Both groups show precisely the same blackish quadruped (with the same position of its tail), precisely the same red snake, a rooster, and an animal associated with water (fish in front of the Judge, and crab in the mirror). Thus, there are four types of animals both in the mirror and in front of the Judge: quadrupeds, reptiles, birds and aquatic animals. Since the mirror does not show any aggression between the animals (which would be possible but which would play no role in the judgment of the human figure), this corroborates that the animals shown in

〔1〕Theoretically, further possible explanations can also be offered, but I found the one described above the most convincing.

the mirror are the sufferers of the various crimes committed by the human being, just like the animals shown in Ten Kings paintings. However, the animals in the Manichaean karmic mirror do not stand for themselves but denote the entire world of animals by referring to the four basic types. Nevertheless, as explicated above, the karmic mirror apparently cannot depict vegetation, therefore it is put aside, and the Righteous Judge applies the more reliable and more comprehensive method of listening to the witnesses, who are at the same time the sufferers of the crimes, and thus the Judge confronts the naked human figure with these witnesses.

5.2.5 The naked person and the monster ward

Sine the judgment scene in the CP, as shown above, is obviously based on the Ten Kings of Hell iconography,[1] I think that all motifs, whenever possible, should be first assigned a Buddhist reading. After this Buddhist interpretation is clear, one can proceed to deciphering the Manichaean meaning of the Buddhist reading. Buddhism can be regarded as the "linguistic" (iconographical) medium through which Chinese Manichaeans expressed their views. Except for such general motifs like the Manichaean divinities as seated buddhas or Mount Sumeru, the CP judgment scene is perhaps the most conspicuously Buddhist scene in the entire CP.

Thus, based on the Dunhuang and Ningbo Ten Kings of Hell paintings, it is clear that the figure whom the monster ward seizes and holds firmly is the person who is being or going to be judged. Among others, the following cases can be cited: [Dunhuang-type:] Or.8210/S.3961, P.4523, Huangyan Bowuguan;[2] [Ningbo-type:] Lu Xinzhong [NNM],[3] Lu Xinzhong

[1] Naturally, it does not mean that the original painting had the same type of scene. On the contrary, if the CP can indeed be traced back to the *Eikōn*, it is evident that the Ten Kings of Hell iconography entered the CP in order to accommodate it to the Chinese context.

[2] NNM 2009: 84.

[3] NNM 2009: 86.

[Shiga–Eigenji], [1] Metropolitan Museum of Art painting. [2] To my knowledge, there is no exception, all these paintings unanimously apply this motif in this sense, and the monster ward never takes hold of any other figures, only the deceased sinner.

The monster ward grabs the hair of the naked person with his left hand, which is a recurring motif, for example, in the court of the fifth king, Yama, where the ward holds the hair of the sinner in order to force him to look at the karmic mirror in front of him. As cited above, this feature is also mentioned in the *Ten Kings sūtra*: "During the fifth seven, Yama rāja puts an end to sounds of dispute, but in their hearts sinners are resentful and unwilling, with their hair yanked and their heads pulled up to look in the mirror of actions." [3] As demonstrated above, the Righteous King in this particular CP scene can be identified as Yama because of the presence of the karmic mirror on the onlooker's right side of the building. Thus, interestingly, the motif of a monster ward who grasps the hair of a sinner is preserved in the CP scene, but the mirror, the ultimate reason to grab the hair, is not placed in front of this figure.

In contrast to other figures in the Ten Kings paintings, the deceased sinners under judgment are usually depicted as almost completely naked; what they usually wear is a cloth around their loins (S.3961, P.2003, P.2870, P.4523, Huangyan Bowuguan 黄岩博物馆 Ten Kings scroll, [4] Sandōzu painting). This usage of the motif is also clearly present in the Sandōzu painting where the two figures under judgment wear these loincloths and nothing else. The depiction is similar, though not identical, in the CP where one can discern only one human figure who can potentially be judged (on

〔1〕NNM 2009: 90.

〔2〕NNM 2009: 83.

〔3〕Teiser 1994: 213–214. X01n0021: p0409c03–04: 五七阎王息诤声，罪人心恨未甘情，策发仰头看业镜…

〔4〕NNM 2009: 84.

the three other figures, see later on). This completely naked figure has neither male, nor female genitals.[1] I interpret this figure without any sexual characteristics as potentially referring to male and female alike, i.e. this figure represents the entire humanity, or at least both male and female sinners.

> The judge is here, he judges each man.[2]
>
> The second power whom Jesus summo[n]ed is the gre[at Jud]ge, who gives judgement on all the souls [of] mankind, [his] dwelling being established in the atmosphere under [.../...] the wheel [...] stars.[3]
>
> [the Judge] who judges everyone who is bound to flesh.[4]

It should be noted that naked figures do appear in the CP in other cases as well, and they never exhibit their gender. They appear twice in the firmaments,[5] and in the "snake-world" scene two naked persons, whose lower part is only visible, are devoured by a red- and green-headed snake, while a third figure on the left upper part of the same scene seems to have just sprung out from the mouth of another snake.[6] It seems highly probable that thc naked figure under judgment and the naked figures in the snake-world are interrelated, perhaps after a detrimental judgment, the

---

[1] Similarly to other traditions, the Righteous Judge as the judge of the individual soul is mentioned several times in the Chinese Manichaica (T307–309; H099, H255, H394–396).

[2] *Psalmbook* 157,31: ⲡⲕⲣⲓⲧⲏⲥ ⲙ̄ⲡⲓⲙⲁ ϥϯϩⲉⲡ ⲁⲡⲟⲩⲉ ⲡⲟⲩⲉ.

[3] Trans. Gardner 1995: 39–40. *Kephalaia* 35,24–27: ⲧⲙⲁϩⲥⲛ̄ⲧⲉ ⲛ̄ϭⲁⲙ ⲉⲧⲁ ⲓ̄ⲏ̄ⲥ̄ ⲧⲁϩ/ [ⲙ]ⲉⲥ ⲡⲉ ⲡⲛⲁ[ϭ ⲛ̄ⲕⲣⲓ]ⲧⲏⲥ ⲉⲧϯϩⲉⲡ ⲁⲛⲯⲩⲭⲁⲩⲉ ⲧⲏⲣⲟⲩ / [ⲛ̄]ⲛ̄ⲣⲱⲙⲉ ⲉⲣ[ⲉ ⲧⲉϥ]ⲥⲕⲏⲛⲏ ⲥⲙⲁⲁⲛⲧ̄ ϩⲛ̄ ⲡⲁⲏⲣ ϩⲁ . . . / [. .] ⲧⲣⲟⲭⲟⲥ . [. .]ⲥⲓⲟⲩ.

[4] *Homilies* 86,12: [ⲡⲉⲧϯϩⲉⲡ ⲁⲟⲩⲁⲛ]ⲛⲓⲙ ⲉⲁⲩⲙⲁⲣϥ̄ ⲁⲧⲥⲁⲣⲝ.

[5] In the third firmament, a naked figure is lying prone in front of a menacing warrior, while in the fifth firmament a divine figure stretches out a small naked one. On the left part of the fifth earth in the lower register, there is an almost naked figure who wears the remnants of armour around his loins. I identified this latter figure as the Primal Man emerging from the depth after the battle with Darkness (see Kósa 2014: 72–74).

[6] Despite being very close in style, the baby Mānī figure in the "Birth of Mānī" painting (Yoshida 2012: Pl. 1.) does not seem to be "semantically" related to the naked figure in the judgment scene, it simply follows the Buddhist iconography of the birth of the historical Buddha scenes.

snakes devour the soul, but such a link could currently be only hypothetical.

The "clothing accessories" of the monster ward, especially the reddish headband and the object around his neck, resemble those of the wards of the Ten Kings paintings.[1] Moreover, grabbing the hair of the naked human figure, as mentioned above, can also be traced back to the *Ten Kings sūtra* and its various pictorial representations, where with this movement the ward forces the sinner to look at the mirror. For reasons expounded in the previous part, here the ward seems to force the human person to listen to the witnesses lining up in front of him.

On the other hand, the ward might also have another function: if the naked person is a sinner (and for various iconographical reasons, to be detailed later on, this is highly probable), then the ward might have the function of taking the sinner to hell.

> The deeds he [the soul] himself has done are revealed... The soul *(qut)* of earth grieves, it is said. The soul of fire and water weeps, it is said. The soul of shrubs and trees lament, it is said. The Just Judge [officer] appears as in a mirror[2] and seizes the denying soul. (...) When the grey she-demon, covered with hair, comes, when she seizes the denying soul, she will drag it into the dark Hell, it is said.[3]
>
> When death comes to an evil man who is enslaved by craving and lust, the devils attend him, taking hold of him, chastising him and

---

[1] E.g. P.4523.

[2] This mirror most probably has nothing to do with the karmic mirror.

[3] Klimkeit 1993: 292, modified according to Wilkens' (2009: 337) translation. T II D 178 §2–7, §11–13 (Wilkens 2009: 336 [and also see his remarks on pp. 338–339], cf. Le Coq 1919: 22, Yoshida 2010: 18b–19a): k(ä)ntü kılmiš kılınčı közünür {t} teyür. yer suv kutı erinür teyür . ot suv kutı ıglayur teyür . ı ıgač kutı ulıyur teyür . köni buryuq közüŋüčä közünüpän tanmiš öz[ü]tüg tutupan (…) t(ä)trü sačl(ı)γ kurtga yäk kälipä*n*in tanmiš özütlärig tut*u*panın . tünärig tamuka tartar teyür. It is to be noted that the *Šābuhragān* (MacKenzie 1979: 509) credits angels with this role: "Then he appoints angels over those evil-doers, and they will seize them and cast them into hell."

showing him terrible things. [1]

Interestingly, Jens Wilkens interprets the role of the elements and the plants in this Uighur text as accusers of the sinner in front of the Just Judge. [2]

5.2.6 A group of three arriving at the judgment scene

On the lower left side of the judgment scene, there is a red cloud with a green outline, on which three figures stand in *añjali mudrā*. All three figures wear a golden crown; two of them are depicted in profile, while the third in the middle is in a full frontal view (Fig. 7). Based on the analogy with the Sandōzu painting from the Yamato Bunkakan, Y. Yoshida identifies this group as that of Daēnā and her two attendants. [3] This is, of course, a possibility, [4] but, in contrast with the Sandōzu painting, here I do not see any visual motif that would suggest that the three figures consist of a main figure and two followers.

[1] *Al-Fihrist* (Dodge 1970: 796).

[2] Wilkens 2009: 339.

[3] Yoshida 2010: 12b. On Daēnā, see e.g. Yoshida 2010a, Gulácsi 2008, Woschitz 1989: 130–134.

[4] Notwithstanding the considerations that are to be outlined later, it might be still meaningful to suppose that this group of three figures is indeed Daēnā and her attendant(s), who appear at the act of judgment. If this were indeed so, this would again draw our attention to the fact that the Virgin of Light (represented on the left middle side of the painting) and Daēnā are two separate figures.

Fig. 7. The three crowned figures arriving on a red cloud on the Judge's right are contrasted with the naked figure on the Judge's left side
Cosmology painting (detail)

In all other cases in the CP, as well as in the Sandōzu painting, such a main figure has a specific mark which differentiates him/her from his/her attendants. Mānī, followed by two other figures, is depicted altogether ten times with a white robe and a green halo, while five times one encounters a group of three where the main figure is smaller than the attendants (on the four continents around Mount Sumeru and a fifth one above the firmaments). A further group of three figures can be discerned above the Sun: the main figure here has a green halo, while the two attendants have no halo or crown. The last type of triad is represented by a group in the middle of the "snake world", another one on the top of Mount Sumeru, and the seated Righteous Judge with a halo plus a crown, and his two standing attendants without either of them. In this type, the central figure is seated (in two cases on a lotus throne), while the attendants are standing beside him which can be considered a typical Buddhist arrangement of the figures. Thus, unlike this group in the judgment scene, all other nineteen groups of three figures include a main figure who is visibly different from the attendants. In the majority of the cases, this distinctiveness is provided by the presence of a halo or a crown.

GROUPS OF THREE IN THE COSMOLOGY PAINTING

1. [Above the Moon:] Mānī with green halo, two attendants without halo or crown, both in ¾ view;

2–3. [Mānī in the Moon and the Sun:] Mānī with green halo, two attendants without halo or crown, both in ¾ view;

4. [Above the 10th firmament on the right side:] Mānī with green halo, two attendants without halo or crown, one frontal view, one ¾ view;

5. [7th firmament, left side:] Mānī with green halo, two attendants with crown only, both in ¾ view;

6. [7th firmament, right side:] Mānī with pink halo, two attendants without halo or crown, one frontal view, one ¾ view;

7. [1st firmament, left side:] Mānī with green halo, two attendants without halo or crown, both ones in ¾ view;

8. [On the left side of the snake-world:] a seated Mānī with green halo, two attendants [seated] without halo or crown, both ones in ¾ view;

9. [beside the Virgin of Light:] Mānī with green halo, two attendants with crown;

10. [Judgment scene:] Mānī with green halo, two attendants with crown;

11. [A group above the Sun:] main figure with green halo, attendants without halo or crown;

12. [A group of three above the 10th firmament:] the main figure is

smaller; all have a halo;

13. [A group of three on Mount Sumeru:] all have a halo, but the central figure is seated on a lotus throne, the attendants are standing;

14. [The Righteous Judge:] seated with halo and crown, the two attendants: standing, without halo or crown;

15. [A figure in the centre of the "snake world":] seated, with a green halo, the attendants without halo or crown are standing;

16–19. [Four groups of three figures:] the apparently main figure is smaller than the attendants, and does not have a halo or a crown, while the attendants have a crown.

While the robes that these figures wear do not differentiate them from other figures related to the Realm of Light, the golden crown they wear narrows down the potential identifications. As for the headgear of the non-demonic figures, there are four types: 1. the complete lack of headgear; 2. golden crown with a red lower part; 3. halo (of various colours); 4. the combination of halo and crown. Halo (Type 3) and halo–crown (Type 4) is typical only of divinities *in stricto sensu*, i.e. the main divine figures, who play an important part in the Manichaean cosmogony.〔1〕 One exception is Mānī himself, who almost invariably has a halo, and another one is an important divine figure without halo, who stands on the fifth earth, and whom I identified with the Primal Man.〔2〕 In the case of this highly important divine figure, the lack of halo can be justified by his state. This scene

〔1〕Only halo: e.g. the Twelve Aeons, the four faces of the Father of Greatness, three-three gods in the Sun and the Moon. Combination of halo and crown: the Father of Greatness, some unidentified divine figures in the Realm of Light (one seated on a lotus throne behind Mānī, two groups of figures on the two sides of the Realm of Light), Splenditenens above the firmaments in the middle, three-three (cf. Kósa 2011: 23–24) figures seated on the columns on the two sides of the painting, a god in the first firmament, the Virgin of Light, two gods (probably the Living Spirit and the Mother of Living) encountering the Primal Man and Gloriosus Rex on the fifth earth.

〔2〕Kósa 2014: 72–74.

depicts how he will be liberated by the two divine figures in front him, but in the narrative present of the painting he is not liberated yet, therefore he has no halo.[1]

The three figures in question in the judgment scene belong to Type 2, which occurs relatively rarely, and in all cases, this type accompanies a major figure belonging to either Type 1 or 3. Such figures accompany Mānī three times (beside Rex Honoris, the Virgin of Light, and the Righteous Judge); they follow four unidentified small figures descending at the four continents around Mount Sumeru, and a further figure beside Gloriosus Rex. Such accompanying figures might be either angels or humans who for some reason stand at an equal level with them. Neither the two missionary paintings, nor the two Realm of Light fragments contain any similar figure, but the Birth of Mānī painting does.

On the right bottom of the latter painting, one can observe three majestic figures with crown, but without halo. Y. Yoshida associates them with the three magi of the gospel of Matthew.[2] Unlike various divine figures floating on cloud in the air, these respectful figures, standing on the green surface where all other earthly events happen, are obviously human beings, thus, though in another Manichaean painting, we have at least one unambiguous example where figures belonging to Type 2 can also be human beings, not only angels.[3] In the following, I will propose two possible identifications of this group of three: firstly, as a group of angels, and secondly, as a group of humans.

If the three figures are angels, then in theory they might be linked with

〔1〕This visual distinction between figures with halo (liberated) and without halo (not liberated) will play an important role in the further analysis.

〔2〕Yoshida 2012: 5b.

〔3〕However, it cannot be excluded that they represent the three magi as three kings (even if it is only a later Christian tradition), and this is the reason why they wear the crowns.

the three angels appearing in the Manichaean *post mortem* state.[1] The problem with this interpretation is that the three angels occurring in this context invariably accompany a major figure (the Light Form or Light Nous), who is, however, nowhere to be found in the CP judgment scene.

> When death comes to one of the Elect, Primal Man sends him a light shining deity in the form of the Wise Guide. With him are three deities, with whom there are the drinking vessel, clothing, headcloth, crown, and diadem of light. There accompanies them a virgin who resembles the soul of that member of the Elect. (…) Then they take the member of the Elect and garb him with the crown, the diadem, and the garments.[2]
>
> And also the fifth father is this Light Form; the one who shall appear to everyone who will g[o] out from his body, corresponding to the pattern of the image to the apostle; and the thr[ee] great glorious angels who are come with her. One (angel) ho[ld]s the prize in his hand. The second bears the light garment. The third is the one who possesses the diadem and the wreath and the crown of light. These are the three angels of light, the ones who shall come with this Light Form; and they appear with her to the elect and the catechumens.[3]
>
> [When a person died], this God Nom Qutï (the Great Nous) comes, along with the three gods…[4]
>
> The image of my counterpart came unto me, with her three angels.

---

〔1〕Cf. Arnold-Döben 1978: 150–151.

〔2〕*Al-Fihrist* (Dodge 1970: 795).

〔3〕Trans. Gardner 1995: 40. *Kephalaia* 36,12–21: ⲡⲙⲁϩϯⲟⲩ ⲇⲉ ϩⲱⲱϥ ⲛ̄ⲓ̈ⲱⲧ ⲡⲉ ϯⲙⲟⲣⲫⲏ ⲛ̄ⲟⲩⲁⲓ̈ⲛⲉ ⲧⲉⲧⲉ / ϣⲁⲥⲟⲩⲱⲛϩ ⲁⲃⲁⲗ ⲛⲟⲩⲁⲛ ⲛⲓⲙ ⲉⲧⲛⲁⲃ[ⲱⲕ] ⲁⲃⲁⲗ ϩⲙ̄ ⲡⲉϥⲥⲱ/ⲙⲁ ⲁϩⲣⲛ̄ ⲡⲉⲓⲛⲉ ⲛⲧϩⲓⲕⲱⲛ ⲙⲡⲁⲡⲟⲥⲧⲟⲗⲟⲥ ⲙⲛ̄ ⲡϣⲁ[ⲙⲧ] / ⲛⲛⲁϭ ⲛⲁⲅⲅⲉⲗⲟⲥ ⲉⲧⲟⲓ̈ ⲛⲉⲁⲩ ⲉⲧⲛⲏⲩ ⲛⲉⲙⲉⲥ ⲡⲟⲩⲉ ⲉϥⲉⲙ[ⲁϩ] /ⲧⲉ ⲙ̄ⲡⲃⲣⲁⲃⲓⲟⲛ ϩⲛ ⲧⲉϥϭⲓϫ ⲡⲙⲁϩⲥⲛⲉⲩ ⲉϥⲃⲓ ϩⲁ ⲑⲃ̄ⲥⲱ / ⲛ̄ⲟⲩⲁⲓ̈ⲛⲉ ⲡⲙⲁϩϣⲁⲙⲧ ⲡⲉ ⲡⲉⲧⲉⲙⲁϩⲧⲉ ⲛⲧϭⲣⲏⲡⲉ / ⲙⲛ̄ ⲡⲥⲧⲉⲫⲁⲛⲟⲥ ⲙⲛ̄ ⲡⲕⲗⲁⲙ ⲛ̄ⲧⲉ ⲡⲟⲩⲁⲓ̈ⲛⲉ. ⲛⲉⲓ̈ ⲛⲉ ⲡϣⲁ/ⲙⲧ̄ ⲛⲁⲅⲅⲉⲗⲟⲥ ⲛⲧⲉ ⲡⲟⲩⲁⲓ̈ⲛⲉ ⲛⲉⲧⲉϣⲁⲩⲉⲓ ⲙⲛ̄ ϯⲙⲟⲣⲫⲏ / ⲛ̄ⲟⲩⲁⲓ̈ⲛⲉ ⲛⲥⲉⲟⲩⲱⲛϩ ⲁⲃⲁⲗ ⲛⲉⲙⲉⲥ ⲛ̄ⲛ̄ⲉⲕⲗⲉⲕⲧⲟⲥ ⲙⲛ̄ ⲛ/ⲕⲁⲧⲏⲭⲟⲩⲙⲉⲛⲟⲥ.

〔4〕Klimkeit 1993: 321. T II D 175.2/R/1–2 (Le Coq 1922: 31): ötrü antaγ nomqutï tngri / üč tngrilärlügün…

> She gave to me the garment and the crown and the palm and the victory. He took me to the judge without any shame; for what he entrusted to me I have perfected.[1]

The other aspect that makes this identification less probable is the lack of any divine prize (the light garment, the crown, the palm etc.) brought by these figures and always mentioned in the texts.

As for the identity of the three crowned figures as humans, I will refer to Nils A. Pedersen's important study on the Coptic *Sermon on the Great War*.

> It must above all be stressed that the judgment decision is conditioned by mankind's attitude towards the Manichaean Church, specifically its true core, the elect. Three groups are gathered before Jesus. The elect have already been saved at the moment of death and have become "angels". They do not therefore have to be judged but must be assumed to be onlookers; this is quite reasonable, since Jesus makes his judgment dependent upon how the others have treated them. The catechumens are awarded "the victory" because they have nourished the elect. (...) The third group, "the goats" (...) are sentenced to eternal damnation because they did not conduct themselves towards the elect as the catechumens did.[2]
>
> That the elect are present during the judgment proceedings is certainly much clearer in Šābuhragān than in SGW [*Sermon on the Great War*, KG], but it can be seen from *Man. Hom.* 38.28.[3]

We know that one of the most important attributes of the elect after death is

[1] Gardner 1996: 15. T. Kell. Copt. 2: 120–126 (Gardner 1996: 14): ⲁ ⲑⲓⲕⲱⲛ ⲙ̄ⲡ[[ⲁⲥⲁ]] /ⲉⲓϣ ⲉⲓ ϣⲁⲣⲁⲉⲓ ⲙⲛ̄ ⲡⲉⲥϣⲁⲙⲧ ⲛ̄/ⲁⲅⲅⲉⲗⲟⲥ ⲁⲥϯ ⲛⲏⲓ̈ [[ⲛ̄ⲧϩ]]ⲃ̄ⲥⲱ ⲙⲛ̄ / ⲡⲕⲗⲁⲙ ⲙⲛ̄ ⲡⲃⲁⲉ ⲙⲛ̄ ⲡϭⲣⲟ [[//]] / ⲁϥϫⲓⲧ ⲁⲣⲉⲧϥ ⲙ̄ⲡⲉⲕⲣⲓⲧⲏⲥ ⲁϫⲛ̄ / ⲗⲁⲟⲩⲉ ⲛ̄ϣⲓⲡⲉ ϫⲉ ⲡⲉⲧⲁϥⲧⲉⲉϥ / ⲁⲧⲟⲟⲧ ⲁⲉⲓϫⲱⲕ ⲙⲙⲁϥ ⲉⲃⲁⲗ.

[2] Pedersen 1996: 356–357.

[3] Pedersen 1996: 357. n. 576.

the crown he receives as a reward of his pure life.[1] The identification of the group of three crowned figures with the elects as onlookers is, of course, only a hypothesis, but it can be visually supported by three further motifs.

Firstly, they stand precisely on the opposite side of the naked figure, who, according to Pedersen's analysis, can only be a catechumen or a sinner (and it would be indeed strange to imagine that a demon ward grasps firmly an elect who followed Mānī's precepts during his whole lifetime[2]). Secondly, the tail of the red clouds on which these three figures stand is pronouncedly meandering downwards, which means that they seem to arrive from the human world around Mount Sumeru. If they were divine figures, it would be more logical to see them as arriving from the upper part of the painting, as it clearly happens in the Sandōzu painting, where Daēnā, despite the fact that she is the embodiment of the individual's deeds,[3] arrives from the uppermost section (the Realm of Light) on a cloud, the tail of which is meandering upwards, pointing to its origin.

The third interesting feature is that two of the three figures are depicted in profile, which most often seems to occur in connection with human figures. These instantces include four kneeling people around Mount Sumeru, two kneeling figures on the top of Mount Sumeru, two kneeling men in front of a seated Mānī on the onlooker's left side of the snake-world, ten kneeling people travelling on the outer surface of the tenth firmament and on clouds above it, four further kneeling persons seated on clouds above the Moon, and a standing Mānī three times in the Moon, the Sun and the Realm of Light. There are three figures standing at the bottom of the

[1] Arnold-Döben 1978: 155.

[2] Cf. the statement that demons cannot harm a virtuous person (Ch/So 14731 + Ch/So 10051 + Ch/So10052 + Ōtani 7127 + Дх 06957/v/9–10; Reck 2003: 338; Wilkens 2009: 340).

[3] Nevertheless, since Daēnā represents the deeds of the individual, there is no compelling evidence that she must originate from the heavenly realm, thus she might arrive from the human world as well (a remark made by Y. Yoshida, July 30, 2012).

snake-world, three further figures on the two edges of the Realm of Light, and a small figure in front of Mānī on the left side of the Father of Greatness, whose human or divine nature is difficult to determine. Among the definitively human figures in profile, 22 are kneeling, and only Mānī is standing. All figures in profile (including Mānī) are depicted in *añjali mudrā.* All unquestionably divine figures in the CP are depicted in either three-quarter profile or full frontal view, and none of them in profile.

In sum, theoretically, it cannot be excluded that the three figures below the Mānī group might be equated with the victorious electi, who have already been granted their crown of life, and thus they have already become part of the divine world ("And his righteous ones and his virgins he had made like the angels" [*Homilies* 38,15–16] [1]).

It must be added that, besides the pros, there are also some apparent cons against this interpretation. In the two missionary paintings, the elects, similarly to Mānī, invariably wear a white robe with a colour border, the former being attested in other textual descriptions and visual depictions. [2] On the other hand, in the CP, except for the figure of Mānī appearing 13 times, there is nobody who would wear such a robe with a colour border. [3] Consequently, there are three possibilities: either there are no elects depicted in the CP, or the missionary painting and the CP are not congruent in this respect, or this difference has some inner logic not yet expounded. I would opt for the third alternative, and propose an explanation for this

---

〔1〕Trans. I. Gardner (Gardner and Lieu 2004: 225).

〔2〕E.g. *Fozu tongji* 佛祖统计 T2035: 0378c, 0474c, *Da Song Sengshilüe* 大宋僧史略 T2126: 0253c, *Minshu* 闽书 7.32a. MIK III 8259 R, MIK III 6265–4966 R, MIK III 4979a–b V, MIK III 4974 R, MIK III 6368 V, MIK III 6283, MIK III 6286, MIK III 4815a, MIK III 6918, MIK III 4624 (Gulácsi 2001: 60, 64, 71, 84, 93, 177, 179, 183, 200–201, 203).

〔3〕There are two figures standing in a group of others on the left and right sides of the Realm of Light who wear a pure white robe without border, and a similar robe is worn by ten of forty angels on the right edge of the ten firmaments. There are, however, clearly different from those worn by the elects in the two missionary paintings.

phenomenon.

As mentioned above, based on both the Manichaean visual and the non-Manichaean textual sources, it is widely acknowledged that Manichaean elects wore a white robe in their daily life. However, the three figures in the judgment scene are clad in colourful robes, which are the combination of dark green, red and pink, colours often associated with light in the CP. These robes, therefore, can duly be called light-robes, which is a well-known symbol for the elect.[1] In the hymn on the Realm of Light of the Chinese Manichaean *Hymnscroll* (*Tan mingjie wen* 叹明界文), the garments of the saints (elects) are described as bright and clean (H179c: 圣众衣服唯鲜洁), unique, adorned, the colours of which are innumerable (H180d: 奇特庄严色无量).

> If we arrive at the day of impermanence [death] and rid ourselves of this abominable body of flesh, all the buddhas, saints and wise surround us all around. The jewel-boats are prepared, the Good Deed [= Daēnā, GK] herself welcomes us, we arrive directly in front of the King of Justice, we receive the Three Great Victories, which are called the flower-crown, the necklace of precious stones and the ten thousand kinds of wonderful robes with pendants. The good deeds, the meritorious virtues and the buddha-nature are praised and eulogized unceasingly.[2]

At least three of the accessories mentioned in connection with the elects are present on the three figures: they wear a crown (though not strictly speaking a flowery crown [*huaguan* 花冠]), they wear different kinds of wonderful robes (*wan zhong miaoyi* 万种妙衣), and they also have pendants (*chuanpei* 串佩).

---

[1] Arnold-Döben 1978: 151–153, Ferreira 2000.

[2] H393–396: 若至无常之日，脱此可厌宍 / 身，诸佛圣贤，前后围绕；宝船安置，善业自迎，直至平等王前，/ 受三大胜，所谓花冠、璎珞、万种妙衣串佩，善业福德佛性，无 / 穷赞叹。

Consequently, in the Chinese context at least, the robes of the saints (deceased elects) were considered colourful, not homogenously white. All these taken together, it might be hypothetically suggested that the elects wore a white robe in their life, but, according to the Chinese Manichaean imagination at least, wore colourful robes after their death.

If this interpretation were correct, this would interestingly dovetail with a recurring statement in the universal eschatological passages: the righteous stand on the Judge's right side, while the sinners on the left.

> And the religious will say to him, '[O god and] our lord! if it please thee, we shall tell thee something of that which the sinners have [done] to us'. And god Xradešahr will answer them so, 'Look on me and rejoice. Besides, whoever may have harmed you, him I shall bring to justice for you and seek *account (from him). But everything which you wish to tell me, that I know'. Then he blesses them and calms their hearts and sets them on the right side, and with the gods they will be in bliss. And the evil-doers he separates from the religious and sets them on the left side and curses them and speaks thus… (*Šābuhragān*)[1]

> And his righteous ones and his virgins he had made like the angels. On the other hand, the goats, who are to his left side, will see the confidence that he has given the ones to the right side. (*Homilies* 38,15–19)[2]

---

〔1〕MacKenzie 1979: 507. MacKenzie 1979: 506: 'wš dynwr gw'nd kw [yzd] / ['w]m'n xwd'y 'grt pszg ty[s] / ['c] h'n (c)[y] dr(w)nd['n] (pd) 'mẖ / [qyrd] pyš tw gw(')m ['w]š'n / x[rd]yšhr yzd pswx 'wẖ / dyy'd kw mn wynyyd 'wd š'd / bwyyd * 'n'y ky pd 'šmẖ / wn'st h'd h'nt'n d'dys(t)['n] / qwn'n w 'ng'm xw'h'n b[yc] / hrw cy 'šmẖ q'myyd p[yš] / mn gwptn h'n 'n d'nym ** ** / ghyš'n 'pryn qwnd 'wš'[n] / dyl wyw'synyd 'wš'n 'w / dšn ''rg 'ystynyd ** w (')[b']g / yzd'n pd š'dyẖ phryzynd ** / 'wd dwšqyrdg'n'n 'z dy(n)[wr'n] / wc'ryd 'wš'n 'w xwy ''rg / 'ystynyd 'wš'n npryn qwnd '[wd] / 'wẖ gwyd kw …

〔2〕Trans. I. Gardner (Gardner and Lieu 2004: 225). *Homilies* 38,15–19: [ⲛⲉϥⲇ]ⲓⲕⲁⲓⲟⲥ ⲇⲉ ⲙⲛ̄ⲛⲉϥⲡⲁⲣⲑⲉⲛⲟⲥ ⲁϥⲉⲩⲉ ⲙ̄ⲡⲣ[ⲏ/ⲧⲉ ⲛ]ⲛ̄ⲁⲅⲅⲉⲗⲟⲥ/ ⲛ̄ⲃⲁⲙⲡⲉ ϩⲱϥ ⲉⲧⲥⲁϭⲃⲟⲩⲣ ⲙ̄ⲙ[ⲁϥ] / [ⲛⲁⲛ]ⲟ ⲁⲡⲕⲁϩⲧⲏϥ ⲉⲧⲁϥⲧⲉϥ ⲛ̄ⲛⲉⲧⲥⲁ ⲟⲩⲛⲉⲙ.

Both the Middle Persian *Šābuhragān* and the Coptic *Homilies*, the two principal sources of our knowledge on Manichaean eschatology, mention that the righteous stand on the Judge's right side, while the sinners ("goats") on his left. This is precisely what we see in the CP: the three crowned figure, who are indeed similar to angels or other divine figures, stand on the Righteous Judge's right side, while a possible sinner (naked, held by the monster ward) on his left side. While the Mānī group, clearly outside the events, observes the scene from the view of an outsider, the three crowned figures clearly stand in front of the Righteous Judge, thus their involvement in the events can safely be assumed. Their position seems to counterbalance or counterpoint that of the naked figure. While they stand on the Judge's right side, the naked person on the left; while they wear ornate robes with divine attributes, the other figure stands completely naked; while they were brought in front of the Judge by a divine red cloud, the naked person was dragged there by a merciless demon-soldier. Such a dichotomy, especially that of the robes and their absence, can already be detected in the Dunhuang Ten Kings paintings, to which the CP scene can be most probably traced back.

In front of the various kings of the Dunhuang scrolls, one can basically observe two types of figures: the more conspicuous ones are those clad in loincloths only, frequently also wearing a cangue or handcuffs, and often attended by human or demonic wards. Those belonging to the other type are clad in robes and in their hands they usually hold evidence of the merit they (or their relatives) accrued while alive (Buddhist statues or scrolls). While the former group is exposed to various tortures or at least evident violence, the members of the latter group seem to float through the scenes without any harm. One of the examples is the illustration in P.4523 + Ch. cii. 001 [1919, 0101, 0.80] from Dunhuang (Fig. 8). Here a middle-aged man, carrying scrolls in his hands, and a middle-aged woman, holding a small statue of Buddha, simply walk (or float) through the various courts of the

Ten Kings.[1] Both wear complete attire, while the various sinners without merit are clad in loincloth, wear a cangue, and sometimes suffer various tortures. What this scroll suggests is that if someone (or his/her relatives) accrued religious merits, such as commissioning the copy of a sūtra or donating money for a Buddha statue, he/she will go through the ten courts unharmed, while other people without the necessary religious merits must undergo the painful procedure of interrogation and torture.[2]

Fig. 8. Contrast between the naked figures with cangue and the properly dressed couple holding the proof (scrolls and statue) of their religious merit. Handscroll illustrating the apochryphal *Ten Kings of Hell Sutra*, Reg. No. 1919,0101,0.80 (detail of the original image). 10th c., ink and colours on paper, 27.8 cm ×239.9 cm.

In sum, the Dunhuang scrolls already included the dichotomy of the clad and the naked "soul(s)". The former ones, due to their own or their relatives' merit, always belong to the privileged few who do not have to suffer at the various courts. In contrast, the naked figures are severely judged and harshly punished. As suggested above, this dichotomy is perhaps also present in the CP scene: those standing on the Judge's right are beautifully clad and thus represent the deceased elects, who have accrued a great amount of merit with their life of utmost austerity, and who were, therefore, granted the divine crown and the light robe. On the other hand, the naked person, seized by a hideous ward, might have committed several

[1] In the court of Yama, the roles are changed.

[2] The age of the two types of people does not allow the possibility that they would be in parental relation (which is otherwise mentioned in the sūtra).

kinds of sins, therefore must bear its consequences.

Although the Manichaean tradition holds that fundamentally there are three ways after death (that of the elect, the auditor, and the sinner),[1] the *Kephalaia* (234,24–236,6) makes it clear that the *Eikōn* did not show the fate of the auditors. If the CP can indeed be traced back to the *Eikōn*, then what we can expect to be depicted in the CP is the appearance of the elects and the sinners in front of the Righteous Judge.

> You have made clear in that great Picture(-Book); you have depic[t]ed the righteous one how he shall be released and [brou]ght before the Judge and attain the land of li[ght]. [You have] also drawn the sinner, how he shall die. [He] shall be [… / s]et before the Judge and tried […] the dispenser of justice. And he is thrown into gehenna, where he shall wander for eternity.[2]

If the hypothesis above is correct, this might indeed be the case: the elects appear as angels on the right side of the Judge, while the sinners appear on his left side.

It must be emphasized, however, that the two other interpretations of this group (Daēnā and two attendants, as proposed by Y. Yoshida, or the three angels, as described above) are also possible and cannot be excluded. Furthermore, I cannot satisfactorily answer the question why, according to the previously outlined interpretation, one sinner but three elects are depicted.[3] A combination of two of the former interpretations might offer a tentative answer, but this reply would be completely speculative.

According to this interpretation, the three figures would consist of an

---

[1] See e.g. Olsson 1988: 279–283.

[2] Trans. Gardner 1995: 241–242. *Kephalaia* 235, 2/8: ⲁⲕⲟⲩ/ⲱⲛϩ̄ ⲁⲃⲁⲗ ϩⲛ̄ ϯⲛⲁϭ ⲛϩⲓⲕⲱⲛ ⲉⲧⲙ̄ⲙⲉⲩ ⲁⲕⲍⲱⲅⲣⲁ[ⲫ]ⲉ ⲙ̄/ⲡⲇⲓⲕⲁⲓⲟⲥ ⲛ̄ⲧϩⲉ ⲉⲧⲉϣⲁϥⲃⲱⲗ ⲁⲃⲁⲗ ⲙⲛ̄ ⲧϩⲉ ⲉⲧⲉϣ[ⲁⲩϫⲓ]/ⲧϥ̄ ϩⲓⲧⲉϩⲏ ⲙⲡⲕⲣⲓⲧⲏⲥ ⲛ̄ϥⲧⲉϩⲟ ⲧⲭⲱⲣⲁ ⲙ̄ⲡⲟⲩ[ⲁⲓ̈ⲛⲉ. ⲁⲕ]/ⲥϩⲉⲓ̈ ⲁⲛ ⲙ̄ⲡⲣⲉϥⲣ̄ⲛⲁⲃⲉ ⲧϩⲉ ⲉⲧⲉϣⲁϥⲙⲟⲩ ϣⲁⲩ . . [. . . .]/[ⲥⲉ]ϩⲱϥ ⲁⲣⲉⲧϥ ϩⲓⲧⲉϩⲏ ⲙⲡⲕⲣⲓⲧⲏⲥ ⲛ̄ⲥⲉⲧⲁϫⲁϥ . . . . . / ⲡⲣⲉϥϯϩⲉⲡ ⲛⲥⲉⲛⲁϫϥ ⲁⲧⲅⲉⲉⲛⲛⲁ ⲧⲉⲧⲉϣⲁϥⲙⲁϩⲉ ⲛϩⲏ/ⲧⲥ̄ ϣⲁ ⲁⲛⲏϩⲉ.

[3] Y. Yoshida raised this question in our email correspondence (July 30, 2012).

elect (the one depicted in full frontal view), plus Daēnā and her attendant (the figures in profile). In this case, Daēnā would indeed appear but only to prove the virtuousness of the elect standing beside her. Visually, this interpretation would offer a more balanced view of one sinner and one elect, symbolizing all sinners and all elects. Thus, the demon ward can seize the sinner, but he is unable to harm the elect,[1] who is placed in the secure shelter of Daēnā and her attendant.[2] According to this interpretation, this group of three would not consist of Daēnā and her two attendants, but Daēnā (in profile, with a pendant), her attendant behind her (in profile, with a pendant), and an elect (in full frontal view, without a visible pendant).

5.2.7 The animals and the five heads in front of the Judge

As mentioned above, the CP judgment scene is based on the iconography of the Ten Kings of Hell paintings. In this type of painting, one can sometimes encounter animals that stand between the person under judgment and Yama, the judge. Examples include the following ones: P.4523 (cock, snake, boar); Lu Xinzhong [Shiga–Eigenji] (cock, goose),[3] Seigan-ji 誓愿寺 scroll [Kyoto] (cock, duck);[4] Lu Zhongyuan [Saikyō-ji 西教寺, Ōtsu] (cock,

〔1〕Ch/So 14731 + Ch/So 10051 + Ch/So10052 + Ōtani 7127 + Дх 06957/v/9–10; Reck 2003: 338; Wilkens 2009: 340.

〔2〕Cf. the statement in the *al-Fihrist* (Dodge 1970: 795): "When the member of the Elect sees them [the devils], he seeks the aid of the deity who is in the form of the Wise [= Daēnā, GK], and the three deities who come close to him." If this interpretation is correct, then a further, equally speculative, hypothesis can be formulated. *Kephalaia* (344,13–22) is a unique locus which describes the judgment of the elect as the separation of the New and the Old Man. Since the Old Man is closely related to the body, in this respect, the naked person (although not in accordance with the Buddhist iconography) could designate the Old Man, while the person on the Judge's right would represent the New Man. The recurrent references to the separation of the two natures in a judgment situation might also entail the same notion, see *Psalm-book* 26,28–29 (ⲛⲉⲧⲡⲱⲣϫ̄ ⲛ̄ⲧϥⲩⲥⲓⲥ ⲥⲛ̄ⲧⲉ); 28,14–15 (ⲛⲉⲧⲡⲱⲣϫ̄ ⲁⲃⲁⲗ ⲛ̄ⲧϥⲩⲥⲓⲥ ⲥⲛ̄ⲧⲉ); 30,26–27 (ⲁϥⲡⲱⲣϫ̄ ⲁⲃⲁⲗ ⲛ̄ⲧ[ϥⲩⲥⲓⲥ ⲥⲛ̄ⲧⲉ]).

〔3〕NNM 2009: 90.

〔4〕Miya 1992: 55. fig. 37.

duck, pig);[1] Lu Zhongyuan [NNM] (cock, goose);[2] Seikadō 静嘉堂 image (snake, goose, bull, cock, turtle, shell, giant crab),[3] Yuanjue dong niche 60 (84), Anyue, Sichuan (cows, dog, snake),[4] Packard set (boar, duck, cow).[5] Their role is clearly described in the *Ten Kings sūtra*: they had been the victims of the sinner, therefore they appear as witnesses in front of the judge.[6]

> For any serious crimes that require serving in the underground prisons for ten kalpas or five kalpas — killing one's father; injuring one's mother; breaking the fast; breaking the precepts; slaughtering pigs, cattle, sheep, chickens, dogs, or poisonous snakes — a person can during life commission this scripture or the various images of the Honored Ones, and it will be noted in the mirror of actions.[7]
>
> The hymn goes: Breaking the fast, damaging the precepts, slaughtering chickens and pigs are reflected clearly in the mirror of actions – retribution is never void. If one commissions this scripture together with the painting of images, King Yama will decide to release you and wipe away yours sins.[8]

In some cases (P.4523, Lu Xinzhong [Shiga–Eigenji],[9] Seigan-ji scroll, [Kyoto][10]) the animals even have a small scroll of paper that is supposed to

---

[1] Miya 1992: 60. fig. 60.

[2] NNM 2009: 92.

[3] SBB 1999: 44. pl. 6-5.

[4] Zhiru 2007: 155. figs. 29–30.

[5] Kwon 1999: 79, Kwon 2005: 29. fig. 1d. On the scattered Packard set, see Kwon 2005: 28.

[6] For examples on various Song paintings, see Teiser 1994: 34. n.5.

[7] Teiser 1994: 202 (cf. n.60, and Hirasawa 2008: 18). X01,0021: p0408b17–19: 在生之日，杀父害母，破齐破戒，杀猪牛羊鸡狗毒蛇，/ 一切重罪，应入地狱十劫五劫。若造此经及诸尊像，/ 记在业镜。For the Old Turkish version, see Zieme 1996: 407.

[8] Teiser 1994: 203. X01, 0021, p0408b20–22: 赞曰: / 破齐毁戒杀鸡猪，业镜照然报不虚。/ 若造此经兼画像，阎王判放罪销除。Cf. Dudbridge 1998: 387–388 [2005: 146]. n.29.

[9] NNM 2009: 90. Cf. the Ten Kings scroll in the Idemitsu Museum, Tokyo (Takasu 2006: 47. Fig. 6).

[10] Miya 1992: 55. fig. 37.

be their accusation against the sinner.[1] Textual sources also attest to this notion: "Geese and ducks carry formal accusations in their beaks in order to lodge their complaints. Chickens and pigs appeal to the king and demand the death [of those who ate them]."[2] Dai Fu's 戴孚 *Guangyiji* 广异记 records stories containing similar motifs, though these are not directly related to the Ten Kings tradition.[3]

Although the animals in the Ten Kings paintings and the CP scene do not precisely overlap, the textual description of the *Ten Kings sūtra*, the visual representations of the same scene, and the *Ten Kings sūtra* as the source of the CP judgment scene together make it evident that the animals between the judge and the human being in the CP must somehow represent living beings that were harmed by the human figure.

There are altogether five animals in front of the human being, and Y. Yoshida is probably right that they must be somehow related to the five

---

〔1〕Cf. Teiser 1999: 191: "The version in the picture-scroll (seventh scene in fig. 1, P.4523) further underscores the inescapability of karmic law, showing three animals advancing to the king's desk, each carrying in its mouth or beak the legal case outlining the sinner's cruelty."

〔2〕Yan Bing 颜丙 or Layman Ruru (Ruru *jushi* 如如居士, d. 1212): "A General Exhortation [to Observe] the Precept Against Taking Life" (*Pu quan jie sha sheng wen* 普劝戒杀生文): 鹅鸭啣状以诉冤。鸡豚告王而索命。虽作畜生在世，皆曾曩劫为人。 Trans. A.G. Wagner 2008: 148.

〔3〕Story 23 [Dudbridge 1995: 179: Administrator Tian is called to to account in the underworld by the beasts he has killed]; story 180 [Dudbridge 1995: 209: a market official is tried for offences alleged by various animals]; story 182 [Dudbridge 1995: 210: Officer Xue comes before a king to face charges of killing animals]; story 183 [Dudbridge 1995: 210: Deng faces the king's rebuke and the threat of attack from animals accusing him]; story 184 [Dudbridge 1995: 210: Zhang comes before a king who confronts him with the animals he has killed]. Cf. Wagner 2008: 148.n.21: "The *Collected Passages on the Joyous Country* [*Lebang wen lei* 乐邦文类, GK], published in 1200, recounts episodes of a butcher seeing on his deathbed a herd of cattle goring him with their horns, and person who slaughtered chickens seeing on his deathbed a spirit directing a flock of chickens to peck his eyes out." Also see W. L. Idema's remark (1998: 187): "For me one of these interesting details was an illustration from manuscript P. 4523 of the court of the fifth king, showing among others three animals, a boar, a rooster and a snake, laying plaint before King Yama. This reminded me of the *sanqu*-song of Yuan times, devoted to first-person complaints by an animal, such as a buffalo or a sheep, to King Yama, about the unfair treatment they had suffered during their lifetime at the hands of a man."

types of living beings mentioned in the Manichaean sources. [1] While the fish, the cock and the snake evidently represent animals in water, birds and reptiles, respectively, quadrupeds are represented by a white and a dark goat-like animal, which is obviously an asymmetry. Thus, there are five animals representing four classes of animals, while the human figure would theoretically symbolize the fifth living being, the human beings, were he/she not already equated with the person under judgment. This group of five living beings is recorded in several Manichaean sources.

> V A. Fifthly. (About sins) Against the five kinds of living beings. V B. And (that is) firstly, against the two-legged human beings; secondly, against the four-legged living beings; thirdly, against the flying living, fourthly, against the living beings in the water, (and) fifthly, the living beings creeping on the ground on their belly." [2]

> They also say that if anyone walks on the ground he harms the ground, and if he moves his hand he harms the air, because air is the soul of men and animals, birds, fish and reptiles and everything there is in this world. [3]

> They [the Manichaeans, GK] say that the atmosphere is the soul of the animals and the people and the birds and the fish and the reptiles, and everything which is in the universe. [4]

> If for my sake human beings were beaten or imprisoned, or if they

---

[1] Yoshida 2010: 12b.

[2] Trans. J. Asmussen (1965: 195). *X^uāstvānīft* VA–B (Asmussen (1965: 172): bišinč biš türlüg tïnl(ï)γqa / bir ymä äkii adaql(ï)γ kišikä / äkintii tört butluγ tïnl(ï)γqa / üčünč učuγma tïnl(ï)γqa / törtünč suw 'ičräkii tïnl(ï)γqa / bišinč yirdäki baγrïn yorïγma tïnl(ï)γqa.

[3] Trans. M. Vermes (2001: 55). *Acta Archelai* X.8 (Beeson 1906: 17): Et illi dicunt, si quis ambulat in terra, laedit terram, et qui movet manum, laedit aërem, quia aër anima est hominum et animalium et volatilium et piscium et repentium et si quid est in hoc mundo [καὶ εἴ τις περιπατεῖ χαμαί, βλάπτει τὴν γῆν· καὶ ὁ κινῶν τὴν χεῖρα βλάπτει τὸν ἀέρα, ἐπειδὴ ὁ ἀὴρ ψυχή ἐστι τῶν ἀνθρώπων καὶ τῶν ζώων καὶ τῶν πετεινῶν καὶ τῶν ἰχθύων καὶ τῶν ἑρπετῶν. καὶ εἴ τις ἐν κόσμῳ ἐστίν].

[4] Shenoute: "Who speaks through the Prophet" (T41), Paris, BN Copte 131[4]f.158b. Trans. I. Gardner (Lieu–Gardner 2004: 230). Shenoute's source was obviously the *Acta Archelai* (Lieu–Gardner 2004: 230).

> had to endure humiliation or insults; if I should have inflicted injury on four-footed animals while ascending or descending, or by beating or spurring them on; if I should have planned to harm wild animals, birds, creatures in the water or reptiles creeping on the ground, and should have harmed their life.[1]

As for the animals, one question still remains unanswered: the Manichaean pentad of living beings always includes the human state, while in the CP the human figure is the person to be judged, and most probably does not belong to the group of living beings in front of him. A tentative answer can only be offered. In order to follow the Ten Kings iconography, the painter of the CP judgment scene had to separate the person seized by the demon ward and the other living beings witnessing against him/her. Witnesses are always animals, never humans, in the Ten Kings paintings as well. However, since the Manichaean system invariably mentions a pentad of living beings, the painter might have inserted a fifth animal, thus creating a group of five living beings, at this stage already excluding the humans,[2] and another group of five stalks with heads on them. Thus, the painter could meet the requirements of both the Manichaean references to five animals and the traditional Ten Kings iconography.

Despite the asymmetry, we do have five living beings; the question is what they mean in this context. Theoretically, they could refer to the five

---

〔1〕M801/32/504–514 (Henning 1937: 33; Klimkeit 1993: 139): cww mn’ pyδ’r / mrṯxmyṯ xwsṯy βsṯy / nmy’k pṯyδy’ / βyrṯ / δ’rnd p’δyẖ / sṯwrpδyy ’wjγnd / βjγnd pyz pṯšk’f / ṯrγṯz’yy ’kṯwδ’rm / pr nxšyrṯ mrγyšṯ / ”pyk δṯw z’yxyzyy / pr’nyṯ γnd’k šym’rw*w* / jw’n zyryšw. On the five living beings, also see Schmidt 1980: 231, Vermes and Lieu 2001: 55.

〔2〕It seems to me that around the two quadrupeds there is a white silhouette, which might indicate that the figures in this part of the painting were, uniquely in the CP, rearranged after the first composition. This would mean that what we see here is the result of a secondary, but rather conscious, composition. Although it is hardly possible to reconcile with the theory expounded in this paper, nevertheless, it might be interesting to note that the two quadrupeds in front of the naked figure could perhaps be also regarded as distant reminiscence of the duality of the good sheep and the evil goat mentioned in the *Homilies* 38,16–22 (also considering the role of goat as an auspicious animal in Chinese iconography).

types of reincarnations (*wǔqù* 五趣), which is sometimes mentioned in Chinese Manichaean sources.[1] Despite the apparent appropriateness of the Buddhist meaning of *wǔqù*, Chinese Manichaean *wǔqù* means something different: it refers to reincarnation as man, bird, fish, animal, or reptile. We possess Manichaean textual evidence to prove that Manichaeism also possessed a fivefold path of reincarnation, even if it differed from the Buddhist one. Besides the general Eastern expressions (Parthian *pnj cyhrg 'jwn*; Uighur *biš ažun*),[2] the Parthian *Huyadagmān* explicitly lists these five paths:

> The bodies of men, and of birds of the air, of fish of the sea, and four-footed creatures and of all insects — who will take me beyond these and save me from (them) all, so that I shall not turn and fall into the perdition of those hells? So that I shall not pass through defilement in them, nor return in rebirth, wherein all the kinds of plants are taken out in...[3]

This being said, there are two strong arguments against the interpretation that the five animals and the human figure symbolize the possible paths of reincarnations. Firstly, according to the obvious Buddhist iconography, the roles of the animals and human are clear: the human being is judged and the animals are the witnesses. Moreover, the evident identification of the Manichaean Righteous Judge with Yama excludes the possibility that here the future reincarnation paths should be the central theme, since this appears

---

〔1〕H023: 一切魔男及魔女，皆从宍身生缘现。又是三界五趣门，复是十方诸魔口。Tr.051–052: 令升暗船，送入地狱，轮回五趣，备受诸苦。卒难解脱。On *wuqu*, see Kósa 2012.

〔2〕M 869 I V 1–2 (Sundermann 1981: 29), T III D 260 (Bang and von Gabain 1930: 184).

〔3〕Trans. Boyce 1954: 83. *Huyadagmān* IVA.7–9 (M6221/V/3–8, Boyce 1954: 82; http://www.bbaw.de/forschung/turfanforschung/dta/mirtext/wmirtext.html): mrdwhmg'n tnb'r °______° mwrg'n 'ndrw 'zyq / zrhyg m'sy'g'n °____° cwhrb'd'n w: wysp dywg / kym 'ymyn wyd'r'ẖ °__° 'wṯ 'c hrwyn bwj'ẖ / kw ny wrt'n 'wṯ k(f)'n °____° pṯ hwyn nrẖ 'bn 's / 'wṯ gst pṯ hwyn ny wyd'r'n ° pd 'jwn ny 'zw(r)[t'n] / cy wysp zng d'lwg ° (')[z]gryftg pṯ (.)[· · ·]t'n. Also see *Acta Archelai* X.1 (Beeson 1906: 15), cf. Vermes and Lieu 2001: 156, 52. n.60; Casadio 1992: 112, Jackson 1925.

without exception only in the tenth court (Wudao zhuanlun wang 五道转轮王) of the illustrated Ten Kings scrolls (e.g. S.3961, P.2870, P.4523), or the independent Kṣitigarbha paintings (e.g. MG 17793, MG 17662, EO.3580),〔1〕 never in Yama's court. Secondly, if the six figures (five animals and the human) represent the five possible paths of reincarnations, then which figure is being judged in the CP judgment scene, i.e. whose reincarnation is at stake?〔2〕

Thus, based on the Ten Kings of Hell iconography, animals more likely represent the various kinds of living beings against whom the human person has sinned. What do then the five heads on green stalks represent? Y. Yoshida interprets these heads as the light elements.〔3〕 I think that this interpretation is partly correct: human heads do represent light, but there are at least two types of them in the CP, and they can be differentiated. The first type is a human head with a halo, this does refer to the liberated light (halo referring to their being liberated): the heads in the Moon and the Sun (Fig. 9/d), or those in the hands of the Virgin of Light belong to this type (Fig. 9/c). However, in the judgment scene the five heads have no halo (Fig. 9/a), which, in my interpretation, means that they are still bound, not liberated.〔4〕 Similar heads without halo can be seen on two of the four continents around

〔1〕Giès 1996: pls. 61, 63, 66.

〔2〕Cf. Yoshida 2010: 12b.

〔3〕Yoshida 2010: 12b.

〔4〕It should be noted that the human heads in MIK III 7283 (Gulácsi 2001, no. 48), which are interpreted by Y. Yoshida (2010: 22a) as liberated light elements, have no halo. Although the fragmentary nature of MIK III 7283, I think, does not allow a secure identification, nevertheless, if Y. Yoshida is right, it might have two different consequences: either my distinction between the heads with/without halo does not apply to Turfan remains, or liberated light was expressed in a different way in Turfan. As for the second possibility, these heads from Turfan invariably wear a headgear, "which consists of a gold circular disc placed between two upward curving white cloths" (Gulácsi 2001: 112). These headgears, I think, might equally fittingly convey the meaning of liberated light, though this could be naturally only proven if similar heads without this headgear would be discovered in a context that would demonstrably refer to the imprisoned state of light.

Mount Sumeru: in both cases, they appear on a tree with three branches (Fig. 9/b).[1] Another difference between the liberated and the non-liberated light particles is that the former ones have a colour "tail", which provides them with the capability of flying, while the members of the latter category are *per definitionem* bound to something (in these cases, stalk or trunk), which does not allow them to move freely.

Fig. 9/a–d. Human heads without halo in the judgment scene (Fig. 9/a) and on the continent beside Mount Sumeru (Fig. 9/b), and heads with halo in the Virgin of Light scene (Fig. 9/c) and in the Sun (Fig. 9/d). Cosmology painting (details) Copyright © Japanese private collection

〔1〕Cf. the birth of vegetation in the following sources: "And the Adamas of Light was sent against her (= it). He fought with her, and vanquished her, turned her on her back, struck her with (his spear) in her heart, pushed his shield upon her mouth, and placed one of his feet upon her thighs and the other upon her breast. And that (sin) which fell on the dry (earth) sprang up into Five Trees" (*Liber Scholiorum*, Jackson and Johannan 1965: 247); "One of them [sins, GK] is the sea [gi]ant (…) The second figure is the one [that] fell on the earth (…) [The] third figure is the nature that fell on wh[at] is dr[y. It fash]ioned the tree and set itself there" (*Kephalaia* 136,23–137,6; Gardner 1995: 144).

Based on these occurrences, I think that the five non-liberated heads on five green stalks with what can possibly be termed as leaves on them, represent not light *in se*, but light particles imprisoned in vegetation. Their non-liberated nature (they are without halo) and the green stalks to which they are bound, I think, all support this interpretation, just like the fact that in this sense they would perfectly complement the animals behind them. In this reading, the five kinds of vegetation, which *par excellence* carry the light nature, and the various animals behind them, were or could have been subject to the harmful activities of the naked human being (in fact, all potential sinners) under judgment, and therefore have the right to witness against him/her in this final moment. The motif of sins against vegetation and animals is attested in several Manichaean confessional texts. Two quotations below refer to the sin of inflicting injury to vegetation, while the subsequent citations refer to the two large groups of herbs/trees and living beings (four kinds of animals and human being), both consisting of five members, precisely as seen in the CP judgment scene.

> It is proper for the person to watch his step while he walks on a path: lest he trample the Cross of Light with his foot, and destroy vegetation.[1]

> For they [Manichaeans, GK] are convinced that plants and trees possess sentient life and can feel pain when injured, and therefore that no one can pull or pluck them without torturing them. Therefore, they consider it wrong to clear a field even of thorns.[2]

> My God, we are encumbered with defect and sin, we are great

〔1〕Trans. Gardner 1995: 217. *Kephalaia* 208,17–19: ⲥϣⲉ ⲁⲡⲣⲱⲙⲉ ⲁⲧⲣⲉϥϭⲱϣⲧ ϩⲁ/ⲣⲉⲧϥ̄ ⲙ̄ⲡⲥⲁⲡ ⲉⲧϥⲁⲙⲁϩⲉ ϩⲛ ⲟⲩⲙⲁⲓ̈ⲧ ϫⲉ ⲛⲉϥϩⲙ ⲡⲥⲧⲁⲩ/ⲣⲟⲥ ⲙⲡⲟⲩⲁⲓ̈ⲛⲉ ⲛⲣⲉⲧϥ̄ ⲛϥ̄ⲧⲉⲕⲟ ⲛⲣⲱⲧ.

〔2〕*De haeresibus* 46.12 (Gardner and Lieu 2004: 191). Patrologia Latina 42: 37: Herbas enim atque arbores sic putant vivere ut vitam quae illis inest et sentire credant et dolere cum laeditur, nec aliquid inde sine cruciatu eorum quemquam posse vellere aut carpere. Propter quod agrum etiam spinis purgare nefas habent.

debtors. Because of the insatiable and shameless Āz demon we in thought, word, and deed, likewise looking with its (i.e. Āz's) eyes, hearing with its ears, speaking with its tongue, seizing with its hand, (and) walking with its feet, incur constant and permanent agony on the light of the Fivefold God in the dry and wet earth, the five kinds of living beings (and) the five kinds of herbs and trees.[1]

... if we should have somehow have sinned against the dry and wet earth, against the five kinds of living beings, against the five kinds of herbs and trees, (then) we now pray, my God, to be liberated from sin.[2]

... injuring or tearing the five (types of) plants or the five (types of) fleshly beings, be they wet or dry...[3]

If we were negligent in the seven alms, the ten precepts, the three seals, the teachings of the Law, and moreover harmed against the five parts of the dharma body [i.e. the Five Lights of the Living Soul, GK], permanently wasting them, if we sometimes cut and fell the five kinds of grasses and trees, or made the five types of living beings our slaves, and had other innumerable faults, now let them all be washed away as we repent.[4]

You maintain in regard to the vulnerable Jesus (patibilem Jesum) – who, as you say, is born from the earth, which has conceived by the

---

〔1〕Trans. J. Asmussen (1965: 198–199). *X^{u}āstvānīft* XV C (Asmussen 1965: 179): t(ä)ŋrim ägsüklüg yazuqluγ / biz ötägčii birimčibiz / todunčsuz uwutsuz suq / yäk üčün : saqïnčïn sözin / qïlïnčïn ymä közin körüp / qulqaqïn äšidip tilin sözläp / älgin sunup adaqïn yorïp / ürkä üzüksüz ämgätirbiz : / biš t(ä)ŋrii y(a)ruqïn quruγ öl / yirig biš türlüg tïnl(ï)γ(ï)γ biš / türlüg otuγ 'ïγačïγ.

〔2〕Asmussen 1965: 195. *X^{u}āstvānīft* III C (Asmussen 1965: 171–172): quruγ öl yirkä biš / türlüg tïnl(ï)γqa biš türlüg / ootqa 'ïγačqa näčä / yaz(ï)nt(ï)m(ï)z ärsär : amtï t(ä)ŋrim / yazuqda bošunu ötünür / biz m(a)nastar hirza.

〔3〕M801/32/498–501 (Henning 1937: 33, Klimkeit 1993: 139): pnc δ'rwkync δ'm / pnc pṯync δ''m / nβṯyy pṯw'ṯyy 'ngrnd / frkr[nd z]*r*yš pṯryš.

〔4〕H391–393: 有缺七施、十 / 戒、三印、法门，又损五分法身，恒加费用；或斩伐五种草木，或劳役五 /类众生，余有无数愆违，今并洗除忏悔!

power of the Holy Spirit – that he hangs in the shape of produce and fruit from every tree; so that, besides this pollution, he suffers additional defilement from the flesh of the countless animals that eat the fruit.[1]

(The queen of Darkness went into the abyss) and thereupon there came into existence the five (sorts of) trees and (of) animals: the flying ones, the creeping (reptilian) ones, the swimming ones, those with legs, and the insects.[2]

The notion that the five light elements (i.e. the Living Soul, *Jesus patibilis*) suffer differently in the vegetation and in the animals also has a textual parallel: "in the five kinds of trees and plants they [the five elements, GK] are living (…) they [the five elements, GK] become mindless, dead (things) in the bodies of the five kinds of so-called 'living' creatures."[3] This Uighur fragment offers a clue to what we see in the CP: the five green stalks representing vegetation have the light-heads on them, while we do not see them in the animals, possibly because the elements are not conscious, not visible in the animals.

In another paper, I endeavoured to demonstrate that the Turfan fragment MIK III 4959 V visually lists sins committed against animals and vegetation.[4] On this fragment, the person standing closer to the judge has the decapitated head of a horned animal hanging in front of his chest, while the other person under judgment has vegetation and a pair of soles in front of him. These latter motifs, as I argued in that paper, jointly refer to the sin

〔1〕BeDuhn 2000: 79. *Contra Faustum* 20.11: Concipientem de Spiritu sancto dicitis terram gignere patibilem Iesum, quem tamen ita contaminatum omni ex ligno pendere perhibetis in frugibus et pomis, ut innumerabilibus animalibus animalium vescentium carnibus amplius contaminetur…

〔2〕'Abd al-Jabbār: *muγnī* 5.19.16–18 (de Blois 2006: 44, also see de Blois's remarks).

〔3〕Zieme 1975: 34 [German], BeDuhn 2000: 84 [English]. Ch/U 6814[=T/II/T/509].V.2–5 (Zieme 1975: 34): biš türlüg ïda ïγačda tirigin ärürlär (…) biš türlüg tïnlïγlarnïng ät'özlärin ičintä ögsüz ölüg titmiš bolurlar.

〔4〕Kósa 2015: 197-203.

of trampling on vegetation. Thus, in this Turfan fragment, these two persons jointly represent sins committed against animals and vegetation. In the CP judgment scene, one single human being seems to represent the sinner against vegetation (human heads [i.e. light] on green stalks) and animals.

Matthew 25,31–46 is used in the Middle Persian *Šābuhragān* and the Coptic *Sermon on the Great War*, the two main sources available on Manichaean eschatology. In his study on Koustaios' *Sermon on the Great War* in the Coptic *Homilies*, N. A. Pedersen stressed that "the services the catechumens performed for Xradešahr are services rendered to the "elect"."[1] Here I will quote Pedersen's further statements about the relevance of the gospel of *Matthew* in the Manichaean context.

> I referred above to the Manichaean conception that "the living soul", the substance of light imprisoned in nature, must be seen as a suffering Jesus-figure (Jesus patibilis). A number of scholars have indeed also suggested that Xradešahr's [Jesus', GK] statements be interpreted on this basis [n.592. Kraeling 1927: 33–34, Puech 1979: 95, Böhlig 1980: 58, Gardner 1983: 293]. (…) It is thus possible that Xradešahr's [Jesus', GK] statements contain two dimensions: The catechumens' care of the elect is the text's clearest dimension, but a deeper dimension underlying this may be this care is also care of "the living soul", which "is" in fact Xradešahr/Jesus.[2]
>
> We are on the right track when we assume that the Manichaean exegesis of the doomsday pericope implies a Jesus patibilis conception.[3]

In *Šābuhragān*, the catechumens rightly protest against the statement that the active redeemer god, Xradešahr [Jesus, GK], has

[1] Pedersen 1996: 365.

[2] Pedersen 1996: 367.

[3] Pedersen 1996: 368.

needs or suffers, but Xradešahr explains to them that the statements are directed towards his passive, suffering alter ego.[1]

The services performed for the elect were indeed performed for Jesus himself, and there can be no doubt that Koustaios meant that both the Great Splendour from the pure Kingdom of Light and the captive, defiled and suffering soul was "Jesus".[2]

It must be stressed that *Matthew* 25,31–46 must have been extremely important for Mānī, since he incorporated it in the *Šābuhragān*, in which he otherwise avoids references to Jesus (he calls him Xradešahr), and where he basically applies a Zoroastrian terminology.[3] Therefore, if Pedersen is right in seeing the Manichaean concept of judgment as based on the human's attitude towards the suffering Jesus, i.e. the sufferings of light in the created world (foremost in the vegetation, secondly in animals and other natural phenomena), then it might be suggested that the five heads on green stalks (representing light in vegetation) in front of the judge and the animals behind them might be taken as the passive sufferers of the sins committed by the human figure who is held by the demon ward.[4]

Thus, similarly to the Buddhist iconography where various animals appear in front of the judge to accuse the sinner of his sins committed against them, in the Manichaean CP, vegetation and animals, which all contain suffering light nature, appear in front of the Manichaean Righteous Judge to accuse the human person of the injuries he committed against them. If this interpretation is appropriate, we succeeded in matching the Buddhist iconography with the Manichaean message, and by using Pedersen's interpretation, we could also find a textual basis in the available descriptions

[1] Pedersen 1996: 368.

[2] Pedersen 1996: 378.

[3] Colditz 2005.

[4] M. Franzmann (2003: 97) links the compassionate nature of the Judge with his ability to suffer together with the righteous, thus this compassionate nature does not mean indulgence towards the sinners.

of the judgment scene (*Šābuhragān, Sermon on the Great War*).

I based my interpretation on the internal evidence of the Cosmology painting, the currently available Manichaean texts and paintings, and the textual and pictorial tradition of the *Ten Kings sūtra*. Nevertheless, needless to say, this is only one of the many possible interpretations of the judgment scene in the Cosmology painting, and thus any new textual or visual evidence identified in the future might alter the analysis expounded above.

REFERENCES

Allberry, Charles R. C. 1938. *A Manichaean Psalm-Book. Part II.* (Manichaean Manuscripts in the Chester Beatty Collection. Volume II.) Stuttgart: W. Kohlhammer.

Arnold-Döben, Victoria 1978. *Die Bildersprache des Manichäismus.* (Arbeitsmaterial zur Religionsgeschichte 3.) Köln: E.J. Brill.

Asmussen, Jes P. 1965. *X^{u}āstvānīft. Studies in Manichaeism.* (Acta Theologica Danica 7.) Kopenhagen: Prostant apud Munksgaard.

Bang, Willy and Gabain, Annemarie von 1930. *Türkische Turfan-Texte. III.* Berlin: Verlag der Akademie der Wissenschaften – W. de Gruyter & Co.

BeDuhn, Jason D. 2000. *The Manichaean Body in Disciple and Ritual.* Baltimore–London: The Johns Hopkins University Press.

Beeson, Charles Henry (ed.) 1906. *Hegemonius, Acta Archelai.* (GCS 16.) Leipzig: J.C. Heinrichs.

de Blois 2003. "Manes' Twin in Iranian and non-Iranian texts." In: Carlo G. Cereti, Mauro Maggi, Elio Provasi and Gherardo Gnoli (eds.) *Religious themes and texts of pre-Islamic Iran and Central Asia : studies in honour of Professor Gherardo Gnoli on the occasion of his 65th birthday on 6th December 2002.* Wiesbaden: Ludwig Reichert Verlag, 7–16.

de Blois, François 2006. "Glossary of technical terms and uncommon expressions in Arabic (and in Muslim New Persian) texts relating to Manichaeism." In: de Blois, François and Sims-Williams, Nicholas (eds.) *Dictionary of Manichaean texts. Vol. II, Texts from Iraq and Iran (Texts in Syriac, Arabic, Persian and Zoroastrian Middle Persian)*. Turnhout: Brepols, 21–88.

Böhlig, Alexander (ed.) 1966. *Kephalaia. Zweite Hälfte. Lieferung 11–12 (Seite 244–291)*. (Manichäische Handschriften der Staatlichen Museen Berlin 1.) Stuttgart–Berlin–Köln–Mainz: W. Kohlhammer.

Böhlig, Alexander und Polotsky, Hans Jacob (eds., trans., mit einem Beitrag von H. Ibscher) 1940. *Kephalaia I,1. Hälfte (Lieferung 1–10)*. (Manichäische Handschriften der Staatlichen Museen Berlin 1.) Stuttgart: W. Kohlhammer.

Boyce, Mary 1954. *The Manichaean Hymn-cycles in Parthian*. Oxford: London Oriental Series.

Casadio, Giovanni 1992. "The Manichaean Metempsychosis: Typology and Historical Roots." In: Wiessner, Gernot – Klimkeit, Hans-Joachim 1992. *Studia Manichaica. Internationaler Kongress zum Manichäismus. Bonn, 1989. aug. 6.–10.* Wiesbaden: Otto Harrassowitz (Studies in Oriental Religions 23), 105–130.

Colditz, I. 2005. "Zur Adaption zoroastrischer Terminologie in Manis Šābuhragān", in D. Weber (ed.) *Languages of Iran: Past & Present. Iranian Studies in memoriam David Neil MacKenzie*. (Iranica 8) Wiesbaden: Harrassowitz, 17–26.

Dodge, Bayard 1970. *The Fihrist of al-Nadim. A Tenth-Century Survey of Muslim culture*. 2nd vol. (Records of Civilization; Sources and Studies 83) New York: Columbia Press.

Du Doucheng 杜斗城 1989. *Dunhuang ben* 《Fo shuo shiwang jing》 *jiaolu yanjiu*. 敦煌本《佛说十王经》校录研究. Lanzhou: Gansu Jiaoyu Chubanshe.

Dudbridge, Glen 1995. *Religious experience and lay society in T'ang China: a reading of Tai Fu's Kuang-i chi.* New York: Cambridge University Press.

Dudbridge, Glen 1998. "Buddhist images in action: Five stories from the Tang." *Cahiers d'Extrême-Asie* 10: 377–391. [Repr. In: Glen Dudbridge 2005. *Books, Tales and Vernacular Culture. Selected Papers on China.* Leiden: Brill, 134–150.]

Ebine Toshirō 海老根聡郎 1986. "Kin Shoshi fude jūō-zu 金处士笔十王図 [Ten Kings paintings by Jin Chushi]." *Kokka* 国华 1986.10: 20–29.

Ferreira, Johan 2000. "A Comparison of the Clothing Metaphor in the Hymn of the Pearl and the Chinese Manichaean Hymnscroll." In: Ronald E. Emmerick, Werner Sundermann and Peter Zieme (hrsg.) 2000. *Studia Manichaica. IV. Internationaler Kongress zum Manichäismus, Berlin, 14.–18. Juli 1997.* Berlin: Akademie Verlag, 207–219.

Fong, Wen C. 1992. *Beyond Representation: Chinese Painting and Calligraphy 8th–14th Century* (Princeton Monographs in Art and Archaeology, No 48.) New York: The Metropolitan Museum of Art; New Haven–London: Yale University Press.

Franzmann, Majella 2003. *Jesus in the Manichaean Writings.* London–New York: T&T Clark.

Furukawa Shoichi 古川摄一 2010. "Shinshutsu Manikyō kaiga shiron —— seisaku nendai wo megutte. 新出マニ教絵画試論 —— 制作年代をめぐって." [Preliminary study of the newly discovered Manichaean paintings concerning their dating]." *Yamato Bunka* 大和文華 121: 35–52.

von Gabain, Annemarie 1973. "Kṣitigarbha-Kult in Zentralasien, Buchillustrationen aus den Turfan-Funden." In: H. Härtel und V. Moeller (Hrsg.) 1973. *Indologen-tagung 1971. Verhandlung der Indologischen Arbeitstagung im Museum für Indische Kunst Berlin 7–9. Oktober 1971.*

Wiesbaden: Franz Steiner Verlag GMBH, 47–71.

Gardner, Iain 1995. *The Kephalaia of the Teacher: The Edited Coptic Manichaean Texts in Translation with Commentary.* Leiden: E.J. Brill.

Gardner, Iain (with contr. Clackson, S. and Franzmann, M. and Worp, K. A.) 1996. *Kellis Literary Texts. Vol. 1.* (Dakhleh Oasis Project Monograph 4; Oxbow Monograph 69.) Oxford: Oxbow Books.

Gardner, Iain and Lieu, S.N.C. 2004. *Manichaean Texts from the Roman Empire.* Cambridge: Cambridge University Press.

Giès, Jacques (dir.) et al. 1996. *Les Arts de l'Asie Centrale: La Collection Paul Pelliot du Musée National des Arts Asiatiques – Guimet.* Vol. 2. Paris: Reunion des Musées Nationaux.

Gulácsi Zsuzsanna 2001. *Manichaean Art in Berlin Collections.* (Corpus Fontium Manichaeorum, Series Archaeologica et Iconographica 1.) Turnhout: Brepols.

Gulácsi, Zsuzsanna 2008. "A Visual Sermon on Mani's Teaching of Salvation: A contextualized reading of a Chinese Manichaean silk painting in the collection of the Yamato Bunkakan in Nara, Japan." *Nairiku Ajia gengo no kenkyū* 内陸アジア言語の研究 [*Studies on the Inner Asian Languages*] 23: 1–16.

Gulácsi, Zsuzsanna 2009. "The Central Asian Roots of a Chinese Manichaean Silk Painting in the Collection of the Yamato Bunkakan, Nara, Japan." (English version of Gulácsi 2009b, ms.)

Gulácsi, Zsuzsanna 2009a. "Yamato Bunkakan zō Manikyō kaiga ni mirareru Chūō Ajia raigen no yōso ni tsuite. 大和文華館蔵マニ教絵画にみられる中央アジア来源の要素について. " [The Central Asian Roots of a Chinese Manichaean Silk Painting in the Collection of the Museum Yamato Bunkakan, Nara, Japan]. *Yamato Bunka* 大和文華 119: 17–34.

Henning, Walter B. 1937. *Ein manichäisches Bet- und Beichtbuch.* Berlin: Akademie der Wissenschaften – W. de Gruyter & Co. [Repr. In:

Boyce et al. 1977: 417–557.]

Heuser, Manfred 1998. "The Manichaean Myth According to the Coptic Sources." In: Heuser, Manfred – Klimkeit, Hans-Joachim 1998. *Studies in Manichaean Literature and Art.* (Nag Hammadi and Manichaean Studies 46.) Leiden–Boston–Köln: Brill, 3–108.

Hirasawa, Caroline 2008. "The Inflatable, Collapsible Kingdom of Retribution: A Primer on Japanese Hell Imagery and Imagination." *Monumenta Nipponica* 63.1: 1−50.

Idema, Wilt L. 1998. "STEPHEN F. TEISER, The Scripture of the Ten Kings and the Making of Purgatory in Medieval Chinese Buddhism, Kuroda Institute Studies in East Asian Buddhism 9. Honolulu: University of Hawaii Press, 1994. xxxiii and 340 pp. Appendixes, Glossary, Bibliography, Index, Index of Manuscripts and Cave Inscriptions. ISBN 0-8248-1587-4." *T'oung Pao* 84: 184–188.

Jackson, A. V. Williams 1925. "The Doctrine of Metempsychosis in Manichaeism." *Journal of the American Oriental Society* 45: 246–268.

Jackson, A. V. Williams and Johannan, Abraham 1965. "Theodore bar Khoni on Mānī's Teachings, Translated from the Syriac with Notes." In: Jackson, A. V. Williams 1965 [1932]. *Researches in Manichaeism. With Special Reference to the Turfan Fragments*. New York: AMS Press INC., 219–254.

Kajitani Ryōji 梶谷亮治 1974. "Nihon ni okeru jūō-zu no seiritsu to tenkai 日本における十王図の成立と展開." [The birth and evolution of Japanese Ten Kings paintings.] *Bukkyō geijutsu* 仏教芸术 97: 84−95.

Kajitani Ryōji 梶谷亮治 1979. "Riku Shinchū fude jūō-zu 陆信忠笔十王図." [The Ten Kings Paintings by Lu Xinzhong.] *Kokka* 国华 1020: 22−38.

Kanazawa Bunko 金沢文库 1991. *Jigoku to jūō-zu: tēma ten.* 地獄と十王図 : テーマ展. [Images of hell and the Ten Kings: a thematic exhibition.] Yokohama: Kanagawa Kenritsu Kanazawa Bunko.

Klimkeit, Hans-Joachim (trans.) 1993. *Gnosis on the Silk Road. Gnostic Texts from Central Asia.* New York: HarperSanFrancisco.

Kósa Gábor 2011. "Translating a Vision — Rudimentary Notes on the Chinese Cosmology Painting." *Manichaean Studies Newsletter* 25 (2010/2011) 20–32.

Kósa Gábor 2012. "Buddhist and pseudo-Buddhist motifs in the Chinese Manichaean *Hymnscroll*." In: I. Beller-Hahn and Zs. Rajkai (ed.) 2012. *Frontiers and boundaries — Encounters on China's margins.* Wiesbaden: Harrassowitz, 49–69.

Kósa Gábor 2012a. "Atlas and Splenditenens in the Cosmology Painting." In: Michael Knüppel / Luigi Cirillo (eds.) *Gnostica et Manichaica. Festschrift für Aloïs van Tongerloo anläßlich des 60. Geburtstages überreicht von Kollegen, Freunden und Schülern*. (Studies in Oriental Religions) Wiesbaden: Harrassowitz, 63–88.

Kósa Gábor 2014. "Translating the *Eikōn*. Some considerations on the relation of the Chinese Cosmology painting to the *Eikōn*." In: Laut, Jens Peter / Röhrborn, Klaus (Hrsg.) *Vom Aramäischen zum Alttürkischen, Fragen zur Über-set-zung von manichäischen Texten. Vorträge des Göttinger Symposium vom 29./30. Sep-tem-ber 2011*. Berlin, New York: De Gruyter (Abhandlungen der Akademie der Wis-sen-schaf-ten zu Göttingen, N. F.) 49–84.

Kósa Gábor 2015. "Two Manichaean Judgment Scenes — MIK III 4959 V and the Yamato Bunkakan painting." In: Richter, Siegfried G. and Charles Horton and K. Ohlhafer (eds.) *Mani in Dublin: Selected Papers from the Seventh International Conference of the International Association of Manichaean Studies in the Chester Beatty Library, Dublin, 8–12 September 2009*. Leiden: Brill, 196-227. (forthcoming)

Kucera, Karil J. 1995. "Lessons in Stone: Baodingshan and Its Hell

Imagery." *The Bulletin of the Museum of Far Eastern Antiquities* 67: 81–157.

Kwon, Cheeyun 1999. *The 'Ten Kings' from the Seikadō Library*. Ph.D. Dissertation, Princeton University.

Kwon Cheeyun 2005. "The Ten Kings from the former Packard Collection: A Reassessment." *Oriental Art* 55.2: 28–36.

von Le Coq, Albert 1919. *Türkische Manichaica aus Chotscho II.* Berlin: Verlag der Königlichen Akademie der Wissenschaften.

von Le Coq, Albert 1922. *Türkische Manichaica aus Chotscho. III.* Berlin: Verlag der Akademie der Wissenschaften.

Ledderose, Lothar 1981. "A King of Hell." In: *Suzuki Kei Sensei kanreki kinen — Chūgoku kaiga shi ronshū* 铃木敬先生还历记念．中国绘画史论集. Tokyo: Yoshikawa kōbunkan, 33–42.

Ledderose, Lothar 2000. "The Bureaucracy of Hell." In: *Ten Thousand Things: Module and Mass Production in Chinese Art.* Princeton: Princeton University Press, 163–185.

Lin Wushu 林悟殊 1997. *Monijiao ji qi dongjian.* 摩尼教及其东渐. [Manichaeism and its Eastern Spread.] Taibei: Shuxin Chubanshe.

van Lindt, Paul 1992. *The names of Manichaean mythological figures: a comparative study on terminology in the Coptic sources.* (Studies in Oriental religions 26.) Wiesbaden: Otto Harrassowitz.

MacKenzie, D. N. 1979. "Mani's Šābuhragān I." *Bulletin of the School of Oriental and African Studies* 42: 500–534.

Matsumoto Eiichi 松本荣一 1937. *Tonkō-ga no kenkyū. Zuzō hen.* 燉煌畫の研究．圖像篇. [Researches on Dunhuang paintings. Images.] Tōkyō: Tōhō Bunka Gakuin Tōkyō Kenkyūjo.

Miya Tsugio 宮次男 1990. "Jūō kyō e ni tsuite 十王経絵について." [On the Illustrations to the Sutra of Ten Kings] *Jissen Joshidai bigaku bijutsushi gaku* 実践女子大美学美术史学 (Jissen Women's University aesthetics and art history) 5: 81–118.

Miya Tsugio 宮次男 1992. "Jūō kyō e shūi 十王経絵拾遺." [Glenings from the Illustrations to the Sutra of Ten Kings] *Jissen Joshidai bigaku bijutsushi gaku* 実践女子大美学美术史学 (Jissen Women's University aesthetics and art history) 7: 1–63.

Miya Tsugio 宮次男 1993. "Jūō jigoku e 十王地狱絵." [Illustrations to the Ten Kings and Hell] *Jissen Joshidai bigaku bijutsushi gaku* 実践女子大美学美术史学 (Jissen Women's University aesthetics and art history) 8: 5–24.

Nara National Museum [= NNM], Nara Kokuritsu Hakubutsukan 奈良国立博物馆 (ed.) 2009. *Seichi Ninpō. Nihon bukkyō 1300-nen no genryū — subete wa koko kara yatte kita.* 聖地寧波:日本仏教1300年の源流 ~ すべてはここからやって来た. [Ningbo, a sacred place: the 1300 years old source of Japanese Buddhism — Everything came from here.] Nara: Nara National Museum.

Olsson, Tord 1988. "The Manichaean Background of Eschatology in the Koran." In: Bryder, Peter (ed.) 1988. *Manichaean Studies. Proceedings of the First International Conference on Manichaeism, August 5–9, 1987.* (Lund Studies in African and Asian Religions 1.) Lund: Plus Ultra, 273–282.

Pedersen, Nils Arne 1996. *Studies in the Sermon of the Great War.* Aarhus: Aarhus University Press.

Phillips, Quitman E. 2003. "Narrating the Salvation of the Elite: The J ō fukuji Paintings of the Ten Kings." *Ars Orientalis* 33: 121–145.

Reck, Christiane 2003. "Die Beschreibung der Daēnā in einem soghdischen manichäischen Text." In: Carlo G. Cereti, Mauro Maggi and Elio Provasi (eds.), *Religious themes and texts of pre-Islamic Iran and Central Asia. Studies in honor of Professor Gherardo Gnoli on the occasion of his 65th birthday* (Beiträge zur Iranistik 24). Wiesbaden: Ludwig

Reichert Verlag, 323−340.

Reeves, John S. 2011. *Prolegomena to a History of Islamicate Manichaeism*. (Comparative Islamic Studies) Sheffield, UK: Equinox Publishing.

Rui Chuanming 芮传明 2003. "Monijiao »Pingdeng wang« yu »lunhui« kao 摩尼教»平等王«与»轮回«考." [On the Manichaean King of Justice and reincarnation.] *Shilin* 史林 2003.6: 28–39.

Rui Chuanming 芮传明 2009. "Pingdeng wang 平等王." [The Righteous King.] In: *Dongfang Monijiao yanjiu.* 东方摩尼教研究. [Studien on Eastern Manichaeism.] Shanghai: Shanghai Renmin Chubanshe, 126–138.

Schmidt, Hans-Peter 1980. "Ancient Iranian Animal Classification." *Studia Iranica* 5–6: 209–240.

Seikadō Bunko Bijutsukan 静嘉堂文库美术馆 [= SBB] (ed.) 1999. *Bukkyō no bijutsu* 仏教の美術, *Mihotoke no osugata, Buddhist Art from the Seikadō Collection.* Tōkyō: Seikadō Bunko Bijutsukan.

Shi Shouqian 石守谦 1985. "Youguan diyu shiwang tu yu qi dongchuan Riben de jige wenti 有关地狱十王图与其东传日本的几个问题." [On some questions concerning the Ten Kings paintings and its eastward spread to Japan.] *Lishi yuyan yanjiusuo jikan* 历史语言研究所集刊 56.3: 565–618.

Soymié, Michel 1966. "Notes d'iconographie chinoise: Les acolytes de Ti-tsang (I)." *Arts asiatiques* 14: 45–78.

Soymié, Michel 1967. "Notes d'iconographie chinoise: les acolytes de Ti-tsang (II)." *Arts asiatiques* 16: 141−170.

Soymié, Michel 1981. "Un recueil d'inscriptions sur peintures: le manuscrit P. 3304 verso." In: Soymié, Michel (dir.) 1981. *Nouvelles contributions aux études sur Touen-houang.* Genève: Droz, 169−204.

Suchan, Thomas 2003. "The eternally flourishing stronghold: an iconographic study of the Buddhist sculpture of the Fowan and related sites at Beishan, Dazu ca. 892–1155." Ph.D. diss. The Ohio State University

Sundermann, Werner 1979. "Namen von Göttern, Dämonen und Menschen in iranischen Versionen des manichäischen Mythos." *Altorientalische Forschungen* 6: 95–133. [Repr.: Sundermann 2001. Vol. I: 121–163.]

Sundermann, Werner 1981. *Mitteliranische manichäische Texte kirchengeschichtlichen Inhalts (mit einem Appendix von Nicolas Sims-Wiiliams).* (Schriften zur Geschichte und Kultur des Alten Orients; Berliner Turfantexte XI.) Berlin: Akademie-Verlag.

Takasu Jun 鷹巣纯 1993. "Meguri wataru akudō: Chōgakuji-bon rokudō jūō-zu no zuzō wo megutte めぐりわたる悪道 — 長岳寺本六道十王図の図像をめぐって." [Crossing the evil paths – on the iconography of the Six Paths and Ten Kings paintings of the Chōgaku temple]. *Bukkyō geijutsu* 仏教芸术 211: 39–59.

Takasu Jun 鷹巣纯 2006. "Idemitsu bijutsukan bon Rokudō jūō-zu ni miru dentō to chiikisei 出光美術館本六道十王図に見る伝統と地域性 (The tradition and regionality seen in Rokudō jūō-zu possessed by the Idemitsu Art Gallery)." *Nihon shūkyō minzoku gakkai* 日本宗教民俗学会 [Studies of religious folklore] 16: 42–60.

Teiser, Stephen F. 1993. "The Growth of Purgatory." In: Ebrey, Patricia Buckley and Gregory, Peter N. (eds.) 1993. *Religion and Society in T'ang and Sung China*. Honolulu: University of Hawai'i Press, 115–145.

Teiser, Stephen F. 1994. *The Scripture on the Ten Kings and the Making of Purgatory in Medieval Chinese Buddhism.* Honolulu: University of Hawaii Press.

Teiser, Stephen F. 1999. "Picturing Purgatory: Illustrated Versions of the Scripture of the Ten King." In: Drège, Jean-Pierre et al. (ed.) 1999. *Images de Dunhuang. Dessins et peintures sur papier des fonds Pelliot et*

Stein. Paris: École française d'Extrême-Orient (Mémoires archéologiques, 24), 169–197.

Tokushi Yūshō 禿氏祐祥 and Ogawa Kan'ichi 小川貫弌 1963. "*Jūō shōshichi kyō* sanzuken no kōzō 十王生七經讚圖卷の構造." In: Seiiki bunka kenyūkai 西域文化研究會 (ed.) *Chūō Ajia bukkyō to bijutsu* 中央佛教美术. [Seiiki bunka kenyū 西域文化研究 Vol. 5.] Kyōto: Hōzōkan, 255–296.

Vermes, Mark (trans.) and Lieu, Samuel N. C. 2001. *Hegemonius: Acta Archelai. (The Acts of Archelaus).* Turnhout: Brepols.

Wagner, Alan G. 2008. *Practice and Emptiness in the Discourse Record of Ruru Jushi, Yan Bing (d. 1212), a Chan Buddhist Layman of the Southern Song.* Harvard University, Cambridge, Mass., PhD diss.

Watanabe, Masako 1984. "An Iconographic Study of "Ten Kings" Paintings." M.A. thesis, The University of British Columbia.

Wilkens, Jens 2009. "Ein manichäischer Alptraum?" In: D. Durkin-Meisterernst / Ch. Reck / D. Weber (Hrsg.) *Literarische Stoffe und ihre Gestaltung in mitteliranischer Zeit. Kolloquium anläßlich des 70. Geburtstags von Werner Sundermann.* (Beiträge zur Iranistik 31) Wiesbaden: Ludwig Reichert Verlag, 319–348.

Woschitz, Karl Matthäus 1989. "Das Mythos des Lichtes und der Finsternis. Zum Drama der Kosmogonie und der Geschichte in den koptischen Kephalaia: Grundmotive, Ideengeschichte und Theologie." In: Karl M. Woschitz, Manfred Hutter und Karl Prenner 1989. *Das manichäische Urdrama des Lichtes. Studien zu koptischen, mitteliranischen und arabischen Texten.* Wien: Herder & Co., 13–150.

Xu Zangjing 續藏經 [= X]. Taibei: Xinwenfeng, 1968–1970. [Reprint of Nakano Tatsue 中野達慧 1905–1912. *Dainihon zokuzōkyō* 大日本續藏經 (Supplement to the Buddhist Canon Printed in Japan) Kyoto: Zōkyō shoin.]

Yoshida Yutaka 吉田豊 2009. "Ninpō no Manikyō e iwayuru "rokudō-zu" no kaishaku wo megutte. 寧波のマニ教画いわゆる「六道図」の解釈をめぐって." [A Manichaean painting from Ningbo − On the religious affiliation of the so-called *Rokudōzu* of the Museum Yamato Bunkakan]. *Yamato Bunka* 大和文華 119: 3−15.

Yoshida Yutaka 吉田豊 2010. "Shinshutsu Manikyō kaiga no keijijō 新出マニ教絵画の形而上." [The cosmogony (and church history) of the newly discovered Manichaean paintings]. *Yamato Bunka* 大和文华 121: 1−34.

Yoshida Yutaka 2010a. "A newly recognized Manichaean painting: Manichaean Daēnā from Japan." In: Mohammad A. Amir-Moezzi, Jean-Daniel Dubois, Christelle Jullien et Florence Jullien (eds.) 2010. *Pensée grecque et sagesse d'Orient. Hommage à Michel Tardieu.* Turnhout: Brepols, 694−714.

Yoshida Yutaka 吉田豊 2012. "Mani no kōtan-zu ni tsuite マニの降誕図について." [On the "Birth of Mānī" painting]. *Yamato Bunka* 大和文華 124 (Mani kōtan-zu tokushū マニ降誕図特輯): 1–10.

Yoshida Yutaka 2015. "Southern Chinese version of Mani's Picture Book discovered?" In: Richter, Siegfried G. and Charles Horton and K. Ohlhafer (eds.) *Mani in Dublin: Selected Papers from the Seventh International Conference of the International Association of Manichaean Studies in the Chester Beatty Library, Dublin, 8–12 September 2009.* Leiden: Brill. (forthcoming)

Yu Wanli 虞万里. 1995. "Dunhuang Monijiao «Xiabu zan» xieben niandai xintan 敦煌摩尼教《下部赞》写本年代新探." [A new research into the date of the manuscript of the Manichaean *Hymnscroll* of Dunhuang]. *Dunhuang Tulufan yanjiu* 敦煌吐鲁番研究 1: 37–46.

Zhang Zong 张总 and Liao Shunyong 廖顺勇 2007. "Sichuan Anyue Shengquan si Dizang shiwang kanxiang 四川安岳圣泉寺地藏十王龛像."

[The Kṣitigarbha and Ten Kings niche statues at the Shengquan monastery, Anyue, Sichuan] *Dunhuangxue jikan* 敦煌学辑刊 2007.2: 41–49.

Zhiru 2007. *The Making of a Savior Bodhisattva. Dizang in Medieval China*. Honolulu: University of Hawai'i Press.

Zieme, Peter 1975. *Manichäisch-türkische Texte. Texte, Übersetzung, Anmerkungen*. Berlin: Akademie-Verlag.

Zieme, Peter 1996. "Old Turkish Versions of the Scripture on the Ten Kings." In: Giovanni Stary (ed.) *Proceedings of the 38th Permanent International Altaistic Conference (PIAC), Kawasaki, Japan, August* 7–12, 1995. Wiesbaden, Harrassowitz, 401–425. [Repr. In: Simone-Christiane Raschmann und Jens Wilkens (Hrsg.) 2009. *Fragmenta Buddhica Uigurica: ausgewählte Schriften von Peter Zieme*. Berlin: Schwarz.]

6 The Passion of Jesus in Manichaean Painting [1]

Zsuzsanna Gulácsi
(Northern Arizona University, U. S.)

A variety of primary and secondary sources confirm that themes of Christian origin, especially the figure of Jesus, remained significant throughout the 1,400-year history of Manichaeism. The polemical writings of Augustine from the late 4th and early 5th centuries famously document the Manichaeans' devotion to Jesus, noting in the *Confessions* that Jesus' name was never absent from their mouths. [2] Manichaean hymns to Jesus are preserved in a diverse group of languages, mostly in Coptic from 4th-century Egypt, but also in Parthian, Sogdian, Middle-Persian, and Uygur from 8th-11th-century East Central Asia, and even in Chinese from 8th-century northern China. [3] The importance of Jesus, particularly in the western part of the Manichaean world, resulted in a Christian reading of Manichaeism that dominated early studies of this religion. Today, views on the origin of Manichaeism are divided between two opposing interpretations, suggesting either that Manichaeism originated in Christianity with strong Zoroastrian influences or, vice versa, in Zoroastrianism with strong Christian influences.

---

[1] For a longer version of this study that considers Manichaean texts and various Diatessaronic passages in connection with the art, see my forthcoming article titled "The Life of Jesus according to the *Diatessaron* in Early Manichaean Art and Text."

[2] Augustine writes: " … in their mouths were the devil's snares and a glue confected of a mixture of the syllables of the names of you (God) and of the lord Jesus Christ and of the Paraclete, our comforter, the Holy Spirit. These names were never absent from their mouths" (*Confessions* 3.6.10).

[3] For Iranian and Turkic Manichaean hymns to Jesus, see Klimkeit, *Gnosis on the Silk Road*, 63–68. For translated Chinese Manichaean hymns to Jesus, see Tsui Chi, "Mo Ni Chiao Hsia Pu Tsan," 176–83.

No matter which of these two traditional views one holds, it is undisputed that Jesus was integral to Manichaeism. While primary Manichaean texts on Jesus have been well known since the early 20th century from the deserts of Northeast Africa and East Central Asia, recent discoveries revealed the existence of three Manichaean Jesus paintings: two fragments from ca. 10th-century East Central Asia and one well-preserved large hanging scroll from 12th/13th-century southern China.[1]

The goal of this paper is to report about the identification of Manichaean a pictorial cycle with a series of individual scenes in gilded frames that narrate the life of Jesus on a folio that survives from a Manichaean illuminated hymnbook from 10th-century East Central Asia. The two adjacent scenes still discernable from this cycle show *"Judas Paid by Caiaphas,"* and *"Foot Washing."* Their unique sequence and iconography accord with two subsequent events discussed in the *Diatessaron* (Gr. διὰ τεσσάρων, lit. 'through four'). Also known as the *Gospel of the Mixed* (Syr. *da-Mehallete*), the *Diatessaron* is the earliest known gospel harmony, dating from the 170s CE. Composed in Syriac, probably by the early Christian writer Tatian (ca. 120-180 CE), this text remained the standard gospel text in the Syriac-speaking part of the Christian world until the late 5th century. The Manichaeans were exposed to Tatian's work most likely already during the life of Mani in the Mesopotamian phase of their history. Subsequently, they were noted for a continued use and preservation of the *Diatessaron* especially in the Latin-speaking part of the Roman Empire until the late 5th century.[2] Direct

[1] These three Jesus paintings were recently discussed in Gulácsi, "A Manichaean *Portrait of the Buddha Jesus*" and Figs. 1, 11, and 13.

[2] In a series of his study of between 1968 and 1993, Quispel argues that it was the Manichaeans, who preserved the most authentic version of Tatian's *Diatessaron* in the West ("A Diatessaron Reading in a Latin Manichaean Codex," 374–378). Unlike the *Diatessaron* in Syriac Christian use, where its content was gradually brought into greater alignment with the standard texts of the Greek gospels, the Manichaean version of the *Diatessaron* in the Latin west remained "archaic" and "wild," since the Manichaeans were under no pressure to "Vulgatize" or "domesticate" it. For a summary of Quispel's argument, see Petersen, *Tatian's Diatessaron*, 282, 336, and 441.

quotations from Tatian' s prose, given in Parthian translation in an East Central Asian Manichaean text, confirm a continued use of the *Diatessaron* until the early 11th century.

A Manichaean Folio Fragment with Life of Jesus Scenes

The narrative scenes at the core of this study are found on a relatively small piece of paper labeled MIK III 4967a in the collection of the Museum für Asiatische Kunst, Staatliche Museen zu Berlin (**Figs. 1a & 1b**). It is one of the ca. 5000 Manichaean manuscript fragments that were discovered by German expeditions between 1902 and 1914 beneath the ruins of the mud-brick buildings of Kocho.[1] Located near to what is today the Turfan Oasis in the Xinjiang Uygur Autonomous region of the Peoples' Republic of China, Kocho was a major oasis city, a fortified trading and agricultural center along the northern Silk Routes. It that was claimed by the Turkic-speaking Uygurs as the winter capital of their Sedentary Empire (843-1213 CE), which they established following the sudden fall their Steppe Empire (742-842 CE).[2] Due to the patronage of Manichaeism by the Uygur ruling elite (755/762 - ca. 1015 CE),[3] Kocho also functioned as the Manichaean religious center of the region that housed the seats of the highest-ranking regional authorities of the Manichaean Church, including one of the twelve "teachers" (Parth. *mozak*, Lt. *maior*) and one of the seventy-two "bishops" (Parth. *aftadan*, Lt. *episcopus*).[4] Fitting the royal sponsorship of art production at an important locale, the ca. 120 Manichaean artistic remains identified today from Kocho include fragments

[1] Von Le Coq, *Chotscho*. The majority of the ca. 5,000 Manichaean manuscript fragments were written in Manichaean script and Iranian languages, and were cataloged by Boyce (*Catalogue*).

[2] Czeglédy, "The Foundation of the Turfan Uyghur Kingdom," 159–163.

[3] On the conversion of Bügü Khan (r. 760–843 CE), the most prominent ruler of the Uygur Steppe Empire and the first khan to support Manichaeism starting between 755 and 762, see Clark, "The Conversion of Bügü Khan," 83–123. For the end of Manichaeism among the Uygurs, see Moriyasu, *Die Geschichte des uigurischen Manichäismus*, 149–209.

[4] The Manichaean authority structure included the following ranks: the *primate* ("pope," central authority, successor to Mani), the 12 *maiores* ("teachers"), the 72 *episcopi* ("bishops") and the 360 *presbyteri* ("presbyters"), see Tardieu, *Manichaeism*, 56–59.

of exquisite illuminated manuscripts, gilded leather book covers, delicately painted or embroidered didactic and devotional textiles, as well as remnants of wall paintings from two ceremonial buildings and from two caves near Kocho.[1] As all the examples of Manichaean art from Kocho, MIK III 4967a dates from within the ca. 270-year period stretching from the mid-8th to the early 11th century. Within this Uygur era of Manichaean history, a narrower time frame that points to the second half of the 10th century may be argued as the most likely time of production and subsequent use of the illuminated manuscript to which this fragment belonged.[2]

The basic textual and codicological contents of this torn double-sided paper piece have been examined, catalogued, and published together with color facsimiles. The fragment was first discussed in 1962 by Mary Boyce, who focused on its text – bits of letters from four lines of a cantillated hymn written in Manichaean script (a version of the Syriac script used exclusively by the Manichaeans) and in a local language, which cannot be determined, since no complete words only a few letters are preserved and even those are interrupted by extra vowels to signal how to chant this hymn.[3] More recently, the basic codicological characteristics of the fragment were considered within the corpus of Manichaean book art by Zsuzsanna Gulácsi in 1997, 2001, and 2005.[4] The latter studies revealed that we are dealing with a fragmentary codex folio of a now lost, relatively large and luxurious illuminated hymnbook that was adorned with delicate figural scenes painted on a lapis lazuli background and framed with gilded borders. Its recto and verso sides have also been confirmed based a rule of Manichaean codicology that involves *the direction of the writing* (right to left on both sides) in relation to *the side margins* or, in this case, *the direction*

[1] For the first study on the identification of the Manichaean corpus from Kocho, see Gulácsi, "Identifying the Corpus of Manichaean Art."

[2] This date is supported by technical, stylistic, and codicological similarities to a carbon-dated bifolio fragment (MIK III 8259) that also contains the name of a historical figure; see Gulácsi, "Dating the 'Persian' and Chinese Style Remains," 8–12 and *Mediaeval Manichaean Book Art*, 39–58.

[3] Boyce, *Catalogue*, 142.

[4] Gulácsi, "Identifying the Corpus of Manichaean Art," 177–215; *Manichaean Art in Berlin Collections*, 124–125 and 237; and *Mediaeval Manichaean Book Art*, 176, Tabs. 5/10 and 5/11.

of the figures' heads (oriented sideways; towards the outer margins on the full-page scene of the recto, just as in the intracolumnar scene of the verso).[1] The original location of the fragment within the upper half of the folio has also been determined. A more detailed examination, however, leads to even further discoveries.

A pair of reconstruction diagrams sums up effectively the surviving codicological data and its interpretation regarding the original layout of these two subsequent codex pages (**Fig. 1**). The fragment, measuring 7.4 cm×4.3 cm, constitutes a torn portion from the inner half and the upper third of a large folio, as confirmed by the content of its verso (**Figs. 1b and 1d**). This page retains bits of the letters from four lines of the cantillated text and a small portion from the edge of the sideways-oriented intracolumnar scene beneath the text, allowing us not only to confirm that this side of the folio was the verso, but also to calculate the approximate size of the folio in relation to data on better-preserved Manichaean illuminated fragments from Kocho. Accordingly, the height of the folio reached a minimum of ca. 29.6 cm.[2] Its width was a minimum of 16.0 cm.[3] The idea that this fragment derived

〔1〕Images turned perpendicularly, i.e., at 90-degree angles, in relation to the direction of writing is a standard feature of East Central Asian Manichaean book art, observed not only in codex, but also in scroll and pustaka (i.e., "palm-leaf") formats; see "Patterns of Page Arrangement" in Gulácsi, *Mediaeval Manichaean Book Art*, 133–193. Sideways-oriented images are also present in Syriac and Armenian illuminated gospels and, to a lesser degree, in Islamic book art. Gulácsi reported on their codicological study in a recent paper ("Sideways Orientated Images of Eastern Christian and Manichaean Illuminated Manuscripts." *36th Annual Conference on Manuscript Studies*, October 16–17, 2009, Saint Louis University, St. Louis, MO).

〔2〕The estimation of 29.6 cm as the minimum height is based on the following: Above the intracolumnar scene, the text-block contained a minimum of six lines, reaching 5.8 cm. If so, the upper margin with its header was min. 3.0 cm. The area of the intracolumnar painting occupied a little more than 2 times one text-block, ca. 13.0 cm. Beneath the painting the second text-block was 5.8 cm, and the lower margin ca. 2.0 cm. If the text-block had eight lines, the folio height would increase by ca. 10.0 cm, similar to the large size of one of the best-preserved fragments, the illuminated bifolio MIK III 8259. For its reconstruction, see Gulácsi, *Mediaeval Manichaean Book Art*, 142–144 and Fig. 5/7.

〔3〕Although there is not enough codicological data preserved on the fragment to calculate the approximate width of the folio, a minimum of 16.0 cm may be proposed in light of recorded proportions of the better-preserved and fully reconstructable illuminated folia from Kocho; see Gulácsi, *Mediaeval Manichaean Book Art*, Tab. 3.8 and Fig. 3/11.

from one of the largest examples from the "medium-size codices" known from Manichaean Kocho, is indicated already by its relatively large script (0.38 cm, measured at the small letters) and line distance (approximately 1.0 cm, measured between the base of the letters) compared to the writing seen on other Manichaean codex fragments.[1]

The technical details of illumination on this fragment accord with better-preserved examples of what has been called as the "West Asian fully painted style of Uygur Manichaean art."[2] As with many other Manichaean manuscript fragments from Kocho, the surface damage of this paper folio allows us to see the stages of the painter's work. Accordingly, we can see bits of the untouched *blank paper surface* on areas where colors or gold leaf have vanished. Remnants from the *underdrawing*, formed by thicker red-violet lines that were drawn directly onto the blank paper surface, are revealed from beneath vanished paint or gold leaf. Bits from *fully painted figures* (plants, objects, garments, and human beings) and the *red-violet contour lines*, which framed their features, are often discernible against remnants of the blue background. The understanding of these techniques of the Manichaean painter is essential for deciphering what is left from the iconography of these fragmentary paintings.[3]

The placement of the pictorial program within the overall layout on these two pages is analogous to other Manichaean examples known today from East Central Asia. As was customary in the medieval book art of the Manichaeans, these pages contained sideways-oriented figural scenes that were positioned systematically with the heads of the figures closer to the

[1] For a codicological study illustrated with tables and diagrams that summarize the measurements in relation to the five size categories (extra small, small, medium, large, and extra large) of Manichaean codices from East Central Asia, see Gulácsi, *Mediaeval Manichaean Book Art*, 76–83; esp. Tabs. 3/4, 3/8, and Figs. 3/9 and 3/11. Illuminated codices from Kocho are documented in "small" (H: 15.0–20.0 cm, W: 7.0–12.00 cm), "medium" (H: 23.0–30.0 cm, W: 13.0–18.00 cm), and "large" (H: 31.0–50.0 cm, W: 19.0–30.00 cm) sizes.

[2] Gulácsi, "Dating the 'Persian' and Chinese Style Remains," 12–19.

[3] On the techniques of Manichaean book painting, including a discussion on the differences between the lines of the under-drawings and contour drawing in the "West Asian Fully Painted Style of Manichaean art," see Gulácsi "Reconstructing Manichaean Book Paintings," 106–116.

outer margins. The surface of the recto was devoted exclusively to painting (**Figs. 1a and 1c**). It was organized into at least two sections, including *one large scene* (measuring ca. 28 cm × 14 cm) and *a row of a maximum of fourteen evenly sized small vignettes in gilded frames*. Each vignette was ca. 2.0 cm in width and a minimum of 3.0 cm in height (including the frame).[1] It is possible that some of the vignettes were wider, resulting in a total number of 12 scenes. Looking at the reconstructed page from the picture-viewing direction, the one large scene was located beneath a thin outer margin. The row of vignettes was painted beneath the large scene and above the inner margin of the page.[2] On the verso, the main pictorial element of the page was the *intracolumnar figural scene* (**Figs. 1b and 1d**). This scene was located between the upper text-block and the lower text-block. When turned to the picture-viewing direction, the upper text-block is on the right and the lower text-block on the left. In this turned position, the thin inner margin of the page falls beneath the scene.[3] While the verso of this folio fragment retains no traces of any floral decorative design (since the upper and outer margins do not survive), it is most likely that this page contained a header along the middle of its actual upper margin (as most Manichaean manuscript pages do), which was then surrounded with floral motifs as seen on most analogous examples of Manichaean book art.[4]

The two primary scenes surviving from the pictorial program of MIK

---

〔1〕If the vignettes were evenly sized, they must have totaled 14, filling out the available 28.0 cm pictorial space within this page layout (14 cm × 2.0 cm = 28 cm). The pictorial space was flanked by margins (2 cm × 0.8 cm = 1.6 cm). The page width (29.6 cm) was filled out by the row of vignettes (28.0 cm) and the two margins (1.6 cm).

〔2〕Another Middle Persian illuminated folio fragment (M 556) from Kocho also preserves an analogous row of small scenes (each measuring ca. 2.0 cm × 1.5 cm), framed in thin red lines and painted against the inner margin of the page. Here, four frames preserve intact widths – they are evenly sized; see Gulácsi, *Manichaean Art in Berlin Collections*, 126–127; and *Mediaeval Manichaean Book Art*, 209.

〔3〕The margin above the scene was probably narrow as well, since the painting most likely intruded to the area of the margin, as seen in other Manichaean examples. For an analogous layout, see for example MIK III 4974 recto, where the intracolumnar scene also reaches into the area of the outer margin (Gulácsi, *Manichaean Art in Berlin Collections*, 84; and *Mediaeval Manichaean Book Art*, 145).

〔4〕This feature can be seen also on MIK III 4974 recto, mentioned in the previous note 25 above.

III 4967a (the large scene on the recto and the intracolumnar scene on the verso) belong to an iconographically distinct group of Manichaean paintings that reflect a local artistic impact and thus, fall beyond the interest of this study. Although they are very fragmentary, it is clear that these two scenes included figures standing on lotus supports in mandala-like arrangements, which is often seen in the contemporaneous Buddhist art of in East Central Asia. The larger scene (preserved on the recto, see Fig. 1a) retains only bits from of the lotus vines from beneath the now-lost lotus supports and feet of most likely standing figures. The smaller scene (preserved on the verso, see Fig. 1b) retains parts of a faded blue background and a section form a white robe of a standing elect, wider at the knee and tapering gradually narrower towards the now lost area of the feet. Examples of analogous lotus plants and mandala-like layouts of figures standing or sitting lotus plants are numerous within the group of Manichaean paintings that integrate local influence into their visual language.[1] As the letter images show, lotus plants in Manichaean art tend to grow out of a central pool of water, with gilded leafy stems spreading across the painting and concluding in open lotus flowers that hold standing or seated figures and sometimes altar displays.[2] In light of such comparative examples, the poorly preserved portions of the two mains scenes on MIK III 4967a become comprehensible. On the recto, leafy gilded stems of the lotus supports remain close to what was the bottom of the painting, suggesting that a set of figures, most likely five, were show standing on lotus flowers next to one another (see Fig. 1c). On the verso, the lower body of a standing white-robed figure is retained

---

〔1〕As seen for example on a solely pictorial scroll fragment, MIK III 4975 and its reconstruction diagram (Gulácsi, *Manichaean Art in Berlin Collections*, 149–150; and *Mediaeval Manichaean Book Art*, 183–184) and a marginal illumination from the recto of the matched codex folio fragments, MIK III 6265 & III 4966 c (Gulácsi, *Manichaean Art in Berlin Collections*, 62–65). The location of the marginal illumination in relation to the rest of the codex page is similar to the folio fragment M 559 (Gulácsi, *Mediaeval Manichaean Book Art*, 167–169).

〔2〕For examples, see the illuminations on the two folio fragments: MIK III 8259 folio 1(?) recto and MIK III 4974 recto (Gulácsi, *Manichaean Art in Berlin Collections*, 56–61 and 83–86, respectively); and the two scroll fragments: 81 TB 65:01 and MIK III 4614 (Gulácsi, *Mediaeval Manichaean Book Art*, 215).

most likely from an original set of five similar figures (see Fig. 1d). The lotus plants, and their use as supports for displaying figures and altars, as well as a diagram-like arrangement of the figures, all allude to East Central Asian pictorial features for they are used in Buddhist art along the Silk Routes. [1] At the same time, however, such motifs are also frequent in the Manichaean art of the region.

At the core interest of this study is row of vignettes narrating the *Life of Jesus* that formed a secondary group of images in the overall pictorial program of the recto of MIK III 4967a, located beneath the main scene (see Fig. 1a and 1c). The vignettes were painted across the entire page in a left to right sequence, as confirmed by their surviving content. From among the now-lost complete row, remnants of four are preserved (**Fig. 2**). From among these four, the two outer ones retain only minimal, mostly codicological information, such as gilded frames and the edges of indecipherable forms surrounded by blue background inside the frames. The two inner scenes retain meaningful content. With the help of an enlarged reproduction, we can clearly see a blue background and a pair of figures interacting as they face one another in each vignette **(Fig. 2a).** In the vignette on the left, both figures are standing. The one on the right wears a headdress, while the other figure does not. In the vignette on the right, we can make out a man standing and another squatting in front of him. A digitally enhanced reproduction, in which only the blue backgrounds and the gold frames were reconstructed while the figures remained untouched, makes their contents discernable with greater ease **(Fig. 2b).** Somewhat easier to see is the vignette on the right. In it, the standing figure is shown lifting his right arm and his right leg. The squatting figure is touching the lifted leg with both hands. Both figures appear to be nude or semi-nude. Familiarity with the biblical narrative allows us to interpret this somewhat

---

〔1〕Examples from East Central Asia dating from between the 8th and 11th centuries include the Tibetan Buddhist carved "Gilded Sandalwood Triptych Mandala of Vairochana" (44–18) in the Nelson–Atkins Museum in Kansas City and the painted "Silk Mandala with Five Deities" (MG 26466) in the collection of the Musée Guimet in Paris (see Giés and Cohen, *Sérinde, Terre de Bouddha*, 395–396 and 402–403).

enigmatic scene as a depiction of the "Foot Washing" episode well-known from the Gospel of John (13:1) reduced to the two main characters: Jesus and Peter. In the vignette on the left, the figure with the headgear wears a red-orange robe and holds a large bowl in front of his chest. The other figure seems to be lesser ranking, since he is shown without headgear and from a profile view. He also wears a cloak, hanging from his right shoulder as he reaches towards the bowl, as if he is about to take (or has just taken) something out of it. Bits of gold flakes visible in the interior of the bowl suggest that it (and/or its contents) was gilded. In association with the previously identified scene, these clues bring to mind another biblical episode – Judas being paid for his betrayal of Jesus. This preliminary identification seems to be supported by the distinct headdress, which may signal here the Jewish high priest, Caiaphas. If so, the event familiar form the Gospel of Matthew (26:14) may be shown here abridged again to the minimal number of figures: Judas and the high priest, Caiaphas. Therefore, this scene may be titled "Judas Paid by Caiaphas."

There are, however, problems with the assumption that these two scenes reflect the canonical gospels. Their sequence, just as the nude (or semi-nude) bodies in the iconography, is clearly not biblical. They reflect an alternative narration of Jesus' life story used by the religious community that created this work of art. *Judas Paid* precedes directly the event of *Foot Washing* in the Manichaean painting. This is not the case in the canonical gospels of the New Testament. The event of *Foot Washing* is not mentioned in any of the three synoptic gospels. It is discussed only in John (13:1-13:11), who does not mention Judas being paid. The latter event is discussed in only two of the gospels: in Luke (22:2-22:6), who mentions Caiaphas, but not the thirty pieces of silver; and in Matthew (26:14-26:26), who mentions the silver, but not the high priest. The fact that none of the gospels could possibly have been illustrated with the sequence of these two scenes confirms the use of a gospel harmony, rather than one of the New Testament gospels. The Manichaeans are well known for their employment of one such gospel harmony – Tatian' s *Diatessaron*. This is not surprising, since as noted before, this text was used exclusively in place of the canonical gospels in Syro-Mesopotamia prior to the early 6th century. Therefore, the text of the *Diatessaron* is the logical first place to look for a narrative with this particular sequence.

The continued use of Tatian' s *Diatessaron* among the Manichaeans during the East Central Asian phase of their history (mid 8th-early 11th centuries) has been confirmed first by Werner Sundermann in 1968. At that time, Sundermann identified two diatessaronic passages in a Parthian language text among the Manichaean manuscript fragments discovered at the archeological site of Kocho (near the Turfan Oasis in the Xinjiang Uygur Autonomous region of the PRC), which corresponded with two sections of the *Diatessaron,* as seen in the Arabic version, generally considered as reliably preserving the sequence of Tatian' s original.

The research I have presented here, in turn, provides *visual* evidence on the artistic impact of the *Diatessaron* by exploring a Manichaean painting from ca. 10th-century Kocho with a previously unidentified subject matter. More specifically, I have argued that two adjacent scenes, remaining from a set of probably 14 small vignettes on a fragmentary folio of a Manichaean illuminated hymnbook (MIK III 4967a recto) depict two events discussed in subsequent passages of the Arabic *Diatessaron*. One of the scenes shows "Judas Paid by Caiaphas," while the other the "Foot Washing." The unique sequence of the two events together with certain iconographic details of the painting cannot be explained in light of the canonical gospels. Their harmonized pictorial narration distinctly corresponds with Tatian' s account—the very gospel harmony used by the Manichaeans.

Unlike other Manichaean depictions of Jesus,[1] this diatessaronic

〔1〕Other Manichaean depictions of Jesus are distinctly of their time and place. In 10th–century East Central Asia, they contain lotus seats, mandala–like arrangements, and sometimes are in a medium and style associated with artists trained in Tang dynasty China. The large and well–preserved Manichaean silk hanging–scroll of Jesus from ca. 13th–century southern China features a lotus thrones and an overall positioning identical to Song and Yuan dynasty Buddhist art, see Gulácsi, "Images of Jesus in Manichaean Art."

painting appears archaic for its time and place. It show no signs of contemporaneous East Central Asian artistic features otherwise common in Manichaean art produced during this era; and instead displays a West Asiatic character in subject matter (Life of Jesus), iconography (lack of halo, short hair), and painting style (fully painted West Asian Style of Uygur Manichaean art). The presence of such an antiquated visual language in a Manichaean diatessaronic painting, together with the use of an equally dated Parthian *lingua sacra* in Sundermann' s diatessaronic passages, suggests that neither this diatessaronic Manichaean painting nor the diatessaronic Manichaean text originated in East Central Asia, but were integrated into Manichaean art and text already during an earlier phase in the history of this religion.

Concerning the Manichaean pictorial roots of this painting, I hypothesize that its prototype was a product of early Manichaeism in a medium independent from the illuminated book, originating in Syro-Mesopotamia between the mid 3rd and early 6th centuries. During this time and in this region, Tatian' s *Diatessaron* was used exclusively in place of the canonical gospels and the Manichaeans were also exposed to it. Based on the importance of Jesus in Mani' s teachings (including both Jesus' life in general and particularly his Passion as an allegory for the suffering of the Divine Light), it seems reasonable to assume that the Life of Jesus was one of the subjects depicted in early Manichaean didactic art and used in the course of Mani' s teaching during the mid 3rd century. The existence and use of didactic paintings displayed in the course of oral instruction is a distinctly Manichaean phenomenon in the second half of the 3rd and the 4th centuries, as documented by various Manichaean and Christian polemical accounts. Therefore, it is reasonable to assume that in this early era, a Manichaean artist committed the content of the *Diatessaron* to painting by creating a narrative cycle in a solely pictorial medium—

physically independent from the text of the *Diatessaron*.[1] After the early 6th century, the *Diatessaron* was no longer the preferred text on the life of Christ in the Syriac Church, and the Manichaeans were increasingly disappearing due to the resurgence of anti-Manichaean legislation by the emperor Justinian (r. 527-565). It is most likely that the emergence of the Manichaean depiction of the Life of Jesus was closer to the earliest possible date, sometime after the mid 3rd century. By that time, narrative Christian art was being made in Syro-Mesopotamia. Similarity with the early Christian pictorial art surviving from Dura-Europos (seen in the short hair and lack of halo for Jesus) also supports the likelihood of an earlier date of origin. Moreover, by the 240's Mani had started to proselytize in southern Mesopotamia, in the course of which he is known to have consciously employed didactic paintings to aid the teachings of his doctrine. Given the evidence pointing to the doctrinal content and didactic function of pictorial art employed by Mani, it is quite likely that the Life Jesus was one of the subjects depicted among the images of Mani's *Picture-Book*.[2]

Future research will have to take on the task of exploring the possible early Christian roots behind this Manichean art. This task is complex. Such a project must begin with the identification of diatessaronic Christian art that the early Christians most likely also produced along and beyond the eastern frontiers of the Roman Empire. As a working hypothesis, one may assume that such very early and very eastern Christian art may have played a role in shaping Manichaean representations of the Life of Jesus in mid 3rd century southern Mesopotamia, and the western regions of Sasanid Iran, from where Mani and a distinctly Manichaean Christology emerged.

[1] John Lowden put forward a convincing hypothesis that considers the origins of full-page narrative and devotional biblical images found in prefatory cycles separately from their biblical texts, see his "The Beginnings of Biblical Illustration (from 2007)," 125-128.

[2] For recent studies on this subject, see Gulácsi's forthcoming monograph, *Mani's Picture-Book*; and a Web journal article, "Searching for Mani's *Picture-Book* in Textual and Pictorial Sources."

Bibliography

Boyce Mary Boyce, *A Catalogue of the Iranian Manuscripts in Manichaean Script in the Berlin Turfan Collection* (Berlin: Akademie Verlag, 1960).

Clark Larry V. Clark, "The Conversion of Bügü Khan," in *Studia Manichaica: IV. Internationaler Kongress zum Manichäismus*, ed. Ronald E. Emmerick, Werner Sundermann, and Peter Zieme (Berlin: Akademie Verlag, 2000), 83-123.

Czeglédy Károly Czeglédy, "The Foundation of the Turfan Uyghur Kingdom," in *Tibetan and Buddhist Studies Commemorating the 200th Anniversary of the Birth of Alexander Csoma de Korös*, edited Lajos Ligeti (Budapest: Akadémiai Kiadó, 1984), 159-163.

Giés & Cohen Monique Cohen and Jacques Giès, *Sérinde, terre de Bouddha : dix siècles d'art sur la route de la soie* (Paris : Réunion des musées nationaux) 1995.

Gulácsi Zsuzsanna Gulácsi, *Mani's Picture-Book: Canonical Didactic Images of the Manichaeans from Mesopotamia to China*. Leiden: E. J. Brill (2013, forthcoming).

________, "The Life of Jesus according to the *Diatessaron* in Early Manichaean art and Text," *Bulletin of the Asia Institute* 22 (2008/2012): 143-169 and color plates 2-4.

________, "Images of Jesus in Manichaean Art." In *STUDIA MANICHAICA: Proceedings from the 7th International Congress of Manichaean Studies, September* 8-14, 2009, *Dublin, Ireland*, edited by S. Richter. Nag Hammadi and Manichaean Studies (Leiden: Brill) 2013, forthcoming.

________, "Searching for Mani' s *Picture-Book* in Textual and Pictorial Sources," *Transcultural Studies* (Thematic issue: *Byzantium beyond its Eastern Frontier*), Peer-reviewed E-Journal of the University of Heidelberg Research Cluster "Asia and Europe in a Global Context," see http://archiv.ub.uni-heidelberg.de/ojs/index.php/transcultural/article/vie

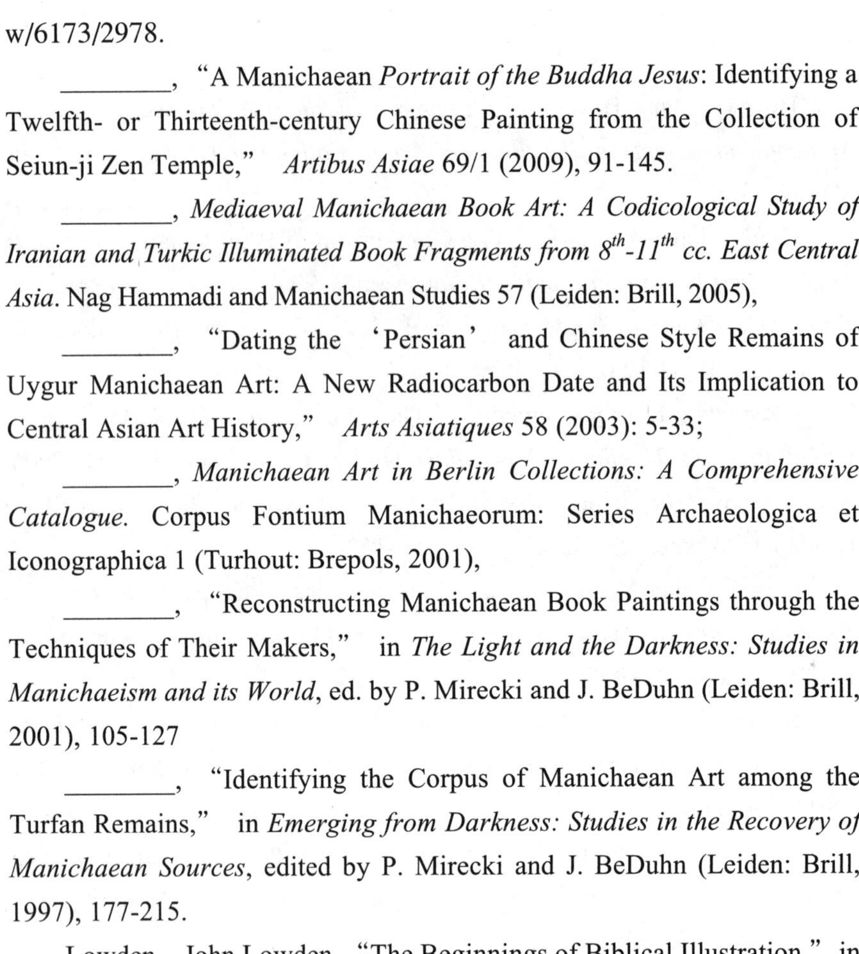

w/6173/2978.

________, “A Manichaean *Portrait of the Buddha Jesus*: Identifying a Twelfth- or Thirteenth-century Chinese Painting from the Collection of Seiun-ji Zen Temple,” *Artibus Asiae* 69/1 (2009), 91-145.

________, *Mediaeval Manichaean Book Art: A Codicological Study of Iranian and Turkic Illuminated Book Fragments from* 8th-11th *cc. East Central Asia*. Nag Hammadi and Manichaean Studies 57 (Leiden: Brill, 2005),

________, “Dating the ‘Persian’ and Chinese Style Remains of Uygur Manichaean Art: A New Radiocarbon Date and Its Implication to Central Asian Art History,” *Arts Asiatiques* 58 (2003): 5-33;

________, *Manichaean Art in Berlin Collections: A Comprehensive Catalogue*. Corpus Fontium Manichaeorum: Series Archaeologica et Iconographica 1 (Turhout: Brepols, 2001),

________, “Reconstructing Manichaean Book Paintings through the Techniques of Their Makers,” in *The Light and the Darkness: Studies in Manichaeism and its World*, ed. by P. Mirecki and J. BeDuhn (Leiden: Brill, 2001), 105-127

________, “Identifying the Corpus of Manichaean Art among the Turfan Remains,” in *Emerging from Darkness: Studies in the Recovery of Manichaean Sources*, edited by P. Mirecki and J. BeDuhn (Leiden: Brill, 1997), 177-215.

Lowden John Lowden, “The Beginnings of Biblical Illustration,” in *Late Antique and Medieval Art of the Mediterranean World*, edited by Eva R. Hoffman (Oxford: Blackwell, 2007), 117-134.

MoriyasuTakao Moriyasu, *Die Geschichte des uigurischen Manichäismus an der Seidenstrasse*, trans. Christian Steineck (Wiesbaden: Harrasowitz Verlag, 2004).

Petersen William L. Petersen, *Tatian’s Diatessaron: Its Significance, Dissemination, Significance and History of Scholarship* (Leiden: Brill) 1994.

Quispel Gilles Quispel, “A Diatessaron Reading in a Latin Manichaean Codex,” *Vigiliae Christianae*, 47/4 [1993], 374-378.

Tardieu Michel Tardieu, *Manichaeism* (Urbana: University of Illinois Press, 2008).

Tsui Chi Tsui Chi, "Mo Ni Chiao Hsia Pu Tsan," *Bulletin of the School of Oriental and African Studies* 11 (1943-44), 176–83.

von Le Coq Albert von Le Coq, *Chotscho: Facsimile-Wiedergabe der Wichtigeren Funde der ersten Königlich Preussischen Expedition nach Turfan in Ost-Turkistan* (Berlin: Dietrich Reimer, 1913; reprint, Graz: Akademie Druck, 1973).

1a. MIK III 4967a recto

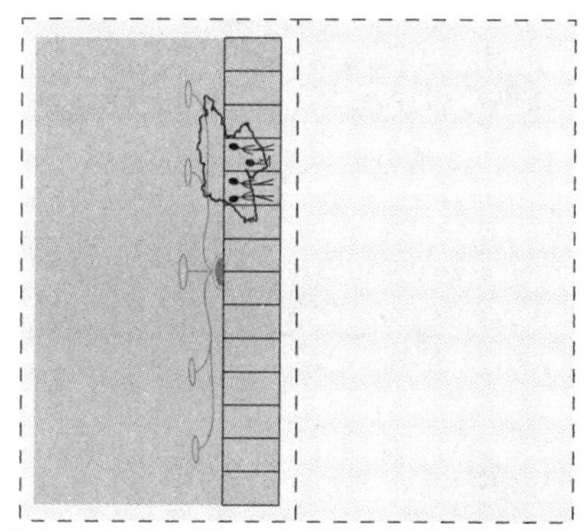

1c. Reconstructed layout of MIK III 4967a recto (H: min. 29.6 cm, W: ca. 16.0 cm)

1b. MIK III 4967a verso (H: 7.3 cm, W: 4.3 cm)

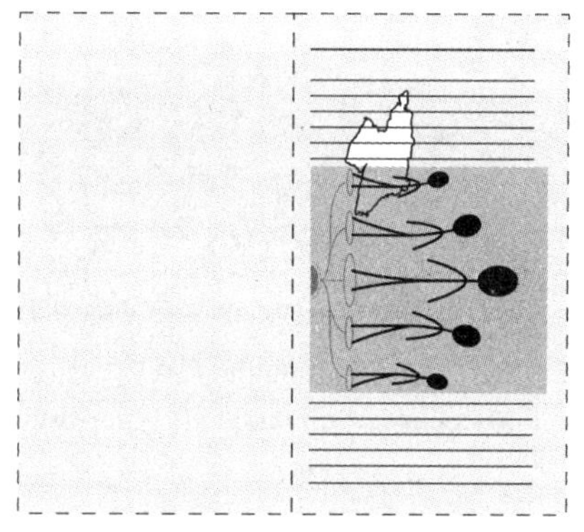

1d. Reconstructed layout of MIK III 4967a verso (H: min. 29.6 cm, W: ca. 16.0 cm)

Fig. 1. Reconstruction of a Folio Fragment from a Manichaean Illuminated Hymn-Book (MIK III 4967a)ca. 10th century Kocho, Museum für Asiatische Kunst, Staatliche Museen zu Berlin

2a. Row of vignettes in actual condition, detail of MIK III 4967a recto (Fig. 1a)

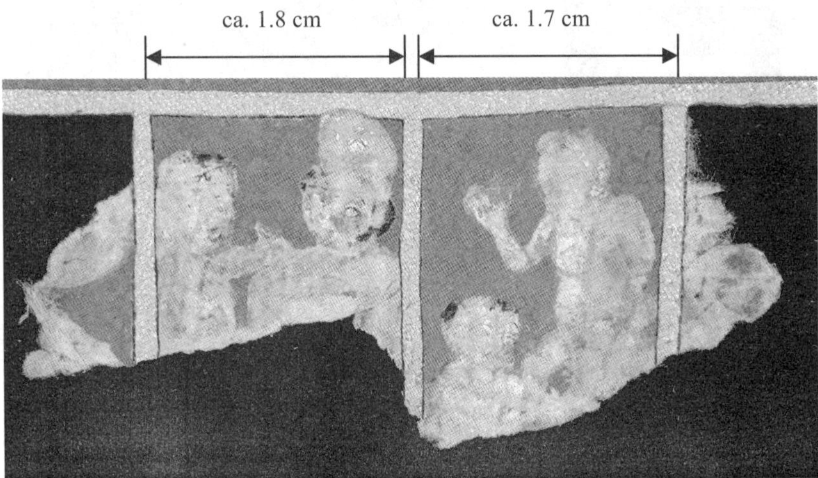

2b. Row of vignettes shown with digitally enhanced background and gold frames

Fig. 2. Scenes from the Life of Jesus Depicted on a Folio Frgament of a Manichaean Illuminated Hymn-Book (detail of MIK III 4967a recto)

7 Charisma of Mildness: Goddess Artistic Images and the Female Followers of Chotcho Manichaean Church

Wang Yuanyuan
(Department of History, Sun Yat-sen University)

There are many female images in Manichaean artworks unearthed in Turfan, including goddesses in religious myth, as well as the worldly female elects and auditors. The difference between them lies in halo and garments: goddess with halo usually wear colorful dress, while the female elects always in white without halo. This paper focuses on the former, but an important point to realize here is that goddesses in discussion not only include the Mother of Life and the Maiden of Light, but also some female images whose identities cannot be determined temporarily, especially the images in the manuscript labeled MIK III 7283 (Fig.1) [1].

7.1 Headgear on the Manuscript MIK III 7283

MIK III 7283 was discovered in the site of α temple in Chotcho. On one side of it, five script lines in Middle Persian still remain which are too fragmentary

〔1〕Z. Gulácsi, *Manichaean Art in Berlin Collection*, Brepols, 2001, pp.112–113.

to judge its topic[1]. A section of a miniature survives on the other side. In the left part of the miniature, we can still see a part of reddish-brown halo and mandorla, which should be a part of a Manichaean deity with his (or her) black hair and white scarf still visible. There are a few head images beside this deity, and one of them is quite clear: it's a black-haired lady with a headgear. The headgear has a golden disk in the middle, surrounded with upward curving white accessory which is in the shape of crescent. The appearance of other head images is similar, so we have no doubt that they are all female heads. These heads are all placed on golden plates. In the column next to the deity there are two plates, with a female head on each. But from the white remnants under the second plates of this column, we can tell there must be another plate with a female head. In the vertical row farther to the deity, there are three plates with two female heads on each, but in a smaller size. We can also find remnants of two headgears under the third plate of this row. Probably, the arrangement of the plates and female heads shows a regular pattern. Therefore, from the decreasing size of plates and heads as well as the increasing number of heads, we may assume in the right missing part of this miniature there might be some plates with three or more heads on them. That is to say, such plates with female head on them might be surrounding the deity.

This strange scene is hard to understand for observer familiar with Chinese culture, because in traditional religious paintings or folk drawings

〔1〕M. Boyce, *A Catalogue of the Iranian Manuscripts in Manichaean Script in the German Turfan Collection*, p.144. According to Prof. Boyce, the side with Manichaean script lines in Middle Persian is the recto of fragment MIK III 7283, but Prof. Gulácsi holds the opposite view. Those Middle Persian lines can only be recognized (see Z. Gulácsi, *Manichaean Art in Berlin Collection*, Appendix I, p.236.) as:

Line 1: ……

Line 2: …… ear]th and sk[y……

Line 3: ……light or (?)……

Line 4: ……was……

Line 5: ……

in China, head on a plate is usually a bloody and horrifying image. It has nothing to do with goodliness or positiveness, let alone holiness. In Chinese tradition, using human head as decoration is likely to represent the evil side. The motif of human head can be found in Tibetan Buddhist arts. For example, some gods hold human heads in hands or wear garlands decorated with human heads (Kapalamala in Sanskrit), but the human heads here represents "heads of evil spirit" or "lust"; some Buddhist instruments such as Kila (Phur-pa in Tibetan) or Khatvanga (Kha-tam-ga in Tibetan) are often decorated with three human heads, which represent lust, evil and imbecility[1]. On the contrary, in late antique and early Mediaeval West Asian arts, architectures or mosiacs with human heads were common, and they are apparently not symbol of evil[2]. Miniature in MIK III 7283 demonstrates an art style closer to the birthland of Manichaeism[3]. The original author of this miniature might be from West Asian Church because the human heads in the golden plates are, judging from their headgears, divine beings rather than evil spirits.

This kind of headgear is common in Manichaean artworks unearthed in Turfan, for instance the miniature on the recto of fragment MIK III 4965 (Fig.2)[4]. The main figure of this picture is a Manichaean god with multi-layered haloes. These layers are in colors of golden, blue, reddish-brown, green from inner to outer, and there is a golden

---

〔1〕Robert Beer (tr. by 向红笳 Xiang Hongjia), 藏传佛教象征符号与器物图解 (*The Handbook of Tibetan Buddhist Symbols*), Beijing, Press of Chinese Tibetan Studies, 2007, pp.108, 111, 170–172.

〔2〕Female heads as decorative motifs are common in Parthian and early Islamic royal architecture. See Z. Gulácsi, *Manichaean Art in Berlin Collection*, p.112, n.2; Idem, *Mediaeval Manichaean Book Art: A Codicological Study of Iranian and Turkic Illuminated Book Fragments from 8th–11th Century East Central Asia*, p.44.

〔3〕Prof. Gulácsi has already pointed out the West Asian painting style in this miniature (see Table4/1), Z. Gulácsi, Mediaeval Manichaean Book Art: A Codicological Study of Iranian and Turkic Illuminated *Book* Fragments from 8th–11th Century East Central Asia, p.112.

〔4〕H.-J. Klimkeit (tr. by 林悟殊 Lin Wushu), 古代摩尼教艺术 (*Manichaean Art and Calligraphy*), Taipei, Shuxin Press, 1995, Plate 33b; Z. Gulácsi, *Manichaean Art in Berlin Collection*, p.106.

crescent-shaped halo in the outermost layer. We can see eight heads clearly in the god's reddish-brown halo. Although their headgears are not well-preserved, it can be still recognized the golden disks surrounded with accessories in the shape of crescent, which are almost identical with that of MIK III 7283. So they are also female divine figures in spite of their unclear facial features. Prof. Klimkeit believes there should have been twelve heads symboling twelve light crowns, and the main god in the middle might be the Father of the Light Kingdom[1]. According to Prof. Z. Gulácsi, they are twelve Virgins (or Maidens) surrounding the Third Messenger[2]. There is one figure with halo on each side of the main god, who are also likely to be divine beings from the Realm of Light[3]. They are holding a huge golden crown over the head of the main god. Both of them wear headgear with a main part similar to that of MIK III 7283, but there is a blue fan-shaped ornament with golden edging behind the main part. The fan-shaped ornament looks like "Qitou 旗头" of Manchurian women (a typical women hairstyle of the Qing Dynasty with the hair coiled on top of the head and put a fan-shaped hair coronet on it). Such headgear with a blue fan-like ornament also appears on the verso of the fragment (Fig.3)[4]. In the verso, the main god with dark hair has unclear facial feature, and is surrounded with two layers of halo. The main part of the god's headgear is also the same as that of MIK III 7283, but with a blue fan-shaped ornament

〔1〕H.-J. Klimkeit (tr. by Lin Wushu), 古代摩尼教艺术 (*Manichaean Art and Calligraphy*), p.74.

〔2〕Z. Gulácsi, Manichaean Art in Berlin Collection, p.104; Idem, Mediaeval Manichaean Book Art: A Codicological Study of Iranian and Turkic Illuminated *Book* Fragments from 8th–11th Century East Central Asia, p.204. 8 heads are extant in the halo, and most believed there should be 12 heads originally. But from the space between 8 heads, we cannot deny the possibility there may be 13 heads originally, if these heads are painted at equal distance.

〔3〕Maybe they are "flying victories" which can be found in late antique Roman and Parthian art and mediaeval Persian royal art. See Z. Gulácsi, *Mediaeval Manichaean Book Art: A Codicological Study of Iranian and Turkic Illuminated Book Fragments from 8th–11th Century East Central Asia*, p.44.

〔4〕H.-J. Klimkeit (tr. by Lin Wushu), 古代摩尼教艺术 (*Manichaean Art and Calligraphy*), Plate 33a; Z. Gulácsi, *Manichaean Art in Berlin Collection*, p.105.

embellished with Pearl Roundel on the edge; and more interesting, there is a small head image with the same headgear atop the fan. Behind the small head, there is another fan-shaped ornament tri-colored in brown, golden and blue. As to this small head, Prof. Klimkeit believes it's an accessory on the main god's headgear, but Prof. Gulácsi thinks it a part of the tricolor fan-shaped ornament as a replacement of a golden disk usually seen[1]. From the shape of the tricolor fan, it might be a headgear. But the small head is more likely to be a part of the main god's headgear. This head is painted at the lower part of the tricolor fan and closer to the Pearl Roundel edge of the main god's headgear, which makes it more like an integral part of the god's headgear. In addition, from the pattern of the blue fan-shaped headgear we know that the golden disk is usually set in the center of the fan. So if the small head is just a replacement of golden disk, it should be in the center, not at the lower position. There is a divine being with golden wing on each side of the tricolor fan. The main part of their headgears is similar to that of MIK III 7283, also with a gilded blue fan-shaped ornament. On the right side of the main god, there is a flanking divine being with the same fan-shaped headgear.

There are two gods on the verso of miniature MIK III 134 (Fig.4) [2]. The one dressed in red on the right has a headgear. The main part of this headgear is the same as that of MIK III 7283, but the central golden disk is styled as a flower. It is noteworthy that behind the main part of the headgear, there is a dark red remnant with black decorations. It's hard to tell if it is also the same fan-shaped ornament, but in different color.

We find another god's headgear painted at the bottom of the recto of

〔1〕H.-J. Klimkeit (tr. by Lin Wushu), 古代摩尼教艺术 (*Manichaean Art and Calligraphy*), p.74; Z. Gulácsi, *Manichaean Art in Berlin Collection*, p.107.

〔2〕Z. Gulácsi, Manichaean Art in Berlin Collection, p.101.

MIK III 4959 (Fig.5)[1], which can be matched with that of MIK III 7283. Without a fan-shaped ornament, this headgear only has a golden disk in the middle surrounded with upward curving white accessory, and the white accessory is outlined in black. The god with this headgear is identified as the Maiden of Light[2]. At the margin of fragment M 23 (Fig.6)[3], there is also a headgear in similar shape as that of MIK III 4959. On the recto of M 23, a footed round plate is drawn with some symbolic food on it[4], and a headgear placed in the middle: a flower-shaped disk surrounded with upward curving white accessory outlined by black lines. At the margin of the recto of *Hūyadagmān* fragment M 223, there is a round plate, but only the foot remains (Fig.7)[5]. With the same pattern of the foot, this plate may be similar to that of M 23, so perhaps there is also a similar headgear on the plate.

The headgears in above-mentioned miniatures are either identical or share a similar main part with that of MIK III7283. We can't judge the identity, title or gender of the headgears' owners, but they are apparently all gods from the Light Kingdom, and some are goddesses. Therefore, the head images on plates in MIK III 7283 should be light beings, even if they have no haloes. Such headgears are often seen in Manichaean artworks of Chotcho. Though the overall appearance of them is not completely identical, their main parts are the same. It's believed that the headgear motif of MIK

[1] Z. Gulácsi, Manichaean Art in Berlin Collection, p.80; idem, Mediaeval Manichaean Book Art: A Codicological Study of Iranian and Turkic Illuminated *Book* Fragments from 8th–11th Century East Central Asia, p.193.

[2] H.-J. Klimkeit (tr. by Lin Wushu), 古代摩尼教艺术 (*Manichaean Art and Calligraphy*), p.67.

[3] M. Boyce, A Catalogue of the Iranian Manuscripts in Manichaean Script in the German Turfan Collection, p.3; Z. Gulácsi, Manichaean Art in Berlin Collection, p.19.

[4] Z. Gulácsi, "Dating the 'Persian' and Chinese Style Remains of Uygur Manichaean Art: A New Radiocarbon Date and Its Implications for Central Asian Art History", *Arts Asiatiques*, Tirage à part, Tome 58-2003, pp.5-33.

[5] Z. Gulácsi, Manichaean Art in Berlin Collection, p.23.

III 7283 must be typical and important in Chotcho Manichaean arts, which were apparently not created randomly by the painters. It should carry some special connotations, and has its own religious source. The prototype of Mani's headgear can be traced back to the headgear of Uighur aristocrat[1], and the headgear discussed here may have something to do with the Manichaean cult of "the Sun and Moon".

The headgear of MIK III7283 consists of two parts: a golden disk in the middle, and a white crescent-shaped ornament supporting it. The colors of the two parts correspond to those of the sun and the moon. And the shape of the headgear is like, a motif with the sun resting on the crescent moon (for convenience, we call it pattern A in this paper). The sun and the moon not only have significance in Manichaean teachings[2], but also stand for the light gods: the sun for the Third Messenger, the moon for Jesus the Splendor and Mani[3]. The importance of "the sun and the moon" in religious teachings will be certainly reflected in art, just like the cross symbol of Nestorianism. In a Nestorian portrait of Jesus Christ found in Dunhuang (Fig.8), cross motifs are shown on his headgear, necklace and staff, which verifies the narrations preserved in the inscription of Daxingguo Monastery in Zhenjiang that the cross symbol should be set up in the house, painted in the chapel, worn on the head and hung on the

〔1〕王媛媛 Wang Yuanyuan, 庇麻与头冠——高昌摩尼教圣像艺术的宗教功能（"Bema and Headgear: Religious Function of Manichaean Iconic Images of Chotcho"）, 张广达先生八十华诞祝寿论文集 (*Festschrift for Prof. Zhuang Guangda's 80th Birthday*), Taipei, 2010, pp.1085–1129.

〔2〕马小鹤 Ma Xiaohe & 芮传明 Rui Chuanming, 摩尼教"朝拜日夜拜月"研究——粟特文 myδry（密思拉）和'yšw（耶稣）考释（"On Manichaean Ritual of Worshipping the Sun in the Morning and the Moon in the night: Studies on Sogdian Terms myδry and 'yšw"）, 学术集林 (*Xueshu Jilin*)15, 1999, pp.263–281; idem, 摩尼教"朝拜日夜拜月"研究（下篇）（"On Manichaean Ritual of Worshipping the Sun in the Morning and the Moon in the night(II)）, 学术集林 (*Xueshu Jilin*)16, 1999, pp.326–343.

〔3〕W. Sundermann, Mitteliranische manichäische Texte kirchengeschichtlichen Inhalts (Berliner Turfantexte XI), Berlin, 1981, pp.45–49; H. –J. Klimkeit, Gnosis on the Silk Road. Gnostic Texts from Central Asia, pp.209–211.

breast[1]. Similarly, the sun and moon in Manichaean context will also provide artistic inspiration to the painters of Chotcho. Moreover, crown decorated with the motif of the sun and moon has a long history in Persia, the cradle of Manichaeism. Some deities worshipped in Central Asia also had headgears with the sun and moon, and it' s even believed that the Khans of the First Turkish Khanate also had such crown[2]. It' s unknown whether Manichaean headgear decorated with the sun and moon was inspired by that.

What's worth noting is that the motif of the sun and moon is common in Chotcho Manichaean art. In the above-mentioned fragment MIK III 4965, there are three golden motifs of the sun and moon and two golden disks along the margin of the miniature. Furthermore, in Manichaean murals and illustrations unearthed in Turfan, we notice some haloes shaped as the sun and moon, but in a slightly different form from pattern A. It's usually painted as , in which the sun is bigger and the moon is more slim and curving, almost encircling the whole sun (we call it pattern B here). The typical example is the halo of Mani showed in the large-scaled mural MIK III 6918 (Fig.9) found in the site of K temple in Chotcho. On the recto (?) of fragment MIK III 4965, the main god is surrounded by five-tiered haloes, and the outermost layer is shaped as a golden crescent, thus making the whole five-tier in the form of pattern B. Such halo is also seen on the recto of manuscript MIK III 6626 & MIK III 6379c (Fig.10)[3]. In this fragment, the main god's facial feature is unclear but we can figure out the shape of

[1] 至顺镇江志 *History of Zhenjiang of Zhishun Era*, Vol.9, Nanjing, Jiangsu Chinese Classics Publishing House, 1999, p.365.

[2] 陈凌 Chen Ling, 突厥王冠考——兼论突厥祆教崇拜的有关问题（"Turkish Crown: Some Problems Concerning Turkish Zoroastrian Belief"), 欧亚学刊 (*Euroasian Studies*) 8, 2008, pp.127–157. It's concluded in this paper the crown of Turkish Khan decorated with the sun and moon pattern has something to do with Zoroastrian Belief .

[3] Z. Gulácsi, Manichaean Art in Berlin Collection, p.109.

the halo from the remaining golden pigment. The main god is surrounded by a red halo. Outside of it, a golden crescent is still traceable. In a textile fragment MIK III 6270 (Fig.11)[1] unearthed in K Temple, there is an elect in white who has an oval-shaped mandorla and a halo styled in pattern B. But the crescent stretches up much longer, which makes the pattern not very standardized. Art is a creative activity, and allows exaggeration and deformation. Motifs of the sun and moon in Chotcho Manichaean arts, although not in a very uniform style, share the same religious connotation and inspiration. Therefore, the important role of the sun and moon in Manichaean teachings and artworks may be a key factor that forms the pattern of headgear in MIK III 7283.

7.2 Goddess image of MIK III 7283 and the Badges Decorated with Goddess Portraits on the Elects' Gowns

As to the symbolic meaning of female heads in MIK III 7283, Prof. Gulácsi is of the view that it can be interpreted to personify the presence of light in food offerings[2].We agree with this view because the golden plate under the head indeed conveys such religious idea.

In Chotcho Manichaean miniatures, plates piling with food or symbolic food are usually depicted. For example, in the scene of Bema Festival on the verso of MIK III 4979 (Fig.12)[3], there is a footed golden round plate in the center, with fruits on it. The verso of MIK III 6257 may also be a celebration scene of Bema (Fig.13)[4]: two elects in white facing a pile of pomegranates and grapes, with a reddish-brown plate filled with breads on

〔1〕H.-J. Klimkeit (tr. by Lin Wushu), 古代摩尼教艺术 (*Manichaean Art and Calligraphy*), Plate 46; Z. Gulácsi, *Manichaean Art in Berlin Collection*, p.173.

〔2〕Z. Gulácsi, Manichaean Art in Berlin Collection, p.112.

〔3〕H.-J. Klimkeit (tr. by Lin Wushu), 古代摩尼教艺术 (*Manichaean Art and Calligraphy*), Plate 21; Z. Gulácsi, *Manichaean Art in Berlin Collection*, p.71.

〔4〕Z. Gulácsi, Manichaean Art in Berlin Collection, p.77.

one side. Judging from some golden pigments barely visible on the plate, it was gilded originally. On the recto of fragment MIK III 4959 (Fig.5)[1], there is a god on the upper right, holding in his right hand a golden plate very similar to that of MIK III 7283, with a fish on it. On the recto of fragment MIK III 6258a (Fig.14)[2], we see a topless figure holding a golden plate in his right hand. This plate is also outlined with red color, just as that of MIK III 7283, but it's a pity we cannot tell if there is anything on the plate. On the recto of MIK III 4974 (Fig.15)[3], there are two elects in white and two auditors, and a plate is shown at the lower part of this picture, possibly with food on it too. Besides, plates also appear on the margin of some manuscripts as decorations, such as the footed carved plates in M23 and M223, the simple round plates (with feet) in M 171 (Fig.16)[4], MIK III 7266 (Fig.17)[5], MIK III 4981a (Fig.18)[6] carrying with some flower or disk patterns possibly as symbolistic food. Of course, there is one exception, an illustration in a Sogdian Manichaean letter (81TB65:1) found in Grotto No. 65 of Bezklik (Fig.19)[7]. In this illustration, there are two goddesses standing on lotus, and a line of golden words is written vertically between them. There is a semi-elliptical blank space formed by red ribbon above the words, and atop the blank space placing a golden plate in the same pattern with that of MIK III 7283. In the plate is a crown, not food or symbolic food. This exception, however, is not enough to challenge the point that plates in

---

[1] H.-J. Klimkeit (tr. by Lin Wushu), 古代摩尼教艺术 (*Manichaean Art and Calligraphy*), Plate 23; Z. Gulácsi, *Manichaean Art in Berlin Collection*, p.80.

[2] Z. Gulácsi, Manichaean Art in Berlin Collection, p.82.

[3] H.-J. Klimkeit (tr. by Lin Wushu), 古代摩尼教艺术 (*Manichaean Art and Calligraphy*), Plate 28; Z. Gulácsi, *Manichaean Art in Berlin Collection*, p.84.

[4] Z. Gulácsi, Manichaean Art in Berlin Collection, p.27.

[5] Z. Gulácsi, *Manichaean Art in Berlin Collection*, p.54. Prof. Gulácsi thinks the red footed plate on this fragment contains food. But it may be symbolistic food.

[6] Z. Gulácsi, Manichaean Art in Berlin Collection, p.167.

[7] As to the plate of this letter, please refer to the first page of 吐鲁番新出摩尼教文献研究 (*Studies on Manichaean Manuscripts Newly-discovered in Turfan*), Beijing, Cultural Relics Press, 2000.

Manichaean arts are usually for carrying food or symbolic food. We think the female heads on golden plates in MIK III 7283 may also be a symbol of food. Using heads with divinity to represent food perhaps imply the divinity of food, and such divinity is obviously light particle, because Manichaean elects firmly believe their food contains rich light particles[1].

In Manichaean myth, incarnation of the light particles in the world is the five sons of "the First Man" (Ohrmizd in Iranian texts, or in the Turkish Xormuzda), who are named as "五明 (the Five Lights)" in Chinese Manichaean texts. To fight the invading Darkness, the Father of Light called forth the Mother of Life, who then evoked "the First Man". The First Man participated in the battle equipped with five divine powers as his sons or arms. These divine powers are five light elements, namely Ether, Wind, Light, Water and Fire. The First Man offered himself up as a bait for the Darkness in order to temporarily satisfy their greed and annihilate them for ever. The forces of Darkness seized the light elements, tore them apart and devoured them. After that, a mixture of light and darkness appeared, and that, is the actual state of the World[2]. Such scene is not only described vividly in Chinese Manichaean *Traité*[3], but also preserved in some Manichaean manuscripts unearthed in Turfan. Parthian fragment M 710 & M 5877(= T II D 138c) records the battle between the First Man and the forces of Darkness:

> Out of pity…
> He (First Man) put on a body…
> The first garb of [the God] Ohrmizd;

---

[1] M. Boyce, A Reader in Manichaean Middle Persian and Parthian, p.107, n.2.

[2] H. –J. Klimkeit, Gnosis on the Silk Road. Gnostic Texts from Central Asia, p.10.

[3]〈摩尼教残经〉释文 (Text of *Traité*), See Lin Wushu, 摩尼教及其东渐 (*Manichaeism and Its Eastward Expansion*), Taipei, Shuxin Press, 1997, p.268; as to the latest version of the text of *Traité*, please refer to Lin Wushu, 敦煌文书与夷教研究 (*Dunhuang Documents and Studies on Persian Religions*), Shanghai Chinese Classics Publishing House, 2011, pp.409–410.

When he had clothed the enemy with (his) five sons,
He surrendered (his) soul to the Darkness;
He sacrificed his own soul;
He scattered (his limbs) for the sake of (his) sons.
He bound the enemies, he brought (his) sons to life,
And with gentleness he redeemed the Kingdom.
[Then] came the beneficent Father [with his] brothers
And [saved] his own Light.[1]

From the above we know the five sons of the First Man are also his own soul, or the Living Soul[2]. In Parthian text M7, there is a conversation between Zarathustra and his own soul. Zarathustra here is one of the prophets in Manichaean myth and has nothing to do with Zoroastrianism. His soul is the light elements imprisoned in the world:

When the saviors, the righteous Zarathustra, spoke with his soul (*grīv*), (he said):

"Deep is the drunken stupor in which you sleep; awake and look at me.

From the World of Peace, from which I have been sent for your sake: "Hail!"

And it (the Living Soul), answered, "I, I am the tender, innocent son of Srōshāvd.

I am in the state of impurity, and I endure suffering. Lead me out of the grasp of death."

Zarathustra said: "Hail", and out to it the age-old question: "Are you my limb? "

[1] M. Boyce, A Reader in Manichaean Middle Persian and Parthian, pp.97–98; H.–J. Klimkeit, Gnosis on the Silk Road: Gnostic Parables, Hymns & Prayers from Central Asia, p.37.

[2] Also see M. Heuser, "The Manichaean Myth according to the Coptic Source", M. Heuser & H.–J. Klimkeit, *Studies in Manichaean Literature and Art*, pp.36–37.

"The power of the living and the salvation of the highest worlds come upon you, from your home.

Follow me, son of mildness, and set the wreath of Light upon your head,

You son of mighty ones that has become so poor that you must go begging in every place…"[1]

Here, Zarathustra calls the light elements "son of mildness", while the light elements addresses itself as son of Srōshāvd, probably to emphasize its origin in the Light Kingdom. In a Parthian hymn to the Living Soul, the light elements in divine meal is called "the Son of God"[2]. There are many other verses on the light elements which cannot be quoted all, but we can summarize that in the eyes of Manichaean followers, light elements (or "五明子" in Chinese, namely the Five Light Sons) are sons of the First Man. Logically, it's assumed the light elements should be a male image in Manichaean arts, but as MIK III 7283, it's depicted as female instead. Although the Maiden of Light was regarded as "Fire", one of the First Man's sons in early Manichaean Coptic literatures, it cannot be taken as the religious basis for depicting the light elements as female images. First, we shall not apply the situation of Coptic Manichaean churches in the 4th century to Uighur Manichaean communities in 8/9-11 centuries; secondly, "Fire"is just one of the five sons of the First Man, and therefore cannot represent all the light elements. Moreover, depicting the light elements as

---

〔1〕F.C. Andreas & W. B. Henning, "Mitteliranische Manichaica aus chinesisch-Turkestan III", Sitzungsberichte der (Königlich-) Preussischen Akademie der Wissenschaften Philosophisch-Historische Klasse, Berlin, 1934, p.872; M. Boyce, A Reader in Manichaean Middle Persian and Parthian, p.108; H.-J. Klimkeit, Gnosis on the Silk Road: Gnostic Parables, Hymns & Prayers from Central Asia, pp.47–48.

〔2〕The original sentence in M7 is: Invite the Son of God as a guest to the divine meal. "The Son of God" here refers to the Living Soul, namely the light elements. See F.C. Andreas & W. B. Henning, "Mitteliranische Manichaica aus chinesisch-Turkestan III", p.870; M. Boyce, *A Reader in Manichaean Middle Persian and Parthian*, p.107 and n.2; H.-J. Klimkeit, *Gnosis on the Silk Road: Gnostic Parables, Hymns & Prayers from Central Asia*, p.47 and p.53, n.28.

female images contradicts with the constant attitude of the Manichees towards women.

There are two eminent goddesses in Manichaean myth, the Mother of Life and the Maiden of Light, and some hymns to them were found in Turfan. They are, however, the only two female deities in this religion[1], far too few compared to other religions. Generally, the Manichaeans were warned to keep away from women, even with a sense of revulsion at women. Prof. Rui Chuanming points out the Manichaeans, consciously or unconsciously, attributes all evils to feminine or female characters[2]. This must result from an idea that the Demoness *Āz* was "the mother of all devils", who captured light particles and imprisoned them in the human body:

> *Āz*, (the Demoness of Greed), [that] evil mother of all demons, grew angry, and she stirred up great turmoil to aid her own soul.
>
> And from the impurity of the demons and from the filth of the she-demons she fashioned the body and entered into it herself.
>
> Then she formed the good soul from the five Light Elements, the armor of the Lord Ohrmizd, and bound it within the body.
>
> She (*Āz*) made him (the first person) as though blind and deaf, senseless and confused so that he might not know his origin and his family.
>
> She created the body as the prison, she fettered the miserable soul.

---

[1] P. Bryder, The Chinese Transformation of Manichaeism. A study of Chinese Manichaean Terminology, p.91.

[2] 芮传明 Rui Chuanming, 摩尼教性观念源流考 ("On the Origin of Manichaean Sexual Attitude"), 社会科学(*Social Sciences*) 2 (2006), pp.76–87; idem, 摩尼教 Hylè、Âz、贪魔考 ("On Manichaean Hylè, Âz, and the Demon of Greed"), 史林 (*Shi Lin*) 5 (2006), pp.88–99. Occasionally, Manichaean literatures reflect some non-negative features of women. Please refer to M. Franzmann, "Beyond the Stereotypes: Female Characters and Imagery in Manichaean Cosmology and Story", *The Australian Academy of the Humanities. The Trendall Lecture 2007*, Canberra: The Australia Academy of the Humanities, 2008, pp.145–159.

(It cried out): "The captors, the demons, she-demons and all the she-devils, are cruel to me."

She fettered the soul firmly to the accursed body; she filled it with hate and sin, anger and vengeance.[1]

This paragraph describes the creation of Man by *Āz*, and "the first person" refers to Adam. As we all know, salvation is the core tenet of Manichaeism. The reason gods were called forth to come to the world and rescue people is that *Āz* imprisoned light elements within the human body, which is the very root of all evils. This concept is also presented in Manichaean literatures. A Middle Persian parable M46 tells a story that a daughter of a king had lovesickness for an outstanding young man, and the king then sent people to catch the youth hiding in the tree. Finally the youth was tricked by an old woman down to the ground, and imprisoned by the king[2]. This young man stands for soul imprisoned in the human body or light elements in the world, the princess stands for greed[3], and the old lady may be embodiment of the Realm of Darkness[4]. There is no doubt that all females in this story, old and young, are symbols of greed and evil.

---

[1] W. B. Henning, "Ein manichäischer kosmogonischer Hymnus", Nachrichten der Gesellschafte der Wissenschaften in Göttingen, Berlin, 1932, pp.214–228; M. Boyce, A Reader in Manichaean Middle Persian and Parthian, p.100; H.-J. Klimkeit, Gnosis on the Silk Road: Gnostic Parables, Hymns & Prayers from Central Asia, pp.38–39. The creation of Man is detailed in Parthian manuscript M7980–7984, see M. Boyce, A Reader in Manichaean Middle Persian and Parthian, pp.71–74; H.-J. Klimkeit, Gnosis on the Silk Road: Gnostic Parables, Hymns & Prayers from Central Asia, pp232–233.

[2] W. Sundermann, Mittelpersische und parthische kosmogonische und Pararabeltexte der Manichäer mit einigen Bemerkungen zu Motiven der Parabeltexte von Friedmar Geissler (Berliner Turfantexte IV), Berlin, 1973, pp.84–86; H.-J. Klimkeit, Gnosis on the Silk Road: Gnostic Parables, Hymns & Prayers from Central Asia, pp.187–189.

[3] Schmidt-Glinzer, Chinesische Manichaica. Mit textkritischen Anmerkungen und einem Glossar, Wiesbaden, 1987, p.79.

[4] H.-J. Klimkeit, *Gnosis on the Silk Road: Gnostic Parables, Hymns & Prayers from Central Asia*, p.188. Prof. M. Franzmann argues that the old lady is a key role driving the plot. Though she is a representative of Darkness, she exhibits a kind of wisdom even more powerful than the Light. See M. Franzmann, "Beyond the Stereotypes: Female Characters and Imagery in Manichaean Cosmology and Story", p.157.

Mani's early missionary activity includes sending his disciple Addā to the Roman Empire. A Sogdian manuscript records Mani's commandment for the disciple: first, Addā is commanded to "take of nothing more than you need, you should rather remain in poverty and blessedness which is the foundation of all bliss", and then Mani "spoke of association with women and gave exhaustive instructions concerning this matter"[1]. Therefore, we can see how important it is to properly deal with women in the view of the Manichaeans, and what they do is keep themselves away from women. Middle Persian fragment M2 is on Ammō, another disciple of Mani, who was sent on a mission to the East. When Ammō arrived at the border of Kushan, a goddess of Xwārāsān named Bagārd appeared in front of him, trying to stop him. In reply to the question by the goddess, Ammō mentioned the commandments of Manichaeism: "we don't eat meat nor drink wine. We also keep away from women"[2]. Parthian manuscript M 4577 warns the male elects when they occasionally need women to cook, they should treat them as servants, avoiding drawing fire on themselves[3]. In Chinese Manichaean *Traité*, we also find a similar precept: "远离调悔、戏笑及以诤论……能于女人作虚假想，不为诸色之所留难，如鸟高飞，不殉罗网 (und die Frauen vermögen sie als leere und trügerische Erscheinungen anzusehen; die sinnlichen Ein-drücke können sie nicht ablenken oder hindern, wie ein hochfliegender Vogel finden sie nicht in

〔1〕See fragment labeled So.13,941(=T II K)&So.14,285(=T II D 136), W. Sundermann, Mitteliranische manichäische Texte kirchengeschichtlichen Inhalts, pp.34–36; H.-J. Klimkeit, Gnosis on the Silk Road: Gnostic Parables, Hymns & Prayers from Central Asia, pp.203.

〔2〕F. C. Andreas & W. B. Henning, "Mitteliranische Manichaica aus Chinesisch-Turkestan II", pp.302–306; M. Boyce, *A Reader in Manichaean Middle Persian and Parthian*, pp. 39–42; H. -J. Klimkeit, *Gnosis on the Silk Road: Gnostic Parables, Hymns & Prayers from Central Asia*, pp.203–205.

〔3〕W. Sundermann, Mitteliranische manichäische Texte kirchengeschichtlichen Inhalts, p.61.

Netzen der Torheit den Tod)."[1]

Given the Manichaean negative attitude towards women, it's quite unbelievable that the light elements can be personified as female. This is not only contradictory with the image of light particles which should be male in the original teachings, but also inconsistent with the negative attitude towards women. As sons of the First Man, light elements are from the Light Kingdom, with divinity inborn. Even after they are mixed with darkness, they are still holy. But Manichaeism always takes women as symbol of lust, greed and other evil natures. The contradiction between religious teachings and arts is reflected not only in written works, but also in Manichaean garment decoration of Chotcho Church.

In the large-scale wall painting MIK III 6918 found in Chotcho, there is a square badge (*segmentum*) depicting a bust of a goddess under the left shoulder of Mani[2]. Another fragmentary wall-painting MIK III 6917 (Fig.20) found in ruin K shows a white gown decorated with a round badge (*orbiculum*), also bearing a head of a goddess[3]. What's more, Prof. Jorinde Ebert published a cotton-painting MIK III 6606 (Fig.21a and b) in her paper, and she thinks in this fragment there is a *segmentum* with a portrait of a goddess under the left should of the figure. In his archeological report, Grünwedel offered a line drawing of a wall painting discovered in Chotcho (Fig.22). On the gown of the main figure, under the right shoulder, there is

---

〔1〕《摩尼教残经》释文 (Text of *Traité*), See Lin Wushu, 摩尼教及其东渐 (*Manichaeism and Its Eastward Expansion*), p.280; also in idem, 敦煌文书与夷教研究 (*Dunhuang Documents and Studies on Persian Religions*), p.425. German translation see Schmidt-Glinzer, *Chinesische Manichaica. Mit textkritischen Anmerkungen und einem Glossar*, p.100.

〔2〕Jorinde Ebert, "Segmentum and Clavus in Manichaean Garments of the Turfan Oasis", D. Durkin-Meisterernst, S.-Ch. Raschmann, J. Wilkens, M. Yaldiz, P. Zieme (eds.), *Turfan Revisited-The First Century of Research into the Arts and Culture of the Silk Road*, Berlin, 2004, p.75.

〔3〕H.-J. Klimkeit (tr. by Lin Wushu), 古代摩尼教艺术 (*Manichaean Art and Calligraphy*), pp.58-59; Z. Gulácsi, *Manichaean Art in Berlin Collection*, p. 205.

also a *segmentum* of a goddess[1]. With reference to the badges on Christian ceremonial gowns, Prof. Ebert concludes that the above-mentioned *segmenta* or *orbicula* are symbols of the ranks or positions of Manichaean elects, and those bearing the badges are church dignitaries, i.e., 慕阇 (Teacher, MP *hammōzagān*), 拂多诞 (Bishop, MP *ispasagān*) and 默奚悉德 (Presbyter, MP *mahistagān*), the first three grades listed in Chinese Manichaean *Compendium*.

Ceremonial garments decorated with a badge of female head are rarely found in other religions. Western Christian costume has badges but barely with a female portrait, and no female Bodhisattva or immortal can be found on Buddhist kasaya or Taoist robe too. It's reasonable to assume that unless the goddess is acknowledged as a very important one in and outside the religion, it will be against the commandment for a monachal person to wear a gown with female portrait on it. Such practice, if we take Buddhism for example, undoubtedly makes a mockery of that famous terminology "yad rupam sa sunyata, yad sunyata sa rupam".

To sum up, personifying the light elements as female which is against Manichaean tradition and precepts might reflect that, the status of goddess (especially the Maiden of Light) in Chotcho Church was improved compared to the earlier period. No matter what the followers' actual attitude towards women was, they at least showed respect to goddesses. That may be also related to the increasing number of female followers in Chotcho Manichaean communities.

7.3 Worship of the Maiden of Light and the Female Manichaeans

As to the identity of the goddess on those *segmenta* or *orbicula*, there are

[1] Jorinde Ebert, "Segmentum and Clavus in Manichaean Garments of the Turfan Oasis", pp.73, 77.

two speculations: the personification of the Manichaean church as a "heavenly queen" in Chotcho or a representation of the Maiden of Light[1]. We are inclined to view it an image of the Maiden of Light.

As previously mentioned, there are only two goddesses in Manichaean myth. The Mother of Life is comparatively less influential than the Maiden of Light in the process of salvation[2]. The Maiden of Light was called forth by the Third Messenger, who seduced the male demons with her naked body. She then resided in the moon with Jesus the Splendor and the First Man, forming a triad of redeeming deities[3]. We learn from some Turfan manuscripts that the Maiden of Light not only enjoyed a high position in the pantheon of Chotcho Church, but also had some special spiritual relations with church leaders, including Mani himself.

In fragment M 38, a Parthian prayer, Mani is invoked as Maitreya, uniting with the dual divinity of Jesus and the Maiden of Light:

> ...Great Maitreya, noble Messenger of the gods, interpreter of the religion, ...Jesus—Maiden of Light, Mār Mani, Jesus—Maiden of Light—Mār Mani, have [mercy] upon me, oh merciful Bringer of Light! Redeem my soul from this cycle rebirth, redeem my soul from [this] cycle of rebirths...[4]

In the prayers to the church dignitaries, followers should first invoke the

---

[1] Jorinde Ebert, "Segmentum and Clavus in Manichaean Garments of the Turfan Oasis", pp.72–83,77.

[2] P. Bryder, The Chinese transformation of Manichaeism. A study of Chinese Manichaean Terminology, p.92.

[3] M. Heuser, "The Manichaean Myth According to the Coptic Source", M. Heuser & H.-J. Klimkeit, *Studies in Manichaean Literature and Art*, pp.43, 99.

[4] F. W. K. Müller, Handschriften-Reste in Estrangelo-Schrift aus Turfan, Chinesisch-Turkistan II. Teil, (Abhandlungen der (Königlich) Preussischen Akademie der Wissenschaften, Philosophisch-Historische Klasse, 1904/2, pp. 7–117), Berlin, 1904, p.77; M. Boyce, A Reader in Manichaean Middle Persian and Parthian, p.196; H.-J. Klimkeit, Gnosis on the Silk Road: Gnostic Parables, Hymns & Prayers from Central Asia, pp.162–163.

Father, and then Jesus, the Maiden of Light and Vahmen[1]:

Highest God, immortal Lord, (you) kings, (you) two enthroned luminaries, strong and mighty Srōshahrāy, redeemer of souls, Lord Mani, you three divinely created rulers: [1] eternally loving redeemer Jesus, [2] beautiful, noble Maiden of Light, [3] highest of those that come, bright Vahman: these almighty gods, endowed with wondrous power, these strong deities, may they bestow powerful new blessing, cheerfulness and new joy upon us…(and furthermore) happiness and new salvation! [2]

Jesus, the Maiden of Light and Vahmen, who could bless the church dignitaries and the followers, are often evoked as a triad of redeeming deities in Chotcho Manichaean hymns. In this group, the Maiden of Light is the one and only female deity. Similar invocation can be found in another hymn:

May love, redemption and divinity, wisdom, insight and knowledge of the Father, of the Son and of the Holy Spirit come from the Messenger of Light, and from Jesus, the Maiden (of Light) and Vahman. [3]

M 31 is a Middle Persian hymn to the Teacher. It says:

May [blessing] come from the three who are to come, the

〔1〕Vahmen was usually evoked during the enthronement of the dignitaries in Chotcho Church. See H.-J. Klimkeit, *Gnosis on the Silk Road: Gnostic Parables, Hymns & Prayers from Central Asia*, p.91; idem, "Manichaean Kingship: Gnosis at Home in the World", M. Heuser & H.-J. Klimkeit, *Studies in Manichaean Literature and Art*, p.212.

〔2〕Please refer to manuscript M 74, F. W. K. Müller, Handschriften-Reste in Estrangelo-Schrift aus Turfan, Chinesisch-Turkistan II. Teil, p.75; M. Boyce, A Reader in Manichaean Middle Persian and Parthian, p.194; H.-J. Klimkeit, Gnosis on the Silk Road: Gnostic Parables, Hymns & Prayers from Central Asia, pp.161-162.

〔3〕See fragment M 729, F. C. Andreas & W. B. Henning, "Mitteliranische Manichaica aus Chinesisch-Turkestan II", pp.330-333; M. Boyce, *A Reader in Manichaean Middle Persian and Parthian*, p.150; H. -J. Klimkeit, *Gnosis on the Silk Road: Gnostic Parables, Hymns & Prayers from Central Asia*, p.96.

redeemers of our souls. Brothers, messengers and spirits, bless this teacher of exalted name whom Vahman has sent us. [1]

In addition, the Maiden of Light was related to some important ceremonies of Chotcho Church, especially the church leader's inauguration. She was evoked in a hymn for the installation of a Teacher:

> (Praise to) you, new teacher of the East and the leader of those of the good religion. For, in the race of rulers, you are born under a happy star. The three [who are to come]: Jesus, the Maiden (of Light) and Vahman... [2]

In these texts, the Maiden of Light appears to be the only female deity that is closely related to Mani, the church leaders and daily religious practice. So we have reason to believe that the female figure on those *segmenta* or *orbicula* is the Maiden of Light. According to Prof. Ebert, the gowns decorated with female portrait were displayed on the occasion of grand festive gatherings. [3] A Teacher's inauguration is certainly such an important occasion. Since the Maiden of Light is evoked in the installation hymn, it's no better choice for the Teacher than wearing a ceremonial cloak with the goddess image on this occasion. Choosing the portrait of the Maiden of Light as decoration is probably due to her eminent position in the pantheon.

The worship of goddess was very popular in ancient times, because the Mother God played an important role in the psychological world of

---

〔1〕F. C. Andreas & W. B. Henning, "Mitteliranische Manichaica aus Chinesisch–Turkestan II", pp.328–329; M. Boyce, *A Reader in Manichaean Middle Persian and Parthian*, p.147; H. –J. Klimkeit, *Gnosis on the Silk Road: Gnostic Parables, Hymns & Prayers from Central Asia*, p.94.

〔2〕Please refer to Middle Persian manuscript M 543, F. W. K. Müller, Handschriften–Reste in Estrangelo–Schrift aus Turfan, Chinesisch–Turkistan II. Teil, p.79; M. Boyce, A Reader in Manichaean Middle Persian and Parthian, p.149; H.–J. Klimkeit, Gnosis on the Silk Road: Gnostic Parables, Hymns & Prayers from Central Asia, p.95.

〔3〕Jorinde Ebert, "Segmentum and Clavus in Manichaean Garments of the Turfan Oasis", p.81.

primitive man[1]. Female deity was respected as the origin of all creatures, and viewed as the key power associated with seasonal changes and the cycle of life and death[2]. Many goddesses are recorded in ancient Chinese classics, and they can be grouped into three types: primitive goddess, goddess of sorcery and goddess as human ancestor[3]. Under the patriarchal system, however, female deities were gradually subordinate to male deities. In Manichaean myth, as the first goddess in the process of salvation, the Mother of Life was emanated from the Father of Light. Female deity being issued from the male deity and the asexual means of emanation show that Manichaeism didn't attach importance to goddess from the start, which resulted in the secondary position of goddess. It's imaginable that in early Manichaean Church the worship of the Maiden of Light was not valued. But in the Church of Chotcho, mainly thanks to her religious function, the Maiden of Light played a more important role than before. In other words, some religious functions of the goddess became more attractive to the followers of Chotcho, and as long as she performed the functions, the followers would be blessed or their wishes would become true. Only in this way could the Maiden of Light have more adherents, hence upgrading her status in the pantheon.

Among the religious functions of The Maiden of Light, besides bringing bliss to the church and its leaders, the charisma to the Chotcho Manichees is surely not her beauty as the seduction to demons, but her

〔1〕Erich Neumann (tr. by 李以洪 Li Yihong), 大母神——原型分析 (*The Great Mother: an Analysis of the Archetype*), Beijing, Orient Press, 1998, p.89.

〔2〕Marija Gimbutas (tr. by 叶舒宪 Ye Shuxian etc.), 活着的女神 (*The Living Goddesses: Religion in Pre-patriarchal Europe*), Guilin, Guangxi Normal University Press, 2008, pp.11, 120.

〔3〕谢选骏 Xie Xuanjun, 中国古籍中的女神——她们的生活、爱情、文化象征("Goddesses in Ancient Chinese Classics: Their life, Romance and Cultural Symbol"), in 王孝廉 Wang Xiaolian &吴继文 Wu Jiwen (eds.), 神与神话 (*Gods and Mythology*), Taipei, 1988, pp.177-190.

releasing the soul of the dead to the Realm of Light[1]. This divine power is described in the hymn on the verso of a Middle Persian fragment M 727 a. It' s stressed that the soul can only go to the heaven with the help of the Father and the Maiden of Light:

> ...the corrupt heresies and (false) teachers,
> Mantle, garment, monochrome and multicolored damask,
> The coquetry of women and the songs of joy,
> The truly lovely appearance of orchards and gardens,
> Presents, gifts and promises:
> ——they can not help on the day of distress.
> The image of the Father, of the Maiden of Light,
> This alone can help on the day [of distress].[2]

Here, "the day of distress" refers to the last minute for a dying person, and at that time the Maiden of Light will appear[3]. The main figure on the embroidered textile MIK III 6251 (Fig.23) is identified as the Maiden of Light[4]. She stands under a waning crescent moon, holding an unknown object in her hand. The whole picture can be interpreted as the transmission of the liberated light. Such image reflects precisely the religious function of the goddess as guiding the soul into heaven. The return of redeemed soul to the Realm of Light after death is not only the ultimate purpose of salvation, but also the greatest desire of those Manichaeans. To the followers in

---

[1] Ch. Reck, "Die Beschreibung der Daēnā in einem soghdischen manichäischen Text", C. G. Cereti et al.(eds.), *Religious Themes and Texts of Pre-Islamic Iran and Central Asia*, Wiesbaden, 2003, pp.323-338. Such image is borrowed from goddess Daēnā in Zoroastrianism, See W. Sundermann, "Zoroastrian Motifs in non-Zotroastrian Traditions", *Journal of the Royal Asiatic Society*, Series 3, 18, 2 (2008), pp.160-162.

[2] M. Boyce, A Reader in Manichaean Middle Persian and Parthian, p.173; H.-J. Klimkeit, Gnosis on the Silk Road: Gnostic Parables, Hymns & Prayers from Central Asia, p.126.

[3] C. G. Schmidt & H. J. Polotsky, Ein Mani-Fund in Agypten. Originalschriften des Mani und seiner Schüler, p.72.

[4] H.-J. Klimkeit (tr. by Lin Wushu), 古代摩尼教艺术 (*Manichaean Art and Calligraphy*), plate 47a and p.82; Z. Gulácsi, *Manichaean Art in Berlin Collection*, p.194.

Chotcho Uighur Kingdom, if their motivation behind the cult of the Maiden of Light is mainly because of her function of releasing souls, they are thought to be more interested in eschatology, with keen anticipation for the future world.

Moreover, the virtues of the Maiden of Light may win herself more adherents. According to Manichaean teachings, twelve light gods correspond to different virtues, and the Maiden of Light is related to the virtues of harmony and mildness[1]. A Parthian hymn for the gods on the Moon says:

> Merciful Mother, Maiden of Light, soul of the God Zurvān,
> beloved of the Lights, — (you are) eternally (holy)![2]

The Maiden of Light is also a deity of goodness, which is noted in a hymn to the Light Kingdom:

> Goodness, which is the living spirit, the wisdom of the Father and the splendor of all the gods. You are the revelation of the life of the World of Light, and the first of those revelations, that are full of wondrous power and wisdom. And you caused the spirit of Zurvān to be strengthened.[3]

As a goddess, the Light Maiden's genial nature appears to be charisma to those adherents. We take the worship of Avalokitesvara as an example, which is undoubtedly one of the most popular beliefs in China. In Indian

[1] H.-J. Klimkeit, Gnosis on the Silk Road: Gnostic Parables, Hymns & Prayers from Central Asia, p.78.

[2] Please refer to fragment M 90, E. Waldschmidt & W. Lentz, "Manichäische Dogmatik aus chinesischen und iranischen Texten", *Sitzungsberichte der (Königlich) Preussischen Akademie der Wissenschaften, Philosophisch-Historische Klasse*, 1933, pp.586–588; H. -J. Klimkeit, *Gnosis on the Silk Road: Gnostic Parables, Hymns & Prayers from Central Asia*, p.129.

[3] Please refer to Middle Persian fragment M738, E. Waldschmidt & W. Lentz, "Manichäische Dogmatik aus chinesischen und iranischen Texten", pp.561–562, 599–603; M. Boyce, *A Reader in Manichaean Middle Persian and Parthian*, p.135; H. -J. Klimkeit, *Gnosis on the Silk Road: Gnostic Parables, Hymns & Prayers from Central Asia*, p.80.

Buddhism, Avalokitesvara was represented as a male deity, and then gradually changed into a female after its spread into China. The viewpoint concerning when the change happened is varied. Most think Avalokitesvara in female image appeared late in the period of the 3rd-6th centuries, and after several hundred years, such image prevailed widely in the Song Dynasty〔1〕. After being portrayed as a female deity, Avalokitesvara with her mildness and mercy attracted more Chinese followers, especially women. As female deities, both Avalokitesvara and the Maiden of Light are respected as the personification of leniency and goodness. And the Maiden of Light guiding the soul into heaven is, to a certain extent, similar to the power of Avalokitesvara saving mankind from the sea of miserable life. In terms of the common ground between these two deities, we can imagine, as the cult of Avalokitesvara became prevailing, the belief of the Maiden of Light could also gain a footing in Chotcho Manichaean Church. But her position cannot be overvalued because decorating the ceremonial gown with her portrait doesn't mean the Maiden of Light had greater divine power than other male gods, such the Father of Light, Jesus the Splendor or Mani. Meanwhile, even if the belief of goddess tended to be more popular in Manichaeism, we cannot identify the female heads symboling the light particles on miniature MIK III 7283 as the Maiden of Light before finding valid evidence. The identification of these female images is unknown, but they at least indicate the prevailing belief of the goddess in Chotcho Manichaean Church.

Along with the boom of the goddess cult, the position and number of the female elects and auditors in Chotcho Uighur Kingdom probably increased too. In manuscripts concerning the early church history, Mani and his disciples are often described as performing healing miracles to save

〔1〕孙昌武 Sun Changwu, 中国文学中的维摩与观音(*Vimalakirti and Avalokitesvara in Chinese Literature*), Beijing , Higher Education Press, 1996, p.314.

female patients. For instance, a girl named Nafshā is recovered after Mani's treatment, and she and her sister, Queen Tadī then convert to Manichaeism:

> [And the Lord Mani], the Apostle, descended in the presence of all, including Nafshā, and he laid his hand on her, and immediately Nafshā was healed, and she was completely free from pain. All the people were amazed at the miracle. Then many people accepted the faith anew. And also Queen Tadī, the sister of Nafshā, the wife or the Emperor, appeared before Mār addā with great … and received the Truth … from him …[1]

Another story is about Gabryab, Mani's disciple, who shows his miraculous medical skill in the Christian community at Revān:

> Then he asked for oil and water and blessed her. And he ordered (them) to write thereon (?), and at the same time he ordered (her) to partake of it (?). And immediately, on the spot, the girl was [healed] from the illness, [and was] completely free of infirmity, and she stood there, [healthy] in body, just as if she … had not been [ill] (at all).
>
> And Gabryab received the … king [of] Revān and his wife, [the mother] of the girl, and also the girl herself in to the community of auditors (by anointing them with) consecrated oil. [And he] commanded (them), "From now on, serve no more … the heretics [and] idols and demons."[2]

From these, we learn that in early period Mani had already concentrated the missionary efforts on females as his target audience. Women are not only

〔1〕Please refer to a Sogdian fragment TM 389c，见 W. Sundermann, Mitteliranische manichäische Texte kirchengeschichtlichen Inhalts, pp.42–45; H. –J. Klimkeit, Gnosis on the Silk Road: Gnostic Parables, Hymns & Prayers from Central Asia, p.209.

〔2〕Please refer to a Sogdian fragment TM 389d，W. Sundermann, Mitteliranische manichäische Texte kirchengeschichtlichen Inhalts, pp.55–57; H. –J. Klimkeit, Gnosis on the Silk Road: Gnostic Parables, Hymns & Prayers from Central Asia, p.210.

more sensitive to religion than men, but also more willing to access and believe in gods[1], and religion can liberate most of them from the aspect of mentality in return[2].

The changes of female followers' status in the Chotcho community are hinted in some Turfan manuscripts. In a hymn for the hierarchy and the community preserved in the Middle Persian fragment M36, the bliss of the god is invoked for the church members by rank:

> May [blessing ever come] anew upon you, teacher [of good name], who have seated yourself on the throne of the prophets....
>
> The 72 bishops of the Truth, the teachers of the path of virtue: May their glory and joy also increase! And may their fame spread with praise to all communities and to every diocese.
>
> The 360 ardent presbyters who raise the children of the gods, the sons of Mani, the Lord: May they delight and be joyful in the constant increase of beneficence and joy.
>
> The wise teachers who teach and reveal the mysteries of wisdom, the flute players of [valiant] Vahman [who play melodies] according to the time of the First Call,
>
> ...the good scribes, the sons of the gods, the strong men, the messengers of the spirit; the pure virgins who execute and fulfill the will of the redeemer: [May they attain] invulnerability...
>
> All the pure elect, the lambs from on high, the white-feathered doves that mourn, lament and are grieved over the highest soul that is the son of Jesus the Friend, and who sing praise to the Holy Spirit: (May they be blessed).

[1] 贺璋瑢 He Zhangrong, 关于女性宗教信仰建立的几点思考 ("Some Points on the Formation of Religious Belief of Women), 华南师范大学学报 (*Journal of South China Normal University*) 3 (2001), pp.45–50.

[2] D.L.Carmody (tr. by 徐钧尧 Xu Junyao &宋立道 Song Lidao), 妇女与世界宗教 (*Women and World Religions*), Chengdu, Sichuan People's Press, 1995, p.5.

Blessed be the sisters, the holy virgins, the brides of the Bridegroom of Light (Jesus). May the right hand of salvation adorn them, and may they enter into the Realm of the Living.

The pious auditors of the living Word, who are the walls of the Holy Church: May they attain fortune and blessing increasingly and may they become perfect by the commandment of the Redeemer. [1]

In this poem, the blessing for church members is invoked rigidly according to their ranks: first for the dignitaries, namely the teacher, bishops and presbyters, and then for the flute players, the scribes, the pure virgins, the elects, the sisters and the auditors. Images of scribes are portrayed on the verso of miniature MIK III 6368 (Fig.24)[2]. Their white garments show that they are also elects. As to the flute players, their identifications are difficult to make certain, because in existing Manichaean artworks found in Turfan there is no white-dressed music players[3]. But in the elect group there must be some music players. Since the hymn of M 36 goes in the order of ranks and presbyters and scribes are all real-person, the flute players between them should be persons in reality too, after all, it seems a little illogical and incongruous to insert a divine being here. So the flute players are probably also elects. Therefore, what preserved in this hymn is definitely not a list of gods, but church members in the real world. It's uncertain whether "the pure

[1] F. C. Andreas & W. B. Henning, "Mitteliranische Manichaica aus Chinesisch-Turkestan II", pp.323-326; M. Boyce, *A Reader in Manichaean Middle Persian and Parthian*, pp.144-145; H. -J. Klimkeit, *Gnosis on the Silk Road: Gnostic Parables, Hymns & Prayers from Central Asia*, pp.92-93.

[2] H.-J. Klimkeit (tr. by Lin Wushu), 古代摩尼教艺术 (*Manichaean Art and Calligraphy*), plate 26; Z. Gulácsi, *Manichaean Art in Berlin Collection*, p.93.

[3] There is a lute (?) player on the recto of fragment MIK III 6368 (Fig.25). He is an auditor judging from his dress. See H.-J. Klimkeit (tr. by Lin Wushu), 古代摩尼教艺术 (*Manichaean Art and Calligraphy*), plate 25; Z. Gulácsi, *Manichaean Art in Berlin Collection*, p.95. There is a flute player on the margin of the verso of fragment So.18700 & M 501e (Fig.26), but he is not an elect. See Z. Gulácsi, *Manichaean Art in Berlin Collection*, p.97. On the above-mentioned illustration of a Sogdian letter (81TB65:1) found in Grotto No. 65 of Bezklik , one of the goddess is playing flute, please refer to the first page of 吐鲁番新出摩尼教文献研究 (*Studies on Manichaean Manuscripts Newly-discovered in Turfan*).

virgins" represents female elects or not, but "the sisters" placed between "the elects" and "the auditors" must refer to the female elects. They appear at the same place in the list of other hymns, for example in fragment M 36:

> And we honor with praise the greater teachers who support and sustain the valiant Vahman, the ruler of the Holy Church.
>
> Furthermore, may the 72 bishops who tend the well-cultivated garden (the Church) be praised.
>
> May salvation and peace, life and happiness [come] upon all presbyters, those who guard the treasure of the praised Mother.
>
> And may the preachers of the secret mysteries be given new power by Vahman, the Redeemer.
>
> Peace and joy upon the good scribes who write the living words of the gods!
>
> Blessing upon the righteous one (the elect), the green tress that bear fruit ...eternally.
>
> Praise to the blessed sisters who wait for the handsome bridegroom.
>
> ...Peace, life and salvation...upon the pious auditors who gather together the community of the oppressed. [1]

Here, "the blessed sisters" being listed between "the elects" and "the auditors" is thought to be related to the wise virgins of Matthew 25:1-13 by Prof. Klimkeit [2]. On the annual Bema ceremony of Chotcho, the church members are also praised according to the same order:

> We honor the great teachers.

---

〔1〕Please see the Middle Persian fragment M11, E. Waldschmidt & W. Lentz, "Manichäische Dogmatik aus chinesischen und iranischen Texten", pp.556–557; M. Boyce, *A Reader in Manichaean Middle Persian and Parthian*, p.146; H. –J. Klimkeit, *Gnosis on the Silk Road: Gnostic Parables, Hymns & Prayers from Central Asia*, p.93.

〔2〕H. –J. Klimkeit, Gnosis on the Silk Road: Gnostic Parables, Hymns & Prayers from Central Asia, p.98, n.14.

We honor the mighty bishops.

We honor the wise presbyters.

We honor the virtuous scribes.

We honor the singers of the melodious hymns.

We honor the pure righteous ones (the elect).

We honor the holy virgins.

We honor and praise the whole Flock of Light which you yourself chose in the spirit of Truth.[1]

In the above three verses, the elects are not specified with their genders, which means they are viewed as a whole including male and female. But the female elects are highlighted alone, being blessed and praised particularly. Such writing style of hymn apparently became a fixed format at that time. It's unknown whether the Manichaeans still stayed away from or even loathed women outside the community, but at least they thought highly of the female followers in the community. They not only paralleled them as the wise Virgins waiting for the coming of Jesus, but also honored and praised them out of the whole group of elects. Thus the female followers in Chotcho Church should be treated with more respect, and such attitude towards them must be associated with their increasing number and considerable influence.

In the postscript of *Mahrnāmag* (M1), a large amount of Manichaean followers' names are listed, including the Khan of the East Uighur Khanate and the governors of the oasis towns along the north rim of Tarim Basin[2]. There are 32 female auditors in it, which are almost the noblewomen from the royal court of the East Uighur Khanate. The total of the male followers

---

[1] Please refer to the Middle Persian and Parthian fragment M 801 concerning Bema ceremony, See W. B. Henning, *Ein manichäisches Bet- und Beichtbuch*, pp.18–32; H. -J. Klimkeit, *Gnosis on the Silk Road: Gnostic Parables, Hymns & Prayers from Central Asia*, p.137.

[2] As to the detailed studies on M1, see Wang Yuanyuan, 从波斯到中国：摩尼教在中亚和中国的传播 (*From Persian to China: the Spread of Manichaeism in Central Asia and China*), Beijing, Zhonghua Book Company, 2012, pp.43–106.

in this name-list is 119, including 16 nobles and courtiers of the court, and 103 officials from the towns along the north rim of Tarim. The number of 32 is twice as much as that of the male followers in the royal court, and it's a significant amount even compared to the totality of 119 males. The same impression can be got from the artworks unearthed in Turfan: there are many female Manichaeans, including elects and auditors, portrayed in the illustrations, textiles and wall-paints[1].

In conclusion, Manichaeans in Chotcho not only personified the light elements which ought to be males as female images instead, but also decorated their ceremonial gowns with the portraits of the Maiden of Light. These practices against the early tradition indicate that the status of the Maiden of Light in Chotcho church was improved. As to the improvement, we cannot consider it in isolation from the following two points: first, certain religious functions and virtues of the Maiden of Light were valued more by the local followers in the Uighur Kingdom; secondly, the status of the female adherents in Chotcho church was improved.

It's interesting that the position of the goddess got further higher as Manichaeism spreading eastward, if we have a look at a Manichaean silk-painting housed in the Yamato Bunkakan of Japan (Fig.27)[2]. This scroll of the 13th century consists of five demarcated layers, and is argued to be conveying a subject concerning Manichaean eschatology[3]. According to the researches of the scroll, a scene of the Light Maiden's visit to heaven is depicted on the top layer, and in the middle of the second layer, a statue of

---

〔1〕Please refer to H.-J. Klimkeit (tr. by Lin Wushu), 古代摩尼教艺术 (*Manichaean Art and Calligraphy*); Z. Gulácsi, *Manichaean Art in Berlin Collection*.

〔2〕泉武夫 Takeo Izumi, "景教聖像の可能性——棲雲寺藏傳虚空藏畫像について",〈國華〉Vol.1330, 2007, pp.10–12.

〔3〕Y. Yoshida, "A Newly Recognized Manichaean Painting: Manichaean Daēn Japan", Mohammad A. Amir – Moezzi, J. – D. Dubois, Ch. Jullien F. Jullien (eds.), *Pensée Grecque et Sagessed'Orient. Hommage à Michel Tardieu*, Brepols, 2010, pp. 694–714.

Mani is seated, then in the fourth and fifth layers, scenes of the Judgement and the hell are shown respectively. Obviously in the scroll, the Maiden of Light, Mani and the Judge are the main figures of the Heaven, the World and the Hell. In Manichaean myth, the Heaven actually refers to the Realm of Light, which is dominated by the Father of Light. In the silk-painting, however, the Maiden of Light appears to be the heroine. Such drawing perhaps reflects the belief of the Maiden of Light in China Proper was more popular than that in Chotcho. Prof. Bryder points out that in Chinese Manichaean manuscripts, the Maiden of Light and the Moon become the focus of all gods and the new Light Kingdom[1]. Presumably, this is the textual base on which the silk-painting was created.

Plates

Fig.1　MIK III 7283

[1] P. Bryder, "On the Sunny Side of the Moon", P. Bilge, H.K. Nielsen, J.P. Sorensen (ed.), *Apocryphon Severini, Presented to Soren Giversen*, Aarhus, 1993, pp.42–49.

Fig.2　MIK III 4965 (recto ?)

Fig.3　MIK III 4965 (verso ?)

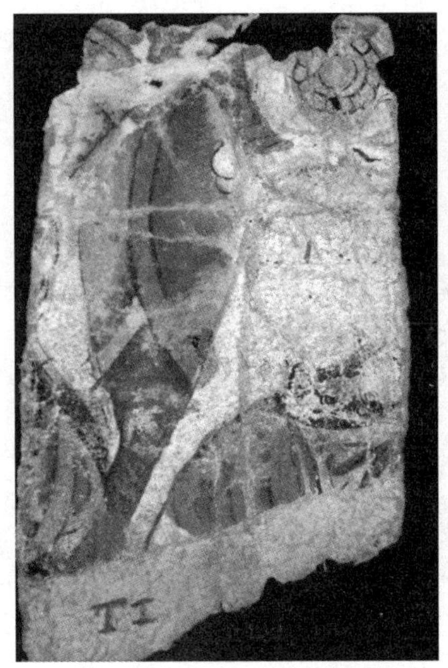

Fig.4 MIK III 134 (verso)

Fig.5 MIK III 4959 (recto)

Fig.6　M 23 (recto)　　Fig.7　M 223(recto)

Fig.8　restored Nestorian paintings of Jesus Christ found in Dunhuang

Fig.9 MIK III 6918

Fig.10 MIK III 6626 & III 6379c (recto)

Fig.11 MIK III 6270

Fig.12　MIK III 4979

Fig.13　MIK III 6257

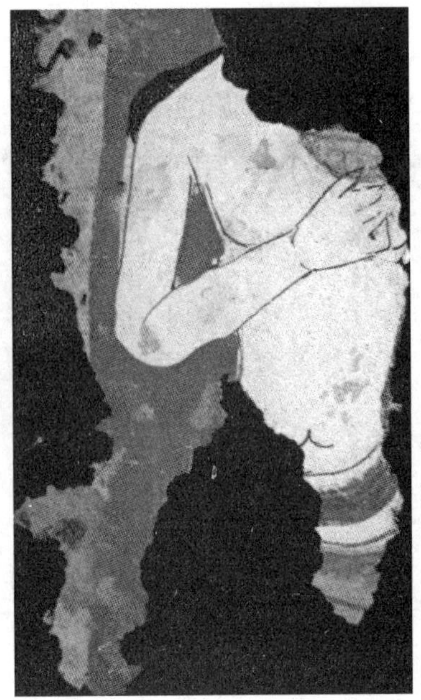

Fig.14 MIK III 6258a

Fig.15 MIK III 4974 (recto)

Fig.16 M 171

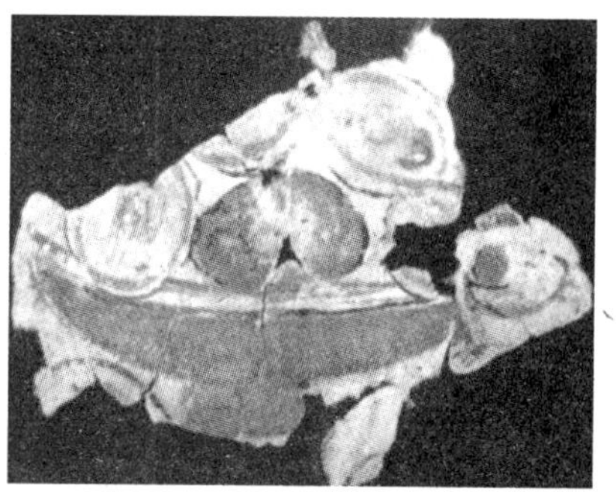

Fig.17 MIK III 7266

Fig.18 MIK III 4981a

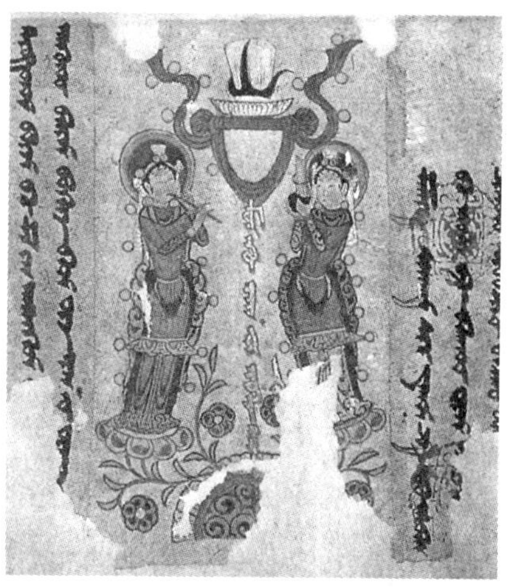

Fig.19 81TB65:1

Fig.20 MIK III 6917

Fig.21a MIK III 6606

Fig.21b line drawing of MIK III 6606

Fig.22　Grünwedel's line drawing of a wall painting in Chotcho

Fig.23　MIK III 6251

Fig.24　MIK III 6368 (verso)

Fig.25　MIK III 6368 (recto)

Fig.26　M 501e

Fig.27 Chinese silk-painting preserved in the Yamato Bunkakan of Japan

8 Letters from Sir Aurel Stein to Gustaf Raquette

Aloïs van Tongerloo (Geel, Belgium) &
Michael Knüppel (Kassel, Germany)

In the archives of the University of Lund (Sweden) there are preserved a substantial number of letters received by Gösta Rikard [Gustaf Richard] Raquette (1871–1945). Although missionary "by profession", he was a scholar as well.[1] In this light he was in scholarly contact with many well-known scholars and explorers who were active during the first three decades of the 20th century. Among them was the famous traveller, archaeologist (or better: archaeological explorer) and historian of Central Asian Buddhist art, Sir Marc Aurel Stein (1862-1943).[2] Eleven letters which were written by him sent to Raquette are preserved in Lunds Universitet, Universitetsbiblioteket under the Signature "Saml. Raquette, Gustav / Vol. 1-2: Brev" (alphabetically), there: Vol. 1 sub "Stein, Sir Marc

---

[1] On life and work of G. R. Raquette (7.2.1871–10.5.1945) see G. W.: Raquette, Gustaf Richard. In: *Svenska Män och Kvinnor. Biografisk Uppslagsbok*. 6. Stockholm 1949, p. 220; Jarring, Gunnar: *Ujgurovedenie v Svecii.* Issledovanija po ujgurskomu jazyku 2. Alma–Ata 1970, pp. 17–20; Eren, Hasan: Raquette, Gustaf Richard. In: *Türk Ansiklopedisi* XXVII.1978, p. 225; Eren, Hasan: Raquette, Gustaf Richard. In: *Türklük Bilimi Sözlüğü*. I: *Yabancı Türkologlar*. Ankara 1998 (TDK, Yayınları, 705), pp. 276–278; Hultvall, John: *Mission and Revolution in Central Asia. The MCCS Mission work in Eastern Turkestan 1892 – 1938*. The authors of this contribution are currently preparing the edition of the letters written by Raquette to W. Bang, W. Bang to Raquette and A. von Le Coq to Raquette. In this publication the text between { } is furnishing the text completion by the editors.

[2] For life and work of Sir M. A. Stein (26.11.1862–26.10.1943) one should consult the literature compiled in Yasuhiro Sueki: *Bibliographical sources for Buddhist studies. From the viewpoint of Buddhist philology*. 2nd ed. Tokyo 2008 (Bibliographia Indica et Buddhica 3).

Aurel". These documents are remains of former broader correspondence exchanges between both travellers and scholars.

While there are a noteable number of works dealing with the life and research of Sir Aurel Stein, the publications about G. R. Raquette are somehow scanty. Gustaf R. Raquette was born on 7 February 1871 in Tolfta in the province of Uppsala. After finishing his school, he attended the Swedish Mission Federation's school (Svenska missionsförbundets mission-sskola) in Stockholm and studied medicine at the Karolinska Institutet in Lund, in 1891—1893. From 1895 to 1896 he served as medical advisor of the Mission Covenant Church of Sweden (*Svenska Missionskyrkan*, MCCS) in Baku (Azerbaijan) and Bukhara (Emirate of Bukhara). From 1896 to 1901 Raquette worked in Kashgar (Chinese Turkistān). In the time between 1901-1904 he travelled to several other places of that region as well as to Great Britain where he obtained the degree of a doctor of tropical medicine of the University of Liverpool in 1903. From 1904 to 1911 he worked in Yarkand, and from 1913—1921 in Kashgar again. After finishing his mission in Uyghuristān he returned to Sweden through Tibet and British India. After his return to Sweden, he worked at Lund University as a lecturer for Oriental languages (especially Eastern Turki [="Modern" Uyghur]). Gustaf [Gösta Rikard] Raquette died on May 10, 1945. During his stay in Chinese Turkistān he achieved a deep knowledge of modern Uyghur language and its various dialects, which was a requirement for his missionary works as well as a necessity for the translation of biblical text into Uyghur language. The result of this efforts has been a complete revision of the full translation of the New Testament undertaken by the British Foreign and Bible Societies (1911) and translations of the book of Job (1921) and the Psalms (1924).

Especially after his return to Sweden, Raquette wrote a numerous series of works on Uyghur language and culture, such as "The accent problem in Turkish" (1927), "English-Turki dictionary" (1927) and "Täji bilä Zohra: Eine osttürkische Variante der Sage von Tahir und Zohra" (1930). He had already worked out an "Eastern Turki grammar" (1912-1914) during his time in Chinese Turkistān.

Document No. 1

page 1: 18 Ms. lines
page 2: 17 Ms. lines
page 3: 5 Ms. lines

[page 1]

Kashgar: July 5, 1915.

Dear Mr. Raquette,

I shall feel greatly obliged if you will kindly accept the enclosed as a small compensation for the trouble you had been good enough to take about medical advice for my men and myself.

I am sorry to have forgotten yesterday to speak to you about the key of the Office Safe which I kept up to the present and which Sir P. Sykes[1] had asked me to hand over to you when leaving.

[page 2]

I hope to hand it to you on my way tomorrow morning when I shall be passing your house.

---

〔1〕This is the soldier and explorer Brigadier-General Sir Percy Molesworth Sykes (28.2.1867–11.6.1945).

I am sorry, the copy of 'Desert Cathay' [1] meant for you was not among the parcels received. I trust it will come by the next Desk and I am arranging that it should be delivered to you by the Clerk. Only it will be well to remind him about it.

In haste

yours sincerely,

A. Stein

[page 3]

I send two more tins of (Plasmon) Arrowroot which Mrs. Raquette [2] may perhaps find useful for your little girl.

Document No. 2

page 1: 16 Ms. lines

page 2: 17 Ms. lines

page 3: 22 Ms. lines

[page 1]

Camp Bostan-arche:

July 10, 1915.

[1] Stein, Aurel: Ruins of Desert Cathay. Personal Narrative of Explorations in Central Asia and Westernmost China. 2 vols. London 1912.

[2] Raquette's wife Evelina Elisabet Björkgren, whom he married on 16 May 1896.

Dear Mr. Raquette,

I hope, you will kindly forgive my troubling you with a request from this distance. I find that my Jodine supply being old has become useless from want of strength. As there is always a chance of some strain or similar little mishap when Jodine would come in usefully, I venture to ask you for the favour

[page 2]

of sending me a ^very small supply of it if you can conveniently spare it. The Kirghiz messenger who takes this to Kashgar would have to carry your reply back here.

I reached this delightful mountain camp day before yesterday and enjoy its peace and coolness greatly. Its height is 10500 ft., just what is needed, and the slopes around me clothed with fir trees which recall Kashmir.

I hope, your little girl

[page 3]

is getting on well and you and Mrs. Raquette are having an easier time now. May you be spared anxiety and great heat.

Please give my best wishes to Mr. Bohlin.[1] The horse he kindly helped to choose carried me very well here. But nature is getting too much for him in these free surroundings with many mares about, and I fear, I shall have to send the animal back for sale to Kashgar before I set out for the

[1] The Swedish missionary Adolf Bohlin (9.3.1873–).

Pamirs.

With kindest greetings for yourself and Mrs. Raquette and best thanks in advance.

Yours very sincerely,

A. Stein

Document No. 3

page 1: 20 Ms. lines

page 2: 18 Ms. lines

[page 1]

Camp Bostan-arche:

July 17, 1915.

Dear Mr. Raquette,

Take my heartiest thanks for the ample supply of Jodine which you so kindly sent me. It arrived quite safely and shall be kept with care.

I am very sorry to think of your little girl still keeping weak. But I hope, your united efforts will help her over this hottest month and then the battle will be won. I wished, you could bring her up to this delightful alpine camping place amidst the firs and juniper trees. But I hope, you will anyhow

[page 2]

come to visit the place before long. It is only circ. 68 miles from Kashgar.

I am starting two days hence for the Pamirs and hope to meet Sir P.

Sykes who is on his way back somewhere near the Ulugh-art Pass.[1]

With renewed heartiest thanks and the warmest good wishes,

Yours very sincerely,

A. Stein

I hope, 'Desert Cathay'[2] has been delivered to you since you wrote. I enclose a 'dedication' slip for the book just to mark it as a souvenir.

Document No. 4

Four typewritten pages numbered 1 to 4

page 1: 23 lines

page 2: 25 lines

page 3: 25 lines

page 4: 20 lines

[page 1]

Camp, P.O. Srinagar, Kashmir: June 6, 1921.

Dear Mr. Raquette,

I hope this letter will find you at Kashgar in full health and as always absorbed in the noble task of aleviating human suffering. The object of my letter is to appeal to your interest as a Turcologist with reference to a

〔1〕The Ulūgh–art–dawān (pass) on the way to Khotan was crossed over by Stein and is described in his account of "Innermost Asia" (Stein, Aurel: *Innermost Asia. Detailed Report of Explorations in Central Asia, Kan–Su, and Eastern Iran*. Carried out and described by Sir Aurel Stein. With descriptive lists of antiques by F. H. Andrews and F. M. G. Lorimer. London 1928).

〔2〕See above.

geographical publication of mine which after years of much labour is now approaching completion.

I mean the new atlas of maps which embodies all the surveys carried out during my three Central-Asian expeditions and which has been under preparation at the Trigonometrical Survey Office, Dehra Dun, since 1916.[1] As it comprises 47 sheets on the scale of 1:500,000 showing all the ground surveyed by myself and my topographical assistants between the Pamirs in the west and the Nan-shan ^ranges in the east and has been executed with abundant detail (in several colours), you will not be surprised at the number of years which the compilation, drawing and reproduction of these maps has needed.

All through my journeys I have taken special care about the record of local names, though, as you will readily understand, no attempt could be made in a publication meant for geographical purposes to reproduce phonetic niceties. All but the simplest diacritical marks are barred by the

[page 2]

rules of the Survey Department.

The publication of this atlas, which is now ready except for a few sheets still in course of printing, is to be accompanied by a special Memoir of mine to be issued in the 'Records of Survey of India'. This Memoir will include a complete index of all local names, numbering of course many thousands. The great majority of them are Turkī and belong to the Tārīm Basin, practically the whole of which as far as inhabited, with big areas of desert in addition, has been surveyed by us.

[1] Memoir on maps of Chinese Turkestan and Kansu from the surveys made during Sir Aurel Stein's explorations, 1900–1, 1906–8, 1913–15 (with appendices by Major K. Mason and J. de Graaff Hunter). Dehra Dun: Trigonometrical Survey Office 1923.

It has occurred to me that a philological examination of these abundant materials of local nomenclature would be an interesting subject for a competent Turkī scholar like yourself. At the same time my Memoir itself would much benefit by such an examination which might determine certain standard forms for local names, necessarily recorded by me in their dialectic forms as actually heard on the spot. I have no doubt that many doubtful names might be cleared up, especially among those names which in the first place were recorded by my assistants possessing no philological training.

I am fully aware that you may not be able to form any definite opinion as to the possibility of furnishing a short essay or other contribution of your own until you have seen the Index or the complete set of the maps. But

[page 3]

perhaps a glance at the map proof which I send herewith as a specimen might enable you to form some provisional idea.

I need not assure how happy I should be if it were possible for you to offer your expert collaboration in one form or other. You are placed in an exceptionally favourable position for ascertaining the true derivation of many of those local names, since Kashgar is a place where traders and others familiar with many of the localities surveyed continually pass. I have no doubt that Colonel Etherton[1] and others at the British Consulate General would be willing to give help in securing competent men for reference.

As regards the eventual publication of your contribution its insertion in

〔1〕Colonel Percy Thomas Etherton (1879-1963) was British Consul at Kashgar (1918-1922). He wrote a number of books of which *Across the Roof of the World. A Record of Sport and Travel through Kashmir, Gilgit, Hunza, the Pamirs, Chinese Turkistan, Mongolia and Siberia*. London 1911 is quite interesting in this context.

the Memoir which will form a separate volume, would perhaps be the simplest solution. But other means could also come under consideration, e. g. the Journals of the Royal Asiatic Society, Asiatic Society of Bengal etc. I am sorry none of the above periodicals offer honoraria; but it might be possible, perhaps, to obtain in your case some reasonable remuneration from Government in view of the direct bearing of such a contribution upon the cartography of Central Asia.

I shall be very glad if you could communicate whatever your view may be as regards the above suggestion as early as possible. The Memoir is not likely to go into

[page 4]

print until the end of the present year, but there would be no difficulty in letting you have a typed copy of the index of names by the time your reply can reach me < ; also a set of maps. >[1]

I was spending most of last year in England for the purpose of seeing through the press Serindia,[2] the final report on my second expedition, filling five bulky volumes 4to. This task is now happily completed, and I hope the work will issue within a few weeks now from Oxford University Press. During my stay at home I spent two happy weeks with Sir George and Lady Macartnay[3] who are now permanently settled in Jersey. Of course, we talked a great deal about bright old days in Kashgar.

---

[1] MS. addition.

[2] Stein, Aurel: Serindia. Detailed Report of Explorations in Central Asia and Westernmost China, carried out and described under the order of H. M. Indian government. Oxford 1921.

[3] Sir George Macartnay (19.1.1867–19.5.1945) was the British Consul–General in Kashgar, his wife Catherine Macartnay née Borland supported Sir Aurel Stein during his archaeological campaigns. Her memoirs were published some decades later (Macartney, Catherine: *An English Lady in Chinese Turkestan.* Hong Kong 1985).

I hope your work is progressing well and conditions in Kashgar are permitting you to gather amply deserved fruits of your devoted labours.

With renewed best wishes for yourself and best regards for Mrs. Raquette,

yours sincerely,[1]

A. Stein[2]

Document No. 5

Two typewritten pages with page number 2

page 1: 27 lines

page 2: 9 lines

[page 1]

P.O. Srinagar, Kashmir: September 7, 1921.

Dear Mr. Raquette,

I wished to thank you before for your letter of July 16th with the unexpected but ^very welcome news of your coming so soon through Kashmir. But I wished to make sure of my reply reaching you en route in Gilgit, and an earlier reply might have missed you.

It is indeed a most pleasant prospect to meet you in Kashmir, and I hope that your journey there will be accomplished according to your programme and in comfort. In any case I know from my own experience that you could not have chosen a better season for crossing the mountains.

[1] Handwritten.

[2] Id.

I fully realize that it would have been easier for you while at Kashgar to offer competent help as regards the Index of Turk~~e~~istān local names. But I also feel sure that with your thorough philological knowledge of Turkī you may be able to investigate those names with considerable advantage even after having returned to your home in Sweden.

I hope your visit to Srinagar will allow us to discuss the matter personally, and this will be quite easy. My camp during October will no longer be on this high mountain top but in an old garden by the shore of the Dal Lake, only some 7 miles from the centre of Srinagar and quite easily accessible by boat. I hope I shall have the great pleasure of receiving your and Mrs. Raquette's visit there soon after your arrival at Srinagar. It will be quite easy for you to come out ~~there~~ for the day and I shall charge myself with all necessary arrangements as soon as I hear from you. A letter addressed Srinagar, Kashmir, will always reach me.[1]

[page 2]

I look forward with much pleasure to the chance of meeting you again and having a long talk about old Kashgar.

I am sending this to the care of Major Lorimer,[2] the Political Agent, Gilgit, for whom as a fellow scholar I have great regard. I hope, he will be able to help you on your way to Kashmir.

With kindest regards for you both

Yours sincerely,

A. Stein[3]

---

[1] Handwritten addition.

[2] This is Lieutenant-Colonel David Lockhart Robertson Lorimer (24.12.1876–26.2.1962), the well known linguist working on Burushāskī. See esp. *The Burushaski Language. I: Introduction and Grammar; II: Texts and Translation; III: Vocabularies and Index.* Oslo: Instituttet for sammenlignende kulturforskning 1935–1938.

[3] Handwritten.

Document No. 6

One page: 23 Ms. lines

[page 1 *recto*]

Camp, P.O. Srinagar: Sept{ember} 21, 1921.

Dear Mr. Raquette,

I have just learned through a telegram of the Political Agent, Gilgit, that after all it had been decided to advise your travelling via Leh. So I enclose now a duplicate of the letter I had sent for you to the care of the P{olitical} A{gent} and wish that it may duly catch you on your arrival from the Kara-Koram. May your journey have been an easy and interesting one, and may you be able to enjoy a good rest with the Mission at Leh where I was so kindly treated after my accident at the end of my second journey in 1908.[1]

It will be a great pleasure to meet you and Mrs. Raquette again and I only wish I had a roof of my own to offer you hospitality.

With kind regards for you both.

Yours sincerely,

A. Stein

Document No. 7

page 1: 23 Ms. lines

page 2: 23 Ms. lines

[1] His second major expedition lasted from 1906–1908 and led him (among other areas of Central Asia) to Kunlun–shan–mountains.

page 3: 7 Ms. lines

[page 1]

Camp, Diwan Amarnath' s
Garden, Ishabar: Oct{ober} 19,
1921.

Dear Mr. Raquette,

It was a fortunate chance which brought me to Srinagar yesterday and made me meet at the Residency Mrs. Riscoe who had just seen your party safely arriving after your long journey. I was delighted to learn the news and trust that all passed off well on your travel and that you did not experience too much anxiety on account of the children. I can realize though what an undertaking it must have meant for you both!

I am still in camp in an old garden on the Dal lake some 7 miles out by road and hope to have the pleasure of receiving a visit from you all here as soon as

[page 2]

the weather clears again and will make the trip out here a pleasant occasion for you both and the children. I shall be able to arrange easily for a boat comfortably to fetch you and take you back.

I am very glad to know that you provided with what I hope are comfortable quarters at the Mission Hospital and trust, you will take a good rest before proceeding further.

Kindly let me know whether I should find you tomorrow or the day after if I came in during the early afternoon. I should, of course, like to see you soon if it did not mean inconvenience to yourselves. I wish, the weather may turn soon into such bright sunshine as we usually enjoy at this season.

Please let me know by the bearer if there is anything I could help to arrange for you locally.

[page 3]

Did you receive the letter I sent you c/o P.O. Leh or the copy of it at the Srinagar P.O.?

With warmest welcome to yourself and Mrs. Raquette

Yours sincerely,

A. Stein

Document No. 8

page 1: 22 Ms. lines
page 2: 23 Ms. lines
page 3: 24 Ms. lines
page 4: 23 Ms. lines

[page 1]

New Delhi: Jan{uary} 19, 1922.
(Address: Srinagar, Kashmir).

Dear Mr. Raquette,

I was greatly pleased to receive while still at Srinagar your interesting letter from the Red Sea and rejoiced heartily at the news of good progress it brought. If I did not thank you for it earlier it was merely because I knew, you would be doing some travelling on the Continent before returning to your home and have your hands full there too after your first arrival. I too spent some weeks over a rapid tour on the N.W. Frontier before and after Christmas, and the correspondence arrears awaiting me here at its close were big.

[page 2]

I was most glad to learn that your journey down to Bombay passed off so well, notwithstanding that great 'rush' at the end. But I knew beforehand that experienced travellers as you all are and with your own thoroughly practical ways you would manage to catch your boat and enjoy some glimpses of India in addition. Still that premature start of your steamer shall be remembered as a warning – in particular to those who have to deal with that Italian line.

I shall think back always with great pleasure to the lucky chance which allowed me to welcome you in that old garden by the Dal shore and to revive in those favoured surroundings common happy memories of Kashgar. I only wish, I could

[page 3]

have offered you hospitality longer, and you had been spared those days of prolonged rain in Srinagar.

It is very kind of you to have asked Miss Svensson for her eventual kind help in the matter of a Badakhshi.[1] My best thanks for it. I shall write to her myself as soon as I can feel fairly sure of my plans beyond the spring. There is just a possibility of my being able to travel northward beyond the Indian frontier before the Kara-Koram route opens and in that case the pony would come too late.

The setting up of the Memoirs on my new maps has just started, and if its printing can be pushed on well at Dohra Dun the Index, too, giving all local names may be in type by the late spring or summer. I shall not fail

[page 4]

to let you have fair proofs in advance so as to enable you to see clearly what you might do as regards your hoped for paper on Turkistan local names. I earnestly wish, you may find yourself in a position favouring this work, and shall feel grateful if you will kindly let me know what you think of it when your plans are matured.

Mr. Skrine[2] who is to officiate for Major Etherton after May has just come to see me. He is a very keen scholarly kind of man and has seen much of Persia. Mrs. Skrine is to go to Kashgar with him.

Please give my best regards to Mrs. Raquette, also Mr. Ahlbert[3] if you see him and take all good wishes for the New Year

from yours very sincerely,

A. Stein

---

〔1〕A native from the province of Badakhshān/ Afghanistān.

〔2〕Sir Clairmont Percival Skrine (1888-1974) entered the Indian Civil Service in 1912, but was transferred soon afterwards to the Political Service. He held appointments in the Indian States, in the Baluchistan Agency and in Kashgar where he was British Consul-General (1922-1924). Here he collected materials for his book *Chinese Turkestan* (1926, repr. 1971). Moreover he served for thirteen years in Iran and wrote *World War in Iran* (1962). Together with Pamela Nightingale he published *Macartney in Kashgar* (1973).

〔3〕This is the Swedish missionary and well-known linguist Gustaf Ahlbert (26.8.1884–14.9.1943).

Document No. 9

page 1: 26 Ms. lines

page 2: 35 Ms. lines: 33 lines written horizontally, two additional lines written vertically

[page 1]

Camp Mohand Marg: Sept{ember} 10, 1922.

Dear Mr. Raquette,

I wish to thank you very heartily for your letter of July 17th and felt very glad for the good news it brought me about yourself and your family. It must have been a great comfort to you and Mrs. Raquette to find yourselves and the children once more safely among your own people after so big a migration.

I am, of course, very sorry that your other labours will not allow you to undertake the analysis of Turkestan local names as recorded in my atlas. But I fully understand the circumstances, and your propable absence from the country would in any case have made it difficult for you to test meanings, etymologies, etc., by local enquiries. I am now doubly glad that I could arrange to get the whole Index of local names printed in my <u>Memoir</u> on the maps, though it fills some 40 pp. foolscap, in double columns. It will thus be available to any Turcologist student who cares to take up the subject; whether in Europe or in Turkestan itself. I have informed Prof. v. Lecoq[1] about the materials thus recorded.

[1] The German archaeologist, turcologist, indologist, manichaean scholar and buddhologist Albert August von Le Coq (8.9.1860–21.4.1930).

In April I had the pleasure to see a good deal

[page 2]

of Mr. and Mrs. Skrine while they stayed at Srinagar on their way to Kashgar. Him I had met before at Delhi. He is a very keen and capable young man and will, no doubt, make the most of his opportunities also in the geographical line.

I was sorry to miss Col. Etherton when he passed through Srinagar as I had by then moved into my mountain camp. But I hope to fare better in the case of Mr. Fitzmaurice[1] who is now travelling down from Leh and whom I have invited to stay with me here. He was most good to my dear old friend Chiang Ssŭ-yeh who breathed his last in March. I feel his loss deeply, but have at least the satisfaction to know that the transfer of his mortal remains to his home in Hu-nan is assured in accordance with his last wishes, through a charitable grant made by Government on Col. Etherton's and my own recommendation and with the help of contributions from his English friends. – Enver Pasha's latest revolt has collapsed,[2] as was to be expected, and he himself is reported to have died. But this may be a mere rumour. That stormy petrel who is responsible for so much human suffering, may yet turn up in some fresh quarter.

I wish you all success in your educational career and hope, your successors in the work at Kashgar and elsewhere will benefit by your teaching for many years. I myself am busy on the report of my third journey.[3]

[1] This is Nicholas Fitzmaurice Esq. (1887–1960) the Vice-Consul at Kashgar 1918–22 and Consul-General in 1922 and from 1931-1933.

[2] The former Ottoman Turkic general and minister of war, Enver Pasha (22.11.1881–4.8.1922), who travelled to Bukhara in 1920 and tried to unify the Turkic peoples of Central Asia to found a new Turkic empire and Khalifat.

[3] His third major expedition lasted from 1913–1916.

Serindia, that on the second is reported to be nearly sold out since its publication last December.

With kindest regards for yourself and Mrs. Raquette and all good wishes

Yours very sincerely,

A. Stein

Please remember me kindly to Mr. and Mrs. Högberg if you have occasion to write to them.[1]

Document No. 10

One typewritten page

page 1: 27 lines

[page 1]

Quetta: April 24, 1927.

(Address: Srinagar, Kashmir).

Dear Mr. Raquetta [sic],

Your very kind present of your English-Turki Dictionary[2] has just reached me in the course of a prolonged archaeological tour on the Baluchistan border. Pressed by many urgent tasks I can send you only with these few lines my warmest thanks for this proof of your remembrance.

---

〔1〕Written vertically.

〔2〕Raquette, Gustaf Richard: *English–Turki dictionary. Based on the dialects of Kashgar and Yarkand.* Lund 1927 (Lunds Universitets Årsskrift Avd. 1, N.F. 23: 4).

I appreciate the scholarly value of your work quite as much as the proof of your continued friendly interest. Even a few glances at your Dictionary have sufficed to show me that this work has been done with the same scholarly care and devotion as your previous publications. I have often wished for such a Dictionary in the course of my travels and feel sure that I should benefit greatly by it if I had a fresh opportunity of visiting that region to which I am attached by so mant happy [1] recollections.

I was very glad to see that you are now holding an ecademic [sic] position in the University of Lund and earnestly wish that your special qualifications may secure you there all the furtherance which you deserve.

With kindest regards for yourself and Mrs. Raquette and best wishes for you both

Yours sincerely

Docent G, Raquetta [sic], Esq., A. Stein

Clemenstorget 12,

Tel. 2370, Lund.

Document No. 11

One typewritten page

page 1: 27 lines

[page 1]

Camp, Hoshap, Makran: February 27, 1928.

Address: c/o Postmaster, Quetta.

[1] Ms. correction.

Dear Mr. Raquette,

Just a few lines written in the course of an archaeological tour in Makran and other parts of Southern Baluchistan which is keeping me very busy ever since November, to thank you for the kind gift of your important paper. Though I have no claim to being a Turcologist I can fully appreciate the interest attaching to that problem of the Turkish accent.[1]

I am very glad to know that you are able in Europe, too, to continue your devoted philological labours. I hope that you will continue to receive all the help you deserve from your University.

I am glad to have seen before my start on this journey the very last proofs of the detailed report, Innermost Asia, on my third Central-Asian expedition. Its four volumes, I hope, will be published at Oxford in the course of the present year.[2] Meanwhile various tours on the Indian North-west Frontier have claimed much of my time.

With best regards and all good wishes

Yours sincerely

A. Stein

Revd. G. Raquette,

University, Lund,

Sweden.

---

〔1〕*The accent problem in Turkish*, Lunds universitets årsskrift. N. F. 1: Teologi, juridik och humanistiska ämnen 24,3, Lund 1927.

〔2〕Innermost Asia. Detailed Report of Explorations in Central Asia, Kan–su and Eastern Īrān, Oxford 1928. 4 vols.

9 Some Remarks on the Old Uigur Report on the Destruction of a Manichaean Monastery

Peter Zieme
(Berlin Free University, Germany)

Since W. B. Henning's first edition, the Sogdian letter of M 112[1] written in Manichaean script aroused great interest among scholars[2]. The verso side of this leaf bears also an interesting text in Old Uigur and was for the first time summarised by K.-H. Menges[3] in the afore-mentioned article. In 1985 Geng Shimin and H.-J. Klimkeit edited the complete Old Uigur text of the verso side of M 112.[4] Later T. Moriyasu published the text again in his book on Uigur Manichaeism.[5] The main progress of his research was the result that he was able to date the text precisely through interpreting the astronomical data contained in it. The data in line 12 can thus be related to the year 983 A.D. This date fits into the general picture of the history of Manichaeism among the Uigurs: "Wir können also als gesichert festhalten, daß die Ruine α einerseits 983 noch ein manichäisches Kloster war. Andererseits stammt die Pfahlinschrift I, die besagt, daß ein adliges uigurisches Ehepaar dort einen buddhistischen Tempel errichten ließ, aus

[1] Henning 1936, pp. 14–18.

[2] Sundermann 1980.

[3] Henning 1936, p. 17 fn. 4.

[4] Geng/Klimkeit 1985.

[5] Moriyasu 2004, pp. 174–183.

dem Jahre 1008. Daher sind wir wohl berechtigt, das letztgenannte Jahr für den Zeitpunkt zu halten, an dem das manichäische Kloster, das die untere Schicht von Ruine α bildet, absichtlich zerstört und ein buddhistischer Tempel an seine Stelle gesetzt wurde."[1]

As L. V. Clark includes this Old Uigur text into his re-edition of the Manichaean corpus in Old Uigur,[2] I will give in the following only some remarks on the leaves related to M 112 in one or the other way.

M 112 is a rather large sheet. Other fragments written in the same or a similar script were regarded as belonging to the letters, but in his re-edition of the Manichaean letters W. Sundermann excluded the fragments M 858a and SI KR IV 852 because of the different spacing between the lines.[3] Doubtlessly his observations are correct, but nevertheless the similarity of the script leads to the assumption that they may have been written by the same scribe.

The fragments M 858a and SI Kr IV 852

In his catalogue J. Wilkens described M 858a and regarded it as belonging to the manuscript M 112[4], although he, too, remarked that the lines run in the opposite direction of M 112.[5] About the contents he writes: "Möglicherweise ein historisches Dokument".[6] The recto side of SI Kr IV

---

〔1〕Moriyasu, 2004, p. 181 (= Moriyasu 1991, p. 151: さて、遺跡 α が 983 年にはまだマニ寺であったこと、 然るに ウイグル貴人夫妻がそこに仏寺を建てさせたことを示す第一棒杭が1008年のものであることが確定したからには、まさしくこと1008年こそが遺跡 α の下層を成すマニ教寺院が意図的に破壊されて仏教寺院に取って替わられた 年と考えてよい で あろう.). K.-H. Menges apud Henning 1936, p. 17 fn. 4 thought that the text was written in the late Mongol period.

〔2〕Clark forthcoming.

〔3〕Sundermann 2007, p. 405.

〔4〕Wilkens 2000, cat.-no. 45.

〔5〕Wilkens 2000, p. 67 (cat.-no. 41).

〔6〕Wilkens 2000, p. 69.

852 displaying the Sogdian text was edited by A. N. Ragoza.[1] As already mentioned, the Old Uigur lines on the verso side run in the opposite direction to M 112. W. Sundermann recognised the joinability of M 858a and SI Kr IV 852.[2]

Remarks on the main text (M 112 etc)

The fragments M 112 and M 119 did not only survive one millennium, but also a temporary being lost. W. Sundermann used for his first edition good photographs, but in 2006 S. Raschmann informed him that the pieces re-appeared.[3] Additionally it should be mentioned that Geng Shimin and H.-J. Klimkeit wrote in a footnote[4] that the fragment was seen in 1984 in the compartment of the Institute of the Academy in Berlin. But this cannot be true as M. Boyce had not seen it while she was working when she prepared the catalogue of the Iranian Manichaean texts[5]. The same authors write in their introduction that they received a photograph from D. Gropp in Hamburg. Chao Huashan's remark that the fragment is in Cologne may be due to some misunderstanding.[6]

The originally separate pieces M 146a and M 336c were later physically joined with M 112 and afterwards glassed so that they form today one unit. Since this reconstructed fragment bears on its verso side the final portion of the Old Uigur text, all other mostly small fragments that are similar in script and shape should be placed before the large one without any further criteria for an exact arrangement.

W. Sundermann's order is as follows:

---

〔1〕Ragoza 1980, pp. 75, 154.

〔2〕Sundermann 2007, p. 405.

〔3〕Sundermann 2007, p. 404.

〔4〕Geng/Klimkeit 1985, p. 10 fn.*. Cp. Sundermann 1984, p. 292.

〔5〕Boyce 1960, pp. 10, 12, 23.

〔6〕Chao 1996, p. 298.

1. fragment M 336a (lacuna of uncertain length).

2. M 112 + M 146a + M 336c.

3. M 336b (position unknown).

4. M 162a (position unknown).

At this point one should consider that possibly also the fragments M 336b and M 162a should be placed before the main text.

Arrangement of the verso sides

Thus the preliminary order of the Old Uigur texts on the verso sides can be established as follows:

a = 4) M 162a (T I D 51), fragment from the right margin.

b = 3) M 336b, fragment from the middle of the sheet.

c = 1) M 336a.

d = 2) M 112, M 146a and M 336c.

Fragment a = 4) M 162a (T I D 51)

Only word remnants of four lines are preserved. In line 2 the word *[ni]zvani-lar* "*kleśa*s" can be read, but the missing context does not allow any further conclusion.

Fragment b = 3) M 336b

The extant words in line 5 *[ön]gdün kedin yıŋ[ak]* "eastern and western direction" can be related to the location data mentioned also in M 112 verso, line 1. Otherwise no decisive words are preserved.

Fragment c = 1) M 336a

The 18 fragmentary lines of M 336a contain some remarkable phrases which regrettably cannot be brought into a continuous text. Line 4 introduces apparently an account about a picture. We read: *otra t(ä)ŋri mani burx[an ...]*, and line 5 *[ik]i elig künki t(ä)ŋ[ri ...]*. The first phrase "in the middle the godly Mani Buddha" may refer to a painting, followed by "sun-god". Also this expression can be part of a picture description, similarly also the phrase *kedin yıŋak yanınta* "on its western side" in line 6. Later in line 13 we read *öŋdünintä* "on its eastern (side)".

Line 10 contains a reference to Jesus: 10 *m(a)šixa burxan tugm[ıš ....]* "(when, or: where) the Buddha Messiah [was] born".

Fragment d = 2) M 112, M 146a and M 336c

The fragment d with its 21 lines is the best preserved piece of this group of fragments. It is the only one that was edited completely so far, as mentioned above. Here I discuss only one word group in line 14 which is of general interest: *üč č'kkwr-lug v(a)rhar*. Geng Shimin and H.-J. Klimkeit translated: "drei Stockwerk hohen (?) Vihāra"[1], similarly T. Moriyasu: "das dreitürmige buddhistische Kloster"[2]. The word *v(a)rhar* is, of course, one of the words for the Buddhist monastery ultimately derived from Sanskrit *vihāra*.

But what is *č'kkwr*[3]? In the dictionaries there is no Turkic word like **čaŋur* with the meaning of "Stockwerk" or "Turm".

T. Moriyasu gave a long explanation in his study on the Stake Inscriptions.[4] He translated the compound *sutup č'kwr* as "a spire of a stūpa"[5] and referred to P. Pelliot's article of 1934 where the latter traced a

〔1〕Geng/Klimkeit 1985, p. 9.

〔2〕Moriyasu 2004, p. 176 (= Moriyasu 1991, p. 148: "三塔（？）のある仏寺").

〔3〕Cp. pict. 1.

〔4〕Moriyasu 2001.

〔5〕Moriyasu 2001, p. 169. Cp. Röhrborn 1996, p. 271 where he refers to the occurrence in the stake inscriptions. According to his note *čäkür* is a synonym to *sutup*< Skt. *stūpa*.

possible lost Tokharian word **čäkür* "tower" in several Chinese transcriptions like 雀梨 *queli* and others, but mainly in 柘厥 *zhejue*〔1〕.

In the Old Uigur Biography of Xuanzang several times the word *č'kwr* occurs. K. Röhrborn supports on one side Pelliot's derivation from a Tocharian word〔2〕, on the other he thinks that "Die Wahl von *čäkür* als Äquiv[alent] von chin[esisch] *lun* (G. 7476) zeigt aber, daß unser Übers[etzer] dieses Wort zu skr. *cakra* 'Rad' gestellt hat."〔3〕 A further example for such an association is HT VIII 1859 where the word is a translation of Chin. 轮奂 *lunhuan* "brilliant"〔4〕. Although obviously the examples in this Old Uigur translation show a relation to Skt. *cakra*, the word obviously is different from the "correct" loan-word *čakir* which can be derived from Sanskrit *cakra* "wheel". Since in such examples we always encounter the spelling *č'kyr*〔5〕, never **č'kwr*, it is advisable to differentiate between the two words as already T. Moriyasu did〔6〕. I quote here the example of HT IV 664-669 *han ävi yanınta azıg šarir-lıg v(a)rhar ol : : edizi yüz čıg : üküš türlüg ärdini-lär üzä etiglig ol : üzäsintä č'kwr turgurup č'kwr bašınta p(a)tmarag atl(ı)g (...)*〔7〕 "Beside the palace of the *han* there is a *vihāra* with a tooth *śarīra*. Its height is 100 feet. It is decorated with many jewels. Above it one built a *č'kwr* . On the top of the *č'kwr* [a big jewel] by name *padmarāga* (...)" = 王宫侧有佛牙精舍，高数百尺，以众宝庄严，上建表柱，以钵昙摩罗伽大宝置之刹端，光曜映空，静夜无

〔1〕Pelliot 1934, pp. 96 sqq.; Moriyasu 2001, pp. 169-170.

〔2〕Röhrborn 1991, p. 219.

〔3〕Röhrborn 1991, p. 220.

〔4〕Röhrborn 1996, pp. 262, 271.

〔5〕Some spellings are given in Moriyasu 2001, p. 170 fn. 49.

〔6〕Moriyasu 2001, p. 170: "we should remember that this *čäkür / čakur* might have been easily confused with another word *čkr / čkir / čakr / čakir / čakar* derived from Skt. *cakra* 'a wheel, circle'."

〔7〕The following lines are too damaged.

云，虽万里同睹。[1] This example clearly shows that the word *č'kwr* is a translation of Chinese 柱 *zhu* which is the equivalent of Skt. *yaṣti*[2], but it cannot be derived from that one.

The spelling *č'kkwr* as mentioned above might be crucial for the search of the origin of the word. Putting together *č'kkwr* and *č'kwr* one can propose for both a spelling like **č(a)ŋgur* or **č(a)ŋur*. In a text of Istanbul (No. 20) there is probably a further occurrence in the following sentence (ll. 6-7): *čaŋur-ug*[3] *sol-tın sıŋar elgintä tutmak üzä / suradı üdkätägi küzädilmiš bodun vin(a)y-lıg* "By holding a stick in the left side hand / one is for ever with the people protected."

Even if there might be a slight possibility to relate this word to the term "roof-ring" of a yurt attested in some Turkic languages as in Kazak *čagarak / čaŋarak*[4] or Kirgiz *čamgarak* "gnutye paločki, vstavljaemye krest-nakrest v tündük (…) i zaveršajuščie derevjannyj ostov jurty"[5], it is not excluded that the word in question is yet of foreign origin. I have to leave the question to further research[6], but I would like to underline that there were in Old Turkic two different, but both phonetically and semantically interrelated words: *čakir* and **čaŋ(g)ur*.

The text ends with an admonition for later generations: *kenki kičiglär y(ä)mä ukzunlar* "the later novices should understand (it)!" Is it foolhardy to

---

〔1〕T. 2053, 242c4-7. Translation Li 1995, p. 119: "Beside the king's palace was the Buddha Tooth Temple, which was several hundred feet high and decorated with various valuable objects. On the temple was erected an ornamental post with a big *padmarāga* ruby set on its spire, which shone brilliantly in the air and could be seen at a distance of ten thousand *li* on a calm and cloudness night."

〔2〕Cp. DDB. See also Kottkamp 1992, p. 61.

〔3〕The last letter is not a clear *-r*, but also not a clear *-z*. Cp. pict. 2.

〔4〕Róna-Tas 1961, pp. 94-96.

〔5〕Judachin 1965, p. 344.

〔6〕There is a Sanskrit word which phonetically could serve as the etymon: *caṅkura*, hypothetically > **čaŋkur,* but semantically it is not very probable, because Monier-Williams has only three meanings "a carriage; a tree; any vehicle" (MW 382b). I could not find this rare word in a meaning related to *stūpa* or other *vihāra* buildings.

believe that it addresses also us?

References

Boyce, Mary. *A Catalogue of the Iranian Manuscripts in Manichean Script in the German Turfan Collection*, Berlin 1960.

Chao Huashan. "New evidence of Manichaeism in Asia: A description of some recently discovered Manichaean temples in Turfan", in: *Monumenta Serica* 44 (1996), 267–315.

Clark, Larry V. *Reedition of the Manichaean Turkic texts* (forthcoming).

DDB. Digital Dictionary of Buddhism (Charles Muller, Tokyo).

Geng Shimin & Klimkeit, Hans-Joachim. "Zerstörung manichäischer Klöster in Turfan", in: *Zentralasiatische Studi*en 18 (1985), 7–11.

Henning, Walter Bruno. "Neue Materialien zur Geschichte des Manichäismus", in: *Zeitschrift der Deutschen Morgenländischen Gesellschaft* 90 (1936), 1–18.

Judachin, K. K. *Kirgizsko-russkij slovar'*. Moskva 1965.

Kottkamp, Heino. *Der Stupa als Repräsentation des buddhistischen Heilsweges. Untersuchungen zur Entstehung und Entwicklung architektonischer Symbolik*, Wiesbaden 1992.

Li Rongxi. *A Biography of the Tripiṭaka Master of the Great Ci'en Monastery of the Great Tang Dynasty*, Berkeley 1995.

Monier-Williams, M. *A Sanskrit-English Dictionary*, Oxford 1899.

Moriyasu, Takao. "Uighur Buddhist Stake Inscriptions from Turfan", in: *De Dunhuang à Istanbul. Hommage à James Russell Hamilton*, ed. by L. Bazin and P. Zieme, Turnhout 2001 (Silk Road Studies V), 149–223.

ウイグル=マニ教史の研究. A Study on the History of Uighur Manichaeism. Research on Some Manichaean Materials and their Historical

Background, Kyoto 1991.

Die Geschichte des uigurischen Manichäismus an der Seidenstraße. Forschungen zu manichäischen Quellen und ihrem geschichtlichen Hintergrund, Wiesbaden 2004.

Pelliot, Paul. "Tokharien et koutchéen", in: *Journal asiatique* 1934, 23-106.

Ragoza, A. N. *Sogdijskie fragmenty central'no-aziatskogo sobranija Instituta Vostokovedenija*, Moskva 1980.

Röhrborn, Klaus. *Die alttürkische Xuanzang-Biographie VII. Nach der Handschrift von Leningrad, Paris und Peking sowie nach dem Transkript von Annemarie von Gabain*, Wiesbaden 1991.

Die alttürkische Xuanzang-Biographie VIII. Nach der Handschrift von Leningrad, Paris und Peking sowie nach dem Transkript von Annemarie von Gabain, Wiesbaden 1996.

Róna-Tas, András. "Notes on the Kazak Yurt of West Mongolia", in: *Acta Orientalia Academiae Scientiarum Hungaricae* 12 (1961), 79–102.

Sundermann, Werner. "Probleme der Interpretation manichäisch-soghdischer Briefe", in: *Acta Antiqua Academiae Scientiarum Hungaricae* 25 (1980), 289–316 (reprinted in: *From Hecataeus to al-Ḫuwārizmī. Bactrian, Pahlavi, Sogdian, Persian, Sanskrit, Syriac, Arabic, Chinese, Greek, and Latin sources for the history of pre-Islamic Central Asia*, ed. J. Harmatta, Budapest 1984).

"Eine Re-Edition zweier manichäisch-soghdischer Briefe", in: *Iranian Languages and Texts from Iran and Turfan. Ronald E. Emmerick Memorial Volume*, ed. by M. Macuch, M. Maggi and W. Sundermann, Wiesbaden 2007, 403–421.

Toalster, John Peter Claver. *Die uigurische Xuan-Zang-Biographie. 4. Kapitel mit Übersetzung und Kommentar* (Inaugural-Dissertation), Giessen 1977.

Wilkens, Jens. *Alttürkische Handschriften Teil 8: Manichäisch- türkische Texte der Berliner Turfasammlung*, Stuttgart 2000.

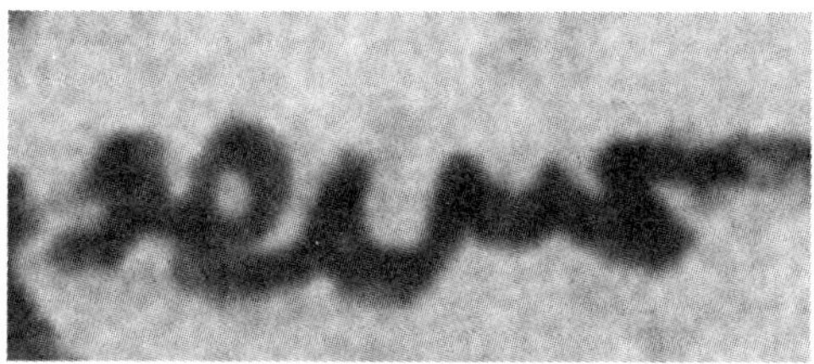

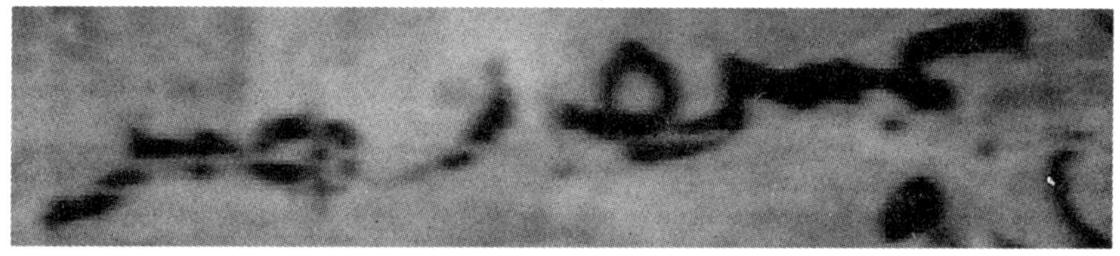

10 景教与明教的七时礼忏

马小鹤
（美国哈佛大学哈佛燕京图书馆）

近年来，引起学界重视的霞浦文书中，有一份《摩尼光佛》。这份文书称颂了佛、法、僧三宝，讲到僧时说：

> 皈依僧，罗汉真人上佺，同光性降十天。广游苦海驾明船，涝漉无价珍宝至法筵。救拔无数真善明缘；善明缘，五戒三印俱全。微妙义最幽玄，光明众广宣传。七时礼忏，志意倍精专，流传正法相继万年。[1]

我们先对这段文字中的若干摩尼教因素略作梳理。“僧”是佛教术语，借指摩尼教僧侣。“罗汉”出自梵文 arhat，佛教术语，原意是应受尊敬、供养的人；此处当指摩尼教圣人。京藏《摩尼教残经》第 11—16 说：“以是义故，净风明使以五类魔及五明身二力和合，造成世界十天八地。”“十天”是摩尼教神祇净风及善母创世时所建立的十层天。敦煌摩尼教文献《下部赞》〈普启赞文〉说“具足善法五净戒”（第 137 行），“五戒”即“五净戒”，是摩尼教僧侣应该遵守的五种戒律：不打诳语、不杀、贞洁、素食、乐贫。“三印”即口印——不说谎话、手印——不杀生、胸印——不淫。《下部赞》〈此偈你逾沙忏悔文〉中，摩尼教平信徒——听者忏悔说：“于七施、十戒、三印法门，若不具修，愿罪销灭！”《摩尼光佛》这段文字很可能受《下部赞》〈叹五明文第二叠〉影响：“复告善业明兄弟，用心思惟诠妙身，各作勇健智船主，渡此流浪他乡子。……幽深苦海寻珍宝，奔奉涅槃清净王。……

[1] 元文琪：《福建霞浦摩尼教科仪典籍重大发现论证》，载于《世界宗教研究》2011年第5期，第173页。

法称所受诸妙供，庄严清净还本主。……过去诸佛罗汉等，并为五明置妙法。”（第249—256行）按照摩尼教教义，人的灵魂乃光明分子，犹如“无价珍宝”沉沦“苦海”，僧侣“驾明船”，把这些灵魂“救拔”出来。

本文主要探讨所谓“七时礼忏”，这是指明教僧侣每天七个时段进行祈祷。这有助于我们确定《大秦景教流行中国碑》上的“七时礼赞”的含义。

景教碑论圣洗瞻礼祈祷等部分写道：“七时礼赞，大庇存亡。七日一荐，洗心反素。”“七日一荐”指基督教传统中于主日的礼拜仪式。但对“七时礼赞”的诠释，则有颇为相左的解说。徐谦信认为，七时礼赞：每天七时有礼拜赞美。按“七时”系古时所指的一天十二时之七时（午时），并不是伟烈、理雅各所说的“每天七次”。[1]段晴教授详细分析了“时”在《全唐诗》中的用例，可以得出三种解释：（一）“七时”指季节。（二）“七时”指一日中的一段时光。（三）“七时”指第七个时辰。在唐诗中数字与“时”搭配表示某一时辰的用法仅有一例，而且前后皆有限定词语，才不至于产生误会。[2]因此，“七时”应该不是指午时，徐信谦“七时”指午时之说难以成立。

段晴详细引用了Kannoonkadan关于东叙利亚教会的年历分为七个循环期的研究，认为“七时”之说，除了可以解释为“日七次”以外，似乎又可以释作“一年的七个时令”。不过，她承认，历史上遗留下来的关于中国景教的文献实在稀少，在没有寻得其他坠绪佐证之前，妄下定论，难免武断。[3]本文即尝试在叙利亚文景教资料与明教的祈祷礼仪中寻一些坠绪佐证，以支持“日七次”之说。

---

〔1〕徐谦信：《唐朝景教碑文注释》，载于刘小枫主编：《道与言：华夏文化与基督文化相遇》，上海：上海三联书店，1995年，第19页；翁绍军：《汉语景教文献诠释》，北京：三联书店，1996年，第52页。

〔2〕任希古：玉署三时晓。指一日的第三时，即寅时，如现代所谓三点钟。段晴：《景教碑中“七时”之说》，载于叶奕良编：《伊朗学在中国论文集》（第三集），北京：北京大学出版社，2003年，第24-25页。

〔3〕中国宗教历史文献继承编纂委员会编纂：《东传福音》第一册，合肥：黄山书社，2005年，第69-70页；段晴：《景教碑中“七时”之说》，第23-29页。

段晴指出：白居易的《偶作》之一说明“时”标明一日中的一段时光：“日出起盥栉，振衣入道场。……日高始就食，食亦非膏粱。……日午脱巾簪，燕息窗下床。……日西引杖屦，散步游林塘。……日入多不食，有时唯命觞。……一日分五时，作息率有常。”[1]此诗中“五时”指日出、日高、日午、日西、日入，景教碑“七时”的用法应该与此相仿，“七时”乃指日出（早晨）、日高（第三时）、日午（第六时）、日西（第九时）、日入（晚餐之时）、晚间、夜间。

将景教碑上的“七时”理解为每天七个时段，源头是明末李之藻（1565—1603），他作于天启五年（1625）的《读景教碑书后》写道：“十字之持，七时礼赞，七日一荐，悉与利氏西来传述规程吻合。”[2]耶稣会士阳玛诺（Manuel Dias，1574—1659）崇祯辛巳（1641）所撰的《景教流行中国碑颂正诠》认同李之藻之说，对“七时礼赞，大庇存亡”注释道：“斯举其益之六，言圣教修士，既登圣会品级之尊，诵经之工，每日七次，不得少缺。其诵经之益，不特施及在教生人，并及在教亡者。或在炼所，未获升天，因赖修士礼赞之工，获拯厥苦年。”[3]威烈（Alexander Wylie，1885—1887）[4]、理雅各（James Legge，1815—1897）[5]、佐伯好郎（1871—1965）[6]等均将“七时”理解为每日

---

〔1〕http://www.zwbk.org/zh-tw/Lemma_Show/15853.aspx （2012/6/14）。段晴：《景教碑中“七时”之说》，第24页。

〔2〕http://jesus.tw/Nestorian_Stele (2012/6/14)

〔3〕《东传福音》，第一册，第91页。

〔4〕A. Wylie, The Nestorian monument; an ancient record of Christianity in China, with special reference to the expedition of Frits v. Holm, ed. by Dr. Paul Carus. Containing: Mr. Holm's account of how the replica was procured, the original Chinese text of the inscription, A. Wylie's English translation, and historical notes on the Nestorians. Chicago, The Open court publishing company, 1909. http://books.google.com/books?vid=HARVARD:32044024460842&printsec=titlepage#v=onepage&q&f=false (2012/6/14)

〔5〕James Legge, The Nestorian monument of Hsî-an Fû in Shen-hsî, China, relating to the diffusion of Christianity in China in the seventh and eighth centuries; with the Chinese text of the inscription, a translation, and notes, and a lecture on the monument with a sketch of subsequent Christian missions in China and their present state, by James Legge. London, Trübner, 1888. New York, Reprinted by Paragon Book Reprint Corp., 1966, p.9.

〔6〕Yoshirō Saeki, *The Nestorian Documents and Relics in China*, Tokyo, Toho Bunkwa Gakuin: Academy of Oriental Culture, Tokyo Institute, 1951, p.56.

七次（seven times a day）。莫尔（A. C. Moule，1873—1957）将“七时”英译为“七个时段（at the seven hours）”。[1] 朱谦之说明：“所谓‘七时礼赞’者，言每日七时祈告歌诗，即昧爽、日出、辰时、午时、日昳、日晡、亥时是。”[2]

伯希和（P. Pelliot，1878—1945）也将“七时礼赞，大庇存亡”理解为：每日七个时段，他们礼拜赞歌，对生者和死者都大有助益。他在注释中说明：“每日七次祈祷（Ces sept prières journalières）后来减少到四次，至少对在俗人士来说是如此。”他所根据的资料包括巴杰（G. P. Badger，1815—1888）所著的《景教徒》（*The Nestorians*），巴哲（E. A. Wallis Budge，1857—1934）编辑、英译的《修道院司事长之书》（*The Book of Governors*）以及他自己与沙畹（Ed. Chavannes，1865—1918）于 1913 年合撰的研究摩尼教的论文。[3]

巴杰《景教徒及其仪式》（*The Nestorians and their rituals*）中关于 19 世纪景教徒祈祷时间的记载如下：[4]

> 景教徒与其它东方信徒一样，一天是从日落后开始算起的，这个时段的礼拜被称为 *d'Ramsha*，即晚祷（Vespers）。此后集会就散了，在黄昏时分再回到教堂里来做夜祷(Compline)，称为 *Soobaa*。但是，后者完全停止了，只用于封斋期（Lent），纪念尼尼微人（Ninevites）谦卑的三天，以及一些节日的前夕，那时夜祷与晚祷结合在一起，共同形成一个礼拜。按照顺序，下一个祈祷是 *Slotha d'Lilya*，即宵祷（Nocturns），在宵祷时，指定念一组称为 Moutwé

---

〔1〕A. C. Moule, *Christians in China before the year 1550*, London, Society for Promoting Christian Knowledge; New York and Toronto, The Macmillan Co., 1930, p.38.

〔2〕朱谦之：《中国景教：中国古代基督教研究》，北京：东方出版社，1993年，第169页。

〔3〕P. Pelliot, *L'inscription nestorienne de Si-ngan-fou*, by Paul Pelliot ; edited with supplements by Antonino Forte. Kyoto : Scuola di studi sull'Asia orientale ; Paris : Collège de France, Institut des Hautes Etudes Chinoises, 1996, pp.175, 219.

〔4〕George Percy Badger, The Nestorians and their rituals with the narrative of a mission to Mesopotamia and Coordistan in 1842-1844, and of a late visit to those countries in 1850 : also, researches into the present condition of the Syrian Jacobites, papal Syrians, and Chaldeans, and an inquiry into the religious tenets of the Yezeedees. London : Joseph Masters, 1852, v. II, p.16. http://nrs.harvard.edu/urn-3:HUL.FIG:002465254 (2012/6/16)

的祈祷文［字面意思是“施恩座”；在念这组祈祷文时，集会的信徒均坐着］。这之后是 *Shahra*，即晨祷（Lauds），在拂晓时开始进行；在这些祈祷之后是 *Slotha d' Sapra*，即早课（Prime）。但是，这种晚上起来参加公共礼拜的习惯已经过时很久了，现在霄祷、晨祷和早课形成一个礼拜，一般被称为 *Slotha d' Sapra*，即早晨祈祷（Morning Prayer）。

巴杰从末·阿布德·耶舒（Mar Abd Yeshua）13 世纪末辑录的历次宗教会议文献中，摘录一些文字，说明以前景教徒所采用的祈祷时间，以及后来发生的那些改变的原因：

耶稣基督，我们至善和仁慈的神和主，他知道我们凡人的脆弱，先知们展示了他的神性，使徒们说明了他统一的神性与人性，吩咐我们做七次祈祷，适合我们的状况。普世宗教父们（Catholic Fathers）自己遵循这条规矩，以此要求僧侣与修士，他们的继承者规定七次礼拜的每一次都应该由三部赞美组诗（*hoolâlé*［一部 *hoolâlé* 由一定数量的赞美诗组成］）这个规矩仍然由比较热衷祈祷的圣洁的牧师和义人所遵循。但是后起的教父们认为，并非所有的人同样倾心于神圣的崇拜，此外，他们平常的工作并非总是允许他们根据法规完成这种崇拜，规定俗人只要做四次礼拜，即晚祷、夜祷、霄祷和晨祷，他们以我主的言辞印证这个规矩。

晚祷和晨祷的规定具有经典性的权威，不能增减。根据高等修道院（*Deir Alleita*）的做法，夜祷和宵祷的规定如下：夜祷由一部赞美诗组（*hoolâla*）、一曲圣歌（anthem）、一首短的赞颂上帝的赞美诗（doxology）、一篇短祈祷文（collect）以及一篇连祷文（litany）组成。霄祷由五或七部赞美诗组、一曲圣歌、一首短的赞颂上帝的赞美诗、一篇短祈祷文以及一篇连祷文组成。考虑到俗人必须从事世俗职业，允许他们自愿参加这些礼拜；但是晨祷和晚祷是经典规定不可有间断的。

末·阿布德·耶舒说明了上述祈祷时段的理由：

第一次祈祷是晨祷，……因为这些理由，晨祷排在第一。

第二次祈祷是晚祷，其合适的时间是日落前一刻。……

第三次祈祷被称之为 *Soobaa*，［字面的意思是“饱餐”］，得名于圣人终日斋戒，［他们只在夜里才吃饭；］但是对俗人来说，它意为“睡前的祈祷”……

第四次礼拜是宵祷，其时间由每一个信徒根据其对此神圣礼仪的热诚来决定。有的人在头遍鸡叫，其他人在第二遍鸡叫，其他人在第三次鸡叫时祈祷；但是现在遵循的普通时段是在教会里集会进行神圣崇拜的时候。[1]

麦克莱恩（A. J. MacLean）在其译注的《东方叙利亚日课》的导言中概括了《教典（*Book of Canon Law*）》的规定：对所有的人要求一日四次祈祷——晚祷、夜祷、夜间祈祷（Night Service）和晨祷。它承认的第一次和最后一次祈祷的规定具有最大的权威，它说，它们的时间长度不可增减；但是其他两次则“根据修道院的规矩”，对俗人来说，则时间长短不拘。（第 5 章第 2 节）夜祷现在几乎取消了，只在一年中某些特定的日子举行，一般夜祷与晚祷合二为一了。《教典》（第 6 章第 1 节）要求修道士与“优秀牧师和俗人”每天做七个时段（seven hours）的祈祷。[2]

上述《教典》记载的修士一日祈祷七次的规定起源古老。一种难以确定年代的《关于僧侣在其小室中的责任的教规》的第 6 条写道：“每天他将完成 300 次坚实的 būrkē，……这些是在修道院集会固定的七次祈祷（时段）之外的。”[3] 这部教规并非为个别的隐士制定的，而是为修道院中的修士制定的。

马鲁达（Mārūdā）大约在 399—410 年间是亚美尼亚与叙利亚边境上迈弗卡特（Maipherqaṭ）的主教，他代表拜占庭皇帝出使波斯，建立

〔1〕摘自末·阿布德·耶舒13世纪末辑录的 Sinhadòs，即《教典》。Badger, 1852, v. II, pp.16–18.

〔2〕Nestorian Church. *East Syrian daily offices*, translated from the Syriac with introduction, notes and indices, and an appendix containing the lectionary and glossary by Arthur John Maclean. Piscataway, NJ : Gorgias Press, c2003, 1894., pp.xii–xiii.

〔3〕Arthur Vööbus, Syriac and Arabic documents regarding legislation relative to Syrian asceticism. Edited, translated and furnished with literary historical data. Stockholm, Etse, 1960, pp.105, 107.

了两国之间的友好关系。他以其能力、律己和医学知识，赢得了波斯国王耶兹德格德一世（Jazdgard I，399—420）的信任，于 410 年 2 月 1 日在首都塞琉西亚–泰西封（Seleucia- Ctesiphon）主持了一次宗教会议，重新组织了波斯教会，标志着其发展的新阶段。这次会议的文献提及一些教规，73 章教规归诸马鲁达，不过其中可能有若干后来加上去的资料。其第 54 章教规写道：[1]

> 此外，一天应该完成七次礼拜：一次在早晨，第三、第六和第九小时（各一次），在晚餐（时间一次），在晚间（一次），在夜间（一次），从而（僧侣）能完成圣大卫（David）说的："一天七次我赞美你，因为你的律法，噢，正义者！"[2]

迦施加尔的亚伯拉罕（Abraham of Kaškar）是 6 世纪东方亚述教会（Assyrian Church of the East）修道院复兴之父，约 492 年生于美索不达米亚的迦施加尔，先在阿拉伯人中传教，后至埃及修习修道院制度。他回到萨珊波斯后，在尼西比斯（Nisibis，在今土耳其东南部）附近的伊兹拉（Izlā）山，建立大修道院，并制定了教规。现存的《迦施加尔的亚伯拉罕教规》撰于 571 年 6 月，其第三条是关于祈祷的，其中写道：[3]

此外，关于祈祷礼拜的时间（times），赞美诗作者写道："我因你公义的典章，一天七次赞美你。"

拜斯阿布赫（Bêth Âbhê）修道院可谓伊兹拉山大修道院最重要的支脉，约于 6 世纪末建于底格里斯河的支流大萨卜河（Great Zab river）

---

〔1〕Ibn aṭ-Ṭaiyib 这样写道："他必须每日七次礼拜、祷告、祈祷，即早晨、三点钟、中午、九点钟、晚间（evening）、一天结束之际（apodeipnon）和夜间（night）。" Maruthas, v.2, pp.v–xi, 82; 参阅 Arthur Vööbus, 1960, pp.115–118, 142.

〔2〕《旧约》《诗篇》（Psalm）119：164，参阅 Peshitta. The Holy Bible from ancient Eastern manuscripts. Containing the Old and New Testaments, translated from the Peshitta, the authorized Bible of the church of the East, by George M. Lamsa. Philadelphia, A. J. Holman Co. [1957], p.650.

〔3〕Arthur Vööbus, 1960, pp.150–151, 157–158. 参阅 E.A. Wallis Budge, The book of governors: the Historia monastica of Thomas, bishop of Marga, A. D. 840, edited from Syriac manuscripts in the British museum and other libraries by E.A. Wallis Budge. London, K. Paul, Trench, Trübner & co., ltd., 1893, I, p.cxxxvi–cxxxvii. http://nrs.harvard.edu/urn-3:HUL.FIG:002233460 (2012/6/17)

右岸的一座山上。此修道院拥有大量地产，被称为“修道院之王”，与波斯贵族有密切联系，其修士学识渊博，人才辈出，在 595—850 年间教育出来的修士中有成百人出任美索不达米亚、阿拉伯、波斯、亚美尼亚、库尔德斯坦和中国的景教主教辖区的主教、大主教和司事长。马尔加的托马斯（Thomas of Marga）于 9 世纪上半叶撰成《修道院司事长之书》，记载了拜斯阿布赫修道院的历史及其历任司事长，是景教历史最宝贵的史料之一。英译本作者巴哲在导言中概述拜斯阿布赫修道院：〔1〕

教会每日进行七次祈祷，僧侣们认真仿效《诗篇》作者所说的：“一天七次我赞美你，因为你公义的典章。”

从以上资料中可以看到，至少 5—9 世纪之间，甚至晚至 13 世纪末，景教修士遵奉《诗篇》之说，每天做七次祈祷。伯希和已经注意到景教的“七时礼赞”与明教的“七时作礼”之间的联系。早在 1913 年，沙畹、伯希和合著的《中国发现的一部摩尼教经典》引用了《佛祖统纪》卷 48 转引的洪迈（1123—1202）著《夷坚志》：“……明教会……其修持者正午一食，裸尸以葬，以七时作礼。”〔2〕

《宋会要辑稿》刑法二记载，宣和二年（1120）十一月四日，臣僚言：“一、温州等处狂悖之人，自称明教，号为行者。……一、明教之人所念经文及绘画佛像，号曰：……《七时偈》……”〔3〕意大利学者富安敦（A. Forte）1973 年用法文翻译了这段资料，作了评注，关于《七时偈》，他认为可能与洪迈说的摩尼教徒“以七时作礼”有关。〔4〕

笔者根据霞浦宋明教徒林瞪与雷法有关，而南宋道士白玉蟾（1194

〔1〕E.A. Wallis Budge, The book of governors: the Historia monastica of Thomas, bishop of Marga, A. D. 840, edited from Syriac manuscripts in the British museum and other libraries by E.A. Wallis Budge. London, K. Paul, Trench, Trübner & co., ltd., 1893. Piscataway, NJ : Gorgias Press, 2003, v.1, p.lv. http://nrs.harvard.edu/urn-3:HUL.FIG:002233460 (2012/6/17)

〔2〕É. Chavannes & P. Pelliot, “Un traité manichéen retrouvé en Chine”, *Journal Asiatique,* 1913, p.338, n.6; p.339, p.355, note.

〔3〕《宋会要辑稿》一六五册《刑法》二之七八，徐松辑，北京：中华书局1957年版（2006年重印），第6534页。

〔4〕Antonino Forte, “Deux etudes sur le manichéisme chinois”, *T'oung pao* LIX, 1973, p.241.

一？）精通神霄雷法，且其语录有涉及明教的内容，遂将《海琼白真人语录》通读一遍，果然发现其《万法归一歌》中涉及明教徒七时作礼："明教专门事灭魔，七时功德便如何？不知清净光明意，面色萎黄空自劳。"〔1〕

元代陈高（1315—1366）所撰《竹西楼记》记述温州平阳明教寺宇潜光院："明教之始，相传以为自苏邻国入流中土，瓯闽人多奉之。其徒斋戒持律颇严谨，日一食，昼夜七时咏膜拜。"〔2〕林顺道先生认为："'昼夜七时'既非指现在所说的七点钟，也不是指昼夜分为七时，不能解读。'昼夜七时，呗咏膜拜'可解释为'昼夜做七次礼拜'。"〔3〕林悟殊先生认为：《夷坚志》说的"以七时作礼"，《宋会要辑稿》"宣和二年十一月四日臣僚言"历数"明教之人所念经文及绘画佛像"中的《七时偈》者，可能就是用于七时作礼。《竹西楼记》作"昼夜七时，咸瞑拜焉"，当同。〔4〕

明教的"七时作礼"、《七时偈》、"七时功德"、"七时咏膜拜"和"七时礼忏"自然与摩尼教选民每天七次祈祷的规矩一脉相承。亨宁（W. B. Henning）1936 年刊布的《摩尼教祈祷忏悔书》的粟特文"祈祷与［赞美诗］"中，选民忏悔道："我有缺七次祈祷（VII 'frywn），七首赞美诗，七次忏悔和七'施'，罪孽深重。"亨宁已经指出，每天选民要做七次祈祷，而听者则做四次祈祷。〔5〕

根据阿拉伯图书馆学家奈迪木（al-Nadīm，995 年卒）的《群书类述》（*al-Fihrist*）记载，摩尼教徒每天要做 7 次祈祷（ṣalawāt sabʿ）或

〔1〕Ma Xiaohe, "Remanis of the Religion of Light in Xiapu (霞浦) County, Fujian Province"，刊于《欧亚学刊》，第9辑，北京：中华书局，2009年，pp.103–104, 108 note 57.

〔2〕陈高：《不繫舟渔集》，哈佛燕京藏精抄本，卷12，叶24。其他版本的校勘见林悟殊《中古三夷教辨证》，北京：中华书局，2005年，第147页。

〔3〕林顺道：《苍南元明时代摩尼教及其遗迹》，载于《世界宗教研究》1989年第4期，第108页，注释4。

〔4〕林悟殊、殷小平：《〈夷坚志〉明教纪事史料价值辨识》，载于《中华文史论丛》2012年第2期，第279页。

〔5〕Henning, W. B. *Ein manichäisches Bet- und Beichtbuch*, APAW, 1936, 10 (*BBB*),pp.38, 16; Klimkeit, H.-J. *Gnosis on the Silk Road. Gnostic Parables, Hymns and Prayers*, Harper San Fransisco, 1993, p.141.

者 4 次祈祷。选民要做 7 次祈祷，听者则只要做 4 次祈祷。听者的 4 次祈祷的时间是：第一次祈祷是太阳刚偏西时（*al-zawāl*）[1]，第二次祈祷是太阳刚偏西与日落之间，然后在太阳落山之后是日落祈祷，日落后三小时是黄昏（*'atamah*）[2]祈祷。每一次祈祷和拜倒，祈祷者都像第一次祈祷时那样做，第一次祈祷是福音使者（*al-Bashīr*）的祈祷。[3]

1948 年，在印度出版了比鲁尼（al-Bayrūnī，973?—1048）研究通过测量阴影来计算时间的专著（Ifrād al-maqāl fī amr al-ẓilāl）。此书清楚地描述了摩尼教选民每天祈祷七次的时间：

> 摩尼教徒的祈祷对选民（ṣiddīqūn）来说是七次，其中第一次是中午的柱祈祷（*ṣalātu l-'amūd*），三十七拜（*rak'ah*），但是在星期一他们将其减少两拜。然后下午三时左右（*'aṣr*），二十一拜。然后黄昏（*'atamah*），二十五拜。然后入夜半小时，同样（数量）。然后子夜，三十拜。然后拂晓，五十拜。然后夜晚已尽、白天开始（即日出），福音使者（*al-bašīr*）（的祈祷），二十六拜。他们当中的听者（sammā'ūn），即忙于世俗事务者，在中午、黄昏（'išā'）、拂晓和日出，作四次祈祷。[4]

我们可以把景教与摩尼教的祈祷时段列为下表：

---

〔1〕al-zawāl，指正午太阳达到最高点后，刚刚开始偏西的时候。

〔2〕'atamah，日落以后，夜晚的前三分之一。

〔3〕Ibn al-Nadim, tr. B. Dodge, *The Fihrist of al-Nadīm. A Tenth-Century Survey of Muslim Culture*, New York and London, 1970, v.2, pp.790-791.

〔4〕Kennedy, E.S. *The exhaustive treatise on shadows*, by Abu al-Rayḥān Muḥammad b. Aḥmad al-Bīrūnī ; translation & commentary by E.S. Kennedy. Aleppo, Syria : Institute for the History of Arabic Science, University of Aleppo, 1976, I, pp.225-226; François de Blois, "The Manichaean Daily Prayers", *Studia Manichaica: IV. Internationaler Kongress zum Manichäismus, Berlin, 14.-18. Juli 1997*, herausgegeben von Ronald E. Emmerick, Werner Sundermann und Peter Zieme. Berlin : Akademie Verlag, 2000, pp.49-54.

景教与摩尼教的祈祷时段表

景教			摩尼教		
马鲁达	《教典》	巴杰	比鲁尼		奈迪木
修士（410 年）	平信徒（1298 年）	19 世纪	选民	听者	听者
早晨	晨祷	拂晓 Shahra 晨祷	拂晓（50 拜）	拂晓	
第三时		Slotha d' Sapra 早课	日出（26 拜）“福音使者”	日出	
第六时（中午）			中午（37 拜）“柱”	中午	正午过后
第九时			下午三点左右（21 拜）		下午三点（12 拜）
晚餐（时）（晚间）	晚祷	日落后 d' Ramsha 晚祷	黄昏（25 拜）	黄昏	日落后（12 拜）
晚间（一天结束之际）	夜祷	黄昏 Soobaa 夜祷	半小时后（25 拜）		黄昏（12 拜）
夜间	鸡鸣之时 霄祷	Slotha d' Lilya 霄祷	子夜（30 拜）		

通过上表的比较，我们可以看到，虽然具体的时间有所不同，但是景教与明教的日课次数仍然有一些共同之处。僧侣（修士、选民）与俗人（平信徒、听者）每天祈祷次数不同，僧侣是 7 次，俗人是 4 次。根据欧洲人的观察，19 世纪波斯景教对信徒每天祈祷次数的要求比较宽松，大约只要 4 次就行了。在中国，直到明代，甚至更晚，明教僧侣每天祈祷 7 次的特点仍然相当引人注目。

参考书目

Badger, George Percy, *The Nestorians and their rituals with the narrative of a mission to Mesopotamia and Coordistan in 1842—1844, and of a late visit to those countries in 1850 : also, researches into the present condition of the Syrian Jacobites, papal Syrians, and Chaldeans, and an inquiry into the religious tenets of the Yezeedees*. London: Joseph Masters, 1852. http://nrs.harvard.edu/urn-3:HUL.FIG:002465254 (2012/6/16)

Budge, E.A. Wallis, *The book of governors: the Historia monastica of Thomas, bishop of Marga, A. D. 840, edited from Syriac manuscripts in the British museum and other libraries by E.A. Wallis Budge*. London, K. Paul, Trench, Trübner & co., ltd., 1893. Piscataway, NJ: Gorgias Press, 2003. http://nrs.harvard.edu/urn-3:HUL.FIG:002233460 (2012/6/17)

Chavannes, é. & P. Pelliot, "Un traité manichéen retrouvé en Chine", *Journal Asiatique,* 1911, 1913.

陈高：《不繫舟渔集》，陈候官校，据明成化元年序刊本抄，哈佛燕京图书馆藏 http://nrs.harvard.edu/urn-3:FHCL:2559567

De Blois, François, "The Manichaean Daily Prayers", *Studia Manichaica : IV. Internationaler Kongress zum Manichäismus, Berlin, 14.-18. Juli 1997*, herausgegeben von Ronald E. Emmerick, Werner Sundermann und Peter Zieme. Berlin: Akademie Verlag, c2000. pp.49–54.

中国宗教历史文献继承编纂委员会编纂：《东传福音》，合肥：黄山书社，2005 年。

段晴：《景教碑中"七时"之说》，载于叶奕良编：《伊朗学在中国论文集》（第三集），北京：北京大学出版社，2003 年，第 21–30 页。

Fihrist, Ibn al-Nadim, tr. B. Dodge, *The Fihrist of al-Nadīm. A Tenth-Century Survey of Muslim Culture*, New York and London, 1970, 2 vols.

Forte, Antonino, "Deux etudes sur le manichéisme chinois", *T'oung pao* LIX, 1973, pp.220–53.

Henning, W. B. *Ein manichäisches Bet- und Beichtbuch*, APAW, 1936, 10 (*BBB*). In Henning, 1977, I, pp.417–557.

Henning, W. B. *Selected Papers* I-II, Leiden et al., 1977.

Kennedy, E.S. *The exhaustive treatise on shadows*, by Abu al-Rayḥān Muḥammad b. Aḥmad al-Bīrūnī ; translation & commentary by E.S. Kennedy. Aleppo, Syria : Institute for the History of Arabic Science,

University of Aleppo, 1976.

Klimkeit, H.-J. *Gnosis on the Silk Road. Gnostic Parables, Hymns and Prayers*, Harper San Fransisco, 1993.

Legge, James, *The Nestorian monument of Hsî-an Fû in Shen-hsî, China, relating to the diffusion of Christianity in China in the seventh and eighth centuries; with the Chinese text of the inscription, a translation, and notes, and a lecture on the monument with a sketch of subsequent Christian missions in China and their present state*, by James Legge. London, Trübner, 1888. New York, Reprinted by Paragon Book Reprint Corp., 1966.

林顺道：《苍南元明时代摩尼教及其遗迹》，载于《世界宗教研究》1989 年第 4 期，第 107–111 页。

林悟殊：《中古三夷教辨证》，北京：中华书局，2005 年。

林悟殊、殷小平：《〈夷坚志〉明教纪事史料价值辨识》，载于《中华文史论丛》2012 年第 2 期，第 255–283 页。

Ma Xiaohe, “Remanis of the Religion of Light in Xiapu (霞浦) County, Fujian Province”，刊于《欧亚学刊》，第 9 辑，北京：中华书局，2009 年，第 81–108 页。

Maruthas, Saint, Bishop of Martyropolis, *The canons ascribed to Mārūtā of Maipherqaṭ and related sources*, edited by Arthur Vööbus. Lovanii : E. Peeters, 1982.

Moule, A. C. *Christians in China before the year* 1550, London, Society for Promoting Christian Knowledge; New York and Toronto, The Macmillan Co., 1930.

Nestorian Church. *East Syrian daily offices*, translated from the Syriac with introduction, notes and indices, and an appendix containing the lectionary and glossary by Arthur John Maclean. Piscataway, NJ : Gorgias Press, c2003, 1894.

Pelliot, P. *L'inscription nestorienne de Si-ngan-fou*, by Paul Pelliot ; edited with supplements by Antonino Forte. Kyoto: Scuola di studi sull'Asia orientale ; Paris : Collège de France, Institut des Hautes Etudes Chinoises, 1996.

Peshitta. The Holy Bible from ancient Eastern manuscripts. Containing the Old and New Testaments, translated from the Peshitta, the authorized Bible of the church of the East, by George M. Lamsa. Philadelphia, A. J. Holman Co. [1957]

Saeki, Yoshirō, *The Nestorian Documents and Relics in China*, Tokyo, Toho Bunkwa Gakuin: Academy of Oriental Culture, Tokyo Institute, 1951.

《宋会要辑稿》，徐松辑，北京：中华书局，1957 年（2006 年重印）。

Vööbus, Arthur. Syriac and Arabic documents regarding legislation relative to Syrian asceticism. Edited, translated and furnished with literary historical data. Stockholm, Etse, 1960.

翁绍军：《汉语景教文献诠释》，北京：三联书店，1996 年。

Wylie, A. *The Nestorian monument; an ancient record of Christianity in China, with special reference to the expedition of Frits v. Holm, ed. by Dr. Paul Carus. Containing: Mr. Holm's account of how the replica was procured, the original Chinese text of the inscription, A. Wylie's English translation, and historical notes on the Nestorians*. Chicago, The Open court publishing company, 1909. http://books.google.com/books?vid=HARVARD:32044024460842&printsec=titlepage#v=onepage&q&f=false (2012/6/14)

徐谦信：《唐朝景教碑文注释》，载于刘小枫主编：《道与言：华夏文化与基督文化相遇》，上海：上海三联书店，1995 年，第 3–42 页。

元文琪：《福建霞浦摩尼教科仪典籍重大发现论证》，载于《世界宗教研究》2011 年第 5 期，第 169–180 页。

朱谦之：《中国景教：中国古代基督教研究》，北京：东方出版社，1993 年。

11　敦煌景教文献写本的真与伪

荣新江
（北京大学中国古代史研究中心）

11.1　小岛文书辨伪

1991 年 2 月，笔者自日本东京飞抵伦敦，应英国国家图书馆的邀请，做敦煌写本编目工作，在图书馆中文部主任吴芳思的安排下，住进伦敦南边一个简陋的公寓里面，除了公共的客厅、厨房，有四个卧室，我居其一，另外两间是新朋友，而最后一个房间里，居然住的是老相识——中山大学林悟殊教授。

于是，从 2 月到 8 月，我有比较充裕的时间向林先生问学，平日我去英国图书馆工作，他去挂单的伦敦大学亚非学院做研究，周末的时候我们常常一起去亚非学院图书馆，各取所需，收集资料，然后一起打道回府。我们之间无所不谈，但最中心的话题，是进入中国的三夷教，也就是祆教、摩尼教、景教。此时的林先生已经出版大著《摩尼教及其东渐》，在继续关注摩尼教之外，领域扩展到祆教和景教。我在做敦煌、吐鲁番文书研究的同时，在汉文文书之外，也关注胡语文献，对外来宗教问题也颇感兴趣。

从敦煌写本的来源上说，英、法、俄所藏和中国北京图书馆（今国家图书馆）所藏为直接从敦煌藏经洞获得的，除此之外的敦煌写本我们统称之为散藏文献。一般来说，一类文献的主体应当在前者当中，而比例较小的部分在后者之中，如佚书郑玄注《论语》，大多数都收藏在英、法两国，因为斯坦因、伯希和是先挑的，只有极少数在后者中。而且前者基本上没有真伪问题，后者中间虽然大多数应当是真品，但也有近人的伪造。有一天，我从敦煌学的角度向林先生提问：学界一般都认为敦煌的景教写本有7件（有的上面写不止一种文献），可是只有1件是伯希和收集品，而其他6件属于散藏文献，这从概率上来说是很难成立的。不仅如此，伯希和编号P.3847《大秦景教三威蒙度赞》和《尊经》，文字都是很短，纸幅不过两叶[1]；而散藏写本如《一神论》《序听迷诗所经》，则都是长卷，这也是很不符合逻辑的事情。因此我怀疑，这些散藏的所谓景教写本中是不是存有伪造的呢？

这一问题也引起林先生的兴趣，经过他的选择，我们打算以日人小岛靖号称得自李盛铎旧藏的《大秦景教大圣通真归法赞》与《大秦景教宣元至本经》为突破口，来看个究竟。林先生负责从景教的历史、教义出发来看小岛文书的内容是否符合景教的历史和教义，我则负责从写本的来龙去脉、其上的印章和题跋等敦煌学方面来看写本是否可信。经过很长一段时间的收集、分析、讨论，最后合作完成《所谓李氏旧藏敦煌景教文献二种辨伪》一文，在确定李盛铎收藏有敦煌真本景教文献的基础上，进一步发现，李氏所藏敦煌写本在其1937年去世之前已经出售，不可能迟到1943年为小岛靖获得；又从写本上的李氏印鉴、题跋看出其伪造之迹；再由前人已经怀疑的开元题记写天宝四载才有的"大秦寺"之名，进而看出其内容也不符合景教教义，甚至抄译《老子道德经》。我们最后的结论是："小岛文书很可能是某一或某些古董商人在李盛铎去世后伪造出来的。综合本文所揭示的种种疑点，我们至少可以说：从严谨的科学态度出发，对于名为小岛文书的《大秦景教大圣通真归法赞》和《大秦景教宣元至本经》这两件写本，我们不能轻信其为出自敦煌藏经洞的唐代景教文献，也不应在有关景教史或敦煌史的研究中无条件地引以为据。"

8月我回国后，又核对了部分北京大学图书馆所藏李盛铎原藏宋元善本书上的李氏印鉴和题记，最后定稿。我们的文章转年发表在饶宗颐

〔1〕见《法藏敦煌西域文献》第28册，上海：上海古籍出版社，2004年，第356-357页。

教授主持的《九州学刊》第 4 卷第 4 期“敦煌学专号”上。这本杂志是香港中华文化促进中心出资，美国郑培凯教授组织人审稿编辑，最后在台湾印刷出版，因此一般学者并不易见到，我们把一些抽印本和杂志送给相关的敦煌学研究者，文章得到饶宗颐、池田温、姜伯勤、项楚、徐文堪等先生的首肯。三四年后，陶步思（Bruce Doar）创办英文杂志《中国考古与艺术摘要》，把这篇文章翻译成英文，发表在 1996 年 5 月出版的第 1 卷第 1 期上，列为头篇文章。[1]陶步思翻译的时候跟我说，他看这篇文章，像是看侦探小说。虽然这篇文章的观点受到了学界不少认同[2]，但由于文章中所批驳的两位研究小岛文书的学者，一位是日本东洋史学的权威羽田亨教授，一位是世界闻名的景教史专家佐伯好郎先生，因此，许多日本学者不愿意公开表明自己的态度。在西方，则有一些积极的反响，全面介绍了我们的观点，并给予充分肯定。[3]当然，这一结论可说是对景教研究的“致命打击”，一些宗教学者特别是景教研究者确实是一时难以认同。[4]

考虑到《九州学刊》发行范围有限，而且不久刊物又停刊，学人不易见到这篇文章，所以林先生把文章略作修订，附录于他翻译的克里木

〔1〕Lin Wushu and Rong Xinjiang, “Doubts concerning the Authenticity of Two Nestorian Christian Documents Unearthed at Dunhuang from the Li Collection”(tr. by Bruce Doar), *China Archaeology and Art Digest*, 1.1, May 1996, pp. 5–14.

〔2〕比较重要的补充是陈怀宇《所谓唐代景教文献两种辨伪补说》，荣新江主编：《唐研究》第3卷，北京：北京大学出版社，1997年，第41–53页。

〔3〕P. Riboud, “Tang”, *Handbook of Christianity in China, vol. One: 635–1800*, ed. N. Standaert, Leiden – Boston – Köln: Brill, p. 7; M. Nicolini-Zani, “Past and Current Research on Tang *Jingjiao* Documents: A Survey”, *Jingjiao. The Church of the East in China and Central Asia*, eds. R. Malek and P. Hofrichter, Sankt Augustin: Institute Monumenta Serica, 2006, pp. 26–29, 36.

〔4〕曾阳晴：《小岛文书真伪考——李盛铎氏旧藏敦煌景教文献二种辨伪再商榷》，载于《中原学报》第33卷第2期，2005年，第253–272页；同作者《唐朝汉语景教文献研究》第二章《小岛文书真与伪》，台北：花木兰文化工作坊出版，2005年，第7–38页；S. Eskildsen, “On the Two Suspect ‘Nestorian Documents’”, Appendix to his “Parallel Themes in Chinese Nestorianism and Medieval Daoist Religion”, *Jingjiao. The Church of the East in China and Central Asia*, pp. 86–91。但这些文章的反驳依据基本上是假设，参看王兰平：《唐代敦煌汉文景教写经研究述评》，载于郝春文主编：《2007敦煌学国际联络委员会通讯》，上海：上海古籍出版社，2007年，第98–99页。

凯特《达·伽马以前中亚和东亚的基督教》的书后。[1]笔者也把此文收入拙著《鸣沙集——敦煌学学术史与方法论的探讨》中，并把补记改入正文；[2]在出版《鸣沙集》的增订本《辨伪与存真——敦煌学论集》时，又将图版略作调整。[3]

1991年8月以后，我们各奔东西，林先生一度在泰国，联系不便，再也没有合作的机会，但当年的话题，分别成为此后若干年两人的研究课题之一。林先生按照当时的想法，一件接一件地清理敦煌景教文献，包括P.3847《景教三威蒙度赞》《尊经》，李盛铎旧藏的《志玄安乐经》《宣元本经》，富冈谦藏旧藏《一神论》和高楠顺次郎旧藏《序听迷诗所经》，考其经文正确含义，辨其写本真伪，发表了一系列论文（详下）。笔者则重点在李盛铎旧藏写本真伪的考察，1997年发表《李盛铎写卷的真与伪》，判断李氏原藏的432号写本为敦煌真品，而坊间冒称的李氏藏卷则需要仔细辨别，其中有真品，也有伪卷。[4]2007年又发表《追寻最后的宝藏——李盛铎旧藏敦煌文献调查记》，总结学界就笔者发现的京都大学羽田亨纪念馆中的李氏旧藏敦煌写本照片所做的研究。[5]

噫！遥想当年在伦敦，正是爱尔兰共和军与英国政府恶斗之时，由于共和军引爆了藏在一个地铁站的炸弹，所以一遇到恐吓电话，伦敦警察局就通知地铁停运。林先生出生潮州，不辨方向，每次从地铁中升到地面，就给我打电话，报告路名。我随即乘巴士前往迎驾，一路返程，又多了许多问学的时光。回忆起来，在英伦与林先生相从切磋学问的日子，那可真是一段美好的时光。

---

〔1〕台北：淑馨出版社，1995年，第189–211页。又收入林悟殊《唐代景教再研究》，北京：中国社会科学出版社，2003年，第156–174页。

〔2〕台北：新文丰出版公司，1999年，第65–102页。

〔3〕上海：上海古籍出版社，2010年，第28–46页，图版5–8页。

〔4〕《敦煌学辑刊》1997年第2期，第1–18页。收入《辨伪与存真——敦煌学论集》，第47–73页，改题“李盛铎敦煌写卷的真与伪”，其英文本“The Li Shengduo Collection: Original or Forged Manuscripts?”载 *Dunhuang Manuscript Forgeries* (The British Library Studies in Conservation Science 3), ed. Susan Whitfield, London: The British Library, 2002, pp. 62–83 + pl. 1.

〔5〕载刘进宝、高田时雄主编：《转型期的敦煌学》，上海：上海古籍出版社，第15–32页；收入《辨伪与存真——敦煌学论集》，第74–90页。

11.2 洛阳新出石本《宣元至本经》

林悟殊先生对敦煌景教写本的个案研究，是从李盛铎旧藏《大秦景教宣元本经》开始的。1995 年，他发表《敦煌遗书〈大秦景教宣元本经〉考释》，根据《羽田博士史学论文集》下卷所刊图版做了释文，并就其篇幅、来源及作者问题加以探讨。[1]大概因为有我们前面合作的文章，林先生在本文中没有特别谈真伪问题。

P.3847《尊经》所列唐代翻译的景教文献中有“宣元至本经”，李氏旧藏的《大秦景教宣元本经》标题虽然漏掉一个“至”字，但从内容、字体、格式诸方面来看，当为敦煌真本。而小岛靖所得《大秦景教宣元至本经》虽然有“至”字，但其他伪迹显示其不是真本。这两个写本，也不可能像某些研究者所说的那样是一种文献的一前一后，其实两卷一真一伪，判然有别。

真正确定《宣元至本经》写本真伪的材料，是 2006 年洛阳发现的唐代景教经幢。先是张乃翥先生独具慧眼，在洛阳古董商店中发现这件景教经幢的拓本，略作考释，以“跋河南洛阳新出土的一件唐代景教石刻”为题，介绍了其重要的学术价值。[2]随后，罗炤先生又先后发表《洛阳新出土〈大秦景教宣元至本经及幢记〉石幢的几个问题》[3]、《再谈洛阳隋唐景教经幢的几个问题》[4]，据原石进一步校正经幢的文字，并讨论了相关的问题。冯其庸先生在得到此经幢拓本后，撰写了

〔1〕原载《九州学刊》第6卷第4期敦煌学专辑，1995年，第23–30页；附录于《达·伽马以前中亚和东亚的基督教》，第212–224页。后收入林悟殊《唐代景教再研究》，第175–185页；又收入《林悟殊敦煌文书与夷教研究》，上海古籍出版社，2011年，第248–258页，改题《敦煌本〈大秦景教宣元本经〉考释》，前言略有增订。

〔2〕载《西域研究》2007年第1期，第65–73页。又《补正说明》，载《西域研究》2007年第2期，第132页；收入葛承雍主编《景教遗珍——洛阳新出土唐代景教经幢研究》，北京：文物出版社，2009年，第5–16页；文后附有英文翻译：“Note on a Nestorian Stone Inscription from the Tang Dynasty Recently Unearthed in Luoyang”，同书，第17–33页。张先生在研究新出经幢时，与我有通信往还，已知有惊人发现，诧为国宝。

〔3〕载《文物》2007年第6期，第30–42、48页；收入《景教遗珍——洛阳新出土唐代景教经幢研究》，第34–59页。笔者在中国人民大学举办该经幢专题报告会场外面，曾匆匆帮罗先生校对一遍录文。

〔4〕载《世界宗教研究》2007年第4期，第96–104页。

《〈大秦景教宣元至本经〉全经的现世及其他》一文[1]，除了以经幢本对勘敦煌本以确定李氏旧藏敦煌本的真实无疑外，还指出小岛所得《宣元至本经》也由此可以确定为伪经。

综合以上三位先生的研究成果，简单来说，这座经幢现只残存上半截，前面刻录的是《大秦景教宣元至本经》，后面刻《大秦景教宣元至本经幢记》，记录唐宪宗元和九年（814），一些粟特亲属及洛阳大秦寺粟特出身的教士，为埋葬一位本出安国的安氏太夫人，竖立经幢，希望借此获得景福，并希望合家亲属没有诸障。张、罗两位先生已经指出：经幢上的《宣元至本经》文字，与李盛铎旧藏敦煌写本没有太大差别，经幢部分的文字有 19 行，但残缺了下半；敦煌写本的文字只保存了相当经幢前 11 行的文字，但每行都抄到行末；所以两者可以相互补充，若经幢现存文字是经文全部，则我们现在可以看到《宣元至本经》的大部分内容。洛阳经幢是不法分子盗掘所得，随后拓本流入古董市场，其价值才为学者发现。随后，经幢本身被公安部门追回，存洛阳市第二文物工作队，现陈列在洛阳市丝绸之路博物馆。从这一情形来看，洛阳经幢的盗掘者是不可能见到过敦煌本《宣元至本经》，即使见过，也不可能编造出敦煌本 11 行后面的景教经文。况且后面的《幢记》也完全是唐朝的语境，后人无法模仿。因此，经幢的真实性丝毫无疑。这样反过来看李氏旧藏的《宣元本经》，其内容和经幢所刻文字无大差别，因此，其为唐朝文献也确凿无疑了。再和“小岛文书”所谓《宣元至本经》对比，两者文字完全不同，可以确证其为近人伪造。

洛阳景教经幢不仅证明了林先生与笔者十多年前在伦敦合作研究所得的结论，也为唐代景教研究提供了新的素材和思路。林先生与其弟子殷小平合撰《经幢版景教〈宣元至本经〉考释——唐代洛阳景教经幢研究之一》[2]、《〈幢记〉若干问题考释——唐代洛阳景教经幢

[1] 2007年9月27日《中国文化报》“国学专栏”，转载于《新华文摘》2007年第23期；收入《景教遗珍——洛阳新出土唐代景教经幢研究》，第60-66页。

[2] 载于《中华文史论丛》2008年第1辑，第325-352页；收入《景教遗珍——洛阳新出土唐代景教经幢研究》，第68-91页；又收入林悟殊《中古夷教华化丛考》，兰州：兰州大学出版社，2011年，第168-191页；《林悟殊敦煌文书与夷教研究》，第259-283页。

研究之二》[1]，并自撰《经幢版“三位一体”考释——唐代洛阳景教经幢研究之三》[2]、《唐代景僧名字的华化轨迹——唐代洛阳景教经幢研究之四》[3]，极大深化了唐代景教教义和历史研究[4]。

11.3 杏雨书屋新刊李盛铎旧藏景教文书二种
——再论李盛铎藏卷的真伪

对于李盛铎旧藏中的另一种景教文献《志玄安乐经》，林悟殊先生也做了个案研究。2001 年，他发表《敦煌本景教〈志玄安乐经〉佐伯录文质疑》，指出后人所依据的佐伯好郎对该经前 10 行录文的臆补是不可依据的。[5]10 年后，他又发表《景教〈志玄安乐经〉敦煌写本真伪及录文补说》，根据杏雨书屋刊布的全卷照片，从该经的承传关系、《尊经》之著录、写本篇幅及内容、作者的推测等角度，推断写本为唐代景教徒真迹。又据原件照片，参考羽田亨录文，做出新的释文本。[6]

关于李盛铎旧藏写本为真品的问题，笔者上述论文从其他角度也有论说，因此对于林先生就《志玄安乐经》写本所做的论证，完全赞同。

在笔者发表《李盛铎写卷的真与伪》之后，又有一些有关李氏藏卷

[1] 载《中华文史论丛》2008年第2辑，第269–292页；收入《景教遗珍——洛阳新出土唐代景教经幢研究》，第92–108页；又收入林悟殊《中古夷教华化丛考》，第192–210页。

[2] 载于《中华文史论丛》2009年第1辑，第257–276页；收入《景教遗珍——洛阳新出土唐代景教经幢研究》，第109–121页；又收入林悟殊《中古夷教华化丛考》，第213–225页。

[3] 载于《中华文史论丛》2009年第2辑，第149–194页；收入林悟殊《中古夷教华化丛考》，第226–268页。

[4] Cf. M. Nicolini-Zani, “The Tang Christian Pillar from Luoyang and Its *Jingjiao* Inscription. A Preliminary Study”, *Monumenta Serica*, 57, 2009, pp. 99–140; Li Tang, “A Preliminary Study on the *Jingjiao* Inscription of Luoyang: Text Analysis, Commentary and English Translation”, *Hidden Treasures and Intercultural Encounters. Studies on East Syriac Christianity in China and Central Asia*, Wein: LIT Verlag GmbH & Co. KG, 2009, pp. 109–132.

[5] 载于《中山大学学报》2001年第4期，第1–7页；收入林悟殊《唐代景教再研究》，第146–155页；《林悟殊敦煌文书与夷教研究》，第284–293页。参看 G. B. Mikkelsen, “Haneda’s and Saeki’s Editions of the Chinese Nestorian *Zhixuan anle jing*. A Comment on Recent Work by Lin Wushu”, *Jingjiao. The Church of the East in China and Central Asia*, pp. 143–148.

[6] 饶宗颐主编：《华学》第11辑，广州：中山大学出版社，2014年，第156–172页；收入《林悟殊敦煌文书与夷教研究》，第294–323页。

的材料发表，其中重要的是罗振玉与王国维的往来通信。现将《罗振玉王国维往来书信》[1]中有关信件转录如下：

六〇二　罗振玉致王国维（1919年7月2日）：

李木斋藏有敦煌古籍，多至四五百卷，皆盗自学部八千卷中者，已展转与商，允我照印，此可喜可骇之事。弟当设印局印之，此刻且勿宣为荷。（459页）

六〇四　罗振玉致王国维（1919年7月3日）：

木斋处之石室书籍，已与约，待渠检出，弟当入都一观。异日检视后，再陈其概略。闻其中有《汉书》数卷、六朝写本无注《论语》一卷，其断简不知书名者无数，必有奇物也。李请弟不咎既往，弟已诺之，故此事且勿披露为荷。（460页）

六〇五　罗振玉致王国维（1919年7月中旬）：

木老所藏，必有奇物，不知何时乃能寓目耳。（461页）

六一七　罗振玉致王国维（1919年9月17日）：

弟前日往看李木斋藏书，敦煌卷轴中书籍，有《周易》单疏（贲卦），有《左传》，有《尚书》（帝典），有《本草序列》，有《开蒙要训》，有《史记》（张禹孔光传），有《庄子》（让王篇），有《道德经》，有七字唱本（一目连救母事，一记李陵降虏事），有度牒（二纸，均北宋初），有遗嘱。卷中印记，有归义军节度使新铸印。其写经，有甘露二年（当是高昌改元）、麟嘉四年（后凉吕光）及延昌、大统、景明、开皇、贞观、显庆、仪凤、上元、至德、天宝、证圣、乾宁等。其可补史书之缺者，有敦煌太守且渠唐儿之建始二年写《大般涅槃经》，其《华严经》有《志玄安乐经》及《宣元本经》（其名见《三威蒙度赞》中），以上诸书乃木斋所藏。渠言潜楼藏本有《刘子》。以上诸书颇可宝贵，恨不得与公共

[1] 王庆祥、萧文立校注，罗继祖审订：《罗振玉王国维往来书信》，北京：东方出版社，2000年，页码随注引文后。

一览之也。（470 页）[1]

六二〇　王国维致罗振玉（1919 年 9 月 20 日）：

李氏诸书，诚为千载秘笈，闻之神往。甘露二年写经，君楚疑为苻秦时物，亦极有理。景教经二种，不识但说教理，抑兼有事实，此诚世界宝笈，不能以书籍论矣。（473 页）[2]

这些过去秘不示人的书信，带给我们许多新的消息。

第一，早在 1919 年 7 月，罗振玉等人就知道李盛铎家藏的敦煌写本是"盗自学部八千卷中者"，这和笔者据松本文三郎《敦煌石室古写经之研究》所记京都大学赴清国调查团所见和李氏藏敦煌写本目录的对比而得出的结论，即"李氏等人实际上是在经卷入学部后才攫取到手的"，完全吻合。特别是罗振玉说"李请弟不咎既往"，则说明李盛铎本人也在私下承认他是从学部偷走的敦煌写卷。这也就证明了李氏旧藏敦煌写卷主要来自清政府从敦煌藏经洞调运来的卷子，所以其真实性基本上没有什么可怀疑的。现在，杏雨书屋刊布了全部属于李氏的 432 号写卷[3]，其中只有《志玄安乐经》尾题说是"丙辰秋日，于君归自肃州，以此见诒"，为其他来路，但时间很早，民国五年（1916），又来自距敦煌不远的酒泉，从来历上也不必质疑。从李氏藏卷的照片看，这些写本和现藏北京国家图书馆的所谓"学部八千卷"的外观、内涵都没有什么差别。其实"学部八千卷"只是当时知道的约数，后来随着整理工作的进行，国家图书馆又找到很多来自藏经洞的残片。多年前，笔者曾发现国家图书馆原编作"临 2371"号（现编号 BD12242）的《新修本草》卷首小纸片，应当可以和冈西为人《本草概说》（创元社，1983 年）书前图版 6 所刊李盛铎旧藏《新修本草》写本（现编号羽 040）首

〔1〕按，本书札整理者录文有误，"唐儿"原录作"唐光"，"志玄"原作"志立"，"三威"原作"三藏"，均据理正之。"其《华严经》有《志玄安乐经》"也不通，或许《华严经》后有缺文。

〔2〕按，《王国维全集》书信卷此札系在1919年7月7日，现在看来，应在9月20日。过去笔者与林先生合撰《所谓李氏旧藏敦煌景教文献二种辨伪》时，只从《全集》看到上引最后一札，现在看到了罗振玉的信件，才能更确切地认清它的含义。

〔3〕杏雨书屋所藏西域出土文献以《敦煌秘笈》之名，自2009年3月由武田科学振兴财团杏雨书屋编集发行。

部直接缀合，并将此比定结果告诉日本友人岩本笃志，岩本氏考察原件后撰写了《唐〈新修本草〉编纂と“土贡”——中国国家图书馆藏断片考》[1]。现在，两件照片都已公布[2]，笔者请国图古籍馆的刘波先生帮忙，将两个写本用电脑缀合起来，可以说是严丝合缝（见图 11–1）。这个例子说明，李盛铎等人的写卷出自学部从敦煌调运的敦煌文献，而在瓜分之时，把一些写卷一分为二，自取较佳的一半，而留下文字较少的一半充数，国图所藏《新修本草》只有标题的半行和下面属衔部分残文，就是这样的结果。

第二，罗振玉说李氏藏卷“多至四五百卷”，这是在看到李氏藏卷之前所得到的消息。我们知道李盛铎 1935 年最后出售给日本时的写本数是 432 号，从 1919 年到 1935 年，作为私家藏卷难免有送礼之类的变动，但这两个数字之间，可以说是大致吻合的。从李盛铎生前对自家写本的珍藏程度来看，一般情况下他是不舍得出手送人的。

第三，罗振玉 1919 年 9 月 15 日到李家看敦煌写本，李盛铎看来是盛情款待，给他看了所藏大多数精品。笔者把罗氏所记与李家最后出售前编的目录——《李木斋氏鉴藏燉煌写本目录》相对照，其见到的写本应当有以下这些（其中年号重复者只选目录首见者，未必准确）：

一　摩诃衍经第八　魏大统八年

二　维摩义记第二　甘露二年

三　十戒经　首尾全　至德二载

四　华严经第廿四　延昌二年　有蓝印

五　未曾有因缘经卷下　开皇十一年官书

六　妙法莲华经卷四　上元二年十月廿八日门下省群书公孙仁约写

七　妙法莲华经卷五　仪凤二年正月秘书省书手田玄徽写

〔1〕载《东洋学报》第90卷第2号，2008年，第1–31页。参看拙文《追寻最后的宝藏——李盛铎旧藏敦煌文献调查记》，载于《辨伪与存真——敦煌学论集》，第87–88页。

〔2〕《国家图书馆藏敦煌遗书》第110册，北京图书馆出版社，2009年，第344页；武田科学振兴财团杏雨书屋编《敦煌秘笈　影片册》一，大阪：武田科学振兴财团，2009年，第271页。

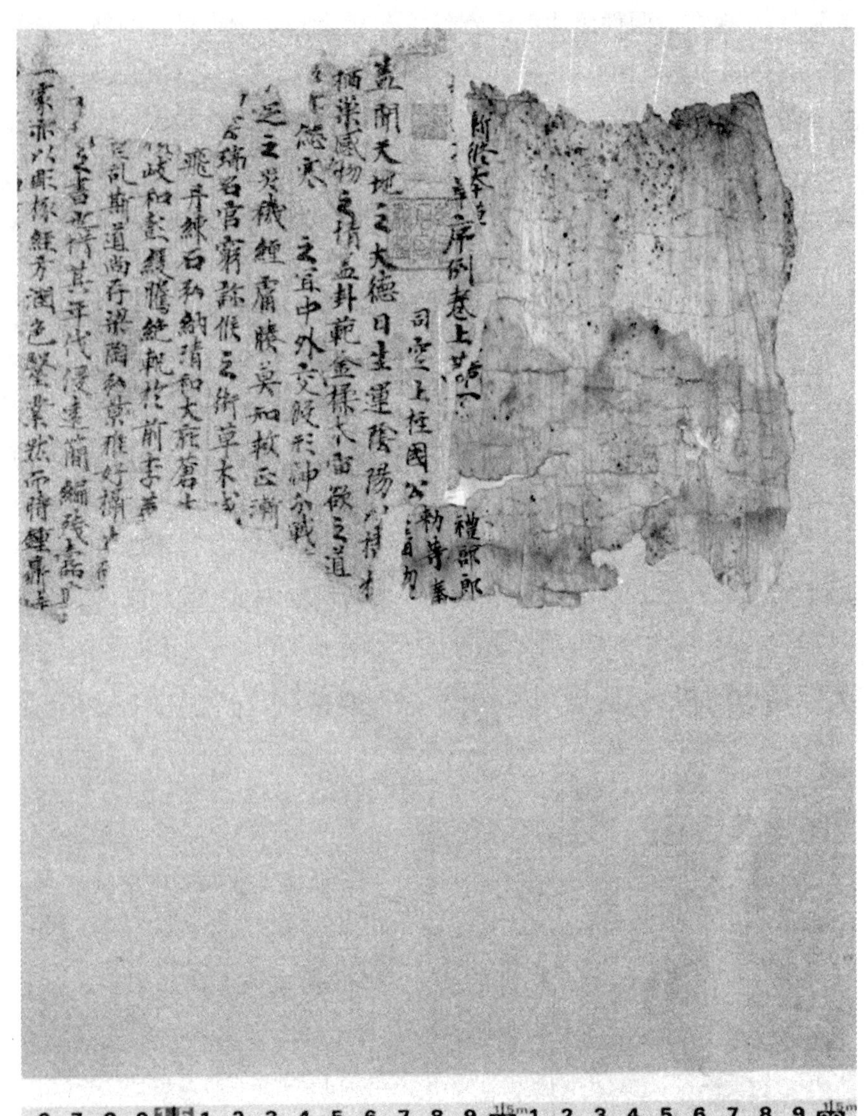

图 11-1:《新修本草》BD12242 与羽 040 缀合图

八　解深密经卷七　贞观二十二年

十　妙法莲华经卷一　证圣元年五月

十三　景教志玄安乐经

十六　左传

十八　尚书

十九　庄子让王篇

廿四　燉煌县龙勒乡户册　天宝八载

廿六　三界寺住奴戒牒　太平兴国八年

廿九　开蒙要训一卷

四十　本草　背写历日

五二　大云寺牒　雍熙五年十月

七十一　目连传七字句小说　背有僧太上父叔状

百七九　华严经卷五十　尾全

四百二九　大般涅槃经卷第卅四　建始二年大且渠唐儿供养苏仲祖写

四百三一　宣元至本经　首全

四百三二　汉书残卷　避世字

罗氏提到的《周易》《史记》《道德经》《李陵变文》，麟嘉、景明、显庆、乾宁写经，未见于《目录》。但就上列写卷来看，也可以说是李盛铎藏品的精华了，其中包括两种景教写本。

自 2009 年 3 月开始，收藏李盛铎旧藏敦煌写本的武田科学振兴财团杏雨书屋开始编集发行《敦煌秘笈　影片册》，包括其所藏全部敦煌、西域出土文献，其中前 432 号就是《李木斋氏鉴藏燉煌写本目录》著录的李氏旧藏，一件都不少。

2009 年 10 月出版的《敦煌秘笈　影片册》第一册刊布了《志玄安乐经》全卷的彩色图版（129—132 页）。这是该经全卷图版的首次发布，过去我们只是看到 1928 年羽田亨在李盛铎家所录的文本，真迹也只有首尾部分照片刊布在《羽田博士史学论文集》下册的卷首，因此新影印本的学术价值不言而喻。林悟殊先生立刻撰写了上述《景教〈志玄安乐经〉敦煌写本真伪及录文补说》，为学界提供了最新的校录文本。

2011年11月出版的《敦煌秘笈　影片册》第五册，又刊布了《宣元本经》的彩色图版（397页），与《羽田博士史学论文集》下册所刊黑白照片对照，两者完全相同，都是26行文字。过去从《羽田论文集》发表的图版来看，不知道后面是否还有保存，现在可以确定，李氏所藏也只有这么一纸。写本最后一行没有抄到最底下即止，或许表明这是没有抄完的一件写本。无论如何，洛阳景教经幢的发现和李氏旧藏写本彩色图片的发表，都给我们带来确凿无疑的信息，即这件是确凿无疑的唐代景教写本。

11.4　杏雨书屋新刊
高楠、富冈旧藏景教文书二种

对于最后2件景教写本，我们在伦敦时也有不少讨论。林悟殊先生往巴黎游学时，把《所谓李氏旧藏敦煌景教文献二种辨伪》一文呈送给吴其昱先生，向他请教。吴先生说，《一神论》和《序听迷诗所经》“这两个文书是假的”。由此，林先生做了详细的研究，先后发表《富冈谦藏氏藏景教〈一神论〉真伪存疑》[1]、《高楠氏藏景教〈序听迷诗所经〉真伪存疑》[2]、《景教富冈高楠文书辨伪补说》[3]，指出这2个写本来历不明，但出自一人手笔，文书结构混乱，题目书写不规范，内容和题目不对应，文字十分工整，但错漏百出。《序听迷诗所经》不仅经题写错，而且用亵渎的词汇“移鼠”来指称基督教的教主耶稣，如此等等，都是匪夷所思。不过，林先生的看法前后也略有变化，2000年

〔1〕载于荣新江主编：《唐研究》第6卷，北京：北京大学出版社，2000年，第67–86页；收入林悟殊《唐代景教再研究》，186–207页；《林悟殊敦煌文书与夷教研究》，第324–346页。

〔2〕载于《文史》第55辑，2001年，第141–154页；收入林悟殊《唐代景教再研究》，第208–228页；《林悟殊敦煌文书与夷教研究》，第347–368页。

〔3〕季羡林、饶宗颐主编：《敦煌吐鲁番研究》第8卷，北京：中华书局，2005年，第35–43页；收入林悟殊《中古三夷教辨证》，北京：中华书局，2005年，第215–226页；《林悟殊敦煌文书与夷教研究》，第369–380页。参看 Lin Wushu, “Additional Notes on the Authenticity of Tomioka’s and Takakusu’s Manuscripts”, *Jingjiao. The Church of the East in China and Central Asia*, pp. 134–142.

发表对富冈所藏《一神论》的辨伪时，认为“富冈文书并非敦煌本真迹，而是20世纪初叶时人所抄写；但其并非凭空赝作，而是由古本可依。这古本，当然不排除明季清初耶稣会士的作品；但更有可能是，在当年问世的敦煌遗书中，除了众所周知的景教写本外，还有类似《一神论》之类内容的一些景教写经，落入骨董商人之手，但过于残烂，在当时难以鬻得好价，遂由造假高手重新加以缮写制作”。[1]到2001年他发表高楠藏《序听迷诗所经》辨伪时，就怀疑这2件写本并非敦煌真迹，很可能同属现代人的精抄赝品，没有再提抄自敦煌古本的可能，最后说：“窃以为，在疑点未能作出较合理的解释，吾人的疑虑未能消除之前，学界对这两件写本的使用，采取较为谨慎的态度，似属必要。”[2]已经将这2件写本排除在景教研究之外。到了2005年，林先生又发表对这2件写本《辨伪补说》，结论是：“到目前为止，我们尚只能说，这两个文书来历不明，文书本身又暴露了诸多疑点，很可能是赝品。”指出它们不一定来自敦煌古本，也可能把明清时期来华耶稣会士的汉文神学著作当作伪造的参考。[3]作为一位宗教史家，林先生抱着极其严谨的态度，从内容上一步步深入剖析这2个写本的疑点，指出它们很可能是今人伪造的赝品。对于林先生的上述观点，景教研究者有些持迟疑态度[4]，有些不愿意接受[5]，有些置若罔闻，不予理睬，继续利用这2种

〔1〕《林悟殊敦煌文书与夷教研究》，第342–343页。

〔2〕《林悟殊敦煌文书与夷教研究》，第364页。

〔3〕《林悟殊敦煌文书与夷教研究》，第378页。

〔4〕Max Deeg, “Towards a New Translation of the Chinese Nestorian Documents from the Tang Dynasty”, *Jingjiao. The Church of the East in China and Central Asia*, pp. 115–131.

〔5〕参看王兰平：《以“十愿”、“十观”为例——看唐代景教与佛教的交涉融合》，载于李金强、吴梓明、邢福增主编：《自西徂东——基督教来华二百年论集》，香港：基督教文艺出版社，2009年，第145–159页；Lanping Wang, “Review of *The Chinese Face of Jesus Christ. Volume I*”, 载于《近代中国基督教史研究集刊》2004/2005年第6期，第87–88页。

写本来做唐朝景教的研究[1]。

笔者完全赞同林先生的观点，在他论证的基础上，笔者想强调以下三点：

第一，唐朝对于外来宗教经典的翻译有着一套严格的制度，从一些敦煌写本佛经保留的译场列位题记就可以看出，如P.3709《佛地经》题记[2]：

贞观廿二年八月十九日直司书手臣郗玄爽写
凡五千五百二言
装潢手臣辅文开
总持寺沙门辩机笔受
蒲州普救寺沙门行友证文
玄法寺沙门玄赜证文
总持寺沙门玄应正字
弘福寺沙门灵闰证义
弘福寺沙门灵范证义
弘福寺沙门惠明证义
弘福寺沙门僧胜证义
沙门玄装（奘）译
银青光禄大夫行太子左庶子高阳县开国男臣许敬宗监阅

可见，正规的译经有笔受、证文、正字、证义等一套严格的程序，有不少经典是经过文学修养很高的学者来润色的，如元和六年（811）所译《大乘本生心地观经》卷一题记[3]：

元和五年七月三日内出梵夹，其月廿七日奉诏长安醴泉寺，至

---

〔1〕Tang Li, A Study of the History of Nestorian Christianity in China and Its Literature in Chinese: Together with a New English Translation of the Dunhuang Nestorian Documents, Peter Lang: Frankfurt am Main, 2002；唐莉：《唐代景教阿罗本文献——〈序听迷诗所经〉及〈一神论〉》，载于刘楚华主编：《唐代文学与宗教》，香港：中华书局，2004年，第665–682页；黄夏年：《景经〈一神论〉之“魂魄”初探》，收入作者《西来东去：中外古代佛教史论集》，北京：中国社会科学出版社，2006年，第359–373页；王兰平博士论文《唐代敦煌汉文景教写经研究》，兰州大学敦煌学研究所，2006年。

〔2〕池田温：《中国古代写本识语集录》，东京：大藏出版株式会社，1990年，第191页。

〔3〕池田温：《中国古代写本识语集录》，1990年，第335页。

六年三月八日翻译进上。

罽宾国三藏赐紫沙门般若宣梵文

醴泉寺日本国沙门灵仙笔受并译语

经行寺沙门令謩润文

醴泉寺沙门少諲回文

济法寺沙门藏英润文

福寿寺沙门恒济回文

总持寺沙门大辨证义

右街都勾当大德庄严寺沙门一微详定

都勾当译经押衙散兵马使兼正将朝议郎前行陇州司功参军上柱国赐绯鱼袋臣李霸

给事中守右补阙云骑尉袭徐国公臣萧俛奉敕详定

银青光禄大夫行尚书工部侍郎充皇太子及诸王侍读上柱国长洲县开国男臣归登奉敕详定

朝请大夫守给事中充集贤殿御书院学士判院事臣刘伯蒭奉敕详定

朝议郎守谏议大夫知匦使上柱国赐绯鱼袋臣孟简奉敕详定

右神策军护军中尉兼右街功德使扈从特进行右武卫大将军知内侍省上柱国剡国公食邑三千户臣第五从直

其中的刘伯蒭即刘伯刍，他的自撰墓志铭近年出土，志文称："明年，有西国竺乾僧奉敕翻译《大乘本生心地经》十卷，诏公详润其文，御制序引。"[1]可见题记中的"详定"应当是负责详细润色其文字、最后定稿的意思。而这里负责详定的大臣萧俛、归登、刘伯蒭、孟简，都是当时重要的文臣，足见宪宗对于翻译佛经的重视。据陈怀宇研究，

〔1〕胡戟、荣新江主编：《大唐西市博物馆藏墓志》，北京：北京大学出版社，2012年，第792-794页，No. 368。

这部佛经和景教经典有着密切的关系[1]。

抄写经典也有一套正规的做法，如 S. 312《妙法莲华经》卷 4 题记[2]：

咸亨四年九月廿一日门下省群书手封安昌写

用纸廿二张

装潢手解集

初校大庄严寺僧怀福

再校西明寺僧玄真

三校西明寺僧玄真

详阅太原寺大德神符

详阅太原寺大德嘉尚

详阅太原寺主慧立

详阅太原寺上座道成

判官司农寺上林署令李德

使太中大夫守工部侍郎摄兵部侍郎永兴县开国公虞昶监

在抄写之后，有初校、再校、三校和各位高僧大德的详阅，不论译经还是抄经，最后都有官员监阅，审查合格才能够流传。当然，上举是最严格的唐朝皇家宫廷写经的样本，大多数写经不一定经过这么多程序，但国家对于译经、抄经的管理和监督是不可或缺的。

如果说《一神论》和《序听迷诗所经》像前人所说是贞观时期景教最早的译经的话，那么唐朝对于这样一种外来宗教的经典翻译活动，一定是要加以监督和校阅的，更何况景教以贞观九年初次传入长安，十二年才被太宗允许立寺，度僧 21 人[3]。此时如果翻译像《一神论》和《序听迷诗所经》这样长篇的经典，一定应当是像上举贞观年间的译本《佛地经》一样经过仔细的翻译、润色程序。现在我们在这两种景教经典上

〔1〕Chen Huaiyu, “The Connection Between *Jingjiao* and Buddhist Texts in Late Tang China”, *Jingjiao. The Church of the East in China and Central Asia*, pp. 93–113；陈怀宇：《从比较语言学看〈三威蒙度赞〉与〈大乘本生心地观经〉的联系》，载于朱玉麒主编：《西域文史》第1辑，北京：科学出版社，2006年，第111–119页

〔2〕《中国古代写本识语集录》，第217–218页。

〔3〕《唐会要》卷49“大秦寺”条，上海：上海古籍出版社，1991年，第1011–1012页。

看到的林先生所说的现象，即结构混乱、文不对题、文字错漏百出等，完全无法将之看做是唐朝正规的景教经典。

第二，由于唐朝对外来经典的翻译有着严格的管理，翻译过程十分谨严，因此一些专门名词往往高度统一。唐朝新译的佛经是这样，其他外来宗教经典的翻译也是这样，当然景教也不例外。比如救世主 Meshiha 或 Messiah 一词的翻译，在目前可以肯定属于唐朝时期的景教文献中，不论是建中二年的《大秦景教流行中国碑》、元和九年的《大秦景教宣元本经》经幢，还是敦煌发现的《大秦景教三威蒙度赞》《尊经》《宣元至本经》《志玄安乐经》，都是用完全一样的“弥施诃”三个字[1]，甚至唐朝的道经《老子化胡经》卷 2 所说的第五十种外道，也用同样的名字“弥施诃”[2]。

我们知道《老子化胡经》是一部官方色彩浓厚的道经，虽然曾几次被禁毁，但也有统治者着意宣传的时候。武则天万岁通天元年（696），僧惠澄上言乞毁《化胡经》，武后敕秋官侍郎刘如璇等议此事[3]，结果刘如璇等人建议不毁《化胡经》[4]。P. 3404《老子化胡经》卷 8 首题下有“奉　敕对定经本”字样[5]，刘屹先生已经指出这一卷应当就是万岁通天元年武后下敕对定之本[6]。笔者曾推测写有“弥施诃”的卷 2 可能是万岁通天元年奉敕对定后的文本，也可能是玄宗时编纂《开元道藏》的产物[7]。因此可以说，《化胡经》的“弥施诃”一词，代

〔1〕林悟殊：《景教〈志玄安乐经〉敦煌写本真伪及录文补说》，载于《林悟殊敦煌文书与夷教研究》，第302页。

〔2〕大渊忍尔编：《敦煌道经・图录编》，东京：福武书店，1979年，第662页。参看拙文《唐代の佛·道二教から见た的外道——景教徒》（高田时雄译），京都大学人文科学研究所编《中国宗教文献研究》，京都：临川书店，2007年，第436页。

〔3〕《新唐书》卷59《艺文志》三《神仙家类》著录《议化胡经状》一卷下注文，北京：中华书局，1975年，第1521页。

〔4〕部分议状见《混元圣纪》卷8，《道藏》第17册，上海书店、文物出版社、天津古籍出版社影印，1994年，第859-860页；《全唐文》卷165，北京：中华书局影印本，1983年，第1686页。

〔5〕大渊忍尔编：《敦煌道经・图录编》，东京：福武书店，1979年，第668页。

〔6〕刘屹：《敦煌十卷本〈老子化胡经〉残卷新探》，载于《唐研究》第2卷，北京：北京大学出版社，1996年，第106页。

〔7〕拙文《唐代の佛・道二教から见た的外道——景教徒》（高田时雄译），第431-433页。

表了唐朝的官方文本，而各种现在确定为真迹的景教文献，不论来自长安、洛阳，还是出自西陲敦煌，都采用这一写法，暗示着这些景教文献的官方背景，即《大秦景教三威蒙度赞》《尊经》《宣元至本经》《志玄安乐经》，都是官方认可的景教译经。长安的《大秦景教流行中国碑》，也是在伊斯协助朔方军平定安史之乱后，景教得到朝廷大力支持的背景下竖立的[1]；元和九年的《大秦景教宣元至本经》经幢，虽然是私家行为，但有"敕东都右羽林军押衙陪戎校尉守左威卫汝州梁川府""义叔上都左龙武军散将兼押衙宁远将军守左武卫大将军置同正员"等官员身份的中外亲族参与，其《宣元至本经》的文字来历也应当是官方文本。

中唐的大历九年（774）后不久，在四川禅宗僧人所编《历代法宝记》中，把禅宗祖师所灭两个外道名之为"末曼尼"和"弥师诃"。这里的"弥师诃"虽然完全是禅僧编造的故事中的人物，但其来历应当借用了《老子化胡经》教化外道的说法，"弥师诃"是抄自《化胡经》而误写其中一字的结果，这和《序听迷诗所经》的用法完全不同。

笔者推测，之所以用"迷诗所"，很可能是谐"迷失所"的音，其并非是"弥施诃"的另一种音译，编造者的目的是要把基督教的救世主说成是"迷失所"，但为遮人耳目，改其中"失"为"诗"罢了。可以说，"弥施诃"是唐朝景教的官方译语，不可能被改作"迷诗所"，从这一点上来说，《序听迷诗所经》的可信度就大打折扣了。

再看《序听迷诗所经》用"移鼠"、《一神论》用"翳数"来译写"耶稣"，这也是无法成立的。我们现在虽然未在确定的唐朝景教文献中见到耶稣的译音词，但唐朝汉译的摩尼教文献，不论是所谓《摩尼教残经》（中国国家图书馆藏宇字 56 号，新编 BD. 00256 号），还是摩尼教《下部赞》（英藏 S. 2659），都统一用"夷数"来音译"耶稣"，推测《摩尼光佛教法仪略》（S. 3969+P. 3884）也应当相同，而《仪略》是"开元十九年六月八日大德拂多诞奉诏集贤院译"，其他两种经典统一、规范的做法也说明是在官方的监督下完成翻译的。从《老子化胡经》

〔1〕参看拙文《〈历代法宝记〉中的末曼尼和弥师诃——兼谈吐蕃文献中的摩尼教和景教因素的来历》，载于拙著《中古中国与外来文明》，北京：三联书店，2001年，第364–365页。

与景教文献用词的相同来看，唐朝景教经典如果用音译来翻译耶稣的话，那么最有可能的词汇就是“夷数”，而不可能是“翳数”或更不雅观的“移鼠”。

因此，从唐朝翻译外来宗教经典的专有名词的统一性，《序听迷诗所经》和《一神论》不应当是唐朝的景教文献。

第三，《序听迷诗所经》和《一神论》两个卷子的真迹，早在1931年就由羽田亨影印发表[1]，影本极佳，可惜是黑白版，对于原卷的一些情形还是不太清楚。自羽田氏发表以后，此两卷藏本不知是仍在富冈、高楠家，还是已经转手他人。笔者1990—1991年间在日本期间，曾多方查找，也无所获。现在我们终于从《敦煌秘笈》中得知，这两个写本后来都归羽田亨本人所有，最后入藏大阪武田科学振兴财团所属的杏雨书屋，编为羽459和羽460号。2012年，这两个卷子的彩色图版刊布在《敦煌秘笈　影片册》第6册中，《序听迷诗所经》在84–87页，《一神论》在89–96页，黄麻纸，十分美观。

遗憾的是，我们现在还无缘看到原件，无法和敦煌纸做对比。据《敦煌秘笈》的编者记录，《一神论》的第一纸为“麁纸，柴色”，与以下其他纸染为黄橡色的上质麻纸不同[2]。这种现象也不是正式的官方写经所应当出现的情况，如果是正常情况下，一个写经的用纸应当是统一的，特别是开头第一纸更应当是尚好的麻纸，怎么可能先用粗纸再用上等的好纸呢？只有近世的伪造物，才比较好解释这种现象。如果伪造者使用原本出自敦煌的素纸而又存货无多，那伪造者可能就用一些粗纸代替。如果使用现代制作的纸，则在使用的时候，不小心开始用了次纸，然后才转用好纸。林先生从写作者对宗教的态度来看这两个写本的真伪，笔者从用纸上来看，制作者缺乏对神圣经典的崇敬之心，所以才会如此随意用纸，这是我们在敦煌写经中很少见到的情形，唐朝僧侣是把

〔1〕羽田亨编：《一神论卷第三　序听迷诗所经一卷》（影印本），京都：东方文化学院京都研究所，1931年。

〔2〕武田科学振兴财团杏雨书屋编：《敦煌秘笈　影片册》第6册，大阪：武田科学振兴财团，2012年，第88页。

经书当作“三宝”来对待的，如此随意，几无可能。

以上从三个方面，对《一神论》和《序听迷诗所经》提出进一步质疑。笔者比较倾向于认为这些写本杂抄自明清以来的汉文基督教文献，抄者并不熟悉基督教教义，为不让人看破马脚，又编造一些从来没有存在过的词汇来替换相应的专有名词，因此要直接找到这些伪本依据的文本着实不易，但这些疑点已经足以质疑这两种所谓唐朝景教写经的真实性了。笔者同意林先生的观点，在这些疑点能够圆满解说之前，最好不要把这两种经典当作唐朝的景教文献来使用。

11.5　结论：重新书写唐代景教研究的“退步集”

总而言之，笔者在林悟殊先生研究的基础上，补充若干新的证据，希望强调如下结论：

一、伯希和自敦煌藏经洞所得 P. 3847《景教三威蒙度赞》《尊经》，为敦煌写本真品无疑；李盛铎旧藏的《志玄安乐经》《宣元本经》，应当来自清朝学部自敦煌藏经洞直接调运的写本，也没有问题。

二、富冈谦藏旧藏《一神论》和高楠顺次郎旧藏《序听迷诗所经》，没有清楚的来源交代，从文字到词汇都有很多疑点，很可能是今人依据明清以来的基督教文献伪造出来的。

三、小岛靖号称得自李盛铎旧藏的《大秦景教大圣通真归法赞》与《大秦景教宣元至本经》，则完全是赝品，没有任何学术价值。

目前，我们所读到的所有唐朝景教史、中国古代基督教史，乃至亚洲基督教史，不论中外，都是建立在以佐伯好郎整理和翻译的上述所有八种景教写本基础上的，现在我们要从中拿掉四种，包括被认为是景教入华后首批翻译的、相对篇幅较长的《一神论》和《序听迷诗所经》，这对于宗教史家可说是巨大的打击。但是，一部宗教史要让人信服，让人感到神圣，就应当建立在真实的材料基础之上，因此，不论接受起来多么痛苦，唐代的景教史都要“倒退”，都需要重写。

这让我想起陈丹青《退步集续编》腰封上写着："一退再退，所为者何？退到历史深处，借一双眼，邀请我们更清晰地照看今日种种文化情境。"在我看来，今日的唐代景教研究，必须书写"退步集"，要从佐伯好郎时代"完美"的景教史往后退，退到一个能够更清晰地照看出唐朝景教文化面相的历史深处，那画面不论多么破碎，但却是更加真实的历史情境。

12　从两件德藏吐鲁番文书看景教与道教之联系

陈怀宇
（美国亚利桑那州立大学）

引　言

1904—1905 年德国探险家勒柯克（Albert von Le Coq）领导了第二次吐鲁番探险活动，其助手巴尔图斯（Th. Bartus）在布拉依克地区发现了一座景教遗址，从中获得大量景教文书，但其中一些文书直到很晚才被公布并编入目录。最近读到 2012 年辛姆斯-威廉姆斯（Nicolas Sims-Williams）教授出版的目录《柏林吐鲁番藏品中的叙利亚文字所写伊朗语写本》，注意到一些新编入该目的文书，并通过"国际敦煌项目"（IDP）柏林网站数据库找到了这些文书的照片，得以细细研读。本文所要讨论的两件吐鲁番文书编号分别为 T II B 66 No. 17 和 T II B 66 No. 18，均是正面为汉文、背面为叙利亚文的双语文书。〔1〕

迟至 1999 年，T II B 66 No. 17 号文书正面汉文部分才由日本学者西胁常记公布，〔2〕2001、2002 年西胁又先后以德文、日文出版了柏林

〔1〕Nicolas Sims-Williams, *Mitteliranische Handschriften Teil 4: Iranian Manuscript in Syriac Script in the Berlin Turfan Collection*, Stuttgart: Franz Steiner Verlag, 2012, p. 53: E 11 Liturgy, SyrHT 3 (=1749=T II B 66 No. 17), and E 11, n296 (1750=T II B 66 No. 18). 德藏叙利亚文文书的综合目录正在由亨特（Erica C. D. Hunter）及其学生狄更斯 (Mark Dickens) 编辑中，尚未出版。

〔2〕西胁常记，"ベルリン・トルファン・コレクション道教文書，"《京都大学総合人間学部紀要》第6号，1999年，第47-66页，该文书见第49-50页，注记为 Syr1749v 号文书，这一标记见于文书本身。他根据残片中的"神思存真""导引三光"之语指出此残片带有道教色彩，但未能比定出其来源。

吐鲁番藏品中所见汉文文书的目录，也注记了这件文书。[1]而 T II B 66 No. 17 号文书的背面叙利亚文部分因为带有粟特文标记迟至 2012 年才由辛姆斯-威廉姆斯编入他出版的中古伊朗语文书目录。辛姆斯-威廉姆斯同时注记了 T II B 66 No. 18 号文书，认为它们均是叙利亚文祈祷文，而正面部分应来自同一件汉文文书，即叙利亚文文书实际上是利用了原来的汉文文书在其背面书写祈祷文。西胁先生注意到 T II B 66 No. 17 是带有道教色彩的文书，但并未说明出其来源。

本文将首先考察两件文书之内容出自《本际经》卷 3，再依据其内容以及所来源的道教文献并结合日本京都杏雨书屋公布的《志玄安乐经》来考察道教与景教之联系。本文将主要根据两件文本使用的词汇、用语及其所反映的意义进行比较，找出其中具有学术旨趣的相似性，从而提供一种新解读，以一窥两者之间的联系。这也是比定这两件吐鲁番出土残片的重要意义。

景教汉文文献与佛教和道教文献之关系，历来深受学界重视。一般学界从分析景教汉文文献和佛道文献相类似的内容和文字入手，将两者进行比较，从而讨论景教汉文文献所受到的佛道影响。[2]至于中古时代景教社区与佛道社区的具体接触，我们知之甚少，但也有一些个案非常有意思，比如高楠顺次郎在 19 世纪末检出《贞元新定释教目录》中所记载的景净与般若三藏进行合作之例，[3]从而增加了一个景教与佛教僧人实际接触互动的例子。吐鲁番出土的一些双语文书，特别是正面是佛道文献而背面为景教文献的文书，至少可以说明当地的景教社区从

〔1〕Nishiwaki Tsuneki, Chinesische und Manjurische Handscriften und Seltene Drucke, Teil 3: Chinesische Texte Vermischten Inhalts aus der Berliner Turfansammlung, beschrieben von Tsuneki Nishiwaki, übersetzt von Christian Wittern, herausgegeben von Simone-Christiane Raschmann, Stuttgart: Franz Steiner Verlag, 2001, p. 133; 日文，《ドイツ将来のトルファン漢語文書》，京都：京都大学出版会, 2002年。

〔2〕有关景教与道教的比较研究，见 Stephen Eskildsen, "Parallel Themes in Chinese Nestorianism and Medieval Taoist Religion," in Roman Malek ed., *Jingjiao: The Church of the East in China and Central Asia*, Sankt Augustin: Institut Monumenta Serica (2006), pp. 57–91. 但该文未涉及本文讨论的两件吐鲁番文书。

〔3〕Takakusu Junjiro, "The Name of 'Messiah' found in a Buddhist Book: The Nestorian Missionary Adam, Presbyter, Papas of China, Translating a Buddhist Sutra," *T'oung Pao* vol. 7 (1896), pp. 589–591.

佛教和道教社区回收写经用纸，用于抄写他们的景教文献。1995 年辛姆斯-威廉姆斯公布了一件粟特文文书，即粟特文本《三威蒙度赞》，其正面便是《法华经》抄本。[1]两者之间在思想、内容、写作风格上并无直接联系。

现在本文又揭示出一件正面是道教《本际经》而背面是景教叙利亚文祈祷文的文献，虽然两者在思想、内容和文本写作风格上也并无直接联系，但这件写本的发现至少说明当时吐鲁番地区的景教徒回收了道教文献用纸。因为在吐鲁番目前没有发现汉文的景教文书，所以目前尚难判断当地的景教徒是否能阅读汉文，也很难判断当地景教徒在何种程度上了解文书正面所抄写道教文献的内容。不过，这件文书能告诉读者的历史信息当然远不止于此。

唐代宗教文献的翻译、书写可能反映出一些跨越不同宗教鸿沟的共通性，特别体现在他们使用相似的词汇和表达。尽管不同宗教社区有不同的信仰，但他们均和当时唐朝的文士有所过从，这使得一些比较流行的宗教词汇和表达能够通过各种管道进入不同的宗教文献，以同样或类似的语言形式而反映不同的宗教意义和内容。换言之，当时不同的中外宗教团体所熟悉的唐代汉文语言文化其实是相当接近的，特别是长安地区的宗教团体所接触的文士和文献，应该属于同一个语境。据敦煌出土的《尊经》，景教文献《志玄安乐经》，应该是在长安景教社区出现的。《本际经》则是唐代高宗、玄宗下敕传写的道教文献，其在长安地区的广泛流通亦不言而喻。基于这样一个大背景，如果以道教《本际经》和景教《志玄安乐经》做一比较，可以获知一些有价值的新信息。

12.1　T II B 66 No. 17 和 No. 18 号文书汉文部分的内容

首先应指出的是，可以在传世文献中找到 T II B 66 No. 17 号文书的

〔1〕Nicolas Sims-Williams, “A Sogdian Version of the ‘Gloria in excelsis Deo’,” in: *Au Carrefour des grandes religions. Hommages a Phillippe Gignoux.* Ed. R. Gyselen, Bures-sur Yvettes, (Res Orientales VII), pp. 257-262. 吉田丰帮助他比定了正面的《法华经》残片。

文本来源。在成书于983年的宋初大型类书《太平御览》卷673《道部》十五可以找到和这件文书内容一致的文字。该文书略存八行，但第八行不可读，实际能读出的部分只有七行，四十余字，几乎难于句读，更不易理解，好在找到了对应文字，可以补入缺失的文字，并进行句读和解释。不过，《太平御览》中的对应文字只有六行可与这件文书所存文字对应，第七行也没有。《太平御览》中的文字也是引用一小段道经文献，很可能本身就没引全，所以第七行缺失了。下面将这件文书进行录文，并对比《太平御览》中所对应的文字，用方括号增补如下：

（1）重科条，防检［过失也，威仪自然经者，具示斋戒，奉法俯］

（2）仰，进止容式，轨［范节度也；方法者，众圣着述，丹］

（3）药秘要，神草灵［芝，柔金水玉，修养之道也；术数者］，

（4）明辩思神，存真念［道，神心虚志，游空飞步，餐吸］

（5）元和，导引三光，仙［度之法也；记传者，众圣］

（6）载述学业，得［道成真，证果众事之迹也

（7）圣之辞，巧芳章句，称［

下面是《太平御览》的文字：

《太微黄书经》曰：天真三皇藏八会之文于委羽山，太微天帝藏一通于龟山。其灵书八会，字无正形，趣究乎奥，难可寻详。得为天书，自然至真。斯八会之气，全五和之音，非浅近者所能洞明。天真皇人，竭其所见，注解其意。八会多文者，生天立地，开化人神。万物之本，主召九天。上帝校定神仙图录，政天分度，安国息民，摄制酆都，降魔伏鬼，敕命水帝，召龙上云。论天地劫期，辩圣真名氏。所理城台种种，因缘广宣，区别五方，元精服御，求仙化形之法，皆演玄妙，自然虚无，正真妙趣，明瞭具足也。又有玉诀者，天真上圣述释天书八会之文，以为正音。又有灵图者，玄圣表化，示以灵变象形述理，令物易悟也。玉皇谱录者，众圣纪述圣君名姓，宗本继嗣，神官位绪也。诫律者，玄圣制敕，诠量罪福，轻重科条，防检过失也。威仪自然经者，具示斋戒，奉法俯仰，进止容式，轨范节度也。方法者，众圣著述丹药秘要，神草灵芝，柔

金水玉，修养之道也。术数者，明辩思神，存真念道，神心虚志，游空飞步，餐吸元和，导引三光，仙度之法也。记传者，众圣载述学业，得道成真，证果众事之迹也。[1]

虽然这段话引了《太微黄书经》，但实际上这段话并非全部来自这部书，[2]来自这部书的内容仅仅包括“天真三皇藏八会之文于委羽山，太微天帝藏一通于龟山”这一句话而已，这句话见于《洞真太微黄书九天八箓真文》，[3]即现存的《太微黄书》第八卷。太微天帝也出现在《皇天上清金阙帝君灵书紫文上经》一文中。[4]

《太平御览》中这段引文接下来说到“其灵书八会，字无正形，趣究乎奥，难可寻详。得为天书，自然至真。斯八会之气，全五和之音，非浅近者所能洞明。天真皇人，竭其所见，注解其意”，这些文字则似来自《太上洞玄灵宝诸天内音自然玉字》的节录，因其内容几乎一致，而文字与现存《道藏》版本颇有些差异。现存版本第三卷《大梵隐语无量洞章》云：“天尊普问四座大众：灵书八会，字无正形，其趣宛奥，难可寻详，天既降应，妙道宜明，便可注笔，解其正音，使皇道既畅，泽被十方。天真皇人稽首作礼，上白天尊：自随运生化，展转亿劫，屡经侍座，未有今日遭值圣道，开诸法门，得见天书，自然至真。斯八会之气，合五和之音，非愚情短思所能洞明。今既厕座次，仰睹玄妙，被命狼狈，不敢藏情，逆用张惶，若无神守，辄竭所见，解注其音，冀万

〔1〕《太平御览》卷673，北京：中华书局，1963年，第3000页。这段话所引用的道教文本基本上出自古灵宝经类文献。

〔2〕经过与柏夷（Stephen R. Bokenkamp）教授反复讨论，清理这段引文的来源。这里要感谢他帮助提供线索，最终找出这段引文来自三部道经。我们也将另外合撰一文讨论这两件吐鲁番文书相关的道教史问题。

〔3〕《中华道藏》第二册, No. 053，北京：华夏出版社，2004年， 第452页中栏。相关提示见朱越利 《黄书考》,《中国哲学》第19期，1998年，第167–188页。贺碧来（Isabelle Robinet）对此书的解题见 Christopher Schipper and Franciscus Verellen eds., *The Daoist Canon: A Historical Companion to the Daozang*, vol. 1, Chicago: University of Chicago Press, 2004, p. 192.

〔4〕见 Stephen R. Bokenkamp, *Early Daoist Scriptures*, Berkeley: University of California Press, 1997, pp. 328–330, also p. 312 导论部分。

有合，开示来生不及之体。惟蒙曲悯。”[1] 至少从内容上来看，《太平御览》所引文字似乎是《诸天内音自然玉字》卷3部分内容的节录。

而剩下的部分起自“八会多文者”，终于“证果众事之迹也”，也即是和本文所讨论的吐鲁番出土文书在内容上相对应的文字，实际来自《太玄真一本际经》卷3，但文字有异。《太玄真一本际经》并不见于传世道藏，但在敦煌出土了很多件《太玄真一本际经》写本，有些品以不同的题名出现。[2]据姜伯勤先生的提示，675—693年间沙州的冲虚观、神泉观均派人去长安参加官府组织的写一切道经活动，以追悼上元二年死去的太子李弘，而其中《本际经》的一些写本也因此传至敦煌。[3]

在敦煌出土的道教文献中，目前已知《本际经》写本有140多件，在数量上是比较突出的一种道教文献，可能也反映了唐代此经因受到高宗、玄宗的支持而一度非常流行，唐代道士常常将这一经文用于发愿祈

〔1〕见《中华道藏》第三册，第220页上栏；该文见于《正统道藏》洞真部，也有敦煌写本残片（P. 2431）。《云笈七签》卷7《三洞经教部》也引了《诸天内音自然玉字》并作解说：“《内音玉字经》云：天皇真人曰：《诸天内音自然玉字》，字可一丈，自然而见空玄之上，八角垂芒，精光乱眼。灵书八会，字无正形。其趣宛奥，难可寻详。皆诸天之中大梵隐语，结飞玄之气，合和五方之音，生于元始之上，出于空洞之中，随运开度，普成天地之功。天尊命天皇真人注解其正音，使皇道清畅，泽被十方。皇人不敢违命，按笔注解之曰：形魂顿丧，率我所见，聊注其文。五合之义，其道足以开度天人也。和合五方无量之音，以成《诸天内音》，故曰五合之义也。”

〔2〕敦煌出土《本际经》写本很早便引起国际学界的注意，实际上最早对英、法所藏《本际经》进行全面整理、编辑、校订、研究的是吴其昱先生，见 Chiyu Wu, *Pen-tsi king: Livre de terme original. Ouvrage taoïste inédit du VIIe siècle. Manuscrits retrouvés à Touen-houang*, reproduits en fac-similé. Introduction par Wu Chi-yu, Paris: Centre Nationale de la Recherche Scientifique, 1960；据山田俊提示，吴先生的研究出版后，后来镰田茂雄、陈祚龙、大渊忍尔、康德谟（Max Kaltenmark）、砂山稔、尾崎正治、荣新江、中田笃郎、卢国龙等先生又续有讨论；山田俊《唐初道教思想史研究：「太玄眞一本際經」の成立と思想》（京都：平乐寺书店，1999年）一书在该经文本及其所反映的道教史、道教思想与实践的讨论等方面均十分详尽，可谓集大成者。尽管后来又发现了一些《本际经》的吐鲁番写本，但均很零散和残碎。

〔3〕很多学者均研究过此经的流传，见姜伯勤先生文章中的提示；姜伯勤《〈本际经〉与敦煌道教》，《敦煌研究》1994年第3期，第1-16页。姜先生也提示了该经的道性论，即道性作为真空与众生性特别是中道真空的意义。

福、治病度亡仪式[1]。敦煌出土的《本际经》卷3《圣行品》写本中有与我们这里讨论的吐鲁番道教文书相对应的文字，其文如下：

自然本文者，天书八会，凤篆龙章，是为天地万物之本，开化人神，成立诸法，主召九天神仙上帝，校订图录，调政璇玑，摄制酆都，降魔伏鬼，敕命水帝，召龙上云。天地劫期，圣真名讳。所治城台，众圣境界，广宣分别，种种阶差，服御元精，化形之法，皆演玄妙，自然虚无，正真妙趣，明瞭具足。神符者，云篆之文，神真之信，召摄众魔，威制神鬼，总炁御运，保命留年。玉诀者，天真上圣述释天书八会之文，以为正音，开示大道。灵图者，众圣化迹，应现无方，图写变通，令物悟解。谱录者，众圣纪述神真名讳，宗本冑胤，神官位绪。诫律者，条制敕约，防非检过，诠量罪福，分别轻重。威仪者，具示斋戒，进退楷模，俯仰节度，轨式容止。方法者，众圣著述丹药秘要，神草灵芝，柔金水玉，修养之道。术数者，明辩思神，存真念道，心斋虚忘，游空飞步，餐吸六炁，导引三光，练质化形，仙度之法。记传者，是诸众圣载述学业，得道成真，通玄入妙，修因方所，证果时节。赞诵者，众真大圣巧饰法言，称扬正道，令物信乐，发起迴向，生尊重心。章表者，师资授受，妙宝奇文，登坛告盟，启誓传度，悔谢请福，关告之辞。[2]

这段文字尽管和吐鲁番出土文书的文字有较多不同，但可以看出内容上基本一致。这段文字的内容主要讲道教文献的十二种分类，即如该道经所说："三洞妙文，天书玉字，云篆龙章，金篇宝秘，皆悉具受。所受诸法，虽复无边，总括条疏，唯十二事，部类分别，随根不同。一者自然本文，二者神符，三者宝诀，四者灵图，五者谱录，六者戒律，

[1] 王卡：《敦煌道教文献研究——综述、目录、索引》，北京：中国社会科学出版社，2004年，第36页；敦煌出土《本际经》写本目录见该书第193–210页，其中卷3著录了15件。

[2] 张继禹主编：《中华道藏》第五册，北京：华夏出版社，2004年，第228页。据整理者王卡先生统计，此卷抄本在敦煌出土至少有15件，底本为P. 2795，参校本为P. 2398号文书。此经亦称《太玄真一本际妙经》。此经初有万毅辑录本，即《敦煌道教文献〈本际经〉录文及解说》，《道家文化研究》第十三辑，1998年，第367–484页；后又有叶贵良更为详尽的辑校本，见《敦煌本〈太玄真一本际经〉辑校》，成都：巴蜀书社，2010年。

七者威仪，八者方法，九者术数，十者记传，十一者赞诵，十二者章表。”而这里所谓十二事，实际上是继承了敦煌出土文书中所谓宋文明《通门论》记陆修静对古灵宝经进行整理分类的思想。在《通门论》系统中，这 12 种道教文献包括自然本文、神符、玉诀、灵图、谱录、戒律、威仪、方诀、众术、记传、赞颂、表奏。[1]道教文献这种 12 类的分法，当然是受到佛教十二部经分类思想的影响，有关这一议题的讨论此处不赘。

敦煌文书中的“所治城台”在吐鲁番文文书中以“所理城台”出现，“治”变为“理”，当是避唐高宗李治之名讳，显见此件吐鲁番文书的道教写经应出自唐代，很可能是在高宗为追悼太子李弘下令写的一切道经中的一种，也可能来自开元时期的官方写经。因为《册府元龟》云开元二十九年（741）十二月玄宗敕令天下诸观自来年正月一日至年终以来常转《本际经》以便富国安民。天宝元年（742）又下诏“宜令天下道士及女道士等，待至今岁转经讫，各于当观设斋庆赞，仍取来年正月一日至年终已来，依前转《本际经》，兼令讲说”。[2]而安史之乱以后道教在敦煌乃至整个河西地区逐渐衰落。[3]

鉴于这件道教文书文字更接近《太平御览》，而非敦煌《本际经》写本，而它的文字又反映其避唐高宗名讳，书法比较规整，或可推知这件吐鲁番（当时为西州）道教抄本出自唐代前期官方写经，不过其所依据的《本际经》版本是一个流行于唐代而被北宋初期《太平御览》所借

〔1〕大渊忍尔 Ōfuchi Ninji, “On Ku Ling-pao-ching,” *Acta Asiatica* No. 27 (1974), pp. 33–56，《道教とその经典》，东京：创文社，1997年，第596–600页；王承文：《敦煌古灵宝经与晋唐道教》，北京：中华书局，2002年，第756页；之后续有王卡、王宗昱、马承玉、刘屹等学者对大渊之说提出质疑，其相关讨论见刘屹《敦煌本〈通门论〉卷下(P. 2861.2+2256)定名再议》，《文献季刊》2009年第4期，第47–55页。

〔2〕《册府元龟》卷53《帝王部·尚黄老》一；卷54《帝王部·尚黄老》二；参见雷闻先生的相关讨论，见《国家宫观网络中的西州道教：唐代西州的道教补说》，《西域文史》第二卷，2007年，第117–127页，收入孟宪实、荣新江、李肖主编：《秩序与生活：中古时期的吐鲁番社会》，北京：中国人民大学出版社，2011年，第279–292页。

〔3〕王卡先生认为敦煌出土的大部分道教写经来自安史之乱前的时代，因为安史之乱造成道教在敦煌地区出现衰落的局面，也使得留下的文献较少，根据他的介绍，似乎敦煌地区并无写于安史之乱后的《本际经》出土；见王卡《敦煌道教文献研究——综述、目录、索引》，第9–15、36页。

鉴的底本，而这个底本与敦煌抄本所依据的《本际经》底本似乎略有文字的不同。如果称敦煌抄本所据版本为 A，吐鲁番抄本所据版本为 B，可知 A 版本似乎更为流行，而 B 版本也流通，甚至宋初的《太平御览》中的引文也据以为用。为何在唐代会有两种不同的《本际经》版本流传，尚需以后进一步研究。

吐鲁番出土 T II B 66 No. 17 号文书第四行的“神思”应为“思神”之误，抄写者后来意识到这个错误，加了一个调转次序的标号 Z，就变成“思神”。因为这一句结合后来一句“存真念道”，可知“思神”实为道教文献中常见的专有名词，即对道教之“神”和“真”进行“思”和“存”实践，这种存思术在道教传统中有很长的历史。下面举两个例子予以说明。比如《无上秘要》卷 57 有“次回还东向，向香炉三捻香，称玄都大洞三景弟子小兆真人某岳先生臣某甲今建斋立直，明灯诵经，思神念真，行道求仙，飞腾九天”。《太上洞玄宝元上经》有 “研经内观者，诵咏灵章，解了妙义，临目思神，与真合也”之句。

如果我们结合 T II B 66 No. 18 号文书的内容，可知 No. 17 与 No. 18 实际来自同一件文本，也即属于同一部道经，即《太玄真一本际经》。我将 T II B 66 No. 18 号文书的内容列出如下，方括号中增补的文字出自敦煌出土《太玄真一本际经》卷 3《圣行品》的内容：

（1）一乘［道。既从明师，禀受尊教，具得要诀，闻已］

（2）思惟，洞解玄妙，通达［明了，觉悟俗境，皆非真实，］

（3）分析观察，知世俗相，［皆悉空寂，入无相门，离］

（4）爱染心，断灭烦恼，到［解脱地，诣长寿宫，常住］

（5）清净，自在无碍，［安隐快乐，非身离身，亦不不］

（6）身，而以一形，周［遍六道，现一切相，随类色像。］

（7）非心离心，亦［不不心，而以一念，了一切法，以］

（8）圆通眼，照［道真性，深达缘起，了法本源，解众生性即真道性。］

这段文字主要讲道教所谓“世俗之相皆悉空寂”而“众生性即是真道性”的道性论，同样的思想也出现在中古时期其他一些道教文献中，比如《太上一乘海空智藏经》，只是文字略有不同。吐鲁番出土的这件 T II B 66 No. 18 文书与敦煌出土文书《本际经》写本在文字上并无不同。

总而言之，从上面的讨论不难得出一个结论，即 T II B 66 No. 17 与 No. 18 应该是出自同一个《本际经》文本的两个残片，因其避唐高宗名讳而应归为唐代道经。背面则是叙利亚文祈祷文，并带有粟特文标记。这两件残片的比定有两点意义。其一，可以帮助我们了解更多关于道教在唐代西州地区流行的情况，即《本际经》卷 3 也出现在这一地区；其二，可以帮助我们从一个新角度来看待当时敦煌吐鲁番地区景教与道教之关系。有关第二点本文第二部分再进行详细阐说。第一点这里提示一下，有关唐代吐鲁番地区的道教，前人多所论说。[1]当地流行的道教文献也在吐鲁番文书发现多种，其中即包括《太玄真一本际经》卷 5（日藏大谷文书 4085 号）和卷 8《最胜品》（德藏吐鲁番文书 Ch 243 = T III T 514 + Ch 286 = T II 1178）。[2]现在本文又提供了一个证据，说明有一件文书来自《本际经》卷 3（T II B 66 No. 17 + 18），而这一卷写本的书法与日藏大谷文书极为接近，似乎来自同一批写经。

〔1〕小笠原宣秀:《吐鲁番出土の宗教生活文书》，载于《西域文化研究》第三卷，1960年，第249–278页；荣新江:《唐代西州的道教》，载于《敦煌吐鲁番研究》第四卷，1999年，第127–144页；雷闻:《国家宫观网络中的西州道教：唐代西州的道教补说》，载于《西域文史》第二卷，2007年，第117–127页，收入孟宪实、荣新江、李肖主编《秩序与生活：中古时期的吐鲁番社会》，北京：中国人民大学出版社，2011年，第279–292页。雷闻先生的文章在脚注四提供了日本所藏吐鲁番道教文书研究的新进展，如陈国灿、刘安志主编《吐鲁番文书总目·日本收藏卷》，武汉大学出版社，2005年；张娜丽《西域出土文书の基础的研究》第 IV 部《大谷文书中に见られる佛典·道书断片——吐鲁番出土の遗文》，东京：汲古书院，2006年，第387–463页；都筑晶子等《大谷文书の整理と研究》二《大谷文书の道经写本断片》，龙谷大学《佛教文化研究所纪要》第44集，2005年，第84–110页。其他散藏中也许还有道教文献残片，值得留意。

〔2〕著录见王卡《敦煌道教文献研究——综述、目录、索引》，第204、207页；卷五见小田义久编《大谷文书集成》卷贰图版80，录文和校订见都筑晶子等《大谷文书の整理と研究》二《大谷文书の道经写本断片》，龙谷大学《佛教文化研究所纪要》第44集，2005年，第94–95页；后者由万毅比定。已知吐鲁番道教文书见王卡书第282–283页。

12.2 景教《志玄安乐经》与道教《太玄真一本际经》

上文讨论确定了这件T II B 66 No. 17 和No.18文书来自《本际经》，继而可以提供给我们一个新信息，即唐代抄写的《本际经》写卷流传到高昌地区，其一部分抄本作为回收利用的纸张进入了当地景教社区。背面祈祷文的年代应该较晚，可能出自高昌回鹘时期，当时道教早已衰微，因而其写经被当成废物再利用。考虑到当时敦煌、吐鲁番的景教徒之间存在联系，[1]也不排除这件文书从河西地区流入高昌地区的可能性。只是敦煌的《本际经》抄本与这里的抄本所据底本不同，使得这种可能性降低了。

有趣的是，因为日本京都杏雨书屋公布了其所收藏的敦煌文书，我们终于得以一窥敦煌出土景教文献《志玄安乐经》的全貌。[2]如果仔细阅读此经，可以发现其文字和思想颇有可与佛、道文献进行相互比较研究之处。唐初出现的《太玄真一本际经》是中古时期相当重要的一部道经，至少从敦煌出土很多写本来看，这部道经在西北地区颇为流行，实际上其中所反映的道性思想在道教思想史上也的确非常重要。而这部经书中的所谓“道性”一说也出现在敦煌出土景教文献《志玄安乐经》之中，[3]这是相当有意思的一件事，值得在这里略加提示。

《本际经》成立的年代肯定早于《志玄安乐经》。《本际经》最初

〔1〕我曾讨论过敦煌、吐鲁番两地景教的联系，见《高昌回鹘景教研究》，《敦煌吐鲁番研究》第四卷，1999年，第165–214页。

〔2〕之前林悟殊先生已对此经的早期研究史有所提示，见《唐代景教再研究》，北京：中国社会科学出版社，2003年，第146–155页。

〔3〕Stephen Eskildsen 提示了《志玄安乐经》所说十观与《本际经》卷2中十种法印类似，见“Parallel Themes in Chinese Nestorianism and Medieval Taoist Religion,” 2006, p. 66。但实际《本际经》卷2所说的并非十法印，而是十二法印；后来王兰平又提示了《志玄安乐经》中言及世人要达到安乐境界需要借助梯橙，而十种观法的表述与道经《太玄真一本际经》卷2《付嘱品》中的说法类似，因而他认为两者异曲同工，但两经之内容与内涵没有关联。见王兰平《以〈志玄安乐经〉十观为例看唐代景教与佛道之间的关系》，载于《敦煌学辑刊》2008年第1期，第160–161页。实际上，这个梯橙的说法，也见于吐鲁番文书，如阿斯塔那509号墓《唐西州道俗合作梯橙及钟记》(《吐鲁番出土文书》第九册，北京：文物出版社，1990年，第137页）提及道士康鸾；参见前引荣新江的论文。

肇源于隋代道士刘进喜的五卷本，后经唐代道士李仲卿增补为十卷本。而《志玄安乐经》译出的年代应该晚于《本际经》，据敦煌出土的《尊经》，《志玄安乐经》应是景净所译，则其年代应在 8 世纪后半叶。不过，该经的文字与风格与《大秦景教流行中国碑》和《三威蒙度赞》非常不同，这三者也许不是成于一人之手，景净或许只是因为身为景教教会领袖被挂上译者之名而已。无论如何，由于高宗、玄宗等人相继下敕令人抄写《本际经》，此经在长安地区大概广为人知，而同样在长安建寺度人译经的景教社区应该不会对这部经典感到十分陌生。简言之，《本际经》不会脱出景教社区所处的语境之外，而相当可能成为其僧人译经参考的语言、文字乃至思想资源。

《本际经》和《志玄安乐经》两者有些用语的表达确实也极为接近。比如《本际经》卷 3 也多次提到了"安乐"，前文提到的 T II B 66 No. 18 残卷中有"知世俗相，［皆悉空寂，入无相门，离］爱染心，断灭烦恼，到［解脱地，诣长寿宫，常住］清净，自在无碍，［安隐快乐］"之说，其实卷 3 里面还有这样的话："未开度者，誓使开度；未安乐者，誓使安乐；未解脱者，誓使解脱；未升玄者，誓使升玄。"[1]"安乐"在两个文献中均与清净、解脱、自在等概念联系在一起。

不过，本文特别关注的是《本际经》和《志玄安乐经》都提及"道性"，而它们对道性的解释很值得进行比较，因为两者均对这一概念有比较相近的描述。《志玄安乐经》里讲到所谓四种修行的胜法，即无欲、无为、无德、无证。其中无证部分说，

> 四者无证，于诸实证，无所觉知，妄弃是非，泯齐德失，虽曰自在，邈然虚空。何以故？譬如明镜，鉴照一切，青黄杂色，长短众形，尽能洞徹，莫知所宜。人亦如是，悟真道性，得安乐心，遍见众缘，患能通达于彼，觉了忘尽无遗，是名无证。

该经后文又说："若有男女，依我所言，勤修上法，昼夜思惟，离诸染污，清净真性，湛然圆明，即知其人终当解脱，是知此经，所生利

[1]《中华道藏》第五册，第228页下栏。

益，众天说之，不穷真际。”　这两段里的所谓“悟真道性”与“清净道性”实际上指的是相同的状态。前者“悟真道性”可以得安乐心，也就是“自在”和“邈然虚空”的状态。后者所谓清净道性，也即是“离诸染污”，不受污染的清净状态，也可以说是“邈然虚空”。所以《志玄安乐经》也说道：

> 若有知见，则为有身；以有身故，则怀生想；怀生想故，则有求为；有所求为，是名动欲；有动欲者，于诸苦恼，犹未能免，况于安乐？而得成就，是故我言，无欲无为、离诸染境、入诸净源、离染能净，故等于虚空，发惠光明，能照一切。照一切，故名安乐道。

这段话很明显指出“离诸染境、入诸净源、离染能净”就是“虚空”的状态，达到这种状态便是得安乐道。而所谓无证，即是无诸实证，“无所觉知”，换言之，不能以通常的实际的经验的感觉去体会，这是一种不证自明的精神上的状态。这里的所谓真道性也见于《本际经》卷4《道性品》，其文云：“弃贤世界太上道君，放此光明，如前圣法，必欲开演真一本际，示生死源，说究竟果，开真道性，显太玄宗。”[1]

前文讨论的《志玄安乐经》有关道性的部分主要讲一种得安乐道的无证状态。而所谓得安乐道也可以在《本际经》中找到类似的表达，这便是“得道”。什么是得道呢？《本际经》卷1云：

> 所谓得道，得无所得；所谓断灭，断无所断。何以故？烦恼性空，执计为有，以执为心，故名为烦恼。若知烦恼，本性是空，心无所着，诸计皆尽，名断烦恼。烦恼病除，故名得道。虽名得道，实无所得。无得无断，假名方便，为化众生，名为得道。[2]

得道实际上是“得无所得”的状态，是断灭的状态，即得到没什么需要得到的，所谓“得道”只是为了方便教化众生而暂且使用的名字，其实并无所谓得到什么，只是一种性空的状态。这和前文《志玄安乐经》所说的“邈然虚空”表述也相当类似。

---

〔1〕《中华道藏》第五册，第233页下栏。

〔2〕《中华道藏》第五册，第215页中栏。

《志玄安乐经》中所谓“离诸染污，清净真性”也能在《本际经》卷2中找到类似的说法：

夫念道者，通能制灭一切恶根，犹金刚刀无所不断，犹如勐火无所不烧。念有二种，一念生身七十二相、八十一好，具足微妙，人中天上三界特尊，是我归依复护之处。二念法身犹如虚空，圆满清净，即是真道，亦名道身，亦名道性。常以正念，不闻馀心，是名念道。[1]

这里的第二念即指法身犹如虚空，圆满清净，也即是“真道”“道身”“道性”。[2]这和《志玄安乐经》所谓清净真性的表达也几乎一样。

《本际经》所谓道性，实际上也以“真性”一词出现，[3]而真性的性质也是“空”。比如《本际经》卷2说：“正道真性，不生不灭，非有非无，名正中道。” 之后，《本际经》卷2继续解释说：

始学之人，精修十行，为方便道，学相似空，能解众生，无真实体，渐悟微尘，亦无真性，悉皆虚假，入一相门，坚固不退，是名登顶。如上高山，至顶得住，而无退堕；知不退已，进更修习，转得胜明，能生真道，力用增益，似于无欲。体滞着故，故名为似，入真法门，故名无欲。甚深正教，能通众生，入无欲道，复名法门。无欲增长，洞解真性，正见诸法，无生灭相，转出生死，破诸魔众，心如琉璃，映彻无碍，正中之正，毕竟永断，名转法轮。[4]

前半段主要讲“真性”实际也是“空”。后半段主要讲作为一种修

〔1〕《中华道藏》第五册，第225页中栏。

〔2〕对于《本际经》道性论的研究，除了前引姜伯勤先生的论说外，还可参见砂山稔：《隋唐道教思想史研究》，东京：平河出版社，1990年；卢国龙：《中国重玄学：理想与现实的殊途与同归》，北京：人民中国出版社，1993年；山田俊：《唐初道教思想史研究：「太玄眞一本際經」の成立と思想》，京都：平乐寺书店，1999年；许汶相：《〈太玄真一本际妙经〉与佛典关系之研究》，台湾辅仁大学宗教学系硕士论文，2011年；黄崑威：《敦煌本〈太玄真一本际经〉思想研究》，成都：巴蜀书社，2011年。

〔3〕而“真性”一词在《景教三威蒙度赞》中出现了两次：“人元真性蒙依止”以及“善护真性得无繇”。不过，这里出现的“真性”意思与《本际经》中的“真性”似无相似之处，也与《志玄安乐经》中的“真性”不同。这一差异可能暗示《三威蒙度赞》与《志玄安乐经》似不是出自同一译者之手，甚至不是出自同一时代。如果真是如此，则至少《志玄安乐经》似非景净所译。

〔4〕《中华道藏》第五册，第223页上栏。

行法门的“无欲”，无欲适用于刚开始修行的人，这些人必须精修所谓“十行”，以便了解众生并无真实体，而无欲是为了了解诸法无生灭相，这样才能洞解真性。这里的“无欲”概念又和《志玄安乐经》中所谓四种胜法的第一种“无欲”表达一样，而且特别强调所谓“无欲”的“增长”。《志玄安乐经》中所谓“无欲”作为四胜法之第一条出现，也是为了服务初学者。《志玄安乐经》是这样解释“无欲”的：

一者无欲，所谓内心有所动欲，求代上事，作众恶缘，必须制伏，莫令辄起。何以故？譬如草根，藏在地下，内有伤损，外无见知，见是诸苗稼，必当凋萃，人亦如是，内心有欲，外不见知，然四肢七窍，皆无善气，增长众恶，断安乐因，是故内心，行无欲法。

这主要讲的是制伏心中的动欲，而且也特别强调要压制四肢七窍被内心之欲所造成的坏影响，而让善气“增长”。我想这种“无欲”之“增长”表达如此接近，绝非偶然，显然存在文本上的某种联系。有趣的是，《志玄安乐经》所讲的四种胜法是接着“十种观法”的修行讲的，这和《本际经》说的作为始学之人精修所谓作为阶梯的“十事”或“十行”然后方可进入到“无欲修行”可能也存在某种相似性。[1]

更有趣的是，《本际经》卷2的末尾部分有一首学道弟子们献给太上大道君的偈诗：

无上净妙真智身，寂灭无相莫能睹。
但见应体还本源，是故各怀大忧苦。
仰赖太上无极尊，犹如失母依慈父。
我等没在忧火中，唯愿时注甘露雨。
断绝倒想恋着心，消除诸见灭邪取。[2]

里面有些表达也可以在《景教三威蒙度赞》中找到相似句子，甚至看上去比佛教文献还更接近景教文献。[3]如《本际经》第一句“无上

〔1〕王兰平已经指出“十观”与“十事”之相似，但惜未提“无欲”在两经中的表达。

〔2〕《中华道藏》第五册，第226页上栏。

〔3〕对于《景教三威蒙度赞》与佛教《大乘本生心地观经》词汇和句式的比较，参见拙撰《从比较历史语言学看两件景教与佛教文献的联系》，载于朱玉麒主编：《西域文史》第1辑，2006年，第111–119页。

净妙真智身，寂灭无相莫能睹”与《三威赞》中“自始无人尝得见，复以色见不可相”等语较为相似。类似的表达还见于《本际经》卷4《道性品》中的颂语“无形五色可瞻视，无说无声可闻听”。[1]“仰赖太上无极尊，犹如失母依慈父”也与《三威蒙度赞》中“大师是我等慈父”相似。而“我等没在忧火中，唯愿时注甘露雨”则与《三威蒙度赞》中的“复与枯燋降甘露，所有蒙润善根滋”一联相似。但是《三威蒙度赞》中的这些词汇并不见于《志玄安乐经》，也因此可以看出虽然《景教三威蒙度赞》与《志玄安乐经》可能均借鉴了唐代流行的道教《本际经》，但看来这两种景教文献却并非出自同一译者之手，显然景净只是作为教会领袖而挂名译者。

前文已经讨论了《志玄安乐经》所说四种胜法中“无证”“无欲”与“道性”之关系及其与《本际经》卷2中表达的相似。而《志玄安乐经》中所谓“无为”也同样见于《本际经》卷4。在《本际经》卷4中有太上道君揭示道性与无为、自然之关系的一段话：

> 言道性者，即真实空，非空不空，亦不不空；非法非非法，非物非非物，非人非非人，非因非非因，非果非非果，非始非非始，非终非非终。非本非末，而为一切诸法根本。无造无作，名曰无为。自然而然，不可使然，不可不然，故曰自然。悟此真性，名曰悟道。了了照见，成无上道。[2]

道性其实便是无为、自然，悟到这点便是悟到真性，可以称为悟道。但这个说法显然与《志玄安乐经》对“无为”的说明差距较大。《志玄安乐经》文云：“二者无为，所谓外形，有所为造，非性命法，逐虚妄缘，必当舍弃，勿令亲近。何以故？譬如乘船，入大海水，逐风摇荡，随浪迁移，既忧沉没，无安宁者。人亦如是，外形有为，营造俗法，唯在进取，不念劬劳，于诸善缘，悉皆忘废，是故外形，履无为道。”据山田俊先生研究，《本际经》除了卷2、3、4讨论了道性，卷6、9也涉及道性思想，卷6讨论道性与究竟、毕竟两种净土之关系，卷9讨论

[1]《中华道藏》第五册，第232页中栏。
[2]《中华道藏》第五册，第234页中栏。

道性与道身思想之联系。[1]但卷6、9中的讨论似乎与《志玄安乐经》中的道性说法差距较远，兹不赘论。

总之，尽管前文所说的景教“无证”“无欲”两种胜法概念可在《本际经》中找到相似的表达，但“无为”概念的表达则差别很大。而《志玄安乐经》中所谓第二种胜法“无德”则似乎不见于《本际经》，或许可见景教汉文经典对道教文献有借用，亦有自己的坚持和发明。

12.3 结 语

综上所述，德国柏林吐鲁番藏品中的T II B 66 No. 17 与No. 18两件文书正面汉文文书大致可确定为《本际经》卷3的一种异本，避唐高宗讳，可知其系唐代道教写经。从其书法风格来看，与日本所藏大谷文书4085号残片《本际经》卷5实际属于同一批写经，很可能是唐代前期西州地区的官方写经。而这两件文书背面是利用道教写经用纸书写的叙利亚文景教祈祷文，并带有粟特文标记，可能是高昌回鹘时期该地景教教会粟特人所用的礼仪文书。这两件文书的道教写经文字与《太平御览》卷673所引道经文字基本一致，但与敦煌出土的道教《本际经》写经略有差异，反映出在唐代流行的《本际经》可能存在两个版本，敦煌抄本与吐鲁番抄本分别来自这两种版本，因而两地写本存在文字上的细微差异。当然，对T II B 66 No. 17号文书的研究也可帮助重新检视《太平御览》卷673所引一段道经文字，可知其实际出自《太微黄书九天八箓真文》《诸天内音自然玉字》和《本际经》三部道经。《太平御览》所引用的《本际经》与吐鲁番出土《本际经》抄本似来自同一种版本。

这两件德藏吐鲁番文书的比定和研究可以帮助我们进一步认识道教与景教之关系，提供了景教徒对道教了解的新证据，至少可知景教徒利用了道教写经的用纸，可能也意识到了道教写经的内容。如果将景教和道教在唐代长安的发展放在一个更大的历史语境中考察，可以推知当时长安地区多种宗教之间互相了解对方社区及其文献的存在应不成问

〔1〕山田俊:《唐初道教思想史研究 : 「太玄眞一本際經」の成立と思想》，第351–362页。

题。《本际经》首先是隋代道士刘进喜造出五卷本，随后唐初道士李仲卿又增补为十卷。武德四年（621），佛教僧人法琳看到刘进喜和李仲卿等人攻击佛教的言论，撰文进行论战。刘进喜和李仲卿在隋末唐初所居住的道观即587年隋文帝设立的清虚观，位于长安西侧的丰邑坊。清虚观正北方向经过崇化、怀德、群贤、居德四坊，即义宁坊，此处后来在638年建立了一座景教寺。总之，道观和景寺之间距离不是很远。鉴于《本际经》在唐高宗、玄宗统治时期因为皇室的尊崇和敕令流行于长安地区，景教社区应该对这部皇室尊崇的经典不会十分陌生。根据敦煌出土的《尊经》，《志玄安乐经》出自景净领导下的长安景教社区，其利用当时长安地区流行的其他宗教的文本、词汇表达等文字资源亦属自然而然之事。考虑到这样的历史语境，我们除了看到景教徒除了废物利用道教写本的用纸之外，也能看到景教徒对道教文献在内容表达上的借鉴。

本文通过比较敦煌吐鲁番地区较为流行的《本际经》写本与敦煌出土的《志玄安乐经》写本的通用词汇与相似表达，可以看到唐代景教徒可能借用了道教《本际经》中的“道性”以及相关的词汇，并赋予景教解说。同时景教《志玄安乐经》中所揭示的四种胜法中“无证”“无欲”等文字皆可在《本际经》中找到类似的表达，可知其或许也有借用道教词汇以及相关表达和解释的因素。尽管敦煌出土的《本际经》长达十卷，但上述这些相似的词汇和表达主要出现在卷2、卷3、卷4部分。无论如何，这一研究可知景教与道教之间存在一些之前并不知晓的联系，帮助读者进一步了解唐代景教文献中所借用的道教表述。

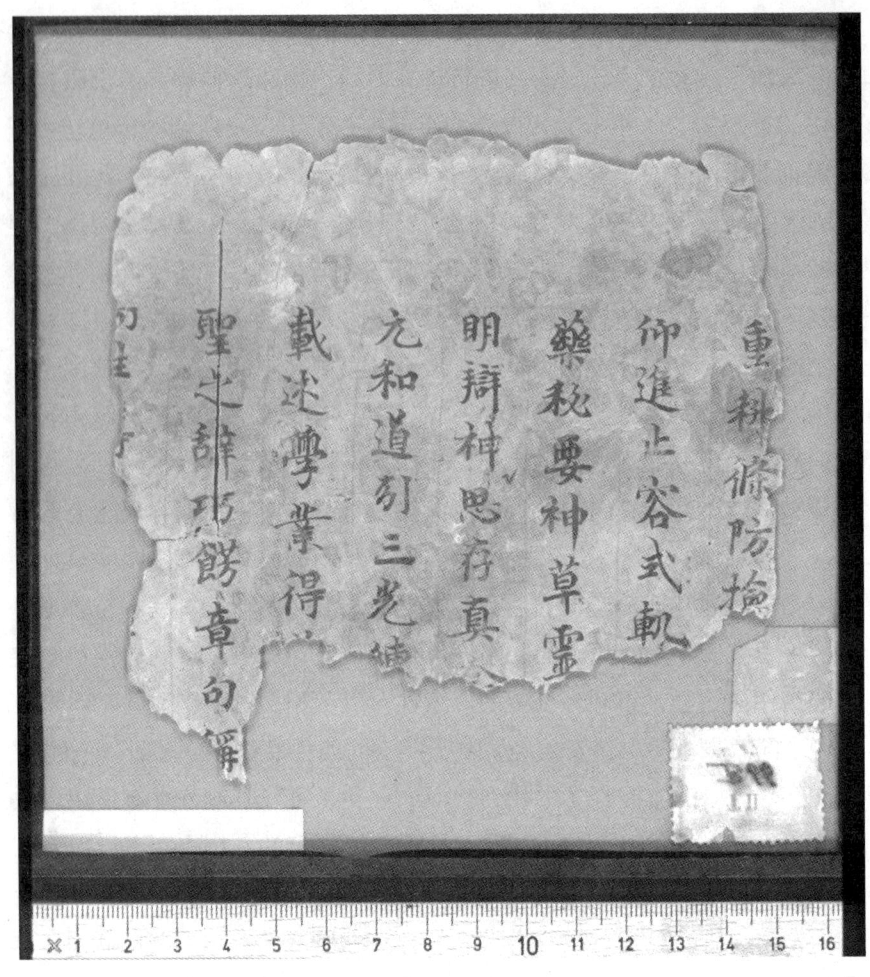
仰進止容式軌
藥秘要神草靈
明辯神思存真
元和道引三光
載述學業得
聖之辭巧餝章句

图版一：T II B 66　No. 17 号文书正面

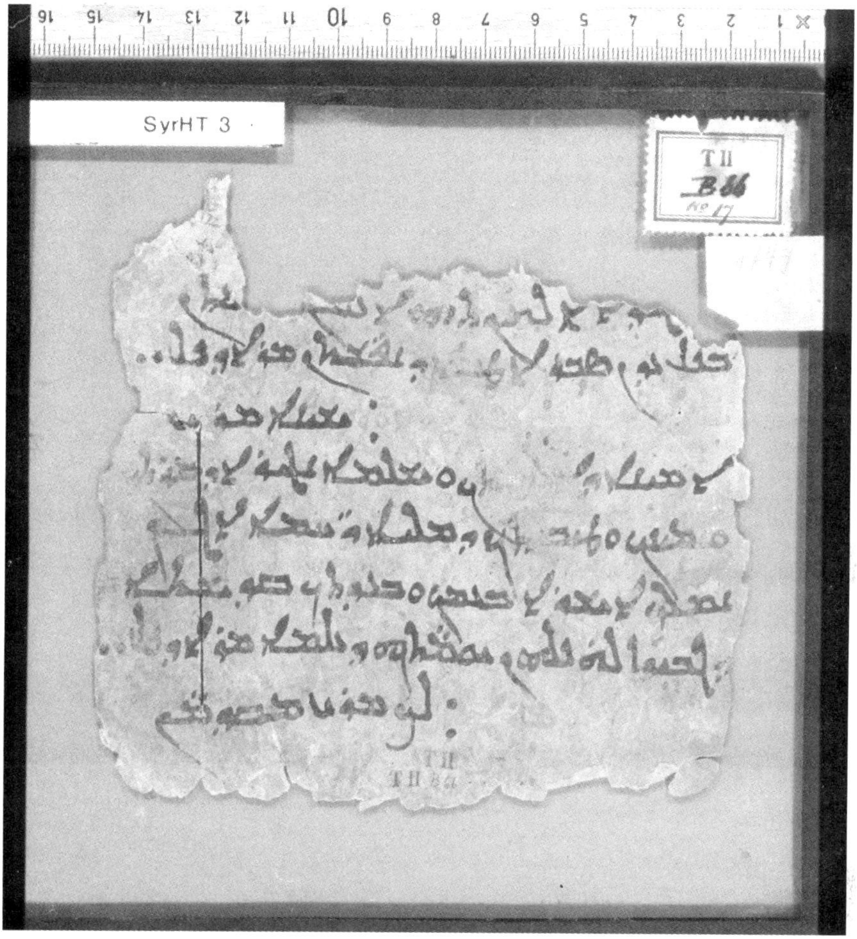

图版二：T II B 66　No. 17 号文书背面

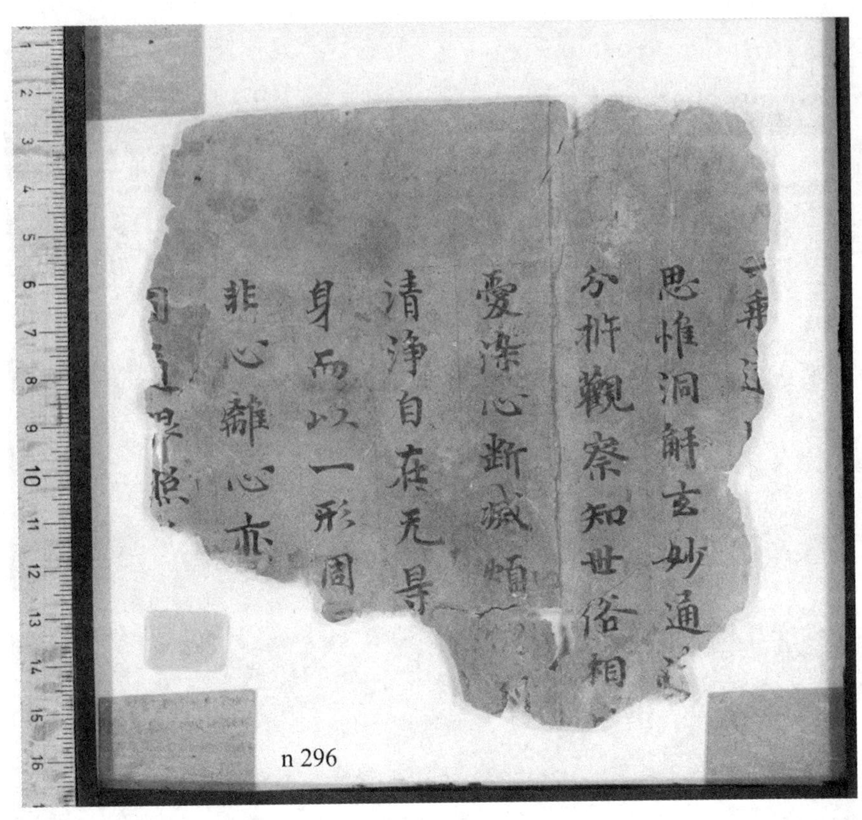
思惟洞解玄妙通
分析觀察知世俗相
愛染心斷滅煩
清淨自在无导
身而以一形固
非心離心亦

n 296

图版三：T II B 66 No. 18 号文书正面

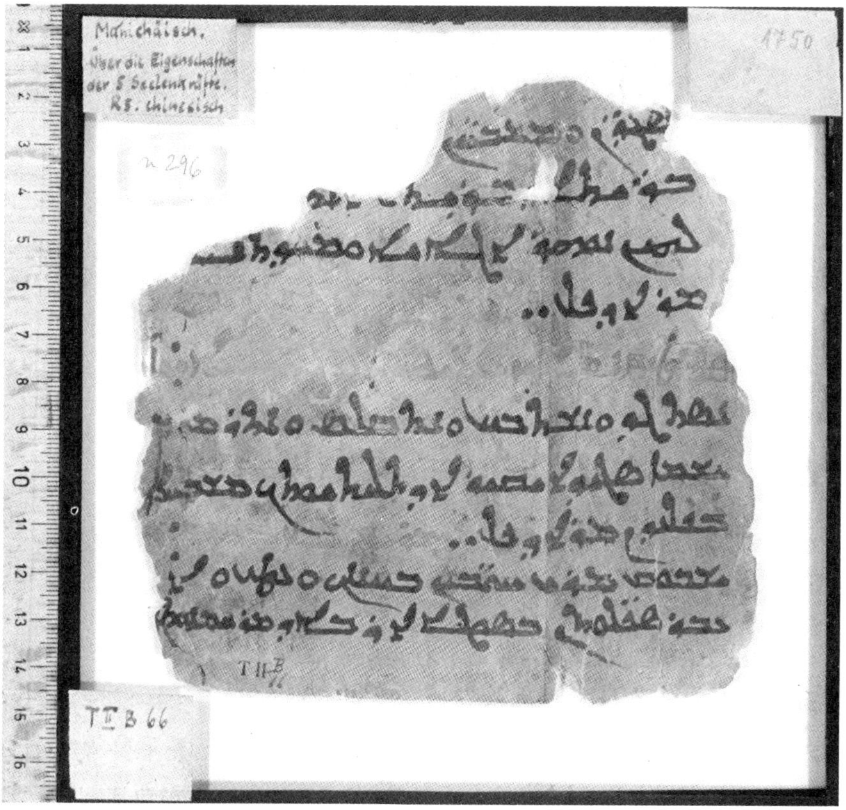

图版四：T II B 66　No. 18 号文书背面

13　唐代基督宗教的宗教多元化策略

Matteo Nicolini-Zani　著
(Comunità Monastica di Bose, Italy),
殷小平　译
（华南农业大学历史系）

13.1　引言
——文献综述

那些希望从历史、文学和神学等角度深入考察唐代中国景教——东叙利亚语基督宗教，亦常被称为“聂斯脱里教”者[1]——的学者，面临的一个主要难题是史料和考古资料的匮乏。即便至关重要的文书资料，数量也非常有限，与唐代大量的儒学、道教和佛教经典比起来，真可谓聊胜于无。[2]

总的看来，7 到 9 世纪的汉文基督宗教文书主要是有关教会、教仪和神学的内容。它们基本上不涉及基督宗教对其他宗教以及宗教多样性的看法，也不详细阐述宗教理论和学说要旨，这些我们今天的基督徒称

〔1〕其教名源自5世纪君士坦丁堡大主教聂斯脱里斯（Nestorius），其学说成为聂斯脱里教会神学的基础。有关东方教会的教义与历史，参见: E. Tisserant., s.v. “Nestorienne (l’église)”, in *Dictionnaire de Théologie Catholique*, vol. XI/1, Letouzey et Ané, Paris 1931, pp. 157–323; R. Le Coz, *Histoire de l’église d’Orient*, Cerf, Paris 1995; W. Baum, D. W. Winkler, *The Church of the East. A Concise History*, Routledge Curzon, London 2003; H. Teule, *Les Assyro–Chaldéens*, Brepols, Turnhout 2008. 有关该教会的误称，参阅 S. Brock, “The ‘Nestorian’ Church: A Lamentable Misnomer”, in *Bulletin of the John Rylands University Library of Manchester* 78/3 (1996), pp. 23–35.

〔2〕有关唐代基督宗教文书的介绍，参见 M. Nicolini–Zani, “Past and Current Research on Tang *Jingjiao* Documents: A Survey”, in R. Malek (ed.), *Jingjiao. The Church of the East in China and Central Asia*, Institut Monumenta Serica, Sankt Augustin 2006, pp. 23–44.

之为“宗教神学”（theology of religions）或“宗教多元主义神学”（theology of religious pluralism）的概念。

在考察唐代基督徒的宗教多元化时，有一点应该明确，即唐代基督宗教是由少数的一群胡人所信奉的这一历史定位。正如9世纪初期的记录所揭示的：

> 国朝沿近古而有力焉，亦容杂夷而来者。有摩尼焉，大秦焉，火祆焉。合天下三夷寺，不足当吾释寺一小邑之数也。[1]

即便如此，在某些史书中景教仍被记载为受官方支持的宗教，从公元781年西安景教碑上的颂词部分来看，这显然是确切的。不过，作为一种外来宗教，它的夷教身份没有改变。对基督徒而言，这是一种积极的区别对待，它把景教与其他宗教划分开来；而对唐朝统治者而言，这只是一种区别而已，其施行不过是为了把景教正确地纳入其政治统治之下。这一点在8世纪圆照《贞元新定释教目录》所摘录的一条敕令中明确无疑地反映出来，其载曰：

> 释氏伽蓝大秦僧寺。居止既别行法全乖。景净[2]应传弥尸诃教。沙门释子弘阐佛经。欲使教法区分人无滥涉。正邪异类泾渭殊流。[3]

由于史料和在华基督徒都为数极少，所以，有关唐代中国基督宗教如何看待其他宗教以及宗教多元化的考察，很大程度上只能是一种推测，并不可避免地陷入片面论断的风险当中。在此先不论文献方面的欠缺，笔者拟从唐代基督宗教汉文经典入手，集中从三个方面讨论基督徒如何看待中国宗教多元性的问题：社会/种族（social/ethnic）、文学/语言（literary/linguistic），以及思想/理论 （ideological/theoretical）。本研究将揭示基督宗教在现代化以前的中国如何遭遇宗教多元化，以及基

[1] 舒元舆：《重巖寺碑序》，载于《全唐文》卷727。录自 F. S. Drake, “Nestorian Monasteries of the T’ang Dynasty and the Site of the Discovery of the Nestorian Tablet”, in *Monumenta Serica* 2 (1936–1937), p. 305（英译）, footnote 43（中文）. 英译文并参见 A. C. Moule, *Christians in China before the Year 1550*, Society for Promoting Christian Knowledge, London–New York–Toronto 1930, pp. 69–70.

[2] 景净是波斯景教僧 Adam 的汉文名，他是公元781年立于长安的《大秦景教流行中国碑》的作者。

[3]《贞元新定释教目录》卷17。

督徒对宗教多元性看法的转变。

13.2 基督教宗教多元化的社会/种族途径

作为一种沿丝绸之路从波斯经中亚而入华的外来宗教，唐代基督宗教被认为是一种在种族上有别于本土道教、儒教的异族宗教。其很自然地与当时入华的外来族群联系在一起，譬如琐罗亚斯德教和摩尼教，或者像最早传入的佛教。

因此，在官方记载中，这一时期的基督宗教称谓总被标明其外来背景。它首先被称作“波斯教”，公元745年以后则被冠以“大秦教”。“大秦”是中国人用来指称罗马帝国东部地区的一个专有术语。同样的，这一时期的基督宗教教堂一开始被称作“波斯寺”，然后被称为“大秦寺”。改名通过公元745年唐玄宗的谕令来强制推行，圣谕曰：“其两京波斯寺，宜改为大秦寺。”〔1〕两京即长安和洛阳。

基督宗教总是与西域地区密切相连，这毫不奇怪，因为唐代中国的基督宗教传教士几乎都是外族身份——波斯人或者中亚人，他们或是由东方教会直接派遣而来的教士，或是那些定居中国的基督宗教世家成员。〔2〕唐帝国的基督宗教社区主要位于国内的政治性或商业性的移民

〔1〕最基本的记载参见《唐会要》卷49，第1012页，并参见《通典》卷40，第1103页；《册府元龟》卷51，20a9–b2 (1.575)。并参见《改波斯寺为大秦寺诏 》，收入《全唐文》32.7a (1.428)。英译文参见 A. Forte, “The edict of 638 allowing the diffusion of Christianity in China”, in P. Pelliot, *L'inscription nestorienne de Si-ngan-fou*, ed. with supplements by A. Forte, Scuola di Studi sull'Asia Orientale, Kyoto and Collège de France/Institut des Hautes études Chinoises, Paris 1996, pp. 349–373 (in particular, pp. 353–355).

〔2〕波斯裔景教徒的两个例子：一位是西安景教碑的作者 Adam，他在唐代基督宗教僧侣中最为人所熟知，汉名“景净”。在两份8世纪晚期的佛教文献《大唐贞元续开元释教录》（卷1）和《贞元新定释教目录》（卷17）中，他被明确记作“大秦寺波斯僧”。另一位是阿罗本，他极可能来自于波斯，其名字也可能是从波斯人名 Ardab ā n（意为“被法律保护的人”）汉译过来的。新近发现的粟特人米姓（见《米继芬（714—805）墓志》）、安姓、康姓基督徒（见立于815年的洛阳景教经幢），则为那些定居中国的伊朗裔基督徒提供了证据。相关研究参见：葛承雍:《唐代长安一个粟特家庭的景教信仰》，载于《历史研究》2001年第3期；笔者译注本见 *Annali. Istituto Universitario Orientale di Napoli* 64 (2004) pp. 181–196；另参见 Matteo Nicolini-Zani, “The Tang Christian Pillar from Luoyang and Its *Jingjiao* Inscription. A Preliminary Study”, in *Monumenta Serica* 57 (2009), pp. 99–140.

聚落。因此，我们发现无论是偏远地区如吐鲁番的基督宗教修道院，还是在中心位置的大都市如长安和洛阳的教堂，都有伊朗人聚居，他们建立起自己的聚落。

由于上述原因，基督宗教很可能被官方看成是一种异端宗教。对此我们是有证据的。唐武宗（840—846）时期的会昌法难（843—845）中，颁发了反对佛教、摩尼教、祆教和基督宗教等诸外来宗教从业人员的敕令。敕令明确提到基督宗教和祆教是一种“夷教”（heretical doctrine），并勒令“大秦穆护、祆三千余人还俗”，以使“不杂中华之风”。[1]

然而，还有一些别的因素，让我们看到了不同于官方记载的内容。这启发我们去思考有关唐代基督宗教的胡裔身份(外来性“foreignness”)问题。这些因素反映了基督徒并不是一个封闭的族群。他们其实很乐意把基督徒的外来出身，通过吸收其他本地元素，铸造其（新的）宗教身份。

史料并未提到基督徒对其他宗教代表的态度以及与之竞争的插曲。我们也看不到基督宗教社区与其他宗教信徒之间存在的分裂。相反，在7到9世纪大都市长安的社会、宗教环境中，基督宗教僧侣与其他宗教信徒的联系应当十分密切。[2]我们至少有一个有关基督徒与佛教僧侣合作翻译各自经典的例子。公元782年基督徒景净来到了大唐帝国的首都长安，[3]在之后的某段时间，景净曾帮助北天竺毕迦国僧般若三藏，把七卷《六波罗蜜经》(*Ṣaṭpāramitāsūtra*)从中亚伊朗语（最有可能是粟

---

〔1〕《唐会要》卷47，第841页。

〔2〕参见 A. Forte, “The Chongfu-si in Chang’an. A neglected Buddhist monastery and Nestorianism”, in P. PELLIOT, *L’inscription nestorienne de Si-ngan-fou*, pp. 429-472; S. Holth, “The Encounter between Christianity and Chinese Buddhism during the Nestorian Period”, in *Ching Feng* 11/3 (1968), pp. 20-29；谢颖男（I. S. Seah）：“Nestorian Christianity and Pure Land Buddhism in T’ang China”，刊《台湾神学论刊》第6卷，1986年，第75-92页。

〔3〕《贞元新定释教目录》卷17有载：“[般若]与大秦寺波斯僧景净，依胡本《六波罗蜜经》译成七卷。时为般若不闲胡语，复未解唐言；景净不识梵文，复未明释教。虽称传译，未获半珠。”参见 J. Takakusu, “The Name of ‘Messiah’ Found in a Buddhist Book; the Nestorian Missionary Adam, Presbyter, Papas of China, Translating a Buddhist Sūtra”, in *T’oung Pao* 7 (1896), pp. 589-591; J. W. Inglis, “The Nestorian Share in Buddhist Translation”, in *Journal of the North China Branch of the Royal Asiatic Society* 48 (1917), pp. 12-15.

特语）译成了汉文。我们还知道，在同一时期，这位景教僧景净还在佛经影响下，撰写了西安景教碑颂的铭文，以及一些其他的景教文献。[1]

此外，毫无疑问的是，唐代中国的基督宗教社区在一定时期内应当有一些汉人信徒。从基督宗教汉文经典的撰写和翻译来看，这是不争的事实。笔者认为，汉文宗教经文采用“景教”一词，也是一个确证，它反映了唐代基督宗教自觉融入本土宗教社会的愿望。中国的基督徒本来可以称其教为“基督教”（意为“基督的教导”），就像佛教徒称他们的宗教为“佛教”（意为“佛陀的教导”）、摩尼教称他们的宗教为“摩尼教”（“摩尼的教导”）一样。然而，基督徒却用了“景教”（Luminous Teaching），将象征基督新生的“光明”和佛教象征“启发智慧”的“光明”巧妙嫁接起来。[2]同样的情况还有基督宗教传教士采用了佛教的名字和头衔，以及佛教的一些职能。[3]

上述种种表明，唐代基督宗教已做好应对宗教多元化的准备，通过与其他宗教代表的接触与合作，为了吸引和欢迎汉人加入其基督宗教团体，他们克服了宗教外来性和种族中心主义的挑战。

13.3 基督宗教宗教多元化的思想/理论途径与文学/语言途径

正如文章开篇所提到的，唐代基督宗教汉文经典中只有极少数篇幅直接论及基督徒如何看待其他宗教及其共处情况。可以预料，这些内容

---

〔1〕A. Forte, “A literary model for Adam: the Dhūta monastery inscription”, in P. Pelliot, *L'inscription nestorienne de Si-ngan-fou*, pp. 473–487; Chen Huaiyu, “The Connection between *Jingjiao* and Buddhist Texts in Late Tang China”, in R. Malek (ed.), *Jingjiao*, pp. 93–113; Id., “The Encounter of Nestorian Christianity with Tantric Buddhism in Medieval China”, in D. W. Winkler & Li Tang (eds.), *Hidden Treasures and Intercultural Encounters. Studies on East Syriac Christianity in China and Central Asia*, LIT, Münster 2009, pp. 195–213.

〔2〕有关这一问题的详细讨论，参见 M. Nicolini -Zani, La via radiosa per l'oriente. I testi e la storia del primo incontro del cristianesimo con il mondo culturale e religioso cinese (secoli VII–IX), Qiqajon–Comunità di Bose, Magnano 2006, pp. 75–83.

〔3〕见781年西安景教碑下半截所录的70位景僧名录（汉文/叙利亚文），注有其尊贵的头衔。其他景僧名字和头衔见815年洛阳景教经幢碑铭文。

多是用论辩的口气来书写的。在景教看来，异教即各种形式的偶像崇拜，充满谬误和虚假，没什么可与“无元真主阿罗诃”相比拟的。以下引述其中一些相关段落：

其神力无余神，唯独一神既有。（《一神论》）[1]

无别道人须向天堂，唯识一天尊亦处分。其人等，人受一神处分者。若向浪道行者，恐畏人承事日月星宿，火神[2]礼拜。恐畏人承事恶魔鬼，夜叉[3]罗刹[4]等。随向火地狱里常住所。为向实处，亦不须信大作信业，不依一神处分。唯有恶魔，共夜叉罗刹诸鬼等。（《一神论》第381—385行）[5]

多有无知之人，唤神比天尊之类，亦唤作旨尊旨乐。人人乡俗语舌，吾别天尊多常在，每信每居。（《序听迷诗所经》18—20行）[6]

弥师诃既似众生，天道为是天尊处分。处分世间下，众生休事属神。即有众[生]，当闻此语，休事属神，休作恶，遂信好业。（《序听迷诗所经》137—139行）[7]

诸人间，施行杂教，唯事有为，妨失直正。譬如巧工，克作牛畜，庄严彩画，形貌类真，将为天农，终不收获。（《志玄安乐经》

---

〔1〕林悟殊:《唐代景教再研究》，北京：中国社会科学出版社，2003年，第351-352页。

〔2〕琐罗亚斯德教，汉文称“祆教”，源于其崇奉的重要对象“火神”（祆）。例如，《旧唐书》卷198有载：“波斯俗事天地日月水火诸神，西域诸胡事火祆者，皆诣波斯受法焉。”《新唐书》卷221载：“波斯国祠天地日月水火……西域诸胡受其法以祠祆。”如是等等，汉文史料中此类记载并不乏见。

〔3〕夜叉，梵文 *yakṣa*，在印度文化中，夜叉是生活在森林中的不作恶的神。而在佛教文化中，他们成为暴烈的魔鬼，他们出现在苦行者居住的幽僻角落，不断打扰苦行者的沉思默想。

〔4〕罗刹，梵文 *rākṣasa*，指“避之免受其害者”，在印度教和佛教神学中，其指一种在黑夜活动的恶鬼，呈动物或人形。[译注，罗刹，又作罗刹娑（罗刹婆为误写）、罗叉娑、罗乞察娑、阿落刹娑。意译为可畏、速疾鬼、护者。女则称罗刹女、罗叉私乃印度神话中之恶魔，最早见于梨俱吠陀。相传原为印度土著民族之名称，雅利安人征服印度后，遂成为恶人之代名词，演变为恶鬼之总名。具神通力，可于空际疾飞，或速行地面，为暴恶可畏之鬼。男罗刹为黑身、朱发、绿眼，女罗刹则如绝美妇人，富有魅人之力，专食人血肉。参见丁福保《佛学大辞典》“罗刹”条，电子版。]

〔5〕林悟殊:《唐代景教再研究》，第384-385页。

〔6〕林悟殊:《唐代景教再研究》，第388页。

〔7〕林悟殊:《唐代景教再研究》，第211页。

108-111 行)〔1〕

在此对上引的正确译文略作评述。经文中被攻讦者，不仅仅是佛、道等东方宗教，也包括了来自闪语世界和伊朗语世界的异端宗教(如琐罗亚斯德教和摩尼教，它们在中国都有了各自的圣祠)，偶像崇拜是它们主要的崇拜形式。〔2〕

然而，与这一“理论框架”形成鲜明对比的，是基督宗教采用了佛道教等异教的术语、图像和观念。这令那些初读汉文文献的读者，尤其基督徒们感到诧异。不过，从这个角度开展对该等文献的研究还不够深入。

当代学者确信，唐代汉文景教经典仿效了道教和佛教的经典。中外学者近来对其文本所用术语及概念的语言学研究，也同样表明大量借鉴同时期佛道教经典词汇的情况存在。〔3〕学者们得出的这一结论，其实早在 1939 年福斯特(John Foster)就已提出过：

> 景教在各方面均采用其他宗教的术语，其中佛教术语最为重要。但这并不意谓着信仰的融合(syncretism)，而只是一种语汇上的借词，即在相似思想背景下对其教义的一种表述，而在远东这一大环境下，这是表达其基督教信仰的惟一方法。〔4〕

---

〔1〕羽田亨:《景教经典志玄安乐经に就いて》，载于《羽田博士史学论文集》卷2，京都大学东洋史研究会，京都，1958年，第278页。

〔2〕有一点值得注意，在解读有名的西安景教碑时，有一铭文历来为学界所误解，其内涵直到最近才被阐明。《大秦景教流行中国碑》第五行有曰:“三百六十五种，肩随结辙，竞织法罗。或指物以托宗，或空有以沦二，或祷祀以邀福，或伐善以矫人。”(P. Pelliot, *L'inscription nestorienne de Si-ngan-fou*, p. 498)此处抨击的不是佛教和道教，也不是儒教，而是摩尼教信徒和基督宗教的异端宗派如马西翁(Marcionites)和梅萨良(Messalians)。参见 M. Tardieu, “Le schème hérésiologique de désignation des adversaires dans l'inscription nestorienne chinoise de Xi'an”, in *Chrétiens en terre d'Iran*, vol. II: Ch. Jullien (ed.), *Controverses des chrétiens dans l'Iran sassanide*, Association pour l'avancement des études iraniennes, Paris 2008, pp. 207-226, in particular p. 221.

〔3〕相关研究参见 M. Nicolini-Zani, “Past and Current Research on Tang *Jingjiao* Documents”, pp. 42-44.

〔4〕J. Foster, The Church of the T'ang Dynasty, Society for Promoting Christian Knowledge, London 1939, p. 112. 相同的观点也见于 TANG LI 唐莉, A Study of the History of Nestorian Christianity in China and Its Literature in Chinese. Together with a New English Translation of the Dunhuang Nestorian Documents, P. Lang, Frankfurt-am-Main 2002, p. 142:“即使景教徒在其经文中采用许多佛教和道教术语，也不能就此认定出现了宗教的融合”。

同样的，陈怀宇曾指出：“景教经典的翻译是准确而规范的，虽然借用了大量佛典中的术语，但其所反映的景教概念非常严格。”[1]黄夏年持相同观点。他很肯定地指出景教以其他宗教为“载体”进行传播。他写道，“佛教成为景教传入中国的载体”。[2]换句话说，“据我们所理解，景教的尝试，是一种宇宙性宗教（即基督宗教）如何在另一种宇宙性宗教（即佛教）的习惯和气质影响下，发展出崭新的亚洲身份。基督宗教的救世神学，在佛教或道教术语所建构的世界观的框架内进行阐述，从而发展成一种以道教或佛教/观音菩萨为模式的佛道化的基督论（Buddho-Daoist Christology）”。[3]

在此宗教化（与“本土化”相对）尝试下创作的经典，尤其是那些最后写成的文书，其主要术语几乎都来自佛教和道教，内容则反映出极鲜明的本土信仰色彩。[4]换句话说，这一时期的汉文景教文献可作为基督宗教在异教环境中被塑造和改变的明证。不过，笔者推测，使用异教的语言并非弱化基督徒身份的威胁，而更应是一种在多元宗教环境下基督徒表达其基督宗教信仰的方法。[5]

13.4　从释经方法的转变看基督宗教的宗教多元化

最后谈谈本文的主要观点。这些观点，笔者在前述几个层面的讨论中早有述及。

---

〔1〕陈怀宇：《所谓唐代景教文献两种辨伪补说》，载于《唐研究》第3卷，1997年，第41–53页；引文见第41–42页。

〔2〕黄夏年：《景教与佛教关系之初探》，载于《世界宗教研究》1996年第1期，第83–90页，引文见第 84页。

〔3〕 R. Malek, “Faces and Images of Jesus Christ in Chinese Context. Introduction”, in R. Malek (ed.), *The Chinese Face of Jesus Christ*, vol. I, Institut Monumenta Serica–China–Zentrum, Sankt Augustin 2002, p. 36.

〔4〕参阅翁绍军：《汉语景教文典诠释》，香港：基督教文化研究所，1995 ；北京：三联书店，1996年。

〔5〕我们别忘了，在7到9世纪的中亚和中国，佛教词汇是一套主流的宗教语言符号。事实上，景教经文采用佛教术语和表达的做法难以避免。由于基督宗教没有一套业已存在的宗教语言系统可资利用，那么，其首批基督徒就只好采用佛教这种主流的宗教语言符号了。

只要唐代基督教开始用汉语表述，这一点无法避免，那么，它最好还是采用阐释经文的办法来适应宗教的多元化，这是所有东方宗教都曾经历过的情况。只是景教尤为明显，它甚至在理论上也借用了佛教来发展自我。这种办法，用佛家的语言来讲，就是“方便”（梵文 *upāyakauśalya*）和“本地垂迹”[1]，通过对佛教教义的改造，使景教学说符合那些认同佛教的人们的思想、文化和宗教立场。说它是一种有选择的整合或许更为恰当，即把那些有别于其他宗教传统的特有要素，根据情形之不同，予以整合，使其达到与自身宗教体系的统一。[2]大乘佛教在向东亚和中亚地区迅速传播的过程中，就被改造成一种与印度背景——其发源于斯，初传于斯——截然不同的宗教文化。[3]用这种诠释经文的方法（hermeneutical approach），中国的佛教吸收了许多道教思想及教义理论，把“道”看成是“谛”之下的一种真理，从而有效地把佛教的观念传到了华夏世界。[4]佛教也因此转变为一种“中国式的佛教”。[5]

摩尼教亦如此。摩尼教在其东渐过程中，以同样的诠释经文的原则，去适应唐代中国——主要是佛教和道教——的文化和宗教环境；摩尼教

---

〔1〕“本地垂迹”，又云“本迹”，意思是佛菩萨为度众生，由自己的实身变化出诸多分身，垂世以度化众生；实身为本地，分身为垂迹。地，为能生义，以利物而自本身垂万化，故为能现之本，称本地；所现之末，称垂迹。在日本，则专指传统固有“神道”中之神。例如，天台、真言等宗，以佛为本，以神为迹，每一神均有一佛或菩萨与之搭配，其神祇皆为佛、菩萨之垂迹。（参《佛光大辞典》，佛光出版社，1989年，第1956页。）

〔2〕参阅 D. S. Lopez jr. (ed.), *Buddhist Hermeneutics*, University of Hawaii Press, Honolulu 1988.

〔3〕参阅 M. Pye, *Skilful Means. A Concept in Mahayana Buddhism*, Duckworth, London 1978; J. W. Schroeder, *Skilful Means. The Heart of Buddhist Compassion*, University of Hawaii Press, Honolulu 2001.

〔4〕参阅 A. Matsunaga, *The Buddhist Philosophy of Assimilation. The Historical Development of the Honji–Suijaku Theory*, Charles E. Tuttle, Vermont–Tokyo 1969, in particular pp. 98–138 (“Buddhist Assimilation in China”).

〔5〕参阅 K. K. S. Ch’ en, *The Chinese Transformation of Buddhism*, Princeton University Press, Princeton 1973; E. Zürcher, *The Buddhist Conquest of China*. The Spread and Adaptation of Buddhism in Early Medieval China, 2 vols., Brill, Leiden 1972.

因此转变成一种“中国式的摩尼教”（a Chinese Manichaeism）。[1]基督宗教同样如此。当基督宗教越过大唐帝国的边陲地区之后，它毫无顾虑地用佛教和道教的那套词汇来表达基督教信仰，从而把自己变成一种“中国式的基督宗教”（a Chinese Christianity）。

唐代景教徒之采用经文诠释，是其适应宗教多元化的重要途径，此为东亚地区所独有。这种途径与圣经翻译学及其后来的发展，是否属于一脉相承的基督宗教传统，在当前还是一个极具挑战性的难题。对广义的基督宗教而言，要进一步讨论和评估历史上教会传统对宗教多元化的看法和态度，还应该从神学和现象学等途径进行考察。

唐代基督徒用诠释经文的办法实现宗教的多元化，这一途径的利弊，有待神学家们进一步考察并做出评价。笔者只想指出，当前的圣经学研究已经充分地说明，除去《圣经》中有关大量反偶像崇拜的记载，世上一切宗教圣书的核心内容，其实都是阐述有关“天主”的计划。在教会看来，其计划就是在复活的上主实现的，为全人类建立天主的国。[2]这是当今一切基督宗教神学所持之共识，其借鉴了不同的宗教体验中都曾表述过的“圣言之种”（semina Verbi）的理论；这一理论最初由早期教会的教父们[3]提出，到“梵蒂冈第二届大公会议”

---

〔1〕米凯森（G. B. Mikkelsen）在其博士论文 *Manichaean Skilful Means. A Study of Missionary Techniques Used in the Introduction of Manichaeism into China*（Århus University, 1999）细致考察了中国摩尼教所使用的佛教借词情况，阐明了这一观点。米凯森指出这种传教策略，使摩尼教得以折衷处理“技术性佛化”（skilful Buddhistization）和 “虔诚传教”（faithful transmission）之间的平衡。并参考 P. Bryder, *The Chinese Transformation of Manichaeism. A Study of Chinese Manichaean Terminology*, Plus Ultra, Löberöd 1985; H. Schmidt–Glintzer, “Das buddhistische Gewand des Manichäismus. Zur buddhistischen Terminologie in den chinesischen Manichaica”, in W. Heissig & H.–J. Klimkeit (eds.), *Synkretismus in den Religionen Zentralasiens. Ergebnisse eines Kolloquiums vom 24.5 bis 26. Mai 1983 in St. Augustin bei Bonn*, Harrassowitz, Wiesbaden 1987, pp. 76–90; S. N. C. Lieu, *Manichaeism in the Later Roman Empire and Medieval China*, J. C. B. Mohr, Tübingen 1992; Id., *Manichaeism in Central Asia & China*, Brill, Leiden 1998.

〔2〕参阅 G. Odasso, Bibbia e religioni. Prospettive bibliche per la teologia delle religioni, Urbaniana University Press, Roma 1998.

〔3〕参阅 J. Dupuis, Christianity and the Religions. From Confrontation to Dialogue, Orbis Books, Maryknoll 2001; M. Dhavamony, Christian Theology of Religions. A Systematic Reflection on the Christian Understanding of World Religions, P. Lang, Bern 2001; Id., Ecumenical Theology of World Religions, Pontificia Università Gregoriana, Roma 2003.

（the Second Vatican Council）时进一步发展并最终确立。在50年前，教会发表了以下宣言：

天主公教绝不摒弃这些宗教里的真的和圣的因素，并且怀着诚恳的敬意，考虑他们的作事与生活方式，以及他们的规诫和教理。这一切虽然在许多方面与天主公教所坚持、所教导的有所不同，但往往反映着去普照全人类的真理之光。……因此，教会劝告其子女们，应以明智与爱德，同其他宗教的信徒交谈与合作。……同时承认、维护并倡导那些宗教徒所拥有的精神与道德，以及社会文化的价值。[1]

至少，这是个良好的开端，它有利于将来进一步讨论基督宗教接受其他宗教教规教义的可能性和可行性。第二届梵蒂冈大公会议所提倡的这些价值观，被认为是"善举"和"真理之光"。

从现象学的角度来看，唐代中国景教为基督宗教的"杂合"（hybridization）提供了一个典型的例子。汉学家和宗教研究学者历来就很清楚，宗教传统的发展和依存与其他宗教息息相关。通过融入新环境的种种努力，它重塑了其宗教传统的内涵和外延；而且，在一多元文化环境下，宗教间的接触与交流常导致"宗教的杂合"（religious hybridization），还有一些其他形式的结合。"宗教杂合"出自社会学领域，它侧重描述不同宗教体验的相互作用和适应改变的趋势（而非宗教自身的情况），它主张果断吸收并同化那些能够丰富其宗教传统的宗教和文化因素。[2]它虽然和"信仰融合"有些关联，但却是不同的概念。[3]像任何宗教运动一样，基督宗教的历史从一开始就是一部有关宗

〔1〕第二届梵蒂冈大公会议：《教会对非基督宗教态度宣言》（Second Vatican Council, *Nostra Aetate* 2.）

〔2〕参阅 W. E. Biernatzki, Roots of Acceptance. The Intercultural Communication of Religious Meanings, Pontificia Università Gregoriana, Rome 1991; Ph. Stockhammer (ed.), Conceptualizing Cultural Hybridization. A Transdisciplinary Approach, Springer, Berlin 2011.

〔3〕参阅 C. Stewart, "Syncretism and Its Synonyms. Reflections on Cultural Mixture", in *Diacritics* 29 (1999), pp. 40–62.

教与文化相互融合的过程的历史。[1]

从某个方面来讲，中国基督徒之身份，与其他地区一样，只有通过与本教以外的其他宗教、文化、语言传统乃至观念的不断融合和同化，才能壮大拓展。不管景教徒为维持其基督徒身份的纯正性付出了多少努力，也不论他们为与其他宗教有所区别展开了多少论辩，整部中国基督宗教史即是这一宗教和文化融合的过程。[2]

〔1〕 R. Aguirre,"The Multiple Heritages in Christianity: Jerusalem versus Athens?", in *Concilium* 45/2 (2009), pp. 15–23.

〔2〕M. Nicolini –Zani, "Religious Heritages in the Christianity of Eastern Asia: Some Examples from the Christian History of China and Japan", in *Concilium* 45/2 (2009), pp. 68–78.

14 Commemorating the Martyrs and Saints at Turfan.[1]

Erica C.D. Hunter
(SOAS, University of London)

The recently completed cataloguing of the 519 Syriac manuscripts that were discovered at the monastery site of Bulayïq, between 1904 and 1907 by the second and third German Turfan Expeditions, now divided between three repositories in Berlin, will release a wealth of material and open new horizons in our understanding of the offices and services of the Church of the East at Turfan.[2] As the liturgical language of the Church of the East, Syriac acted in the same way as Latin that was used by the Roman Catholic church until the pronouncements of Vatican II and was a vital trajectory connecting Turfan with the 'mother church' in Mesopotamia. Many of the fragments which were discovered at Turfan come from the various liturgical books, notably the Hudra and Beth Gazza that were used to celebrate the cycle of offices and commemorations within the Church of the East. Of particular interest are fragments that invoke Mary and various martyrs whose commemoration in the liturgy sheds important insight into their public remembrance, whilst a handful of prayer-amulets, provide rare

[1] The author is grateful to the *Staatsbibliothek zu Berlin–Preussicher Kulturbesitz* for access to the relevant fragments. Low resolution images of the SyrHT signature numbers are available on the International Dunhuang Project website (http:id.bl.uk/ enter the signature number in the search box).

[2] Syrische Handschriften, Teil 2. Texte der Berliner Turfansammlung. Syriac texts from the Berlin Turfan collection, edited by Erica C D Hunter and Mark Dickens will appear as part of the VOHD series.

insight into private devotions associated with the saints. In both their public and private capacities, the martyrs were invoked to provide protection to the faithful, upholding a heritage that was inherent within the Church of the East, and maintained at Turfan.

SyrHT 279-284 is a series of six leaves being prayers devoted to Mary. Although their sequence has not been determined, since the upper parts of the leaves are missing, they are unique in the collection.[1] They eulogise: ܛܘܒܝܟܝ ܒܬܘܠܬܐ ܩܕܝܫܬܐ ܛܘܒܝܟܝ ܐܡܗ ܕܡܫܝܚܐ"blessed are you holy virgin, blessed are you, mother of Christ".[2] In addressing Mary as the "Mother of Christ" i.e., the Christotokos, rather than as the "Mother of God" i.e., the Theotokos, they uphold the Diophysite theology of the Church of the East. Mary's integral place –and her celebration– in the liturgy are recalled by the exhortation: ܢܚܕܘܢ ܫܡܝܐ ܘܬܪܘܙ ܐܪܥܐ ܒܝܘܡ ܕܘܟܪܢܗ ܕܒܬܘܠܬܐ ܩܕܝܫܬܐ "may the heavens rejoice and the earth exalt on the day of the holy virgin's commemoration".[3] The protective powers that Mary bestowed on the faithful through her prayer are enunciated: ܢܛܪ ܒܥܘܕܪܢܐ ܕܨܠܘܬܟܝ ܡܢ ܟܠ ܒܝܫܢ "may he be? protected from all evil by the aid of your prayer".[4] Here one might have expected to readܢܬܛܪ instead of ܢܛܪ i.e. 3rd masculine singular Imperfect Ethpa'el rather than the 3rd masculine singular Imperfect Pa'el. However, irrespective of this orthographic peculiarity, the prophylactic role of Mary's prayer is explicit.

The martyrs were also frequently invoked. Various fragments cite Sergius and Bacchus, the Roman soldiers who were put to death in the early fourth century during the reign of Emperor Diocletian. Their proper names [ܒܟܘܣ ,]ܘܡܪܝ ܣܪܓܝܣ ,ܡܪܝare written in rubric in n. 164, a partial folio

[1] SyrHT 279–284 is housed in the Staatsbibliothek, Berlin.

[2] SyrHT 280 side (a) ll. 5–7.

[3] SyrHT 279 side (a), ll.4–7.

[4] SyrHT 280 side (b) ll. 4–6.

composed of three separate fragments from a Sogdian gospel lectionary, but written in Syriac script.[1] Immediately following the citation of names is the incipit Matthew 16:24 which introduces the gospel reading for their commemoration. The juxtaposition of [ܡܪܝ] ܣܪܓܝܣ ܘܡܪܝ, ܒܟܘܣܐ][2] in SyrHT 155 may be from a Commemoration for Sergius and Bacchus within the Hudra, the principal liturgical book of the Church of the East that contained "the variable chants of the choir for the divine office and the Mass for the entire cycle of the liturgical year".[3] The traditional connection of the martyrs may be sustained by the phrase ܒܪܗܘܡܝܐ "in the Roman [Empire]" that occurs in the preceding line.[4] The combination of [ܡܪܝ] ܣܪܓܝܣ ܘܡܪܝ, [ܒܟܘܣ] is also cited in the small fragment SyrHT 385.[5] The occurrence in the preceding line of [ ]ܡܛܠ ܗܘ ܕܐܬܩܛܠܘ "they were killed because ..." appears to be unrelated to Mar Sergius and Mar Bacchus, but suggests that SyrHT 385 is from a commemoration liturgy remembering the martyrdoms of various saints.

MIK III 45, a 61-folio manuscript that is the most complete codex of the Hudra to have been found at the monastery site of Bulayïq, also mentions Mar Sergius and Mar Bacchus, albeit in conjunction with Mar George. The latter was perhaps the most popular saint at Turfan since versions of his *vita* occur in Syriac, Sogdian and Uighur–the only saint to do so.[6] The manuscript has, on the basis of palaeographic analysis, been

[1] The fragment, which is in the collection of the Turfanforschung, Berlin, is torn at the left edge, but the proper name Bacchus can be reconstructed.

[2] SyrHT 155 side (b), l.5.

[3] W. Macomber, "A List of the Known Manuscripts of the Chaldean Hudra", *Orientalia Christiana Periodica* XXXVI: 1 (1970) 120.

[4] ܪܗܘܡܝܐ 'Roman', R. Payne Smith, *A Compendious Syriac Dictionary* (Clarendon Press, Oxford: 1903) 531, R. Payne Smith, *Thesaurus Syriacus* (Clarendon Press, Oxford: 1868–1901) 3830. Syr HT 155 side (b), l.4. The loss of the left-hand side of the folio does not allow the intermediate text to be reconstructed.

[5] SyrHT 385 side (a) ll. 4–5.

[6] MIK III 45 is housed in the Museum für Asiatische Kunst, Dahlem, Berlin.

dated to the 9th or 10th century, making it one of the earliest extant Hudras.[1] The intent of the invocation to Mar Baccus and Mar Sergius, together with that of Mar George, is clear, requesting their protection and support through their prayer:[2]

1 ܡܪܝܐ ܒܚܝܠܟ ܒܚܝܠܐ

2 ܘܒܥܘܕܪܢܐ ܕܡܠܟܐ ܫܡܝܢܐ ܗܘ ܕܡܢ ܩܕܝܡ

3 ܐܬܛܘܒܗܝ، ܕܒܘ ܡܪܝ، ܡܪ ܒܟܘܣ ܘܡܪܝ، ܣܪܓܝܣ

4 ܡܪܝ، ܓܘܪܓܝܣ ܠܒܟܘܪܐ ܙ ܨܠܘܬܗܘܢ

5 ܢܗܘܐ ܠܓܘܣܐ ܘܫܘܪܐ ܪܡܐ ܠܢܦܫܬܢ ܘܗܝ،

6 ܬܩܘܡ ܠܢ ܒܝܘܡܐ ܕܒܘܚܪܢܐ

(1) Lord, by your power. By the power (2) and assistance of the heavenly King who was from aforetime (3) the blessed Mar Bacchus and Mar Sergius and Mar George (4) conquered. May their prayer be (5) a refuge and a lofty fortress for our soul and (6) raise us up on the day of trial.

The military backgrounds of Mar Sergius and Mar Bacchus is recalled by the terminology ܙܟܘ "they conquered" and ܫܘܪܐ ܪܡܐ "lofty bulwark", which is applied in the cycle of liturgy pertaining to a season of prayer and petition in a spiritual, rather than a temporal, vein. Similarly, 'victory' terminology also occurs in SyrHT 140, a liturgical fragment that commemorates Mar Cyriacus and his mother, Julitta, whose celebrated martyrdoms purportedly took place at Tarsus in the early fourth century on the orders of the governor,

[1] E. Sachau, "Litteratur-Bruchstücke aus Chinesisch-Turkistan", *Sitzungsberichte der Königlich Preussischen Akademie der Wissenschaften* (Sitzung der philosophisch-historischen Classe von 23. November) XLVII (1905), 964-973, specifically 964. H. Engberding, "Fünf Blätter eines alten ostsyrischen Bitt- und Bussgottesdienstes aus Innerasien", *Ostkirchliche Studien* 14 (1965) 121-48, specifically 123 has compared its palaeography with Add. 12138 in the British Library which is dated to 899 CE. For details of B.L. Add 12138 see, W. Wright, *Catalogue of Syriac manuscripts in the British Museum: acquired since 1838*, 3 vols. (London, Trustees of the British Museum: 1870-2), v. I, 101-108.

[2] MIK III 45 fol. 13, side (b) ll. 1-6.

Alexander.[1] The death of Mar Cyriacus, by being thrown into a cauldron of heated pitch, is counterpointed in SyrHT 140 by the exaltation that expresses the martyr's 'victory':[2] ܘܐܒܗܬܬ ܐ[ܢܬܝ] ܠܪ̈ܕܘܦܘܗܝ ܟܕ ܐܬܝܗܒ ܟܠܝܠܐ ܕܙܟܘܬܐ "But you shamed his persecutors when the crown of victory was borne".[3] Whilst Julitta's method of execution is not specified by SyrHT 140, the fragment makes an explicit mention of the protection bestowed by the prayers which she and her son uttered -presumably at their point of death: ܕܨܠܘܬܗܘܢ ܫܘܪܐ ܬܗ[ܘܐ] ܠܢ ܘܬܛܪ̈ܢ ܡܢ ܡܪ̈ܘܕܐ "their prayer might be a bulwark for us and protect us from the rebellious ones".[4] As with Bacchus and Sergius, the prayers that Mar Cyriacus and Julitta, uttered at the moment of their execution, acted as a catalyst unleashing forces to protect the faithful in all the trials of life.

Although the 'prayer at the point of death' imparted protection, the martyrs' potency could be exercised long after their execution, through their relics. Drawing on the *Qale de-'Onyata Sahide* "Chants of the Martyrs' Responses", an early work wherein various martyrs are cited, SyrHT 140

〔1〕SyrHT 140 and SyrHT 141 are single leaves, 16–17 lines per side. The upper and lower margins have been lost, as has one of the side margins. SyrHT 144 is a corner fragment of a leaf with upper and outer margins, measuring 8.0 cm × 5.2 cm, 7 lines per side. For publication of the text and translation of SyrHT 140 see E.C. D. Hunter, "SyrHT 140: Commemorating Mar Cyriacus and Julitta", in MORE MODOQUE. *Die Wurzeln der europaïschen Kultur unde deren Rezeption im Orient und Okzident. Festschrift für Miklós Maróth zum siebzigsten Geburtstag*. ed. Pál Fodor (et. al), (Forschungszentrum für Humanwissenschaften der Ungarischen Akademie der Wissenschaften, Budapest: 2013) 225–233.

〔2〕N. Sims–Williams, "Cyriacus and Julitta, Acts of ", *Encyclopedia Iranica* VI:5, 512. The story of Cyriacus and Julitta circulated in many languages including Latin, Armenian, Syriac, Arabic, Coptic and Sogdian. The Sogdian version from Turfan has been recently published by N. Sims–Williams, "A Sogdian fragment from the martyrdom of Cyriacus and Julitta", in MORE MODOQUE. *Die Wurzeln der europaïschen Kultur unde deren Rezeption im Orient und Okzident. Festschrift für Miklós Maróth zum siebzigsten Geburtstag*, ed. Pál Fodor (et.al), (Forschungszentrum für Humanwissenschaften der Ungarischen Akademie der Wissenschaften, Budapest: 2013) 235–239.

〔3〕SyrHT 140 side (b), l. 5.

〔4〕SyrHT 140 side (b), ll. 8–9.

makes explicit reference to the bones of Mar Cyriacus[1] offering the paradigm of Exodus 17:1-7: [ܠܡܘܬܐ ܥܡܐ] ܚܕ ܓܪ̈ܡܘ ܕܩܘܪܝܩܘܣ ܠܒܪܢܫܘܬܐ[ܢܒܥܘܢ] ܕܣܝܡܝܢ ܒܥܕܬܐ ܠܒܢܝܢܫܐ ܡܘܫܐ ܪܫܐ [ܕܥܒܪ̈ܝܐ] ܐܪܕܝ ܡܝܐ ܡܢ ܟܐܦܐ ܘܐܫܩܝ ܠܥܡܐ

"Moses, the leader [of the Hebrews] made water flow from the rock and gave <it> to the [faithless] people to drink. [How much] indeed, may the bones of Mar Cyriacus, that are placed in the churches ... discharge for mankind".[2] The passage in *Qale de-'Onyata Sahide:* ܕܣܝܡܝܢ ܒܥܕܬܐ. ܡܘܫܐ ܐܪܕܝ ܡܝܐ ܡܢ ܟܐܦܐ ܘܐܫܩܝ ܠܥܡܐ ܠܡܘܬܐ ܥܡܐ ܚܕ ܓܪ̈ܡܘ ܕܩܘܪܝܩܘܣ ܕܣܗܕܐ ܥܘܕܪܢܐ ܠܒܢܝܢܫܐ ܪܫܐ ܕܥܒܪ̈ܝܐ specially mentions ܥܘܕܪܢܐ "assistance" imparted for mankind by the saint's bones. Although the word is absent in SyrHT 140 –which has a textual lacuna at this point– the direct comparison made with Moses, highlights the life-giving and prophylactic qualities which were attributed to Mar Cyriacus' bones. By contrast, Julitta's remains receive no mention.

SyrHT 140 has inserted the reference to Mar Cyriacus within ܓܪ̈ܡܘ ܕܩܘܪܝܩܘܣ .. ܕܣܝܡܝܢ ܒܥܕܬܐ "the bones that are placed in the churches" as it appears in the *Qale de-'Onyata Sahide*. This specific reference may be generic, but it may also suggest that holy relics of Mar Cyriacus' (and other saints) were actually venerated at Turfan. Relics could be transported over enormous distances. The remains of Mar Thomas, the celebrated founding father of Christianity in India were, according to tradition, brought back from Mylapore (near Madras) where he was martyred in 68 CE to Edessa where his bones were enshrined in a silver reliquary until the city fell to the

[1] T. Darmo (ed.), *Ktaba da-Qdam wad-Batar wad-Hudra wad-Kashkol wad-Gazza w-Qala d-'Udrane 'am Ktaba d-Mazmure,* 3 vols. (Trichur, Kerala: Church of the East, 1960-2). In the printed Darmo Hudra that is largley based on post-sixteenth century manuscripts, this follows the Psalter, but its place in earlier Hudras has not yet been determined.

[2] SyrHT 140 side (a), ll. 9-12. For this quotation in *Qale de-'Onyata Sahide,* see the lemma *Thirteenth Qale for the morning of the first Sunday.* Darmo, I, 453.

Turks in 1144 CE.[1] This removal or 'translation of the martyrs' was in keeping with a major trend that emerged in the fourth century, especially in the Byzantine territories, following the cessation of the 'great age' of persecution when the remains of martyrs were exhumed from their original burial-places and were brought to the great imperial cities to be housed in sumptuous reliquaries.[2] Such secondary burials, encapsulated not only the potency of the martyr, but also embellished the patron church or monastery by their prestigious association. If some remains of the celebrated Mar Cyriacus had been brought to Turfan, the church at Chocho might be considered to have been the repository of such a reliquary.

In addition to the very public 'cult of martyrs' at Turfan, a handful of prayer-amulets give rare glimpses into individual, private devotions. SyrHT 99 and SyrHT 330, two dislocated fragments, begin with the quotation of John 1 : 1-2 "In the beginning was the Word and the Word was with God and the Word was God…", that introduces the prayer of]ܡܪܝ ܬܡܣܝܣ ܣܗ]ܕܐ "Mar Tamsis, the]martyr]":

4]ܡܪܝ[ܐ ܐܠܗܐ ܫܠܝܛܢܐ ܗܒ ܠܝ ܫܐܠܬܐ

5 [ܟܘ̈ܪܗ]ܢܐ ܐܘ ܟܘܪܗܢܐ. ܘܢܬܕܟܪ

6 ܐ ܕܢܨ̈ܚܬܐ ܥ̱ ܠܘܬܐ ܗܕܐ

7 ܘܠܐ ܕܐܬܚܫܒ. ܘܡܪܚܡܢܘܬܐ

8 ܘܒܐ ܒܥܠܕܒܒܐ ܘܕܝܢܐ ܘܡܪܟ

9 ܠܝ ܘܡܪܘܬܟ ܬܬܒܪ ܪܘܚܬܟ

(4) … [Lord] God Almighty, grant me the request, (5) … [diseases] or illnesses. And may it be commemorated (6) … of

[1] They were then transferred to the island of Chios and subsequently in 1258 CE to Ortona on the Adriatic coast. The practice still continues. At the consecration of the Syrian Orthodox Church in Ealing, London on Sunday July 3rd, 2010 by The Syrian Orthodox Patriarch, His Holiness, Mar Ignatius Zakka I Iwass, relics of St. Thomas were brought from Mosul for the occasion.

[2] B. Kötting, *Der frühchristliche Reliquienkult und die Bestattung im Kirchengebäude* (Opladen, Westdeutscher Verlag, Cologne: 1965) for discussion of this phenomenon in the East Roman Empire.

sorceries/magic. This prayer (7) … that is recalled and by mercy/alms (8) … [crucifixion] suffering and holy. And bless (9)… to it? and your dominion. Your greatness shall be increased.

Cut down from a much larger manuscript, the still visible folding of SyrHT 99 into three indicates that the leaf was carried as a personal possession, as an amulet protecting the bearer.[1] Regrettably, unlike the celebrated 'mega'-martyrs who achieved international fame, very few biographical details are known about Mar Tamsis, a northern Mesopotamian saint, who appears to have lapsed almost into complete obscurity. However, he is still occasionally commemorated in the East Syrian liturgy.[2]

Protection from illness and disease were foremost amongst private concerns as seen in a leaf pieced together from three fragments: SyrHT 206, SyrHT 235 and SyrHT 316:[3]

1 ܘ[...]ܦܘ ܘܬܪܘܣ[...]

2 ܡܚܘܗ ܡܪ̈ܥܐ ܘܟܘܪ̈ܗ[ܢܐ]

3 ܘܐܣܝܘܬܐ ܘܒܘܪ̈ܟܬܐ

4 ܘܡܠܢܟܘܠܝܐ[4] ܘܚܫܐ

5 ܒܝܫܬܐ ܘܟܠܗܘܢ ܚܫܐ

6 ܘܟܐܒܐ ܀ ܐܡܝܢ ܀

7 ܘܐܢܫܐ ܕܠܝ ܒ

---

[1] For full discussion of SyrHT 99 and SyrHT330 see E.C.D. Hunter, "Traversing Time and Location: A Prayer-Amulet to Mar Tamsis from Turfan", in *From the Oxus River to the Chinese Shores. Studies on East Syriac Christianity in Central Asia and China* [Orientalia–patristica–oecumenica v. 5] (Lit. Verlag: Salzburg, 2013) 23–41.

[2] The commemoration of Mar Tamsis falls on the 8th Wednesday after Epiphany. In most years, however, there are only seven weeks after Epiphany.

[3] SyrHT 206, side (a), SyrHT 235, side (a) and SyrHT 316, side (b).

[4] Misspelling of ܡܠܢܟܘܠܝܐ "melancholy [black bile, gloom, madness]" (Greek, μελαγχολία) – see R. Payne Smith, *Thesaurus Syriacus* (Clarendon Press, Oxford: 1868–1901), 2147. M. Sokoloff, *A Syriac Lexicon. A translation from the Latin, Correction, Expansion and Update of C. Brockelmann's Lexicon Syriacum* (Eisenbrauns, Winona Lake; Piscataway, NJ, Gorgias: 2009), 720 lists ܡܠܢܟܐܘܠܝܐ..

8 [1] ܡܪܝܐ ܐܠܗܐ ܦܪܕܝܣܐ

(1)… and may you remove (2) from him illnesses and diseases (3) and fevers and seizures (4) and melancholy and the Evil Eye (5) and all sufferings (6) and pains, Amen. (7)-(8) And as the Lord God planted Paradise. [2]

Due to lacunae and also the incomplete nature of the text, the martyr or saint who is addressed in this prayer remains unknown, but is intimated by the 3 masculine singular imperative ܘܬܪܚܩ "may you remove" as well as the supporting paraphrase of Genesis II:8-14 that continues on the reverse side of the leaf.

Martyrs, continued to be invoked for assistance and protection long after their deaths. However, the living saints could also be approached. SyrHT 45-46, a badly water-stained and deteriorated bifolium relates an account of Mar BarShabba's life, the traditional founder of Christianity at Marv, whose acolytes included Mart Shir, a member of the Sassanian royal family who was exiled to the garrison city in the fourth century, due to her renunciation of Zoroastrianism. [3] Her adoption of Christianity, at the behest of Mar BarShabba had incurred the Sassanian monarch's ire since conversion to Christianity amongst the royal echelons was prohibited. Members of the royal family who thus lapsed were often martyred, the most

〔1〕Only part of downstoke (or upstroke) visible. If the character is not final Aleph ܐ, it could be upstroke from a final Yodh.

〔2〕A paraphrase of Genesis II:8–14 naming the four rivers of Paradise follows on SyrHT 206, side (b), SyrHT 235, side (b) and SyrHT 316, side (a).

〔3〕H.-J. Polotsky's translation was published in F.W.K. Müller–W. Lentz, "Soghdische Texte II". *Sitzungsberichte der Preussischen Akademie der Wissenschaften* 21 (1934) 559–64. Mart Shir's pronouncement: ܐܦ ܠܝ ܠܡܐ ܚܠܘܦ ܡܢܗ ܘܗܫܐ: ܩܕܡܝܗܘܢ ܗܘܐ ܐܡܝܢܐ. ܕܠܒܪ ܡܢ ܚܕ ܐܠܗܐ ܠܝܬ ܐܠܗܐ ܐܚܪܢܐ ܘܟܠ ܕܠܢܘܪܐ ܘܫܡܫܐ ܘܫܪܟܐ ܕܐܣܛܘܟܣܐ "Apart from the one God there are no others and whoever honours and worships fire and sun, and the rest of the elements or graven images will perish with them" (SyrHT 46, side (b), ll. 5-6.). Polotsky, 562 records: ܐܣܛܘܟܣܐ *sic, lies* ܐܣܛܘܟܫܐ.

celebrated pair being Behnam and his sister Sara.[1] In this instance, the king decided to banish Mart Shir, his sister along with her ladies. Mar BarShabba, also went to Marv and, when Mart Shir fell ill, he was approached possibly by a eunuch, who was probably a court official. To the latter's request for healing, Mar BarShabba replied explicitly:[2]

4 ❖ ܐܡܪ ܠܗ ܡܪܝ ܒܪ
5 ܫܒܐ ܐ ܐܢ ܟܘܪܗܢܐ ܗܘ❖ ܦܓܪܢܝܐ ܕܥܠ ܡܠܟܬܐ. ܠܐ
6 ܐܣܝܐ ܐܢܐ ܕܟܐܒܐ ܦܓܪܢܝܐ. ܐ ܐܢ ܟܐܒܐ ܗܘ ܕܪܘܚܢܝܐ
7 ܐܝܬ ܠܢ[4] ܚܝܠܐ ܡܢ ܫܘܠܛܢܐ ܐܠܗܝܐ ܠܡܛܪܕ ܕܝܘܐ[3] ܘܗܘܝܐ
8 [5]ܫܘܠܡܐ ܓܡܝܪܐ ܕܢܦܫܬܐ ❖

(4) Mar BarShabba said to him, (5) "If it is a bodily illness concerning the queen, (6) I am not a physician of bodily pains. However, if it is a disease of the spirit, (8) we have the power for the divine authority to drive away demons and there will be (8) a full recovery of the soul.

The request indicates that the long-standing practice of Christians acting as physicians to the royal Sassanian household in Seleucia-Ctesiphon appears also to have been continued at distant Marv.[6] Yet, as SyrHT 45-46

[1] The existing monastery of Mar Behnam in northern Iraq was founded in the fourth century upon the site of their martyrdom. For further discussion, see S. Rassam, "Der Mār Behnam. The monastery of Saint Behnam", in Erica C.D. Hunter, *The Christian Heritage of Iraq. Collected papers from the Christianity in Iraq I–V Seminar Days* [Gorgias Eastern Christian Series 13] (Gorgias Press, Piscataway, NJ: 2009), 77–86.

[2] SyrHT 45, side (a), ll. 4–8.

[3] Polotsky, 559 read ܕܝܘܐ. i.e. singular "demon".

[4] Or ܐܝܬܝ?

[5] Polotsky, 559 read ܕܢܦܫܬܐ.

[6] Amongst the many Christian (Church of the East) physicians to the Sassanid court, perhaps the most notorious was Gabriel of Sinjar, the personal physician to Khusrau II (590–628 CE). His treatment led to the monarch's favourite –and Christian– wife, Shirin giving birth to a healthy son, after many years of infertility. Like most of the physicians to the Sassanid monarchs, Gabriel belonged to the Church of the East, but when he divorced his Christian wife and took up with two Zoroastrian women, he was excommunicated from the Church of the East for dissolute behaviour. In pique, Gabriel converted to the Miaphysite Church and, exercising his power at the court, persuaded Shirin likewise to do so. See Christoph Baumer, *The Church of the East: an illustrated history of Assyrian Christianity* (IB Tauris, London: 2008), 84.

articulates, the source of the healing and prophylactic powers possessed by the saint were 'gifted from above'.

Concluding Comments:

The public and private commemoration of the saints and martyrs in the Syriac fragments demonstrates that the hagiographical traditions of the 'mother church' in Mesopotamia –and indeed wider Christendom– were maintained at Turfan. Whilst some of the characters, notably Mar BarShabba and Mart Shir, who were inextricably connected with the advent of Christianity to Marv, 'the gateway to Central Asia and China' might be considered 'local' figures, the 'mega'-martyrs, such as Mar Bacchus and Mar Sergius, as well as Mar Cyriacus and his mother, Julitta originated from the East Roman territories. The shrine of Mar Bacchus and Mar Sergius was at Sergiopolis (Resafe) on the Euphrates,[1] whilst Mar Cyriacus and his mother were, according to tradition, put to death at Tarsus in Cilicia.[2] The celebrated martyrs all hail from the late third and early fourth centuries, the time when martyrdom peaked -especially during the reigns of Emperors Decius and Diocletian, but preceded the Christological schisms of the fifth century.

Despite the ensuing sectarianism of the subsequent centuries that isolated the Church of the Eaṣt from the main branches of Christendom, it upheld robustly the 'classical' heritage of martyrdom. At Turfan, this legacy was also expressed by the rich repertoire of hagiographies that have emerged amongst the Sogdian Christian fragments which provided reading material for the monks. Commemorating the martyrs and their remains were

---

〔1〕For the development of Sergiopolis as a shrine and pilgrimage centre see, J. Spencer Trimingham, *Christianity amongst the Arabs in pre–Islamic times* (Longman, London: 1979), 235–8.

〔2〕Sims–Williams (2013) 235 points out the martyrdoms of Cyriacus and Julitta were declared spurious by the Gelasian Decree and refers to E. von Dobschütz, *Das Decretum Gelasianum de libris recipiendis et non recipiendis. Texte und Untersuchungen zur Geschichte der altchristlichen Literatur* XXXVIII/4. Leipzig 1912. Despite this official decree, the stories still retained a great popularity.

undoubtedly already practices familiar to the Uighur monk, Rabban Sauma when he visited Constantinople in 1287 CE *en route* to Rome. Touring the Byzantine capital city, amongst the sights that he saw were "many shrines of the holy fathers" and also "many amulets and images figured in bronze and stone".[1] He also viewed ܓܠܘܣܩܡܐ i.e. the "shrine" or "reliquary",[2] of an unnamed holy woman, who was reputed to have miraculous healing powers.[3] Rabban Sauma may have marvelled at the reliquaries whose opulence embellished the magnificent imperial city, yet he would have felt very much 'at home' with the protection and healing which the saints provided for the faithful – and indeed may have even offered his own intercessory prayers.

BIBLIOGRAPHY

Badger, G. P. *The Nestorians and their rituals*, 2 vols (London, Joseph Masters: 1852).

Baumer, C. *The Church of the East: an illustrated history of Assyrian Christianity* (IB Tauris, London: 2008).

Borbone, P.-G. (trans.), *Storia di Mar Yahballaha e di Rabban Sauma : un orientale in Occidente ai tempi di Marco Polo* (Zamorani, Turin: 2000).

Darmo, Th. (ed.) *Ktaba da-Qdam wad-Batar was-Hudra wad-Kashkol wad-Gazza w-Qala d-'Udrane 'am Ktaba d-Mazmure*, 3 vols. (Trichur,

[1] J. Montgomery (trans.), The history of Yaballaha III, Nestorian patriarch, and of his vicar, Bar Sauma, Mongol ambassador to the Frankish courts at the end of the thirteenth century (Columbia University Press, New York: 1927), 54.

[2] ܓܠܘܣܩܡܐ Payne-Smith (1903) 70 notes that this is a Greek loan-word γλωσσόκομον meaning "case, money-box, coffin esp. a case where the remains of saints were preserved, i.e. a shrine or reliquary". Sokoloff, 234 "chest, box".

[3] P.-G. Borbone (trans.), *Storia di Mar Yahballaha e di Rabban Sauma : un orientale in Occidente ai tempi di Marco Polo* (Zamorani, Turin: 2000), 171; citing Anthony of Novgorod (1200) identifies her as Theodosia of Constantinope who was martyred for protecting an icon of Christ during the first phases of the first iconoclast controversy in 729.

1960-1962). = Darmo HUDRA.

Engberding, H. "Fünf Blätter eines alten ostsyrischen Bitt- und Buss-gottesdienstes aus Innerasien", *Ostkirchliche Studien* 14 (1965), 121-48.

Hunter, E.C.D. "SyrHT 140: Commemorating Mar Cyriacus and Julitta" in *MORE MODOQUE. Die Wurzeln der europaïschen Kultur unde deren Rezeption im Orient und Okzident. Festschrift für Miklós Maróth zum siebzigsten Geburtstag*, ed. Pál Fodor (et. al), (Forschungszentrum für Humanwissenschaften der Ungarischen Akademie der Wissenschaften, Budapest: 2013) 225-233.

Hunter, E.C.D. "Traversing Time and Location: A Prayer-Amulet to Mar Tamsis from Turfan"in *From the Oxus River to the Chinese Shores. Studies on East Syriac Christianity in Central Asia and China* [Orientalia-patristica-oecumenica v. 5] (Lit. Verlag: Salzburg, 2013), 23-41.

Hunter, E. C.D. and M. Dickens (eds.), *Syrische Handschriften, Teil 2. Texte der Berliner Turfansammlung. Syriac texts from the Berlin Turfan collection*, Stuttgart:VOHD, forthcoming.

Kötting, B. *Der frühchristliche Reliquienkult und die Bestattung im Kirchengebäude* (Opladen, Westdeutscher Verlag, Cologne: 1965).

Macomber, W. "A List of the Known Manuscripts of the Chaldean Ḥudra", *Orientalia Christiana Periodica* XXXVI:1 (1970), 120-134.

Montgomery, J. (trans.), *The history of Yaballaha III, Nestorian patriarch, and of his vicar, Bar Sauma, Mongol ambassador to the Frankish courts at the end of the thirteenth century* (Columbia University Press, New York: 1927).

Payne Smith, R. *A Compendious Syriac Dictionary* (Clarendon Press, Oxford: 1903).

Payne Smith, R. *Thesaurus Syriacus* (Clarendon Press, Oxford: 1868-1901).

Polotsky, H-J. in Müller, F. W. K. & W. Lentz, "Soghdische Texte II",

Sitzungsberichte der Preussischen Akademie der Wissenschaften (1934), 559-564.

Rassam, S. "Der Mār Behnam. The monastery of Saint Behnam", in E.C.D. Hunter, *The Christian Heritage of Iraq. Collected papers from the Christianity in Iraq I-V Seminar Days* [Gorgias Eastern Christian Series 13] (Gorgias Press, Piscataway, NJ: 2009), 77-86.

Sachau, E. "Litteratur-Bruchstücke aus Chinesisch-Turkistan", *Sitzungsberichte der Königlich Preussischen Akademie der Wissenschaften* (Sitzung der philosophisch-historischen Classe von 23. November) XLVII (1905), 964-973.

Sims-Williams, N. "Cyriacus and Julitta, Acts of", *Encyclopedia Iranica* VI:5, 512.

Sims-Williams, N. "A Sogdian fragment from the martyrdom of Cyriacus and Julitta" in *MORE MODOQUE. Die Wurzeln der europaïschen Kultur unde deren Rezeption im Orient und Okzident. Festschrift für Miklós Maróth zum siebzigsten Geburtstag*, ed. Pál Fodor (et. al), (Forschungszentrum für Humanwissenschaften der Ungarischen Akademie der Wissenschaften, Budapest: 2013) 235-239.

Sokoloff, M. *A Syriac Lexicon. A translation from the Latin, Correction, Expansion and Update of C. Brockelmann's Lexicon Syriacum* (Eisenbrauns, Winona Lake; Piscataway, NJ, Gorgias: 2009).

Spencer Trimingham, J. *Christianity amongst the Arabs in pre-Islamic times* (Longman, London: 1979).

Wright, W. A *Catalogue of the Syriac manuscripts preserved in the library of the University of Cambridge*, 2 vols. (Cambridge, Cambridge University Press: 1901).

15 A Note on the Place Name "City of Royal Residence" (Wangshe-zhi-cheng 王舍之城) in the Xi'an Stele

Max Deeg
(Cardiff University, UK)

After the famous"explorations"of Zhang Qian (张骞) between 138–125 B.C., which occurred during the Former Han dynasty (前汉; 206 B.C. –8 A.D.) considerable curiosity concerning the areas lying west of the Chinese sphere of influence developed. Indeed, there was probably no period in Chinese history in which the interest in the "Western Regions" (*xiyu* 西域) was greater than during the Tang (唐) dynasty (618–907). The historical setting for such an interest is well known: in the early period of the Tang it was the conflict with the Turks — inherited from previous dynasties such as the Sui (隋 581–618) — and the expansion of the Tang empire into Central Asia, while, in the later period, it was the presence of relatively large diasporic communities; these included traders and refugees from the collapsed Sasanian empire (with the assassination of the its last ruler, Yazdegerd II, in Merv in the year 651 A.D.) and Central Asians, Indians and Arabs as well, which stimulated the interest in, and the flow of, information in China as to the regions lying west of the Gansu corridor.

Belonging to these diasporic groups – about whom the honoured recipient of this Festschrift has furthered our knowledge considerably – are the Christian communities of the Tang period, called "Nestorian" in older secondary literature, as well as the"Church of the East" or, more recently, using the name given in the Chinese documents, "Brilliant (or Luminous) Teaching" (Jingjiao 景教). This religious group left a historical document that attracted the attention of early Western missionaries such as Matteo Ricci / Li Madou (利玛窦, 1552–1610) in the late Ming (明, 1368–1644) and early Qing (清, 1644–1912) period. This text was that of the famous stele from Xi'an (西安), the Jingjiao-liuxing-zhongguo-bei (景教流行中国碑), the "Stone Inscription about the Diffusion of the Luminous Teaching in the Middle Kingdom". This document has been translated over and over again and contains extremely useful information about the first one and a half century of history of these early Christian communities in China.[1] It contains, however, also some riddles which have, despite all the efforts invested in the translation and interpretation of the stele and its text, not been completely solved; one of these unanswered questions is whether or not the early Christians of the Tang period were a largely Iranian diasporic community or one which contained Chinese converts. While the latter part of the question cannot be answered with certainty, it is clear that the majority of the adherents were of Iranian origin. The recent discovery of another stele, the so-called *dhāraṇī* pillar from Luoyang[2], shows that the community in the eastern capital of the empire was dominated by Sogdians, although this, of course, does not exclude the possibility of quite a high number of other Iranian (or/and Central Asian) Christians, who had fled from the Sasanian empire after its breakdown, Arab invasion and final conquest.

The Xi'an stele presents us with the names of some leading figures of the Christian community in the Tang capital of Chang'an (长安), which was

〔1〕On the reception story of the stele see Keevak 2008.

〔2〕For a collection of articles about this new find see Ge 2009; a tentative English translation is given in Li 2009.

based in the Yining (义宁) ward in the northwest of the capital. Beside the list of names at the end of the document, which contains the Chinese and the Syro-Iranian names of members of the Christian community, who were mainly monks and priests, we gain information about the persons directly involved in the production and erection of the stone tablet: these include the priest Adam / Jingjing (景净), who authored the inscription, and his father Yazadbozid / Yisi (伊斯), who allegedly commissioned the inscription and in whose honour the stone was erected. The Chinese text gives their family's (non-Chinese) place of origin as Wangshe-zhi-cheng (王舍之城), "City of Royal Residence":

> The great lord of donations, the "Great Lord of Radiant Fortune, [Bearer] of the Golden [Seal] and of the Purple [Ribbon]", simultaneously vice military commander of Shuofang, director of the palace administration on probation, receiver of the purple *kāṣāya*, the monk Yisi was friendly and loved generosity, had heard of the Dao and strove to practice [it]; [he] came from afar to China from the "City of Royal Residence" to China; [his] skills were more highly [developed than those] of the Three Dynasties, [his] art was more comprehensive [than] the ten perfections [of the art of healing].〔1〕

The Syriac passage at the end of the Chinese text helps to clearly identify the"City of Royal Residence" as Balkh〔2〕, one of the major cities in what was called historically Bactria or Tokharestan, a region south of the Oxus / Amu Darya river (in today's northern Afghanistan). This part of the inscription has been translated several times and recently has been discussed

〔1〕大施主，金紫光禄大夫，同朔方节度副使，试殿中监，赐紫袈裟，僧伊斯，和而好惠，闻道勤行。远自王舍之城，聿来中夏。术高三代，艺博十全。

〔2〕According to Moule 1930: 43, note 34, this identification was first made by Claude de Visdelou 1760: 399, called Pathien (based on the Chinese Badiyan, see below), and then taken over by T.–J. Lamy et A.Gueluy 1897.

in detail by Erica Hunter[1] and Samuel Lieu[2]. Neither of them comment, however, on the relation – or rather the difference – between the Syriac form of the place name, Balh/Balkn, and the obvious Chinese equivalent, Wangshe-zhi-cheng (王舍之城), "City of Royal Residence". For reasons given below, I would like to concentrate on this topic in some more detail. The Syriac passage in question reads, in translation:

> In the year 1092 of the Greek[3] the lord Yazadbōzīd[4], priest and chorespiscopus of Kumdān, the imperial city, son of the late Mîlês, priest from Balkh, the city in Taḥorèstân[5], had this stone stele erected, on which is written the divine order of our savior and the predicament of our fathers to the rulers of China. … Adam, deacon, son of Yazadbōzīd, chorepiscopus.[6]

Two points may be noted and stressed immediately when comparing the Chinese with the Syriac passage: firstly that the Syriac is geographically more specific, not only in giving the place name Balkh, but also the wider

---

〔1〕Hunter 2009.

〔2〕Lieu 2009: 229ff.

〔3〕This is the usual chronological scheme of the Eastern Church which starts counting from the twelfth year after the death of Alexander the Great and the first conquest of Syria through the Seleucids (311 BC). The year 1092 lasted from the first day of the month October 780 to the 30th September 781, and the corresponding Chinese part of the inscription specifies that the stele was erected on Sunday, 4th February 781: see Dauvillier in Pelliot 1984: 56, note 4; Lieu 2009: 231f. The use of the Seleucid chronology is not the only one used by followers of the Church of the East – see the Greek beside the Sasanian one in a Sogdian Christian document: Sims–Williams1985: 31, or, in a Chinese–Parthian bilingual inscription of the later Tang the Sasanian (Yazdgird [sic!]), the Arabic and the Chinese–dynastic ones: Humbach 1988: 80f.

〔4〕"Saved by God" 19: Jazdbōzēḏ ; cp. Middle–Iranian Yazdan–buxt (Gignoux1986: 192, no.1061). On Yisi / Yazadbōzīd see Deeg, forthcoming.

〔5〕Bailey (quoted in Black 1936–37: 25, note 10) thinks that the Syriac is based on a Sogdian form of the name.

〔6〕(in Dauvillier's vocalized transcription) Baš^{e}nat^{h} 'àlèp^{h} w^{e}t^{h}èš'în w^{e}t^{h}artên d^{he}Yàunàyê Màr(i) Yazdbôzêd qaššîšâ w^{e}k^{h}ôr'appèsqôpâ dh^{e}K^{h}ûmdân m^{e}d^{h}înat^{h} malkût^{h}â bar nîḥ nap^{h}šâ Mîlês qaššîšâ d^{he}mèn Balḥ m^{e}d^{h}î(n)ttâ d^{he}T^{h}aḥôrèstan 'aqqîm lûḥâ hànâ d^{he}k^{h}êp^{h}â d^{h}ak^{he}t^{h}îb^{h}àn bèh m^{e}d^{h}ab^{h}rànût^{h}éh d^{e}p^{h}àrôqan w^{e}k^{h}àrôzût^{h}hôn d^{e}'ab^{h}àhain dal^{e}wàt^{h} malkê d^{he}Ṣinàyê … 'Ad^{h}àm m^{e}šamm^{e}šànâ bar Yazdbôzêd kôr'appèsqôpâ. See also the most recent discussion of the passage by Hunter.

region of Taḥorèstân (To(k)arestan); secondly, in the Chinese passage it is stated that Yisi / Yazadbōzīd came from Balkh, while in the Syriac it is Yisi's father Mîlês' place of origin. Taken together, both passages seem to imply that it was Yisi who emmigrated from Tokharestan to China. Since Yisi served under the Chinese general and high official Guo Ziyi (郭子仪, 697–781) during the An Lushan (安禄山，755–763) rebellion, he must have arrived and established himself in China some time before these events. It is quite likely that he had fled from Balkh during or after the Arab final conquest of the city in the year 734.

It seems obvious that for a Chinese reader of the stele, who was not familiar with either the identity of the name "City of the Royal Residence" (Wangshe-zhi-cheng 王舍之城) or the content of the Syriac part of the inscription, it would have been hard – and was hard, indeed, for the earliest Western translators of the text – to know what and where this place was. For an educated Chinese reader of the Chinese text of the inscription, however, there was a way to localize the place by means of earlier textual references; the most well-known one being, for a Tang readership, the description of Balkh in the famous Buddhist traveler Xuanzang's (玄奘) "Records of the Western Regions" (Xiyu-ji 西域记; submitted to emperor Taizong in the year 646, one year after Xuanzang's return)[1], in which Balkh is given the epithet "Minor City of Royal Residence" (Xiao-wangshe-cheng 小王舍城):

Going in [a] western [direction from Khulm], [one] arrives in the

〔1〕On the Xiyu–ji and its history see Deeg 2009, and Deeg 2012.

kingdom of Fuhe[1]. The kingdom of Fuhe measures more than eight hundred miles from the east to the west [and] more than four hundred miles from the south to the north. On [its] northern [side it] is adjacent to the river Fuchu. The great capital of the kingdom has a circumference of more than twenty miles, [and] all the people call it the minor city of "Royal Residence". Although this city is strongly [fortified], its population is small. The kinds of products grown on its soil are extremely numerous, [so that] it is difficult to list all the plants growing on land and in the water. There are more than one hundred monasteries and more than three thousand monks [who] all practice and study the teaching of the Small Vehicle (Hīnayāna).[2]

Xuanzang's place name "Minor City of Royal Residence" (Xiao-wangshe-cheng 小王舍城) has been interpreted as being connected to the Chinese "standard" translation of the ancient Central-Indian Magadhan capital of Rājagṛha in Buddhist translations and texts[3]. This resulted in a quite blurred interpretation of the name of the Central Asian city, which is best seen in Saeki's comment on the stele:

---

〔1〕Fohe 缚喝/ **bua*^{h}*-xat*, or, with an alternative reading of the first character, Fuhe 缚喝/ **buak-xat*, clearly refers to Balkh, but Xuanzang's transliteration is not directly representing this form of the toponym. The older Iranian name forms for the greater region and the city are Old-Persian Bāxtriš, Avestan Bāxdi, Pahlavi Bākhal or Bakhli (see Mizutani 1999: 109f., note 1; Ji 1985: 115f., note 1; Leriche, Grenet 2011; *baxlo* / βαχλο on Hephtalite coins and in Bactrian manuscripts: Kurbanov 2010: 105; Sims-Williams 2007: 202a), probably in Skt. Vāhlika (in the Bṛhatsaṃhitā; see Watters 1903-1904: I, 109). Although there is no direct correspondence to either forms of Xuanzang's name, it seems that the second reading (**bua*^{h}*-xat*) comes closer to an assumed regional toponym (**baxt*), although Mizutani, with caution, suggests the alternative reading (**buak-xat*) as corresponding to a form like Bākhal(a). The rich variety of Chinese transliterations of the toponym referring to Balkh seems to reflect a considerable number of different autochthonous names as well: Weishu 魏书 102, 西域传: Boti 薄提 / **bak–dεj*; 北史: Boluo 薄罗 / **bak–la*; Xin–Tangshu 新唐书, 43b, Dili 2: Bozhi 薄知 / **bak-triă*; in the Biography of Dharmagupta in the Gaoseng-zhuan 高僧传: Boqieluo 薄怯罗 / **bak-k*^{h}*iap-la* (see Ji 1985: 116, note 1).

〔2〕T.2087.872c.1ff. (quoted after Ji 1985: 115): 缚喝国东西八百余里, 南北四百余里, 北临缚刍河。国大都城周二十余里，人皆谓之小王舍城也。其城虽固，居人甚少。土地所产，物类尤多，水陆诸花，难以备举。伽蓝百有余所，僧徒三千余人，并皆习学小乘法教。

〔3〕Saeki 1916: 237f.

There were at least two places known by the name of "the Royal City." The first was the royal residence of Magadha, the Kingdom of Central India. Rajagriha, "Royal City," was the first Metropolis [sic!] of Buddhism. Of the second, we read in the famous "Buddhist Records of the Western World" by Hsuan-chuang … He usually calls it "Little Rajagriha" (i.e., Royal City). This "Little Rajagriha" is no less a place than the city of Balkh in Bactria, which is some 20 *li* in circumference. We think that "the Royal City" mentioned on the Stone is this "Little Rajagriha," because in the Syriac part of the Inscription we find that many of the Nestorian priests, – above all, the father of Yazedbouzid – came from Balkh. It is not very difficult to imagine why the adjective "little" was dropped. Its omission before "Royal City" in this case was something like adding the adjective "great" before the name of the country, … … in the case of "Rajagriha," the author attained his purpose of glorifying the city by simply dropping the prefix "little." He could not call Balkh the "great Rajagriha," because the title belonged to the Royal City in Magadha.[1]

What is wrong with this statement – the gist of which has been repeated by several other scholars[2]? Beside the historical inaccuracies – for instance, the fact that Rājagṛha had already been replaced as the capital of Magadha by Pāṭaliputra in the Buddha's lifetime – I would suggest that, by overemphasizing and generalizing Xuanzang's linking of Balkh and the the old capital of Magadha, Rājagṛha, a major point in the interpretation of the function of the name "City of Royal Residence" in the stele has been missed. It must be interpreted as propaganda by the early Christian community, who wished to forge links with the glories of historic Balkh; the epithet of Balkh, "Royal Residence", which sometimes may have been used as a real

[1] Saeki 1951: 97f.

[2] See e.g. Nicolini–Zani 2006: 205, note 87.

toponym (see below), has, in my view - at least originally - nothing to do with a desire for parallelism with the famous old Buddhist city. It is an ancient name for the city of Balkh, although Xuanzang may have thought of Rājagṛha when he heard the local name (or rather ephithet) of the city. Such a connection might have been based on several factors: such as the important Buddhist community, as well as the influential monastic site and *stūpa* of Navavihāra ("New Monastery" or Nau Bahār in Muslim sources), which was probably very influential in the 7th and 8th - as the connection between monastery's leaders and the later Muslim dynasty of the Barmakids shows; and the important Buddhist pilgrimage sites dedicated to the two merchants Trapuṣa and Bhallika – the latter name having been brought up in connection with the name of Balhk – and their *stupas*, which were in the vicinity of the city.

In his monumental *translatio cum commentario* of the stele, posthumously edited by Antonino Forte, Pelliot, in a short note - the elaboration of which is missing- raises doubts about the equation of the two cities of"Royal Residence"[1].The great French scholar also reemphasizes this doubt in his notes on the text of Marco Polo, where he suggests that "City of the Royal Residence"does not refer to the Indian name Rājagṛha, the old capital of the kingdom of Magadha, "but is another name of Balkh". Here, again, however, he does not provide further explanation.[2]

The oldest Chinese notion of a city called "Royal Residence" in the region of Tokharestān is the capital of the Hephthalites / Yeda (嚈哒), which is already found in Wei Shou's (魏收, 506-572) Weishu (魏书)120 (compiled 551–554). The transliteration of the autochthonous name is

〔1〕Pelliot, Forte 1996: 280, note 205: "J'ai expliqué plus haut (cf. supra, p. [manque]) pourquoi il fallait y voir non pas Rājagṛha de Magadha comme on l'a fait généralement, mais Balkh au Tokharestan." On this missing part see Forte's note, p.343.

〔2〕Pelliot 1959: 72.

Badiyan(拔底延) / **bat-tɛj'-jian*:

> The kingdom of Yeda: [the population is of] Great Yueshi stock, [which is] also called a special tribe of the Gaoche; [their] origin is from the north of the Śakas (Sai). [The kingdom lies] south of the Jinshan, to the west of Khotan, [and] the capital [is] two hundred [Chinese] miles south of the river Oxus [and] 10100 miles from Chang'an. Its capital [is called] Badiyan city, that is city of the "Royal Residence". [It measures] more than ten miles [each] side, [and there are] many monasteries and *stūpa*s [which] are all adorned with gold.[1]

Identical or almost identical passages are found in the Beishi (北史) 97 (completed by Li Yanshou (李延寿) in 659) and in the Suishu (隋书)83 (compiled by Wei Zheng 魏徵, 629–636). But there is also, again in chapter 97 of the Beishi, the following note, which makes it probable that the name may indeed have been taken in a contemporary context as referring to Balkh:

> At the time of the emperor Yang [of the Sui] the attendant censor Wei Jie[2] [and] the metropolitan commandant retainer Du Manxing were sent as envoys to all the kingdoms of the Western Fan, [they] went to Jibin and received a bowl [made of] agate, [they] received Buddhist *sūtra*s in the city of "Royal Residence", [they] received ten dancing girls, lion skins [and] hair of the fire mouse[3] in the kingdom of Shi[4] and returned [to China].[5]

---

〔1〕嚈哒国，大月氏之种类也，亦曰高车之别种，其原出于塞北。自金山而南，在于阗之西，都马[emend to 乌]许水南二百余里，去长安一万一百里。其王都拔底延城，盖王舍城也。其城方十里余，多寺塔，皆饰以金。 See also the German translation of the Beishi-version in Markwart 1938: 38f.

〔2〕On Wei Jie see Kuwayama 2002a: 136f.

〔3〕The "fire mouse", *huoshu* 火鼠, is the mythical salamander-like animal of whose hair the Chinese thought asbestos was produced.

〔4〕史: Keš on the upper Kaška Darya: see Stark 2009: 43, note 138.

〔5〕炀帝时，乃遣侍御史韦节、司隶从事杜行满使于西蕃诸国，至罽宾得玛瑙杯，王舍城得佛经，史国得十舞女、师子皮、火鼠毛而还。

The city of Badiyan has been identified with several places[1], *inter aliud* with Bādhaghīs (Bāḏĝīs) or Bāmyin of the Muslim sources near Herat[2], or with Warwālīz (Walwālīz), east of Balkh and in the vicinity of modern Qunduz[3]. Uchida Ginpū's (内田吟风) explanation that Xuanzang's transliteration Fohe respresents an Iranian toponym Patiyan[4] which is supposed to mean, following the Chinese sources (see above), "Royal Residence"[5], is not supported by any known source[6]. Uchida's note is therefore a distorted and reified continuation of Markwart' s assumption that the Chinese Badiyan may be related to a Persian name[7]. It is also, for my purpose, not important whether the "real" – in the sense of historical at a certain point in time – Badiyan can be identified with Balkh or some other place east or west of it, since it is rather the cultural memory of Balkh as the city of "Royal Residence" that I am concerned with. It is still, however, worthwhile to point out the possibility that the Chinese historical identification of such a city in the Tang period – and this is the only important point of my rather lengthy discussion – was indeed Balkh. Since the name refers to the capital of the Hephthalites, it is quite possible that the

---

〔1〕An overview is given by Kuwayama 2002a: 137.

〔2〕Chavannes 1903: 224, note 5. Because of this identification, which was first made by Specht in 1883, Chavannes even assumed that Yisi came from Bādhagīs. There is no evidence for a prominent position of the city in medieval times: see Bosworth 1988a., and already Markwart 1938: 39, strongly opposed this identification.

〔3〕Markwart 1938: 44. This also seems to be the opinion of Kuwayama 2002a: 138.

〔4〕This equation was already made by Visdelou in 1760: 349, note 2.

〔5〕Repeated by Ji: 116, note 1.

〔6〕I am grateful to Prof. Nicholas Sims-Williams for confirming that there is not such an Iranian toponym or word.

〔7〕Markwart 1901: 309 (appendix), where he hesitantly suggests an identification with Paikand / Paikent in the Bokhara oasis on the basis of an audacious etymology of the place name *Patkand / *Patikanta, "Stadt, bezw. Haus (eig. Grube, **kanta*, *kand*, syn. *kata*, *kat*) des Herrschers" ("city, resp. house (literally pitch, *...) of the ruler"); see also Markwart 1938: 43f., where he suddenly proposes Iranian *paδijān*, "das oberherrliche" ("the ultimate splendid"). It may suffice to note that these reconstructions do not fit to the Middle-Chinese reconstructed pronunciation of the place name at all; see already Kuwayama 2002a: 137. Earlier Markwart 1901: 240, however, is more reluctant to identify the location of the city.

name underlying Chinese Badiyan had the meaning "Royal Residence" in the Hephthalite language.

The stress which both quoted passages make on a flourishing Buddhism makes it rather unlikely that any other urban centre than Balkh in the region could have been meant. Also the projected route of Wei Jie's journey could suggest that the city of "Royal Residence" must have been positioned on the way between Jibin, probably "Greater Gandhāra" at that time, and the kingdom of Shi (史), i.e. Keš, should have taken the new route – especially if one follows Kuwayama's theory[1] – across the Hindukush and via Bāmiyān, and the natural point of transition in the northwestern direction towards Shi would have been, indeed, Balkh. Furthermore, the distance given from the river Oxus and the route in southern direction, two hundred Chinese miles (*li* 里), makes rather more sense in the case of Balkh (ca. 70 km as the crow flies) from modern Termez than of a place around modern Qunduz (ca. 50 km, without a clear starting point at the Oxus).

It is, in any case, not very likely that the parallelization with the Indian Rājagṛha was the origin of the name. The name is rather an autochthonous one. Balkh has been, for centuries, since the Achaemenid period, the capital of the region. The city was then the capital of the Graeco-Bactrian rulers[2], and under the Hephtalites the ruler of Balkh bore the Bactrian title *šāva*, "king"[3]. Under the Sasanians, the city was the capital of one of the four *marzubān*s / *marzpān*s (military governor) of the province of Khorasan[4], but came under the control of the Western Turks in the second half of the 6th

〔1〕Kuwayama 2002b.

〔2〕Barthold 1968: 76.

〔3〕Harmatta, Litvinsky 1996: 371.

〔4〕Barthold 1968: 77. The Sasanians may have opened a mint in Balkh in the second half of the 6th century as coins with the signature *blh* minted during the reign of Ohrmazd IV (579–591) could suggest; see Vondrovec 2010: 181.

century[1]. Wherever the capital of the Western Turks in Bactria / Tokharestan – and before that of the Hephthalites in Bactria – has to be looked for[2], the report in Xuanzang's record that the son of the Turkic ruler Tong *yabghukhagan* / Tong *yehukehan* (统叶护可汗), Si *yehu* (肆叶护), had planned an attack on the city's famous Buddhist monastery, the Navavihāra[3], – a piece of information which probably means an attack on the city itself – shows the central position of Balkh under the Western Turks. In 652 the city was first conquered, together with the cities of Merv, the seat of a Christian bishop, and Heart, by the Arabs. Still later in Arabic sources it bore the epithet "the Royal [City]"[4]. Balkh resisted Arab control several times[5] and could temporarily retain its relative independence under local rulers[6]. The main and central mosque in the centre of the city (*šahristān*) was built, according to Muslim sources, in the year 742[7]. This was some years after the final Muslim occupation of the city, in the year 734.[8] The city was destroyed by Dschingis Khan after an uprising against the Mongols.

As an archaeological site Balkh has been quite well excavated through the Franco-Afghan archaeological initiatives, starting with Alfred Foucher

---

[1] The importance of the city under the Sasanians is also underlined by the description of the siege imposed on it by the Turks, a description of which is given in the Armenian chronicle of Sebēos: see Stark 2008: 210, note 1166. The name "Royal Residence", *mnyst'n šḥyky*, is attested on Sasanian coins of Šāpūr found in Merv (see De la Vaissière 2005: 99), without claiming here that this was indeed referring to Balkh.

[2] The Turkic *yabghu* around 630 seems to have resided in the region of Huo, the Warwalīz of the Muslim sources; Stark 2008: 211.

[3] See Chavannes 1903: 196.

[4] Marquart 1901: 91.

[5] See Bosworth 1988b.

[6] On the events in the second half of the 7th century and the beginning of the 8th century, focused on the attempts of Tarkhan Nīzak to establish himself as ruler of Tokharestan with Balkh as ist centre which ended with his death in the year 710, see Esin 1977. At the beginning of the 8th century (712/713) the ruler bore the title Ispahbadh; see Barthold 1968: 77.

[7] Barthold 1968: 78.

[8] Lieu 2009: 236.

(Foucher 1942), from the thirties of the last century[1]. While no archaeological traces of Christianity have been found in Balkh so far, there is textual evidence for the existence of Christian communities in the city, which is not very surprising considering its strategic value in military and economic terms[2]. The so-called Bar-Šabba-fragment in Sogdian from the Berlin Turfan collection[3] tells the legend of the bishop Bar Šabba of Merv who, in this version, set up Christian communities in different places, e.g. in Margiana, Merv and Balkh[4]. In my opinion, this source has been underrated in relation to the stele of Xi'an. Since Balkh is not mentioned in the standard version of the legend it seems to be a localised version into which regional names were added because of the existence of local Christian communities. At the time when Yazbozid's father Mîlês must have lived there (in the first decades of the 8th century?), the city definitely had a multi-ethnic and multi-religious community[5], and it probably still had a rich historical memory, which left traces in the local version of the Bar-Šabba-legend.

The Muslim sources contain a lot of information on Balkh (see Markwart 1901: 87ff.): the city is praised and lauded as e.g. "the Mother of

〔1〕Foucher 1942: 55ff.; Ball 1982: 47ff., no.99; Ball 2008: 154ff.

〔2〕Saeki's 1951: 106, assumption that the city was one of the twenty-four metropolitan sees of the Church of the East is obviously based on a misinterpretation: see Dauvillier, in Pelliot 1984:64 .

〔3〕With a Syriac correspondent fragment which does, however, not contain the passage with the place name.

〔4〕Müller, Lentz 1934: 525, translation of lines 28ff.: "Und er siedelte dort dienende Brüder und dienende Schwestern an: in den Gegenden von Fars bis hin nach Gurgan und in der Gegend von Tus, in Abarschahr und in Serachs und Merwrod und in Balch und in Herat und in Seistan. Er erbaute dort Gotteshäuser und bereitete alles, was nötig ist. Und auch Presbyter und Diakonen siedelte er dort an." ("And he settled serving brothers and serving sisters there: in the region of Fars all the way to Gurgan, and in the region of Tus, in Abarschahr and in Serachs and Merwrod and in Balch and in Heart and in Seistan. He built houses of God and everything needed. And he also settled presbyters and deacons there.") See also Sims-Williams 1988; Gillman, Klimkeit 1999: 211.

〔5〕Lieu 2009: 235f. On the presence of Jewish traders in the region see De la Vaissière 2005: 184f.

All Cities"(*umm al' bilād*)[1], or as "Balkh the Splendid" (Pahlavi: Bahl-i-bāmīk, etc.)[2]. The Ḥudūd-al-'Ālam's has a rather lengthy description which reflects the importance of the city, and some of the details given correspond with Xuanzang' s report:

> Balkh, a large and flourishing town which was formerly the residence of the Sasanian kings (...). In it are found buildings of the Sasanian kings with paintings (*naqsha*) and wonderful works (*kārkird*), (which) have fallen into ruins. (That place) is called Nau-bihār. (Balkh) is a resort of merchants and is very pleasant and prosperous. It is the emporium (*bār-kadha*) of Hindūstān. There is a large river in Balkh that comes from Bāmiyān and in the neighborhood of Balkh is divided into twelve branches. It traverses the town and is altogether used for the agriculture of its districts. ... (Minorsky 1970: 108)

What is important in this passage is that it emphasizes that Balkh was the residence of kings and, although this was not really the case historically, it seems to reflect the old epitheton of the city, "Royal Residence". The Chinese *wang* 王 was an appropriate rendering and *interpretatio-sinica*-like rank for the Hephthalite ruler, the Sasanian governor and the Western Turkic *yabghu*. If we take the Chinese translation of Badiyan in the Weishu and other sources – even if the city denoted by the name did not necessarily refer to Balkh at all times – for granted, we have a match with the name of the city in the Chinese part of the stele. It is also understandable why Xuanzang had to add the attribute "small" or "minor": probably not only because he, as a committed Buddhist and a traveler, clearly knew the ancient capital of the kingdom of Magadha, Rājagṛha, as the "real" city of "Royal Residence" (Wangshe 王舍), but also because of the real position of Balkh in the administrative structure of the Sasanian empire, in which the

〔1〕Barthold 1968: 76.

〔2〕Markwart 1901: 87.

capital, Seleukia-Ktesiphon, had the pre-right to be called "(City of) Royal Residence". This is despite Balkh not being under direct Sasanian control any more[1]. Be this as it may, the legacy of Balkh being called the city of "Royal Residence" is a long one, which was not restricted to the actual status of the city at a certain point in its history. It is very probable, then, that the epithet was used in the Chinese text of the stele on purpose and with a specific intention. But, to come back to my initial question, what may have been the motivation to use the name "City of Royal Residence" for Balkh in the Chinese part of the inscription?

The answer to this question, substantiated by the information given and discussed above, can, of course, only be speculative. But the close relationship of Jingjing and especially of his father Yisi with the Tang court may have prompted the author of the text – be it Jingjing himself or an unmentioned writer – to emphasise the significance of the place of origin of the family for the sake of the person for whom the inscription was committed in the first place - Jingjing's father (and his grandfather Mîlês) - as a royal city in the Chinese text, although the glory days of Balkh were long over when the first generation of the family had emigrated to China, which is reflected in the Syriac part of the textwhere Balkh is just called $m^{e}d^{h}$*îna*. The use of the name then would, in a certain way, reflect and symbolize the Persian Christian family's position in the Tang hierarchy: while the imperial city Chang'an (Khumdan) is called the "Royal (or Imperial) City" ($m^{e}d^{h}$*înat*^{h} *malkût*^{h}*â*)[2], the city of origin of Jingjing's /

---

〔1〕It is possible that this title was upheld under Western Turkic predominance of Bactria / Tokharestan and belonged to the historical self–identity and –image of the city.

〔2〕In Syriac the difference between an imperial and a royal or princely city could not be – and in the context needed not to be – differentiated. In Chinese such a difference would also not be made since *jing* 京, "capital", is the normal word for the imperial capital. There were, however, also more specific terms like *huangdu* 皇都, "imperial capital", or, even more corresponding to *wangshe* 王舍, *huangcheng* 皇城 for the imperial palace area.

Adam's father Yisi, who held a relatively high position as a direct advisor of the *wang* 王 ("prince") of Fenyang 汾阳, Guo Ziyi, was appropriately and aptly designated by its well-known Chinese name: the city of the "Residence of a Prince"[1].

Bibliography

T. Taishō-shinshū-daizōkyō 大正新修大藏经, ed. Takakusu Junjirō 高楠顺次郎 & Watanabe Kaikyoku 渡辺海旭.

Ball, Warwick. 1982. *Archaeological Gazetteer of Afghanistan / Catalogue des sites archéologiques d'Afghanistan*, vol.1. Paris: Édition de Recherche sur les civilisations.

—. 2008. *The Monuments of Afghanistan. History, Archaeology and Architecture*. London, New York: I.B.Tauris.

Barthold, W[asilij]. 1968. *Turkestan down to the Mongol invasion* (Third edition). London: Luzac and Company Ltd.

Bosworth, C.E. 1988a. "Bāḏĝīs. i. General and the Early Period". *Encyclopædia Iranica* (online version, url: http://www.iranicaonline.org/articles/badgis-region, accessed 05-01-2013).

—. 1988b. "Balḵ. ii. History from the Arab Conquest to the Mongols".*Encyclopædia Iranica*(online version, url: http://www.iranicaonline.org/articles/balk-town-and-province#pt6, accessed 05-01-2013).

Chavannes, Édouard. 1903. *Documents sur les Tou-Kiue (Turcs) Occidentaux – recueillis et commentés suivi de notes additionelles*. St.Petersburg: Adrien-Maisonneuve (Nachdruck Taibei 1969).

Deeg, Max. 2009. "Writing for the Emperor – Xuanzang Between Piety, Religious Propaganda, Intelligence, and Modern Imagination". In:

[1] It may have come handy that the Iranian did not make a clear-cut difference between royal capital and bigger city (*šahristân*).

Martin Straube, Roland Steiner, Jayandra Soni, Michael Hahn, Mitsuyo Demoto (eds.).*Pāsādikadānaṃ. Festschrift für Bhikkhu Pāsādika*. Marburg: Indica et Tibetica Verlag: 30-60.

—. 2012. "'Show Me the Land Where the Buddha Dwelled …' – Xuanzang's 'Record of the Western Regions' (Xiyu ji): A Misunderstood Text?"*China Report* 48: 89-113.

—. 2013. "A Belligerent Priest – Yisi and his Political Context". In: Li Tang, Dietmar W. Winkler (eds.). *Fran the Oxus River to the Chinese Shores. Studies on Syriac Christianity in China and Central Asia*. Wien. Berlin: LIT Verlag: 107-121.

De La Vaissière, Étienne. 2004. *Histoire des marchands Sogdiens*. [2]Paris: De Boccard (Bibliothèque de l'Institut des Hautes Études Chinoises, Volume XXXII) (quoted in its English translation: 2005. *Sogdian Traders: A History*. Leiden: Brill).

—. 2010. "The Last Bactrian Kings". In: Alram, Michael; Klimburg-Salter, Deborah (eds.). *Coins, Art and Chronology, II. The First Millennium C.E. in the Indo-Iranian Borderlands*. Vienna: 213-218.

Esin, Emel. 1977. "Tarkhan Nīzak or Tarkhan Tirek? An Enquiry Concerning the Prince of Bādhghīs Who in A.H. 91 / A.D. 709-710 Opposed the 'Omayyad Conquest of Central Asia". *Journal of the American Oriental Society* 97.2: 323-332.

Foucher, Alfred. 1942. *La vielle route de l'Inde de Bactres à Taxila*. Paris: Les Éditions d'art et d'histoire (Mémoires de la Délégation Archéologique Française en Afghanistan, tôme 1).

Ge Chengyong 葛承雍 (ed.). 2009. *Jingjiao yizhen – Luoyang xinchu Tangdai jingjiao jingchuang yanjiu* 景教遗珍—洛阳新出唐代景教经幢研究/ *Precious Nestorian Relic – Studies on the Nestorian Stone Pillar of the Tang Dynasty Recently Discovered in Luoyang*. Beijing: Wenwu-chubanshe 文物出版社.

Gignoux, Philippe. 1986. *Iranisches Personennamenbuch (hrsg.v. M. Mayrhofer u. R. Schmitt), Band II: Mitteliranische Personennamen, Faszikel 2: Noms propres Sassanides en moyen-Perse épigraphique*. Wien: Verlag der Österreichischen Akademie der Wissenschaften (ÖAW, Phil.-Hist.Kl.).

Gillman, Ian; Klimkeit, Hans-Joachim. 1999. *Christians in Asia Before 1500*. Ann Arbor: The University of Michigan Press.

Harmatta, J.; Litvinsky, Boris A. 1996. "Tokharistan and Gandhara under Western Türk rule (650-750)". In: Litvinsky, Boris. A.; Zhang Guang-Da; Samghabadi, R. Shabani (eds.). *History of civilizations of Central Asia, Volume III: The crossroads of civilizations: A.D. 250 to 750*. Paris: UNESCO (Indian reprint Delhi 1999): 367-401.

Humbach, Helmut (unter Mitwirkung von Wāng Shìpíng). 1988. „Die Pahlavi-Chinesische Bilingue von Xi'an". In: *Acta Iranica* 28, *Hommages et Opera Minora, vol. XII, A Green Leaf. Papers in Honour of Professor Jes P. Asmussen*. Leiden: E.J. Brill: 73-82.

Hunter, Erica C.D. 2009. "The Persian contribution to Christianity in China: Reflections in the Xi'an Fu Syriac inscriptions". In: Winkler, Tang. 2009: 71-85.

Ji Xianlin 季羡林, and others (eds.). 1985. *Datang-xiyuji-xiaozhu* 大唐西域记校注 (*„Kommentar zum Datang-xiyuji"*). Beijing: Zhonghua-Shuju(Nachdr. Taibei 1987).

Keevak, Michael. 2008. *The Story of a Stele. China's Nestorian Monument and its Reception in the West*, 1625-1916. Hong Kong: Hong Kong University Press.

Kurbanov, Aydogdy. 2010. *The Hephthalites: Archaeological and Historical Analysis*. Berlin (PhD. thesis, Freie Universität).

Kuwayama, Shōshin. 2002a. "The Hephtalites in Tokharistan and Gandhara". In: Kuwayama, Shōshin. *Across the Hindukush of the First*

Millenium. A Collection of Papers. Kyoto: Institute for Research in Humanities, Kyoto University: 107-139 (originally published 1991 in: *Zinbun: Annals of the Institute for Research in Humanities*, Kyoto University: 89-134).

—. 2002b. “Two Itineraries concerning the Emergence of the Colossi in Bamiyan”. In: Kuwayama, Shōshin. *Across the Hindukush of the First Millenium. A Collection of Papers*. Kyoto: Institute for Research in Humanities, Kyoto University: 140-155 (originally published 1987 in: G.Gnoli, L.Lanciotti (eds.). *Orientalia: Iosephi Tucci Memoriae Dicata*. Roma, Serie Orientale Roma 57/2: 703-727).

Lamy, Thomas-Joseph; Gueluy, Albert. 1897. *Le monument Chrétien de Si-ngan-fou. Son texte et sa signification*. Bruxelles: Hayez.

Leriche, P.; Grenet, F. 2011. “Bactria”. *Encyclopædia Iranica*(online version, url: http://www.iranicaonline.org/articles/bactria, accessed 05-01-2013).

Le Strange, G. 1905. *The Lands of the Eastern Caliphate. Mesopotamia, Persia, and Central Asia from the Moslem Conquest to the time of Timur*. Cambridge: Cambridge University Press.

Lieu, Samuel. 2009. “Epigraphica Nestoriana Serica”. In: Sundermann, Werner; Hintze, Almut; de Blois, François (Hrsg.). *Exegisti monumenta. Festschrift in Honour of Nicholas Sims-Williams*. Wiesbaden: Harrassowitz (Iranica, Bd.17): 227-246.

Lin Wushu 林悟殊. 2003. Tangdai-jingjiao-zai-yanjiu 唐代景教再研究 (Neue Studien zum Nestorianismus der Tang-Zeit). Beijing: Zhong guo- She hui-Ke xue-Chu ban she.

Markwart, Josef. 1901. *Ērānšahr nach der Geographie des Ps. Moses Xorenac'ci – mit historisch-kritischem Kommentar und historischen und topographischen Excursen*. Berlin: Waldmannsche Buchhandlung (Abhandlungen der Königlichen Gesellschaft der Wissenschaften zu Göttingen,

Philologisch-Historische Klasse, Neue Folge Band 3, Nro.2: 3-358).

— (ed. Hans Heinrich Schaeder). 1938. *Wehrot und Arang. Untersuchungen zur mythischen und geschichtlichen Landeskunde von Ostiran*. Leiden: E.J. Brill.

Minorsky, V[ladimir]. 1970. *Ḥudūd-al-'Ālam, 'The Records of the World', A Persian Geography 372 A.H.-982 A.D.*^{2}Cambridge: Cambridge University Press.

Mizutani Shinjō 水谷真成. 1999. *Daitō-saiiki-ki* 大唐西域记. Vol.1. Tokyo: Heibonsha 平凡社 (Tōyō-Bunko 东洋文库 653)

Moule, A.C. 1930. *Christians in China Before the Year 1550*. London: Society for Promoting Christian Knowledge.

Müller, F.W.K.; Lentz, W. 1934. "Sogdhische Texte II". In: *Sitzungsbericht der Preussischen Akademie der Wissenschaften* 1934: 504-607.

Nicolini-Zani, Matteo. 2006. *La via radiosa per l' oriente. I testi e la storia del primo incontro del cristianesimo con il mondo culturale e religioso cinese (secoli VII-IX)*. Magnano: Edizioni Qiqajon.

Pelliot, Paul. 1959. *Notes on Marco Polo I (Ouvrage Posthume).* Paris : Imprimérie Nationale.

—. 1984. *Recherches sur les chrétiens d'Asie Centrale et d'Extrême-Orient, tôme II, 1 La stèle de Si-ngan-fou*. Paris: Éditions de la Fondation Singer-Polignac (Œuvres posthumes de Paul Pelliot, présenté par Jean Dauvillier).

Pelliot, Paul; Forte, Antonino (ed.). 1996. *L'inscription nestorienne de Si-Ngan-Fou, Edited with Supplements by Antonino Forte*. Rom / Paris: Scuola di Studi sull'Asia Orientale / Institut des Hautes Études Chinoises (Italian School of East Asian Studies Epigraphical Series 2 / Collège de France, œuvres posthumes de Paul Pelliot).

Saeki, Peter Yoshirō. 1916. *The Nestorian Monument in China.*

London: Society for Promoting Christian Knowledge.

1951. *The Nestorian Documents and Relics in China*. Tokyo : The Maruzen Company Ltd.

Sims-Williams, Nicholas. 1985. *The Christian Sogdian Manuscript C2 (With 207 Facsimiles on 95 Plates)*. Berlin: Akademie Verlag (Schriften zur Geschichte und Kultur des Alten Orients, Berliner Turfantexte XII, Akademie der Wissenschaften der DDR, Zentralinstitut für Alte Geschichte und Archäologie).

—. 1988. Article "BARŠABBĀ". In: *Encyclopædia Iranica* 3: 829 (online: http://www.iranicaonline.org/articles/barsabba-legendary-bishop-of-marv-and-founder-of-the-christian-church-in-eastern-iran, access 16-12-20120.

—. 2007. *Bactrian documents from Northern Afghanistan. Vol.2: Letters and Buddhist texts*. Oxord, New York: The Nour Foundation in association with Azimuth Editions (Studies in the Khalili Collection).

Stark, Sören. 2008. *Die Alttürkenzeit in Mittel- und Zentralasien. Archäologische und historische Studien*. Wiesbaden: Dr. Ludwig Reichert Verlag (Nomaden und Sesshafte, Sonderforschungsbereich Differenz und Integration, Band 6).

—. 2009. *Transoxianien nach dem Tang Huiyao des Wang Pu, Übersetzung und Kommentar*. Norderstedt: Books on Demand GmbH.

Tang, Li. 2009. "A Preliminary Study on the *Jingjiao* Inscription of Luoyang: Text, Analysis, Commentary and English Translation". In: Winkler, Tang. 2009: 109-132.

Tubach, Jürgen. 1999. „Die nestorianische Kirche in China". *Nubica et Æthiopica IV / V* (*Internationales Jahrbuch für Koptische, Meroitisch-Nubische, Äthiopische und verwandte Studien*). Warszawa: 61-193.

Uchida Ginpū 内田吟风. 1972. "Tokara(Tukhāra)kokushi-kō" 吐火羅(Tukhāra) 國史考. In: *Tōhō-gakuhui-sōritsu-nijūgo-shū'nen-ki'nen Tōhōgaku-*

ronshū 東方學會創立二十五紀念東方學論集 / *Tōhōgaku Ronshū, Eastern Studies Twenty-fifth Anniversary Volume*. Tokyo: Tōhō Gakkai (The Institute of Eastern Culture): 91-110.

Visdelou, Claude de. 1760. "Éloge de la Religion admirable établie dans le Royaume de la Chine, composé par King-tcing, Bonze du Temple de Ta-tsin & gravé sur la pierre". *Le journal des sçavans*, Juin 1760: 342-352.

Vondrovec, Klaus. 2010. "Coinage of the Nezak". In: Alram, Michael; Klimburg-Salter, Deborah; Inaba, Minoru; Pfisterer, Matthias (eds.). *Coins, Art and Chronology II: The First Millenium C.E. in the Indo-Iranian Borderland*. Wien: Verlag der Österreichischen Akademie der Wissenschaften: 169-187.

Watters, Thomas. 1904-05. *On Yuan Chwang's Travels in India*. 2 vols. London: Royal Asiatic Society.

Winkler, Dietmar W.; Tang, Li. 2009: *Hidden Treasures and Intercultural Encounters. Studies on East Syriac Christianity in China and Central Asia*. Wien, Münster: LIT Verlag (orientalia – patristica – oecumenica, Vol.1).

16 Epigraphica Nestoriana Serica (II)*

Samuel N. C. Lieu 刘南强
FRAS, FRHistS, FSA, FAHA
Inaugural Distinguished Professor (Ancient History)
Macquarie University, Sydney, Australia

16.1 Background

In 2009 I published in the Festschrift of Professor Nicholas Sims-Williams FBA an article on the bilingual aspects of the famous Nestorian Monument from Xi'an (*Da Qin Jingjiao liuxing Zhongguo bei* 大秦景教流行中国碑 'Stele on the diffusion of the 'Luminous' Religion of Da Qin (i.e. the Church of the East, more popularly known as Nestorian Christians) in the Middle Kingdom (i.e. China)').[1] My 2009 article is intended to be the first of an ongoing series of studies contributing to a new edition and translation of this seminal epigraphical text together with a full commentary - linguistic, historical and theological. The research for these studies is carried out under the aegis of an international and inter-academy collaborative project: 'China and the Mediterranean World - archaeological sources and literary documents up to the 10th Century CE (La Chine et le Monde Méditerranéen:

* The author is grateful for financial support for the research for this article from the Australian Research Council and from the Chiang Ching Kuo Foundation for Scholarly Exchange.

[1] S.N.C. Lieu, "Epigraphica Nestoriana Serica" in W. Sundermann, A. Hintze, F. de Blois (eds.) *Exegisti Monumenta. Festschrift in Honour of Nicholas Sims-Williams*. Iranica 17 (Wiesbaden 2009, 227–246.

sources archéologiques et documents écrits jusqu' au 10e siècle)'sponsored by the Union Académique Internationale (International Union of Academies) and of which I am the current co-ordinator. A bilingual (English and Chinese) web-page detailing the aims of the project can be found at: http://www.vitterhetsakad.se/uai

The official statement on the project is as follows:

> The UAI has decided to launch this project (in collaboration with the Chinese Academy of Social Sciences and any academy who would like to participate). The aim of the project is to produce a series of volumes, which will demonstrate the mutual knowledge of the respective cultures during these periods, the mutual relations between them and influence they exerted on each other. The time frame shall be from ancient times until the Tang Dynasty in China.
>
> Volumes shall be produced which document mutual contacts and influence, but there shall also be publications containing studies of more synthetic character.
>
> Concrete tasks shall be (i) to collect a corpus of European, Chinese and Central Asian texts, which contain references to the other culture, and publish these in their original as well in translations into Chinese, English and French; (ii) to publish archaeological charts of objects from one culture found in another culture: silver and gold objects, pottery ceramics, silk, numismatic objects etc.; (iii) to produce synthetic studies of cultural, religious, philosophical, social and linguistic influence of one culture upon the other. This project was adopted by the UAI in 2004 as a category B Project.

The main results of the project which had received funding from both the Australian Research Council and from the Chiang Ching Kuo Foundation for Scholarly Exchange from 2010-2012 can be found at the 'SERICA' website: http://www.mq.edu.au/research/centres_and_groups/ancient_cultures_research_

centre/ research/ cultural_ ex_ silkroad/serica/

As epigraphical evidence, i.e. data from inscriptions, is of paramount importance to the project, the research team based at Macquarie University, Sydney (Australia), under my direction has chosen a number of inscriptions to showcase the genre. The Xi'an Monument, the most 'Roman' of all documents discovered in China, deserves pride of place as it is more than a long and well preserved Chinese inscription. It includes also lists of proper-names and titles as well as colophons giving important historical details in the Syriac language – a Semitic language comprehensible to many Romans and Byzantines from Syria and Christians in regions beyond the Euphrates, especially those in Sasanian Iran and in South India. Since the publication of my article in 2009, a number of important studies germane to the topic had appeared and I also had the opportunity to report on my findings at international conferences and discuss them with a number of leading scholars. I have therefore decided to honour the lifetime contribution of Professor Lin Wushu to the history of Iranian religions in China with further thoughts on some of the issues I raised in my 2009 study and also to report on the progress in the preparation of the edition and translation of the text of the monument for on-line publication. I would also like to express here my personal thanks and those of my wife, Professor Judith Lieu, currently Lady Margaret's Professor of Divinity at the University of Cambridge, to Professor Lin and his family for their generous hospitality and kindness to us and our daughter during our two visits to China in the 1980s.

16.2 Text and Translation

The 'Nestorian Monument', as we all know, is now exhibited at the Xi'an Forest of Inscribed Stelae Museum (*Xi'an beilin bowuguan* 西安碑林博物

馆) which is part of the Shanxi (or Shaanxi) Provincial Museum (*Shanxisheng bowuguan* 陕西省博物馆). Since its discovery *circa* 1623 CE,[1] the text of the 'Nestorian Monument' has no shortage of translations into European languages although printed editions of the Chinese (and Syriac) are considerably fewer in comparison. Of the translations listed below (in chronological order according date of first publication) only those by Legge, Saeki and Pelliot are accompanied by editions of the original Chinese text and the text-edition accompanying the translation of Pelliot does not give the sections in Syriac:

Legge, J. *The Nestorian monument of Hsî-an fû in Shen-hsî, China: relating to the diffusion of Christianity in China in the seventh and eighth centuries with the Chinese text of the inscription, a translation, and notes, and a lecture on the monument, with a sketch of subsequent Christian missions in China* (London, 1888), pp. 2-31.

Wylie, A. *apud* Charles F. Horne, ed., *The Sacred Books and Early Literature of the East*, Vol. XII, *Medieval China* (New York, 1917), pp. 381-392.

Moule, A.C. *Christians in China before the Year* 1550 (London, 1930), pp. 35-52.

Foster, J. *The Church of the T'ang Dynasty* (London, 1939) pp. 134-151.

Saeki, P.S. *The Nestorian Monuments and Relics in China* (Tokyo, 1937, revised, 1951), pp. 320-33, and Chinese Text Section, pp. 1-13.

Pelliot, P. *L'Inscription nestorienne de Si-ngan-fou*, edited with supplements by A. Forte (Kyoto-Paris, 1996), pp. 173-180 and 497-503 (Chinese text).

[1] For an excellent study of the impact of the discovery on western attitude to China and her culture see M. Keevak, *The Story of a Stele: China's Nestorian Monument and Its Reception in the West, 1625–1916* (Hong Kong, 2008).

Palmer, M. *The Jesus Sutras – Rediscovering the lost religion of Taoist Christianity* (London, 2001), pp. 224-32.

Xu Longfei, *Die Nestorianische Stele in Xi'an. Begegnung von Christentum und chinesischer Kultur* (Bonn, 2004), pp. 95-101.

Fortunately rubbings of the text of the inscription (of both Chinese and Syriac sections) are on sale at the souvenir shop of the museum. As the rubbing is a faithful reproduction of the original inscribed text, it is of immeasurable value to scholars who need regular access to the text in Chinese and Syriac scripts. As the inscribed lines of the main (i.e. Chinese) part of the inscription are exceedingly long, a photographic reproduction of the text is of limited value to scholars. A recent edition of the text in a Chinese publication including segmented photographic reproductions of the text is fiendishly difficult to consult as the vertically inscribed lines are not numbered at the top of each photograph.[1] The need to arrive at an agreed system of numbering of the lines of the text, both Chinese and Syriac, has long been felt. The translation of Pelliot is the only modern one that includes line-numbers (in egregious Roman numerals) and the same applies to the appended text of original in Chinese script. As Pelliot's translation and edition is still little used by scholars in China because the translation and commentary are both in French, I have made available on-line a preliminary edition of the original Chinese and Syriac text based on that of Saeki and my own copy of the rubbing of the inscription with the same line numbers as given in Pelliot's translation and edition but in less obtrusive Arabic numerals. This can now be found under 'Inscriptions' at the SERICA website at:

---

〔1〕Lu Yuan 路远, *Jingjiao yu Jingjiao bei* 景教与"景教碑" (Nestorianism and the "Nestorian Monument") (Xi'an, 2009) 330–348. I am grateful to Dr Sally Church, Fellow of Wolfson College Cambridge, for drawing my attention to this recently republished and important work on the history of the Church of the East in China and for lending me her own copy of the work.

http://www.mq.edu.au/research/centres_and_groups/ancient_cultures_research_centre/research/cultural_ex_silkroad/serica/inscriptions/

As the accompanying text in Pelliot's posthumously published volume does not include the sections of the text in Syriac, I have ventured to number the latter in my 'on-line' edition with capital letter 'S' (for Syriac) before the line-numbers also in Arabic numerals. I have used standard transliteration for the Syriac text rather than experimenting with Estrangelo fonts as the transliterated version in uni-code will permit easy word-searches. The SERICA research team at Macquarie University has currently applied for funding from the Chiang Ching Kuo Foundation for International Scholarly Exchange to compile a lexical index / concordance (covering both the Chinese and Syriac texts) of this important bilingual text with the intention of expanding such a research tool to cover eventually all Chinese and Syriac texts and inscriptions of 'Nestorian' (i.e. Church of the East) provenance found in China.

16.3 Fapshy, Papshy or Fapsh' = Fashi 法师?

The Syriac text of the inscription, consisting mainly of names and titles,[1] could have been read with ease by a Syriac-speaking Christian except for a small number of place-names which will be discussed later in this study. Two titles, though, which might have caused problems had their meanings not been provided by someone who knew them are P'PŠY or P'PŠ' in line (S)1 and ŠY'NGTSW' in line (S)64 of the Syriac respectively. There is general agreement on the latter as transliteration for the Chinese term *shang-zuo* 上座"(on) high seat" (i.e. office of an abbot). Scholarly opinion,

[1] On proper names in Syriac found on the 'Monument' and other Christian texts from the Tang period see now the important study of Hidemi Takahashi, 'Transcribed Proper Names in Chinese Syriac Christian Documents' in G.A. Kiraz (ed.) *Malphono w-Rabo d-Malphone. Studies in honor of Sebastian P. Brock* (Piscataway NJ, 2008), 631–662.

however, is still very divided over the first title occupying an eminent position at the beginning of the text.

The two most common explanations of this puzzling word in Syriac script are:

(1) It is a transliteration of the commonly encountered Chinese religious title *fashi* 法师 (lit. 'teacher *or* master of the law'). For such a solution to work, a reading of P'PŠY is preferable to P'PŠ'. However, as I have pointed out in my earlier study,[1] I made a close inspection of the relevant word on the 'Monument' itself when I visited Xi'an in 2007, and I am fairly certain that the inscribed text gives P'PŠ' and not P'PŠY. It is not impossible that the stone-cutter or epigrapher had made a mistake as it is very easy to confuse a final –y (Yūdh) with a final -' ('Ē) in the Estrangelo Syriac script in which the Syriac text on the 'Monument' was inscribed. On the other hand, the inscriber made few, if any, mistakes in inscribing the Syriac text on the 'Monument'. But if he was not proficient the Syriac language, then mistakes could not have been completely prevented and once a mistake was made on the stone itself, it would have been next to impossible to make corrections. There is also the annoying problem of the medial –P- which is completely redundant to the phonetic transliteration of the Chinese term *fashi*. Moule, a strong proponent of the *fashi* solution, states in a foot-note: 'Dr L.D. Barnett has very kindly found the sounds in question written *phab shi* in a contemporary bilingual MS in the Stein collection.'[2] Unfortunately Moule did not tell us what languages were used in this bilingual text nor did he give us its manuscript signature.

(2) P'PŠ' is a variant form of the Syriac title P'P'S, i.e. 'Pope' (<Gr. πάππας <Lat. *Papa*). Such a solution certainly fits the context as its holder Adam (Chin. Jingqing 景清) was effectively the Archbishop of China

[1] Lieu, *op. cit.* 230.

[2] A.C. Moule, *Christians in China before the Year 1550* (London, 1930), 35, n. 12.

(CYN(Y)STN *v. infra*).[1] I was inclined towards accepting such a solution in my earlier study because of the double 'P' in the transliterated form of the title. The title of 'Papa (i.e. Pope) of China' would have been highly suitable for a cleric made very senior by the geographical coincidence of his archdiocese with a vast empire (i.e. Tang China) and its isolation from the main body of the Church of the East. However, for a completely normal Syriac title (i.e. P'P'S) to appear in such an unconventional manner (i.e. P'PŠ'), a historical explanation is needed and I have surmised that the original Syriac term P'P' or P'P'S was transliterated into Chinese at an early stage of the diffusion of Syriac Christianity in China. The title took root in the Chinese language of the Church of the East and it was this 'native' Chinese form (now lost) that found its way back into the Syriac text inscribed on the 'Monument'. However, I also drew attention to another problem in adopting the Papas-solution viz. that the form of the 'pontifical' title P'P'S is derived originally from Greek (πάππας) and the final -ς in the title would normally have been transliterated into the Syriac script with an S and not with a Š.[2] The problematic use of the Š in P'PŠY / P'PŠ' and the addition of what appears to be a suffix (either –y or –') remain almost impossible to explain unless the title had been adopted into a language which employs suffices before being re-transliterated into Syriac.

Since 2009, I have discussed the 'Papa(s)' solution with a number of scholars in Syriac studies and a problem which quickly surfaced from these discussions concerns the very late date of the 'Monument' (erected in 781 CE) for the use of the term P'P' in Syriac as a title for a senior bishop of the

[1] On translating the title as 'papas of China' see E.C.D. Hunter, 'The Persian contribution to Christianity in China' in D.W. Winkler and Tang Li 唐莉 (eds.) *Hidden Treasures and Intercultural Encounters. Studies on East Syriac Christianity in China and Central Asia* = Orientalia–Patristica–Oecumenica 1 (Vienna and Münster, 2009) 73. For earlier discussions see Saeki, *op. cit.* 82–83 and for a useful summary of different views among Chinese scholars see Lu Yuan, *op. cit.*, 101–02.

[2] Lieu, *op. cit.*, 230.

Church of the East. In my earlier article I have suggested that P'PŠ' might have been transliteration for the Chinese term *fazhu* 法主 (lit. 'Lord of Law') which is used to translate the term Patriarch (Syr. PṬRYRKYS) in a bilingual section of the 'Monument'[1] - a title still in use for the most senior cleric of the Greek Orthodox Church with virtual papal status – would have well suited the position of Adam as the head of the Church of the East in China. However it remains hard to explain why the monk who scripted the Syriac sections of the inscription and who was obviously a Syriac-speaker did not simply write PṬRYRKYS, i.e. the conventional form for Patriarch, as he had done on the second line of the Syriac text on the 'Monument'. His intended readership would have almost certainly been Syriac-speaking and he would have only used a non-Syriac term unless the relevant title had become so Sinicized that it had to be 're-transliterated' into the Syriac from the Chinese.

Sinological scholars with whom I had discussed the issue cautioned against abandoning the *fashi*-solution too readily. There is no doubt that P'PŠ' or P'PŠY is not a conventional Syriac word and to see it as a corruption or variant of P'P'S or P'P' begs too many questions both scribal and linguistic and it is easier to explain it as the phonetic transliteration of a Chinese term. The term *fashi* is widely used of priests in a variety of religions in China and had come to be seen as a reverential rather than status term. It is therefore not out of place for Adam to be styled '*the* priest of China' and using a term which is of Chinese origin to underscore the fact that it was over the Church of the East *in China* that he exercised his authority.

---

[1] Line 2 of the Syriac text of the 'Monument'. See Saeki, *op. cit.* ('The Chinese Text' section) 9. Cf. Lieu, *op. cit.* 230–31.

16.4 Ṣyn(y)stan, Kwmd'n and Srg

The Syriac part of the document contains three place-names which are of Iranian origin, viz. ṢYNST'N, KWMD'N and SRG. All three are attested with more or less the same spelling in the second of the so-called 'Ancient Sogdian Letters' (British Library Ms. Or. 8212/95) composed by Sogdian merchants between 307 and 311 CE.[1] The letters were and found in 1907 by Aurel Stein in a Chinese watch-tower just west of the Jade Gate, a fortified outpost guarding the western approaches to the Dunhuang 敦煌[2] – a name which though famous among the Chinese as the gate-way to the Silk Road was probably of foreign origin.[3] The collection consisted of a small dossier of five letters written to friends and relatives at Loulan and Samarkand by Sogdian merchants who traded along the land-routes between Loulan 楼兰 (Sogd. *kr'wr'n*) and a number of key Chinese cities including Dunhuang (Sogd. *drw''n*),[4] Luoyang 洛阳 (Sogd. *srγ*),[5] Chang'an 长安 (Sogd. *'xwmt'n*),[6] Guzang (Sogd. *kc'n*),[7] Yeh 邺 (Sogd. *'nkp'*), Jiuquan

〔1〕Ed. and trans. N. Sims-Williams, 'The Ancient Sogdian Letter II', in M.G. Schmidt and W. Bisang (eds.) Philologica et Linguistica – Historia, Pluralitas, Universitas. Festschrift für Helmut Humbach zum 80. Geburtstag am 4 Dezember 2001 (Trier, 2001), 267–280.

〔2〕The standard edition of all five letters remains H. Reichelt (ed.), *Die soghdischen Handschriften-reste des Britischen Museums*, 2 vols. (Heidelberg, 1928–1931), ii, 1–35. New editions of the letters are currently being published by Prof. Nicholas Sims-Williams. Colour photographs of the manuscript of Letter II can be found in A. L. Juliano & J. A. Lerner, *Monks and Merchants: Silk Road Treasures from Northwest China* (London and New York, 2001) 47–48. On the dating of the letters see F. Grenet and N. Sims-Williams, "The historical context of the Sogdian Ancient Letters", in *Transition periods in Iranian history, Actes du Symposium de Fribourg-en-Brisgau (22–24 Mai 1985)* (Leuven, 1987) 101–122.

〔3〕On the various forms of the name see J. Harmatta, 'Origin of the name Tun-huang', in A. Cadonna, *Turfan and Tun-huang: The Texts – Encounter of Civilizations on the Silk Route*, Orientalia Venetiana IV (Florence, 1992) 15–20.

〔4〕Ancient Letters II.23, ed. cit. 270.

〔5〕*Anc. Lett.* II.11, 268.

〔6〕*Anc. Lett.* II.15, 268.

〔7〕*Anc. Lett.* II.6, 268.

酒泉 (Sogd. *cwcn*)[1] and Jincheng 金城 (Sogd. *kmzyn*).[2]

The Syriac part of the inscription interestingly uses two names for China. The first of these, ZŸNY' which is found on line 12 of the Syriac,[3] is abridgement for *bt zÿny'* ('the land of the Chins') which is standard designation for China in Syriac literature.[4] More prominent however is the form ṢYN(Y)ST'N which is given on line 1 of the Syriac at the head of the document as part of the title of Adam and which is clear from its ending that it was of Iranian, especially Sogdian, origin. While there is little doubt that Sogdian *cyn(y)stn* and the Syriac *ṣyn(y)st'n* both designate China, there is some reluctance among Chinese scholars in embracing the generally accepted supposition that the '*cyn-*' part of the state-name is derived from the notorious but powerful, albeit short-lived, Qin 秦 (Ch'in in Wade-Giles System) Dynasty (221–206 BCE) and thereby admitting that the most popular modern western names for the Middle Kingdom (i.e. China, Chine, Cina, Kina) too were all derived from the dynastic title of the Qin (Ch'in) Empire. Most Chinese scholars simply translate *cyn(y)stn* as Zhongguo 中国 'Middle Kingdom' – the official title of China which is stated in large characters in the header of the 'Monument'. Some scholars have ventured to transliterate it, and to my mind correctly, as Qinisitan 秦尼斯坦.[5] However, one alternative suggestion is that *cynst'n* is derived phonetically not from the Qin Dynasty but Jinguo 晋国 i.e. 'State of Jin'[6] (265–420 CE) – Jin being the title of the dynasty ruling at the time when the 'Ancient

[1] *Anc. Lett.* II.5, 268.

[2] *Anc. Lett.* II.23, 270.

[3] Line S12 = line 11 of the edition of the text of Saeki. See Saeki, *op. cit.* ('The Chinese Text' section) 11.

[4] Cf. Lieu, *op. cit.,* 231–232.

[5] Lu Yuan, *op. cit.*, 100.

[6] Suggested by Wang Jiqing 王冀青 *ap.* Bi Bo 毕波, 'Sutewen gu xinzha Hanyi yu zhushi 粟特文古信劄汉译与注释 (Ancient epistolary document in Sogdian language: Chinese translation and commnetary)', *Wenshi* 文史 67 (2004/ii) 82.

Sogdian Letters' were written. However, attention must be drawn to an important article by the late Dr James Hamilton in which has convincingly demonstrated that the title of Qin 秦 totally dominated the nomenclature for China in Central Asian languages and even seemingly unrelated but popular names such as *Seres* ('People of Silk') and *Serica* ('Land of Silk') in Latin and *Σῆρες* ('People of Silk') and *Σηρική* ('Land of Silk') in Greek all derive ultimately from Qin 秦 and not from the Chinese word for silk (*si* 丝) because of the final -n/-r switch frequently encountered in Central Asian languages.[1] While the term Qinren 秦人 'men of Qin' is not as commonly attested as Hanren 汉人 'men of Han' (i.e. a Chinese), it is nevertheless found in ancient Chinese texts[2] and the terms *Qinshamen* 秦沙门 'monk from Qin' and *Qin(wen)* 秦(文) 'the Qin = Chinese (language)' are found in a collection Buddhist colophons from the 4th to the 5th Centuries CE and in contexts which unambiguously involve the state or language of China.[3]

Also unmistakably Sogdian are the names of the two Chinese capital cities of Chang'an 长安 (Syr. *kwmd'n* <Sogd. *'xwmt'n*) and Luoyang (Syr. *srg* <Sogd. *srγ*) given in the Syriac part of the inscription – names which are also found in the Ancient Sogdian Letters.[4] As the name of a major city in China, *kwmd'n* has long been known to Western scholars through the

[1] J. Hamilton, 'East-West Borrowings via the Silk Road of Textile Terms', in Diogenes – A quarterly publication of the International Council for Philosophy and Humanistic Studies 171 (1995) 25–33.

[2] Cf. P. Pelliot, *Notes on Marco Polo*, I (Paris, 1959) 264–45.

[3] *Taishō shinshu daizōkyō* 大正新修大藏经 (Tokyo, 1936–) 55.64c29: 秦沙门道养; 64c4: 转胡为秦. The brief revival of (Later) Qin 后秦 as a dynastic title from 399–416 during the Five Dynasties and Sixteen Kingdoms period (304–439 CE) might have helped to perpetuate the equation of Qin = China and the Chinese. On this see Tsui Chung-hui, *A study of early Buddhist scriptural calligraphy: based on Buddhist manuscripts found in Dunhuang and Turfan (3–5 century),* (PhD Hong Kong University, 2012) 135.

[4] On Sogdian names of the Chinese principal Silk Road cities see N. Sims-Williams, 'Towards a new edition of the Sogdian Ancient Letter I', in E. de la Vaissière and E. Trombert (eds.), *Les Sogdiens en Chine*, Études Thématiques 17 (Paris, 2005), 181.

Byzantine historian Theophylactus Simocattes who in his history of the reign of the Emperor Maurice composed in the early 7th C. CE tells us that according to his Turkish sources Chubdan (Gr. *Χουβδάν*) was the local name for a major city in China (Gr. *Ταυγάστ* <Turk. Tawγast) founded by Alexander the Great![1] The Greek form of the name *Χουβδάν* (which has a manuscriptal variant: *Χουμαδάν*) is an excellent example of the b/m switch due to nassalisation widely attested in Altaic languages. Chumbdan (Sogd. *'xwmt'n* or *γwmt'n*),[2] however, is clearly not a phonetic transliteration of the Chinese name Chang'an – the western capital of Tang China - but most scholars are agreed that it was the transliteration of Xianyang 咸阳, the capital of the more ancient Qin Dynasty (221−206 BCE) which was situated only a few kilometres upstream (west) from Chang'an.[3]

For Luoyang 洛阳 the Eastern capital of Tang China in the modern Henan 河南 Province, and the seat of a Chorepiscopos of the Church of the East, the Syriac text of the 'Monument' gives *SRG* which is identical to *srγ*, the standard form for Luoyang in Sogdian.[4] Given her great importance as the final terminus of the Silk Road, the presence of a Nestorian community in the capital city of Luoyang has long been assumed

[1] Theophylcatus Simocattes, *Historiae*, VII,9,8–9. Text and translation in J. Sheldon (trans.) G. Coedès, *Texts of Greek and Latin Authors on the Far East From the 4th C. B.C.E. to the 14th C. CE,* Studia Antiqua Australiensia 4 (Turnhout, 2010) 137.

[2] The adjectival form *γwmt'ncw* is found in É. Benveniste (Ed. and trans.) *Textes sogdiens* (Mission Pelliot en Asie Centrale, 3. Série, Paris 1940), Vol. 2, 58, Texte 2, line 1233.

[3] E. de la Vaissière (translated by J. Ward), *Sogdian Traders – A History* (Handbuch der Orientalistik, Section 8, Vol. 10; Leiden 2005), 22. See also Moule, *Christians* 48–49, note 45.

[4] The Sogdian version of the name srγ is found in Buddhist Sogdian writings in the form of srγc'nch knδh 'the town of Saraγ'. Cf. *Sūtra of the condemnation of intoxicating drink*, l.34, ed. D.N. Mackenzie (ed. and trans.), *The Budhist Sogdian Texts of the British Library*, Acta Iranica 3 (Leiden–Teheran, 1976), 10. Cf. I. Gershevitch, *A Grammar of Manichaean Sogdian*, Publication of the Philological Society (London, 1954) 156 (§1023).

by scholars.[1] The close connection between the Church of the East and Sogdian mercantile settlements in Tang China is now confirmed by the historical information provided by the newly discovered stele from Luoyang.[2] Like Khumdan, the Sogdian toponym *S(a)r(a)γ* bears little phonetic relation to the original Chinese city-name of Luoyang. Paul Pelliot has suggested that *Saraγ* might have been a phonetic transliteration of the 'luo'part of Luoyang[3] but such a suggestion cannot explain the initial s- unless the Sogdians had experienced difficulty in pronouncing the initial *l*- of the Chinese name and had to transliterate the name *Luoyang* orally into something like *(s)l'a(n)g*. An alternative way of solving the problem is to discover if Luoyang had been historically associated with another name, especially one that might have been in use when the Sogdians first came to know the city through trade. For much of its long history Luoyang was in the prefecture of Henan 河南 and the modern city with the same name is still in a province also with the same name – the association of Luoyang with Henan is therefore of long duration. However, at some point in its long history, the prefecture of Henan was called Sizhou 司州 which under the Jin Dynasty, the period of the Ancient Sogdian Letters, was also known as

〔1〕The discovery of one or more inscribed document similar to the Nestorian Monument from other major Tang cities had already been predicted by a leading scholar of Sino-Western relations more than eighty years ago. Cf. Feng Chengjun 冯承钧, *Jingjiaobei kao* 景教碑考 (*Study on the Nestorian Monument*) (Shanghai 1931) 60.

〔2〕Cf. Zhang Naizhu 张乃翥 "Ba Luoyang xin chutude yi jian Tangdai Jingjiao shike 跋洛阳新出土的一件唐代景教石刻" (*Xiyu yanjiu* 西域研究 2007/1, 65–73). 65f. English translation by P. de Laurentis, "Notes on a Nestorian Stone Inscription from the Tang Dynasty Recently Unearthed in Luoyang", in: Ge Chengyong 葛承雍 (Ed.) *Jingjiao yizhen* 景教遗珍 (Precious Nestorian Relic), *Luoyang xinchu Tangdai jingjiao jingchuang yanjiu* 洛阳新出唐代景教幢研究 (Studies on the Nestorian Stone Pillar of the Tang Dynasty Recently Discovered in Luoyang), Beijing 2009, 17–33) 17–18. For the text and English translation see Tang Li 唐莉, 'A Preliminary Study on the Jingjiao Inscription of Luoyang: Text, Analysis, Commentary and English Translation', in Winkler and Tang (eds.) *op. cit.*, 108–132.

〔3〕P. Pelliot, 'L'évêché nestorien de Khumdan et Sarag', *T'oung-pao*, 25 (1928) 91. See also Moule, *op. cit.*, 48–49, note 45.

Sili 司隸.[1] While Sili bears greater phonetic resemblance to Saraγ than Luoyang, its association with Luoyang is tenuous and short-lived and it will not be easy to argue at this stage of our knowledge for a direct onomastic link between Sili and Saraγ. However, we have no idea how *srγ* was vocalized in Sogdian and in Sili we do have the possibility of a new line of historical and linguistic inquiry.

16.5 Jingjiao and Tarsā(g)

In my 2009 study I have made the bold suggestion that the character *jing* 景 in the official title of the Church of the East in China which is often translated as 'luminous' was originally a calque for a Chinese word meaning 'fear' as Christians in Central Asia had long been known by the Middle Persian name of *tarsāg,* Christian Sogdian *ṯrs'q* or New Persian *tarsā* 'fearer, shaker'.[2] Shortly after my article was published, I was able to elaborate on my hypothesis with further supporting evidence in a conference paper delivered to the Third International Conference: 'Research on the Church of the East in China and Central Asia' held in Salzburg in 2009.[3] I am grateful to the many positive comments on my main hypothesis – especially to Dr Penelope Riboud for pointing out to the participants of the conference in her own lecture that the character *xian* 祆 used for Zoroastrianism in Tang China is a specially devised character used to transliterate the Middle Persian word *dyn* 'religion'. The term *tarsā* is

[1] Cf. Shi Jangru 石璋如 *et al.* (eds.) *Zhong-guo li shi di li* 中国历史地理, 3 vols. (Taibei, 1954), i, 278c.

[2] Lieu, *op. cit*. 241–46. NB error on p. 24, line 18 – delete the term '*jing ming* 景命' from the list of terms with the word *jing* 景 as it was not used in a theological or ascetical sense in the context of the 'Monument'. On different forms of the word *tarsāg* in Middle Iranian languages see Gershevitch, *op. cit.*, 150 (§990).

[3] S.N.C. Lieu, 'The 'Romanitas' of the Xi'an Inscription', has appeared in Tang Li 唐莉 and D. W. Winkler (eds.), *From the Oxus River to the Chinese Shores: Studies on East Syriac Christianity in China and Central Asia* (Vienna and Münster, 2013) [Publication announced on 5th February 2013, *non vidi.*] .

found in phonetic transliteration in the Chinese text of the 'Monument': *dasuo* 达娑 and in a literary context which draws direct comparison between it and the *jingshi* 景士 i.e. priests of the *jing* teaching:[1]

> Among the dasuo 达娑 (*tarsā*) with their rule of purity, such excellence has not yet been heard of; but we see this among the white-robed *jingshi* 景士.

What amazed me was that the term *tarsā* remained in vogue as a designation for Christians who had come to China from Central Asia right down to Modern period. On 26th July 1605, after a long and seemingly unfruitful search for the survival of Christian communities at Kaifengfu 开封府 where there was still a thriving Jewish community with its own synagogue, Matteo Ricci wrote:[2]

> A few days ago we came to know for certain that there have been a good number of Christians in China for the past five hundred years and that there are still considerable traces of them in many places. ... Now we know that in the middle of China, half a month from here and the same distance from Nanchino (*Nanjing*), in the province of Honan (*Henan*) and in the capital which is called Caifun fu (*Kaifengfu*) there are five or six families of Christians who have now lost almost all the

---

[1] *Xi'an Monument* (Chin.) l. 26, ed. Saeki, *op. cit.* ('The Chinese Text' section) 8; trans. Moule, *op. cit.*, 45 (altered).

[2] Matteo Ricci, *Lettere (1580–1609)*, in P. Corradini and F. D'Arelli (eds.) *Lettere (1580–1609) Matteo Ricci* (Macerata, 2001) 412–13: Puochi giorni sono venessimo a sapere per cosa certa che dentro della Cina, vi fu da cinquecento anni in qua buon numero de christiani, e che anocora ve ne resta grande vestigio in molti luoghi. ... Adesso sapessimo che nel mezzo della Cina, longi da qui mezzo mese, et altre tanto di Nanchino, nella provincia di Honan, e nella metropoli che si chiama Caifun fu, vi sono cinque o sei era di christianità, per avere già parecchi anni che della chiesa fecero tempio di un iolo, che si chiama Quanguam. Quello che ci impeditte a saperlo sin hora fu non si nominare loro per nome de christiani, ma per gente de *Terza*; pare nome del regno donde vennero alla Cina, e dalla lege de *xezu*, che vuol dire della lettera di dieci, che nella lettera cina è una croce perfetta, di questo mono +; perché nella figura e fisonomia del viso e in non adorar idoli erano simili ai Mori e Giudei; solo erano diversi, che mangiavano carne di porco ed ogni carne, facendoli sopra di essa una croce con la mano. English translation by Moule, *op. cit.*, 6–7 (all words in Chinese have been given in *Pinyin* in the translation cited above).

little Christianity they had, because several years ago they turned the church into the temple of an idol called *Quanguam* (*Guanwang*, i.e. Guan Yu). What has hindered us from knowing of them until now is that they are not called by their race of *Terza* (i.e. *Tarsā*), which seems to be the name of the country from which they came to China, and by the religion of the *xezu* (*shizi*), which means 'of the sign of ten' which in Chinese writing is a perfect cross like this †; for in appearance and features and in not worshipping idols they were like the Moors and Jews and were only distinguished by the fact that they ate pork and all kinds of flesh, making over it a cross with the hand.

This important reference to the survival of both the Christian community in Kaifengfu and its use of the term *Tarsā* as its mark of identity, now studied mainly by scholars of Matteo Ricci[1] rather than of the Church of the East in China, would have further strengthened my faith in my hypothesis that the character *jing* is a calque for *tarsā* had I discovered it earlier.

16.6 Nestorian Inscriptions from Yangzhou (扬州) and Quanzhou (泉州)

It was my original intention to include a second section in my 2009 study detailing some of the research conducted by an Australian team of scholars under my direction which had visited China on a regular basis between 2000 and 2008 to conduct research on Christian (both Nestorian and Catholic) and Manichaean Remains in Quanzhou 泉州 and neighbouring Jinjiang 晋江, both in the Province of Fujian 福建, as well as the

〔1〕See e.g. the important and highly informative study of A. Dudink, 'Zhang Geng, Christian Convert of Late Ming Times: Descendant of Nestorian Christians?', in C. Jami and H. Delahaye (eds.), *L'Europe en Chine: interactions scientifiques, religieuses et culturelles aux XVIIe et XVIIIe siècles: actes du colloque de la Fondation Hugot (14–17 octobre 1991)* (Paris, 1993), 57–86.

results of a short visit by the team to Yangzhou 扬州. I wished in particular to discuss the emblematic and problematic term *Yelikewen* 也里可温 which was widely used to designate the Church of the East in Chinese sources. However, lack of time prevented me from completing the section on time, hence the enigmatic and misleading footnote 71 on p. 245: 'On the probable derivation of the term (i.e. *Yelikewen*) see below' which refers unfortunately to the deleted second part of the article.

In 2008, the Australian team visited Yangzhou 扬州 and Quanzhou, both being important centres of the Church of the East (Nestorian Christianity) under Mongol rule. At Yangzhou, the team was able to view the bilingual (Turco-Syriac and Chinese) tombstone of 'Lady' Elizabeth (Chin. *yelishiba* 也里世八) (*d.* 20th May 1317), one of the best-preserved examples of Nestorian epigraphy and first discovered on 14 November 1981.[1] Editions and translations of the text have been published by Professor Geng Shimin 耿世民[2] and by Professor Niu Ruji 牛汝极.[3] It soon became obvious to me from discussing the history of the discovery of the inscription with Mr. Zhang Zhijun 张志军, the Deputy-Director of the Storage Department of the Yangzhou Museum which had just moved to its new premises, that ours was the first 'Western'-trained research team to have actually viewed this much cited and oft reproduced tomb-stone in person. Professor Majella Franzmann, the chief Syriac epigraphist of the

〔1〕Wang Qinjin 王勤金, 'Yuan yanyou sinian yelishiba mubei kaoshi 元延祐四年也里世八墓碑考释 (Research on the epitaph of Elizabeth (Yelishiba) from the fourth year of the Yanyou Reign-Period)', *Kaogu* 考古, 1989, pt. 6, 553–554 and 573. A photograph of the squeeze is given on p. 554.

〔2〕Cf. Geng Shimin, H.-J. Klimkeit and J.-P. Laut, 'Eine neue nestorianische Grabinschrift aus China', *Ural-altaistische Jahrbücher* 14 (1996) 164–75, and Geng Shimin, 'Reexamination of the Nestorian Inscription from Yangzhou' in R. Malek (ed.), *Jingjiao – The Church of the East in China and Central Asia,* Collectanea Serica (Sankt Augustin, 2006), 243–56.

〔3〕Niu Ruji 牛汝极, *Weiwuer guwenzi yu guwenxian daolun* 维吾尔古文字与古文献道论 (*Research Studies on Old Uighur Language and Documents*) (Ürümqi 1996), 119–26, and idem, 'Nestorian inscriptions from China (13th–14th C.)' in Malek (ed.), *op. cit.* 232–33.

team, therefore carefully checked the published text of Geng against the inscription itself and she quickly noticed that the last word on the third line is not the commonly attested Turkish word S'KYŠ or S'QYŠ 'reckoning' (in a calendrical sense) but the less common word S'NY which has a similar meaning.[1] The team's new reading, approved by Professor Peter Zieme, has now been published in its final report on Christian and Manichaean remains in Quanzhou[2] and the new reading should be quite clear to all who can read the Estrangelo Syriac script from the colour photograph of the inscribed stone taken by Dr Gunner Mikkelsen which the team has now also published.[3] Even though only one new reading was made, it nevertheless demonstrates the need to examine inscriptions in person and not to rely entirely on published photographs of squeezes. It is also necessary to draw special attention to the team's emended new text of a famous Christian inscription from Yangzhou as it is published in a collection otherwise devoted totally to epigraphical finds from Quanzhou.

As for *Yelikewen*, my original intention was to draw attention to the important discovery made by Professor Peter Zieme of the equivalent word in a Syro-Turkic text and to explore the possibility that, like the character *jing*, it too might have etymologically or historical links with the word *tarsā(g)*. The text in question is a blessing-formula used at weddings by Turkish-speaking Christians and in this the term occurs first in line 7 of the Verso as 'RK'GWN (*ärkägün*) and in line 13 in the abridged as 'RK (*ärk*).[4]

---

[1] Cf. G. Clauson, An Etymological Dictionary of Pre-Thirteenth-Century Turkish (Oxford, 1972) 830-31 (s.v. sa:n).

[2] S.N.C. Lieu, L. Eccles, M. Franzmann, I. Gardner and K. Parry, *Medieval Christian and Manichaean Remains from Quanzhou (Zayton)*, Corpus Fontium Manichaeorum: Series Archaeologica et Iconographica 2 (Brepols, 2012) 172-74.

[3] Ibid. 172.

[4] P. Zieme, 'Ein Hochzeitssegen uigurischer Christen', in K. Röhrborn and H.W. Brands (eds.), Scholia. Beiträge zur Türkologie und Zentralasienkunde, Annemarie von Gabain zum 80. Geburtstag am 4. Juli 1981 dargebracht von Kollegen, Freunden und Schülern (Wiesbaden, 1981) 223.

The form in which the word appears in the Estrangelo script reminds one of the accusative-form of the Greek word *ἀρχηγός* viz. *ἀρχηγό ν* 'founder, leader' – a word more often associated with Manichaeism as Mani' s successor was often styled 'archegos' than with the Church of the East. This new discovery will certainly open new lines inquiry as one needs to know whether the Turco-Syriac form given in this blessing-formula was the original Mongol(?) word of which *Yelikewen* was its Chinese transliteration or *vice versa*.

Since my decision to delay publishing my own views on the subject as they were still at their formative stages, a number of important new studies germane to the same topic have appeared. The most important of these are:

Moriyasu Takao 森安孝夫 'The Central Asian Roots of a Chinese Manichaean Silk Painting in the Collection of the Yamato Bunkakan, Nara, Japan', in J. van den Berg, A. Kotzé, T. Nicklas and M. Scopello (eds.), *In Search of Truth. Augustine, Manichaeism and other Gnosticism: Studies for Johannes van Oort at Sixty*, Nag Hammadi and Manichaean Studies Series 74 (Leiden, 2011), 315-337 + pls. 5, esp. 352-57.

Tang Li 唐莉, 'A New Investigation into Several East Syrian ("Nestorian") Christian Epitaphs Unearthed in Quanzhou: Commentary and Translation', in D.E. Bumazhnov, E. Grypeou, T.B. Sailors and A. Toepel (eds.) *Bibel, Byzanz und Christlicher Orient, Festschrift für Stephen Gerö zum 65. Geburtstag*, Orientalia Lovaniensia Analecta, 187 (Leuven, 2011), 343-61, esp. 348, n. 24.

___ *East Syriac Christianity in Mongol-Yuan China*, Orientalia Biblica et Christiana 18 (Wiesbaden, 2011), esp. 55-57.

The new studies show ways of tackling the age-old '*Yelikewen*- problem' from different perspectives and it is fair to say that a major break-through, let alone a consensus of opinions, in explaining its origin still lies very much in the future.

16.7 Conclusion and Congratulation

The modern study of Iranian religions (Zoroastrianism, Manichaeism and Nestorian Christianity) in China began only with the discovery of genuine Manichaean and Christian texts and Zoroastrian inscriptions in Middle Iranian languages from Central Asia in the last century. For the second half of that century, Professor Lin Wushu's copious and outstanding scholarship has helped to significantly push back the frontier of knowledge in his chosen field of research. In an area of study where new knowledge continuously and rapidly fills gap and challenges old assumptions, Professor Lin is unlikely to remain inactive in his retirement. His friends and admirers will continue to look forward to his well-informed and sagacious comments in his future publications.

17 *Chongfu Si* and *Zhangjiao Si*: On the Christian Administration in Yuan China

Yin Xiaoping
(History Department, South China Agricultural University)

Deng Zhicheng 邓之诚 noted in his *History of China during Two Thousands Years* 中华二千年史 that, "Religious officers are considered more significantly valuable than those of previous dynasties in China".〔1〕 It has been proved exactly correct that the religious institutions established in the Yuan Dynasty were more in number and greater in power. The Department of *Xuanzheng* (宣政院 i.e., Commission for Buddhist and Tibetan Affairs) was in charge of Buddhism and Lamaism; the Department of *Jixian* (集贤院 i.e., Academy of Scholarly Worthies) administered Taoism; and the Bureau of *Chongfu,* or *Chongfu Si* 崇福司, was responsible for all Christian affairs throughout the country. Of these three religious institutions, the Department of *Xuanzheng* enjoyed the highest grade of the court rank. However, neither Department of *Xuanzheng n*or *Jixian* was confined to those religious affairs. Actually, the former managed all Tibetan affairs at the same time, and the latter mainly administered schools in the empire and *yin* and *yang* matters, etc..〔2〕 *Chongfu Si* was the only

〔1〕Deng Zhicheng, Zhonghua Erqiannian Shi 中华二千年史 (History of China during Two Thousands Years), vol. 4, Beijing: Zhonghuashuju, 1983, p. 371.

〔2〕*Yuan shi* 元史 (ab.,*YS, History of the Yuan Dynasty*),Beijing: Zhonghuashuju, 1978, vol. 87, pp.2193, 2192.

organization completely dealing with religious affairs.

17.1 The foundation of *Chongfu Si*

Chongfu Si was set up as an office of a lower grade of second court rank under Kublai Khan's reign (1260–1294), and became a department of second court rank in the middle Yuan Dynasty, which was eventually equal to the Department of *Jixian*. This is recorded in *Yuan shi* 元史, *the History of the Yuan Dynasty*:

> The Bureau of *Chongfu*, or *Chongfu Si,* shall enjoy the fixed salary of the second court grade. The Bureau has the jurisdiction over Ma'erhaxi 马儿哈昔 (*mar*, the honorable title given to a Nestorian Bishop)[1], *Lieban* 列班 (*rabban*, lit., the great religious teacher), *Yelikewen* 也里可温 (Arkehum or ärgägün, mainly refers to the Eastern Syriac Christians),[2] and duties engaging in the sacrifice and other similar ceremonies in *Shizi Si* 十字寺 (the Cross Monastery). [The Bureau consists of] four directors of the lower grade of the second court rank, two associate directors of the lower grade of the third court rank, two subordinate directors of the lower grade of the fourth court rank, two deputies of the lower grade of the fifth court rank, one chief secretary of the lower grade of the sixth court rank, one assistant secretary of the lower grade of the seventh court rank, one commissary of records of the upper grade of eighth court rank, besides two

[1] Samuel. N. C. Lieu, "Nestorians and Manichaeans on the South China Coast", *Vigiliae Christianae*, 34,1980, p. 73, 84, n. 13, 14. P. Pelliot, "Chrétiens d'Asie Centrale et D' extrême-Orient". *T'oung Pao*. Vol. 15, No. 5, 1914, p. 637.

[2] As to the Chinese word "Yelikewen" 也里可温, it originally referred to the Christians under the Mongol Empire and appeared frequently in the official documents at that time. Chen Yüan 陈垣 considered that it referred to all Christians of different schools, including Catholicism and Eastern Syrian Christianity, but in the author's opinion, Yelikewen mostly referred to those Eastern Syriac Christians, especially the Nestorians. See "On the interpretations of Yelikewen in Chinese context". *Ouya Yanjiu* 欧亚研究 [*Eurasian Studies*], vol. 9.

annalists, one translator, one interpreter, one seal-keeper and two couriers. The Bureau was founded in 1289, the 26th year in the *Zhiyuan* period (1264–1294). In the 2nd year in the *Yanyou* 延祐 period (1314–1320), It was promoted and expanded to a Department (*Chongfu Yuan* 崇福院) with one President over it to direct the whole affairs. To this Department all affairs of *Yelikewen* were transferred after seventy-two offices of *Zhangjiao Si* 掌教司 across the Empire were abolished. Seven years afterward, however, the Department was made the Bureau again, and the above-mentioned officials were attached to it.〔1〕 崇福司，秩〔从〕二品。掌领马儿哈昔列班也里可温十字寺祭享等事。司使四员，从二品。同知二员，从三品。副使二员，从四品。司丞二员，从五品。经历一员，从六品。都事一员，从七品。照磨一员，正八品。令史二人，译史、通事、知印各一人，宣使二人。至元二十六年置。延佑二年，改为院，置领院事一员，省并天下也里可温掌教司七十二所，悉以其事归之。七年，复为司，后定置已上官员。

As cited firstly in this recordation, the basic obligation of *Chongfu Si* involved controlling the affairs of *mar-hasia*, *rabban*, *Yelikewen,* or *rabban-ärkägün*，and supervising the ceremonies of sacrifice and prayers which were held in *Shizi Si* 十字寺. *Shizi Si* was the common name for the church or the monastery in Yuan China, for the Chinese word "十"（lit., the number ten）looks like a Christian Cross hanging inside the monasteries. However, each monastery in China had its own Chinese name, such as the Monastery of *Daxingguo* 大兴国寺, the Monastery of *Yunshan* 云山寺 and the Monastery of *Jumingshan* 聚明山寺 in Zhenjiang 镇江, and the Monastery of *Xingming* 兴明寺 in Quanzhou 泉州. Besides, the monastery at that time was also called *humra* ("missionary" in turkic)〔2〕 in some

〔1〕*YS*, p, 2273.

〔2〕Liu Yingsheng, "About Mar Serghis", *Yuanshi Luncong*, vol. 8, 2001, p. 15.

circumstances. In a word, *Chongfu Si* dealt with all affairs about monks, Christians and churches in Yuan China.

As for the history of this institution, *Chongfu Si* was created in the twenty-ninth year under Khbilai's reign (1260–1294). It consisted of twenty officers and belonged to the central governmental system, which had a higher grade of the second court rank, and all these positions were finally established in 1320. Below the central authority were the local offices of *Zhangjiao Si* (Office for Christian Affairs), which dealt with the religious matters about the local *Shizi Si* and Christians in each circuit. Therefore, it could be argued that a two-level bureaucratic administration had been formed in the earlier Yuan Dynasty.

In 1315, *Chongfu Si* was promoted to a higher ranking Department *Chongfu Yuan*; meanwhile, seventy two *Zhangjiao Si* around the country were cancelled and abolished. Considering most offices of *Zhangjiao Si* were founded inside the local cross monasteries, it could be speculated that the number of these local monasteries had reached to more than seventy two till 1315. It reveals the fact that the new religion of Christianity had greatly expanded in China during several decades (1289–1311/1315)[1] and was officially equal to the traditional religion Taoism. There is no doubt that Christianity had advanced rapidly in the earlier period, which I partly attribute to the support and motivation from *Chongfu Si*. On the other hand, the expansion of the local *Zhangjiao Si* was sacrificed by the promotion, as it was recorded, "seventy-two offices in the empire were abolished at the same time". It seems that the promotion of the official status for Christians caused an inverse consequence.

As a newly introduced religion, Christianity in Yuan China was taken

---

〔1〕Here the article uses another year of 1311. According to an imperial edict in the fourth year of Zhida 至大 period, all local religious offices controlled by Buddhists, Taoists and Yelikewen were abolished. See *Yuan dian zhang* 元典章, repr. Beijing: Zhonghuashuju, 2011, vol. 33, p.1128.

seriously. Some argue that it could ascribe to the tolerant and liberal religious policy of the Yuan government that all religions were respected and utilized by the Mongol rulers. As a result, most leading religious institutions were established, and all religious groups, like Buddhist monks, Taoists, *Danishmand* (答失蛮, the teacher of Islam) and *Yelikewen* 也里可温 were authorized no trade tax or any forced labor or all requisitioned service that other secular groups must take. *Chongfu Si* was created in such circumstances.

However, if we compare the policy with that of the early-mid Tang China, the conclusion could not be made so easily. Before the *Huichang* Period (841–846 A.D.), the Tang government also adopted the policy of treating the foreign religions like *Jingjiao* tolerantly. We could find the closest relations between Nestorian monks and the royal court; according to the well known Xi'an stele, emperors of Tang Dynasty treated Nestorians with great respects. Nevertheless, the government never set up an official institution for Nestorians, both *Jingjiao* and Manichaeism were under the supervision of *Honglu Si* 鸿胪寺 (Court of State Ceremonial), and later by Board of Rites 礼部, the authority dealing with the Buddhist and the Taoist affairs. Among the three foreign religions in the Tang Dynasty, only the Zoroastrianism, or Religion of *Xian* 祆教, had founded its religious office, *Xianzhu* 祆祝 in the office of *Sabao* 萨宝府 (*Sārthavāk*), to manage their religious affairs and obtained a higher political position. The reason why the Tang government set up this institution was as follows: on one hand, the Zoroastrianism was the dominant faith in those Iranian or Sogodian immigrants and descendants in China; on the other hand, the office of *Sabao* and *Xianzhu* had existed in the official system since the Northern Dynasties. The Tang government set up *Xianzhu* for Zoroastrians in China out of both political and institutional concerns. [1] As for the Nestorianism in China, in other words, there was no institutional example for the Yuan government to set up an office to conduct the Christian affairs; *Chongfu Si* was totally an original creation. The basic reason, I think, was that there were much more believers in Yuan China, not only lots of Christians in the upper ruling class like the Golden Family itself and the noblest families from Nestorian Kerait, Ongut tribes, but also a large number of Central Asian Christians who belonged to the second senior class in Yuan society. [2] It was understood that the government took the benefits and religious rights of these Christians into concern. Therefore, it witnessed the most tolerant religious policy in Yuan China; even the newly introduced Christianity could attain a higher political status. The support of the ruling class was what the Nestorianism in Tang China lacked.

17.2 The Officers of *Chongfu Si*

As a newly created institution, *Chongfu Si* is the key to understanding the religious and political position of Christianity in Yuan China. Gao Tietai did a primary textual study and collected the records of fourteen officials of *Chongfu Si*. [3] Like other governmental authorities, all posts of *Chongfu Si* were confined to the routine affairs. Four directors, two associate directors, two subordinate directors and two deputies were senior civilian officials; one chief secretary, one assistant secretary and one correspondence secretary were *Shoulingguan* 首领官, or staff supervisors, who dealt with

---

[1] Lin Wushu, *Tangdai Jingjiao Zaiyanjiu* 唐代景教再研究[*New Reflections on Nestorianism of the Tang Dynasty*], Beijing: Zhongguo shehui kexue chubanshe, 2002, p.110.

[2] Cf. Yin Xiaoping, *Study on Yelikewen in the Yuan Dynasty*, Lanzhou: Lanzhou University Press, 2012.

[3] Gao Tietai, *Study on the Bureau of Chongfu*, master thesis of Northeast university of China, 2011.

the general and clerical affairs. [1] All these officials, enjoying a certain grade of the court rank, were mainly selected through hereditary and imperial examinations, [2] paid by the government and supervised by the Censorate. The lower *Liyuan* 吏员, or the petty officials with no court rank, like two annalists, one translator, one interpreter, one seal-keeper and two couriers, handled the routine affairs of financial income and expense, translating and keeping official documents, managing the seals, reporting to the superior institutions and conveying the imperial edicts, etc.. Nothing related to the unification of faith or modeling the religious rituals. The official rank was irrelevant to their hierarchical status in the Church, not to mention many of them were not Christians at all.

As to the scale, *Chongfu Si* could not compare to *Xuanzheng Yuan* and *Jixian Yuan*, furthermore, it was only confined to engaging in the religious affairs, while *Xuanzheng Yuan* and *Jixian Yuan* were not, especially *Xuanzheng Yuan,* it enjoyed a higher grade of the court rank and played a more important role as an imperial central authority for Buddhists and Tibetan affairs; "it selects the officials freely", which means the Department had a certain self-autonomy, and its officials were selected from both Buddhist and secular circles. [3]

Unlike Buddhists authorities, most directors of *Chongfu Si* were not collected from the priests or missionaries in the Church. The most significant one was Ai Xue 爱薛, besides Ai Xue, there were other five leading directors of *Chongfu Si* recorded in Chinese sources; none of them was a priest.

Three directors were recorded in the official history *Yuan Shi* 元史, Ai

[1] Xu Fan, *Yuandai lizhi yanjiu* 元代吏制研究 [*Study on Official Institutions in the Yuan Dynasty*],Tianjin: Laodong renshi chubanshe, 1987, pp. 41-46.

[2] Gao Tietai, *op. cit.*, pp. 32-33.

[3] *YS*, vol. 87, p.2193.

Xue 爱薛 (Isa, 1227–1308), Yeliya 也里牙 (Eliah)[1] and Ma Mouhuozhe 马某火者. Saeki considered Ma Mouhuozhe was a bishop; therefore he translated his Chinese name as Mar Moses, [2]as we know, "mar" means the bishop in the church and Moses is a common name among Christians. While Moule considered Ma Mouhuozhe as a Muslim, he pointed out that, "Ma-mou-huo-chê, probably Mahmud Khoja, suggests a Moslem and it is surprising to find him as President of the Christian Ch'ung fu ssŭcho 崇福司, but there is no reason to doubt the accuracy of the text." [3] In spite of the correctness of these two points, whether or not Ma Mouhuozhe was a priest was still discussable.

Ai Xue, or Isa, was a profound Nestorian from Western lands of Fulin 拂菻, or Phurom. Pelliot believed that he was an Arabic-speaking Syrian.[4] Ai Xue was recommended by a Nestorian missionary Rabbanata 列班・阿答 to the court of Guyuk Khan in 1240s, since then he had been serving in the Mongol court till he passed away in 1308. Before he was sent to Ilkhan Empire in the diplomatic mission to have an audience with Il-khan Arghun in 1283, Ai Xue had served in court as a translator for his proficiency in western languages for almost forty years, and as the chief of the Offices of Western Astronomy and of Arabian Medicine for about twenty years. On his return from western lands of two-year hard journey in 1287, he was immediately appointed some vital posts, firstly the President of *Mishu Jian*

---

〔1〕*YS*, vol. 134, pp. 3248-3249; Cheng Jufu, "Fulin Zhongxianwang Shendaobei"拂菻忠献王神道碑 [Tombstone of Loyal Prince of Fulin], in *Quan yuan we*n 全元文, vol. 535. Nanjing: Jiangsu Guji Chubanshe, 1999, pp. 325-326; Han Rulin, "Restudy on Ai Xue", in *Qionglu Ji* 穹庐集, Shijiazhuang: Hebei jiaoyu chubanshe, 2000, pp. 93-108.

〔2〕In the 18th year of Zhi-yuan Period (1358), Ma Mouhuozhe was appointed Canzhi Zhengshi 参知政事. But in the 11th lunar month he resigned the Presidency of the Department of *Chongfu*. *YS*, vol. 113, p.2856, also see Yoshiro Saeki, *The Nestorian Documents and Relics in China*, 1937, p. 498.

〔3〕A.C. Moule, Christians in China before 1500, London, New York and Toronto, 1930, p. 228, note 22.

〔4〕P. Pelliot, "Chrétiens d'Asie Centrale et D' extrême-Orient", *T'oung Pao*. Vol. 15, No. 5,1914, p. 639.

秘书监(Palace Library), two years later the Director of *Chongfu Si,* then *Pingzhang Zhengshi* 平章政事 (Minister of State) and *Qinguogong* 秦国公 (Duke of Qin) in 1298. His son Eliah inherited his post in *Chongfu Si*. Both Chinese and Persian documents did not reveal any priest post about Ai Xue. In Rashid al-Din's *Jami'al-Tavārikh,* Ai Xue was described as a radical Christian who always persecuted Muslims, however he was not declared as a missionary. 〔1〕 If he was, it was not necessary to neglect this important fact in Persian sources or the history of the East Church.

Another probable director of *Chongfu Si*, Ashikedai 阿实克岱, who might be the eldest son of Ai Xue and might have accompanied his father to Ilkhan Empire, was entitled the Director of *Chongfu Si* in a memorial text, 〔2〕 but his name was not recorded in two biographies of Ai Xue, one being the official biography in *Yuan shi*, the other "*Fulin zhongxianwang shendaobei*" 拂菻忠献王神道碑 by Cheng Jufu 程鉅夫.

Besides the above mentioned figures, there were other two directors of *Chongfu Si* in private sources, Dulin Timur 笃麟铁穆尔 and Liu Zeli 刘则礼, and it is still discussible whether they were Christian or not. 〔3〕

---

〔1〕Rashid al-Din, *Jami'al-Tavārikh*, vol. 2, Yu Dajun trans., Beijing: the Commercial Press, 1998, p. 347.

〔2〕Yao Sui 姚燧. "Kao Chongfu Shi Ashikedai zhuifeng Qingonggong Zhongyigong zhi"考崇福使阿实克岱追封秦国公忠翊公制, in *Quan yuan wen*, vol. 300, pp. 360-361.

〔3〕According to Liu Zeli's biography in Li Jiben's corpus *Yishan Wenji*, Liu was the descendant of famous Confucian scholar Shentu Zhiyuan 申屠致远 who lived in the period in the latter half of 13th century. In the 24th year of Zhizheng Period (1363) Liu was granted the director of *Chongfu Si* for his military deeds of putting down the peasants rebellion, he himself being impossible a Christian. Timur was a Mongol, his Grandmother was a Kerait noblewoman, but it was not clear whether Timur was a Yelikewen or not. Timur's primitive name was Yinyanashuoli 音牙纳硕理,When he was at the age of eleven, Emperor Wenzong found him extraordinarily beautiful among the guardsmen, so the emperor put him in the important posts from then on. He was entitled a new name Dulin Timur 笃麟铁穆尔 by Wenzong, and was appointed the director of Chongfu Si 崇福司使, the Ritual Observances Commissioner 太常院使, the Grand Judge of the Court Imperial Clan 大宗正府也可札鲁花赤, the Associate Military Affairs Commissioner 知枢密院事, the Palace Provisions Commissioner 宣徽使, etc. See Huang Jin 黄溍, *Huang Wenxian Ji* (黄文献集, *Corpus of Huang Wenxian*), in *Quan yuan wen*, vol. 967, Jiangsu Guji Chubanshe, 1999, p. 151.

One fact cannot be ignored when discussing the status of all above officials: although most directors of *Chongfu Si* were not priests, some even not Christian, they administered all affairs of priests and monks and monasteries in the Metropolitan of China. Comparing the position of priests in Tang Dynasty, it seemed the same that the priests and monks in both Tang and Yuan dynasties were under the supervision and administration of the central government.

Although few names of *mar-hasia* or *rabban-ärkägün* were recorded in Chinese sources, we know they had formed a close relationship with the Mongol rulers. According to the recordation of John of Plano Carpini and William of Rubruck, during the reigns of Khubilai's predecessors like Guyug and Mongke, there were many Nestorian priests in Khan's court.[1] We even know that one *mar-hasia* ever leaded the followers to pray in the court in 1320s according to *Zhishun Zhenjiang zhi* (至顺镇江志 *the Gazetteer of Zhenjiang in the period of Zhishun*) by Yu Xilu 俞希鲁.[2] He might be the Nestorian physician Shabi 撒必 from Samarqand who cured Tuluy and then got a post of the Court physician and an honorable title of *darqan*. Mar Serghis 马薛里吉思, who built seven monasteries in South China, was one of his grandsons. Since Mar Serghishad devoted himself to the spread of Christianity in China, he was accordingly considered a bishop in the Church.[3] Nevertheless, Mar Serghis never served in *Chongfu Si*.

It could be concluded farther that *Chongfu Si* had no organizational relation with the East Church on the one hand, for its officers were not selected from the priests or missionaries in the Church; on the other hand, the missionizing activities of the East Church in China should be totally

---

[1] P. Pelliot,"Chrétiens d'Asie Centrale et D' extrême-Orient", pp. 627-629.

[2] *Zhishun Zhenjiang zhi* 至顺镇江志, Beijing: Zhonghuashuju, 1990, p. 2740ab.

[3] Yin, Xiaoping, "Origins of Christians in South China during the Yuan Dynasty According toZhishun Zhenjiang zhi (1329-1332)", in *Zhonghua Wenshi Luncong* 中华文史论丛, vol. 89, 2006, No. 4, pp. 289-313.

supervised by *Chongfu Si*. That is to say, if the institution was held by those religious Christian, the Bureau could play an actual role in supporting the missionary career in China, but considering many directors of *Chongfu Si*, especially in the later period of the Yuan Dynasty, were not Christians, its significance in this aspect would greatly decrease.

17.3 The Religious Service Supervised under *Chongfu Si*

The medical and interpreting role of *Yelikewen* in Yuan China has been much valued, while their religious role, which was undoubted the most important, has not been adequately discussed. The religious role of the court priests, i.e., *mar-hasia* and *rabban*, who belonged to the upper class of *Yelikewen*, was to lead the service of *Gaotian* (Prayers for Heavenly God), *Zhushou* (Blesses for the long live) and *Qifu* (Wishes for good fortunes) as *Yuan shi* and *Yuan dian zhang* point out clearly.

> In the 4th lunar month of 4th year in the Zhida period (1311 A.D.), in the divine decree of the Emperor, Buddhist monks, Taoists, *Yelikewen* and Dānishmand are not to be charged with any requisition, they pray for God for the long lives. 至大四年四月，钦奉圣旨：和尚、先生、也里可温、荅失蛮不教当差发，告天咱每根底祝寿者么道来。[1]

Actually, *Gaotian* and *Zhushou* were the obligations of all religious people in Yuan China, as a repay, they were privileged no corveé or trade tax. We consider that the sacrifice service held in the Cross Monastery consisted of these religious rites of *Qifu*, *Zhushou* and *Gaotian*.

Little was mentioned about the activities of *mar-hasia* and *rabban* in Chinese documents. Judging from the limited remained sources, I speculate

[1] *Yuan dian zhang*, vol. 33, (repr., Beijing), p. 1127.

roughly that the Nestorian rituals in China had been influenced by Buddhism and Confucianism. For example, in the first year during the Tianli 天历 period (1329), Kocho monks 高昌僧 were requested to offer the Buddhist service at Pavilion of *Yanchun* 延春阁, and at the same time the *Yelikewen* priests were requested to hold a similar service at the Shrine of Empress Dowager *Xianyi zhuangsheng* 显懿庄圣皇后.[1] Both the Pavilion and the Shrine were associated with the upper Mongol noblewomen. The former was the main part of the Palace of *Yanchun*, where the emperor's wives and concubines lived; the latter was sacred to Empress Dowager *Xianyi zhuangsheng* and belonged to the Imperial Ancestral Temples. As we know, many imperial women in the Mongol court were Nestorian, the most famous one, Empress Dowager *Xianyizhuangsheng*, or Sorghaghtani Beki 唆鲁禾帖尼, was the wife of Tuluy Khan, the mother of Kublai, Mongke and Hulagu, and was from the famous Nestorian Kerait 克烈 tribe. Her shrine was neither a chapel nor an imperial church; indeed it was an imperial ancestral temple that was founded in the early Yuan Dynasty. When the Mongols established the dominion in China, they accepted some Chinese or Confucian rituals for a better adaptation on these grand conquered civilized lands. In the 3rd year during the *Zhishun* 至顺 period under Kublai Khan's reign, the Imperial Ancestral Temple was finally set up, with seven deceased emperor and empresses being given the honorary posthumous titles and *Zhuangsheng* being the title of Sorghaghtani Begi. As one of the greatest and most powerful women, she helped her sons to be the great Khans, and was consequently memorized honorably by the whole empire during the Yuan Dynasty. Later in Wuzong's reign, "*Xianyi*" was added into her posthumous name that formed her complete posthumous title "X*ianyi zhuangsheng*".[2]

[1] *YS*, vol. 32, p. 711.

[2] *Ibid*, vol. 74, pp. 1831-1832, 1836.

Building the imperial ancestral temple and fulfilling the ancestor worship was an important transformation in the ruling pattern after the Mongols entered the Central Plains of China. The religious rituals held in the noblest Sorghaghtani's temple were influenced by the Chinese ones. Sorghaghtani Beki enjoyed great honor among the *Yelikewen* in the Mongol Empire. In the 3rd lunar month, the 1st year during the Later Zhiyuan period (1336), as *Yuan shi* records: "the Central Ministry asks the instruction of sacrifice ritual in the Cross Monastery in Ganzhou, Gansu Province, for commemorating the honorable Empress Dowager Beqi, the mother of Emperor Shizu (Kublai). 甘肃甘州路十字寺奉安世祖皇帝母别吉太后于内，请定祭礼" [1] Sorghaghtani Beki was undoubtedly the most powerful Nestorian woman in the Mongol Empire. The conduct of cherishing her memorial tablet in the local monastery seemed political and realistic, and it was similar to that in the monastery of Tang China, as recorded by the missionaries in the Christian Monument at Xi'an: "The most religious Emperor Hsüan Tsung ordered the prince of Ning-kuo and the four other princes to go in person to the Temple of Happiness to build and set up the altars and courts... At the beginning of T'ien-pao he ordered Kao Li-shih, the commander in chief, to take the portraits of the five sages (emperors) which were placed in the monastery, and to present a hundred rolls of silk, which were reverently received with salutations to the portrait of wisdom. 玄宗至道皇帝，令宁国等五王，亲临福宇，建立坛场……天宝初，令大将军高力士，送五圣写真，寺内安置，赐绢百匹，奉庆睿图。" [2]

In the earlier period when it was in the charged of the devout Christian Ai Xue, *Chongfu Si* really played a significant role in the spread of Christianity in China. In the first year of *Yuanzhen* 元贞 period (1295), Ai Xue, the director of *Chongfu Si,* delivered an application to the Grand

〔1〕*Ibid*, vol. 38, p. 826.

〔2〕A.C. Moule, *op. cit.*, p. 41.

Council to ask for the tax reduction for Mar Serghis.[1] Councilor-in-chief Wan Ze 完泽, who was a Kerait and might be a Nestorian,[2] reported to Emperor Chengzong 成宗 (Temür) and obtained a letter of protection under the imperial seal, which was recorded in *Zhishun Zhenjiang zhi* that besides thirty *qing* 顷 (about 500 acres) of official land, thirty-four *qing* of civilian land was further granted to seven temples (the cross monasteries) as their perpetual maintenance. 奏闻玺书护持，仍拨赐江南官田三十顷，又益置浙西民田三十四顷，为七寺常住。[3] With the support of Wan Ze and Ai Xue in the court, Mar Serghis was consequently approved to reduce and postpone paying the tax.[4] As may be imagined, Mar Serghis could not have made such great missionary achievements without the aid and support in the court.

A counterevidence was that two of these cross monasteries were attacked and occupied by Buddhists afterwards when Ai Xue died in 1308. In around 1311, the *Juming* Monastery 聚明寺 and the *Yunshan* Monastery 云山寺 were occupied by the Buddhists and were renamed Prajna Temple 般若寺. New Buddhist statues were re-carved and re-painted; furthermore, the Crosses inside the monastery were destroyed by force.[5] In this case, thc Buddhist monks were aided by the government, it was announced that, "the offspring of *Yelikewen* were warned not to take back the monasteries, or they would be punished".[6] During the competition between Buddhists

---

〔1〕After conquering the South Song Dynasty, the Buddhists, Taoists and Yelikewen should pay commercial and land taxes. Chen Yuan, "Yuan Yelikewen Jiao Kao" 元也里可温教考 [Study on Yelikewen in the Yuan Dynasty], in *Chen Yuan Xueshu Lunwenji* 陈垣学术论文集, vol. 1, Beijing: Zhonghuashuju, 1980, pp. 22-24.

〔2〕Liu Yingsheng, *op. cit.*, pp. 16.

〔3〕*Zhishun Zhenjiangzhi*, 1990, vol. 9, p. 366.

〔4〕*Tong zhi tiao ge* 通制条格, *Xuxiu Siku Quanshu* 续修四库全书, Shanghai Ancient Books Publishing House, p. 855; Fang Linggui, (anno.), *Tongzhi Tiaoge Xiaozhu* 通制条格校注, vol. 29, Beijing: Zhonghuashuju, 2001, pp. 720-721.

〔5〕Zhishun Zhenjiangzhi, p.2748a.

〔6〕*Ibid*, p. 2748a.

and Christians for about three decades, *Yelikewen* failed in the end.

As a governmental authority, *Chongfu Si* was restricted to the religious affairs and was supervised by the Grand Council and the Censorate, any arrogating conduct being not permitted. One example is recorded in *Yuan dian zhang*:

> In the 7th lunar month of 4th year of the Yanyou Period (1317 A.D.), the Provincial Governor of the Huaidong (i.e., the provinces lying in the east of the River Huai) had the honor to receive an instruction from the Grand Council that the imperial Censorate had received a report from the Judicial Commissioner of Huaidong, which was as follows: "On the 30th of January of the 4th year of the Yanyou Period, the Imperial gifts were ordered. Hereupon, (General) Chechedu (i.e., Tchiktchito) 彻彻都 and General Shansiding 苫思丁 (i.e., Justin) rode four horses to Yangzhou to send forth the incense to the Yelikewen's Cross Monastery and bestowed the silk cloth, wine and other things on the donors of Merit and Virtue. On the second day of the following month, when Toktokhos 脱脱禾孙(i.e., The officer inspecting the official documents and luggage of the envoy at the courier station of the courier route) Wu Yexian got the decree that carried by the courier of *Chongfu Yuan*, he argued the matter against it that the imperial gifts of wine and sweet wine were not mentioned in the decree at all, and according to the sacred command from the Emperor, only silk cloth was ordered to be given to Aolahan (奥剌憨 i.e., Abraham) and Lülü 驴驴, the wine was excluded. It shall be informed that every reward and punishment must be carried out appropriately in the way of governing, and with regard to the way of rewards, everything must be put on faithfully of the laws and observance…However, Aolahan was only a *Yelikewen*, with neither literary pursuits worthy of name of culture nor military merits (to

deserve such imperial gifts). He was a mere rich tradesman in Yangzhou and a very common fellow. It is true that his father had a name for building monasteries, but that was so many years ago. At first, by means of false representations Aolahan managed to be engaged in the service of the public work, and then he begged Hucha 忽察 (i.e., Khoitcha) in *Xuanwei* 宣慰 (i.e., the Pacification Commission) for undertaking the power to collect the wine taxes. Being greedy by nature and coveting after large profits, he made great fortune at the expense of the people in general. He was then arrested, and was sentenced for fifty-seven lashes after admitting all his crimes. However, he succeeded in presenting a petition to the Throne by making manifest his innocence, and the Emperor benevolently declared the general pardon and remitted Aolahan's punishment. Despite these, he did never share the honor to serve in the presence of His Majesty, nor was he born in a ranking family. The Emperor should neither be informed of the name of this man. Then the *Chongfu Yuan* had transmitted to the officials the sacred command that Shansiding and his men rode four horses to carry two bottles of wine and sweet wine to Yangzhou. Shansiding delivered them (to Aolahan) because he believed they had the honor to receive these things, while it was only a case that people received reward without proper merit, not to mention it was clear that the two bottles of wine were not mentioned in the sacred command at all, and *Chongfu Yuan* had never applied for the imperial wine in advance. Therefore, we delivered the copy of the sacred command and got hold of the instruction letter in question, which had already been reported to the superior authorities and made the case very clear. " Nevertheless, on the 10th of January of the 4th year of the Yanyou period, the very timely imperial proclamation for his pardon was issued...*Chongfu Yuan* was just authorized to award the imperial gift incense in the name of the Emperor's command which never included the sweet wine for Aolahan, and this was illegal with no permission of the Grand Council and the Department of *Xuanhui*. [1]

延祐四年七月，行省准中書省咨：御史台呈："淮东廉访司申：'延祐四年正月三十日，有御位下徹徹都、苫思丁，起马四疋，前来也里可温十字寺降御香，赐与功德主段疋、酒等。至初二日，有脱脱禾孙吴也先，赍到崇福院元差苫思丁等差札，赴司覆说：苫思丁差札内别无御赐酒醴。照得崇福院奏奉圣旨，奥刺憨、驴驴，各与一表里段子，别无御赐酒醴。看详：为治之道，必先信其赏罚，为赏之道，尤宜重其典礼……彼奥刺憨者，也里可温人氏，素无文艺，亦无武功，系扬州之豪富，市井之编民。乃父虽有建寺之名，年已久矣。本以影射差徭，营求忽察宣慰等，包办扬州酒课，贪图厚利，害众成家。取讫招伏，拟决五十七下。申覆宪台照详，来奉明降，钦遇诏恩释免。较之，此辈未尝御前进侍，又非阀阅之家，圣上亦不知识。今崇福院传奉圣旨，差苫思丁等起马四疋，赍酒醴二瓶，前来扬州，传奉圣旨恩赐，是乃无功受赏。况崇福院奏奉圣旨事意内，别无御酒二瓶，不见崇福院端的曾无奏赐酒醴。为此，卑司今抄崇福院答札在前，申乞照详。'得此。照得延祐四年正月初四日钦遇诏赦。钦此……本台看详，崇福院官当元止是奏奉御香，别无所赐奥刺憨酒醴，又不经由省部、宣徽院，有违定例。"

As above mentioned, *Chongfu Yuan* was sentenced illegal for its wrongly official conduct. All official affairs should be carried out in accordance with laws. Shansiding was sent to Yangzhou in order to award the imperial gifts of silk, wine and incense to Aolahan and Lülü for their great donation to the local Cross Monastery. However, among the imperial gifts the wine and sweet wine were exclusively managed by the Department of *Xuanhui* 宣徽院, which were therefore called *Xuanhui* wine 宣徽酒. *Chongfu Yuan* had no authority to award *Xuanhui* wine for *Yelikewen*

[1] *Yuan dian zhang*, vol. 36,(repr., Beijing), pp. 1280-1281.

without the permission of the Grand Council and the Department of *Xuanhui*. It seemed very insignificant but really intolerant because of its illegal procedure, even just for two bottles of wine. That's why *Chongfu Yuan* was accused officially by the Judicial Commissioner of Huaidong 淮东廉访司.

17.4 The Operation and Cancellation of *Zhangjiao Si*

Now it comes to the issue of local institution *Zhangjiao Si*.

In 1315, seventy-two *Zhangjiao Si* or the Office of Christian affairs around the country were totally abolished, meanwhile *Chongfu Si* was promoted to a higher ranking authority *Chongfu Yuan*. Besides the recordation in *Yuan shi* there is no further information about *Zhangjiao Si* in official documents. Only two records discovered in an archeological finding and a private epitaph were relevant, one is about Wu Antonius 吴咹哆呢嗯, the chief of *Zhangjiao Si* in Quanzhou circuit, the other is about Sao Ma 骚马 (Sauma), the chief of *Zhangjiao Si* in Jining circuit. [1]

Sauma was from the Mongol Qarluq tribe, and his brief biography was recorded in "the Gravestone of Sir Leshan". It was said that in the earlier times he was appointed the chief of *Zhangjiao Si*, and in his service period he reconstructed a Cross Monastery. [2]

Sauma was a very common Nestorian name, and Sao Ma was its Chinese translation. [3] The Chief of *Zhangjiao Si* was his primary post, which, like the Buddhist official, was usually set for monks. I consider

---

[1] Zhang Jiajia, "A study and commentary on a Nestorian Family in Jining Circuit in the Yuan Dynasty: Based on the Stele Inscriptions of the Antanbuhua (按檀不花) Family", *History Study*, 2010 (5), p. 47.

[2] *Ibid*, p.47.

[3] J. Chabot, De Mar Jabalaha III, Patriarche des Nestoriens (1281-1317), et de Moine Rabban Çauma, Ambassadeur du roi Argoun en Occident (1287), Paris, 1895, p.12-13.

Sauma was a monk (probable an abbot) of the local monastery, therefore he got the post in *Zhangjiao Si* and reconstructed the cross monastery later. After *Chongfu Si* had been promoted to *Chongfu Yuan* since 1315, Sauma also lost his post in *Chongfu Si*.[1]

Wu Anduonisi (Antonius) was both the abbot of the *Xingming* Monastery and the chief of *Zhangjiao Si* in Quanzhou circuit. Of course he was appointed this post for his religious status. His name was found in a Chinese-Uighur Nestorian tomb stele discovered in Quanzhou, dated in the tenth year of Dade Period (1306 A.D.).[2]

A famous poet Jin Yuansu 金元素, who was also a Nestorian Christian, had visited the Cross Monastery of Xingming during his official service in Fujian. In one of his poetry "Ji Daxingming Si Yuanming Lieban 寄大兴明寺圆明列班", or "To Rabban Yuanming of the Monastery of Xingming", he wrote a poem as follow (a literal translation):

> The entrance of the Monastery is always closed down; its steps look green with perennial moss.
>
> The altar lamp burns all day long; its flame comes from the shrine in Fulin.
>
> 寺門常锁碧苔深，千载灯传自苐林[3]

Lieban, or rabban, was the respectable title for the priests in *Yelikewen*, although we know nothing about Rabban Yuanming. Yuanming is a typical Chinese expression, and it was his title "rabban" that revealed his high position in the East Church and his knowledge in Syriac. While Fulin was also the homeland of Jin Yuansu, it was not an exact place but vaguely

[1] Zhang Jiajia, *op. cit.*, p. 47.

[2] Wu Wenliang, Wu Youxiong (ed.), *Religious Inscriptions in Quanzhou* 泉州宗教石刻, revised version, Beijing: Science Press, 2005, p. 419.

[3] Jin Yuansu, *Nanyou Yuxing Shiji* (南游寓兴诗集, *Collection of Poems during the Traveling Southward*), quoted from Xiao Qiqing 萧启庆, "the Semu literati Jin Hala and his Nanyou Yuxing Shiji", firstly published in *Hanxueyanjiu* 汉学研究(*Chinese Studies*), vol. 13, No. 2, 1995, pp. 1-14.

referred to the western lands where the flame of Xingming Monastery was taken from. The word *dengchuan* 灯传 is a Buddhist term which means the transmission of religious tradition, therefore, it might imply the religious connection between the Cross Monastery of Daxingming and its mother Church in Western Asia.

The ethnicity of Antonius has not been made clear. He might be a Chinese, or a Uighur or an Ongut who was proficient in Chinese literature.[1] Judging from the nation of *Yelikewen* in Yuan China, it's impossible that Wu Antonius was a Han Chinese. Since he was an abbot of a Cross Monastery, he must be acquainted with Syriac Nestorian classics and the Nestorian rituals, and it was obviously difficult for a local Chinese to grasp such skills. Compared with other Nestorian descriptions discovered in Quanzhou, especially those carved with Chinese characters, this stele seemed more sinicized for its shape, structure, inscription and expression.

For the administrative convenience on local affairs of Yelikewen and the cross monasteries, many *Zhangjiao Si* were established throughout the country. They probably set the office in the monastery and choose the officials from the monks, just like the local Buddhist official system always did. Therefore, the local monasteries got great power in dealing with the missionary affairs. Once the central institution could not supervise *Zhangjiao Si* properly and efficiently, they would gradually expanded out of control.

It might be the reason that caused the conflict between *Yelikewen* and Taoists. In 1304, the 8th year during the Dade 大德 Period, Taoists complained to the Department of Jixian that Yelikewen in Wenzhou circuit set an office to expand their religion; many residents in Wenzhou enlisted themselves as the members of the Yelikewen religion in order to elude their civil duties.

[1] Wu Wenliang, Wu Youxiong, *op. cit.*,pp.418-421.

Besides, Yelikewen gradually usurped both the power and the authority of the Taoism, and they insisted on preceding the Taoists in both the place and the order when they prayed for the Emperor in sacrifice ceremonies.[1] The complaint was forwarded to the Board of Rites eventually, and the decision was made that since then in the sacrifice ceremonies or other similar occasions the right order should be obeyed strictly that the Buddhists and Taoists should precede those of *Yelikewen*'s.[2]

The religion of *Yelikewen* was competitive. Though it actually emerged in 1270's in the Yangtze River district, in 1310's this religion had been able to compete with traditional Taoism. Not only did it strive for the believers but also it preceded the place and the order in ritual service. We could discover the intense relations in religious competition at that time according to the above-mentioned cases.

One illegality that the Taoist priests accused *Yelikewen* was that the latter enlisted many people to its religion. This was just an excuse from the Taoists' side. Actually, all religions in Yuan China expanded their power and influence by striving for more land and people. Owing to the privilege of less corvée and less tax, the religious people formed a privileged class beyond ethnicity in Yuan China, as Meng Siming 蒙思明 pointed out in his research.[3] In consequence, many secular people, including wealthy people, refugees and beggars, enlisted themselves to one religion so as to avoid their corvée.[4] It's not rare that the people eluded their tax and corvée in Chinese history; however, such a strategy went to a peak in the Yuan Dynasty.

In 1310 when Emperor Renzong 仁宗 acceded to the throne, the

[1] *Yuan dian zhang*, vol. 33, p. 1143.

[2] *Ibid*, p. 1144.

[3] Meng Siming 蒙思明, *Yuandai Shehui Jieji Zhidu* 元代阶级制度 (*The Institutions of Classes in the Yuan Dynasty*), Shanghai: Shanghai Renmin Chubanshe, 2006, p. 79.

[4] *Ibid*., pp. 78-81.

Emperor commanded to abolish the religious offices of Buddhism, Taoism, *Yelikewen*, *Dānishmand* and *Baiyunzong* 白云宗 so as to increase the government revenue.[1] The offices of *Zhangjiao Si* were abolished during the period. The cause and the consequence of this policy was recorded in *Yuan dian zhang* ("Abolish the Buddhist and Taoist *yamen* and exempt"革僧道衙门免差发). In the 4th year of Zhida 至大 Period, because the local religious offices of Buddhism, Taoism, *Yelikewen* and Dānishmand had caused so many administrative problems and juridical chaos, therefore, all local *yamen* of them were ordered to be abolished. Only Commission for Buddhist and Tibetan Affairs (*Xuanzheng Yuan*) and Commission of Merit and Virtue remained, and the local governors, *Darughachi* 达鲁花赤, were authorized to draw back the civil and penal jurisdiction.

In 1315 A.D., *Chongfu Si* was promoted to *Chongfu Yuan*, and all local *Yelikewen* affairs were charged directly by this central department. It was in this year that no local *Zhangjiao Si* for *Yelikewen* affairs survived neither did their religious officials.

17.5 Conclusion

Reviewing each period of Christianity in China, only the Yuan government set up the Bureau to manage Christian affairs separately, and many officials in this Bureau were Christians. Furthermore, there were lots of Christians in upper Mongols and central Asian (*semu* 色目) bureaucrats who belonged to the first and the second ruling class. The number of *Yelikewen* in Yuan China was considerable that the government must take their benefits and religious rights into concern. Therefore, it witnessed the most tolerant religious policy in Yuan China; even the newly introduced Christianity could attain a higher political position. The support of the

〔1〕*YS*, vol. 24, p. 542.

ruling class was what the Nestorianism in Tang China lacked.

Chongfu Si was in charge of *Yelikewen* and the religious rituals held in the monasteries by *mar-hasia* and *rabban*. The local religious activities were limited in the Cross Monastery and were supervised directly under *Chongfu Si* in theory. Based on the managerial demand on the local cross monasteries, *Zhangjiao Si* was founded. Usually it was set inside the local cross monastery for the convenience of management, and the abbot were appointed the chief of *Zhangjiao Si*, which was the same as the monk official system of Buddhism.

As a secular governmental authority, the officials of *Chongfu Si* need not be selected from the priests or missionaries in the Church. Although *Chongfu Si* was engaged in the religious service for the ruling class, the missionary career in China was not its responsibility, however, it actually provided great support and helped the cross monasteries in the country to attain more developing opportunities.

On the contrary, *Zhangjiao Si* was the institution dealing with the local religious affairs, their officials were mostly selected from the senior monks, like a Buddhist Chief of Buddhism, especially from the abbots of the cross monasteries. The Chief of *Zhangjiao Si* was possibly an honorable post, yet it actually grasped much autonomy power. Therefore, it was very common that *Zhangjiao Si* took in many people for development. With the conversion to Christianity of these people (even the amount of converts was not very large), they also succeeded in avoiding lots of miscellaneous duties and gaining economic benefit.

It reveals two different religious administrative levels in Yuan China. On the upper level, *Chongfu Si* offered the religious service for the ruling class and supervised the local cross monasteries; it didn't devote itself to the missionary activities. While on the lower level, with the political, economic and religious profits relating to the missionizing activities directly,

Zhangjiao Si had benefited from the expansion of the local cross monasteries and had played a more practical role. However, it was not clear when *Zhangjiao Si* was set up, supposing it was in 1289, the year that *Chongfu Si* was founded, it took only two decades to run the local offices before the year of 1315. During such a short period the number of *Zhangjiao Si*, which was equal to or more than that of the cross monasteries in China, had amounted to seventy-two. *Zhangjiao Si* and local cross monasteries had proved their missionary energy convincingly.

Unfortunately, with the direct intervention of the government, this energy and vitality in the provinces came to an end. In 1315, seventy-two offices of *Zhangjiao Si* were thoroughly abolished; meanwhile *Chongfu Si* was promoted to the Department *Chongfu Yuan*. It meant that *Yelikewen* kept their influence and authority on the upper level, but the missionary energy and self-development in the local regions decreased and gradually faded.

18 A Study of Zurvanite Zoroastrianism: an Edition of *'Ulamā-ye Islām of Another Version* (UI-2) and its Long Quotation in a Book of Āzar Kayvān School

Takeshi AOKI
(Waseda University, Tokyo, JAPAN)

18.1 What is *'Ulamā-ye Islām of Another Version* (UI-2)?

The New Persian treatise known as *'Ulamā-ye Islām* (three versions now extant; UI-1, UI-2 and UI-Kāma Bohra) was supposed to be translated from the otherwise lost fifth century Pahlavi original in the 13th century. The significance of this treatise depends on the fact that it is the only extant Zoroastrian source in any language on the religious idea of Zurvanite Zoroastrianism, the state religion of Sasanian Persia (224-651CE).

Previous studies on *'Ulamā-ye Islām* and its known MSS till 2010 are already reported in Aoki 2014a. In addition to it, the edition of *Ulamā-ye Islām from the Rivāyat of Kāma Bohra* (UI-KB) is available at Aoki 2014a, and the nature of *'Ulamā-ye Islām* (UI-1) as a refutation to the Islamic theology is discussed at Aoki 2014b. But few studies have forcused on *'Ulamā-ye Islām of Another Version* (UI-2) after the time of Zaehner 1955 except Azkā'ī 1990 in spite of the fact that UI-2 is the most famous version of *'Ulamā-ye Islām* among Zoroastrian scholars since the 18th century.

Therefore, the first aim of this paper is to provide a prospect on this treatise with its tentative edition based on some Zoroastrian Persian Codices from Iran. The second aim is to reconstitute its long quotation in the Zoroastrian Persian treatise named *the Book of Mōbedān Mōbed Dādār Dāddukht*, which, in all likelihood, belongs to Āzar Kayvān School Tradition in the 17th century.

18.2 An edition of *'Ulamā-ye Islām of Another Version* (UI-2)

§MSS: As far as I can see, the following five codices – two from Iran and three from India – contain the independent MSS of UI-2 as below:

· The Islamic Republic of Iran, Majles 86908 Codex (for short Majles 86908 UI-2)

· The Islamic Republic of Iran, Majles 87947 Codex (for short Majles 87947 UI-2)

· The Meherjirana Library T-35 Codex (for short MR T-35 UI-2)

· The Mumbai University Library BUL vol. LI Codex (for short BUL UI-2)

· The Molla Feroze Library B-VIII-3 (for short MFL 106 UI-2)

In this paper, the tentative edition is based on Majles 87947 UI-2 and other variants can be seen at footnotes.

§Section Arrangement and Concordance: Section arrangement of UI-2 follows Zaehner 1955. About the concordance with UI-KB and UI-1, see Aoki 2014a.

§System of MS Reproduction: The reproduction system for New Persian spelling here follows the text of Majles 87947 UI-2 literally, which means that any adjustment according to modern Persian writing system has not been done. i.e. آكاهى is not corrected as آگاهى, كنندۀ is not corrected as كنندهٔ and برسيد is not corrected as پرسيد etc.

———————————————————————————————————

علمای اسلام دیکر روش

1) در عهد الدین بعد از ششصد از یزدجردی[1] علمای اسلام[2] یکی از دین آکاهی مثله[3] چند خواست. و در ین معنی سخن کفته است[4] و در ین باب کتابی ساخته اند. و نام این کتاب علمای اسلام[5] نهاده اند یعنی پیدا کنندۀ چکونکی جهان و روح مردم از ازل تا ابد.

2) پرسید که شما انکیزش را چه کوئید[6] وایمان دارید یا نه؟

3) موبدان موبد کفت که ما انکیزش را ایمان داریم و قیامت خواهد بودن.

4) پس علمای اسلام[7] کفت که جهان[8] بوده است؟ وخداي آفرینش مردم و[9] نیستي[10] و باز مردن و[11] زنده[12] باز[13] کردن در ین چه مصلحت است؟

5) و دین دستور آن ایام کفت که آنچه تو مي پرسي بسوي انکیزش نخست بباید دانستن که آفریدن چه بود و میرانیدن چیست و باز زنده کردن چراست.[14] بباید کفتن که جهان بوده است یا آفریده[15].

6) اول از جهان باز کویم وکویم که[16] جهان بوده است یا آفریده. اکر کویند[17] بود " "

[1] MFL 106 UI-2 and MR T-35 UI-2 start here.

[2] BUL UI-2 starts here.

[3] MFL 106 UI-2, MR T-35 UI-2, BUL UI-2: مسله

[4] Majles 87947 UI-2: شد

[5] Majles 87947 UI-2: علما السلام

[6] Majles 87947 UI-2, Majles 86908 UI-2, BUL UI-2: کویند

[7] Majles 87947 UI-2:علما اسلام

[8] MFL 106 UI-2: چون

[9] BUL UI-2: non

[10] MFL 106 UI-2: مردم

[11] MFL 106 UI-2 lacks باز مردم و

[12] BUL UI-2: non, MR T-35 UI-2: زنده باد

[13] Majles 87947 UI-2: زنده and باز are in reverse order.

[14] MFL 106 UI-2: پس

[15] MFL 106 UI-2: است

[16] MFL 106 UI-2: و ~non

[17] MFL 106 UI-2: کوید

آفریده بود[1] این سخن محال[2] بود بسبب آنکه در جهان نو نو چیزها می افزاید و هم در جهان مي کاهد و[3] چون چنین بود که مي کاهد و مي افزاید و نقصان میکیرد و باز زیادت میشود. پس هر چه پدیرندهٔ کون و فساد بود معلول بود[5][4] خدایرا نشاید. پس درست شد که جهان نبوده است و بیافریده اند. پس آفریده را از آفریدکار چاره نیست.

7) و بباید دانستن که در دین پهلوي که زرتشتیان بدان[6] مذهب اند جهانرا آفریده کویند. پس چون کفتم[7] که جهان آفریده است بباید کفتن که که[8] آفرید[9] و کی آفرید و چون آفرید[10] و چرا آفرید[11].

8) در دین زرتشت چنین پیدا است که حد از زمان دیکر همه آفریده است. و آفریدکار زمانست و زمانرا کناره پدید نیست و بالا پدید نیست و بن پدید نیست. و همیشه بوده است و همیشه باشد. و هر که خردي دارد نکوید که زمان از کجا آمد. با این همه بزرکواري که بود کسي[12] نبود که ویرا آفریدکار خواندي. چرا؟ زیرا که آفرینش نکرده بود.

9) پس آتش را و آب را بیافرید. چون بهم رسانید اورمزد موجود آمد. و زمان هم آفریدکار[13] بود و هم خداوند بسوي آفرینش که کرده بود.

10) پس اورمزد روشن و پاك و خوشبوي و نیکوکردار بود و بر همه نیکوئیها توانا بود. پس چون فروشیب[14] تر نکرید نود و شش هزار فرسنك آهرمن را دید سیاه و پلید و کند و بدکردار. و اورمزد را شکفت آمد که خصمي سهمکین بود.

11) و اورمزد چون آن خصم را دید اندیشید که مرا آین[15] خصم ازمیان بر باید کرفت و

[1] MFL 106 UI-2, Majles 87947 UI-2, Salar Jung 3493 UI-2: آفریده ~ non

[2] Majles 86908 UI-2, MR T-35 UI-2: non

[3] MFL 106 UI-2: non

[4] MFL 106 UI-2, BUL UI-2, MR T-35 UI-2: non

[5] Majles 87947 UI-2: و معلول

[6] MFL 106 UI-2: در ان

[7] Majles 87947 UI-2, BUL UI-2: کفتیم

[8] MR T-35 UI-2: جهان

[9] Majles 86908 UI-2, MR T-35 UI-2: non ~

[10] Majles 86908 UI-2: ~ non

[11] MR T-35 UI-2: ~ non

[12] MFL T-35 UI-2: کس

[13] BUL UI-2: افریدکار (redundant)

[14] MR T-35 UI-2: فروسیب

[15] Majles 87947 UI-2: این

اندیشه کرد که[1] بچند و چه اقرار همه باندیشید.

12) و پس آغاز کرد و اورمزد هر چه[2] کرد بیاري زمان کرد و هر نیکي که در اورمز بایست بداده بود. و زمان درنك خداي اورمزد پیدا کرد و بر اندازۀ دوازده هزار سال باشد. و سپهر و نقاش و مینو[3] در وي پیوسته کرد.

13) و اين دوازده برج که در سپهر بسته است هر یك[4] هزار سال تربیت کنند[5] و بر اندازۀ سه هزار سال کار روحاني ساخته آمد و حمل و ثور و جوزا تربیت کننده بودند[6] هر یك هزار سال ببرجي.

14) و پس آهرمن روي ببالا نهاد تا باورمزد جنك کند و لشکري[7] از دیو[8] ساخته وصف کشیده[9] با دوزخ دوارید. و[10] پس از ان پلیدي و تاریکي و کندکي که در وي بود لشکري ساخته کرد. ممکن بوده[11]. و در ین معني سخن بسیار است و مقصود که هم هیچ بدست نداشت هم با دوزخ دوارید.

15) از راستي که در اورمزد دید سه هزار سال نیارست جنبیدن تا این سه هزار سال کار کیتي ساخته شد تربیت کیتي بسرطان و اسد و سنبله رسید. و در ین معني سخن بسیار است.

16) اما سخن چند در ین معني یاد کنیم. در[12] آفریدن کیتي نخست آسمان پیدا کرد و بر اندازۀ بیست و چهار در بیست و چهار هزار فرسنك بالا تا بکروثمان بر شده و بر روي آسمان. و بعد از چهل و پنج روز آب[13] پیدا کرد. و بعد از شصت روز از[14] آب و اسمان زمین[15] پیدا آمد[16]. و بعد از هفتاد و پنج روز[17] نباتهاي بزرك و خورد پیدا

[1] MFL 106 UI-2: non

[2] Majles 87947 UI-2: و جه

[3] MFL 106 UI-2: نقاش and مینو are in reverse order.

[4] MFL 106 UI-2: یکی

[5] Majles 87947 UI-2, MFL 106 UI-2: کرد

[6] MFL 106 UI-2:بود

[7] BUL UI-2: لشکی

[8] MFL 106 UI-2: دید

[9] MFL 106 UI-2:و

[10] MFL 106 UI-2: non

[11] MFL 106 UI-2: کمی بود← ممکن بوده

[12] Majles 86908 UI-2, MR T-35 UI-2: non

[13] MFL 106 UI-2: اسمان

[14] MFL 106 UI-2: non

[15] Majles 87947 UI-2, MFL 106 UI-2, BUL UI-2: non

[16] MFL 106 UI-2: زمین~ non

[17] MFL 106 UI-2: زمین

كرد [1]. و بعد از سي روز [2] كاو كيومرث [3] پيدا آمد. و بعد از هشتاد روز [4] آدم و هوا [5] پديد آمده بود. [6]

17) و چون اين سه هزار سال كه ياد كرده آمد بكدشت مردم و جهان و ديكر آفرينشها كه ياد كرده آمد موجود شد و [7] ديكر باره اهريمن دروند [8] بجنبيد و آسمانرا و كوه را و زمين را سوراخ كرد و در كيتي داوريد [9]. و هرچه در كيتي بود از بدي و پليدي خوَيش آلوده كرد.

18) و چون بار روحاني چيزي بدست نداشت در كيتي نود شبان روز جنك كرد و سپهر بشكست. و مينوان بياري كيتي آمدند.

19) و هفت ديو كه بتر بودند [10] بكرفتند و بر سپهر بردند و بر بند مينوي ببستند. و آهرمن هزار درد بر كيومرث نهاد تا كذشته شد و از او چند چيزها در وجود آمد. در ين معني سخن بسيار است. و از كاو هم چند [11] چيزها و حيوانات موجود شد. در ين معني سخن بسيار است [12].

20) و پس آهرمن را بكرفتند و [13] هم بدان سوراخ كه در دنيا آمده بود با دوزخ بردند و بر بند مينوي ببستند. پس دو فرشته چون ارديبهشت امشاسفند و ورهرام [14] ايزد بموكل وى [15] ايستاده اند.

---

〔1〕MFL 106 UI-2: نباتهاي ~ non

〔2〕MFL 106 UI-2: نبات بزرک و خرد

〔3〕MFL 106 UI-2: كاو ~ non

〔4〕MFL 106 UI-2: كاو كيومرث

〔5〕MFL 106 UI-2: آدم ~ non

〔6〕Majles 86908 UI-2:

و بهفتاد و پنچ روز تمام شد چون تربيت بسرطان رسيده بود آدم و هوا پديد آمده بود.

MFL 106 UI-2:

و بعد از هفتاد و پنچ روز آدم و هوا پديد آمد تا سال سيصد و شصت و پنچ روز اينها تمام جمله شد و چون ترتيب بسرطاب رسيده بود آدم و هوا پديد آمده بود.

〔7〕MFL 106 UI-2: اهرمن دروند

〔8〕MFL 106 UI-2: اهريمن ~ non

〔9〕Majles 87947 UI-2: دواريد

〔10〕MFL 106 UI-2: بود

〔11〕MFL 106 UI-2:كانه

〔12〕Majles 86908 UI-2, MFL 106 UI-2, BUL UI-2, MR T-35 UI-2: در ~ non

〔13〕MFL 106 UI-2: non

〔14〕MFL 106 UI-2: بهرام

〔15〕MFL 106 UI-2:او

21) و اكر كسي كويد كه چون اين همه رنج از وي است و چون بكرفتند او را چرا نكشتند؟ ببايد دانستن كه كسي جانوري بكشد و كويد كه فلان جانوري بكشتم و چون جانور بكشت آتش وي بآتش شد و آب او [1] بآب شد و خاك او با خاك شد و باد او با باد شد. و در وقت انكيزش انكيخته شود و در ميان چيست كه كسسته شود؟

22) معلوم شد كه هيچ از ين كه كفته آمد نيست نشده [2] است اما هر يك چون [3] از [4] جوهر چهار كانه [5] جدا شده اند. پس آهريمن در ين سطبري چون [6] كشته شود جز [7] چنين كه ميكشندش بساكتي و درنك و بدي با نيكي آورند و تاريكي با روشني [8] و پليدي با پاكي تا استادي باشد نه كين و خصومت.

23) اكر كويد كه چون اينهمه استادي داشت [9] آهرمن خود چرا ميداد؟ ما در اول كفته ايم كه اورمزد و اهرمن هر دو از زمان موجود شده اند و هر كروهي كه بركونه ديكر ميكويند.

24) قومي كويند كه اهرمن را از ان داد تا اورمزد داند زمانه بر همه [10] چيز توانا ست. و هر [11] كروهي ميكويند كه نبايست داد با اورمزد بكفت [12] كه من چنين مي توانم كرد و اورمزد را و ما را در رنج نبايست انداخت. و ديكري كويد [13] كه زمان را [14] از بدي آهرمن و از نيكي اورمزد [15] چه رنج يا راحت؟ و كروهي كويند كه اورمزد را و اهرمن را بداد تا نيكي و بدي در هم [16] آميزد و چيزها از رنك رنك در وجود مي [17] آيد. و كروهي كويند كه اهرمن فرشتهٔ مقرب بود و [18] بسبب نا فرماني كه كرد نشانه لعنت شد.

---

[1] MFL 106 UI-2, MR T-35 UI-2: وى

[2] MR T-35 UI-2: شده

[3] Majles 86908 UI-2, MFL 106 UI-2, MR T-35 UI-2: non

[4] Majles 86947 UI-2: در

[5] MR T-35 UI-2: كانه (redundant)

[6] MFL 106 UI-2:كه

[7] MFL 106 UI-2, BUL UI-2: چون

[8] MFL 106 UI-2:روشنائى

[9] MFL 106 UI-2:راست

[10] Majles 87947 UI-2: non

[11] Majles 87947 UI-2: non

[12] Majles 87947 UI-2:كفت

[13] Majles 87947 UI-2: كو

[14] MR T-35 UI-2: non

[15] MFL 106 UI-2:چه اورمزد

[16] MFL 106 UI-2:ب

[17] Majles 87947 UI-2, BUL UI-2: non

[18] MFL 106 UI-2: non

در ین معني سخن بسیار است.

25) اکنون با سر حکایت خویش شویم پس چون مینوان آهرمن را در دوزخ ببستند و دیوان هفتکانه بر سپهر ببستند [1] نام دیوان اینست که ثبت شد زیرج نیرح و ناانکیش و ترمد و حشم و سبیح و بیسژ. و هورمزد هر یکي را از [2] هفتکانهٔ روشني کرد آورده است و نام هورمزدي کرده توانند کرد کیوان هورمزد و بهرام و شید و ناهید و تیر و ماه.

26) چون اینکارها راست آمد سپهر بکشت و خورشید و [3] ستارکان بر آمدن و فروشدن آغاز کردند [4] و ساعات و روز و شب و سال و ماه پیدا شد و دهندکان پدید آمدند. در ین معني سخن بسیار است.

27) و سه هزار سال مردم بودند [5] و دیو نیز آشکارا بود. و جنك مردم با دیوان بودي. و در مردم چند چیز اورمزي است و چند اهریمني و در کالبد آتش است و آب و خاك و باد. و دیکر روان است و هوش است و بوي است و فروهر است. و دیکر حواص [6] پنچکانه چون بصر و سمع و ذوق و شم و لمس [7] است.

28) و کر کسي کوید کاین همه از روانست نه چنانست بسبب آنکه بسیار کس باشد که کنك باشد یا لنك باشد. اکر کسي کوید روان چون این همه ساز و برکیها ندارد چه تواند کرد؟ نه چنانست که ما مي ینیم که آتش دهن ندارد خورشن میخورد و پاي ندارد [8] چنانکه هیزم نهي از بوي هیزم برود و چشم ندارد و چشمها را روشنائي دهد. این [9] سبب آنرا [10] کفته آمد تا دانیم که با این همه ساز و برکیها که بما داده است بي نظر او چیزي نباشیم و با این همه کبر و مني که با یکدیکر داریم. چون [11] چیزهای اورمزدي یاد کردیم [12] آهرمني هم یاد کنند [13] تا دانند و [14] آز و نیاز و رشك و کین و ورن و دروغ و خشم است در دیوان

〔1〕MFL 106 UI-2: و

〔2〕MFL 106 UI-2:دین

〔3〕MFL 106 UI-2:ماه و

〔4〕Majles 86908 UI-2: کرد

〔5〕Majles 86908 UI-2, MFL 106 UI-2: بود

〔6〕Majles 87947 UI-2, Majles 86908 UI-2, MR T-35 UI-2: حواس

〔7〕MR T-35 UI-2: ماس

〔8〕MFL 106 UI-2:و

〔9〕MFL 106 UI-2:ان

〔10〕MFL 106 UI-2: non

〔11〕Majles 86908 UI-2: چو, MR T-35 UI-2: چه

〔12〕Majles 87947 UI-2:و

〔13〕MFL 106 UI-2:کنیم

〔14〕Majles 86908 UI-2, MFL 106 UI-2, MR T-35 UI-2: non

کالبد داشتند. طبایع چهار کونه بودي.

29) [1]

30) بسبب آنرا که قوت آهرمن بدان دیوان فلکي میرسد از ان ایشان را نو نو بدي جهان میرساند تا قوت آهرمني نقصان میشود و بدي آهرمن بدو کم[2] شود تا قیامت را همه بدي وي بکاهد و نیست شود.

31) و مردم آن ایام براه راست میرفتند و دیوانرا[3] میزدند تا آن وقت که پادشاهي جمشید رسید. ششصد[4] سال و شانزده سال و ششماه و[5] پادشاهي کرد و خشم دیو بر وي راه یافت و بخدائي دعوي کرد. و ده ااء[6] تازي ویرا بکرفت و بکشت و بدر پادشاهي بنشست.

32) و هزار سال براند و دیو و مردم بهم بر آمیخت بسیاري جادوئي در جهان بکرد تا بآن وقت که فریدون اتفیان بیامد و او[7] را[8] ببست. ده ااء[9] یعني ده عیب اکنون ضحاك میخوانند[10] [11]. بعد از ان در میان مردمان جنك پدید آمد زیراکه بهري[12] با دیو آمیخته شده بودند و بعضي کمراهي دیده بودند. پس فریدون جهد میکرد تا مردمانرا براه راست خواند چون[13] از نژاد وي افراسیاب پدید آمد آشوب زیادت شد چون کیخسرو پدید آمد جهانرا از بدان پاك کرد.

33) پس زراتشت اسفنتمان به پیغمبري آمد و اوستا و زند و پازند بیاورد. کشتاسپ شاه قبول در جهان کرد و چهار یکي از جهان دین زراتشت قبول کردند و در جهان روا کرد. و سیصد سال کار دینداران هر روز بهتر بود. تا اسکندر رومي بیامد دیکر باره کفتکوي زیادت شد.

34) بعد از ان اردشیر بابکان آن کفت کوي کم کرد تا پانصد سال بر آمد. بعد از ان لشکر عرب

---

[1] The section order of Zaehner 1955 lacks the 29th section.

[2] MFL 106 UI-2:مى

[3] BUL UI-2: non

[4] MFL 106 UI-2:شسصد

[5] Majles 87947 UI-2: non

[6] MFL 106 UI-2:ده اك

[7] MR T-35 UI-2: non

[8] MR T-35 UI-2: non

[9] MFL 106 UI-2: ده اك

[10] MFL 106 UI-2: اكنون ~ non

[11] MFL 106 UI-2:

زشت منكرى و كوتائى و بيشريرمى و بسيار خورى و بدزبانى و دروغ كوى و شتاب كارى و بد دى و بيخردى عرب لفظ دهاك معرب كردند ضحاك كفتند

[12] MR T-35 UI-2: بهر

[13] Majles 86908 UI-2, MR T-35 UI-2: چو

بجنبيد و عجم را زير دست كرد و هر روز ضعيف تر ميشد[1]. تا[2] آن وقت كه بهرام هماوند آيد و[3] تخت ساسانيان مملكت بكيرد.

35) پس اوشيدر بامي بيايد و اوستا و زند نسكي زيادت از انكه زرتشت اسفنتمان آورده است بياورد و بهرام هماوند در جهان روا كند[4]. و آن سه بهره كه در روزكار زرتشت نپذيرفته باشند سه[5] يكي زيادت قبول[6] كند و بچهار صد سال زيادت روا باشند. پس ديكر بار كفتكوي پديد آيد. در ين معني سخن بسيار است.

36) و ديكر باره اوشيدر ماه آيد و كفتكوي از ميان[7] بر[8] كيرد و نسكي اوستا زيادت از انكه[9] اوشيدر بامي بياورد و در جهان روا كند.[10] از مردمان كه بي دين باشند يك نيمه دين به قبول كند. و ديكر باره زمانه نيكي بكذرد و زمانه بدي در آيد و هم بكذرد.

37) بعد از ان سياوشاني نسكي اوستا زيادت از اوشيدر ماه بياورد و جهانيان همه دين به[11] قبول كند[12] و كفتكوي از جهان بر خيزد و پنجاه و هفت سال بر آيد رستاخيز باشد. در ين معني هم سخن بسيار است. كوتاه تر[13] كرفتم تا خوانند را ملالت نيفزايد.

38) و آمديم با سر حكايت خويش آنكه ميكويند كه كسي بمرد يا بكشند[14] باد وي با باد پيوست و خاك وي با خاك و آب وي با آب و آتش وي بآتش پيوست و روان و هوش و بوي هر سه يكي شوند و با فروهر پيوندند همه يكي شود. اكر كناه زيادت بود عقوبت دهند و اكر مزد زيادت دارد[15] ببهشت رسانند. پس ديوان كه با اين شخص بوده باشند همه فرسوده كشته باشند.

39) بجهت عقوبت كه كشيده بود ارديبهشت امشاسفند ميانجي عقوبت بود نكذارد كه عقوبت

[1] Majles 87947 UI-2, MFL 106 UI-2, MR T-35 UI-2: شود

[2] Majles 87947 UI-2, BUL UI-2: non

[3] Majles 87947 UI-2, BUL UI-2: آن

[4] MR T-35 UI-2: كنند

[5] Majles 87947 UI-2, BUL UI-2: باره اوشيدر ماه

[6] Majles 87947 UI-2, BUL UI-2: non

[7] MFL 106 UI-2:جهان

[8] BUL UI-2: دارد

[9] MFL 106 UI-2: non

[10] Majles 86908 UI-2, MFL 106 UI-2: و

[11] MR T-35 UI-2: non

[12] Majles 86908 UI-2, MFL 106 UI-2: كنند

[13] BUL UI-2: non

[14] MFL 106 UI-2: كشتند

[15] MFL 106 UI-2: بود

زيادت از كناه دهندش و اكر بهشتي بود ببهشت و اكر كروثماني بود بكروثمان و اكر همستاني[1] بود بهمستان[2] برندش تا[3] رستخيز.

40) زور ديوان بسوده بود و از بدي نيست كشته بسبب آنكه مردم عقوبت كشند و ديوان كه با مردم اند بسودند.

41) بعد از ان بهشتي و دوزخي را كالبد بر انكيزند هم از ان جوهر نخستين از مينوان[4] آتش آتش و از[5] آب آب و از خاك خاك و از باد باد جمع كنند و روان باز بتن آيد.

42) و بدي كه در تن مردم است آنزمان چون رستاخيز بود بدي نماند و مردمان بي مرك و[6] پيري و[7] نياز باشند همچنين هميشه زنده باشند.[8]

43) و چهار پاي و مرغ و ماهي ايشانرا روان نبود و مينو چهار كونه باز ايشان[9] پيوندد. بدان سبب ايشانرا شمار و حساب نيست كه ايشان روان و فروهر ندارند. و دليل بر ين كه مردم خرد دارد و دانش و راستي و بالا و سخن كفتن بزبان و كار كردن بدست[10] روانست. و اكر نه همه جانوران از ين چهار طبايع بهره دارند. پس مردم اين همه زيادت دارد[11] بسبب روان حساب و شمار مردم را بود و ديكر جانوران ندارند.

44) و آنچه كفته آمد كه آفريدون[12] چه بود و ميرانيدن چيست و باز اميد زنده كردن چراست؟ ببايد دانستن كه آفريدون[13] از سر رحمت و فضل وي بود. و ميرانيدن بسبب آنست[14] كه ما چون[15] امشاسفندان بودي كه نمردي آهريمن در ما نتوانستي كميخت[16] بدي و تاريكي و پليدي و كنده وی هميشه بماندي. خون[17] ما در كميخت ما مي رنجاند و مي

---

[1] Majles 87947 UI-2: همستکانی

[2] Majles 87947 UI-2: همستکانی

[3] Majles 86908 UI-2, MFL 106 UI-2:روز

[4] BUL UI-2: از

[5] MR T-35 UI-2: non

[6] MFL 106 UI-2:بی

[7] MFL 106 UI-2:بی

[8] MFL 106 UI-2:و هيچ بدی نماند

[9] MR T-35 UI-2: را

[10] MFL 106 UI-2:همه بدست

[11] BUL UI-2:دارند

[12] Majles 87947 UI-2: آفريدن

[13] Majles 87947 UI-2: آفريدن

[14] MFL 106 UI-2:اين است

[15] Majles 86908 UI-2: non, MR T-35 UI-2: با

[16] Majles 87947 UI-2: و

[17] Probably چون ? But all MSS show this spell.

كشود و مي پندارد كه ما را نيست ميكند نميداند كه آن بدي خويش است كه بر مي اندازد ميرانيدن اينست[1].

45) و زنده باز كردن بر وي فريضه است بسبب آنكه ما[2] بسياري رنج كشيده ايم چه در كيتي چه در مينو. پس فريضه باشد از سر رحمت و كرم خويش كه ما را زنده كند اكر چه كه در ميانه چيزي مرده نيست و ليكن پراكنده جمله كند شخص را بر انكيزد و پاداش دهد از نيكوئيهاي خويش.

46) و آن بيست و يك نسك اوستا كه ميكويند[3] اوستا زبان[4] اورمزد است و زند زفان ما و پازند آنكه هر كسي بدانند كه چه ميكويد.

47) و اين بيست و يك نسك[5] را[6] اوستا[7] [8] زند و پازند اينست كه پيدا[9] كنيم. و هفت نسك را زند و پازند اينست كه[10] ياد كرديم و هفت نسك را زند و پازند اينست كه[11] شايست و ناشايست و كن و مكن و كوي و مكوي و ستان و مستان و خور و مخور و پاك و پليد و پوش و مپوش و مانند اين. اكر همه ياد كنيم[12] كتاب بنهايت رسد كوتاه كرفتم. و هفت نسك را زند و پازند طبيعي و نجوم است. در اين معني هم[13] سخن بسيار است.

48) ميكويند كه خورشيد كرد زمين بر ميكردد و بهر جا كه خورشيد ميرود چون اينجا كه مائيم آسمان و ستاركانست و خواه در زير زمين خواه در پهلوي زمين تواند بود كه ما خود در زير زمين ايم و ميكويم با بالاي زمين ايم. و در اوستا و زند چنين ميكويد كه هر مردم كه بودند و آنچه اند و آنچه باشند همه بهشتي شوند و عقوبت روانرا باشد[14] پيش از رستخيز.

---

[1] MFL 106 UI-2:است

[2] MR T-35 UI-2: non

[3] MFL 106 UI-2: ميكوييم

[4] MFL 106 UI-2:زفان

[5] Majles 86908 UI-2, BUL UI-2: اوستا

[6] MLF 106 UI-2, MR T-35 UI-2: non

[7] Majles 86908 UI-2, BUL UI-2: non

[8] MR T-35 UI-2: را

[9] MR T-35 UI-2: ياد

[10] MR T-35 UI-2: non ~

[11] MR T-35 UI-2: ~ non

[12] MFL 106 UI-2: كنم

[13] MFL 106 UI-2, BUL UI-2: non

[14] MFL 106 UI-2: و

49) [1] شكفت تر اينكه فرزند بدبيرستان مي فرستيم و نيكي شان مي آموزيم و از بدي شان دور ميكنيم چون بنكري هنوز بدي پيش دانند كه نيكي و نيكي هم در پيش خداي نيكو است و هم در پيش خلق. بدي هم در پيش [2] آفريدكار بد است هم در پيش مردم. و در مردم نيكي و بدي است و در كيتي نيكي و بدي است و در سپهر نيكي و بدي هست [3] و در مينو بهشت و دوزخ است.

50) و ما آفريدۀ آفريدكار ايم و باز كشت همه بدوست. و اكر نبايستي آفريدكار نيافريدي و در ين كه [4] بدي نميبايد و هست ستري هست يا خرد ما بدان نمي رسد پس چون چنين است كار خدا بخدا مي [5] بايد كذاشت.

51) و آنچه كفته است كه ميبايد كرد همي بايد كرد و آنچه فرموده [6] است كه نمي بايد كرد نمي بايد كرد و آنچه كفته است كه انديش مي انديشد و آنچه كفته است كه [7] نميبايد انديشيد نمي بايد انديشيد و آنچه كفته است كه كوي ميكوي و آنچه كفته است كه مكوي نبايد كفت و آنچه فرموده [8] است خور ميخورد و آنچه فرموده است كه مخور نبايد خورد و آنچه كفته است كه [9] پوش مي پوش آنچه كفته است كه مپوش نبايد پوشيد مانند اين. شرط ما آنست كه به بندكي مشغول باشيم.

52) و درود و آفرين بر پاكان و نيكان و رهنمايان باد نيكي باد ايدون باد. تمام شد كتاب علماى اسلام. [10]

18.3 a Long Quotation of '*Ulamā-ye Islām of Another Version* (UI-2)

§Majles 13522 Codex: In this chapter, a long quotation of *'Ulamā-ye Islām*

[1] Majles 86908 UI-2, MFL 106 UI-2: و

[2] MR T-35 UI-2: خلق ~ non

[3] Majles 86908 UI-2: در ~ non

[4] MFL 106 UI-2: non

[5] Majles 87947 UI-2, Majles 86908 UI-2, MR T-35 UI-2: همي

[6] Majles 87947 UI-2, BUL UI-2: كفته

[7] Majles 86908 UI-2, MR T-35 UI-2: non

[8] MFL 106 UI-2: كفته

[9] BUL UI-2: كه

[10] Majles 86908 UI-2, BUL UI-2: تمت تمام شد

of Another Version (UI-2) in a Zoroastrian Persian treatise belonging to Majles 13522 Codex will be dealt. This codex consists of the following six treatises:

fol. 1r-fol. 6r: without the opening head and title

fol. 6v-fol. 8r: *Dāstān-e Khvān Nāme*

fol. 8r-fol. 50r: without any title, but its incipit is "In the time of Khusraw Anūshirwān…"

fol. 50v-fol. 88r: *Dāstān-e Mōbedān Mōbed Dādār Dāddukht va Keyfīyat-e ān*

fol. 88r-fol. 90v: *Sougand Nāme* (for this treatise, see Aoki 2011 and 2012)

fol. 90v-fol. 96v: *Zand Bahman Yasht va Jāmāsbī* without its latter part

Several factors prevent to investigate this codex. Firstly, pages in the codex are out of order due to an error in binding, perhaps, by the Majles library. For example, the fourth treatise which we will discuss here later seems to occupy fol. 50v-fol. 88r, though, strangely enough, the Majles catalogue reports it consists only of fol. 66v-fol. 88r (Hā'erī 1305-1377AH, pp. 271-272). But if we go on reading this treatise in both of those orders, it does not make sense. As far as I can see, the fourth treatise consists of fol. 50v-fol. 64v and fol. 81r-fol. 88r, although I could not identify the contents of the interval 14 fols between fols 66-88.

Secondly, this codex is badly damaged, especially in its first 33 fols. For example, one of third of fols 3, 7, 12 and 13 are lost. In addition to this, the first treatise lacks its opening head and sixth treatise has only 6 fols. Comparing its ordinal amount of *Zand Bahman Yasht va Jāmāsbī* (Dhabhar 1932, pp. 481-493), it certainly lacks consideble part of the text.

No colophon covering the whole codex can be found within the text, but three interval colophons are shown at the ends of the each treatise as below:

fol. 4v: "Bahrām Mehrabān Bahrām Goshtāsb wrote (this MS) at Shahrīvar day (without month and year)"

fol. 8r: "Bahrām Mehrabān Bahrām Goshtāsb wrote (this MS) at Ohrmazd day, Bahman month, 1000 and 14 year"

fol. 50r: "Bahrām Mehrabān Bahrām Goshtāsb wrote (this MS) at Shahrīvar day, Khordād month, 1000 and 14 Jalālī year"

Guessing from those colophons, at least till the third treatise, this codex was written by the same copyist named Bahrām Mehrabān Bahrām Goshtāsb in the middle of the 17th century CE.

This codex has four impressed ownership stamps of "Majles 1302 year" at fol. 1r, fol. 7r, fol. 37r and fol. 96v. Probably this date depends on the Iranian Solar calendar, it is very likely that this codex was possessed by the Majles library after 1302 Sh. = 1944 CE. But there is no clue to know the owner before the Majles.

§*the Book of Mōbedān Mōbed Dādār Dāddukht*: the fourth treatise of this codex is entitled *the Book of Mōbedān Mōbed Dādār Dāddukht*, the MS of which has not included in any known Zoroastrian Rivayats collected by Hormazyar Framroz in 1644 CE (see Unvâlâ 1922; Dhabhar 1932). But after the 19th century, this treatise was reported three times as below:

The first MS was brought from India by Martin Haug (d. 1876) in 1866 CE. It is the 13th treatise named *the Book of Dādār bin Dāddukht* (fol. 188-fol. 213) in the M Codex No. 7, die Bayerische Staatsbibliothek, copied in 27, Janunary, 1809 CE (Haug 1884, p. 113).

The second MS was indicated by Edward West (d. 1905) as the Or. 8994 (fol. 104-fol. 139), the British Library (West 1896-1904, pp. 123-124).

The third MS is the second treatise of F52 Codex, the Meherjirana Library (Navsari, India). Although it is named *Ārāste* (Dhabhar 1923, p. 31), insofar as I read it, its content corresponds to *the Book of Mōbedān Mōbed Dādār Dāddukht* exactly (Aoki 2003, p. 2). This codex has a colophon as

"Dastūr Īrachjī copyed (it) at 1247 Yazdegirdī (=1877CE) from the MS copyed by Goshtāsb Ardashīr in the order of Mollā Kāūs Rostam at 1155 Yazdegirdī (=1785CE)." Arguably this Dastūr Īrachjī is the famous copyist Dastūr Īrachjī Sohrābjī Meherjīrānā (1826-1900), and Mollā Kāūs Rostam may be the leader of the Kadmi School, Mollā Kāūs Rostam Jalāl (1733-1802).

I suppose this treatise was one of the MSS brought from Iran by this Mollā Kāūs Rostam Jalāl, who stayed in Iran between 1768 and 1780 then reportedly carried several Zoroastrian MSS back to India. Unfortunately those MSS he brought from Iran were doubted in its authenticity by the Shahanshahi school, then the most part of them got be scatterd afterwards.

§*the Book of Mōbedān Mōbed Dādār Dāddukht* and *Āzar Kayvān School*: This treatise should be divided to three parts according to its contents, and the last third part (fol. 63, l. 16-fol. 64v, l. 17, fol. 81r, l. 1- fol. 87v, l. 16) corresponds to UI-2 (section1-section44). Before analyzing this long quotation, however, it might be useful to show the whole structure of this text.

The main subject of the first part (fol. 50v, l. 3-fol. 51r. l. 14) is "Dādār Dāddukht and a (fictional) Intellectual History of Ancient Iran." According to the text, "Among Persian and Pahlavi books of Mānī (certainly the Prophet of Manichaeism!), there is a book which justifid him (Mānī) as an Orthodoxy (of Zoroastrianism!). Dādār Dāddukht was a Mōbedān Mōbed of the time of Shāhānshāh Shāpūr…Because that book (one of the Mānī's books) was written in Darī language, Mōbedān Mōbed Abū Nasr bin Sorūshyār bin Āzar Kharrād translated it…" This Āzar Kharrād might be the same person who was one of the disciple of the 17th century Zoroastrian Mythtic Āzar Kayvān (d. 1618), and this book's highly affirmative estimation on Mānī, a heresy from view point of average Zoroastrians, might reflect a religious idea of Āzar Kayvān School, which has a special book for Prophet Mānī named *Arzhang-e Mānī* (Mānī's picture book). Therefore, we can conjecture with some confidence that this treatise was written by a member of Āzar Kayvān School, or at least under the strong influence of them after the 17th century.

The main subject of the second part (fol. 51r, l. 14-fol. 63r, l. 16) is a "Discussion between Dādār Dāddukht and Greek Doctors." According to the explanation of Dādār Dāddukht, the origin of Greek medicine was the Ancien Persian Wisdom – quite popular theory among medieval Zoroastrians. But he continues that the origin of those wisdoms is the *Avesta va Zand* in Persian, which is also called *Qur'an* in Arabic, then he got its contents back from Greek libraries and retranslated into Persian again. This means that Islam also belongs to Ancient Persian Intellectual Tradition. Unquestionably this view of the sacred book is common with Āzar Kayvān School.

The main subject of the third part (fol. 63, l. 16-fol. 64v, l. 17, fol. 81r, l. 1- fol. 88, l. 7) is a "Discussion between Dādār Dāddukht and Muslim Doctors" till fol. 87v, l. 16, but this part is an extract from UI-2,§1-44. One of the significances of UI-2 depends on the fact that this is the only traditional Zoroastrian Persian treatise to be quoted in the books of Āzar Kayvān School.

§an Example of the Quotation of UI-2: As is cleared from the abovementioned, this long quotation of UI-2 is obviously copied after the 17th century when Āzar Kayvān School began to spread their syncretism of Zoroastrianism and Islam through their unique literary activety. Therefore, Majles 13522 Codex is inefficient for the study of *'Ulamā-ye Islām of Another Version* (UI-2) itself. Interestingly, however, it shows UI-2 still remain in use by a 17th century mystical thinker to express his religious idea in the context of traditional Zoroastrianism.

It is not necessary here to show the whole quotation of UI-2, but its example makes clear which MSS tradition the author of *the Book of Mōbedān Mōbed Dādār Dāddukht* consulted. See the quotation between section 8 and section 13 as below.

8）در دین زراتشت چنین پیدا ست که چندان زمان دکر همه آفریده است. آفریدکار زمان است زمان را کناره پدید نیست و بالا بدید نیست و بن پدید [illegible]. همیشه بوده است و هر که خردي دارد نکوید که زمان از کجا آمد. با این همه بزرکواري که بود کسي نبود که ویرا آفریدکار خواندي. چرا؟ زیرا که هنوز آفرینش نکرده بود.

9）پس آتش را و آب را بیافرید. چون بهم رسانید [illegible] موجود آمد. و زمان هم آفریدکار بود و هم خداوند سوي آفرینش که کرده بود.

10）پس هورمزد روشن و پاك و خوش بوي ونیکوکردار بود و بر همه نیکوئیها توانا بود. پس چون هورمزد بیش تر نکرید نود و شش [illegible] فرسنك آهرمن دید سیاه و کنده وپلید و بدکردار. پس دادار اورمزد را شکفت آمد که خصم سهمکین بود.

11）و اورمزد چون آن خصم را دید اندیشید که مرا این خصم ازمیان بر باید کرفت و اندیشه کرد که بچند وچه قرار باندیشید.

12）و آغاز افرینش کرد و [illegible] هر چه کرد بیاري زمان نتواند[1]کرد پس هر نیکي که اورمز را بایست بداده بود. و زمان و[2]درنك خداي[3]پیدا کرد و بر اندازه دوازده [illegible] باشد. و سپهر و مینو و نقاش[4]در وي پیوسته کرد.

13）و این دوازده برج که بر سپهر بسته است هر یك را هزار سال تربیت کنند و بر اندازه ج [illegible] کار روحاني ساخته حمل و ثور و جوزا تربیت کننده بودند هر برجی مدت [illegible]

From this partial quotation, we can draw three conclusions as below:

1）The author of *the Book of Mōbedān Mōbed Dādār Dāddukht*, probably a member of Āzar Kayvān School, extracted the third part of his

[1] This word can be found only at Majles 13522 Codex.

[2] This و can be found only at Majles 13522 Codex.

[3] Other MSS of UI-2: ورمزد

[4] This order corresponds only with MS of MFL 106 Codex.

treatise from a MS of UI-2 in the line of MFL 106 Codex, which is a grand daughter Codex copied in 1876 CE from the lost Collection of Persian Rivayats edited by Barzu Kamdin in 1636 CE. I hope this fact contributes to the study of Āzar Kayvān School in some manner.

2) The author of *the Book of Mōbedān Mōbed Dādār Dāddukht* revised the text partially, but he seems not to intend to delete the Zurvanite nuance within the text. Supposedly he quoted UI-2 without any recognition that it belongs to the tradition of Zurvanite Zoroastrianism.

3) Some Persian words are replaced with Pahlavi synonyms, but it is not clear who did it. Maybe the author himself or copyist(s) did.

I would like to pay my respects by this small article to Prof. Lin Wushu, one of the precursors of the studies on Iranian religions in the Far East. Although I have never been recognized by him personally, I learnt much about Zoroastrianism, Manichaeism and Nestrianism in Medieval China through his vast amount of Chinese writings. His disciple Dr. Zhang Xiaogui kindly called for me to contribute this Festschrift for Prof. Lin's 70 years old to express my homage to him. So I am also indebted much to Dr. Zhang, one of my best colleages since 2006 when we first met at a hotel in Guangzhou to discuss about Iranian religions in China and Japan.

Bibliography

MSS

The Islamic Republic of Iran, Majles 13522 Codex

The Islamic Republic of Iran, Majles 86908 Codex

The Islamic Republic of Iran, Majles 87947 Codex

The Meherjirana Library T-35 Codex

The Mumbai University Library BUL vol. LI Codex

The Molla Feroze Library B-VIII-3

MSS Catalogues

Dhabhar, E. B. N. 1923: *Descriptive Catalogue of all Manuscripts in the First Dastur Meherji Rana Library*, Navsari, Bombay.

Hā'erī, 'Abd al-Hoseyn et als. (eds) 1305-1377AH: *Fehrest-e Noskhe-hā-ye Khattī-ye Ketābkhāne-ye Majles Showrā-ye Eslāmī*, vol. 37, Tehrān.

Editions

Aoki, Takeshi 2014a: "Zoroastrian Persian Manuscripts on Zurvanism in Iran and India with an edition of *'Ulamā-ye Islām from the Rivāyat of Kāma Bohra* (UI-KB)," *Navsari Zoroastrian Studies Conference (January / 12-15 / 2013) Proceedings*, Mumbai (forthcoming)

– 2014b: "A Zoroastrian Refutation to the Mu'tazilite Theology with an Edition of *'Ulamā-ye Islām* (UI-1)," *Journal of Central Eurasian Studies*, vol. 4, Seoul National University (forthcoming)

Azkā'ī, Parviz 1990: "Resāle-ye Zorvānī 'Olamā-ye Eslām," In: *Cheste*, No. 3, pp. ٣٤١-٣٥٧. (reprint: In: *Mīrāth-e Eslāmī-ye Īrān*, No. 4, 1997, pp. ٥٨١-٦٠٠)

Unvâlâ, Ervad Manockji Rustamji 1922: *Dârâb Hormazyâr's Rivâyat*, 2vols, Bombay.

Studies

Aoki, Takeshi 2003: 「インド・ゾロアスター教徒の思想形成」、小林フェローシップ 2002 年度研究助成論文、富士ゼロックス小林節太郎記念基金 (in Japanese).

–2011: 「ミトラ教ペルシア語文献研究 1～『シャープール・バルージーのミトラ教についての書簡』の写本蒐集と校訂翻訳～」、『慶應義塾大学言語文化研究所紀要』、第 42 号、pp. 29-45 (in Japanese).

–2012: 「ミトラ教ペルシア語文献研究 2～『シャープール・バ

ルージーのミトラ教についての書簡』の写本蒐集と校訂翻訳〜」、『慶應義塾大学言語文化研究所紀要』、第 43 号、pp. 1-18 (in Japanese).

Dhabhar, E. B. N. 1932: *The Persian Rivayats of Hormazyar Framarz,* Bombay (reprint, 1999).

Haug, Martin 1862: *Essays on the Sacred Language, Writings, and Religion of the Parsis*, Bombay.

West, E. W. 1896-1904: "Pahlavi Literature," *Grundriss der iranischen Philologie*, zweiter Band, pp. 75-129.

Zaehner, R. C. 1955: *Zurvan: a Zoroastrian Dilemma*, Oxford.

19 吉美博物馆所藏石重床的几点思考

沈睿文
（北京大学中国考古学研究中心）

2004年，法国吉美博物馆根据德凯琳（Catherine Delacour）、黎北岚（Pénélope Riboud）的复原方案展出某收藏家的一石棺床。〔1〕参校已有相关石葬具构图，可知该复原方案符合其内在理路。在此基础上，两位学者也对石屏图案的内涵做了有益的探讨。〔2〕只是其中结论或有可商处，犹需重加讨论。本文拟对此再做辨析，并对相关问题略作申论。

19.1 墓主人身份

北朝隋粟特裔贵族墓葬基本可依照葬具分作两大系统，即石重床（俗谓石棺床）的现实纪功图像系统和石堂的神性图像系统。后者间或会以图像表现形式或少数的图像以为纪功之符号，由此而呈现出统一性和多样性的特征。〔3〕据此吉美石棺床宜称之为“石重床”，其所属亦应同为域外种落之首领。但从其图像特征判断，它跟其他相关葬具既有

〔1〕Guimet, Musée éd. , Lit de pierre, sommeil barbare, Présentation, après restauration et remontage, d’une banquette funéraire ayant appartenu à un aristocrate d’Asie centrale venu s’établir en Chine au VIe siècle, Paris, Musée Guimet, 2004。

〔2〕德凯琳、黎北岚著，施纯琳译：《巴黎吉美博物馆展围屏石榻上刻绘的宴饮和宗教题材》，载山西省北朝文化研究中心《4~6世纪的北中国与欧亚大陆》，北京：科学出版社，2006年，第108–125页。黎北岚：《袄神崇拜：中国境内的中亚聚落信仰何种宗教》，载荣新江、华澜、张志清主编《法国汉学》第十辑“粟特人在中国——历史、考古、语言的新探索”专号，北京：中华书局，2005年12月，第416–429页。相关研究尚有：万毅《巴黎吉美博物馆展胡人石棺床图像试探》，载于《艺术史研究》第十二辑，广州：中山大学出版社，2010年，第15-37页。案，本文所用考古资料皆径取自原考古发掘简报、报告或复原者的编号，恕下文不再指出。

〔3〕沈睿文：《论墓制与墓主国家和民族认同的关系——以康业、安伽、史君、虞弘诸墓为例》，载朱玉麒主编《西域文史》第六辑，北京：北京大学出版社，2012年12月，第221–226页。

相似之处，也有不同。

为宦中土王朝，自约束于后者之体制。根据北朝丧葬体制中“夫妇宴乐+出行”的墓葬壁画构图程式，可推知吉美石重床背屏之4、5（图19–1、19–2）应为该墓主夫妇的图像。其中第4屏的中心位置图像为：在一曲盖之下一左手握拄三叉戟、舒腿坐于筌蹄[1]之上的男子。依墓葬壁画构图之常情，此人应即该墓主人。在已经发现的其他同样性质的石质葬具，如虞弘墓石堂以及山东青州傅家画像石中，便有墓主人坐于筌蹄之上的形象。

虞弘墓石堂椁壁浮雕之八（图19–3）的中心图像是一男子头戴波斯王冠，架腿坐于一筌蹄之上。[2]该男子形象在石堂椁壁图案中多处出现，且皆位于所在图像的中心位置。故可推断该形象表现的便是墓主人虞弘。根据虞弘墓志知，他曾任检校萨宝府、仪同三司、领左帐内等职，并非国王或者国王之苗裔，为何得以头戴王冠？其原因在于，虞弘任检校萨宝府，为该种落政教首领，亦即为其种落在隋王朝的最高领导者，可视作“王”。如，其背光为“王者灵光”[3]可证。另外，冠以波斯王冠恐亦意在彰扬墓主人生前出使波斯的功绩，是为记功符号。

---

〔1〕孙机：《唐·李寿石椁线刻〈侍女图〉、〈乐舞图〉散记》（上），原载《文物》1996年第5期，第39–40页；后收入所撰《中国圣火——中国古文物与东西文化交流中的若干问题》，沈阳：辽宁教育出版社，1996年12月，第209–211页。

〔2〕山西省考古研究所、太原市考古研究所、太原市晋源区文物旅游局：《太原隋代虞弘墓清理简报》，载于《文物》2001年第1期，第27–52页；山西省考古研究所、太原市考古研究所、太原市晋源区文物旅游局：《太原隋虞弘墓》，北京：文物出版社，2005年。

〔3〕王小甫：《拜火教与突厥兴衰——以古代突厥斗战神研究为中心》，载于《历史研究》2007年第1期，第30页；后收入所撰《中国中古的族群凝聚》，北京：中华书局，2012年8月，第26–27页。

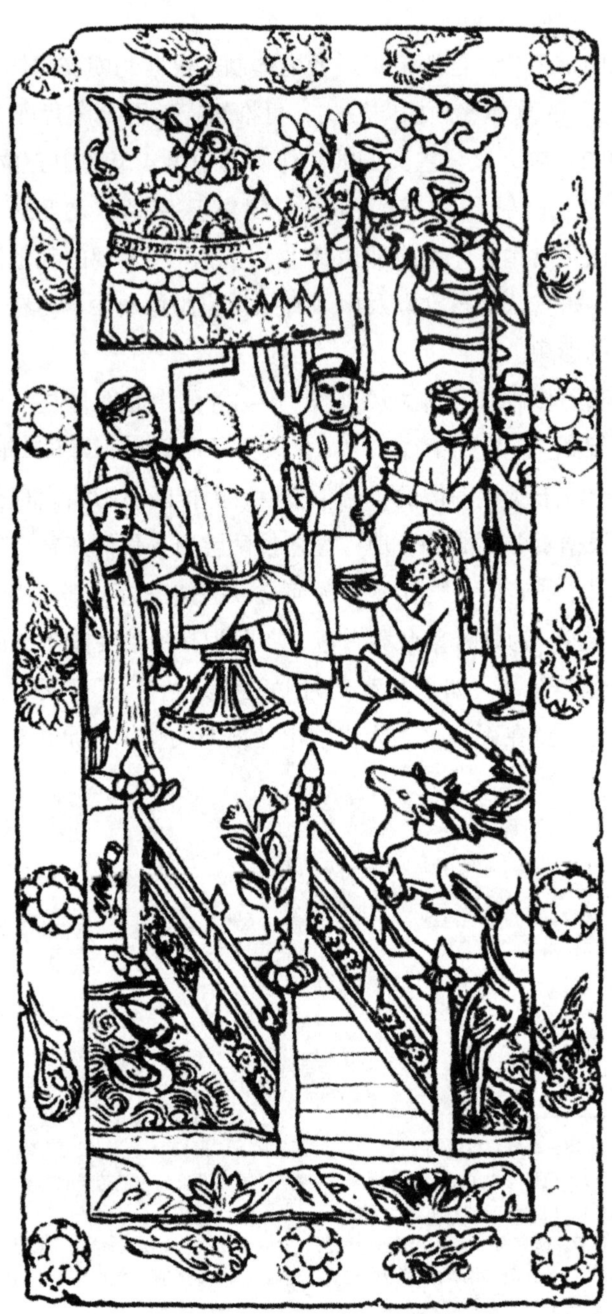

图 19–1　吉美石重床背屏第四石

图 19–2　吉美石重床背屏第五石

图 19–3　虞弘墓石堂椁壁浮雕之八

另一筌蹄图像见于山东青州傅家画像石[1]，其中第二石所谓“商谈图”（图 19–4）中，一头戴纶巾男子架腿坐于筌蹄之上。该男子同样在这批画像石中多次出现，且居诸图像的中心位置。如此亦可判断该男子为墓主人。

图 19–4　山东青州傅家画像石第二石

〔1〕夏名采：《益都北齐石室墓线刻画像》，载于《文物》1985年第10期，第49–54页；夏名采：《青州傅家北齐线刻画像补遗》，载于《文物》2001年第5期，第92–93页。由于安伽等粟特裔墓葬的发掘，这批画像石的内涵得以发覆。可参郑岩：《粟特祆教美术东传过程中的转化——从粟特到中国》，原载巫鸿主编《汉唐之间文化艺术的互动与交融》，北京：文物出版社，2001年，第73–112页；后题作《青州傅家北齐画像石与入华祆教美术》，收入所撰《魏晋南北朝壁画墓研究》，北京：文物出版社，2002年，第236–284页；又题作《青州北齐画像石与入华粟特人美术——虞弘墓等考古新发现的启示》，收入所撰《逝者的面具——汉唐墓葬艺术研究》，北京：北京大学出版社，2013年2月，第266–307页。姜伯勤：《青州傅家北齐画像石祆教图像的象征意义——与粟特壁画的比较研究》，载中山大学艺术学研究中心编《艺术史研究》第5辑，广州：中山大学出版社，2003年，第169–188页；后收入所撰《中国祆教艺术史研究》，北京：三联书店，2004年，第63–76页。

从虞弘和青州的案例来看，推断此类葬具图像中坐于筌蹄之上的人物多为墓主人形象，应大体不误。据此，吉美石重床第 4 屏曲盖下之男子应为墓主人。显然，背屏 6（图 19–5）中手持来通（rython）的男子亦为同一人物。也就是说，墓主人在背屏中两度出现。其图像的重复出现无疑也是对上述判断的有力支持。

但是，该人物（墓主人）个体生命的旅程为何，因墓志等文字资料的缺憾而无从得知。所幸，石重床背屏中与该人物共存的一些图案特质给我们提供了线索。在背屏 4 中，他手持三叉戟，坐于曲盖之下，该曲盖之上饰有两只相对头部往外（正面）扭转的动物，惜已难辨识。同样地，在背屏 6 中，墓主人"头帐"之上也有两只相对头部往外扭转的动物纹样（图 19–6）。这两只动物形象为尖喙、头顶有冠，头颈下有垂肉（俗称"鸡坠子"）。毋庸置疑，这正是对公鸡的如实写照。由此推论，背屏 4 墓主人曲盖顶部两侧所饰动物很可能也是公鸡。

图 19–5　吉美石重床背屏第 6 石

图 19-6　吉美石重床背屏第 6 石上部“金鸡帐”

正是三叉戟以及公鸡的装饰样式披露了墓主人身份的某些信息。此二者究竟所指为何？1994 年，统万城出土的翟曹明石墓门给我们提供了解读的重要线索。该墓石墓门构件（图 19-7）也有此两种装饰样式。〔1〕

翟曹明墓石门楣在龙头两侧阴线刻一对公鸡（图 19-8、19-9、19-10），而非常见的朱雀或者凤凰。其石门扉上各彩绘一手持三叉戟的武将。究其原因，在于墓主人的种族文化与政教身份。该墓所出《夏州天主仪同翟曹明墓志》（北周大成元年/579 年撰）记志主：“君讳曹明，西国人也。祖宗忠烈，令誉家邦。受命来朝，遂居恒夏。君幼怀歧嶷，长有才雄。咢咢当官，恂恂乡邑。伤魏载之衰泯，慨臣下之僭凌。

〔1〕陕西历史博物馆编：《三秦瑰宝——陕西新发现文物精华》，西安：陕西人民出版社，2001年6月，第133页图。

是以慕义从军，诛除乱逆。巨猾摧峰，六军振振。”也就是说，他原本在乡邑当官，任职“天主”，则其必为当地粟特聚落领袖；在北魏灭亡之际，加入北魏军队，任“仪同”职，即为国家所授之乡团统帅称号。[1]墓志署葬日为“大周大成元年岁次已亥（579）三月癸四日”。大成元年二月辛巳已改大象，夏州据京城遥远，尚未得消息。可见翟曹明并非如“三秦瑰宝”展览说明所言为唐人，而是和安伽葬于同一年的西国胡人。[2]通过对翟曹明墓志以及隋唐时期翟姓胡人姓名、婚姻以及文化特征的比照分析，可推断统万城一带的稽胡中应有不少源于粟特的胡人，他们大量进入这一地区，可能与北魏灭北凉而迁徙大量粟特胡人前往平城地区有关，也可能是粟特商团东渐的结果。[3]而翟曹明当是这些粟特种落的政教、军事领袖。墓主人“天主”的政教身份提醒我们可从祆教的角度解读上述装饰纹样。

在祆教中，公鸡为斯劳沙（Sraosha）的圣禽。[4]斯劳沙不仅是阿胡拉·马兹达的使者，而且是恶魔的惩治者（fiend-smiter），是世界的化身，最有力的矛以及高贵的神。[5]斯劳沙为古伊朗神话中宗教虔诚和秩序之精灵，其中古波斯称之为“斯罗什”。斯劳沙取代一较为古老之神（似为埃里雅曼或密特拉）。斯劳沙确信查拉图什特拉之说正确无讹，遂向其祝福。[6]另外，斯劳沙在护卫、辅佐墓主人灵魂方面也起着重要的作用，此见下文。

---

〔1〕荣新江：《从聚落到乡里——敦煌等地胡人集团的社会变迁》，载高田时雄编《敦煌写本研究》第三号，2009年3月，第28页。按，翟曹明墓志文录自荣新江：《新出石刻史料所见粟特人研究的动向》，载于《关西大学东西学术研究所纪要》第44辑（2011年4月1日），第103页。

〔2〕荣新江：《学术训练与学术规范》，北京：北京大学出版社，2011年，第134页。

〔3〕罗丰、荣新江：《北朝时期统万城的西国胡人——翟曹明墓出土文物初探》，2003年“沙漠古都统万城学术研讨会”论文。

〔4〕魏庆征编：《古代伊朗神话》，太原：北岳文艺出版社/山西人民出版社，1999年，第374–375页。

〔5〕关于斯劳沙的记载可参：*The Zend-Avesta*, Part Ⅱ, in *Sacred Books of the East*, vol.23, Translated by James Darmesteter, The Oxford University Press, 1882, pp.159–167; *The Zend-Avesta*, Part Ⅲ, in *Sacred Books of the East*, vol.31, Translated by L. H. Mills, The Oxford University Press, 1887, pp.305–306.

〔6〕魏庆征编：《古代伊朗神话》，第374–375页。

图 18-7　统万城翟曹明石墓门

图 19-8　翟曹明石门楣中间龙头

图 19-9　翟曹明墓石门楣左侧金鸡

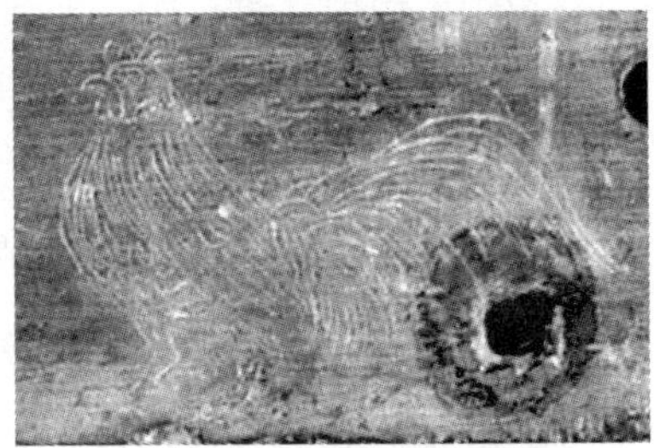

图 19-10　翟曹明墓石门楣右侧金鸡

翟曹明墓石门楣线刻的公鸡斯劳沙在祆教中代表的战斗力以及对宗教的忠诚，跟墓主“天主”的身份以及墓志文称其“慕义从军，诛除乱逆。巨猾摧峰，六军振振”——突出其从军经历恰可吻合。应无疑义。如此，在其石门扉上阴刻一对手持三叉戟的武将应也意在强调翟曹明的战将身份及其军功。这跟公鸡斯劳沙的内涵是一脉相承的。北朝隋墓葬石门武士形象多拄仪刀，少数另有执盾的，尚不见手执三叉戟者。而祆教风神的一个典型形象便是手执三叉戟（图 19-11、19-12），如此似乎也就意味着三叉戟与信奉祆教的战将之间的某种联系。

图 19-11　片吉肯特出土壁画 Weshparkar

图 19-12　史君石堂 E1 风神

翟曹明墓志的发现，使得该墓石门楣上线刻金鸡的祆教内涵得以解开，并可明晰其石门扉上彩绘武士所持三叉戟是跟墓主人战将的身份紧密相连的。据此便可辨析吉美石重床墓主人的政治身份。

吉美石重床背屏4中，墓主人左手持三叉戟。由翟曹明墓石门的构图，同样可以推知战将应该是吉美石重床主人的一个重要身份。而其曲盖、“头帐”上端两侧的公鸡应也是斯劳沙的圣禽。那么，在汉语文献中装饰有斯劳沙圣禽的“头帐”是否有专有名称？而“斯劳沙”的圣禽是否也有相应之称呼？

《安禄山事迹》卷上载：

> 玄宗尝御勤政楼，于御座东间设一大金鸡帐，前置一榻，[安禄山]坐之，卷去其帘，以示荣宠。每于楼下宴会，百僚在座，禄山或拨去御帘而出。〔1〕

金鸡帐，文献亦有写作“金鸡障”的。如，李德裕《次柳氏旧闻》载：

> 天宝中，安禄山每来朝，上(玄宗)特异待之，每为致坐于殿，而偏张金鸡障其下，来辄赐坐。〔2〕

《开元天宝遗事》卷下“金鸡障”条载：

> 明皇每宴，使[安]禄山坐于御侧，以金鸡障隔之。〔3〕

又《资治通鉴》卷215载：

> 上(玄宗)尝宴勤政楼，百官列坐楼下，独为[安]禄山于御座东间设金鸡障，置榻使坐其前。仍命卷帘以示荣宠。〔4〕

李德裕、司马光所载与《安禄山事迹》同，唯金鸡帐作“金鸡障”〔5〕。胡三省注云：“障，坐障也，画金鸡为饰。”也就是说金鸡障上画有“金

---

〔1〕〔唐〕姚汝能撰，曾贻芬点校《安禄山事迹》，《开元天宝遗事·安禄山事迹》，北京：中华书局，2006年3月，第78页。

〔2〕〔唐〕李德裕编，丁如明校点《次柳氏旧闻》，载《唐五代笔记小说大观》(上册)，上海：上海古籍出版社，2000年3月，第471页。

〔3〕〔五代〕王仁裕撰，曾贻芬点校《开元天宝遗事》，《开元天宝遗事·安禄山事迹》，第54页。

〔4〕《资治通鉴》卷215玄宗天宝六载春正月“戊寅，以范阳、平卢节度使安禄山兼御史大夫”条，第6877页。

〔5〕白居易《胡旋女》诗亦云：“梨花园中册作妃，金鸡障下养为儿。禄山胡旋迷君眼，兵过黄河疑未反。”见朱金城笺注《白居易集笺校》卷3，上海：上海古籍出版社，1988年12月，第161–162页。

鸡”的装饰。安禄山的种族与祆教信仰与翟曹明同，此已为定谳。[1]故唐玄宗所设金鸡障之金鸡当即斯劳沙圣禽之谓，显然唐玄宗是依照安禄山的种族文化习惯安排接见礼仪。

不过，“金鸡障”之“障”应指行障。从上述语境来看，恐是李德裕、司马光等人将它与行障混同[2]，这种误解直到明代张居正《帝鉴图说》仍是（图 19–13）。换言之，“金鸡障”为“金鸡帐”之误，而其准确的形象应是吉美石重床背屏 6 中的“头帐”。

图 19–13　张居正《帝鉴图说》宠幸番将图

〔1〕如，Edwin G. Pulleyblank, *The Background of the Rebellion of An Lu–shan*, London, Oxford University Press, 1955. 陈寅恪：《唐代政治史述论稿》，载所撰《陈寅恪集·隋唐制度渊源略论稿·唐代政治史述论稿》，北京：三联书店，2001年4月，第210–234页。荣新江：《安禄山的种族与宗教信仰》，原载《第三届唐代学术研讨会论文集》，1997年；收入所撰《中古中国与外来文明》，北京：三联书店，2001年12月，第222–237页；后增订以“安禄山叛乱的种族与宗教背景”为题，收入中国社会科学院历史所隋唐宋辽金元史研究室编《隋唐辽宋金元史论丛》第一辑，北京：紫禁城出版社，2010年11月，第86–103页。Rong Xinjiang, “The Religious Background to the An Lushan Rebellion,” in *Chinese Scholars on Inner Asia,* ed. by Luo Xin, Bloomington, Indiana University, 2012, pp.97–138. 钟焓：《安禄山等杂胡的内亚文化背景——兼论粟特人的“内亚化”问题》，载于《中国史研究》2005年第1期，第67–84页；王小甫：《拜火教与突厥兴衰——以古代突厥斗战神研究为中心》，载于《历史研究》2007年第1期，第24–40页；后收入所撰《中国中古的族群凝聚》，第1–36页。沈睿文：《安禄山身世之推测》，载中国人民大学国学院主编《国学的传承与创新：冯其庸先生从事教学与科研六十周年庆贺学术文集》，上海：上海古籍出版社，2013年3月，第1057–1074页。但是，信仰祆教的安禄山也服食道教之丹药。此详悉沈睿文：《安禄山服散考》，载宁夏文物考古研究所编《丝绸之路上的考古宗教与历史》，北京：文物出版社，2011年8月，第73–89页。

〔2〕扬之水：《行障与挂轴》，载所撰《终朝采蓝：古名物寻微》，北京：三联书店，2008年11月，第28–41页。

至此，金鸡帐的形貌已经清晰，亦可知圣禽斯劳沙在汉文献中被称为“金鸡”。那上引文献中金鸡帐前之“榻”又为何物？

吉美背屏 6 的图像恰是“设一大金鸡帐，前置一榻，坐之”的写照。这显然是中亚粟特显贵的习俗。既然唐玄宗是以安禄山的种族文化习惯来接见，也就是说，“营州杂胡”的安禄山在范阳日常也是如此。

那么，历史文献对如此场景下的安禄山是如何记叙的呢？史载：安禄山在范阳时，“潜遣贾胡行诸道，岁输财百万。至大会，禄山踞重床，燎香，陈怪珍，胡人数百侍左右，引见诸贾，陈牺牲，女巫鼓舞于前以自神”[1]。也就是说，安禄山经常坐在“重床”上接受罗拜，发号施令。《旧唐书·安禄山传》亦载：

> ［安］禄山欣荷，无所隐，呼［李林甫］为十郎。［刘］骆谷奏事，先问“十郎何言？”有好言则喜跃，若但言“大夫须好检校”，则反手据［重］床曰：“阿与，我死也！”[2]

可见安禄山在其种落的特定场景中，代表其身份的坐具为重床。对此，张广达考辨道：中亚西亚的显贵除了冠冕之外，普遍以床座体现其身份，王公的座床即是王座。而上引文中所载“营州杂胡”安禄山所坐之“重床”和“反手”所据之“床”应当就是中亚西亚的王公显贵所坐的 g’s/gāh/座/王座。安伽墓出土的石榻当是与安伽身份相应的“重床”[3]。如此视之，唐玄宗在勤政殿的赐座之所以在文献中称为“榻”，在于这只是唐玄宗所赐的一个坐榻（具）而已，而非如同安禄山在范阳时的王座。

器物的名称不仅跟它的样式有关，而且也跟它的功能相契。这无疑增添了辨析名物的难度，幸有吉美石重床背屏 6 的图像，使得我们可窥伺安禄山情状之一斑。

Avesta 中的《诸神颂》第 14 部 *Bahrâm* Yašt，叙述了祆教战神韦雷

[1]《新唐书》卷225上，北京：中华书局点校本，1975年，第6414页。

[2]《旧唐书》卷200上《安禄山传》，北京：中华书局点校本，1975年，第5368页。

[3] 张广达：《再读晚唐苏谅妻马氏双语墓志》，原载《国学研究》第10卷，北京：北京大学出版社，2002年，第18–19页；此据所撰《张广达文集·文本、图像与文化流传》，桂林：广西师范大学出版社，2008年，第268–269页。

斯拉格纳 Verethraghna(Warahrān/Bahrâm)的十种化身，分别是：疾风(Wind，§2)、牡牛（Bull，§7）、白马（Horse，§9）、骆驼（Camel，§11）、野猪（Boar，§15）、青年（Youth，§17）、隼雀（Vareghna/Hawk，§19）、牡羊（Ram，§23）、牡鹿（Buck，§25）、男子汉（Man， §27）。[1]在吉美石重床背屏 6 石重床的壸门上尚浮雕有一小鸟，很可能便是隼雀，即祆教战神的化身。这跟该屏的整体意蕴是相吻合的。同理，这也是该石重床背屏第四石右侧雕绘一牡鹿的原因。

另外，在吉美石重床背屏 6 上部墓主人手持来通做饮状，其左下角则有一犬在进食。我们知道，严格的正统要求琐罗亚斯德教信徒不仅应该喂食饿狗，而且每个家庭至少一天要喂一次，且应在家人吃饭前喂。其原因便是为家中的亡灵积德。[2]由此视之，吉美石重床背屏 6 该场景恐正是琐罗亚斯德教徒和狗之间的这种特殊关系的真实写照。

19.2 背屏 1、2 的内容及装饰图案

德凯琳、黎北岚将背屏 2 中上部图像的神祇（图 19-14）判读为立在太阳中央的苏利耶神（sūrya），而背屏 1 中无人乘骑之马（图 19-15）则多被解释成水神 tishtrya。[3]但是，如果将此二屏的内容与史君石堂东壁三屏（E1-3）的图像内容比较，实不难发现此二者是表达共同之祈愿，只不过其具体表现形式略有不同而已。而在此比较中，吉美石重床背屏 1、2 的内容也可得以重新解读。

[1] *The Zend-Avesta*, Part Ⅱ, in *Sacred Books of the East*, vol.23, pp.231-238.其中隼雀（Vareghna），原文作“Raven”（p.236），即“渡鸦、大乌鸦”。Mary Boyce 则译作“hawk”，即隼雀。详 Mary Boyce, *Textual Sources for the Studies of Zoroastrianism*, Edited and Translated by Mary Boyce, The University of Chicago Press,1999, p.30.王小甫曾专文梳理辨正，详所撰《拜火教与突厥兴衰——以古代突厥斗战神研究为中心》，载《历史研究》2007年第1期，第24-40页，特别是第25-27页；又收入所撰《中国中古的族群凝聚》，第16-19页。

[2]〔英〕玛丽·博伊斯著，张小贵、殷小平译：《伊朗琐罗亚斯德教村落》，北京：中华书局，2005年7月，第155-157页。

[3] 对相关研究的总结详悉荣新江：《Miho 美术馆粟特石棺屏风的图像及其组合》，载于《艺术史研究》第四辑，广州：中山大学出版社，2002年，第207-210页。

图 19-14　吉美石重床背屏 2

图 19-15　吉美石重床背屏 1 无人乘骑之马

根据北朝隋“夫妇宴乐+出行”的墓葬壁画构图程式，可断该马表示出行。若依汉文化出行仪仗的制度，则该马为诞马。[1]这在北朝墓葬壁画中也有见，如娄叡墓墓道壁画（图 19–16）。但是，这个问题至此并未完全了结。

图 19–16　太原娄叡墓墓道东壁上层壁画中的诞马

在 Miho 美术馆石重床的 B 屏图像中，这匹受人供奉的马匹占据主要空间，且其上有一巨大的伞盖——常常是用来遮盖主人公或各国王的，显然这是一匹不同寻常的马。[2]确实，Miho 美术馆石重床背屏 H 上部，I、J 左侧下部图像（图 19–17 至 19–19）的构图足以证明，上述背屏图像的中心人物身后皆有一曲盖。在史君石堂西壁 W2 中，一位侍者更是持一曲盖侍立于马侧，恭候亭中对坐的主人（图 19–20）。史君石堂北壁 N3（图 19–21）中，史君夫妇皆各依曲盖乘骑出行。换言之，该曲盖的出现足可表明该诞马乃墓主人抑或某位神祇所骑乘。但是，若将该“诞马”置于整个背屏的构图程式之中，并将它跟史君石堂东侧三屏的内容比较，则不仅可断定其乘骑者为墓主人，而且亦可理解为何在上述背屏图像中将墓主人略去。

〔1〕相关文献的梳理，可参见沈睿文：《唐陵的布局：空间与秩序》，北京：北京大学出版社，2009 年4月，第138–142页。

〔2〕荣新江：《Miho 美术馆粟特石棺屏风的图像及其组合》，第208页。

图 19-17 Miho 美术馆石重床背屏 H 上部图像

图 19-18 Miho 美术馆石重床背屏 I 图像

图 19-19 Miho 美术馆石重床背屏 J 左侧下部图像

图 19-20　史君石堂西壁 W2

图 19–21　史君石堂北壁 N3

史君石堂东壁 E1（图 19–22）中间以山和云朵将画面分为上、下两部分。上部正中为一正面盘坐于 3 头牛之上的主神，其头戴宝冠，右手握三叉戟，上举于头右侧，左手拄腰，手腕皆戴镯。主神有背光，背光上部覆有拱形飘带（风袋？），两侧各一带翼飞天执其两端。主神下方有 5 位神祇，中间神祇大体居中，其头戴宝冠，右手置于胸前，左手拈花，亦仅露出半身。右边一位，身穿圆领窄袖长裙，腰束带，肩生翼，右手拄腰，左手曲臂，跣足，双脚交叉，左脚腕戴镯。该神祇的右后方尚有 2 位头戴宝冠的神祇。右侧一位右手持杯于胸前，左臂抬起，腰部以下隐于山后。中间神祇的左下方尚有一男一女，皆跪坐于椭圆形地毯上，上方为一男子，头戴帽，身穿圆领窄袖长袍，腰束带，右手托一长方形物，左手略上举。下方为一女子，梳髻、着中原式样的交领宽袖长裙，裙腰高及胸部。下部为起伏的山峦，山坡上有两只犬，犬颈下挂铃。山下有一雕栏的拱形桥，桥左侧站立两位口带拍汪（Paiwand）的祭司，桥上方分刻两团火焰。桥面上有向右行进中的一群动物，从左至右依次为 2 只羊、1 只羊羔和 2 头骆驼。最后面的一头骆驼背负高高的货物，货物上站立 2 只鸡。桥梁下有四柱，柱头分别雕作鸟形或兽形，桥下为旋涡状水波纹。

E2（图 19–23）中间的祥云和瑞草将画面分为上、下两部分。画面上部正中为两匹向左飞奔的翼马，其中下面一匹马头顶日月。两匹马的上方为一头戴宝冠的飞天，左手持一物，右手略上举，身穿圆领窄袖长裙，腰束带，跣足。飞天的右边和下方，均刻有莲花图案。下面一匹马的左边有一人，头挽小髻，背面，四肢向上，两手分别握有一物。肩上飘带下垂，似正从空中坠落。下部画面为 E1 桥梁的延伸部分，桥上行进的人和动物亦与 E1 连贯，其中走在最前面的似为 3 个大人和 1 个小孩。最前边一位仅露出半身，中间为一男一女。最左边为一孩童。此 4 人身后为 2 匹马，其后有 5 只动物，有驴和牛等，牛做回首状。桥下水中有莲花和莲叶，水波中间有两水兽，张口上视。

图 19–22　史君石堂东壁 E1

图 19-23　史君石堂东壁 E2

E3（图 19–24）中，墓主人夫妇在女仙的导引下，升入天国的图像，占据了画面的绝大部分。画面正中为一对男女前后各骑一翼马向右前方飞奔，二人双手皆于胸前上举张开，男子头戴宝冠。画面最右上方为 2 个头戴宝冠导引的女仙，上方者肩生双翼，右手持一环形物，左手向上托举。在墓主夫人周围，还有 4 个发髻不同的伎乐女仙，均肩生双翼，居左上方者弹琵琶，右前方者吹奏横笛，右下方者弹箜篌，左下方者吹奏排箫。在伎乐女仙的下面，有 4 个飞奔的动物，从右到左分别为狮子、牛、骆驼、羊，其后半身皆化为回环漫卷的云纹。动物以下为河岸山石，石上点缀少许植物。河水与 E2 图相连，水中有 3 只水禽。

史君石堂东壁从 E1→E3 图像表现墓主人史君夫妇灵魂经过钦瓦特桥升入中界的过程，当无疑义。其 E1 背光圆环内的男神为琐罗亚斯德教的风神（Weshparkar），肩生双翼的女神应该是 Daēnā 女神，至于其身后的两位女子，则是 Daēnā 女神的女侍，她们负责看管属于 Daēnā 的两样东西：杯子和花。[1] 该场景图绘表现的是善士的灵魂于死后第三日拂晓在熏风中走近“筛选之桥”。当有德的死者的灵魂来到“筛选之桥”前，得到手举杯钵的妲厄娜，也就是他的“信仰”化身、体现他的生前行为的“内在自我”的迎接，携犬在身侧的美丽的妲厄娜所持的杯钵中满盛 Zaremaya 月份酿制的乳酪。此后，善士的灵魂则走过宽阔的“筛选之桥”而走进“中界”（天堂）。至于看不到善教的盲人（Kavi）、听不见善教声音的聋子（Karapan）、宗奉魔鬼妲厄娲、依势弄权竭力破坏人类生存的恶人，则到了自食其果的报应时刻，在“筛选之桥”前战栗地承受他们自己的“信仰”的化身——妲厄娲的盛怒。他们走不过窄如薤叶的“筛选之桥”，将沉沦于 Druj（恶魔）的世界——北方（地狱），在那里吃的是毒物，受的是恶魔的折磨，转侧呻吟，永无解脱之

〔1〕荣新江：《佛像还是祆神？——从于阗看丝路宗教的混同形态》，载于《九州学林》第1卷第2期，2003年冬季，第103–110页。F. Grenet, P. Riboud et Yang Junkai, “Zoraoastrian Scenes on a Newly Discovered Sogdian Tomb in Xi’an Northern China,” *Studia Iranica*, 33.2, 2004, pp.282–283. 杨军凯：《西安北周史君墓石椁图像初探》，载《法国汉学》第十辑“粟特人在中国——历史、考古、语言的新探索”专号，第12页；姜伯勤：《入华粟特人萨宝府身份体制与画像石纪念性艺术》，载于《法国汉学》第十辑“粟特人在中国——历史、考古、语言的新探索”专号，第45页。

日。[1] 在 E2 中，自空中往下坠落的人应该表现的是“恶人”坠入地狱，首先等待他们的是“筛选之桥”下水中张口以待的 2 只水兽。

图 19–24　史君石堂东壁 E3

〔1〕张广达:《唐代祆教图像再考——P.4518（24）的图像是否祆教神祇妲厄娜（Daēnā）和妲厄娲（Daēvā）》，原载荣新江主编《唐研究》第3卷，北京：北京大学出版社，1997年12月；此据所撰《张广达文集・文本、图像与文化流传》，桂林：广西师大出版社，2008年9月，第281–282页。

在E1中下部，骆驼“背驮”的2只鸡，应该是斯劳沙的圣禽。《斯劳沙·亚什特》第七章称赞斯劳沙“总是醒着，从不入眠”，夜间负责保护马兹达的创造物，以免遭受妖魔鬼怪的侵害。斯劳沙是亡灵的引导者，故在葬礼开始时必须吟诵；还在每日五个时辰吟咏，以祈求斯劳沙的神佑。[1]斯劳沙接引死者之灵到彼世。《亚斯纳》第五十六章（《斯劳沙·亚什特·哈多赫特》）把斯劳沙称作人死后头三天亡灵的庇护神和第四天清晨亡灵的引路者，在帕拉维语文献《阿尔塔伊·维拉夫》中，当这位虔诚的祭司饮下掺有印度大麻酚浸液的酒后，昏昏然灵魂出窍之际，便是在斯劳沙和火神阿扎尔的引导下游历地狱和天国的。[2]

E3表现的是史君夫妇进入中界（天堂）的情形，可以看到乐伎的普遍存在。由死者灵魂的“良知”化身为美丽少女的Daēnā，在引导灵魂通过钦瓦特之后会引领它进入美好的天国，一个充满诗情画意的美丽花园。那里花香鸟语，枝繁叶茂，硕果累累，仙乐曼妙。而且最后这一点至关重要，琐罗亚斯德教的天国伽尔扎曼(garōdmāna)[3]本意就是“歌声的殿堂”(the House of Welcoming Songs)，因为曼妙的音乐是灵魂欢愉之源。[4]《伽萨》（Yasna L.4）载：“神主马兹达和头三位大天神啊！此时此刻我引吭高歌把你们赞颂，但愿正教徒所梦寐以求的[女仙]，在通往伽尔扎曼（天国）的路上飘然出现。”[5]故而天宫伎乐形象是判断图像内容是否为天国的首要因素。换言之，带翼女仙，只有在中界中才出现。

我们注意到，在史君石堂E3中，升入中界的史君夫妇便骑乘翼马。这恰说明死者亡灵正是乘骑翼马而升入中界的。同样地，在史君石堂E2上部，2匹翼马竭力飞向并试图接住正在下坠的恶者。结合E2、E3

---

〔1〕元文琪：《〈阿维斯塔〉导读》，载〔伊朗〕贾利尔·杜斯特哈赫选编，元文琪译《阿维斯塔——琐罗亚斯德教圣书》，北京：商务印书馆，2005年11月，第370页。

〔2〕元文琪：《〈阿维斯塔〉导读》，载《阿维斯塔——琐罗亚斯德教圣书》，第445页。

〔3〕Ph. Gignoux, “L'enfer et le paradis d'après les sources pehlevis,” *Journal Asiatique*, 256, 1968, pp.219–245.

〔4〕Guitty. Azarpay, “The Allegory of Dēn In Persian Art,” *Artibus Asiae*, Vol.38, no.1, 1976, p.47.

〔5〕*The Zend-Avesta*, Part Ⅲ, in *Sacred Books of the East*, vol.31, p.172. 本文译文据《阿维斯塔——琐罗亚斯德教圣书》，第431–432页。

的场景，可以推知翼马的任务是将死者灵魂载入中界。故可知，无人乘骑的覆盖鞍鞯之马是为墓主人进入中界而备。在史君石堂 E1、E2 下部钦瓦特桥上，紧跟史君夫妇之后的便是 2 匹马，其后才是牛羊、骆驼等，而到了 E3，上述所有动物都长出双翼随史君夫妇一同升天，当然那 2 匹马也随之变成翼马成为史君夫妇升入中界的坐骑。这也是为何在相关图像中在该马之前或有进行供奉的行为，如 Miho 美术馆石重床的 B 屏者（图 19–25），原来缘于该马承担着墓主人灵魂升入中界的神圣使命。有意思的是，类似的情景也见于中亚粟特壁画。在阿夫拉西亚卜（Afrasiab）发现的一幅 7 世纪的粟特大壁画上，绘有一奔赴帝王陵墓的仪仗，其中的两个人之间有一匹佩戴鞍鞯的马，马前面的人将它牵向一位祭司（padām）[1]。可见，在上述石葬具中出现佩戴鞍鞯之马的场景应也是现实出殡仪式的真实写照。而这种情景置于北朝隋的出行程式中恰又可对应诞马，实乃巧思。

幸赖史君墓的发现及其石堂图像的解读，使得此类葬具图像的准确把握成为可能。若将吉美石重床背屏 1、2 的构图与史君石堂东壁 E1、E2、E3 的构图相比较，便可发现二者内容之相似，唯图像表现方式略有变化而已。此下便尝试重新辨识吉美石重床背屏 1、2 的诸元素。

解读图像须基于对其构图诸元素的准确认识。吉美石重床背屏 2 上部的图像（图 19–26），德凯琳、黎北岚描述为“一四臂女神立于莲花之上，其中两臂手持莲花，自一充满妖魔的海面涌出；其背后有一呈四层重叠圆盘状的太阳，其左右各有一射手。上方似为天上世界”[2]。实际上，该图像要表达的是跟史君石堂 E1 相同的内容，即佑护死者亡灵安全通过钦瓦特桥，升入中界。只不过在构图中省去钦瓦特桥的浅浮雕，尽管如此，仍可从其他元素对此进行解读。

〔1〕Marshak.B.I., “La thèmatique sogdienne dans l’art de la Chine de la seconde moitiè du Vi^{e} siècle,” *Académie des Inscriptions & Belles Inscriptions & Belles–Lettres, Comptes rendus des séances de l’année 2001 janvier–mars*, Paris, 2001, p.238.

〔2〕德凯琳、黎北岚著，施纯琳译：《巴黎吉美博物馆展围屏石榻上刻绘的宴饮和宗教题材》，载于《4~6世纪的北中国与欧亚大陆》，第110页。

图 19–25　Miho 美术馆石重床的 B 屏

图 19-26　吉美石重床背屏 2 上部图像

首先，该图像下部在海面上出现的各种怪兽（图 19-27），其中明显可辨者有蛇以及狼等捕食动物，它们都属于毒虫害兽（xrafstar），代表恶神以及恶人在地狱的惩罚方式。[1] 于此可知该情景意在表示地狱，我们不妨称该水域为“地狱之海”。对此，史君石堂 E2 的表现方式可为辅证，该屏径直将有张口等待吞噬恶者的怪兽的水域置于钦瓦特桥之下，而上空则有 2 位未能通过钦瓦特桥的恶者正坠向该水域。同样的场景也出现在史君石堂 N5（图 19-28）画面下部。史君石堂 N5 画面下部为 2 位落水者，水中有荷叶和 2 只水兽，落水的 2 人回首惊恐地看着水兽，两手上举，伸向从天上飞来搭救他们的 2 个女仙，在该女仙身后还有一女仙项戴璎珞，右手托一盛有物品的大盘，左手拿一花瓶，正飞向他们。不难辨识，史君石堂 N5 中的怪兽形象（图 19-28-2）亦见于吉美石重床背屏 2 下部，可见史君石堂该屏下部表现的也是地狱之海及其毒虫害兽。显然，其中落水的 2 人应为堕落的恶者灵魂，而水中的毒虫

〔1〕Mahnaz Moazami, “Evil Animals in the Zoroastrian Religion,” *History of Religions*, Vol. 44, No. 4 (May 2005), pp. 300–317.

害兽则是通过吞噬他们的灵魂来表现对后者的惩罚。由上述史君石堂E2、N5二屏的构图可以确定，在升至中界的过程中，于亡者灵魂而言，地狱之海的毒虫害兽无疑是一致命威胁。

其次，德凯琳、黎北岚将该图像上部描述为日天苏利耶，应该是对该图像构成的误解。从构图来看，该四臂女神并非从下部的海面涌出，其背后亦非四层重叠圆盘状的太阳。这些构图元素可从已发掘或辨识的同类石葬具的图像中寻求佐证。

史君石堂西壁W1（图19–29）画面上部中心位置的神祇交脚盘坐于莲花宝座，[1]其身后有椭圆形背光。安伽墓石门楣的骆驼火坛底座也是莲花（图19–30），法国国立图书馆藏敦煌藏P. 4518（24）号白画左侧的善神妲厄娜（Daēnā）[2]的底座亦饰有莲花（图19–31）。可知底座有莲花装饰的神祇为祆教之善神。对照观察吉美石重床背屏2上部神祇，应该也是坐于莲花座上的善神，其背后为四层背光，而非“一个呈四层重叠圆盘状的太阳”，而且其样式很可能便是类似P. 4518（24）白画中善神妲厄娜（Daēnā）的底座。

图19–27　吉美石重床背屏2下部图像

〔1〕西安市文物保护考古所：《西安市北周史君石椁墓》，载于《考古》2004年第7期，第41–42页；西安市文物保护考古所：《西安北周凉州萨保史君墓发掘简报》，载于《文物》2005年第3期，第10–11页。姜伯勤：《北周粟特人史君石堂图像考察》，载于《艺术史研究》第7辑，广州：中山大学出版社，2005年，第281–298页。

〔2〕张广达：《唐代祆教图像再考》，所撰《张广达文集·文本、图像与文化流传》，第274–289页。

1

2

图 19-28　史君石堂 N5 及其下部

图 19-29　史君石堂西壁 W1 上部

图 19-30　安伽墓石门楣骆驼火坛

图 19-31　P. 4518（24）白画

新疆和田出土的一些木板画，有学者将它判定为粟特系统的祆教神谱。如，和田出土的木板 D.X.3 正面，为 3 个一组的神祇，从左到右依次绘制的是阿胡拉 · 马兹达（Ohrmazd）、娜娜女神（Nana）和风神

（Weshparkar）。[1]（图 19–32）木板中的风神盘坐于圆毡之上，身后左右胁侍手持弓或箭。吉美背屏 2 上部神祇左右胁侍各张一弓做射箭状，这在构图上跟和田 D.X.3 木板画正面的风神图像大同。据此应可比定该神祇为风神（Weshparkar）。背屏 2 下部海中的怪兽与史君石堂 E2 钦瓦特桥下者同为毒虫害兽，表示地狱，已如前具。如此则吉美石重床背屏 2 的构图意蕴实与史君石堂 E2 同，只不过前者略去钦瓦特桥的表现。但是，需要注意的是，在前者的右下部尚有一位光头神祇，左右手各执一物，做挥舞状。该神祇为何，其详请见下文。

图 19–32　和田出土的木板 D.X.3 正面

如果依照史君石堂 E3 是表现史君夫妇进入中界（天堂）的场景，那么吉美石重床背屏 1 是否也是如此呢？在该背屏的上部同样发现与史君石堂 E1 相同的女仙伎乐场景。吉美石重床背屏 1 上方有一女仙，说明此处已为中界，前已述及。而下方承载墓主灵魂升入中界的诞马的存在，也就确保墓主亡灵可顺利进入中界。或许这是表示墓主灵魂进入中界的一种简化方式？这应该是此类石葬具图像出现诞马以及在现实的丧葬活动中安排该马的宗教内涵吧。尚须注意的是，吉美石重床者有

〔1〕M.Mode, “Sogdian God in Exile– Some iconographic evidence from Khotan in the light of recently excavated material from Sogdiana,” *Silk Road Art and Archaeology*, 2, 1991/92, pp.179–214. 荣新江：《中古中国与外来文明》，第311–315页；姜伯勤：《祆教艺术史研究》，第195–202页。对此，张广达、张小贵等学者则持不同意见。详张广达：《唐代祆教图像再考》，所撰《张广达文集·文本、图像与文化流传》，第285页；张小贵：《中古华化祆教考述》，北京：文物出版社，2010年3月，第80–81页。

一犬坐于马的左后腿根处，当为犬视。这进一步说明该石屏意在表现丧葬行为。于是，此类石葬具中该类图像的象征意义也就皎然。

就目前所知石葬具图像来看，出现此类图像主题的还有虞弘墓石堂椁壁浮雕之一（图 19-33）、青州傅家第四石“出行图之一”〔1〕（图 19-34）以及 Miho 美术馆藏石棺床 B。吉美石重床背屏 1 以及上述前三者在该马的地面部分皆不见鱼和水的表现，此与 Miho 美术馆石重床 B 屏构图不同。

图 19-33　虞弘墓石堂椁壁浮雕之一

〔1〕夏名采：《益都北齐石室墓线刻画像》，载于《文物》1985年第10期，第49–54页。

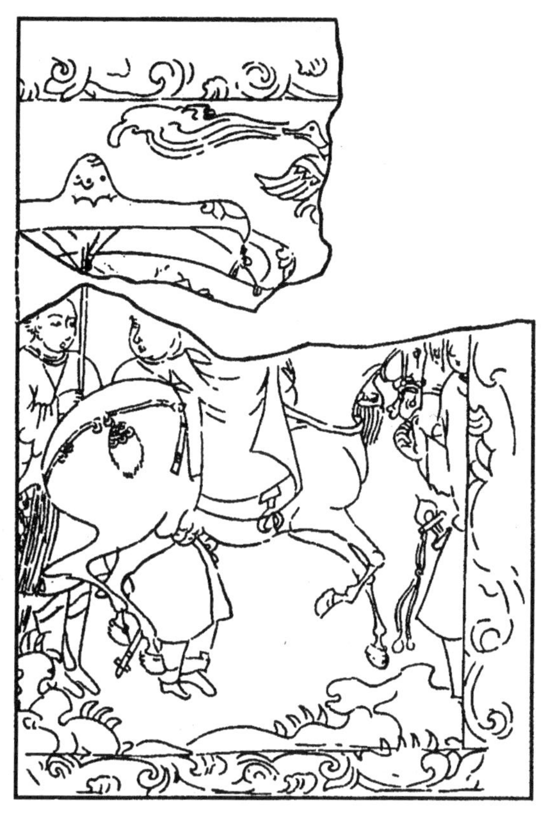

图 18–34　青州傅家第四石

虞弘墓石堂椁壁浮雕之一图像主体为：一驭者在马前手执缰绳，该人与马的前腿之间以及马的前后腿之间各有一犬，马上覆有鞍鞯，其后有 3 位侍立者。最前者曲臂上伸，似做手势；后二者左臂下皆夹一茵褥。[1]该图像位于石堂门的左（西）外侧第一屏，依照北朝隋唐墓葬壁画的构图程式，恰好位于出行队列的最前端。这从与之相对称的石堂门的右（东）外侧第一屏（图 19–35）为骑乘出行的构图可证。同样地，该浮雕中的 2 只犬意味着丧葬的题材。这表明该马应也是丧葬出行仪仗的构成。一如吉美石重床者。

〔1〕《太原隋虞弘墓》，第98–101页。

图 19–35　虞弘石椁椁壁浮雕第九幅

青州傅家石屏的构图为一覆有鞍鞯的马往右做行走状，马身的后侧有2人，其一手持伞盖，另一头转向前者，在马前可辨识有一侍立者手执缰绳。尽管该石屏的具体位置不详，但从刊布的画像石屏来看，可以判断该石屏应与同出的第三石所谓“车御图”（图19-36）分别位于整个画像石构图的东、西两侧，[1]此二石屏共同构成鞍马犊车出行，符合北朝墓葬壁画程式。亦即，可以确定该构图的内涵实际与上述虞弘者大同，表示出行之意。

图19-36　青州傅家第三石

〔1〕沈睿文：《青州北齐傅家画像石的图像组合》，待刊。

Miho 美秀美术馆藏石棺床 B 下部同样为一覆以鞍鞯的马，亦无人骑乘，其前有一男子跪地双手朝着马首举杯做供奉状，马后面有 4 位侍立者。上述场景前面有一水域，水中有 3 条游鱼，其前行方向与马同。因为水和游鱼的存在，该马被推断为得悉神或阿姆河河神之一。[1] 其根据便是阿富汗 Ghulbiyan 石窟 4 世纪壁画中的 Tishtrya（水神）画像下面有水和鱼（图 19–37），可以和 Miho 石棺床 B 屏下面的水和鱼对比。换言之，水及其中的游鱼成为判断与之共存的神祇是否为 Tishtrya 的重要标志。

图 19–37　阿富汗 Ghulbiyan 石窟 4 世纪壁画中的 Tishtrya（图中编号 8）

但是，事实是否如此呢？如果同样梳理这批石葬具中相关水景的图像，则不难发现上述推论犹有可究之处。

史君石堂 W1、E3 二屏亦有水的表现，前者上部的中心图像为一神祇，后者展示史君夫妇进入中界，可知这两块石屏展现的都是神性的空间。在这两屏的下部便都有 2 只鸭子悠闲地凫游于水池的场景（图 19–38、19–39）。

〔1〕有关论述详悉荣新江：《Miho 美术馆粟特石棺屏风的图像及其组合》，第208–210页。

图 19–38　史君石堂 W1 下部水池场景

图 19–39　史君石堂 E3 下部水池场景

德凯琳、黎北岚认为吉美石重床第三石表现坐在大象上的俱吠罗（Kubera）场景。在该画面下部（图 19–40）也有水池的表现，只不过将鸭子、游鱼替换成莲花。而吉美石重床第四石墓主人坐于曲盖之下，画面的左下角也表现 2 只凫游水面的鸭子（图 19–41）。

图 19–40　吉美石重床第三石

图 19–41　吉美石重床第四石左下水池场景

综上，可以得出这样的结论：水中的鱼、鸭、莲花，表示一种祥和、宁静自然的和谐氛围，在表现神祇或者中界的空间中多有之。但是，并非有水域的表现便是表示祥和、自然的氛围。显然，若水域中出现毒虫害兽，便非此意。如，前文所言史君石堂 N5 画面下部中的毒虫害兽正欲吞噬 2 位已落水之人，是为地狱之海。可知毒虫害兽的存在使得相关水域的表现意境迥异，其用意一如前述。

要之，从吉美石重床背屏 1 中上部女仙的雕绘可知该石屏表现的是进入中界的情景，该屏下部无人乘骑的覆以鞍鞯之马在出殡仪式中承担将墓主载入中界的重任。与此同时，该马在此类葬具图像中恰亦位于出行队列之前端，正与北朝隋墓葬图像程式构图同。这种图像布局虽然是现实葬仪的如实写照，但从此布局结果的巧合来看应该也是动过心思。

借此机会尚需言及的是，见诸吉美石重床背屏 3 的大象，在虞弘墓石堂以及青州傅家画像亦可见。它们应该也是表示出行仪仗之一部。

青州傅家画像第八石（图 19-42）为大象载“象舆”，上分饰 6 个摩尼宝。[1] 此石应该与第九石所谓“送葬图”（图 19-43）对称分布于左右两侧，[2] 表示丧葬之出行仪仗。[3]

而虞弘墓石堂内壁浮雕第 6 幅（图 19-44）则表现墓主虞弘乘一大象回首杀狮的场景。从整个石堂浮雕的构图来看，该石屏表现狩猎出行的场景。

---

〔1〕扬之水：《象舆——兼论青州傅家北齐画像石中的“象戏图”》，载于《中国文化》2011年第1期，第40-48页；后收入所撰《曾有西风半点香：敦煌艺术名物丛考》，北京：三联书店，2012年1月，第209-228页。

〔2〕郑岩认为此二石原来的位置可能比较对称。详所撰《逝者的面具——汉唐墓葬艺术研究》，第288-291页。

〔3〕姜伯勤、郑岩误将此屏勘定为祆教“万灵节”。详姜伯勤：《中国祆教艺术史研究》，第70-73页；郑岩《逝者的面具——汉唐墓葬艺术研究》，第288-289页。

图 19-42　青州傅家画像第八石

图 19–43　青州傅家画像第九石

由上述三例的情况可知，这批石葬具中出现的大象亦首在表现仪仗出行之意蕴，所以才会出现其乘骑者可有可无的现象。而从虞弘石堂的情况来看，其骑乘者有可能便是墓主本人。尽管吉美石重床背屏 3 浮雕主体人物已被破坏，但从其构图来看，乘象者为酒神节日场景中的俱吠罗（Kubera）神祇恐无大碍。

19.3 背屏 8 的内容

虽然德凯琳、黎北岚误认为吉美石重床背屏 8（图 19–45）表现的是沼泽场景，但是她们对该场景的描述仍大体客观。该画面的下半部为一大水域，其北岸有一植物。水域中有一人骑于张口露齿的水牛背上，其下部浩大的水面上另有一口中衔鸟的怪兽。骑牛之人昂首双手做张弓拉弦射物状。半空中山岭重重，下承三层之台，恐意在表现重峦叠嶂与画面下半部场景的距离。在山岭后伸出一巨型鸟头，鸟头后方则衬以光芒闪烁的太阳。该背屏表现的内容为何？

图 19–44　虞弘墓石堂内壁浮雕第 6 幅

图 19-45　吉美石重床背屏 8

在伊朗—雅利安神话中，大鸟塞伊纳（Saena），是一只猎鹰，它栖于万种之树（Tree of All Seeds）上面，摇落树上的种子，由风雨带往各地，乌鲁卡萨海（the sea Vouru-Kasha）里有卡拉（Kara）鱼，看守万种之树，时刻提防青蛙之类的害虫侵扰；还有一头“正义的驴子”，三腿、六眼、九嘴，体白，头上长着金角；而统治着乌鲁卡萨海里的居民的乃是一头巨兽瓦西·潘查萨迪瓦拉（Vasi Panca, sadvara）。另外，还有一些生性邪恶的巨兽或巨鸟，如蛇（龙）怪阿日·达哈卡（Azi Dahâka），三首、食人，以及苏鲁瓦拉（Sruvara），有角，浑身青黄，食马与人。[1]可见万种之树生长于乌鲁卡沙海之滨，它亦被视为可医治百病之树。因此，在《阿维斯陀》中又有一说，即生命之树“豪摩”——玛达，也生长于宇宙之山（“胡凯里亚”）的山脚下，位于沃鲁卡沙湖畔或湖中，其侧为阿尔德维泉。[2]

在伊朗—雅利安的宇宙观中，相传世界分为七大境域（大洲），其中最大者为赫瓦尼拉塔（Khvaniratha），面积是其余六洲的总和，为人类所居。赫瓦尼拉塔位于中央，其他六境域分布于其四周，有广阔的水域和茂密的森林相隔。哈拉（Hara）圣山位于赫瓦尼拉塔的中央，太阳环绕此山运行，世界因而一半黑暗，一半光明。[3]从哈拉山顶流下一条大河哈拉瓦底（Harahvaiti），在山脚下一分为二，向东流去的是潘赫维·达提雅（Vanhvi Daitya），向西流去的是郎哈（Ranha），最后注入乌鲁卡沙海。

对照上述伊朗—雅利安神话，吉美石重床背屏 8 的图像意蕴基本可以释读。其中图像下部表现的正是乌鲁卡沙海，其北岸的植物应为万种之树，海中口中衔鸟的怪兽便是看护该树的卡拉鱼。图像上部的大鸟便是猎鹰塞伊纳，山岭则为位于赫瓦尼拉塔中央的哈拉圣山，屏中的太阳表示环绕哈拉山运行。而乌鲁卡沙海中的人与牛，表现的则应是诸神在赫瓦尼拉塔中创造动物原人（Gayomeretan）和原牛（Gavaevodata）。综上可知，吉美石重床背屏 8 图像大体可谓是对伊朗—雅利安关于宇宙起源创始神话的描绘。[4]

19.4 背屏的纹饰

本文这部分拟探讨这套石重床的装饰图案。从收藏品的现状来看，其装饰图案可以分成两大部分，即有关祆教的纹饰和北朝的纹样。前者包括石重床床座前挡及左右两侧壶门内的三对坐伎、背屏 1 上部表现的

〔1〕龚方震、晏可佳:《祆教史》，上海：上海社会科学出版社，1998年，第45页。

〔2〕魏庆征编:《古代伊朗神话》，第373页。

〔3〕魏庆征编:《古代伊朗神话》，第297页。

〔4〕关于伊朗—雅利安人宇宙起源的创始神话，可参见龚方震、晏可佳:《祆教史》，第35–36页。

祆教中界的女仙，以及背屏 2 下部海中的毒虫害兽。后者则包括背屏 2 上部相对的人面鸟身兽和兽首鸟身、背屏 2 下部海中手持鼓槌和束腰状物的神祇，以及石重床座背面壶门内纹饰，还有诸石屏花边中的神兽头像及小团花。关于乐伎在祆教丧葬中的作用，前已撰文讨论，兹不赘述[1]。此部分重点讨论后两种装饰图案。

前已述及，在墓主灵魂升至中界的过程中，于死者而言，地狱之海的毒虫害兽无疑是一致命威胁。这在史君石堂 E2 钦瓦特桥（图 19–46）下便有重点表现。于是，在史君石堂 E1、E2 中的钦瓦特桥下柱头便相应地出现动物头部。E1、E2“筛选之桥”9 根桥柱柱头上的所谓“鸟形”，仔细观察其头部上方有冠状物，因此也很可能是斯劳沙的圣禽公鸡，则其意义在此不言自明。其功能应如同钦瓦特桥上的骆驼背上的公鸡（斯劳沙圣禽）一样。若此，则与之共存的其余桥柱头上的怪兽应也为祆教善神之圣禽。它们共同在护卫、辅佐墓主人灵魂安全通过钦瓦特桥，以免遭水中怪兽，即地狱之海毒虫害兽的吞噬。

图 19–46　史君石堂 E1、E2 钦瓦特桥

〔1〕沈睿文：《论墓制与墓主国家和民族认同的关系——以康业、安伽、史君、虞弘诸墓为例》，第226–229页。

有意思的是，安伽墓石重床的床座前面（图 19-47）以及左右两侧挡板（图 19-48、19-49）也有类似图像。显然，该石重床的制作者有意通过联珠圈把其中的动物区分成两大类。联珠圈中的动物有斯劳沙圣禽，则可知联珠圈中的动物为史君石堂钦瓦特桥下柱头上的动物，而地狱之海中的毒虫害兽则没有围绕以联珠圈。安伽石重床如此使用床座挡板图案的分类表现史君石堂 E1、E2 下部的内容，亦可谓之巧思。

图 19-47　安伽墓石重床的床座前挡

图 19-48　安伽墓石重床的床座左侧挡板

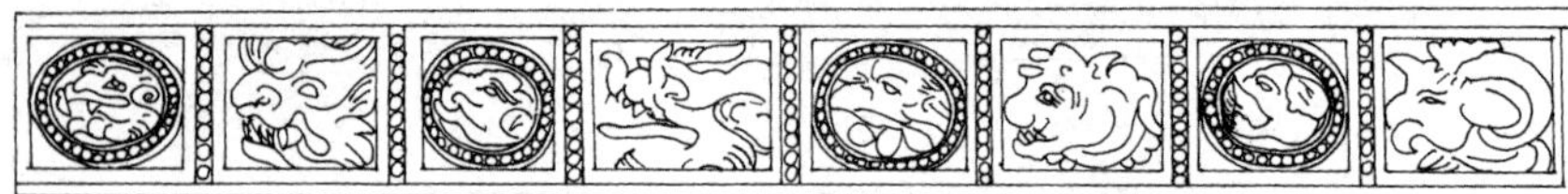

图 19-49　安伽墓石重床的床座右侧挡板

祥瑞图案中的北朝纹样，背屏 2 上部相对的人面鸟身兽和兽首鸟身、背屏 2 下部海中手持鼓槌和束腰状物的神祇，以及石重床座背面壶门内纹饰，还有诸石屏花边中的神兽头像则共同构成北朝的祥瑞图案。这是一套以雷工（公）为核心的出行程式。其构图模式为：四神、祥瑞、雷公、风伯、雨师、河伯（四足鱼）以及跪拜、仰望和迎谒者。其中的祥瑞类后来逐渐集中到千秋、万岁之上，风伯、河伯则分别代替以观风鸟、四足鱼。[1]实际上，在此出行仪仗中，雷公以及风伯、雨师、河伯等具有出行辟兵的意蕴，或也被替代为山精、海若之流。[2]

解开这套纹样的一个关键便是背屏 2 下部双手分持束腰状物和鼓槌的神祇（图 19–50），该神祇应是太一和雷工的合体。所谓束腰状物应即石，该神祇亦见于北魏冯邕妻元氏墓志（图 19–51），自铭“挟石”。《云笈七签》卷 24《日月星辰部》云：

> 北斗君，字君时，一字充。北斗神君本江夏人，姓伯名大万，挟万（石）二千石，左右神人姓雷名机字太阴，主天下诸仙人。又招摇与玉衡为轮，北斗之星，精曜九道，光映十天。[3]

图 19–50　吉美石重床神祇

图 19–51　北魏冯邕妻元氏墓志“挟石”背屏 2 下部

北斗星君挟石二千石。[4]换言之，所谓挟石便是北斗星君，亦即太一。此为汉文化传统之神祇。至迟在汉代便以该形象来表示太一神，如临沂画像石墓横梁（图 19–52），后来在北魏时期得到继承，除了见

〔1〕沈睿文：《唐宋墓葬神煞考源——中国古代墓葬太一出行系列研究之三》，载荣新江主编《唐研究》第十八卷，北京：北京大学出版社，2012年，第199–220页。

〔2〕《隋书》卷69《王劭传》，北京：中华书局点校本，1973年，第1607–1608页。

〔3〕〔宋〕张君房编，李永晟点校：《云笈七签》，北京：中华书局，2003年，第549页。

〔4〕姜伯勤：《敦煌艺术宗教与礼乐文明》，北京：中国社会科学出版社，1996年，第66页。

诸冯邕妻元氏墓志纹饰之外，尚见于陕西户县祖庵北魏石棺构件（图19-53）。可见，吉美石重床者应该是后者的变体，只缘表现手握之便而雕绘成该形状。

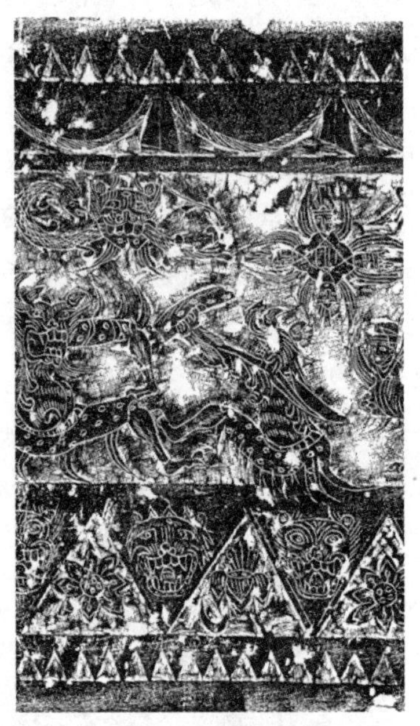

图 19-52　临沂画像石墓横梁“挟石”

图 19-53　陕西户县祖庵北魏石棺构件中的“挟石”

需要注意的是，该神祇还手持鼓槌，这表示他还具备雷工的神性。手持鼓槌、脚踏连鼓的雷工形象在北朝屡见，[1]此不赘述。但是这里需要进一步考量的是，吉美石重床的该神祇是否还有其他来源？

古伊朗神话中有一水灵，这就是"诸水之子"阿帕姆·纳帕特（Apãm Napât），该神祇属善灵。关于该神祇的观念，源于印度—伊朗共同体时期。始于这一时期，阿帕姆·纳帕特作为雷电之化身的观念一直留存；而雷电又与雨水紧密相关。《耶什特》（XIX Zamyâd Yast）中，不乏关于阿帕姆·纳帕特的神话片断，即：阿帕姆·纳帕特曾将王权的表征——"法尔恩"藏于沃鲁卡沙湖深处，以避三首之龙阿日·达哈卡（Azi Dahâka）；阿帕姆·纳帕特曾创造人类；与阿胡拉·马兹达和密特拉同称为"阿胡拉"。此神灵由来颇为古远，且在古代印度·伊朗人神殿中位格颇高。[2]其中阿帕姆·纳帕特最为典型的神格便是雷电化身，在背屏 2 中的神祇身处地狱之海中，颇疑吉美石重床的墓主及制作者将阿帕姆·纳帕特跟汉文化的太一、雷工糅为一体也未可知。

需要说明的是，在北朝至隋的粟特裔石葬具上多出现雷工形象，吉美石重床并非孤例。此如，隋代安备石重床后板右腿，有一神祇左手持一圭状物，右手持一锤子做下砸状（图 19–54）。此形象亦见于敦煌 285 窟窟顶北披壁画，其中"一兽头人身怪人，手持铁钻，砸石发光，大约就是霹电"（图 19–55）[3]，霹电即雷工之礔电。这也见于北魏冯邕妻元氏墓志纹样（图 19–56），只是形象不同。实际上，太一出行在北朝高等级墓葬及其石葬具上的表现已为程式。在此出行程式中，石重床诸石屏花边中的神兽头像（图 19–57），便为山精、海若之流，[4]亦即被习称为"畏兽"者。此在安伽石重床榻腿（图 19–58）以及史君石堂外

〔1〕杨泓对此曾有专文研究，详所撰《雷公怒引连鼓辨》，载杨泓、孙机：《寻常的精致》，沈阳：辽宁教育出版社，1996年，第251–253页；后收入同作者《逝去的风韵——杨泓谈文物》，北京：中华书局，2007年，第271–273页。

〔2〕魏庆征编：《古代伊朗神话》，第371页。

〔3〕段文杰：《道教题材是如何进入佛教石窟的——莫高窟249窟窟顶壁画内容探讨》，所撰《段文杰敦煌石窟艺术论文集》，兰州：甘肃人民出版社，1994年，第21、322–323页。

〔4〕此请见笔者关于太一出行的系列研究。

壁建筑斗拱间（图 19-59）皆可见其完整形貌。

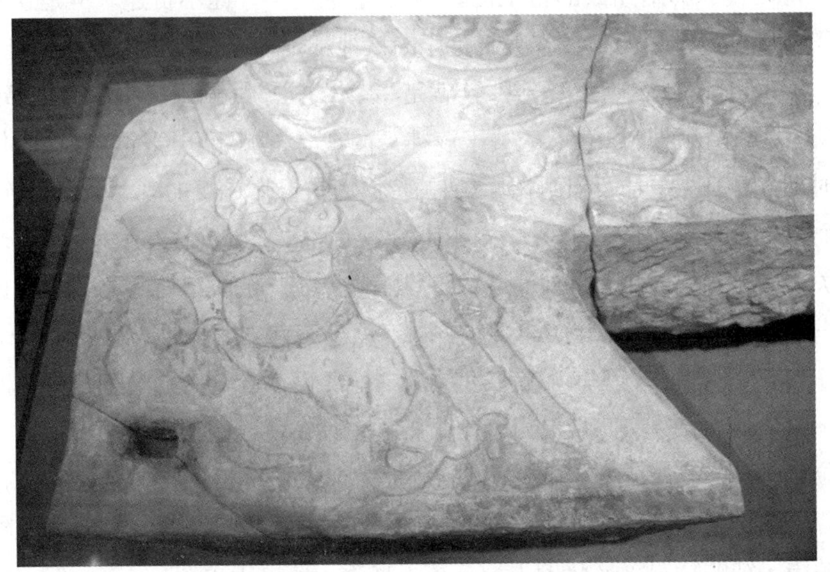

图 19-54　隋代安备石重床后板右腿礔电

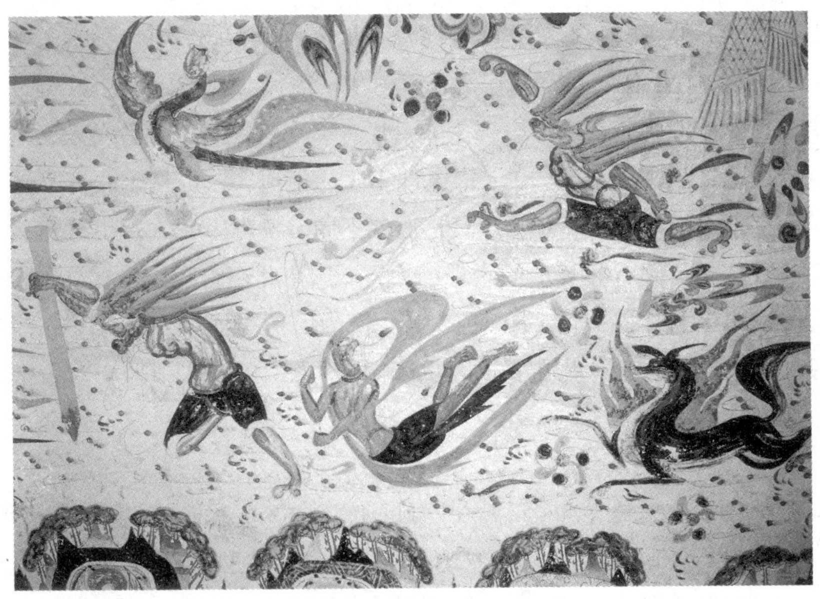

图 19-55　敦煌 285 窟窟顶北披壁画礔电

图 19-56 北魏冯邕妻元氏墓志礔电纹样

1　　　　2

图 19-57　吉美石重床诸石屏花边中的神兽头像

图 19-58　安伽石重床榻腿“畏兽”

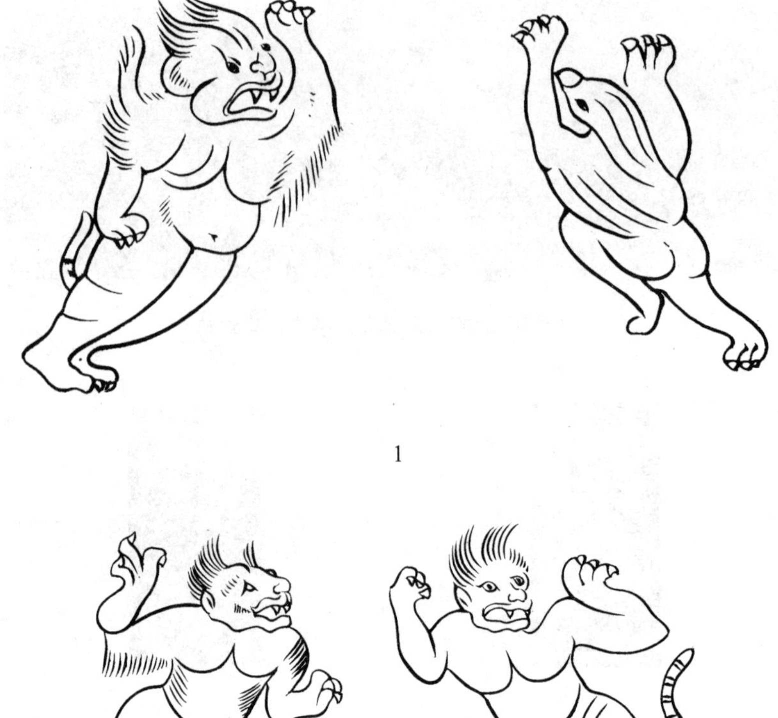

1

2

图 19-59　史君石堂外壁建筑斗拱间“畏兽”

吉美石重床的这套纹样既为太一出行，则其中背屏 2 上部的人面鸟身兽和兽首鸟身便即所谓千秋万岁，[1] 而非中古波斯文化圈流行的一

〔1〕朱岩石：《“千秋万岁”图像源流浅识》，中国社会科学院考古研究所汉唐与边疆考古研究编委会编：《汉唐与边疆考古研究》第一辑，北京：科学出版社，1994年，第131–135页；王去非：《隋墓出土的陶“千秋万岁”及其他》，载于《考古》1979年第3期，第275–276页。

种吉祥神兽“森木鹿”的形象[1]，这在河南邓县学庄画像砖墓的画像砖中有题铭（图 19-60）可证，此自不待言。

图 19-60　河南邓县学庄画像砖墓“千秋”“万岁”铭画像砖

19.5　小结

本文根据同类石葬具对吉美石重床图像内涵重新辩证，可知该石重床图像既有墓主政治身份的表现，又有祆教教义、神话的展示，从而表现出与其他石重床不同的情状。

如上所述，在目前所见相关考古资料，唯靖边翟曹明墓石墓门图案颇为特殊，展示祆教圣禽（金鸡）斯劳沙以及手执三叉戟的门将。这些元素亦见于吉美石重床背屏中的金鸡帐以及墓主人手执三叉戟的形象。进言之，翟曹明墓石墓门与吉美石重床在图像方面的特殊性明显相契。二者出现此种现象并非只是一种巧合，这表明相同的种族文化在丧葬图像上的延续，可能也预示着二者年代相去不远。

〔1〕康马泰（Matteo Compareti）著，毛民译：《对北朝粟特石屏所见的一种神异飞兽的解读》，载《4~6世纪的北中国与欧亚大陆》，第166–189页。

20　中古祆教华化概说

张小贵　曾超颖
（暨南大学历史系）

祆教乃源于波斯的琐罗亚斯德教（Zoroastrianism），中古时期其由中亚传入中国，在唐代中国曾一度流行，与摩尼教、景教一道，被称为三夷教。作为一种外来宗教，其在中国传播必然要受到中土社会政治经济文化因素的制约。唐代会昌灭法，祆教即遭到取缔。然而宋代文献不乏有关祆教的文字记载，其与之前的祆教是否完全等同？宋代以后，祆教鲜见流行。那么，祆教在中古中国的传播特色是什么，其最终走向又是如何？要厘清这一问题，首先要从祆教的性质谈起。

20.1　民俗化：有祆无教

早在 1923 年，陈垣先生即发表《火祆教入中国考》一文，从拜火拜天的角度，将汉文献的祆教、火祆教比定为波斯琐罗亚斯德教，这一结论长期为学界所认同。至于用祆来指代该教的原因，陈垣先生在文中指出：

> 公历纪元前五六百年，波斯国有圣人，曰苏鲁阿士德 Zoroaster，因波斯国拜火旧俗，特倡善恶二原之说：谓善神清净而光明，恶魔污浊而黑暗；人宜弃恶就善，弃黑暗而趋光明；以火以光表至善之神，崇拜之，故名拜火教。因拜光又拜日月星辰，中国人以为其拜天，故名之曰火祆。祆者天神之省文，不称天神而称祆者，

明其为外国天神也。[1]

此段论述表明，古代中国人把琐罗亚斯德教称为祆教，乃因其教徒拜日月星辰而被误解为拜天之故，亦即按其礼俗最明显的特征来命其名。据陈垣先生的考证，在唐之前，乃称其为天神、火神、胡天神，到了隋末唐初，始新造一“祆”字，来专指该教。[2]如此专门为之造字命名，在古代中国的诸多外来宗教中，独此一家。这固然反映了该教在华流播的广度和影响，[3]但更证明了古代在华活动的琐罗亚斯德教徒与波斯本教有所区别，乃以粟特人为主要载体的粟特版琐罗亚斯德教，[4]该版本保持较多的是早期琐罗亚斯德教的成分，拜日月星辰的礼俗特别突出，如是才会造成中国人误解其为拜天；而以萨珊波斯人为主体的琐罗亚斯德教徒，其礼俗乃以祭祀圣火为最突出，通过祭祀圣火来与神沟通，这与拜天显然不可等同。

就目前的研究来看，粟特祆教与波斯本教之间存在着实质性的差异，具体表现在：后者崇拜上神阿胡拉·马兹达，基本上可归为一神教；有系列化的经典和各种清规戒律、礼仪；有完整教会组织等等，具有完整的宗教体系。而前者则是多神崇拜，其自身并无完整的宗教体系，属于以粟特人为主的中亚某些民族的民间信仰，主要表现为民俗的一个组成部分。因此，由粟特地区传入中国的火祆教不可能像佛教那样，也不可能像景教、摩尼教那样，企图以其义理，刻意向中国社会的各层民众传教。但其作为一种习俗，更易以感性的模式为汉人所了解，从而影响汉人社会。也就是说，祆教入华以后，主要是以胡俗的方式影响汉人，因此随着时代推移，其更易走向汉人的民间，汇入中土的民俗。

---

〔1〕陈垣：《火祆教入中国考》，完成于1922年4月，发表于《国学季刊》第一卷第一号（1923年1月），发表后，1923年1月、1934年10月作者进行过两次校订。本文采用1934年10月校订本，据《陈垣学术论文集》第一集，北京：中华书局，1980年，第304页。

〔2〕《陈垣学术论文集》第一集，第308页。

〔3〕详参林悟殊：《火祆教在唐代中国社会地位之考察》，载蔡鸿生主编《戴裔煊教授九十诞辰纪念文集：澳门史与中西交通研究》，广州：广东高等教育出版社，1998年，第169-196页；修订本见其著《中古三夷教辨证》，北京：中华书局，2005年，第256-258页。

〔4〕参阅林悟殊：《〈伊朗琐罗亚斯德教村落〉中译本序》，载余太山主编《欧亚学刊》第4辑，北京：中华书局，2004年6月，第255-259 页。又见林悟殊《中古三夷教辨证》，第432-439页。

尽管入华祆教并无完整的宗教体系，然而在唐代社会，祆教毕竟是作为一种独立的信仰而存在的，主要在来自西域的胡人中流行。唐贞观五年（631），将祆教诣阙闻奏的何禄，就是该教的传法穆护，尽管其并未带来本教经像，也未有向汉人传教的豪言壮语，但随后朝廷即在崇化坊建立祆祠，显然与他的宣传有关。而这座祆祠与前后长安城内所建的其他祆祠一样，都集中在胡人聚居区内，显然乃为满足来华胡人的祆教信仰而设。根据文献记载，唐代的祆教习俗主要表现为西域胡人聚火祝诅、以咒代经、妄行幻法等等。写于光启元年（885）的敦煌文书《沙州伊州地志残卷》（S. 367），述及贞观十四年（640）高昌未破以前敦煌北面伊州伊吾县祆庙的宗教仪式活动：

伊吾县……火祆庙中有素书，形像无数。有祆主翟槃陁者，高昌未破以前，槃陁因入朝至京，即下祆神，因以利刀刺腹，左右通过，出腹外，截弃其馀，以发系其本，手执刀两头，高下绞转，说国家所举百事，皆顺天心，神灵助，无不征验。神没之后，僵仆而倒，气息奄，七日即平复如旧。有司奏闻，制授游击将军。〔1〕

唐张鷟《朝野佥载》卷 3 记载与之类似：

凉州祆神祠，至祈祷日祆主以铁钉从额上钉之，直洞腋下，即出门，身轻若飞，须臾数百里。至西祆神前舞一曲即却，至旧祆所乃拔钉，无所损。卧十馀日，平复如故。莫知其所以然也。〔2〕

张鷟也记录了东都洛阳祆祠祭祀的情况：

河南府立德坊及南市西坊皆有胡祆神庙。每岁商胡祈福，烹猪羊，琵琶鼓笛，酣歌醉舞。酹神之后，募一胡为祆主，看者施钱并与之。其祆主取一横刀，利同霜雪，吹毛不过，以刀刺腹，刃出于背，仍乱扰肠肚流血。食顷，喷水呪之，平复如故。此盖西域之幻

---

〔1〕中国社会科学院历史研究所、中国敦煌吐鲁番学会敦煌古文献编辑委员会、英国国家图书馆、伦敦大学亚非学院编：《英藏敦煌文献》第一卷，成都：四川人民出版社，1990年，第158页；录文参考唐耕耦、陆宏基编：《敦煌社会经济文献真迹释录》第一辑，北京：书目文献出版社，1986年，第40–41页。

〔2〕〔唐〕张鷟撰，赵守俨点校《朝野佥载》（《隋唐嘉话·朝野佥载》，唐宋史料笔记丛刊），北京：中华书局，1979年，第65页。

法也。[1]

由此可以看出，无论是张鷟笔下的凉州、洛阳，抑或敦煌文书所记伊州伊吾县祆庙的仪式活动，都表明这种祭祆方式在入华祆教徒中具有普遍性，从碛西到东都，均曾不同程度流行。这一祭祆活动带有明显的萨满教色彩，与萨珊波斯所规范的琐罗亚斯德教的祭祀仪式是不同的。我们知道，波斯阿契美尼王朝时期流行的琐罗亚斯德教也有许多萨满教的成分，学者们从《希罗多德历史》中找到不少例证。然而在琐罗亚斯德教成为萨珊波斯帝国的国教后，经过统治者的规范，其萨满教成分已经大为减少了。没有文献能够证明萨珊王朝时期的圣火庙里，举行过类似的萨满活动。近代学者对印度琐罗亚斯德教徒，即巴斯人礼仪习俗的田野调查，[2]也未见有萨满教的成分。玛丽·博伊斯教授在对伊朗残存的琐罗亚斯德教村落考察时，发现面对疾病之类的不幸，当地信徒们也偶有采用类乎巫术的方式驱邪者，但因其有违正统琐罗亚斯德教的教导，而为村落领袖所劝止；倒是他们周围的伊斯兰教徒才热衷于这类活动。由此推想，其类乎巫术的活动，当不是本教传统的继承，而是受当地伊斯兰教徒的影响。[3]因此到了萨珊波斯时期，即便萨满教成分在当地民众中尚有遗存，也应是相当边缘化了。唐代祆祠的祭祀活动与萨珊波斯不同，带有中亚祆教浓厚的胡巫之风，更表明中土祆教乃经由粟特人“间接传入”。

不过尽管凉州、伊吾、洛阳祆祠的祭祀皆带有明显的西胡色彩，但随着时间推移，当这些西域胡人深入到中土内地之后，其祭祆的情况也发生着细微的变化。细察有关洛阳祆祠的记载，其祆主乃“招募”而来，与凉州、伊州的祆主是不同的。凉州的祆主如何产生，文献并无特别说明。但是伊吾火祆庙中的祆主翟槃陁却“身世显赫”。据考，“槃陁”

[1]《朝野佥载》，第64–65页。

[2] 详阅 Jivanji Jamshedji Modi, *The Religious Ceremonies and Customs of the Parsees*, 2nd Edition, Bombay 1937.

[3] 详阅 Mary Boyce, *A Persian Stronghold of Zoroastrianism,* Oxford: Oxford University Press, 1977, repr. University Press of America: Lanham · New York · London, 1989, pp.21–22. 中译本见〔英〕玛丽·博伊斯著，张小贵、殷小平译：《伊朗琐罗亚斯德教村落》，北京：中华书局，2005年，第18–21页。

即粟特语 Bntk 的音译，意为“奴”“仆”，[1]其姓翟表明乃为粟特化的高车人。[2]翟氏因为通神灵验，而“制授游击将军”，绝非一般招募可比，其因主事祆祠祭祀而被封官，可能与唐时萨宝府下的祆正、祆祝一样。吾人固知自北朝开始，中原王朝就设有萨宝府兼领西来商胡贩客的民事与宗教事务，但其时尚未有专设祆正、祆祝的记录。而到了唐代，在萨宝府下专设这些官职，主持宗教事务，说明唐朝廷对胡人宗教信仰的重视。即使在开元初罢视品官时，萨宝府及下属祆正、祆祝还得以保留，可见当时祆教势力影响之大，朝廷不得不正视这一现实而采用相应的政策，让祆教得以在胡人中自行传播，直到会昌灭佛时始予取缔。碛西一带与东都洛阳祆主的产生方式存在着不同，表明祆教深入中土后不断华化。其信众为满足自身的祭祀需要，不得不出资来招募祆主，而不像前代那样，有官方任命的祆正、祆祝主持祭祀。

当然，无论是朝廷任命，还是民众招募，负责唐代祆祠祭祀的庙祝都带有浓厚的胡巫色彩。然而到了唐末五代，特别是宋代以后，祆祠祭祀的巫风日益淡化。我们以开封城北祆庙的史世爽家族为例，其家世至迟可上溯至唐咸通三年（862），其初设之时也许是为满足胡人的信仰需要，但会昌灭法，祆教亦受到牵连，势力大减。而在华世代生活数百年的胡人后裔，已与汉人无异。到了史世爽时，他和中国民间社会中的庙祝，已经没有什么实质性差异，所以张邦基将其与池州郭西英济王祠的庙祝连类而书，不加区别。这无疑表明此时祆庙庙祝已和中国传统社会中神庙的庙祝一样了。考察此时有关祆庙的记录，反映的都是地道的汉人信仰，和唐代胡人取火咒诅祭祆的情形已完全不同了。宋代有关祆教祠庙的描述中，已不见请巫通神的记载。如果说唐代祆祠还保有中亚祆教胡巫祭祀的特色，到了宋代，祆庙里面则“有祝无巫”，已经看不

〔1〕蔡鸿生：《唐代九姓胡与突厥文化》，北京：中华书局，1998年，第39页。

〔2〕此点乃为蔡鸿生先生所提示。吉田丰先生认为翟是一两个突厥部落所用的姓，韩森女史认为一些粟特人可能是借用了他们的姓。见韩森（Valerie Hansen）著，王锦萍译《丝绸之路贸易对吐鲁番地方社会的影响：公元500—800年》，提交2004年4月23—25日北京举行“粟特人在中国国际学术研讨会”论文；收入荣新江、华澜、张志清主编《粟特人在中国——历史、考古、语言的新探索》，《法国汉学》第十辑，北京：中华书局，2005年12月，第117，132页注28。

到丝毫胡人色彩了。

另外，从祆祠功能的变化，也可窥见这一外来宗教逐渐华化的历程。祆祠（或祆庙）是祆教徒的主要宗教活动场所，唐初祆祠的建立主要是为群胡祀火祭祀提供场所。发生在祆祠中的聚火祝诅、以咒代经、妄行幻法等等活动，毫无疑问是为满足胡人祆教信仰而举行。到唐末宋初，开封史氏所主持的祆祠虽仍以祠祆神闻名，但却不是为了满足胡人的宗教信仰了。考虑到范鲁公在封丘巷祆庙的遭遇，以及常彦辅在祆庙祈祷病愈的灵验故事，"东京城北有祆庙……京师人畏其威灵，甚重之"表明祆庙已成为满足普通民众祈福禳灾的民间信仰。特别是《宋史》与《宋会要》的记载，表明其已得到中原王朝的许可，与一般汉人的土地、城隍信仰无异了，究其原因，乃是朝廷出于祈雨的需要。到了南宋末年，地方官为了防止兵变而在镇江的祆庙祈祷，并最终得到回报，更符合民间信仰求神纳福的宗教特征。祭祆原为胡人的信仰习俗，宋代成为汉人祈福禳灾的手段。

到了唐末五代，由于胡汉的融合，敦煌地区的祆庙成为游神赛会的娱乐场所，祆神与门神、阿娘神、张女郎神等等，成了民众祈赛的诸神之一，赛祆遂变成地道的汉人风俗。祆神之被祈赛，不过是当地的民俗，完全不是某一宗教门派所专有，而是当地各族居民所共享；其已逐渐失去琐罗亚斯德教固有的宗教意义了。到了宋代，祆神和城隍土地、五龙祠一道被纳入中原王朝祭礼之内，进入了中国民间万神殿。如果说祆教初来之时并未以一个完整的宗教体系向汉人传播，而是以胡俗的方式在中国社会发生影响；那么到了宋代，原属西胡的祆俗已完全变为汉地的民俗。可以说，唐以后，有"祆"无"教"是这一外来宗教进一步民俗化的表现。

20.2 无像、画像与偶像

一般认为到公元前 5 世纪末 4 世纪初，琐罗亚斯德教已明显实行偶像崇拜了。韦勘德（Stig Wikander）曾断言早期的琐罗亚斯德教徒并不知道庙火仪式。[1]德国考古学家施帕曼博士（Dr.Schippmann），对波斯境内的琐罗亚斯德教火庙进行了综合考察研究，他认为琐罗亚斯德教徒于公元前 4 世纪时始接受庙火仪式。[2]玛丽·博伊斯教授（Mary Boyce）肯定了他的观点，并补充道，古伊朗地区首先实行庙火仪式，它与需要使用圣像的阿娜希塔（Anahit）仪式不同，乃为反对圣像崇拜而确立，并逐渐发展成为该教的正统仪式。[3]如此，火逐渐成为琐罗亚斯德教徒唯一崇拜对象，其地位越发重要。

真正意义上的破坏圣像运动，到帕提亚晚期逐渐开展起来，至萨珊王朝时赢得完全胜利。在帕提亚晚期，随着希腊化影响的减退，反对圣像崇拜、支持火坛的情绪日益高涨。伏洛吉斯（Valakhš，Vologeses）一世统治时，在其发行的钱币反面印上火坛，代替了希腊风格的神像；而地方大族，如伊斯塔克尔阿那希塔神庙的保卫者，他们都是波斯的萨珊家族，则把神像从圣祠移出，代之以圣火。[4]

到了萨珊时期，进一步以法律形式禁止圣像崇拜。阿达希尔一世（Ardashir I，A.D.224—240）从掌权之日起就是积极的破坏圣像者。他通过法律，明确反对把圣像作为礼拜对象，认为那是不合法的。萨珊时期的国王们，连同祭司与贵族，都积极建立圣火，用之代替圣像，并为其建造祠庙。当圣像从圣祠移走后，要在圣祠里安置一处火坛，以驱逐潜在圣像中的邪恶。一份中古波斯语文献详细记录了琐罗亚斯德教徒在神庙中移走圣像、放置火坛的情况：

> 在库思老·卡瓦丹（Khusrau ī kawādān）统治时，有两个人，名叫卡卡（kakā）和阿杜尔陀姆（Ādurtōhm），他们在某地拥有一座神庙。他们按照祭司（Mōbeds）的命令，把神像移出神庙，而代

[1] Stig Wikander, Feuerpriester in Kleinasien und Iran, Lund, 1946.

[2] K. Schippmann, *Die iranischen Feuerheiligtüer*, Berlin–New York, 1971.

[3] Mary Boyce, "On the Zoroastrian Temple Cult of Fire", *Journal of the American Oriental Society*, Vol. 95.3, 1975, pp.455–456.

[4] Mary Boyce, "Iconoclasm among the Zoroastrians", *Christianity, Judaism and Other Greco–Roman Cults: Studies presented to Morton Smith at Sixty*, ed. by J. Neusner, Vol. 4, Leiden, 1975, pp.104–105.

之以火坛（’twrlwk）。当被要求把火带回迪瓦·卡达甘（Dīwān ī kardagān）时，他们并不赞同。他们及其后代接到命令，应该负责照管那座庙及里面的火坛。他们成功地把火坛安置在正确的地方；只要还活着，就可以在那里看护火。[1]

由此可见，中古时期波斯正统琐罗亚斯德教，并不行圣像崇拜。不过，传入中土的祆教却屡见行圣像崇拜的记载。上引敦煌文书 S. 367 记载：

伊吾县……火祆庙中有素书，形像无数。

日本学者神田喜一郎曾根据唐代金石文字中常见的“素画”，而怀疑此处素书或为素画之误，认为此座祆庙供奉的乃该教神祇的彩绘塑像。[2]笔者通过考察，认为此处的“素书”，乃指祆神画像，[3]其应来源于中亚祆教传统，缘该地向为中亚粟特人聚居之地。S. 367 记载伊州的建置沿革如下：“隋大业六年（610）于城东买地置伊吾郡。隋乱，复没于胡。贞观四年（630），首领石万年率七城来降。我唐始置伊州。……管县三：伊吾、纳职、柔远。”[4]同卷记载伊州辖下柔远县阿揽神的情况，与伊吾县的情况类似，也是由入华胡人所建：“右相传，隋大业十二年（616），伊吾胡共筑营田。贞观四年，胡归国，因此为县，以镇为名。……柔远镇，镇东七里，隋大业十二年置伊吾郡，因置此镇。……其州下立庙，神名阿览。”[5]伊州的胡人聚落是贞观初年由内迁的粟特人组成，他们入华既未久，华化亦未深，固容易保存本教原始信仰；其祆神信仰是粟特聚落内部的重要精神生活，如是，则供祀祆神画像应

---

〔1〕Mary Boyce, “On the Sacred Fires of the Zoroastrians”, *Bulletin of the School of Oriental and African Studies* (*BSOAS*), Vol.31, 1968, pp.63-64.

〔2〕神田喜一郎：《素画に就いて》，《东洋史研究》第5卷第3号，昭和15年；后收入其著《东洋学说林》，东京弘文堂刊，1948年12月，此据《神田喜一郎全集》第一卷，京都，1986年，第85-88页。

〔3〕张小贵：《唐伊吾祆庙“素书”非塑像辨》，载《中华文史论丛》2008年第2辑，第321-338页；其著《中古华化祆教考述》，北京：文物出版社，2010年，第69-77，91-94页。

〔4〕《英藏敦煌文献》第一卷，第158页，录文参考唐耕耦、陆宏基编《敦煌社会经济文献真迹释录》一，第40页。

〔5〕《英藏敦煌文献》第一卷，第158页，录文参考唐耕耦、陆宏基编《敦煌社会经济文献真迹释录》一，第41页。

为沿袭粟特本土的信仰方式。

到了宋代，祆教祠庙中直将祆神像作摩醯首罗像供奉，事见宋代董逌《广川画跋》卷 4《书常彦辅祆神像》的记载：

> 元祐八年（1093）七月，常君彦辅就开宝寺之文殊院，遇寒热疾，大惧不良。及夜，祷于祆神祠。明日，良愈。乃祀于庭，又图像归事之。属某书，且使教知神之休也。祆祠，世所以奉梵相也。其相希异，即经所谓摩醯首罗。有大神威，普救一切苦，能摄伏四方，以卫佛法。当隋之初，其法始至中夏，立祠颁政坊。常有番人奉事，聚火祝诅，奇幻变怪。至有出腹决肠，吞火蹈刃，故下俚庸人，就以诅誓，取为信重。唐祠令有萨宝府官主司，又有梵祝以赞于礼事，其制甚重，在当时为显祠。今君以祷获应，既应则祠，既祠则又使文传，其礼至矣。与得悉唐国顺大爵宾同号祆神者，则有别也。[1]

从这段记载的行文语境看，祆神祠应是附属于文殊院里面。而佛教寺院所供奉的神像，普遍是塑像，因而，该祆神祠所供奉的祆神当亦为偶像。不过，其之附属于文殊院，则是由于人们把其所奉之神目为摩醯首罗之故。该神既“有大神威，普救一切苦，能摄伏四方，以卫佛法”，自是佛教诸神之一。“祆祠，世所以奉梵相也。其相希异，即经所谓摩醯首罗”一句，表明宋时将二者比附的错误观念依然存在。由于常君所图之像已不存，该像究竟与摩醯首罗有无区别，无从考证；但无论如何，这段记载无疑暗示了宋代的祆神崇拜，已被偶像化了。

宋僧文莹的《玉壶清话》（又名《玉壶野史》）曾提及：

> 范鲁公质举进士，和凝相主文，爱其私试，因以登第。凝旧在第十三人，谓公曰：“君之辞业合在甲选，暂屈为第十三人，传老夫衣钵可乎？”鲁公荣谢之。后至作相，亦复相继。时门生献诗，有“从此庙堂添故事，登庸衣钵亦相传”之句。初，周祖自邺起师

〔1〕〔宋〕董逌撰，陈引驰整理，徐中玉审阅：《广川画跋》卷4，《传世藏书·集库·文艺论评》3，海南：国际新闻出版中心出版，1996年，第2900–2901页。录文可参考景印《文渊阁四库全书》“子部”一一九，艺术类，台湾：商务印书馆发行，813册，第476–477页。

向阙，京国罹乱，鲁公遁迹民间。一旦，坐对正（应为封丘）巷茶肆中，忽一形貌怪陋者前揖云："相公相公，无虑无虑。"时暑中，公执一叶素扇，偶写"大暑去酷吏，清风来故人"一联在上，陋状者夺其扇曰："今之典刑，轻重无准，吏得以侮，何啻大暑耶？公当深究狱弊。"持扇急去。一日，于祆庙后门，一短鬼手中执其扇，乃茶邸中见者。未几，周祖果以物色聘之，得公于民间，遂用焉。忆昔陋鬼之语，首议刑典，疏曰："先王所恤，莫重于刑。今繁苛失中，轻重无准，民罹横刑，吏得侮法，愿陛下留神刑典，深轸无告。"世宗命公与台官剧可久、知杂张湜聚都省详修刊定，惟务裁减，太官供膳。殆五年书成，目曰《刑统》。[1]

同一记事亦见于宋邵伯温《邵氏闻见录》（又称《邵氏闻见前录》）卷7，[2]尽管两段文字略有出入，但有关开封封丘巷有祆庙的记载却是一致的。[3]值得注意的是，该段文字记录了范鲁公质于封丘巷祆庙后门见有一"土偶短鬼"，或以为此土偶可作为祆庙有塑像的证据。[4]按中国主流宗教所崇拜诸神，不乏有异貌者，但毕竟鲜被称"怪陋"。故祆庙所奉"土偶短鬼"，或为华化祆神也未可知。若果真如此，则亦可佐证宋代祆庙之偶像化。这与祆教初传中土时行画像崇拜的情况显为不同，更与波斯正统琐罗亚斯德教崇拜圣火大异其趣。当然，这些偶像虽被人们目为祆神，但并非正统琐罗亚斯德教万神殿的神祇，表明人们对

〔1〕〔宋〕文莹撰，郑世刚、杨立扬点校：《玉壶清话》卷6（《湘山野录·续录·玉壶清话》，唐宋史料笔记丛刊），北京：中华书局，1984年，第57页。

〔2〕〔宋〕邵伯温撰，李剑雄、刘德权点校：《邵氏闻见录》，北京：中华书局，1983年，第62页。

〔3〕神田喜一郎氏在其《祆教杂考》（原刊《史学杂志》第39编第4号，昭和三年四月，第381–394页；昭和四年十月补订，收入其著《东洋学说林》，今据《神田喜一郎全集》第一卷，第73–75页）一文中，以邵伯温记载与《东京梦华录》互证，确认该庙之存在。1933年神田氏在《祆教琐记》一文中进而指出宋僧文莹《玉壶清话》亦有关于范质的记载，并指出其早于《邵氏闻见录》所记。见《祆教琐记》，《史林》第十八卷第一号，昭和八年一月发行，第15–26页；昭和九年十月补订，收入其著《东洋学说林》，此据《神田喜一郎全集》第一卷，第89–101页。此外，刘铭恕先生亦举证宋欧阳玄《睽车志》也有范质祆庙遇鬼的记载，不过内容略简，见其文《元人杂剧中所见之火祆教》，《金陵学报》第11卷1期，1941年，第46–47页；又见《边疆研究论丛》，1942–1944年，第12–13页。可见这一传说在当时的流行。

〔4〕那波利贞：《祆庙祭祀小考》，《史窗》第一〇号，1956年，第16页。

祆教作为外来宗教的真实面目日益模糊，而民众则想当然地来祭祀所谓祆神，这种变化正反映了祆教之日益本土化。

这一变化表明，到了宋代，祆教虽已经不是作为一门独立的宗教存在，然而祆神却因灵验而被人们保留下来。到了宋代，所谓祆神偶像，也汇入了中国传统的民间信仰。之所以产生这种情况，与中国传统的文化环境自是密切相关。中国自古即为圣像，尤其是偶像崇拜的民族，无论掌控国家意识形态的儒家，还是各行各业、各宗各族，无论是作为主流宗教的佛道二家，还是各种民间信仰，都有各自的偶像崇拜。而且古代中华民族乃多神崇拜的民族，对黎元百姓来说，他们并不专宗哪神哪教，并不太关心严格的宗教学说、教条、戒律，而是敬畏崇拜各种神，凡神必拜，只要其灵验就可以。正是在这种历史背景下，祆神“被动”地被汉人所改造，从而演化、嬗变出符合汉人习惯的种种祆神形象。当然，这种祆神与祆教本身已经无所关联了。因此，我们无妨把祆神偶像化看作祆教华化的另一种表现。

20.3　血族内婚与同姓不婚

琐罗亚斯德教婚姻观的一大特征是鼓励血亲婚。如萨珊王朝（Sasanian，公元 224—651 年）时期，开国君主阿尔达希尔（Ardashir，约 226—240 年在位）娶了自己的姐妹丹娜（Denak）为妻；沙普尔一世（Shapur I，公元 239—272 年在位）则娶了自己的女儿阿杜尔・阿娜希特（Adur-Anahid）为后。[1]时任琐罗亚斯德教大祭司的克德尔（Kirder）鼓励这种近亲婚姻，甚至目为虔诚的功德。[2]当时的基督教徒 Basil 也曾报导了这种奇特的婚俗，并认为其是不合法的。[3]萨珊王朝后期，著名的祭司米赫兰（Mihram-Gushnasp）七岁时就熟知琐罗亚斯德教圣

〔1〕Mary Boyce, Zoroastrians：Their Religious Beliefs and Practices, London: Routledge, 2001, p.111.

〔2〕伊藤义教《カルデールの「ゾロアスターのカアバ」刻文について》,《オリエント》，第24卷第2号，1981年，第9页。

〔3〕St Basil, *Collected Letters*, Loeb Classical Library, vol.IV, CCL VIII. 引自 Mary Boyce, *Zoroastrians：Their Religious Beliefs and Practices*, p.111.

经，并虔诚遵守本教近亲结婚的风俗，娶了自己的姐妹为妻。[1]到了10 世纪，帕拉维文（Pahlavi）文书仍然记有琐罗亚斯德教兄妹结婚的例子。[2]14 世纪的文献则记录了祭司们极力主张中表等旁系血亲结婚。此后这种近亲婚渐成为琐罗亚斯德教社区中最为流行的婚姻形式。[3]琐罗亚斯德教实行血亲婚姻，是符合该教教义的，如《亚斯那》（Y.12.9）中记载："我向崇拜马兹达（Mazda）的宗教效忠，摈弃进攻，放下武器，行血缘婚，这是正当的。"[4]

这种血亲婚，也见于汉籍的记载。如《周书·异域传》载：

> ［波斯国］俗事火祆神。婚合亦不择尊卑，诸夷之中，最为丑秽矣。民女年十岁以上有姿貌者，王收养之，有功勋人，即以分赐。[5]

《魏书》卷 102、《北史》卷 97 所载与《周书》略同。[6]《隋书》亦记载波斯国："妻其姊妹。"[7]中亚地区也存在这种婚俗。开元中期（723—727）去天竺巡礼的新罗僧慧超在《往五天竺国传》中记载："又从大食国已东，并是胡国。即是安国、曹国、史国、石骡国、米国、康国等。……又此六国总事火祆，不识佛法。唯康国有一寺，有一僧，又不解敬也。此等胡国，并剪鬓发。爱着白氎帽子。极恶风俗，婚姻交杂，纳母及姊妹为妻。波斯国亦纳母为妻。"[8] 8 世纪中期（751—762）曾被大食人所俘而西行的杜环，在《经行记》中记载："诸国陆行之所经也，胡则一种，法有数般。有大食法、有大秦法、有寻寻法，其寻寻

---

〔1〕G. Hoffman transl. *Auszüge aus syrischen Akten persischer Märtyrer*, Leipzig 1880, repr. 1966, pp.93–95.

〔2〕B. T. Anklesaria ed., *Rivāyat-ī Hēmīt-ī Asavahistān,* Vol.I. *Pahlavi Text*, Bombay 1962, pp.104–107.

〔3〕Mary Boyce, Zoroastrians：Their Religious Beliefs and Practices, p.175.

〔4〕Mary Boyce, *A History of Zoroastrianism*, Vol.I, Leiden/Köln: E. J. Brill, 1975, p.254.

〔5〕《周书》卷50《异域》下，第920页。

〔6〕参阅余太山：《两汉魏晋南北朝正史西域传研究》，北京：中华书局，2003年，第65–94页。

〔7〕《隋书》卷83《西域》，第1856页。

〔8〕〔唐〕慧超原著，张毅笺释：《往五天竺国传笺释》（中外交通史籍丛刊9），北京：中华书局，2000年，第118页。

烝报于诸夷狄中最甚，当食不语。”[1]这里，“烝报于诸夷狄中最甚”的寻寻法，一般被认为是祆教法，[2]可与慧超所记的中亚六国风俗相印证。其中，作为西粟特中心的安国，其婚俗似更引人注目：“［安息国］王姓昭武，与康国王同族。……风俗同于康国，唯妻其姊妹，及母子递相禽兽，此为异也。”[3]此处的安息国显然即粟特安国，有《隋书》的相关记载为证：

> 安国，汉时安息国也。王姓昭武氏，与康国王同族，字设力登。妻，康国王女也。都在那密水南，城有五重，环以流水。宫殿皆为平头。王坐金驼座，高七八尺。每听政，与妻相对，大臣三人评理国事。风俗同于康国，唯妻其姊妹，及母子递相禽兽，此为异也。炀帝即位之后，遣司隶从事杜行满使于西域，至其国，得五色盐而返。[4]

以上所述，主要为中亚粟特地区的祆教婚俗。但根据记载，安国实行的血缘婚，在康国似乎并不存在，表明这一婚姻主要为西粟特所有，东粟特却不见记载。详细情况值得进一步探讨。以上所述为父系集团内婚制的极端例子，亦即父女为婚，母子为婚和兄妹为婚。

当然，我们并没有找到琐罗亚斯德教规定教徒必须父女、母子及兄妹通婚的证据，也未发现处罚不实行此类婚姻的案例。穆格山出土粟特文书 Nov.3 和 Nov.4，是订于康国王突昏十年（710）的婚约，表明康国上层社会的婚姻生活已经具有相当完备的法律形态，[5]与前引史载康国婚俗不同于安国的情况吻合。因此，慧超和杜环笔下“极恶风俗，婚

［1］［唐］杜环原著，张一纯笺注《经行记笺注》（中外交通史籍丛刊9），北京：中华书局，2000年，第21页。

［2］Éd. Chavannes et P. Pelliot, ‘Un traité manichéen retrouvé en chine’, *Janvier Février*, 1913, pp.155–157. 中译本见伯希和、沙畹撰，冯承钧译《摩尼教流行中国考》，载冯承钧译《西域南海史地考证译丛八编》，北京：商务印书馆，1962年重印第1版，第50–51页，收入1995年5月北京第2次影印《西域南海史地考证译丛》第二卷。杨志玖：《寻寻法考》，《边疆人文》第四卷，天津，1947年12月。

［3］［唐］杜佑撰，王文锦等点校《通典》卷192《边防》八，北京：中华书局，1988年，第5239页。

［4］《隋书》卷83《西域》，第1849页。

［5］В. А. ЛИВШИЦА, *ЮРИДИЧЕСКИЕ ДОКУМЕНТЫ И ПИСЬМА*, Москва, 1962, стр.47.

姻杂交，纳母及姊妹为妻”及“烝报于诸夷狄中最甚”之类的血缘群婚残迹，“就只能看作是中亚两河流域婚姻制度发展不平衡在唐人行纪中的反映，而不应当用它来概括唐代九姓胡婚俗的全貌”。[1]可以这样说，血亲婚为波斯琐罗亚斯德教的独特婚俗，但并不能概括粟特祆教婚俗的全貌。这或许也可视为中亚祆教与波斯本教之间的一大区别吧。

从上文论述可以看出，尽管汉文典籍记载其为“诸夷之中最为丑秽”，而正统的琐罗亚斯德教却把这种族内血亲婚目为功德和虔诚的善行。这自是源于两者不同的文化传统所致。中国自古即禁止同姓为婚，其重要考虑即为禁止血族内婚。如唐代法律规定“诸同姓为婚者，各徒二年。缌麻以上，以奸论”。[2]所谓“缌麻”，是丧服五服中最轻的一种，指较为疏远的亲属或亲戚，如高祖父母、曾伯叔祖父母、中表兄弟等等。也就是说，唐朝法律不仅规定同姓不得结婚，而且如果近亲结婚也要以犯奸科罪。唐李回为建州刺史时，因“取同姓女子入宅”及其他事由，被仇人锻成大狱，贬为抚州司马，最后在贬所死去。[3]这是唐代“同姓不婚”的显例。另外，唐代曾任余杭太守的张守信，欲将自己的女儿嫁与富阳尉张瑶，后因人提醒，及时制止了这桩“同姓”婚姻。而任汉州雒县县令的李逢年，也差点娶了蜀中望族李札之妹，后亦因“同姓”而终止婚姻。[4]可见“同姓不婚”观念在时人中之流行。宋代法律规定与唐相同，对同姓不婚的规定也是极为严格的。[5]以后各代也各有对同姓不婚的规定，只是细节略有不同而已。同时，由于中国古代极为重视伦常，因此关于宗亲、中表以及其他亲属之间禁止婚姻的规定也是极其严格的。[6]虽然从历史上看，姓氏有“同名异实”或“姓同源异”的事例，但在相当长的时期内，限制同姓为婚就等于禁止同族为婚，与之相为补充的是繁复严格的“近亲禁婚制”。在这种严格的婚姻

〔1〕蔡鸿生：《唐代九姓胡与突厥文化》，第23–24页。
〔2〕刘俊文撰：《唐律疏议笺解》下，北京：中华书局，1996年，第1033页。
〔3〕〔五代〕王定保撰：《唐摭言》，上海：上海古籍出版社，1978年，第20–21页。
〔4〕〔宋〕李昉等编：《太平广记》卷242，北京：人民文学出版社，1959年，第1872–1873页。
〔5〕周密：《宋代刑法史》，北京：法律出版社，2002年，第210–212页。
〔6〕史凤仪：《中国古代婚姻与家庭》，武汉：湖北人民出版社，1987年，第98–102页。

禁忌下，波斯和中亚粟特人“纳母及姊妹为妻”的祆教婚俗自然容易被汉人目为“诸夷之中最为丑秽”了。[1]

就目前所知，现可确认的入华祆教徒婚例，应是晚唐苏谅与马氏夫妇。据汉文志文，马氏是苏谅之妻；而据婆文志文，首先对之解读的日本著名伊朗学家伊藤义教认为马氏是苏谅的女儿，他曾将这种亦女亦妻的疑难解归结为伊朗的血亲相婚的习俗。[2]但是，许多学者对此未表首肯。时至今日，马氏夫妇是否具有血缘关系，仍未有定论，因而此例婚姻并不能用以证明入华祆教徒曾虔诚地遵循本教血亲婚。考虑到上述的社会背景，亦很难证明马氏夫妇为父女通婚。

由以上论述可以看出，中古时期入华的祆教信徒，是极难保持本教奉为功德的血亲婚的。至于学者们研究的胡汉通婚的例子，虽然很难遽断其已非祆教信徒，但在中土的社会文化背景下，彼等在婚俗方面保持本教传统的信念可谓难上加难。究其原因，当求之于陈寅恪先生的卓识：

> 夫僧徒戒本本从释迦部族共和国之法制蜕蝉而来，今竟数典忘祖，轻重倒置，至于斯极。橘迁地而变为枳，吾民族同化之力可谓大矣。但支那佛教信徒，关于君臣父子之观念，后虽同化，当其初期，未尝无高僧大德，不顾一切忌讳，公然出而辩护其教中无父无君之说者。独至男女性交诸要义，则此土自来佛教著述，大抵噤默不置一语。如小乘部僧尼戒律中，颇有涉及者，因以“在家人勿看”之语标识之。（《高僧传》一《康僧会传》云：“（孙皓）因求看沙门戒，会以戒文禁秘，不可轻宣。”疑与此同。）盖佛藏中学说之类是者，纵为笃信之教徒，以经神州传统道德所薰习之故，亦复不能奉受。特以其为圣典之文，不敢昌言诋斥。惟有隐秘闭藏，禁绝其流布而已。莲花色尼出家因缘中聚麀恶报不载于敦煌写本者，即由于此。[3]

---

〔1〕董家遵著、卞恩才整理：《中国古代婚姻史研究》，广州：广东人民出版社，1995年，第117–201页。

〔2〕伊藤义教：《西安出土汉、婆合璧墓志婆文语言学的试释》，载于《考古学报》1964年第2期，第197–203页+2图版。

〔3〕陈寅恪：《莲花色尼出家因缘跋》，原载《清华学报》第七卷第一期，1932年1月，今据其著《寒柳堂集》，北京：三联书店，2001年，第174页。

通过这段有关文化交流中客体文化如何适应主体文化的宏论，陈先生道出了中国传统道德中的人伦之始亦即“夫妇”之义的重要，正是由于此，佛法初来时虽敢昌言“无父无君”之说，对类乎莲花色尼因“聚麀恶报”而出家的因缘，却大抵噤默不置一语。这样看来，原本崇尚“纳母及姊妹为妻”的祆教徒，在入华以后，自是很难实行这种“聚麀乱伦”之婚。更何况若依陈先生“［吾国中古史］种族之分，多系于其人所受之文化，而不在其所承之血统”的观念，唐宋时代出土墓志所披露多为“世代甚远久”的胡姓居民，对其信仰的观察必须注重世代层次，始能做出更精确的分析。[1]

20.4　弃尸于山与入土为安

有关波斯琐罗亚斯德教葬俗的中文记载，见于《周书·异域传下》波斯国条：

> 死者多弃尸于山，一月治服。城外有人别居，唯知丧葬之事，号为不净人。若入城市，摇铃自别。[2]

今本《魏书·西域传》《北史·西域传》波斯国条所录相同。有关波斯琐罗亚斯德教天葬习俗的文献记载，最早似可追溯到公元前5世纪希腊作家希罗多德（Herodotus）的记录：

> 据说波斯人的尸体是只有在被狗或是禽类撕裂之后才埋葬的。玛哥斯僧（又译麻葛僧等）有这种风俗那是毫无疑问的，因为他们是公然实行这种风俗的。[3]

公元1世纪希腊作家斯特拉波（Strabo）指出，［波斯］王族也实行曝尸：“他们不但承认古波斯的神祇，建筑火祭坛；并且严格遵从琐罗亚斯德教教律，暴弃王族尸体，以供秃鹫和犬，这是连先前的阿契美

〔1〕陈寅恪：《白乐天之先祖及后嗣》，见其著《元白诗笺证稿》，上海：上海古籍出版社，1978年3月新1版，1982年2月第2次印刷，第307–308页；北京：三联书店，2001年，第317页。

〔2〕《周书》卷50，第920页。

〔3〕George Rawlinson transl., *The History of Herodotus*, *Great Books of The Western World*, Vol.6, I.140, The University of Chicago, 1952, p.32. 参阅王以铸译《希罗多德历史》，北京：商务印书馆，1997年，上册，第72页。

尼朝都未能实行的。”[1]到萨珊波斯时期，统治者通过行政力量推行该教，“即使原来没有天葬习惯的波斯人，在这种严刑重罚下，也都得一遵教法，改用天葬，并且逐步习以为常了。”[2]沙卜尔二世（Shapur II A.D. 309-380）统治时，编定了该教经典《阿维斯陀经》，其中《辟邪经》（*vendîdâd*，音译“文迪达德”）第三章第四节从法律上规定了执行天葬。[3]据现有材料，无法确定《辟邪经》的编纂日期，但经文表明其“于帕提亚时期编纂，部分内容甚至更加古老”。[4]由此可以断定，这种葬俗至少在帕提亚晚期琐罗亚斯德教复兴时已经存在，在萨珊时期颇为流行。

7世纪初，隋炀帝派往西域的使者韦节，在《西蕃记》中记录了当时康国的葬俗，是有关粟特火袄教葬俗的珍贵记载。801年成书的杜佑《通典》加以引录：

> 国城外别有二百馀户，专知丧事。别筑一院，院内养狗，每有人死，即往取尸，置此院内，令狗食人肉尽，收骸骨埋殡，无棺椁。[5]

其中，收骸骨埋槟即使用盛骨瓮的习俗，已为中亚考古发现所证实。[6]

而中国古代的丧葬观念明显和波斯及中亚袄教徒的观念相矛盾。如汉代刘熙的《释名》卷8《释丧制》记载了中国人的丧葬观念：

> 葬不如礼曰埋，埋痗也，趋使腐朽而已也。不得埋曰弃，谓弃

[1]〔美〕W. M. 麦高文著，章巽译：《中亚古国史》，北京：中华书局，2004年，第86页。

[2] 林悟殊：《中古琐罗亚斯德教葬俗及其在中亚的遗痕》，见其著《波斯拜火教与古代中国》，第88页。

[3] J. Darmesteter transl., *The Zend-Avesta*, Part I, *The Vendīdād*, in F. Max Müller ed. *SBE*, Vol. IV, Oxford University Press, 1887; repr. Motilal Banarsidass, 1965, 1969, 1974, 1980, pp. 31-32.

[4] Ehsan Yarshater ed., *The Cambridge History of Iran*, Vol 3(2), Cambridge: Cambridge University Press, 1983, p.1159.

[5]《通典》卷193，第5256页。

[6] 香山阳坪《オスアリについて—中央アジア・ゾロアスター教徒の藏骨器》，刊东京《史学杂志》第72编第9号，1963年，第54-68页。G. A. Pugachenkova, 'The Form and Style of Sogdian Ossuaries', *BAI*, new series 8 (The Archaeology and Art of Central Asia. Studies from the Former Soviet Union), 1996, pp.227-243. L. V. Pavchinskaia, 'Sogdian Ossuaries', *BAI*, new series 8, pp.209-226.

之于野也。不得其尸曰捐，捐于他境也。[1]

唐玄宗朝官修的类书《初学记》加以引用，反映了这种观念的持久性：

礼记曰:葬也者藏也，藏也者欲人弗得见也。左传曰:天子七月而葬，同轨毕至，诸侯五月，同盟至，大夫三月，同位至，士逾月，外姻至。释名曰:藏不如礼曰埋,埋痗［趋使腐朽而已］也。不得埋曰弃。不得其尸曰捐［捐于他境］。[2]

在中国历史上最为常见、最为悠久的乃是土葬。[3]这与中国古代传统的伦理道德密不可分。在中国，儒家历来在丧葬上强调"入土为安"，注重尸体的保护，把"慎护"先人发肤作为自己"扬名后世"的孝举。《礼记·祭义》载："宰我曰：'吾闻鬼神之名，不知其所谓。'子曰：'气也者，神之盛也。魄也者，鬼之盛也。合鬼与神，教之至也。'众生必死，死必归土，此之谓鬼。骨肉毙于下，阴为野土。其气发扬于上，为昭明，……圣人以是为未足也，筑为宫室，设为宗、祧，以别亲疏远迩，教民反古复始，不忘其所由生也。众之服自此，故听且速也。"[4]这种"死后归土"的儒家丧葬观，在佛教未传入中国以前，一直左右着中国丧葬民俗的导向。虽然自从佛教传入中国，并在民间广为流传以后，这种传统的儒家丧葬观念和葬式遭到了强有力的冲击，但土葬仍是占主导地位的丧葬模式。例如到了唐代，官府仍然主张埋葬。天宝元年三月甲寅，令葬埋暴骨诏：

移风易俗，王化之大猷；掩骼埋胔，时令之通典。如闻江左百姓之间，或家遭疾疫，因而致死，皆弃之中野，无复安葬。情理都阙，一至于斯。习以为常，乃成其弊。自今已后，宜委郡县长吏严加诫约，俾其知禁，勿使更然。其先未葬者，即勒本家收葬。如或无亲族，及行客身亡者，仰所在村邻，相共埋瘗，无使暴露，庶叶

〔1〕〔清〕毕沅疏证《释名疏证》第三册，王云五主编《丛书集成初编》据经训堂丛书本影印，上海：上海商务印书馆，1936年，第282页。

〔2〕〔唐〕徐坚等《初学记》第二册，北京：中华书局，1962年，第359页。

〔3〕徐吉军、贺云翱著:《中国丧葬礼俗》，杭州：浙江人民出版社，1991年，第181-215页。

〔4〕〔清〕孙希旦撰，沈啸寰、王星贤点校:《礼记集解》卷46，下册，北京：中华书局，1989年，第1218-1220页。

礼经。诸道有此同者，亦宜准此。[1]

宋代以后火葬盛行。然而，类似野葬的“薄俗”，在宋代仍遭到官府的镇压：

范忠宣公帅太原，河东地狭，民惜地不葬其亲，公俾僚属收无主烬骨，别男女，异穴以葬；又檄诸郡仿此，不可以万数计。仍自作记，凡数百言，曲折致意，规变薄俗。时元祐六年（1091）也。淳熙间（1174—1189），臣僚亦尝建议：柩寄僧寺岁久无主者，官为掩瘗。行之不力，今柩寄僧寺者固自若也。[2]

以上事例无非说明，迟至有唐一代，社会上占主导地位的殡葬方式依然是土葬，因此我们考察入华祆教的葬俗时，必须考虑中土传统的丧葬观念。从1999年起太原虞弘墓、2000年西安北周安伽墓、2003年西安史君墓的发现，人们越来越关注于北朝隋唐时期入华粟特人的墓葬。就此类墓葬的性质，目前比较保守的看法似乎是他们采用了汉地固有的使用石葬具的风俗，但是与同期同类墓葬不同，将尸体直接置于石上，这一点倒与祆教教义暗合，缘因大地乃是善的造物，不能受到尸体的污染。[3]这一变革，或不排除受中土丧葬观念制约的可能。

以上我们仅从祭祀仪式、崇拜对象、婚丧礼俗等各个角度对祆教华化的表现进行勾勒。由于火祆教没有汉译经典出土，又缺乏明确的遗址遗物发现，所以国人研究不乏模糊之处。以祆教礼俗为研究对象，无疑有助于我们的立足点落到实处，从而全面和深入地认识祆教“辗转间接”传入中国后，其发生变异的过程及最终命运。以礼俗为题，才能使考察对象落到实处，从而避免言之无物、探讨空疏。正如琐罗亚斯德教史研究的权威英国玛丽·博伊斯（Mary Boyce）教授所说：

西方琐罗亚斯德教研究的一个弱点是过分依赖文书……在对宗教进行纯学术研究时，很可能会主观选择一些看似重要的部分；

---

〔1〕李希泌主编：《唐大诏令集补编》，上海：上海古籍出版社，2003年，第948页。

〔2〕〔宋〕周煇撰，刘永翔校注：《清波杂志校注》卷12，北京：中华书局，1994年，第508页。

〔3〕Mary Boyce, *A Persian Stronghold of Zoroastrianism*, p.148. 中译本参考〔英〕玛丽·博伊斯著，张小贵、殷小平译《伊朗琐罗亚斯德教村落》，第159–160页。

> 而根据与现实信仰的接触，可以使人们了解信徒对本教教义的理解，这些教义可能就体现在主要仪式中。[1]

仪式往往比枯燥的信条更具持久性，我们追踪入华祆教的礼仪习俗，或许更易接近这一中古外来宗教的真相。

[1] Mary Boyce, "The continuity of the Zoroastrian Quest", in W. Foy(ed.): *Man's religious quest: a reader*. London, Croom Helm in association with the Open University Press, 1978, p. 604, 613.

附：

林悟殊先生论著目录

英文论文

—— "Review of Samuel N.C.Lieu, *Manichaeism in the Later Roman Empire and Medieval China*", *Journal of the Royal Asiatic Society* (London), 1986, pp.311-312.

——"Review of Peter Bryder, *The Chinese Transformation of Manichaeism*", *Journal of the Royal Asiatic Society* (London), 1987, pp. 166-167.

——"On The Joining Between The two Fragments of *The Cempendium of the Teaching of Mani, The Buddha of Light*", in P. Bryder (ed.), *Manichaean Studies, Proceedings of the First International Conference on Manichaeism*. Lund Studies in African and Asian Religions I, Lund 1988, pp. 89-94.

——"A New Find of a Manichaean Stone Carving in Fujian, China", in *Manichaean Studies Newsletter*, Leuven 1989.1, pp. 22-27.

—— "The Origin of *the Compendium of the Teaching of Mani, the Buddha of Light* in Chinese", in Tongerloo, A. Van and Soren Giversen (ed.), *Manichaca Selecta. Studies presented to Professor Julien Ries on the occasion of his seventieth birthday*, Lovanii 1991, pp. 225-232.

—— "On the Spreading of Manichaeism in Fujian, China", in Wiessner, G.und H.J. Klimkeit (ed.), *Studia Manichaica. II. Internationaler Kongreß zum Manichäismus, 6-10. August 1989. St. Augustin/Bonn*, Otto Harrassovitz. Wiesbaden, 1992, pp.342-355.

—— "A Discussion About the Difference between the Heaven- God in the Qoco Kingdom and the High Deity of Zoroastrianism", in *Zentralasiatische Studien* 23 (1992/1993), Herausgegeben von Walther Heissig und Michael Weiers, Otto Harrassowitz. Wiesbaden 1993, pp. 7-12.

—— "A Research on the Original Manuscript of Chinese Manichaean Hymnal", in A.van Tongerloo (ed.), *The Manichaean NOYE, Proceedings of the Internatinal Symposium Organized in Louvain from 31 July To August 1991*, Lovanii 1995, pp. 177-181.

——and Rong Xinjiang, "Doubts Concerning the Authenticity of Two Nestorian Christian Documents Unearthed at Dunhuang from the Li Collection", *China Archaeology and Art Digest*, Vol. 1, No. 1, 1996, pp. 5-14.

—— "A General Discussion of the Tang Policy Towards Three Persian Religions: Manichaeism, Nestorianism and Zoroastrianism" , *China Archaeology and Art Digest*, Vol. 4, No. 1, Dec. 2000, pp. 103-116.

—— "Personal views on the Success and Defeat of the Nestorian Mission in Tang Dynasty China", *China Archaeology and Art Digest*, Vol. 4, No. 1, Dec. 2000, pp. 208-209.

——"Notes on the Title of the Dunhuang Manichaean Hymnscroll (S.2659 摩尼教下部赞 Mo-ni chiao hsia-pu tsan) ", *Paper for the Fifth International Conference of Manichaean Studies September* 3-7, 2001, Istituto Universitario Orientale Napoli, Italy.

—— "Additional Notes on the Authenticity of Tomioka's and Takakusu's Manuscripts", *Paper for "Reseach on Nestorianism in China" International Conference*, Salzburg, Austria, 20-26 May, 2003; Roman Malek in connection with Peter Hofrichter ed., *Jingjiao The Church of the East in China and Central Asia*, Sankt Augustin: Institut Monumenta Serica, pp.133-142.

——and Wang Yuanyuan, "Persian Zoroastrianism and the Worship of the God of Xian in Ancient China", Yu Taishan & Li Jinxiu eds., *Eurasian*

Studies, Vol. I, Beijing: The Commercial Press, 2011, pp.328-354.

——《汉文摩尼经与景教经之宏观比较》，呈交 2004 年 1 月 18 日—21 日京都大学人文科学研究所创立 75 周年“中国宗教文献研究国际会议”论文。《中国宗教文献研究国际シンポジウム报告书》，京都，2004 年，第 131–150 页。

译著

——〔德〕克里木凯特撰：《古代摩尼教艺术》，广州中山大学出版社，1989 年；台北淑馨出版社增订版，1995 年。

——〔德〕克里木凯特撰：《达·伽马以前中亚和东亚的基督教》，台北淑馨出版社增订版，1995 年。

译文

——〔澳〕柳存仁撰：《唐前火祆教和摩尼教在中国之遗痕》，刊《世界宗教研究》1981 年第 3 期，第 36–61 页。

——〔英〕刘南强撰：《摩尼教寺院的戒律和制度》，刊《世界宗教研究》1983 年第 1 期，第 24–37 页。经修订附录于《摩尼教及其东渐》，台北淑馨出版社，1997 年，第 107–130 页。

——〔英〕刘南强撰：《华南沿海的景教徒和摩尼教徒》，刊《海交史研究》1987 年第 2 期，第 93-104 页。经修订附录于《达·伽马以前中亚和东亚的基督教》，台北淑馨出版社，1995 年，第 157–177 页。

——〔瑞典〕翁拙瑞撰：《我对晋江摩尼教草庵的考察》，刊《海交史研究》1989 年第 2 期，第 103–105 页。

专著

——《摩尼教及其东渐》，北京：中华书局，1987 年；增订版台北淑馨出版社，1997 年。

——《波斯拜火教与古代中国》，台北：新文丰出版公司，1995 年。

——《泰国大峰祖师崇拜与华侨报德善堂研究》，台北：淑馨出版社，1996 年。

——《唐代景教再研究》，北京：中国社会科学出版社，2003 年 1 月。

——《中古三夷教辨证》，北京：中华书局，2005 年。

——《中古夷教华化丛考》，兰州：兰州大学出版社，2011 年。

——《林悟殊敦煌文书与夷教研究》，上海：上海古籍出版社，2011 年。

——《摩尼教华化补说》，兰州：兰州大学出版社，2014 年。

论文

——《摩尼的二宗三际论及其起源初探》，刊《世界宗教研究》1982 年第 3 期，第 45–56 页。

——《古代摩尼教》外国历史小丛书，北京：商务印书馆，1983 年；收入《世界古今宗教史话》，北京：商务印书馆，1991 年，第 223–263 页。

——《敦煌本〈摩尼光佛教法仪略〉的产生》，刊《世界宗教研究》1983 年第 3 期，第 71–76 页。

——《摩尼教入华年代质疑》，刊《文史》18 辑，1983 年，第 69–81 页。

——《〈摩尼教残经一〉原名之我见》，刊《文史》21 辑，1983 年，第 89–99 页。

——《〈摩尼光佛教法仪略〉的三圣同一论》，呈交 1985 年敦煌吐鲁番学术讨论会论文。

——《摩尼教在回鹘复兴的社会历史根源》，刊《世界宗教研究》1984 年第 1 期，第 136–143 页。

——《本世纪来摩尼教资料的新发现及其研究概况》，刊《世界宗教资料》1984 年第 1 期，第 1–6 页。

——《〈老子化胡经〉与摩尼教》，刊《世界宗教研究》1984 年第 4 期，第 116-122 页。

——《从考古发现看摩尼教在高昌回鹘的封建化》，刊《西北史地》

1984年第4期，第9–16页。

——《摩尼教〈下部赞〉汉译年代之我见》，刊《文史》22辑，1984年，第91–96页。

——《唐代摩尼教与中亚摩尼教团》，刊《文史》23辑，1984年，第85–93页。

——《宋元时代中国东南沿海的寺院式摩尼教》，刊《世界宗教研究》1985年第3期，第103–111页。

——《宋代明教与唐代摩尼教》，刊《文史》24辑，1985年，第115–126页。

——《唐宋〈三际经〉质疑》，刊《文史》25辑，1985年，第109–114页。

——《吃菜事魔与摩尼教》，刊《文史》26辑，1985年，第149–155页。

——《龙门天竺寺非摩尼教寺辨》，刊《中原文物》1986年第2期，第105–110页。

——《慕阇考》，刊《文史》27辑，1986年，第61–66页。

——《唐代长安火祆大秦寺考辨》，刊《西北史地》1987年第1期，第8–12页。

——《印度的琐罗亚斯德教徒》，刊《世界宗教资料》1987年第1期，第1–5页。

——《论高昌“俗事天神”》，刊《历史研究》1987年第4期，第89–97页。

——《火祆教始通中国的再认识》，刊《世界宗教研究》1987年第4期，第13–23页。

——《我与〈文史〉》，刊《书品》1988年第3期，第64、76页。

——《泉州摩尼教墓碑石为景教碑石辨》，刊《文物》1988年第8期，第82–86页。

——《唐人奉火祆教考辨》，刊《文史》第30辑，1988年，第101–107页。

——《祆教的原始经典〈伽萨〉》，刊《世界宗教资料》1987 年第 1 期，第 10–14、19 页。

——《〈阿维斯陀经〉及其研究概况》刊《西南亚研究》1989 年第 1 期，第 46–48 页。

——《近代琐罗亚斯德教研究的滥觞》，刊《百科知识》1989 年第 4 期，第 26–27 页。

——《火祆教的葬俗及其在古代中亚的遗痕》，刊《西北民族研究》1990 年第 1 期，第 61–67，60 页。

——《〈摩尼光佛教法仪略〉残卷的缀合》，载《敦煌吐鲁番文献研究论集》第 5 集，北京：北京大学出版社，1990 年，第 179–201 页。

——《伦敦藏敦煌写本〈下部赞〉原件考察》，刊《季羡林教授八十华诞纪念论文集》，南昌：江西人民出版社 1991 年，第 871–900 页。

——《福建发现的波斯摩尼教遗物》，刊台北《故宫文物月刊》133(第 12 卷第 1 期)，1994 年 4 月，第 110–117 页。

——《祆教净礼述略》，刊台北《辅仁大学神学论集》第 102 号，1994 年，第 619–634 页。

——《从福建明教遗物看波斯摩尼教之华化》，附录于台版《古代摩尼教艺术》，1995 年，第 123–137 页。

——《粟特文及其写本述略》，附录于台版《古代摩尼教艺术》，1995 年，第 109–122 页。

——《敦煌遗书〈大秦景教宣元本经〉考释》，刊香港《九州学刊》第六卷第四期敦煌学专辑，1995 年，第 23-30 页；附录于台版《达·伽马以前中亚和东亚的基督教》，1995 年，第 212–224 页。

——《唐代摩尼教术语“三常”一词考释》，刊台北《敦煌学》第 20 辑，1995 年，第 47–52 页。

——《摩尼教“三常”考——兼论景教碑“启三常之门”一句之释读》，刊饶宗颐主编《华学》第一期，广州：中山大学出版社，1995 年，第 18–24 页。

——《摩尼教研究之展望》，刊台北《新史学》第 7 卷 1 期，1996

年，第 119–134 页；转载于王元化主编《学术集林》，卷 14，上海：上海远东出版社，1998 年，第 334–351 页。

——《金庸笔下的明教与历史的真实》，刊台北《历史月刊》第 98 期，1996 年 3 月，第 62–67 页。

——《一位名不见高僧传的高僧》，刊台北《历史月刊》第 104 期，1996 年 9 月，第 18–22 页。

——《泰国大峰祖师崇拜述略》，刊王见川・柯若朴主编《民间宗教》第 2 辑，台北南天书局发行，1996 年，第 1–17 页；经修订作《宋大峰祖师崇拜流行泰国述略》，刊饶宗颐主编《华学》第 2 辑，广州：中山大学出版社，1996 年，第 180–189 页。

——《治学求真感言》，刊胡戟主编《唐研究纵横谈》，北京：中国社会科学出版社，1996 年，第 169–174 页。

——《书评：*The Manichaean Hymn Cycles Huyadagmān and Angad Rōsnān in Parthian and Sogdian*》，刊《敦煌吐鲁番研究》第 2 卷，北京：北京大学出版社，1997 年，第 379–380 页。

——《潮汕善堂文化及其初入泰国考略》，刊《海交史研究》1997 年第 2 期，第 82–97 页。

——《孙中山为潮侨郑智勇取名事质疑》，刊《韩山师范学院学报》1997 年第 3 期，第 115–117 页。

——《敦煌摩尼教〈下部赞〉经名考释——兼论该经三首音译诗》，刊《敦煌吐鲁番研究》第 3 卷，北京：北京大学出版社，1998 年，第 45–51 页。

——《唐朝三夷教政策论略》，刊荣新江主编《唐研究》第 4 卷，北京：北京大学出版社，1998 年，第 1–14 页。

——《景教在唐代中国传播成败之我见》，刊饶宗颐主编《华学》第 3 辑，广州：中山大学出版社，1998 年，第 83–95 页。

——《火祆教在唐代中国社会地位之考察》，载蔡鸿生主编《戴裔煊教授九十诞辰纪念文集：澳门史与中西交通研究》，广州：广东高等教育出版社，1998 年，第 169–196 页。

——《唐季“大秦穆护祆”考》（上），刊《文史》第 48 辑，1999 年 7 月，第 39–46 页。

——《唐季“大秦穆护祆”考》（下），刊《文史》第 49 辑，1999 年 12 月，第 101–112 页。

——《波斯琐罗亚斯德教与中国古代的祆神崇拜》，刊余太山主编《欧亚学刊》第 1 辑，北京：中华书局，1999 年，第 207–227 页；收入傅杰编《二十世纪中国文史考据文录》下册，昆明：云南人民出版社，2001 年 12 月，第 1892–1907 页。

——《泉州白耇庙属性拟证》，刊《海交史研究》1999 年第 2 期，第 12–22，11 页。

——《关于潮汕善堂文化的思考》，刊《人海灯》，岭东佛学院主编，1999 年第 4 期，第 34–42 页；陈三鹏主编《第三届潮学国际研讨会》，广州：花城出版社，2000 年 8 月，第 465–474 页。

——《陈寅恪先生“胡化”、“汉化”说的启示》，刊《中山大学学报》2000 年第 1 期，第 42–47 页；收入胡守为主编《陈寅恪与二十世纪中国学术》，杭州：浙江人民出版社，2000 年 12 月，第 268–278 页。

——《回忆汪淑钧教授英语教学引发的思考》，刊夏纪梅编《贤母良师 益友》，广州：广东人民出版社，2000 年 2 月，第 127–134 页。

——《史学研究生若干规范训练之我见》，刊《学位与研究生教育》2000 年第 5 期，第 4–6 页。

——《唐代首所景教寺院考略》，刊饶宗颐主编《华学》第 4 辑，北京：紫禁城出版社，2000 年，第 275–285 页。

——《20 世纪中国琐罗亚斯德教研究述评》，刊余太山主编《欧亚学刊》第 2 辑，北京：中华书局，2000 年，第 243–265 页。

——《西安景教碑有关景寺数量词句考释》，刊《国学研究》第 7 卷，北京：北京大学出版社，2000 年，第 97–113 页。

——《盩厔大秦寺为唐代景寺质疑》，刊《世界宗教研究》2000 年第 4 期，第 1–12 页。

——《西安景教碑研究述评》，刊刘东主编《中国学术》第 4 辑，北京：商务印书馆，2000 年，第 230–260 页。

——《陈垣先生与中国火祆教研究》，刊龚书铎主编《励耘学术承习录：纪念陈垣先生诞辰 120 周年》，北京：北京师范大学出版社，2000 年，第 170–179 页。

——《富冈谦藏氏藏景教〈一神论〉真伪存疑》，刊荣新江主编《唐研究》第 6 卷，北京：北京大学出版社，2000 年，第 67–86 页。

——《敦煌景教写本伯 3847 之再研究》，刊《敦煌吐鲁番研究》第 5 卷，北京：北京大学出版社，2000 年，第 59–77 页。

——《书评：柳洪亮主编〈吐鲁番新出摩尼教文献研究〉》，刊《敦煌吐鲁番研究》第 5 卷，北京：北京大学出版社，2000 年，第 361–366 页。

——《高楠氏藏景教〈序听迷诗所经〉真伪存疑》，刊《文史》第 55 辑，2001 年 7 月，第 141–154 页。

——《敦煌本景教〈志玄安乐经〉佐伯录文质疑》，刊《中山大学学报》（社会科学版），2001 年第 4 期，第 1–7 页。

——《值得青年学者取法的西域史研究专著——读〈唐代九姓胡与突厥文化〉》，刊《西域研究》，2001 年第 1 期，第 103–108 页。

——《20 世纪敦煌汉文摩尼教写本研究述评》，刊段文杰主编《敦煌学与中国史研究论集：纪念孙修身先生逝世一周年》，兰州：甘肃人民出版社，2001 年 8 月，第 430–435 页。

——《泰国潮人德教信仰考察》，刊《泰中学刊》（曼谷）2001 年，第 29–37 页。

——《二十世纪唐代火祆教研究述评》，刊胡戟等主编《二十世纪唐研究》，北京：中国社会科学出版社，2002 年 1 月，第 577–585 页。

——《二十世纪唐代摩尼教研究述评》，刊胡戟等主编《二十世纪唐研究》，第 569–577 页。

——《二十世纪唐代景教研究述评》，刊胡戟等主编《二十世纪唐研究》，第 585–611 页。

（注：以上三篇述评编入是书文化卷第二章第三节第 569–611 页，以“三夷教”为题。）

——《敦煌汉文景教写本研究述评》，刊余太山主编《欧亚学刊》第 3 辑，北京：中华书局，2002 年，第 251–287 页。

——《有关“莆田市涵江新发现摩尼教文物古迹”的管见》，刊《世界宗教研究》2002 年第 3 期，第 145–148 页。

——《唐百丈禅师怀海生年考》，刊《中山大学学报》2002 年第 5 期，第 54–60 页。

——《泉州草庵摩尼雕像与吐鲁番摩尼画像的比较》，刊《考古与文物》2003 年第 2 期，第 76–80 页。

——《20 世纪的泉州摩尼教考古》，刊《文物》2003 年第 7 期，第 71–77 页。

——《泉州摩尼教渊源考》，刊林中泽主编《华夏文明与西方世界》，香港：博士苑出版社，2003 年，第 75–93 页。

——《元代泉州摩尼教偶像崇拜探源》，刊《海交史研究》，2003 年第 1 期，第 65–75 页。

——《唐代三夷教的社会走向》，刊荣新江主编《唐代的宗教信仰与社会》，上海：上海辞书出版社，2003 年 8 月，第 359–384 页。

——《从〈百丈清规〉看农禅——试论唐宋佛教的自我供养意识》，刊胡素馨主编《寺院财富与世俗供养》，上海：上海书画出版社，2003 年 12 月，第 380–401 页。

——《陈寅恪热的回归——读蔡鸿生〈仰望陈寅恪〉》，刊《书品》2004 年第 3 辑，39–49 页；第 4 辑，第 48–55 页。

——《福建明教十六字偈考释》，刊《文史》2004 年第 1 辑，第 230–246 页。

——《元〈竹西楼记〉摩尼教信息辨析》，刊饶宗颐主编《华学》第 7 辑，广州：中山大学出版社，2004 年 12 月，第 242–252 页。

——《〈伊朗琐罗亚斯德教村落〉中译本序》，刊余太山主编《欧亚学刊》第 4 辑，北京：中华书局，2004 年 6 月，第 255–259 页。

——《内陆欧亚祆教研究述评》，刊余太山主编《内陆欧亚古代史研究》，福州：福建人民出版社，2005 年，第 399–418 页。

——《景教富冈高楠文书辨伪补说》，刊季羡林、饶宗颐主编《敦煌吐鲁番研究》第 8 卷，北京：中华书局，2005 年，第 35–43 页。

——《福州浦西福寿宫“明教文佛”宗教属性辨析》，刊《中山大学学报》（社会科学版）2004 年第 6 期，第 118–123，264 页。

——《摩尼教入闽路线问题评说》，刊《福建宗教》2005 年第 1 期，第 25–26 页。

——《宋元滨海地域明教非海路输入辨》，刊《中山大学学报》2005 年第 3 期，第 67–71 页。

——《敦煌汉文摩尼教写经研究回顾》，刊《中古三夷教辨证》，第 107–118 页。

——《英法藏敦煌汉文摩尼教写本原件考察》，刊《中古三夷教辨证》，第 119–122 页。

——《明教：扎根中国的摩尼教》，刊《寻根》2006 年第 1 期，第 10–14 页。

——《宋元温州选真寺摩尼教属性再辨析》，刊《中华文史论丛》2006 年第 4 辑（总第 84 辑），第 265–288 页。

——《摩尼教华名辨异》，刊《九州学林》5 卷 1 期（2007 年春季号），第 187–237 页；收入马西沙主编《当代中国宗教研究精选丛书·民间宗教卷》，北京：民族出版社，2008 年，第 28–77 页。

——《李白〈上云乐〉景教思想质疑》，刊《文史》2007 年第 2 辑（总第 79 辑），第 169–186 页。

——《西安景碑有关阿罗本入华事辨析》，刊《文史》2008 年第 1 辑（总第 82 辑），第 149–165 页。

——《泉州晋江新发现摩尼教遗迹辨析》，刊饶宗颐主编《华学》第九、十辑（二），上海：上海古籍出版社，2008 年，第 754–767 页。

——《游子贵有赤诚心——〈游子心〉读后感》，刊〔泰国〕王侨生著《游子心》，香港：博士苑出版社，2008 年，第 218–220 页。

——《经幢版“三位一体”考释——唐代洛阳景教经幢研究之三》，刊《中华文史论丛》2009年第1辑（总第93辑），第257–276页；收入《景教遗珍——洛阳新出土唐代景教经幢研究》，第109–121页。

——《唐代景僧名字的华化轨迹——唐代洛阳景教经幢研究之四》，刊《中华文史论丛》2009年第2辑，第149–194页。

——《为华化摩尼教研究献新知——评粘良图〈晋江草庵研究〉》，刊《海交史研究》2009年第2期，第128–134页。

——《晋江摩尼教草庵发现始末考述》，刊《福建师范大学学报》2010年第1期，第61–65页。

——《宋代明教伪托白诗考》，刊《文史》2010年第4辑（总第93辑），第175–199页。

——《“宋摩尼教依托道教”考论》，刊张荣芳、戴治国主编《陈垣与岭南：纪念陈垣先生诞生130周年学术研讨会论文集》，北京：中国社会科学出版社，2011年，第81–107页。

——《摩尼教“裸葬”辨》，刊刘东主编《中国学术》第32辑，北京：商务印书馆，第244–264页。

——《霞浦科仪本〈下部赞〉诗文辨异》，刊《世界宗教研究》2012年第3期，第170–178页。

——《明教五佛崇拜补说》，刊《文史》2012年第3期（100辑），第385–408页。

——《海外潮人的中间阶层亦值得研究——〈海外潮人文丛〉引发的一点思考》，刊陈春声、陈伟斌主编《地域文化的构造与播迁——第八届潮学国际研讨会论文集》，北京：中华书局，2012年，第8–11页。

——《敦煌摩尼教〈下部赞〉“电光佛”非“光明处女”辨》，刊《文史》2013年第1期（102辑），第175–196页。

——《跋〈乐山堂神记〉再考察》，刊陈春声主编《海陆交通与世界文明》，北京：商务印书馆，2013年，第256–260页。

——《霞浦科仪本〈奏教主〉形成年代考》，刊《九州学林》第31辑，2013年，第102–135页。

——《敦煌摩尼教文书日月神名辨》，刊《敦煌吐鲁番研究》第13卷，上海古籍出版社，2013年，第441–455页。

——《京藏摩尼经开篇结语辨释》，刊《西域研究》2013年第2期，第41–50页。

——《京藏摩尼经音译词语考察》，刊《世界宗教研究》2014年第1期，第1–13页。

——《摩尼教“拂多诞”名辨》，刊《中华文史论丛》2014年第1期（总第113期），第287–309页。

——《景教“净风”考——夷教文典“风”字研究之一》，刊《西域研究》2014年第3期，第50–64页。

——《唐代摩尼教“风”入神名考——夷教文典“风”字研究之二》，刊《西域研究》2014年第3期，第65–76页。

——《摩尼教〈下部赞〉三首音译诗偈辨说》，刊《文史》2014年第3辑，（总第108辑），第5–57页。

——林悟殊、荣新江：《所谓李氏旧藏敦煌景教文献二种辨伪》，刊香港《九州学刊》1992年4月第四卷第四期，第19–34页。

——林悟殊、殷小平：《经幢版〈大秦景教宣元至本经〉考释——唐代洛阳景教经幢研究之一》，载《中华文史论丛》2008年第1辑，第325–352页；收入《景教遗珍——洛阳新出土唐代景教经幢研究》，第68–91页。

——林悟殊、殷小平：《唐代“景僧”释义》，刊《文史》2009年第1辑（总第86辑），第181–204页。

——林悟殊、王媛媛：《泉州草庵遗址明教属性辨识之学理与方法》，《中华文史论丛》2010年第3期（总第99期），第343–369，401页。

——林悟殊、张淑琼：《佛书所载摩尼僧始通中国史事辨释》，刊余太山、李锦绣主编《丝瓷之路：古代中外关系史研究》，I，北京：商务印书馆，2011年，第279–297页。

——林悟殊、殷小平：《〈夷坚志〉明教纪事史料价值辨释》，刊《中华文史论丛》2012年第2期（总第106期），第255–283页。

——林悟殊、王媛媛：《五代陈州毋乙之徒非“末尼党类”辨》，刊《中国史研究》2012年第2期，第91-104页。

——殷小平、林悟殊：《幢记若干问题考释——唐代洛阳景教经幢研究之二》，刊《中华文史论丛》2008年第2辑，第269-292页；收入《景教遗珍——洛阳新出土唐代景教经幢研究》，第92-108页。

欧亚历史文化文库

已经出版

林悟殊著:《中古夷教华化丛考》 定价:66.00 元
赵俪生著:《弇兹集》 定价:69.00 元
华喆著:《阴山鸣镝——匈奴在北方草原上的兴衰》 定价:48.00 元
杨军编著:《走向陌生的地方——内陆欧亚移民史话》 定价:38.00 元
贺菊莲著:《天山家宴——西域饮食文化纵横谈》 定价:64.00 元
陈鹏著:《路途漫漫丝貂情——明清东北亚丝绸之路研究》
定价:62.00 元
王颋著:《内陆亚洲史地求索》 定价:83.00 元
〔日〕堀敏一著,韩昇、刘建英编译:《隋唐帝国与东亚》
定价:38.00 元
〔印度〕艾哈默得·辛哈著,周翔翼译,徐百永校:《入藏四年》
定价:35.00 元
〔意〕伯戴克著,张云译:《中部西藏与蒙古人
——元代西藏历史》(增订本) 定价:38.00 元
陈高华著:《元朝史事新证》 定价:74.00 元
王永兴著:《唐代经营西北研究》 定价:94.00 元
王炳华著:《西域考古文存》 定价:108.00 元
李健才著:《东北亚史地论集》 定价:73.00 元
孟凡人著:《新疆考古论集》 定价:98.00 元
周伟洲著:《藏史论考》 定价:55.00 元
刘文锁著:《丝绸之路——内陆欧亚考古与历史》 定价:88.00 元
张博泉著:《甫白文存》 定价:62.00 元
孙玉良著:《史林遗痕》 定价:85.00 元
马健著:《匈奴葬仪的考古学探索》 定价:76.00 元
〔俄〕柯兹洛夫著,王希隆、丁淑琴译:
《蒙古、安多和死城哈喇浩特》(完整版) 定价:82.00 元
乌云高娃著:《元朝与高丽关系研究》 定价:67.00 元
杨军著:《夫余史研究》 定价:40.00 元
梁俊艳著:《英国与中国西藏(1774—1904)》 定价:88.00 元
〔乌兹别克斯坦〕艾哈迈多夫著,陈远光译:
《16—18 世纪中亚历史地理文献》(修订版) 定价:85.00 元

成一农著:《空间与形态
——三至七世纪中国历史城市地理研究》 定价: 76.00 元
杨铭著:《唐代吐蕃与西北民族关系史研究》 定价: 86.00 元
殷小平著:《元代也里可温考述》 定价: 50.00 元
耿世民著:《西域文史论稿》 定价: 100.00 元
殷晴著:《丝绸之路经济史研究》 定价: 135.00 元(上、下册)
余大钧译:《北方民族史与蒙古史译文集》 定价: 160.00 元(上、下册)
韩儒林著:《蒙元史与内陆亚洲史研究》 定价: 58.00 元
〔美〕查尔斯·林霍尔姆著,张士东、杨军译:
《伊斯兰中东——传统与变迁》 定价: 88.00 元
〔美〕J.G.马勒著,王欣译:《唐代塑像中的西域人》 定价: 58.00 元
顾世宝著:《蒙元时代的蒙古族文学家》 定价: 42.00 元
杨铭编:《国外敦煌学、藏学研究——翻译与评述》 定价: 78.00 元
牛汝极等著:《新疆文化的现代化转向》 定价: 76.00 元
周伟洲著:《西域史地论集》 定价: 82.00 元
周晶著:《纷扰的雪山——20 世纪前半叶西藏社会生活研究》
定价: 75.00 元
蓝琪著:《16—19 世纪中亚各国与俄国关系论述》 定价: 58.00 元
许序雅著:《唐朝与中亚九姓胡关系史研究》 定价: 65.00 元
汪受宽著:《骊靬梦断——古罗马军团东归伪史辨识》 定价: 96.00 元
刘雪飞著:《上古欧洲斯基泰文化巡礼》 定价: 32.00 元
〔俄〕T. Б.巴尔采娃著,张良仁、李明华译:
《斯基泰时期的有色金属加工业——第聂伯河左岸森林草原带》
定价: 44.00 元
叶德荣著:《汉晋胡汉佛教论稿》 定价: 60.00 元
王颋著:《内陆亚洲史地求索(续)》 定价: 86.00 元
尚永琪著:
《胡僧东来——汉唐时期的佛经翻译家和传播人》 定价: 52.00 元
桂宝丽著:《可萨突厥》 定价: 30.00 元
篠原典生著:《西天伽蓝记》 定价: 48.00 元
〔德〕施林洛甫著,刘震、孟瑜译:
《叙事和图画——欧洲和印度艺术中的情节展现》 定价: 35.00 元
马小鹤著:《光明的使者——摩尼和摩尼教》 定价: 120.00 元
李鸣飞著:《蒙元时期的宗教变迁》 定价: 54.00 元

〔苏联〕伊·亚·兹拉特金著，马曼丽译：
《准噶尔汗国史》(修订版) 定价：86.00 元
〔苏联〕巴托尔德著，张丽译：《中亚历史——巴托尔德文集
第 2 卷第 1 册第 1 部分》 定价：200.00 元（上、下册）
〔俄〕格·尼·波塔宁著，〔苏联〕B.B.奥布鲁切夫编，吴吉康、吴立珺译：《蒙古纪行》 定价：96.00 元
张文德著：《朝贡与入附——明代西域人来华研究》 定价：52.00 元
张小贵著：《祆教史考论与述评》 定价：55.00 元
〔苏联〕K．A．阿奇舍夫、Г．A．库沙耶夫著，孙危译：
《伊犁河流域塞人和乌孙的古代文明》 定价：60.00 元
陈明著：《文本与语言——出土文献与早期佛经词汇研究》
定价：78.00 元
李映洲著：《敦煌壁画艺术论》 定价：148.00 元（上、下册）
杜斗城著：《杜撰集》 定价：108.00 元
芮传明著：《内陆欧亚风云录》 定价：48.00 元
徐文堪著：《欧亚大陆语言及其研究说略》 定价：54.00 元
刘迎胜著：《小儿锦研究》(一、二、三) 定价：300.00 元
郑炳林著：《敦煌占卜文献叙录》 定价：60.00 元
许全胜著：《黑鞑事略校注》 定价：66.00 元
段海蓉著：《萨都剌传》 定价：35.00 元
马曼丽著：《塞外文论——马曼丽内陆欧亚研究自选集》
定价：98.00 元
〔苏联〕И．Я.兹拉特金主编,M.И.戈利曼、Г.И.斯列萨尔丘克著，
马曼丽、胡尚哲译：《俄蒙关系历史档案文献集》(1607—1654)
定价：180.00 元(上、下册)

华喆著：《帝国的背影——公元 14 世纪以后的蒙古》 定价：55.00 元
П．K.柯兹洛夫著，丁淑琴、韩莉、齐哲译：《蒙古和喀木》
定价：75.00 元
杨建新著：《边疆民族论集》 定价：98.00 元
赵现海著：《明长城时代的开启
——长城社会史视野下榆林长城修筑研究》(上、下册)
定价：122.00 元
李鸣飞著：《横跨欧亚——中世纪旅行者眼中的世界》 定价：53.00 元
李鸣飞著：《金元散官制度研究》 定价：70.00 元
刘迎胜著：《蒙元史考论》 定价：150.00 元
王继光著：《中国西部文献题跋》 定价：100.00 元
李艳玲著：《田作畜牧
——公元前 2 世纪至公元 7 世纪前期西域绿洲农业研究》
定价：54.00 元

〔英〕马尔克·奥莱尔·斯坦因著，殷晴、张欣怡译：《沙埋和阗废墟记》
定价：100.00 元
梅维恒著，徐文堪编：《梅维恒内陆欧亚研究文选》 定价：92 元
杨林坤著：《西风万里交河道——时代西域丝路上的使者与商旅》
定价：65 元
王邦维著：《华梵问学集》 定价：75 元
芮传明著：《摩尼教敦煌吐鲁番文书译释与研究》 定价：88 元
陈晓露著：《楼兰考古》 定价：92 元
石云涛著：《文明的互动
——汉唐间丝绸之路中的中外交流论稿》 定价：118 元
孙昊著：《辽代女真族群与社会研究》 定价：48 元
尚永琪著：《鸠摩罗什及其时代》 定价：70 元
薛宗正著：《西域史汇考》 定价：136 元（上、下册）
张小贵编：
《三夷教研究——林悟殊先生古稀纪念论文集》 定价：100 元
石云涛著：《丝绸之路的起源》 定价：83 元（暂定）
〔英〕尼古拉斯·辛姆斯-威廉姆斯著：
《阿富汗北部的巴克特里亚文献》 定价：163 元（暂定）
许全盛、刘震编：《内陆欧亚历史语言论集——徐文堪先生古稀纪念》
定价：90 元（暂定）
余太山、李锦秀编：《古代内陆欧亚史纲》 定价：122 元（暂定）
王永兴著：《唐代土地制度研究——以敦煌吐鲁番田制文书为中心》
定价：70 元（暂定）
王永兴著：《敦煌吐鲁番出土唐代军事文书考释》 定价：84 元（暂定）
李锦绣编：《20 世纪内陆欧亚历史文化论文选粹：第一辑》
定价：104 元（暂定）
李锦绣编：《20 世纪内陆欧亚历史文化论文选粹：第二辑》
定价：98 元（暂定）
李锦绣编：《20 世纪内陆欧亚历史文化论文选粹：第三辑》
定价：97 元（暂定）
李锦绣编：《20 世纪内陆欧亚历史文化论文选粹：第四辑》
定价：100 元（暂定）
馬小鶴著：《霞浦文書研究》 定价：88 元（暂定）
林悟殊著：《摩尼教華化補說》 定价：109 元（暂定）